Outside
MAGAZINE'S

Adventure Guide to
New England

Also available:

Outside Magazine's Adventure Guide to Northern California

Outside

MAGAZINE'S

Adventure Guide to
New England

BY STEPHEN JERMANOK

Macmillan • USA

MACMILLAN TRAVEL

A Simon & Schuster Macmillan Company
1633 Broadway
New York, NY 10019

Find us online at http://www.mgr.com/travel
or on America Online at Keyword: Frommer's

ISBN 0-02-860900-X
ISSN 1088-2693

Series Editor: Ian Wilker
Cover by Mike Bain, *Outside* Magazine
Design by Amy Peppler Adams, designLab
Digital Cartography by Ortelius Design

Maps copyright © by Simon & Schuster, Inc.

Special Sales
Bulk purchases (10+ copies) of Frommer's
travel guides are available to corporations at
special discounts. The Special Sales
Department can produce custom editions to
be used as premiums and/or for sales
promotions to suit individual needs. Existing
editions can be produced with custom cover
imprints such as corporate logos. For more
information write to: Special Sales, Simon &
Schuster, 1633 Broadway, New York, NY
10019.

Manufactured in the United States of America

Stephen Jermanok has explored
more than fifty countries in the past
decade, but it's New England—his
boyhood stomping grounds—that he
knows best. His many articles on
outdoor recreation, travel, art, music,
and food and wine have appeared in
such publications as the *Washington
Post*, *Travel & Leisure*, *Town & Country*,
New York, the *Miami Herald*, and *Art
& Antiques*. Mr. Jermanok recently
authored a screenplay for the
Academy Award–winning producer
of *Babette's Feast*. He lives in
Brookline, Massachusetts.

Contents

List of Maps xii

What the Symbols Mean xv

Map Legend xv

Introduction xvi

1 The Basics 1

Getting Underway 2

Backpacking 2
Ballooning 8
Bird Watching 8
Boardsailing 9
Canoeing 9
Cross-Country
    Skiing 11
Dogsledding 12
Downhill Skiing/
    Snowboarding 12
Fishing 13
Golf 14

Hang Gliding 14
Hiking 14
Horseback Riding 16
Ice Climbing 16
Ice Fishing 17
Llama Trekking 17
Mountain Biking 17
Powerboating 19
Road Biking 19
Rock Climbing 21
Sailing 21
Scuba Diving 22

Sea Kayaking 23
Snowmobiling 23
Snowshoeing 24
Spelunking 24
Surfing 24
Swimming 24
Tubing 24
Walks & Rambles 25
Whale Watching 25
Whitewater
    Kayaking 26
Whitewater Rafting 26

Outfitters 27

Schools 31

Maps 34

Books 35

Spas 36

Campgrounds & Other Accommodations 37

Features:
◆ *Backcountry Equipment Checklist 6*

2 The Litchfield Hills and Western Connecticut 38

The Lay of the Land   39

Orientation   40

Parks & Other Hot Spots   40

What to Do & Where to Do It   42

Ballooning 42
Bird Watching 42
Boardsailing 42
Canoeing 42
Cross-Country
    Skiing 44
Downhill Skiing 47
Fishing 47

Golf 48
Hiking &
    Backpacking 48
Horseback Riding 50
Mountain Biking 51
Road Biking 52
Sailing 53
Sea Kayaking 53

Snowmobiling 54
Swimming 54
Tubing 54
Walks & Rambles 54
Whitewater
    Kayaking 54

Campgrounds & Other Accommodations   55

3 Eastern Connecticut 57

The Lay of the Land   58

Orientation   59

Parks & Other Hot Spots   59

What to Do & Where to Do It   62

Backpacking 62
Ballooning 62
Bird Watching 62
Canoeing 63
Cross-Country
    Skiing 63

Downhill Skiing 64
Fishing 64
Golf 64
Horseback Riding 64
Mountain Biking 65
Road Biking 66

Sailing 68
Sea Kayaking 68
Snowmobiling 70
Swimming 70
Walks & Rambles 70

Campgrounds & Other Accommodations   73

Features:

◆ *Yankee Doodle Dandy 69*

4 Coastal Rhode Island, Block Island & Beyond 76

The Lay of the Land   77

Orientation   78

Parks & Other Hot Spots   79

What to Do & Where to Do It   80

Ballooning 80
Bird Watching 80
Boardsailing 80
Canoeing 80
Cross-Country
  Skiing 81
Downhill Skiing/
  Snowboarding 81

Fishing 81
Golf 82
Horseback Riding 82
Mountain Biking 82
Powerboating 84
Road Biking 84
Sailing 86
Scuba Diving 88

Sea Kayaking 88
Snowmobiling 89
Surfing 89
Swimming 89
Walks & Rambles 89

Campgrounds & Other Accommodations   91

5 The Berkshires **93**

The Lay of the Land   95

Orientation   95

Parks & Other Hot Spots   97

What to Do & Where to Do It   99

Bird Watching 99
Boardsailing 100
Canoeing 100
Cross-Country Skiing 101
Downhill Skiing/
  Snowboarding 106
Fishing 107
Golf 107

Hiking &
  Backpacking 107
Horseback Riding 113
Mountain Biking 113
Road Biking 114
Rock Climbing 115
Sailing &
  Powerboating 116

Sculling 116
Snowmobiling 116
Snowshoeing 116
Swimming 116
Walks & Rambles 116
Whitewater Kayaking
  & Rafting 117

Campgrounds & Other Accommodations   118

Features:

◆ *October Mountain or Kilimanjaro? 103*
◆ *Herman, I'd Like to Introduce You to Nathaniel 110*
◆ *Leave It to Beaver 112*

6 Greater Boston, Cape Ann & the South Shore **120**

The Lay of the Land   121

Orientation 122

Parks & Other Hot Spots 122

What to Do & Where to Do It 125

Bird Watching 125
Boardsailing 125
Canoeing 125
Cross-Country
  Skiing 126
Downhill Skiing 127
Fishing 127

Golf 128
Horseback Riding 128
Mountain Biking 128
Powerboating 129
Road Biking 129
Sailing 133
Scuba Diving 134

Sculling 134
Sea Kayaking 134
Snowmobiling 134
Surfing 134
Swimming 135
Walks & Rambles 135
Whale Watching 137

Campgrounds & Other Accommodations 137

Features:

◆ *Walden Pond 132*

7 Cape Cod, Nantucket & Martha's Vineyard 139

The Lay of the Land 143

Orientation 144

Parks & Other Hot Spots 144

What to Do & Where to Do It 149

Bird Watching 149
Boardsailing 151
Canoeing &
  Kayaking 152
Cross-Country
  Skiing 153
Fishing 153

Golf 154
Hiking 154
Horseback Riding 155
Mountain Biking 155
Powerboating 157
Road Biking 157
Sailing 161

Scuba Diving 161
Sea Kayaking 161
Surfing 162
Swimming 163
Walks & Rambles 164
Whale Watching 168

Campgrounds & Other Accommodations 169

Features:

◆ *Creature of Habit 153*
◆ *Noted Naturalists of Cape Cod 165*

8 Southern & Central Vermont 171

The Lay of the Land 173

Orientation 175

Parks & Other Hot Spots   178

Southern Vermont ◆ What to Do & Where to Do It   185

Bird Watching 185
Canoeing 190
Cross-Country
   Skiing 193
Downhill Skiing/
   Snowboarding 197
Fishing 203
Golf 204

Hiking &
   Backpacking 204
Horseback Riding 210
Ice Fishing 211
Llama Treks 211
Mountain Biking 211
Powerboating 213
Road Biking 213

Sailing 215
Snowmobiling 215
Snowshoeing 216
Spelunking 216
Swimming 216
Tennis 216
Walks & Rambles 216

Central Vermont ◆ What to Do & Where to Do It   217

Ballooning 217
Bird Watching 217
Cross-Country Skiing 220
Downhill Skiing 222
Fishing 226

Golf 227
Hiking &
   Backpacking 227
Horseback Riding 229
Ice Skating 229

Mountain Biking 229
Road Biking 231
Rock Climbing 233
Snowmobiling 234
Swimming 234

Campgrounds & Other Accommodations   234

Features:

◆ *Southern Vermont Ski & Winter Sport Shops 200*
◆ *The Long Trail 206*
◆ *Central Vermont Ski & Winter Sports Shops 225*

❾ Lake Champlain, the Northern Green Mountains & the Northeast Kingdom 239

The Lay of the Land   240

Orientation   241

Parks & Other Hot Spots   242

What to Do & Where to Do It   245

Bird Watching 245
Boardsailing 246
Canoeing 246
Cross-Country Skiing 248
Downhill Skiing 251
Fishing 254
Golf 255

Hiking &
   Backpacking 255
Horseback Riding 260
Ice Fishing 260
Llama Treks 260
Mountain Biking 260
Powerboating 262

Road Biking 262
Sailing 264
Scuba Diving 266
Snowmobiling 267
Snowshoeing 267
Swimming 267
Walks & Rambles 267

Campgrounds & Other Accommodations   268

Features:

◆ *The Catamount Trail 252*
◆ *Northern Vermont Ski & Winter Sports Shops 253*

10 The White Mountains & Other New Hampshire Highlights 273

The Lay of the Land   274

Orientation   276

Parks & Other Hot Spots   277

What to Do & Where to Do It   281

Bird Watching 281
Boardsailing 282
Canoeing 282
Cross-Country
   Skiing 285
Downhill Skiing/
   Snowboarding 287
Fishing 289

Golf 290
Hang Gliding 290
Hiking 290
Horseback Riding 298
Ice Climbing 299
Ice Fishing 299
Kayaking 299
Mountain Biking 299

Powerboating 302
Road Biking 302
Rock Climbing 304
Sailing 304
Scuba Diving 304
Snowmobiling 304
Snowshoeing 304
Swimming 305

Campgrounds & Other Accommodations   305

Features:

◆ *The Appalachian Mountain Club 292*
◆ *Bullwinkle and Company 297*

11 The Maine Coast **308**

The Lay of the Land   311

Orientation   312

Parks & Other Hot Spots   312

What to Do & Where to Do It   318

Ballooning 318
Bird Watching 318
Boardsailing 321
Canoeing 321

Cross-Country
   Skiing 321
Downhill Skiing 322
Fishing 322

Golf 323
Hiking 323
Horseback Riding 325
Mountain Biking 326

Powerboating 327
Road Biking 327
Rock Climbing 330
Sailing 331

Scuba Diving 332
Sea Kayaking 332
Snowmobiling 334
Snowshoeing 334

Swimming 335
Walks & Rambles 335

Campgrounds & Other Accommodations 336

Features:

◆ *Blue in the Face 318*
◆ *Homer at Home 322*
◆ *Did They Get Bibs and Butter Sauce? 325*
◆ *We're Jammin' 331*
◆ *The Maine Island Trail 333*

12 The Maine Woods 339

The Lay of the Land 340

Orientation 341

Parks & Other Hot Spots 344

What to Do & Where to Do It 349

Ballooning 349
Bird Watching 349
Canoeing 350
Cross-Country
  Skiing 353
Dogsledding 357
Downhill Skiing 358
Fishing 359

Golf 362
Hiking &
  Backpacking 362
Horseback Riding 367
Ice Fishing 367
Mountain Biking 367
Powerboating 368
Road Biking 368

Sailing 369
Snowmobiling 369
Snowshoeing 370
Swimming 370
Walks & Rambles 371
Whitewater Rafting 371

Campgrounds & Other Accommodations 373

Features:

◆ *The Vanishing Wild Woods 354*
◆ *Move Over Milwaukee 359*
◆ *Do You Know the Way to Moosehead Lake? 370*

Index 379

List of Maps

Outside in New England   **4**

The Litchfield Hills   **41**

Block Island   **87**

The Berkshires   **96**

Greater Boston   **123**

Cape Cod   **140**

Martha's Vineyard   **147**

Nantucket   **149**

Southern Vermont   **188**

Central Vermont & The Lower Champlain Valley   **218**

Northern Vermont   **243**

White Mountains   **278**

Cape Ann & The New Hampshire Coast   **282**

Southern Maine Coast   **310**

Acadia National Park   **314**

Downeast & Penobscot Bay   **316**

The Sunrise Coast   **319**

Maine's Western Lakes & Mountains   **342**

The North Woods & Allagash Wilderness Waterway   **346**

The Moosehead Lake Area   **348**

Baxter State Park   **375**

Invitation to the Reader

In researching this book, I criss-crossed New England in search of the very best places to get outside. I'm sure you have your own favorite spots, or at least will find new ones as you explore. Please share your secrets with me, so I can pass them on in upcoming editions. If you were disappointed with a recommendation, I'd love to know that, too. Please write to:

Steve Jermanok
Outside Magazine's Adventure Guide to New England
Macmillan Travel
1633 Broadway
New York, NY 10019

An Additional Note

Please be advised that travel information is subject to change at any time. Every effort has been made to ensure the accuracy of the information provided in this book, but we suggest that you write or call ahead for confirmation when making your travel plans. The authors, editors, and publisher cannot be held responsible for the experiences of readers while traveling. Outdoor adventure sports are, by their very nature, potentially hazardous activities. In doing any of the activities described herein, readers assume all risk of injury or loss that may accompany such activities. The Publisher disavows all responsibility for injury, death, loss, or property damage which may arise from a reader's participation in any of the activities described herein, and the Publisher makes no warranties regarding the competence, safety, and reliability of outfitters, tour companies, or training centers described in this book.

TO LISA

For guiding me on the right path.

Acknowledgments

THIS BOOK WOULD NEVER HAVE COME TO FRUITION WITHOUT KEEN ADVICE and wise guidance from the following people. I'm grateful to my family for their unyielding support, especially to my brother Jim, who kept me laughing on numerous hiking, biking, sea kayaking, and fishing adventures, and to Julie, Neil, and Amielle, who made the transition from New York to Boston easy and exciting. I'd like to thank my editors, Lisa Renaud, for her faith in a first-time author, and Ian Wilker, for his copious patience. Kudos go to my trainer, Tim Embery, for getting my body ready to tackle a virtually impossible challenge. In Massachusetts, I would like to thank Michelle Ellicks, Steven Ziglar, Maurene Campbell, Tracy Bakalar, Arthur Ratsy, Steve Richards, George Roberson, Richard Woller, John Budris, Jon DeBlase, and Jim Prusko. The Vermont chapters owe much of their existence to the diligent work of Christy Warner. Praise also goes to Jamie Cope, Barbara Thompke, and Maya Golomb. In New Hampshire, many thanks to Ann Kennard, Dick Hamilton, Susan Logan, Liz Stearns, Rob Burbank, Len Reed, and Kevin Killourie. Maine's one-woman powerhouse is Nancy Marshall. I'd also like to thank John and B.B. Meader and Dr. Will and Suni Grossman for their suggestions. In Connecticut, Mike Beringer, Carolyn Waesche, Janet Serra, Marilyn Mulholland, Jackie La Bella, Nini Davis, and Susan Crowley all deserve credit. In Rhode Island, I'd like to mention Brenda Farrell and Becky Bovell. Finally, I would like to thank all the park rangers, outfitters, sporting goods store owners, friends, and anonymous outdoorspeople who helped me along the way.

What the Symbols Mean

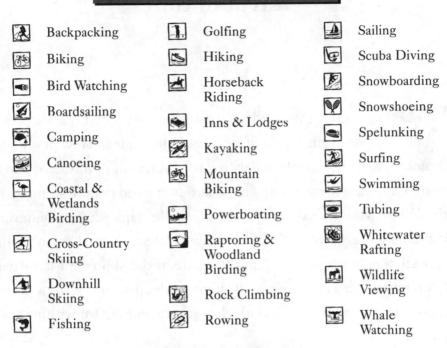

Backpacking		Golfing		Sailing
Biking		Hiking		Scuba Diving
Bird Watching		Horseback Riding		Snowboarding
Boardsailing		Inns & Lodges		Snowshoeing
Camping		Kayaking		Spelunking
Canoeing		Mountain Biking		Surfing
Coastal & Wetlands Birding		Powerboating		Swimming
Cross-Country Skiing		Raptoring & Woodland Birding		Tubing
Downhill Skiing		Rock Climbing		Whitewater Rafting
Fishing		Rowing		Wildlife Viewing
				Whale Watching

Map Legend

===35=== Interstate highway

===53=== Primary road

=27=A16= Secondary road

= =A25= = Unimproved road

===□=== Interchange

········ Specialized trail

········ Trail

+++++++ Railroad

– · – · – State boundary

– – – – – County boundary

────── Park/wilderness area boundary

◨◨◨◨ Metropolitan area

○ ○ City

↗ Beach

⤙ Dam

▲ Peak

■ Point of interest

▢ ♠ National/State/County park

▢ National/State forest

▢ Indian/military reservation

⤫ ✈ Airstrip/Airport

············· Ferry route

Introduction

FEEL LIKE PADDLING A CANOE ACROSS A WILD LAKE TO A lookout on a pair of nesting bald eagles? How about cycling the lonely, lovely roads of Vermont's Northeast Kingdom? Or hiking the windblown, lichen-encrusted granite summits of the White Mountains? Keep on reading. Perhaps you're wondering if there's a beach on the Cape Cod National Seashore that isn't wall-to-wall people when it's 96° in the shade, if the skiing at Mad River Glen's as tough as they say, or if there's a deep-woods walk within a half-hour of Boston. You'll find what you're looking for within these pages.

This is a book about New England's special places, and all the things you can do outside while visiting them. No longer will you have to purchase piles of books on every sport and every region in New England. No longer will you have to make numerous phone calls to find the one outfitter that's ideal for you. This book is all-encompassing, covering all of New England from Connecticut's Litchfield Hills to Maine's vast North Woods. It includes every sport imaginable: walking, biking, fishing, hiking, canoeing, skiing, and swimming—even hang gliding, spelunking, and tubing.

Most important, this guide is for everyone. There's an outing here for you whether you're an average Joe like me who simply yearns to play outdoors, a parent with small children, or a cyclist in training for the Tour de France.

I've cut right to the chase: I've chosen the very best footpaths and watercourses, roadways and backcountry ski trails. For the past year, I have talked to park rangers, outfitters, sporting goods store owners, high school and college coaches, sporting clubs, professional athletes, numerous family members, friends, and locals who have lived their entire lives in New England. I somehow managed, by the power of persuasion or by simply prying, to get these people to reveal their secret trails, fishing holes, and backcountry roads. A big surprise was the number of supposedly laconic New Englanders who were willing to share. No one but a local could possibly know some of the places that appear in print for the first time in this book.

The fun part for me, of course, was rambling my way through the region. With my treasured list of recommended activities, I hiked the trails, walked the beaches, biked the rolling roads, and mountain biked and cross-country skied on remote national forest trails. More than 60 percent of the routes I tried didn't make the cut—all were good exercise, but for one reason or another, I didn't feel that they were among New England's best. I vouch for every one of the featured trails in this book—to me, they are indeed the best New England has to offer. I have also tried to be as honest as possible so you can get a feel of what it's like to take each venture before you begin.

I sincerely hope this book will live in the glove compartment of your car, there to help you steal away from the cares and commotion of the everyday world into nature's quietude.

—Stephen Jermanok, December 14, 1995

The Basics

THIS BOOK IS DIVIDED INTO 11 GEOGRAPHICAL REGIONS, spanning New England from the northeast corner of the Maine Coast to the southwest corner of the Litchfield Hills. All of the regional chapters include an in-depth list of sports, categorized alphabetically from backpacking to whitewater rafting. Under each sports heading, I feature specific trails, routes, and waterways that I personally tried and proved to be the best in the Northeast. These featured activities are described in detail. Time required, level of difficulty, location, and availability of maps are all addressed. Of course, time and level of difficulty are relative terms, but I based these quotients on the average person who works out several times a week and is in relatively decent shape. Level of difficulty varies from sport to sport. For example, I labeled all walks and rambles as easy, but a hike designated as easy is inherently more strenuous than a walk, since hikes denote a climb uphill. An easy cross-country ski trail involves far more work than an easy flatwater canoe jaunt, etcetera, etcetera. I am assuming that you have tried the sport within the last year. If you have not been on a bicycle in the past 12 months, you'll find my easy routes attainable but challenging.

At the other extreme are the bikers, hikers, and skiers who work out religiously. I guarantee that the routes I have listed as strenuous will test your abilities and stamina.

However, I'm not worried about you. I'm worried about the guy who just inhaled a box of chocolate chip cookies, smoked a couple butts, and now wants to climb Mount Lafayette at four in the afternoon. Use common sense. If you haven't climbed a mountain since the Red Sox were in the World Series, don't start with Katahdin. If a mountain climb is listed as easy, it might challenge the casual hiker who has not climbed in a long time. If a mountain climb is listed as strenuous, you better believe that this trail is unrelenting, often grueling, and goes straight up the mountain at a steep pitch.

For sports such as boardsailing, golfing, and surfing, I've simply listed the top courses or beaches as recommended to me by golf pros, local outfitters or owners of sporting goods stores, college sporting clubs, chambers of commerce, other writers, and friends. Also discussed under the regional sport headings are outfitters, schools, and store rentals that cater specifically to that area and outdoor recreation. A complete alphabetical listing of outfitters and schools, as well as some helpful hints regarding options, can be found at the end of this chapter. Each regional chapter concludes with the top campsites, inns, and resorts that cater to sports enthusiasts.

This introductory section will help you plan your trip, whether it's on your own or with an outfitter. I have listed every sport found in the regional chapters, discussing in detail the equipment, logistics, and conditioning necessary to perform that particular activity. I've included the top destinations in New England for each sport. The latter half of this chapter contains information on locating the best maps, additional reading, and an overall list of outfitters and schools.

Getting Underway

BACKPACKING

This is the perfect sport with which to begin this section, since no other activity requires more preplanning than backpacking. You have to eat and sleep for days or weeks without the luxury of a refrigerator, oven, and bed. Obviously, the first items you need are good hiking boots and a backpack. Boots these days have uppers made of either water-resistant (Nubuck) leather or a combination of leather and lighter synthetic fabric; most good boots today have a waterproof Gore-Tex lining sewn into the boot. Basically, if you're going on a short weekend hike with a fairly light load, the synthetic boots are probably okay, but for anything else you'll want the heavy-duty support and rugged durability of the leather models. Wear new boots *before* heading out to the trails to prevent blistering. Preferably, you should also soak the boots and wear them till they dry to break in the leather.

As far as packs go, the debate over the merits of the old-fashioned external-frame pack and the more newfangled internal-frame pack has raged on for years. External-frame packs probably enjoy their greatest continuing popularity on the East Coast: they're generally a little cheaper; they're well-suited to carrying heavy loads on fairly straight-ahead trail like most of the Appalachian Trail, the chief long-distance backpacking route in the Northeast; and finally, experienced AT hikers pare down their loads to the point where they don't really need the carrying capacity of a big internal-frame pack.

But internal-frame packs have clearly outdistanced their rivals in most ways.

They're more stable over rough going—the rock-hopping and steep-and-twisty section of the AT, for example—because they distribute the weight more evenly across your hips and shoulders and cinch more snugly to your back. They let you carry greater loads and they're now easier to use, what with packs that have both top and front zippers, allowing you easy access to the whole sack. I myself prefer internal-frame packs, which can be formed to your back.

Whichever you choose, get a pack that really fits you—don't try to fit yourself to a pack. A good pack will have plenty of padding and support, a wide, firm hip belt, and a lumbar support pad.

Now comes the hard part—trying to pare down your load so you don't feel purely like a beast of burden on your hike. All the essentials are listed in the "Backcountry Equipment Checklist" below. Make sure you pack enough food for at least two more days than you intend to be out, but go for the lightest, dehydrated foods you can find. Take all food out of its bulky packaging and put it instead in resealable bags. Invest in ultralight, multipurpose outdoor clothing—and don't bring more than one change of socks, T-shirts, etc., because long-distance hiking is inevitably a business that brings people out of the woods in an incredibly fragrant, gamey condition. And don't bring Colin Fletcher's *Complete Walker* with you, or any other large, heavy book. Dispensing with these things will make the difference between a 30- and a 50-pound pack, which is the gap between comfort and misery.

Clothing, food, and matches should be kept in plastic bags, tubes, or waterproof stuff sacks so that they stay dry.

Being outside without a refrigerator and a house on your back is a serious impediment to gourmet cookery. Meals on the trail are a mixture of dried foods—rice, beans, lentils, pastas, dried meats, Wasa bread, plastic jars of peanut butter and jelly, cereal, dried fruits, trail mix (nuts, carobs, raisins, etc.), granola bars, salt and pepper, cookies, and pre-made meals such as Lipton's Cup-a-Soups or freeze-dried backpacker dinners. The last are kind of expensive, and I've seen more than a few thru-hikers scoff at them, but what the hey, they're featherweight, easy-to-prepare meals that generally taste like three-star fare next to Kraft Macaroni and Cheese. I buy them all the time.

One of the crucial survival duties of every backpacking trip is to make sure you are carrying enough water to last you a while, and to know exactly where your refills along the trail are going to come. Topo maps can help, and guidebooks to the Long Trail and Appalachian Trail will tell you where you'll find reliable springs. In addition to water, dried milk, tea, and hot chocolate are good to bring, and those new "coffee singles" (coffee bags shaped like tea bags) are, I think, the best bit of new technology for backpackers in a while, but I guess you have to hate instant coffee as much as I do. Depending on the amount of time you plan to spend away from civilization, you might need to send packages of food and fuel to friendly inns or post offices along the way.

In a *Boston Globe* article last summer, there was an article about an obese man who quit his job to lose weight by walking the Appalachian Trail. He was venturing from south to north and had lost 50 pounds by the time he reached the Massachusetts border. The moral of this story is that anyone can backpack (though you'll be a lot more comfortable if you're in shape). Indeed, I meet far more backpackers who start their long hikes out-of-shape than in-shape. If you

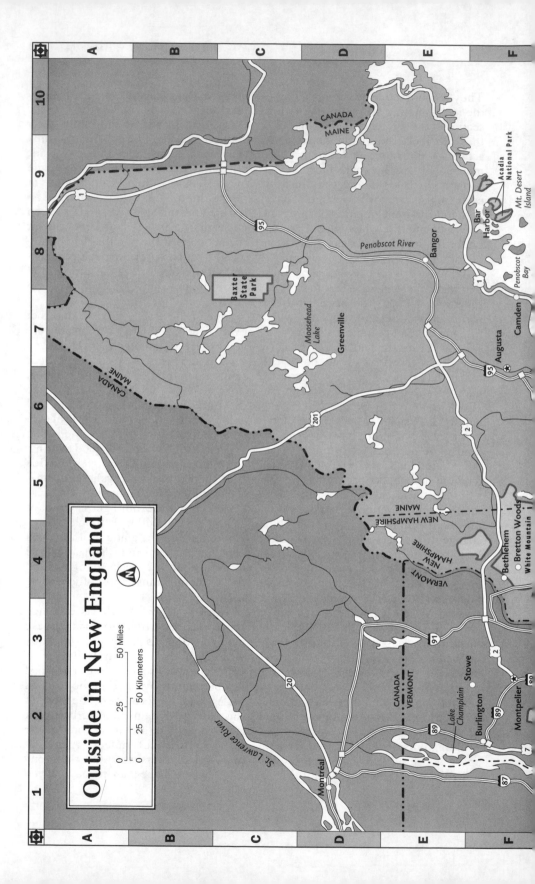

Outside in New England

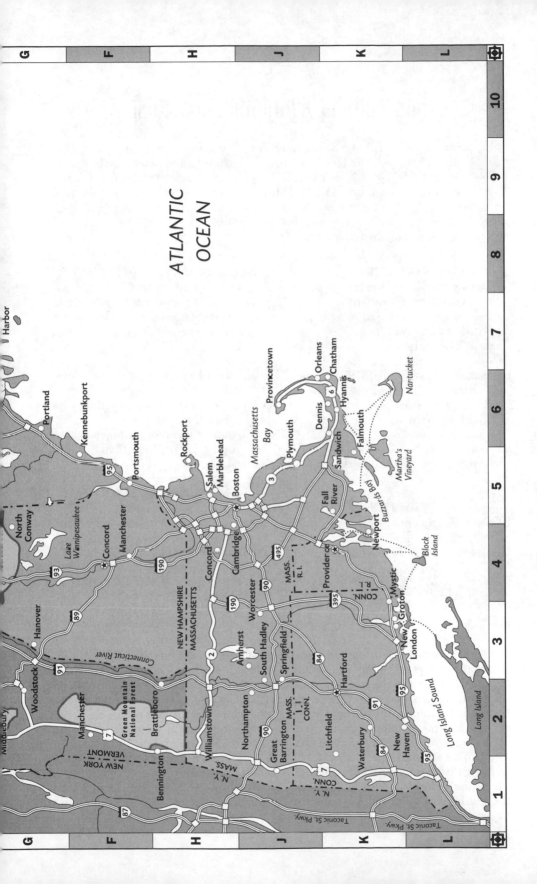

Backcountry Equipment Checklist

Below is a list of things you'll need for a backcountry trip of two or more days. This is more or less a backpackers' list, for a four- to seven-day summer or falltrip on a New England long-distance trail. But the list will also do for canoeing, backcountry skiing, whatever—there will be a few extra items of equipment you'll want for different kinds of trips, but no matter what you're planning, you'll kick yourself at some point if you don't have nearly all of this gear with you (a few things are obviously optional):

KITCHEN

- ☐ lightweight water filter (I suggest the SweetWater Guardian)
- ☐ 2–3 Nalgene quart-size water bottles
- ☐ 5-gallon camp waterbag
- ☐ stainless-steel cookset
- ☐ wooden spoon
- ☐ backpacking stove (like MSR Whisper-Lite)
- ☐ 1.5–2 quarts stove fuel
- ☐ kitchen matches
- ☐ biodegradable soap
- ☐ scouring pad
- ☐ washcloth/potholder/towel

- ☐ trail snacks, like gorp (trail mix), beef jerky, dried fruit, in Ziploc bags
- ☐ dinners—mac'n'cheese, freeze-dried dinners, cous-cous and Knorr gravy, other one-pot meals, in Ziploc bags
- ☐ spices/seasonings
  big chocolate bar (you'll thank yourself)
- ☐ Nalgene bottle o' booze (you'll thank yourself again)
- ☐ separate stuff sacks for lunch/snacks and breakfast/dinner foods

PANTRY

- ☐ coffee singles or tea bags, in Ziploc bag
- ☐ breakfast foods, like instant oatmeal, in Ziploc bag
- ☐ lunch items, such as PBJ, crackers, cheese, hard sausage

BEDROOM

- ☐ waterproof groundcloth
- ☐ tent (roomy 3-season, Moss or Sierra Designs)
- ☐ sleeping bag rated to 20°F
- ☐ cotton sleeping-bag liner
- ☐ sleeping pad (Therm-A-Rests are great)

can somehow make it through the first two to three days of hiking, you should be fine for the rest of the trip. The most important task is to prevent blistering by wearing comfortable shoes and heavy socks—and more important, to do at least a week of fairly heavy walking before you hit the trail.

Long distance backpackers will cherish Maine's **Hundred Mile Wilderness,** the last long reach of the AT—and the most remote section of the entire 2,135-mile trail—before it reaches Baxter State Park and Katahdin. This part of Maine is dense with fir and spruce forests. The hike takes 10 to 14 days to complete. For more information, contact the Maine Appalachian Trail Club, P.O. Box 283, Augusta, ME 04330 (e-mail: Mark Stoffan at mstoff41@maine.maine.edu).

Vermont's 265-mile **Long Trail** runs the length of the state from

CLOTHES CLOSET

- [ ] boots (Vasque Sundowners, Salomon 8's)
- [ ] 2 pairs heavy wool socks
- [ ] polypropylene sock liners
- [ ] polypropylene long johns
- [ ] 2 pairs baggy nylon shorts, w/ sewn-in briefs
- [ ] baseball cap, or other sun hat
- [ ] knit wool cap
- [ ] bandanna
- [ ] water/wind-resistant, breathable shell
- [ ] rain pants
- [ ] cotton/synthetic T-shirt
- [ ] pile pullover
- [ ] pile pants
- [ ] Tevas (camp shoes)
- [ ] clothes stuff sack

ALL-PURPOSE ESSENTIALS

- [ ] maps/compass
- [ ] GPS (global positioning system) device
- [ ] bug dope
- [ ] lighter
- [ ] whistle (for bear country, or rescue)
- [ ] sunglasses
- [ ] watch
- [ ] toothbrush, razor, other toilet gear
- [ ] camera gear
- [ ] binoculars
- [ ] Mini Mag flashlight, or like
- [ ] extra batteries
- [ ] battery-powered or candle lantern
- [ ] Swiss army knife

- [ ] 75–100-foot rope, for hanging food, etc.
- [ ] toilet paper
- [ ] toilet trowel
- [ ] extra quart Ziploc bags
- [ ] extra gallon Ziploc bags
- [ ] extra stuff sack
- [ ] a good book
- [ ] notebook/pen

FIRST-AID KIT

- [ ] 2" x 3" moleskin
- [ ] pair small shears
- [ ] thermometer
- [ ] safety pins
- [ ] acetaminophen/ibuprofen/aspirin
- [ ] diarrhea pills
- [ ] antacid tablets
- [ ] sunscreen
- [ ] sting relief pads
- [ ] iodine solution
- [ ] iodine ointment
- [ ] triple antibiotic ointment
- [ ] antiseptic towelettes
- [ ] single-edge razor blade
- [ ] 1" x 3" fabric bandages
- [ ] fabric knuckle bandages
- [ ] sterile wound closure strips
- [ ] 4" x 4" sterile gauze pads
- [ ] adhesive tape
- [ ] elastic bandage
- [ ] 5" x 9" combine dressings
- [ ] irrigation syringe
- [ ] wire mesh splint

Massachusetts to Canada, and it's wonderful from top to bottom. Any number of section hikes can be made, but the reaches of the trail north of Sherburne Pass (U.S. 4) are a little less crowded. If I had to make one recommendation for a long weekend's hike, I'd say haul yourself up to the northernmost section, from **Jay Peak to State Route 15,** near Johnson. It draws the fewest hikers, and has perhaps the greatest variety of really rugged terrain. Give yourself three to four weeks to walk the entire length of the trail, which is the oldest long-distance hiking trail in the nation. For additional information, contact the Green Mountain Club, P.O. Box 650, Waterbury Center, VT 05677 (tel. 802/244-7037).

For shorter trips, consider the AT in the **White Mountains** and the AT from **Mount Everett,** through the **Berkshires,** to the summit of **Mount Greylock.** The **Pemigewasset Wilderness** between the Franconia Range and Crawford Notch and the **Mahoosuc Range** on the Maine border offer excellent five-day backpacking opportunities in the Whites. Also in the Whites are the **"High Huts,"** eight mountain huts operated by the Appalachian Mountain Club. Strung along 56 miles of the Appalachian Trail, these rustic accommodations offer two hot meals a day and bunk beds. For more information, contact the AMC, 5 Joy Street, Boston, MA 02108 (tel. 617/ 523-0636).

BALLOONING

I haven't the slightest idea how to go up in your *own* hot-air balloon. If you plan on flying with one of the numerous outfitters across New England, all you'll need is a camera, sunglasses, and perhaps a sweater. **Bowland Balloons** in West Fairlee, Vermont, and **Balloon Rides** in Portland, Maine, are two of the better options.

BIRD WATCHING

With the Atlantic Coast to the east and a slew of National Forests and State Parks to the west, birding opportunities in New England are virtually unlimited. More than 300 species have been observed in New England in the past decade. Just during the last year, I have spied bald eagles, peregrine falcons, ospreys, every type of heron imaginable, piping plovers, warblers, snowy egrets, ibis, puffins, terns, rufous-sided towhees, American oystercatchers, razorbill auks, black guillemots, seven different sandpipers, and numerous other birds migrating along the coast from Connecticut to Machias Seal Island in Maine. Inland, I've seen wild turkeys, red-tailed hawks, eagles, owls,

hummingbirds, cackling loons, Canada geese, wood ducks, mallards, and goldfinches with breasts as yellow as the morning sun.

The most essential piece of equipment for any bird watcher is binoculars. It's worth spending the extra money to buy a really good high-power pair, with good close-focus, sharpness of image, and contrast. On the coast, wear a hat or you might get a nasty burn during your outing.

There are so many special places to view birds in New England that it's almost impossible to list them all. Due to the nature of bird watching, on any given day, one spot could be far better than the next. However, you will never go wrong with these six locales:

◆ **Machias Seal Island, Maine** If you can make it up to the northern reaches of the Maine coast, this is a site not to be missed. Walk on a small island shared by puffins, razorbill auks, and terns. Three boat charters will take you there.

◆ **Wellfleet Bay Wildlife Sanctuary, Wellfleet, Massachusetts** In an area of the Cape that's known for its abundance of migratory shorebirds, Wellfleet is a head above the rest. Not surprisingly, the sanctuary is run by the Massachusetts Audubon Society. Birds seem to be instinctively attracted to places run by the Audubon Society.

◆ **Monomoy Island, Massachusetts** Wellfleet Bay Wildlife Sanctuary and the Cape Cod Museum of Natural History arrange trips to this small island off Chatham in Cape Cod. Nestled between those nasty herring gulls are marsh hawks, oystercatchers, terns, and sandpipers. Groups of seals are often found playing offshore.

◆ **Parker River National Wildlife Refuge, Plum Island, Massachusetts** How kind of the Federal Government to shut down the beaches of Plum

Island in the early summer so we can go bird watching. The main reason behind the closing is to protect the piping plover, which can be seen nesting off the Atlantic shores in May and June.

◆ **Umbagog Lake, Errol, New Hampshire** You'll need a canoe to go birding here, but it's worth the extra effort. Loons, Canada geese, and herons line the waters; you eventually reach a dead oak tree where a pair of nesting bald eagles are the main attraction.

◆ **Acadia National Park, Bar Harbor, Maine** Come June, birders flock to the slopes of Champlain Mountain, where nesting peregrine falcons can be observed.

BOARDSAILING

Sailing and boardsailing go hand-in-hand. The same prevailing winds and countless bays that enchant sailors attract windsurfers. Coves on the Atlantic coast like Kalmus Beach on the Cape, Duxbury Bay on the Massachusetts South Shore, and Nantucket's Harbor are the places windsurfers congregate. But don't forget about the hundreds of bays on lakes and ponds that lie inland. Under each regional chapter, I have listed the leading boardsailing locales and places that rent sailboards.

CANOEING

Whether you like to put in to the quiet water of a backwoods pond, run a leisurely float-and-paddle down a flat and mild quickwater river, or take on whitewater rips, the long sinuous rivers, lakes, and hidden ponds that blanket the Northeast make it one of the premier canoeing destinations in the country. Tensions turn to tranquility on waters where loons replace the loonies of the city. There are hundreds of camping sites on the shores and islands, tucked between large evergreens.

BEFORE YOU GO

There's a host of options which lead to many questions:

1. **Should I buy or rent a canoe?** You really don't need to be an expert to answer this question. Purchasing a canoe will increase your canoeing options greatly. Some of the rivers and lakes I've written about are only accessible for people who own canoes. However, most of the waterways have rentals on the shores. If you live close to a river or lake and canoe often, you probably own a canoe already. Obviously, if you only paddle once or twice a summer, renting a canoe will suffice.

2. **What equipment will I need for a day trip? For overnight trips?** For a day trip, the necessary equipment includes a canoe, paddles, life jackets, sunscreen, sunglasses, bathing suit, and water. For overnight trips, you need the above-mentioned items plus all the equipment found in the backpacking section—backpack, tent, sleeping bag, food, stove, fuel, clothes, and so on. Since you're not walking, carrying all your belongings in the canoe is much easier. That is, unless you have to portage. Portaging means balancing the canoe on your shoulder as you walk on land between two bodies of water. Depending on the distance overland, a portage can be a two-second walk or a grueling two-mile journey. This should be taken into account on longer trips. Take a look at the handy backcountry checklist, above.

3. **Should I go with a guide or on my own?** Flatwater canoeists certainly don't need a guide for day trips. The advantage of having a guide or outfitter for longer flatwater canoe trips is that someone is there to assist you with your paddling, set up the tents, help cook the food, and provide you with an intriguing history of the area. It's also nice to share the experience with a large group. With some outfitters, like Vermont Waterways, you don't even have to camp overnight. Similar to many bike-tour operators, they'll bring you to the best day trips in the state and then drive you to a sumptuous inn that evening. Obviously, the major disadvantage with hiring a guide or signing up with an outfitter is the additional cost and the lack of privacy. With a little more work, you can have the water to yourself. On many of the longer jaunts like the Allagash River in Maine, you can hire someone to shuttle you and the canoe back to your car—some of them will even pick you up with a float plane.

Whitewater canoeists who are not completely confident in their skills should consider a guide for day and overnight trips. It's no fun tipping over and watching your canoe get loose and go down the river without you.

4. **Do I need instruction?** Instruction in flatwater canoeing can only help, but is not necessary. Mastering the strokes will help you to guide yourself in the proper direction without exerting more energy than is needed. For whitewater canoeing, lessons should be mandatory. Every year, inexperienced paddlers try their luck on the rapids only to find their canoes or bodies thrashed on the rocks. Don't be foolish. If you're not prepared, whitewater canoeing can be a dangerous sport. Two of the better places to learn are the L. L. Bean Paddling Schools in Freeport, Maine, and Maine Sport Outfitters in Rockport, Maine. (See "Schools" section below for more information.)

THE BEST DAY TRIPS

Here's my list of favorite one-day paddle trips in New England:

◆ **Chesuncook Lake, Northern Maine** An incredibly peaceful and scenic locale. Mount Katahdin looms in the background.

◆ **Umbagog Lake, Errol, New Hampshire** New Hampshire's premier canoeing jaunt is on rivers that lead to and from Umbagog Lake.

◆ **The Lamoille River, Northern Vermont** Weaving through Vermont's green pastures and farmland, the Lamoille is canoeable anywhere from Johnson to Lake Champlain.

◆ **Green River Reservoir, Northern Vermont** A little-known gem surrounded by uninhabited forest.

◆ **The Willimantic River, Eastern Connecticut** Located in the overlooked northeastern corner of the state, the 14½-mile stretch of the Willimantic River from Route 32 to Eagleville Dam is easy whitewater.

THE BEST OVERNIGHT TRIPS

Not surprisingly, all my favorite long-distance, backcountry paddle trips are in Northern Maine, where wildlife outnumbers people:

◆ **The Allagash Wilderness Waterway, Northern Maine** This serene 92-mile waterway, a collection of pristine rivers, lakes, and ponds, deserves its reputation as the finest canoe trip east of the Mississippi. The trip takes between 7 and 10 days to complete, and except for two series of rapids, it is all flatwater.

◆ **The St. John River, Northern Maine** Mostly Class II and III whitewater, the only time to cruise down these rapids is May to mid-June. The trip takes 7 to 10 days.

◆ **The St. Croix River, Northern Maine** Less tumultuous than the St. John, but still whitewater. The 3- to 6-day trip can be taken throughout summer.

◆ **Lobster to Caucomgomoc Lake, Northern Maine** This one- to two-week trip is ideal for families. The trip starts in Lobster Lake, snakes through the West Branch of the Penobscot to Chesuncook Lake, Black Pond, and Caucomgomoc Lake.

CROSS-COUNTRY SKIING

Cross-country skiing in New England is a very broad term. With new skis and new techniques, nordic skiers are no longer confined to the groomed trails of a ski touring center. In fact, the distinction between downhill and cross-country skiing gets hazier every year. The touring centers are still the most popular place for cross-country skiing, with the Trapp Family Lodge in Stowe, Vermont, Jackson Ski Touring Foundation in Jackson, New Hampshire, and Carrabassett Valley in Carrabassett Valley, Maine, leading the pack. Yet, even these premier ski touring centers are devoting more and more space each year to backcountry skiing.

What is backcountry skiing? That's a damn good question. I tend to think of backcountry skiing as any trail that's not groomed or track-set. This includes the carriage path trails at Acadia National Park, the thousands of miles of dirt roads and snowmobile trails that weave through upper New England, former downhill ski slopes like the Teardrop and Bruce Ski Trails built in the 1930s but no longer in use, hundreds of miles of hiking trails through the Green Mountain and White Mountain National Forests, and the renowned Tuckerman, the large cirque or bowl that sits on Mount Washington.

Within this wide web of trails that traverse mountains, skirt lakes, and overlook oceans, is one 280-mile long route that runs the length of Vermont. Called the **Catamount Trail,** it starts in southern Vermont at Readsboro and ends at North Troy on the Canadian border. In between lies some of the finest skiing in the east, from backcountry trails that are etched into Mount Mansfield to ski touring centers located in the Green Mountain National Forest, like Blueberry Hill and Mountain Top. The Catamount is almost 90 percent complete, with over 250 miles of the trail now in service.

Cross-country skiing, mountain biking, and rock climbing are the most demanding sports in this book. Some of the noted telemark trails involve climbing mountains on skis. Even level groomed trails at ski touring centers require that you are in relatively good shape. Many cross-country skiers work out on Nordic Traks or treadmills for weeks in advance. This is good conditioning, but I find the best exercise for cross-country skiing is simply to jog outside in winter. I'm facing the elements, getting acclimated to the cold weather, and unlike working out on the machines at the local health club, I'm propelling myself forward with my own power. To build up arm strength, simply do lightweight curls or push-ups.

If you haven't cross-country skied in a while, you're in for a big surprise. There are now a variety of skis to tackle the variety of terrain. First, there's the old touring ski, good for diagonal striding on groomed trails. Skating skis or racing skis are shorter and more narrow than the traditional track skis and are used with a speed-skating technique for quickness. Backcountry skis are wider than touring skis to aid maneuverability on ungroomed trails. You'll need to purchase telemark skis and learn the telemark technique if you want to try downhill backcountry runs like Tuckerman, the Teardrop Trail, or the Bolton-Trapp Trail from Bolton Ski Touring Center to Trapp Ski Touring Center. Telemarking is a gracefully lunging, turning technique that gives free-heelers something close to the kind of control on steep slopes that alpine skiers have. The telemark ski is like a backcountry ski, but has metal edges to grip hard surfaces and give you control and carving ability. They tend to be heavy and should only be used on difficult trails. Finally, there are *randonée* skies. This is for the telemarker who wants to ski down ungroomed and groomed alpine slopes. This ski bridges the gap between cross-country and downhill skiing.

Away from groomed trails, you should always carry water and food in a backpack. Serious skiers also wear climbing skins and, like a biker, bring a small tool kit to fix skis or bindings. If you think getting a flat is bad on a warm summer day, just wait till your skis snap atop a blustery mountain. Climbing skins are imperative for backcountry skiers who plan to climb mountains before skiing down them. They are strips of fabric that travel the length of the ski and stick to the snow to prevent sliding backwards. Tool kits include a screwdriver, screws, glue, hose clamps and aluminum flashing (to fix broken poles and skis), duct tape, and even an extra binding. Many tele-markers also wear knee pads, just in case you wipe out on a patch of ice or a rock.

Since cross-country skiing is a highly aerobic sport done in a cold climate, I want to discuss the importance of layering clothes. The simple problem with cold weather sports is that if you get too cold, you'll freeze, and if you get too warm, you'll sweat, dehydrate, and also freeze. Layering helps to alleviate this problem. I usually wear three layers of clothing. The first layer is a thin polypropylene or capilene thermal underwear that "wicks" sweat away from your body to the outer layer. The second layer is polar fleece, or pile, to keep you warm, and the final layer is a light Gore-Tex shell and pants, which both "breathe" moisture into the air and protect against harsh winds. Some of my friends also wear a long-sleeve shirt between the capilene and polar fleece jacket, but that's far too much warmth for me. I can't

overemphasize how important it is that you don't sweat profusely. It's much better to be cold when you start skiing and quickly warm up within the first five minutes of exercise than to be over-heated and perspire excessively. Hat, mittens, and a scarf are essential.

Frankly, I have no favorite cross-country ski trails. All the ones that I feature in this book were equally exhilarating. Depending on the amount of snow and skiers, the best trails vary day to day. Under each regional chapter, I have described my favorite backcountry trails and ski touring centers. With such a wide range of routes, the important thing is to stick to your level of competence. Don't attempt to ski Tuckerman or the Bruce Trail unless you know how to telemark or downhill ski.

DOGSLEDDING

Cruising in the Maine woods on a sled behind a line of dogs is the next best thing to entering the Iditarod. Two outfitters in Maine provide this unique thrill. Mahoosuc Guide Service in Newry, Maine, offers daily and overnight trips. T.A.D. Dog Sled Services in Stratton, Maine, offers half-hour trips. Dress warmly with boots, gloves, layered clothes, a hat, scarf, sunglasses, even goggles to protect your eyes from the snow the dogs kick up.

DOWNHILL SKIING/ SNOWBOARDING

New England has a long history of downhill skiing. It is the home of the first U.S. ski trail, first ski school, first tow rope, and first aerial tram (installed at Cannon Mountain, New Hampshire in 1938). From Tuckerman and Wildcat in New Hampshire to Mount Mansfield in Vermont, fearless outdoorsmen would brace themselves for their quick descent on two pieces of wood. They were even foolhardy enough to compete in races. Detachable quad chairlifts and high-speed gondolas whisk people to the top in record times. From there, you have an incredible number of expanding options, from easy trails that wind slowly down the mountain to heart-thumping double diamonds that will have you hurtling down moguls at an electrifying pace. With increased technology, there are more and more trails each year, faster lifts, and better snowmaking.

Conditioning, equipment, and clothing for downhill skiing and snowboarding are far less complex than for cross-country skiing. Learning the skills and practicing is more of an asset than a well-tuned body. Of course, the better shape you're in, the less you risk injury. But I've been on lifts with people who make Pavarotti look like a toothpick but who ski far better than I ever will. They know their techniques and they have time to hone their skills. Schooling is a very important element of this sport. You should always consider signing up for a lesson or two.

Skis range from high performance to the much wider specialty performance skis. High performance skis are used by racers or other adroit skiers, specialty performance skis help you to improve your turns quickly. There are also a variety of snowboards, from the short and wide freestyle, used for trick riding, to the long and narrow freeride, used in deep powder for cruising. Try the different skis and snowboards at a rental shop before you buy.

The Gore-Tex, slimtech, and fleece jackets and ski pants are a lot warmer and more weather-resistant than they used to be. I usually just wear a turtleneck, thermal bottoms, jacket, ski pants, gloves, hat, and scarf. Unlike during cross-country skiing, the only time you really sweat is when you're peering over that double-diamond run, egged on by your buddies

to follow them. Snowboarders tend to wear looser-fitting pullovers and shells for greater freedom of movement.

Skiers are so fond of their particular ski resorts that I'm inevitably going to cause a debate with my Top 10 List, but here goes:

1. Stowe
2. Sugarbush
3. Killington
4. Sunday River
5. Sugarloaf
6. Pico
7. Jay
8. Loon
9. Mount Snow/Haystack
10. Saddleback

My top three choices for snowboarding are Stratton, Stowe, and Killington, in that order.

FISHING

From the trout and landlocked salmon caught in the Battenkill, Penobscot, and Kennebec Rivers, to the stripers, blues, cod, and tuna found in the Atlantic, you have to try hard not to hook anything in the waters of New England. Almost any body of water you venture to, whether it be a pond, river, lake, or ocean, you'll find an assortment of fish. There are so many places to fish and so many different techniques, from fly-fishing to surfcasting to deep sea fishing, that it would be absurd to list my favorites. What I have done in each region is jot down the places where the locals fish. They're not going to be happy with me, but I have exposed their coveted fishing holes—the rivers where fly-fishing anglers are knee-deep in water, the rips in the coastline where ocean stripers and blues swim to saltwater ponds and other estuaries, the small ponds that can only be found if you've lived nearby for years.

Before you break out your pole, make sure you have a fishing permit. Contact the respective Department of Fish and Wildlife, listed under each region. Many of these offices also publish guides offering various techniques to catching the big one. If you don't know the area, it's always worthwhile to go with a guide who can show you around and explain which flys, hooks, and lines to use. Instruction is also beneficial, and almost mandatory when it comes to fly-fishing. Orvis in Arlington, Vermont, and L.L. Bean in Freeport, Maine, are two of the better fishing schools. Most importantly, fishing is fun for everybody, not just the *Field & Stream* subscriber who has been out casting for the past forty years. During the preparation of this book, my brother and I went fishing for the first time in years. We hired a talented guide in Martha's Vineyard named Coop Gilkes, and lo and behold, we both caught stripers within an hour. It was one of the numerous highlights of researching this guide.

GOLF

If I had a decade to write this book, I couldn't try all the courses in New England. What I have done instead is asked golf pros in the region what their favorite courses are—excluding the one at which they're employed. If pros in the region kept naming the same course, I included it in this book. The rest just don't make the grade.

New England golfing varies with the landscape, from ocean courses on the Cape to the more mountainous courses inland. The best courses, like Samoset in Rockport, Maine, Ocean Edge in Brewster, Massachusetts, and Woodstock in Woodstock, Vermont, take full advantage of their scenery.

HANG GLIDING

Morningside Flight Park in western New Hampshire is the most respected place to learn how to hang glide in the northeast. The 250-foot hill gently slopes down to a landing area.

HIKING

I've devoted more space to hiking than any other sport in this book. That's because mountains and hills dominate the landscape of New England. The ridge of mountains starts to rise in the Litchfield Hills, heading north to the Berkshires and Green Mountains, and then east to the White Mountains, Mount Katahdin in Maine, and the highest mountain on the Atlantic shoreline north of Brazil, Cadillac Mountain in Acadia National Park. The network of trails is extensive and impressive. Footpaths climb up the verdant mountains of Vermont, slip through the granite notches of the Whites, meander high above the Rangeley Lakes, venture straight up Katahdin's most precipitous point, the Knife Edge, and keep running till the land runs out on the shores of the Atlantic. Paths are both narrow and wide, soft and springy, rock-littered, leaf-littered, and root-studded. They cross rivers, skirt lakes, find hidden ponds, and overlook the wide blue ocean.

Since the day I climbed Greylock as a kid, I've been attacking these hills and I haven't been bored yet. Even if I've hiked a trail a number of times, I still find something new—a new tree, a better view. I'm not the first hiker to be enthralled. These trails have enticed visitors since hikers were called rusticators, trampers, and trekkers. Even in the 1850s, Thoreau was a second- or third-generation hiker. People have been inscribing their names on the rocks of Mount Monadnock, the most climbed mountain in the world, since 1801.

Climbing any mountain, regardless of height, will make you sweat. However, almost anyone in reasonably fit condition will enjoy the hikes listed as easy in the regional chapters. Even some of the moderate peaks are attainable. You shouldn't try any of the strenuous climbs unless you have climbed at least two moderate mountains or have been working out on a regular basis. I don't care if you were born in the Swiss Alps, climbing Katahdin will make your legs weary.

Most injuries like sprained ankles or sprained knees occur on the hike down, not up. Your legs are already tired from the ascent, and it's easy to slip when you're moving much faster. Take it slowly, and if you have weak ankles or knees like me, bring an ace bandage for extra protection against the pounding. This next suggestion might seem obvious, but don't make the descent first. At the Stony Ledge Trailhead on Mount Greylock, I met a guy who parked his car at Greylock's summit and walked all the way down to the bottom of the mountain. Smoking a cigarette, he asked me how to get back up. What did he think, there was an elevator around the next tree?

In your day pack, always bring at least one 32 ounce bottle of water with you. For strenuous hikes, you'll need two. Also bring nuts, raisins, or trail mix for a quick boost of energy. For longer hikes, there's no better place to have lunch than the top of a mountain. Often, I will bring an extra T-shirt, so I'll have something dry to wear on the way down, and a light Gore-Tex jacket to keep me warm on those windy summits.

More than one-third of the hikes I went on did not make it into this book. They were decent and even challenging, offering views of the surrounding terrain, but for one reason or another were not the best. If I had to write a book called *100 Hikes in New England*, I would be forced to include them and, thus, you wouldn't have any idea which trails are

truly the finest. Out of the hikes that did make it into the book, these are the crème de la crème:

♦ **Mount Katahdin via the Helon Taylor, Knife Edge, Saddle and Chimney Pond Trails** Climbing to Katahdin's 5,267-foot peak is a rite of passage for New England hikers. The Knife Edge is the most thrilling and terrifying hiking trail in the Northeast. Both sides of the narrow path drop dramatically down to the valley floor.

♦ **Falling Waters Trail/Franconia Ridge/Old Bridle Path** This White Mountain trail has it all, from a path along a series of waterfalls to a 1.7-mile ridge walk between 5,108-foot Mount Lincoln and 5,249-foot Mount Lafayette.

♦ **Camel's Hump via the Forestry, Dean, and Long Trails** Foot traffic might be heavy on this 7.2-mile (round-trip) trail, but deservedly so. Walk through the forest and then onto the Long Trail for an exhilarating hike up to the slab of rock known as Camel's Hump.

♦ **Acadia Mountain** While the crowds congregate atop Cadillac Mountain in Acadia National Park, I take the short trail up Acadia Mountain. Situated on Mount Desert Island's western side, the summit has staggering vistas of Somes Sound, the only fjord on the Eastern seaboard.

♦ **Mount Pisgah** One of Vermont's more grueling hikes, the trail climbs swiftly above Lake Willoughby. The reward is Pulpit Rock, a small rocky platform that juts out of Pisgah's plummeting cliffs.

♦ **Zealand Trail** More a walk than a hike, this rambling trail through dense forests of maples, beeches, and birches is ideal for young children. The only climb is up to the AMC's Zealand Hut, where you can have a glass of lemonade and take in the views of the Pemigewasset Wilderness.

◆ **The Appalachian Trail to Mount Greylock** (one-way) This seven-mile trail weaves through the forest on the AT to the peak of Greylock. Very few hikers except the AT through-hikers take this ascent to Greylock.

◆ **Mount Hunger** More often than not, you can have this trail and the summit to yourself. Views of Camel's Hump, Mount Mansfield, and much of the Green Mountain National Forest can be seen from the rocky peak.

◆ **Maiden Cliff** Situated in Camden Hills State Park, the trail climbs through dark forest and open ledges, rewarding the hiker with views of Maine's Penobscot Bay and the town of Camden.

◆ **Welch/Dickey Mountain Trail** A worthy introduction to the granite trails and summits of the White Mountains, this three- to four-hour hike climbs two peaks before looping back to the parking lot.

Honorable Mention: Roaring Brook/ Stony Ledge Loop—Both the Stony Ledge and Roaring Brook Trails lead to Stony Ledge, a group of rocky cliffs that offer majestic views of Mount Greylock's summit and the V-shaped wedge of trees that blankets the valley between the peaks known as The Hopper.

HORSEBACK RIDING

You don't have to venture to the Wild West to go on an overnight riding trip. Kedron Valley Stables in South Woodstock, Vermont, and Vermont Icelandic Horse Farm in Waitsfield, Vermont, offer four- to six-day inn-to-inn trips in the Green Mountain National Forest. You ride four to six hours a day covering an average of 10 to 20 miles, and while the horses rest you can take in the surroundings on foot. Both these trips are for experienced riders only. Contrary to the image presented by the movie *City Slickers*, horseback riding is not a sport where you ride for four days straight, unless you have some idea of what it's like to sit in a saddle. Otherwise, your visions of *High Noon* might turn into great doom, and you could be walking bowlegged for the next month.

Hundreds of stables around New England offer lessons and guided trail rides. The various sites include the shores of Block Island, the steep trails of the White Mountains, and the 200-year-old villages of northeastern Connecticut.

ICE CLIMBING

Ice climbing is not one of those activities where you suddenly scream to your significant other in the car, "Honey, there's an icicle hanging from that mountain over there. Let's do it." No, winter mountaineering is taken very seriously in these parts. The sport involves ascending steep slopes covered with snow and ice, frozen waterfalls, and frosted-over gorges. Intensive instruction is an absolute must. You have to learn how to use an ice axe, wear crampons, and handle the many ice formations. Even with these skills, ice climbing can be a dangerous sport. It seems like each year someone dies at Mount Washington's Huntington Gorge, the top ice-climbing destination in the East. Many of these climbers had the necessary skills, but sometimes even experience is not enough to handle winter's unpredictable weather.

Learn the sport from an expert, **Rick Wilcox,** co-owner of International Mountain Climbing School in North Conway, New Hampshire (see "Schools," below). Head of the White Mountains' Search & Rescue Team, Wilcox is a survivor of Everest.

ICE FISHING

Along with mountain biking, sea kayaking, and backcountry skiing, ice fishing is one of the fastest-growing sports in the region. Anglers are realizing that many of the larger fish are caught during this time of the year. And, with the advent of synthetic winter clothing, you no longer have to wear wool plaids and freeze. Simply drill a hole and drop a line. Many of the larger bodies of water require snowmobiles for access. Contact the respective state's Department of Wildlife for fishing permits.

LLAMA TREKKING

All right, so you can't ride it like a horse, but at least the furry guy helps carry camping equipment and food, allowing you to hike or walk longer distances. You get to pet him, too (when they're not in a testy mood). Each llama can carry up to 100 pounds on a full-day trck, and their padded hooves have no impact on the trails. Look under the Northern and Southern Vermont regional chapters for more information.

MOUNTAIN BIKING

Time and time again, in the regional chapters, I emphasize the exhilarating feeling of freedom this sport gives. I hate to be redundant, but the ability to zip down a narrow mountain trail across a shallow stream, to cruise along the banks of a river on a former railroad bed, or to ride on a dirt road through the farmland of Vermont is a thrill rarely surpassed by any other sport. On most of the trails mentioned, I hardly ever came across another human, let alone another biker. More importantly, I never carried a map and I almost always got lost. This might sound foolish to some of you, but not knowing where you are in a New England forest is like backpacking from village to village in Europe with no destination in mind: You create your own exciting path and your own destiny on most of these rides. That's why I love New England mountain biking. Unlike the West, with its 14,000 foot peaks and vast wide-open spaces, New England's parks and forests are compact and far more gentle. If I take a wrong turn I don't risk death, nor do I spend the night howling with coyotes. Even within the larger national forests, I'm never more than 2 to 3 miles from a dirt road and civilization.

With this in mind, most of the rides featured in the regional chapters have no specific routes. I have led you to the water, now drink! Ironic as it might seem, with regard to mountain biking, this guide book is not going to guide you at all. The worst thing I can do is give you directions. I don't want you to be clutching a map, looking at a network of single-track spiraling in every direction, and saying, "I think this is the way. No, maybe it's this one. . . . Or this one." Weave you own web and you'll soon find your own favorite trails to try again and again.

Single-track, double-track, and dirt roads dominate the mountain biker's terrain. Dirt roads can range from hard-packed gravel logging roads in Maine to the sandy fire roads of Martha's Vineyard State Park. Double-tracks vary in width from snowmobile tracks to former railroad beds to old carriage paths. They are ideal trails for the beginner to intermediate biker. All experienced bikers are in search of the elusive single-track trail. These narrow trails, created by hikers or motorcross bikers, whisk you in and out of the forest, within arm's length of trees and bushes on both sides. So-called "technical" single-track trails are the most challenging. They wind up and down the hills, over rocks, roots, and soft mud that often feels like quicksand. On these trails, it is not uncommon to get off your bike and walk around an obstacle.

Conditioning is of the utmost importance for this sport. A 5- to 10-mile jaunt on a single-track trail is far more exhausting than the same distance on a paved road. The trail becomes even more grueling if it's too advanced for your level and you have to get on and off your bike numerous times. The best way to get in shape for mountain biking is to mountain bike. Start with easy trails around your neighborhood and work your way up. If there are no forests or parks nearby, then opt for a road biking route that takes you up and down hills. Any of the easy dirt roads described in the regional chapters can be tried without much advanced preparation.

Bring lots of water. I can't stress this enough. This is such a strenuous sport that even the short trips require two to three bottles. A spare tube and patch kit, a tire lever, an air pump, a chain rivet tool, a spoke wrench, allen wrenches, a six-inch adjustable wrench, and a small screwdriver are essential to fix flats, broken spokes or chains, and other problems that might arise in the woods. A small first aid kit is also advisable. You can fit this all into a backpack or fanny pack. As for the main piece of equipment, the bike, I simply bought a Trek 950 two years ago and I've been riding it ever since. I added hand grips on the sides of the handlebars to help climb hills and snap-in pedals so that my biking shoes are locked in. This prevents my feet from slipping off the pedals. Most of my friends have Rockshox which help absorb the constant pounding of the bike when you're on technical single-tracks. Since I switch from fat knobby tires to thin slick tires when I go road biking, I don't want to put many

more mountain biking features on my Trek. But believe me, I've felt the need for these biking shock absorbers numerous times.

On a final note, I've mountain biked with people of all ages, from 7 to 70. The preconception that this sport is for crazed kids who like to catch air off mountainous cliffs only applies to a few bikers and stunt men who do Nike and Dr. Pepper commercials. For the rest of us, the only difference between road biking and mountain biking are the tires and the terrain. My favorite trails cater to all levels:

◆ **Ridgepole Trail, New Hampshire** An incredibly strenuous, yet thrilling trail, the Ridgepole climbs high into the Sandwich Mountain range, with views overlooking Squam Lake. The downhill on steep single-tracks will shake you like an earthquake on the San Andreas Fault.

◆ **Bartlett Experimental Forest, New Hampshire** Situated in the heart of the White Mountains, snowmobilers have created a vast network of trails that suit bikers well. The paths cruise up and down mountains across numerous brooks.

◆ **Carriage Path Trails, Acadia National Park** Off limits to motorized vehicles, these wide, hard-packed trails lead bikers to some of the most secluded parts of Acadia National Park. The 43-mile network of trails are ideal for inexperienced mountain bikers.

◆ **Waitsfield, Vermont** One of the three areas in southern Vermont that will entice bikers. The hills north of Rolston Road are laced with trails, but also ask locals about "The Clinic."

◆ **Pachaug State Forest** Located in the eastern part of the state, Pachaug is Connecticut's largest public space. The 23,000-acre state forest plays host to an incredible amount of single- and double-track trails.

◆ **Maple Ridge Sheep Farm, Randolph, Vermont** In an area known for it's road and off-road biking, the 9.8-mile Maple Ridge Trail is arguably the best.

◆ **Arcadia Management Area, Rhode Island** Situated on the western part of the state, the 13,817-acre Arcadia attracts bikers from as far as Boston and New Haven. Over 30 miles of single-tracks, double-tracks, and dirt roads snake through the forest.

◆ **Savoy Mountain State Forest, Massachusetts** In an area of western Massachusetts known for its abundance of state forest, Savoy offers the most extensive network of trails for bikers in the Berkshires. The trails wind through the dense forests to short summits.

◆ **Craftsbury Common, Vermont** This 11-mile dirt road featured in the Northern Vermont chapter is a fine introduction to the area's rolling green meadows and dairy farms. It's also a good warm-up for the single- and double-track trails found at Craftsbury Center.

◆ **Mount Snow, Vermont** The first ski resort to devote itself to mountain biking, Mount Snow now offers more than 140 miles of riding. This is a great place to take courses and train before venturing into the wild woods.

Honorable Mention: Maudslay State Park, Newburyport, Massachusetts—This small park on the banks of the Merrimack River only has a limited amount of trails, but they're all fun. Just be cautious of the hikers.

POWERBOATING

Listings for motorboat and jet ski rentals can be found under each regional chapter.

ROAD BIKING

New England's diversity of terrain, history, and compact size have all helped to create one of the top road biking destinations in the country. Perhaps most significant, the landscape is manageable. The media loves to harp about the spectacular beauty of the Rockies and the West—and there's no denying that. However, most people do not have the leg strength to bike through the mountainous passes of Colorado. Even the most treacherous gaps in the White Mountains are no more than a 2,000-foot climb, and those will challenge the best and fittest bikers. Go East, young man and woman, and you'll find thousands of miles of road that form hundreds of loops ranging from 10 to 110 miles long. And, contrary to what you might be thinking, car traffic is not a problem. Most of the congested roads are found around urban centers, not in the rural countryside.

The main attraction of New England biking is its stunning scenery—the white steeples that dot the rolling green hills and farmland of Vermont, the sweeping mounds of sand that form Cape Cod, the rocky and rugged coast of Maine, the towering granite of New Hampshire's White Mountains, and the Atlantic islands with their moors, bogs, and beaches.

The routes in this book are geared toward every type of biker imaginable. Whether you bike more than 100 miles a week or haven't been on two wheels in two years, whether you want a serious workout or want to go sightseeing at a slow pace, there are rides in each region at your level of biking. I have also taken into account your interests, from enjoying the stunning scenery to learning the local lore and history, to finding a good place to picnic or have lunch. Architecture, geology, wildlife, and art history are a few of the subjects I've touched on to make each ride as intriguing as possible. Thus, if you are expecting to see only terse directions like "turn right at 15.2 miles, veer left at 18.6 miles, etc. . . ," you're in for a surprise. The necessary directions and remarks about terrain have been sprinkled with anecdotes and history that I hope will enrich each ride. I discuss only day trips. However, in many regions, like Vermont, you can simply connect the day loops to ride around the state.

After your bike, water is the most important necessity. I always bring 32 to 64 ounces with me, and usually end up stopping at a store to buy more. Drink often, especially when riding under a hot sun, because it's difficult to realize how dehydrated your body really is. My backpack or fanny pack also holds trail mix or raisins for a quick energy boost, a spare tube and patch kit, a tire lever, an air pump, a chain rivet tool, a spoke wrench, allen wrenches, a six-inch adjustable end wrench, and a small screwdriver. If you think that a basic bicycle repair kit is only essential for mountain biking, you're wrong. I've had flats in the middle of cow country, where the nearest town is 10 to 20 miles away. You don't want to walk that far. On overnight camping trips, you'll need to purchase front and back panniers (packs). Believe it or not, you can fit all your belongings in these packs. Look under "Backpacking" for the list of essential gear needed for overnight jaunts.

For years, I wore loose fitting T-shirts and shorts on all my rides, vowing never to wear brightly colored spandex. Then one day, after a particularly treacherous mountain bike ride, I walked into a bike shop and bought a pair of fluorescent blue shorts. I will never wear loose-fitting shorts on a bike again. Spandex is far more supportive and my voice is now back to its normal tenor range.

The problem with bike riding is that it's too easy a sport to learn. Most people have been biking since the age of five or younger, and think they can hop on a bike and ride 40 miles on any given day. Some of you who haven't pedaled in years will attempt to ride my moderate to strenuous loops, and you might succeed. But I guarantee you won't be happy the next couple days or during the latter part of the ride. If you are not in condition prior to a five-day bike tour, most of your riding will be in the support van (I'll talk about conditioning for guided overnight trips in detail under "Outfitters"). As with all sports, start slow! Prior to going on a long bike trip, I'll ride around Central Park's 6-mile loop, gradually building my stamina to ride twice and three times around the park. If you live in New England, start with an easy bike ride and slowly work your way up to moderate and strenuous trails.

This is just a small sampling of routes featured in the regional chapters. There are many more rides where these came from:

◆ **Gay Head Ride, Martha's Vineyard** The longer, more challenging ride on the Vineyard is this 40-mile round-trip route to Gay Head Cliffs. The loop takes you through the towns of West Tisbury, Chilmark, and Menemsha before returning to Vineyard Haven.

◆ **Islesboro, Maine** A 28-mile bike ride on one of Penobscot Bay's most picturesque islands.

◆ **Randolph, Vermont** Vermont's highly touted green meadows, corn pastures, and farms are nestled in the foothills of the Green Mountains on this 36.5-mile loop. The ride is best taken during fall foliage season when the trees are ablaze in color.

◆ **Lincoln/Concord/Carlisle Loop, Massachusetts** Northwest of Boston, this 26-mile ride was designed with history buffs in mind. Stops include the Minute Man National Historical Park, the Old Manse, Walden Pond, the DeCordova Museum, and the Gropius House.

◆ **Jeffersonville Loop, Jeffersonville, Vermont** You'll need to change your slicks to hybrids to ride over several dirt roads on this short loop. The views of Mount Mansfield and Madonna Peak are well worth it.

◆ **Province Lands, Provincetown, Massachusetts** My favorite bike trail on the Cape is not the 25-mile Rail Trail, but this 8-mile rollercoaster bike path that rolls up and down the dunes of P'town.

◆ **Connecticut River, Essex, Connecticut** A 22-mile ride along the lower Connecticut River that takes you past Victorian mansions to the Goodspeed Opera House and the Gillette Castle. You cross the river on a quick ferry to return to Essex.

◆ **Block Island, Rhode Island** More a tour of the island than a strenuous workout, this 13-mile loop self-guides you through Old Harbor to two lighthouses, cliffs, moors, secluded walks, and long stretches of beach.

◆ **Nantucket, Massachusetts** The only way you should travel on Nantucket is by bike. Start on the cobblestone streets of Nantucket town, taking the 6-mile Milestone bike path to the rose-trellised cottages of 'Sconset.

◆ **Lake Champlain, Vermont** A 27-mile ride that takes you along the southern shores of this long lake. Ride south from Vergennes past Basin Harbor and Arnold's Bay for views of the Adirondacks on the far shores and the Green Mountains to the east.

Honorable mention: East Island Route, Martha's Vineyard—This 20-mile ride takes you to the eastern end of the Vineyard through the towns of Oak Bluffs and Edgartown before reaching the nature preserves on Chappaquiddick Island. Part of the route is a bike path along Joseph Sylvia State Beach.

ROCK CLIMBING

Depending on the region, rock climbing can be just as accessible as mountain climbing. This is certainly the case in the White Mountains of New Hampshire, where faces of rock line the major roads. Numerous rock climbing sites like Cathedral Ledge, Whitehorse Ledge, and Cannon Cliffs exist within the twisted and carved granite that shape these mountains. The Berkshires and the Green Mountains also have several faces of rock to latch onto like Spiderman.

A good rock climbing school will help you spot the hand and footholds in the rock face that, at first glance, may appear too smooth. They will also teach you how to use your ropes and pulley to rappel down safely. The International Mountain Equipment Climbing School in North Conway, New Hampshire, is the largest and one of the most respected rock climbing school in the eastern United States. For private lessons, contact Stephen Lewanick, owner of Ascents of Adventure. When we last spoke, Stephen had just returned from Africa where he guided a group of blind climbers up to the peak of Africa's highest mountain, Kilimanjaro (phone numbers and addresses can be found under the Schools section and in the regional chapters).

SAILING

Home to the America's Cup for more than 50 years, Newport and the rest of the northeastern Atlantic coast deserve their reputation as one of the leading cruising grounds in the world. Almost every day in summer, you'll see numerous rounded sails tacking in and out of legendary bays like Narragansett in Rhode Island and Penobscot off the mid-Maine coast. With reliable winds, there's hardly ever a luff. With hundreds of island anchorages, there are more than enough harbors in which to spend the day or evening. And let's not forget about the large lakes that lie inland. Champlain, Winnipesaukee, Moosehead, Squam, and many smaller bodies of water are just as popular with sailors.

Within each region, I have pointed out remote and picturesque anchorages like Potter's Cove at the north end of Prudence Island in Narragansett Bay, Isle au Haut in Maine's Penobscot Bay, and Tarpaulin Cove on the south side of Naushon Island, one of the Elizabeth Islands off Cape Cod. I have listed the top sailing schools, such as J World in Newport and Bay Island Sailing School in Rockland, Maine. I have also mentioned the top places to bareboat charter like Hinckley Yacht Charters in Bass Harbor, Maine, and Winds of Ireland in Burlington, Vermont. "Bareboat" chartering means renting a large sailboat for day or overnight trips. You play the role of captain, in charge of navigation, provisions, and the safety of the boat. Schooling and prior sailing experience are necessary to bareboat charter, especially on the coast where fog, currents, wide tidal differences, and a merciless shoreline can wreak havoc on the most accomplished sailor and his craft. Less-experienced sailors should consider renting Lasers, Rhodes, or Sunfishes at the rental places listed in the regional chapters.

SCUBA DIVING

This is another sport where schooling is not only suggested, it's mandatory. You must be certified by the National Association of Underwater Instructors (NAUI) or Professional Association of Dive Instructors (PADI) to scuba dive. Once you have your certification or C-card, you can dive with any resort or outfitter in the world. However, some diving operators offer a one-day resort course. I'm not sure how the sport's governing bodies justify this approach, but I don't recommend it. The dive is supposed to take place in a shallow pool to give non-divers a feel of what it's like to breath with a self-contained underwater breathing apparatus (SCUBA) or air tank, but that's not always the case. My brother once took a so-called resort dive in Bali. Within five minutes of instruction, he was diving at a depth of 60 feet with me and the other certified divers, swallowing water between large gasps of air. If you want to dive, get your certification.

Scuba diving is one of the most meditative and mesmerizing sports around. Once you get over your initial fear of breathing from an air tank and having to regulate your ears to the depth, you can relax and take in the wondrous surroundings. Coral of every fluorescent color imaginable play host to a dazzling array of sea life. Tropical fish look you in the eye, manta rays glide above your air bubbles, innocuous sharks thrill you as they swim by. This is what diving is like in the warm waters of the Caribbean and South Seas. New England diving pales in comparison. It has its share of sea life, from harbor seals to porpoises to starfish, but visibility and water temperatures are dramatically reduced. The best feature of New England diving is the 18th- and 19th-century shipwrecks that rest on the lake or ocean floor. In Lake Champlain, divers are still finding boats that were used in the Revolutionary War and the War of 1812.

Dive in New England to sharpen your skills between trips to the

Caymans, Turks & Caicos, or Fiji. I would not go out of my way to take a diving trip here, nor would I register for a course. Start your diving career off on the right foot with an intensive four-day course in the Florida Keys and Caribbean. Once you've whet your appetite for more, try the cold waters of New England.

SEA KAYAKING

I had never attempted this sport before researching this book, but that's in the past now. All it took was one guided trip on Frenchman Bay off the mid-Maine coast and I was hooked. Paddling on the surface of the water, I was eye to eye with seals, porpoises, and chubby birds called black guillemots. Kayaking around the islands of the bay, the mountains of Acadia National Park hovered above the shoreline. It was an incredible experience, one that made me wonder why I had waited so long. In fact, after that fateful day, wherever I traveled along the coast, I would always ask, "You wouldn't happen to know where I could rent a sea kayak?"

Don't make the same mistake I did and overlook the chance to glide over the ocean waters with the sea's myriad creatures. It's far less dangerous than you would imagine. Many of the guided trips are in bays or ocean tributaries where the surf is low or nonexistent. Even when you venture out to the open ocean, the water is usually calm once you break the crest of the waves. However, lessons are still imperative if you plan on renting a kayak on your own. You need to learn proper paddling technique and how to self-rescue. Sea kayaking is surging in popularity, but every year someone tarnishes the image of this sport by being reckless. An owner of a kayak rental operation on the Cape told me about one incident several summers back, when an arrogant man demanded to rent a kayak without the proper training. The owner mistakenly gave in when the man said he was only going to fool around near the shore. That evening, the kayak washed ashore. They never did find the renter. For lessons, Jeff Cooper, owner of H2Outfitters in Orr's Island, Maine, comes highly recommended. He's one of two Northeastern kayakers who are certified to teach other instructors, let alone beginners.

Those who have mastered this sport will treasure the New England coast, where hundreds of spruce-covered islands and protected inlets shelter kayakers from ocean waters. The highlight of Northeast sea kayaking is the 325-mile-long Maine Island Trail. Designed specifically for kayaks and small sailboats, the Maine Island Trail is a necklace of 80 islands that are strung together along the coast from Portsmouth, New Hampshire, to Machias, Maine. Outside of Maine, the trip to Monomoy Island from Chatham on Cape Cod and the paddle from Narrow River to Beavertail State Park in Rhode Island are two popular jaunts.

SNOWMOBILING

Snowmobiling in many areas of northern New England is more than a sport, it's a method of transport. Hundreds of miles of trails snake through secluded woods in Vermont, New Hampshire, Maine, and Quebec. Aroostook County in Northern Maine is consistently rated one of the top five snowmobiling destinations in the country. But you don't have to travel so far north to enjoy this exciting activity. Many of the parks in southern New England are open to snowmobiles, including the Rockwell Road ride up to the summit of Mount Greylock.

If you own a snowmobile, all it usually takes is a phone call to the local snowmobile chapter and the state Department of Parks and Recreation to find the network of trails in the region and to obtain maps. For those of you who don't own snowmobiles, I've listed places to rent and outfitters who arrange guided trips.

SNOWSHOEING

Snowshoeing is essentially winter hiking. Many of the trails that weave through the forests of New England are ideal for snowshoeing once a blanket of white covers the ground. Simply replace your hiking boots with snowshoes. In the regional chapters, I have named stores that rent snowshoes and guided tours by outfitters. One of the most scenic tours is not on a trail but a road closed in winter: Umiak Outfitters in Stowe, Vermont, takes snowshoers through Smugglers' Notch on Route 108.

SPELUNKING

Green Mountain Adventures in Manchester Center, Vermont, escort guests to New England's longest cave. Located at the foot of Dorset Mountain in East Dorset, the cave was discovered in 1967.

SURFING

Hey, dude, this side of the country has waves, too, and we're more civilized. When I lived in Huntington Beach, California, I heard stories all the time about the lowly beginner who had the bad fortune of cutting in front of the local surfing stud on a killer wave. He often went home with fragments of his board imbedded in his scalp. In Hawaii, it can get even uglier. Thankfully, we have proper etiquette on the East Coast. If someone dares to cut a line in front of us, we yell, "Get the f— out of the way!"

Throw on the wetsuit and surf year-round. As with cross-country skiing, it might be a little cold at first, but once you swim back from the shore a couple times, you'll warm up. Rhode Island, the Cape, the Vineyard, Nantucket, and the shores of Eastern Massachusetts are the surfing venues. Check each region for specific beaches.

SWIMMING

Wherever you venture in New England, water is always close by. Whether you're heading east to the Atlantic coast, west to 120-mile-long Lake Champlain, or to the multitude of ponds, rivers, and large lakes that lie in between, you should never have to travel more than 30 minutes to go swimming. That includes the urban areas of Boston, Providence, and Hartford. Your only dilemma is deciding which number sunblock you need to apply to your skin.

I feel somewhat remorseful that clandestine beaches and coveted swimming holes are now public knowledge, but there's more than enough water to go around. Check each chapter to find the swimming holes where locals go in your region. From Cape Cod north, the waters of the Atlantic are frigid year-round. The ponds and lakes are a much better option. South of the Cape, on the Rhode Island and Connecticut beaches, the Atlantic starts to warm up a little, making it bearable to swim for long periods of time.

TUBING

Farmington River Tubing supplies inner tubes for a two-and-a-half-hour journey down the Class I, II, and III rapids of Farmington River, Connecticut. Children must be at least 10 years old and stand at least four feet, five inches tall.

WALKS & RAMBLES

Finally, we arrive at the sports where conditioning is not necessary and your excuses for not attempting them are unconvincing. All you need is a good pair of walking shoes or sneakers, a bottle of water, and off you go. Not surprisingly, the best walks are on the coast where the terrain is flat, nature is abundant, and views are plentiful. The hardest part of many of these walks is finding the trailhead, but now that problem is alleviated. Try these for starters:

◆ **Fort Hill Trail, Massachusetts** Coastal marshes, swamps of red maples, and a former whaleboat captain's home combine to create a majestic walk on the Cape Cod National Seashore.

◆ **Cedar Tree Neck Sanctuary, Massachusetts** You'll inevitably find the combination of forest, bogs, and rocky coastline on this Martha's Vineyard walk enchanting.

◆ **Monhegan Island, Maine** Better known for its unspoiled beauty which has captivated artists for over a century, this small island off the Maine coast has two walking trails that venture to the southern and northern halves of the island. The paths guide you through stunted forests to 160-foot high cliffs above the Atlantic.

◆ **Great Island Trail, Massachusetts** This 7-mile loop is more of a hike than walk. The path follows the perimeter of Great Island, a former whaling port and now one of the most remote parts of the Cape.

◆ **The Greenway Trail, Rhode Island** Even in the heart of summer, you'll rarely find another person on these Block Island trails. The trails weave through forests and moors on their way to the seashore.

◆ **Gay Head Cliffs, Massachusetts** A simple walk on a Martha's Vineyard beach with the multi-colored Gay Head Cliffs rising above you.

◆ **Halibut State Park, Massachusetts** Located on Cape Ann, walk around the large quarry before you venture down to the shores of the Atlantic, where you can rock-hop on large boulders that line the coast.

◆ **Quoddy Head State Park, Maine** Situated at the northeastern-most point of the United States, this walk rambles over 90–150-foot cliffs. Across Lubec Channel is New Brunswick's Grand Manan Island.

◆ **Wellfleet Bay Wildlife Sanctuary, Massachusetts** Run by the Massachusetts Audubon Society, this is the place on the Cape to go bird watching. The trails lead to the beaches and marshes of Cape Cod Bay.

◆ **Cliff Walk, Rhode Island** Who can resist the temptation to peek inside the sprawling lawns once owned by the Vanderbilts and Astors? New England's most popular walk takes you to these famous Newport mansions by way of a path along the rugged Rhode Island shore.

Honorable Mention: Robert Frost Interpretive Trail, Vermont—This 1-mile long dirt path is a worthy introduction to the poet and to the woods where he summered for 39 years. Seven Frost poems are posted at regular intervals throughout the forest setting.

WHALE WATCHING

Whale-watching cruises are big business along the Atlantic coast. Almost everyday, from mid-April to November, boats leave the mainland in search of the biggest mammal on the planet. Many of these boats have naturalists on board to discuss the various species you can see, their migratory patterns, and the dangers fishing nets and oil spills pose to their survival. The majority of these naturalists have been at their jobs for so many years that they not only know the whales on a first-name basis, but they know their parents, grandparents, and children.

One of the most popular whale hangouts is Stellwagen Bank, an 18-mile long crescent-shaped underwater mesa that's located about 7 miles north of Provincetown, 25 miles east of Boston, and 12 miles southeast of Gloucester. Currents slam into the bank, bringing nutrient-rich cold water to the surface. This attracts fish, which in turn attracts numerous species of whales, including humpbacks, the larger fins, and smaller minkes. Cruises leave daily from Provincetown, Gloucester, Plymouth, and Boston.

Bring a jacket on board, and don't make the mistake I did of venturing out to sea on an overcast day when the swells are immense. Pallor will transform your face from its natural color to a shade of green more commonly found on the Vermont hillside.

WHITEWATER KAYAKING

New England's foremost whitewater kayaking rivers are also the leading whitewater rafting rivers. However, that's where the similarities end. Whitewater kayakers need serious instruction, practice, and conditioning. Whitewater rafters can simply sign up for a trip and have an incredible journey down the waterway with no experience whatsoever. There's a vast difference between a large floating object you sit in with eight other people (including a guide) and a small, slender watercraft you essentially wear.

The West Branch of the Penobscot, the Kennebec, and Dead Rivers in Maine are the most turbulent waterways in New England. Kayakers should know how to handle Class III–V rapids (for definitions of Class ratings, see "Whitewater Rafting"). The West River in Vermont, the Housatonic River in Connecticut, and the Deerfield River in western Massachusetts are less volatile and, thus, better places to learn the sport. A good choice for instruction is Bruce Lessels, owner of Zoar Outdoor in Charlemont, Massachusetts. A former World Whitewater Champion and author of the *Whitewater Handbook*, Bruce offers intensive whitewater kayaking classes that last two to three full days. By the end of the second or third day, you will be paddling down Class II–III rapids in the deep pools of Zoar Gap.

WHITEWATER RAFTING

Whitewater rafting is a thrilling experience that everyone can enjoy regardless of age or degree of shape. There's very little danger involved with these rafts, which easily handle high and rough water. Occasionally the craft will tip, but guides are experienced in assisting guests back into the boat, and everybody is required to wear a flotation device.

Rivers are rated by varying degrees of whitewater. Class I is calm with slow moving currents; Class II has moderate rapids or waves with relatively few obstructions; Class III is a swift current with more obstructions; Class IV is a powerful current with drops and many obstacles; and Class V is the most advanced, with series of complex rapids, drops, and challenging obstacles. There is a Class VI rating for those of you who are suicidal. However, these rivers are not considered navigable and you could easily risk death.

The West Branch of the Penobscot, Kennebec, and Dead Rivers in Maine, West River in Vermont, and the Deerfield

River in Massachusetts are the only places in New England to whitewater raft. The Maine rivers are the most tumultuous, with some rapids in the Class V range. A long list of outfitters offer their services. Check each regional chapter and the "Outfitter" section of this chapter to find names and phone numbers. All river trips last one day only.

Outfitters

"Yeah, yeah. All these sports, I love them, but the problem is I don't have time. I don't have time to buy a bike. I don't even have time to pedal. Listen, I get two weeks off a year and then it's back to the floor of the Stock Exchange. For those two weeks, I'd like to breathe in some fresh air while I'm outside. A nice bike trip in Vermont, hiking in the Whites, you know what I mean. And I don't want to take care of a damn thing ... no flat tires, no rentals, no accommodations, no food, nothin'. Ya got it?"

Yes, Type A, I understand your criteria. You want to participate in some sort of outdoor activity in the day and be pampered at night. You want someone to guide you on your sporting excursion and you don't want to be bothered with equipment problems, finding a trail-head, renting a canoe, or setting up a tent and cooking over a fire. You want someone to deal with all your arrangements, but you still want to take the best trips outlined in this book. Then you'll need to find an outfitter.

The choice of outfitters in New England is overwhelming. Pick a sport, any sport? How about an eight-day canoe trip on Maine's Allagash River; a five-day bike trip on Nantucket, Martha's Vineyard, and the Cape; an overnight dogsledding trip on the Maine-New Hampshire border; a week-long hiking tour of the Berkshires; a mountain

biking camp in the White Mountains; a six-day cross-country ski tour through Vermont's Northeast Kingdom; a four-day sea kayaking tour of Maine's coastal islands, including Acadia National Park; a three-day fly-fishing trip on Vermont's Battenkill River; or a weekend kayaking tour of the Lake Champlain islands? If you can't get away for that long, you can always hire a boat to go deep-sea fishing for a day off the Atlantic coast, go whitewater rafting down the Deerfield River in Massachusetts, telemark ski with a guide in the Mount Mansfield area, jump in a boat for a bird watching cruise to Cape Cod's Monomoy Island, take a guided sea kayaking trip from Narragansett Bay to Beavertail State Park, or climb Mount Washington ... in winter.

The irony is that even finding a good outfitter and trip takes time. Hopefully, I've saved you hours of researching by listing my favorite outfitters under each sport heading in the regional chapters. However, some questions should always be asked. Most are common sense. Some are related to specific sports:

1. **What's the cost and what's included in the price?** First and foremost, discuss the type of accommodation and whether all meals are included. Some companies skip lunch or an occasional dinner. Is liquor included? Then ask about shuttles to and from airports, cost of rentals, bikes, skis, etc.

2. **What level of fitness is required?** By far the most important question. Get a feeling for the tour. Is this an obstacle course better suited for Marines, a walk in the park for teetotalers, or somewhere in between? Do you bike 20, 40, or 60 miles a day? Do I have options for each day? Can I go shopping or sightseeing one day while my wife bikes to her legs' delight?

3. **How long have you been in business?** Credentials are important, but not nearly as important as the answer to the next question.

4. What are the age and experience of the guides? Outfitters in desperate financial straits may be tempted to hire young guides on the cheap; you don't want guides who have little experience in that sport or are from an entirely different part of the country.

5. How many people are in the group? What is the guide-to-client ratio? Do I have to compete with 30 or only 5 other people for the guide's attention?

6. Is it mostly singles or couples? Guided tours are a great place to befriend other singles or couples. Make sure you find out which trip best suits your needs.

7. What equipment is required? What type of equipment can I rent? Some fly-fishing companies request you to bring your own equipment. Others will rent you their own poles. Find out what they offer, especially when dealing with bikes. Do they rent 10-speed Raleighs or 21-speed Cannondales and Treks?

8. What happens if it rains? Do you have alternative plans or do you expect me to climb Mount Greylock in a downpour? How much free time do we have? Is every minute of the day accounted for, or should I bring that new novel I've been wanting to read?

9. How far in advance do I need to book? Don't miss out on a limited amount of spaces by waiting to the last minute. Some of these tours are booked a year in advance.

10. Can I bring young children? Most outfitters will usually answer affirmatively to this. A buck is a buck, no matter who hikes or sits on the bike. However, you should take yourself and the other guests into account. Do you want to bike 5 miles when you can bike 50? Do you really want to bring a young child bird watching or fly-fishing so he

can scream and scare off all the birds and fish?

The most important question above is about the level of fitness. Depending on what shape you're in, your trip can be nirvana or a living hell, not to mention a waste of money. Don't wait until the last minute to condition. If you plan on taking a week-long bike trip, start biking or doing an aerobic activity four to six weeks in advance, three times a week. If you can work out on weights or do push-ups or pull-ups, that's even better. I'd even hire a trainer at your local health club to set up a workout schedule for you. A $40 to $60 investment for a one-hour session with a trainer is far less money than the $500 or more you'll lose if you can't keep up or hurt yourself trying.

The pro to hiring a guide is the complete and utter lack of responsibility on your part. Most outfitters will find a way to relieve all your vacation worries, from accommodations to food to equipment. You also have a chance to make new friends. The con is the additional cost. Most of these trips can be done on your own for much less (that's one of the reasons I wrote this book). The other con is the lack of privacy. There's no place better than a mountain top, lonely backcountry road, or tranquil river to collect your thoughts and gain a sense of serenity. This is especially true if you live in a city like I do. On vacation, you've earned a certain amount of peace and quiet. This fragile state can easily be shattered by the loquacious woman with the shrill voice or the garrulous man with the guttural laugh. One way to eliminate this problem is to simply book the whole trip with a group of your friends.

The following is a list of all the outfitters found in the book that offer overnight trips. To locate the more than 100 outfitters who provide day trips, look under the specific sport and chapter.

◆ **Appalachian Mountain Club,** P.O. Box 298, Gorham, NH 03581 (tel. 603/466-2727). I can't possibly list all the overnight trips the AMC offers. Call for a catalog. Here's just a small sampling: a four-day women's canoe trip on Umbagog Lake, an eight-day hike and rock climbing trip in the White Mountains for teenagers, more than 23 guided hut-to-hut hikes in the Whites, and a guided Appalachian Trail hike in the Berkshires.

◆ **Back Country Excursions,** RFD 2, P.O. Box 365, Limerick, ME 04048 (tel. 207/625-8189). Cliff Krolick, owner of Back Country Excursions of Maine, guides mountain bikers on 60 miles of connected trails through the Sebago Lake area, near the New Hampshire/Maine border.

◆ **Backroads,** 1516 Fifth Street, Berkeley, CA 94710-1740 (tel. 800/GO-ACTIVE). Backroads features five-day biking tours of Penobscot Bay, Maine, southern Vermont, northern Vermont, and Cape Cod and the islands. They also offer six-day hiking tours of Vermont's Northeast Kingdom and the Berkshires, and a six-day cross-country skiing tour of the Northeast Kingdom and Mount Mansfield area.

◆ **Battenkill Canoe, Ltd.,** Route 7A, Arlington, VT 05250 (tel. 802/362-2800 or 800/421-5268). Features two-, three-, and five-day inn-to-inn trips on Vermont's finest waterways.

◆ **Berkshire Hiking Holidays,** P.O. Box 2231, Lenox, MA 01240 (tel. 800/877-9656). A variety of walking and hiking tours ranging from 3 to 14 days. Areas include the Berkshires, Cape Cod, and Vermont.

◆ **Bike Vermont,** P.O. Box 207, Woodstock, VT 05091 (tel. 800/257-2226). Offers weekend, three-day, five-day, and six-day tours to all regions of the state.

◆ **Clearwater Sports,** Route 100, Waitsfield, VT 05673 (tel. 802/496-2708). Offers overnight trips on the Winooski, Mad, and White Rivers.

◆ **Country Inns Along the Trail,** RR3, P.O. Box 3115, Brandon, VT 05773 (tel. 802/247-3300). Custom designs self-guided hiking trips where you can walk inn-to-inn.

◆ **Country Walkers,** P.O. Box 180, Waterbury, VT 05676 (tel. 802/244-1387). Offers inn-to-inn walking tours in southern Vermont, some led by natural history grad students at University of Vermont.

◆ **Craftsbury Center,** P.O. Box 31, Craftsbury Common, VT 05827 (tel. 800/729-7751). This mountain biking and cross-country ski center offers three- to six-day guided mountain biking tours.

◆ **Down River Canoes,** CT 154, Haddam, CT 06438 (tel. 203/345-8355). Offers overnight canoe outings on the Connecticut River.

◆ **4 Seasons Touring,** P.O. Box 132, Townshend, VT 05353 (tel. 802/365-7937). Arranges inn-to-inn walking tours with a historical bent in southern Vermont.

◆ **Gilpatrick's Guide Service,** P.O. Box 461, Skowhegan, ME 04976 (tel. 207/453-6959). Author of *Allagash, The Canoe Guide's Handbook* and *Building a Strip Canoe*, Gil Gilpatrick is a canoeing legend in northern Maine. He offers eight-day guided canoe trips on the Allagash River.

◆ **High Country Snowmobile Tours,** Wilmington, VT (tel. 800/627-7533 or 802/464-2108). Arranges guided hourly, half-day, full-day, and overnight snowmobile trips into the Green Mountain National Forest.

◆ **Hiking Holidays,** P.O. Box 750, Bristol, VT 05443 (tel. 802/453-4816). Five five-day hiking trips covering all regions of Vermont, a five-day guided tour of Acadia and the Maine Coast, and a five-day tour of the Berkshires.

◆ **H2Outfitters,** P.O. Box 72, Orr's Island, Maine 04066 (tel. 207/833-5257). Sea kayakers will cherish these two- to five-day trips along the Maine coast. Tours include a four-day trip from Owl's Head to Lamoine State Park, a five-day trip from Lamoine State Park to Eastport, and a two-day trip around Orr's Island and Casco Bay.

◆ **Kedron Valley Stables,** P.O. Box 368, South Woodstock, VT 05071 (tel. 802/ 457-1480). Leads four-day inn-to-inn horseback riding tours in southern Vermont. The horses average 15 miles a day.

◆ **L. L. Bean Outdoor Discovery Program,** Freeport, Maine 04033 (tel. 800/ 341-4341, ext. 6666). L. L. Bean's trips always include instruction, so expect to leave the trip markedly improved in your sport. They feature a vast array of activities, including a five-day canoe trip on the Allagash River, a five-day sea kayaking trip on Penobscot Bay, weekend bike trips to Bethel, Maine, and a five-day fly-fishing trip to Grand Lake Stream, Maine.

◆ **Mahoosuc Guide Service,** Bear River Road, Newry, ME 04261 (tel. 207/ 824-2073). Polly Mahoney and Kevin Slater deserve kudos for their innovative trips. First and foremost are their overnight dogsledding and cross-country skiing trips around Umbagog, Richardson, and Chesuncook Lake. Come summer, they offer canoe trips on the St. John, Allagash, Moose, and Penobscot Rivers. Polly specializes in women-only trips, ranging in sports from dogsledding to flatwater canoeing to whitewater canoeing.

◆ **Maine Sport Outfitters,** P.O. Box 956, Route 1, Rockport, ME 04856 (tel. 800/722-0826). Offers two- to four-day sea kayaking trips on the Maine Is-

lands and four- to eight-day canoe trips on Maine's noted rivers.

◆ **Maine Windjammer Association,** P.O. Box 317, Rockport, ME 04856 (tel. 800/614-6380). Offers overnight to week-long trips to the Penobscot Bay Islands on their fleet of windjammers.

◆ **New England Hiking Holidays,** P.O. Box 1648, North Conway, NH 03860 (tel. 800/869-0949). Trips include five-day hiking tours of Acadia National Park, the White Mountains, or Vermont's Northeast Kingdom.

◆ **Nordic Adventures,** P.O. Box 155, RD 1, Rochester, VT 05767 (tel. 802/ 767-3996). Nordic Adventures guides cross-country skiers on inn-to-inn tours in Vermont.

◆ **Northeast Ventures,** PO Box 185, Newtonville, MA 02160 (tel. 617/ 969-7479). Noted for their hiking, biking, and canoeing trips in the White Mountains, they also feature trips to the Rangeley Lake area and Baxter State Park in Maine.

◆ **Northern Maine Riding Adventures,** P.O. Box 16, Dover-Foxcroft, ME 04426 (tel. 207/564-3451 or 207/ 564-2965). Registered Maine Guide Judy Cross offers a variety of overnight horseback rides in the heart of the Maine Woods.

◆ **North Wind Touring,** P.O. Box 46, Waitsfield, VT 05673 (tel. 802/496-5771). Leads weekend to five-day cross-country ski and walking tours in central Vermont.

◆ **North Woods Ways,** RR2 Box 159A, Willimantic, ME 04443 (tel. 207/ 997-3723). Besides being noted authors and craftspeople, Registered Maine Guides Alexandra and Garrett Conover are trained naturalists and multi-talented guides. Few people know the rivers of Maine like these locals. The couple offers trips on the Allagash and St. John Rivers, and Chesuncook and

Caucomgomoc Lakes. Tours range from five to eight days.

◆ **Outdoor Bound of Vermont,** RR#5-2147, Bear Swamp Road, Montpelier, VT 05602 (tel. 802/223-4172 or 800/639-9208). Arranges four-day cross-country and telemark ski trips to Bolton Valley and Stowe, Vermont.

◆ **Sakonnet Boathouse,** 169 Riverside Drive, Tiverton, Rhode Island (tel. 401/624-1440). Features three-day guided sea kayaking trips to Block Island and along the Rhode Island coast.

◆ **Vermont Bicycle Touring,** P.O. Box 711, Bristol, Vermont 05433 (tel. 800/245-3868). Offers six five-day biking tours and eight weekend tours to every region of Vermont; a five-day trip to Cape Cod and the islands; and three- to five-day tours of Penobscot Bay, Boothbay Harbor, and Acadia National Park.

◆ **Vermont Icelandic Horse Farm,** RR 376-1, Waitsfield, VT 05673 (tel. 802/496-7141). Owner Christina Calabrese offers half- to three-day rides in the Green Mountain National Forest on her pony-sized Icelandic horses.

◆ **Vermont Waterways,** RR 1, P.O. Box 322, East Hardwick, VT 05836-9707 (tel. 800/492-8271). Arranges weekend to five-day canoe trips on the White, Winooski, Connecticut, and Lamoille Rivers. They also offer a kayaking tour through the Lake Champlain islands.

◆ **Walking-Inn-Vermont,** P.O. Box 243, Ludlow, VT 05149 (tel. 802/228-8799). Specializes in self-guided inn-to-inn tours on which they shuttle your luggage to the next accommodation.

◆ **Walking the World 50 Plus,** P.O. Box 1186, Fort Collins, CO 80522 (tel. 800/340-9255). An eight-day walking tour of the Maine coast including Monhegan Island, Mount Battie, and Acadia; an eight-day canoeing and walking tour of Rhode Island; and an eight-day trip to the White Mountains are just a few of the New England vacations. As the name implies, walkers must be over the age of 50.

◆ **Walking Tours of Southern Vermont,** RR2, P.O. Box 622, Arlington, VT 05250 (tel. 802/375-1141). Leads five-day, seven-day, and weekend inn-to-inn walking tours of southern Vermont. They also offer llama treks and tours strictly for women.

◆ **Wild Earth Adventure,** P.O. Box 655, Pomona, NY 10970 (tel. 914/354-3717). Trips include an eight-day guided backpacking trip through the Green Mountain National Forest and a nine-day backpacking trek on Maine's 100-mile Wilderness Trail, as well as numerous day trips.

Schools

Instruction is an important aspect of outdoor recreation. For sports like sailing, scuba diving, sea kayaking, whitewater kayaking, and rock climbing, schooling is imperative. Lessons in cross-country or downhill skiing, mountain biking, horseback riding, golfing, fishing, and canoeing can only improve your skills and make the sport more enjoyable.

The same questions asked to outfitters above apply to schools. Group size is extremely important. You want to be in a small group where you get personalized attention. Be blunt with your questioning. If you want to be able to bareboat charter a sailboat in the Penobscot Bay Islands or whitewater kayak down a Class III river, inquire whether you'll be able to achieve those goals after the course is finished. Also ask how much time is spent in the classroom compared to time spent participating in the activity. From my years of being a swim instructor, I know that you can talk to students until you're blue in the face outside the water, but it's not until they jump into the pool that they learn anything. You retain far more by doing than listening.

Throughout the regional chapters, I have pointed out schools that cater to each activity. I have listed these schools alphabetically below. I omitted downhill ski areas and horseback riding stables, but obviously they all offer lessons.

◆ **Acadia Mountain Guides,** 137 Cottage Street, Bar Harbor, Maine 04609 (tel. 207/288-8186). Rock climbing in Acadia National Park.

◆ **Adventure Learning,** 67 Bear Hill, Merrimack, MA 01860 (tel. 508/346-9728 or 800/649-9728). Sea kayaking clinics off Cape Ann, Massachusetts.

◆ **Appalachian Mountain Club,** P.O. Box 298, Gorham, NH 03581 (tel. 603/466-2727). A long list of courses offered all over New England, from mushroom foraging to canoeing to backpacking. Call for a catalog.

◆ **Ascents of Adventure,** P.O. Box 6568, Albany, NY 12206 (tel. 518/475-7519). Rock climbing instruction in the Berkshires and southern Vermont.

◆ **Atlantic Climbing,** 24 Cottage Street, Bar Harbor, ME 04609 (tel. 207/288-2521). Rock climbing in Acadia National Park.

◆ **The Battenkill Anglers,** P.O. Box 2303, Route 7A, Manchester Center, VT 05255 (tel. 802/362-3184). Fly-fishing lessons on the Battenkill River in southern Vermont.

◆ **Bay Island Sailing School,** 120 Tillson Avenue, Rockland, ME 04841 (tel. 800/421-2492). Sailing on the Maine coast.

◆ **Bigelow Bike Tours,** P.O. Box 75, Stratton, ME 04982 (tel. 207/246-7352). Six-day mountain bike camps in Carrabassett Valley.

◆ **The Block Island Club,** Block Island, RI 02807 (tel. 401/466-5939). Sailing instruction in the waters off Block Island.

◆ **Boston Harbor Sailing School** (tel. 617/523-2619). Sailing school in Boston.

◆ **Boston Sailing Center** (tel. 617/227-4198). Sailing school in Boston.

◆ **Brookside Angler,** Route 7A, Manchester Village, VT 05255 (tel. 802/362-3538). Arranges three- to eight-hour fly-fishing instruction on the Battenkill River in southern Vermont.

◆ **Burlington Community Boathouse,** at the foot of College Street in Burlington, VT 05401 (tel. 802/865-3377). Sailboat lessons on Lake Champlain.

◆ **Charles River Canoe and Kayak Center,** 2401 Commonwealth Ave., Newton, MA 02166 (tel. 617/965-5110). Sculling lessons on the Charles River.

◆ **Clarke Outdoors,** 163 Route 7, West Cornwall, CT 06796 (tel. 860/672-6365). Whitewater kayak instruction on the Housatonic River, Connecticut.

◆ **Coastal Sailing School,** Marblehead, MA 01945 (tel. 617/639-0553). Sailing school on Massachusetts' North Shore.

◆ **Coastline Sailing School,** 8 Marsh Road, Eldridge Yard, Noank, CT 06340 (tel. 203/536-2689). Sailing instruction on eastern Connecticut's Long Island Sound.

◆ **Courageous Sailing Center** (tel. 617/725-3263). Sailing school in Boston.

◆ **Lewis Cuyler,** (tel. 413/496-9160). Sculling lessons in the Berkshires.

◆ **Essex River Basin Adventures,** Main Street, Essex, MA 01929 (tel. 508/768-ERBA or 800/KAYAK-04). Sea kayaking instruction on the North Shore of Massachusetts.

◆ **Fly Fish Vermont,** 804 S. Main St., Unit 4, Stowe, VT (tel. 802/253-3964).

Fly-fishing instruction in the Mount Mansfield region of Vermont.

◆ **The Golf School** (tel. 800/240-2555). Golf classes in Carrabassett Valley, Maine, and Mount Snow, Vermont.

◆ **Gone With the Wind,** Norwalk, CT (tel. 203/852-1857). Offers boardsailing instruction in Norwalk, Connecticut.

◆ **Goose Hummock,** Route 6A, Orleans, MA 02653 (tel. 508/255-0455). Sea kayaking instruction off Cape Cod.

◆ **Great Outdoors Trading Company,** 73 Main Street, Newport, VT 05855 (tel. 802/334-2831). Boardsailing lessons in the South Bay area of Lake Memphremagog, Vermont.

◆ **H2Outfitters,** P.O. Box 72, Orr's Island, ME 04066 (tel. 207/833-5257). Sea kayaking instruction on Orr's Island, Maine; Kittery, Maine; Reading, Massachusetts; Old Saybrook, Connecticut; Riverhead, New York; and Brick, New Jersey.

◆ **International Mountain Equipment,** Main Street, North Conway, NH 03860 (tel. 603/356-6316). Operates the biggest ice climbing and rock climbing school in the East.

◆ **The International Sailing School and Club,** 253 Lakeshore Drive, Colchester, VT 05446 (tel. 802/864-9065). A membership fee entitles you to sailing workshops, clinics, and unlimited use of their sailboats and sailboards on Lake Champlain.

◆ **Island Sport,** 86 Aquidneck Avenue, Middletown, RI 02842 (tel. 401/846-4421). Boardsailing lessons in Newport, Rhode Island.

◆ **J World,** P.O. Box 1509, Newport, RI 02840 (tel. 800/343-2255). Highly regarded sailing school located in Newport, Rhode Island.

◆ **Killington School for Tennis** (tel. 800/343-0762). Offers two, three,

and five-day programs on their eight outdoor courts situated in central Vermont.

◆ **L. L. Bean Paddling,** Fly-Fishing, and Cycling Schools, Freeport, ME 04033 (tel. 800/341-4341, ext. 6666). Canoeing, sea kayaking, fishing, and biking instruction in Maine.

◆ **Longshore Sailing School,** Longshore Club Park, 260 S. Campo Road, Westport, CT 06880 (tel. 203/226-1646). Popular day sailing school on Connecticut's Long Island Sound.

◆ **Mad River Bike Shop,** Route 100, Waitsfield, VT 05673 (tel. 802/496-9500). Offers a five-day mountain bike camp in central Vermont for teenagers.

◆ **Maine Sport Outdoor School,** P.O. Box 956, Route One, Rockport, ME 04856 (tel. 800/722-0826). Sea kayaking, canoeing, and fishing instruction on an island in Muscongus Bay, Maine.

◆ **Main Stream,** Route 44, New Hartford, CT 06057 (tel. 860/693-6791 or 860/379-6657). Whitewater canoe lessons on the Farmington River, Connecticut.

◆ **Morningside Flight Park,** P.O. Box 109, Claremont, NH 03743 (tel. 603/542-4416). Hang-gliding lessons in western New Hampshire.

◆ **Mount Snow,** VT (tel. 800/245-SNOW). Runs one of the top mountain biking schools in the northeast.

◆ **Nauset Sports,** Route 6A, Orleans, MA 02653 (tel. 508/255-4742). Boardsailing and sea kayaking instruction off Cape Cod.

◆ **Northland Trout Tours,** North Fayston, VT (tel. 802/496-6572). Fishing lessons in Vermont's Mad River Valley.

◆ **Orvis,** Manchester, VT 05254 (tel. 800/235-9763). Two to two-and-a-half day fly-fishing courses are taught on the Battenkill River in southern Vermont.

◆ **Sail Newport,** 53 America's Cup Avenue, Newport, RI 02840 (tel. 401/849-8385). Sailing and boardsailing school situated in Newport, Rhode Island.

◆ **Sakonnet Boathouse,** 169 Riverside Drive, Tiverton, RI 02878 (tel. 401/624-1440). Provides sea kayaking clinics on the Rhode Island coast.

◆ **Shake-a-Leg Sailing Center,** Newport, RI (tel. 401/847-3630). Sailing school in Newport for the physically challenged.

◆ **Small Boat Shop,** 144 Water Street, South Norwalk, CT 06854 (tel. 203/854-5223). Sea kayaking instruction on Connecticut's Long Island Sound.

◆ **Stratton Golf School,** Stratton Mountain, VT (tel. 802/297-4114). Golf school in central Vermont.

◆ **Tudhope Sailing Center and Marina,** at the foot of the Grand Isle Bridge in the Lake Champlain Islands (tel. 802/372-5320). Sailing lessons on Lake Champlain.

◆ **Umiak Outdoor Outfitters,** 849 South Main Street, Stowe, VT 05672 (tel. 802/253-2317). Canoeing and snowshoeing instruction in the Stowe, Vermont area.

◆ **Vermont Fly Fishing School,** Quechee Inn, Woodstock, VT (tel. 802/295-3131). Fly-fishing instruction in eastern Vermont.

◆ **Waterfront Diving Center,** 214 Battery Street, Burlington, VT 05401 (tel. 802/865-2771). Scuba diving instruction on Lake Champlain.

◆ **The Watershed,** 409 Main St., Wakefield, RI (tel. 401/789-1954). Teaches surfing lessons every Wednesday at noon at Narragansett Beach, Rhode Island.

◆ **Windsurfing of Watch Hill,** 3 Bay Street, Watch Hill, RI (tel. 401/596-0079). Boardsailing lessons off western Rhode Island's coast.

◆ **Winnipesaukee Kayak Company,** Route 109, Melvin, NH (tel. 603/544-3905). Kayak lessons on the waters of Lake Winnipesaukee and other nearby lakes.

◆ **Winni Sailboarder's School & Outlet,** 687 Union Avenue, Laconia, NH (tel. 603/528-4110). Boardsailing lessons on Lake Opechee, in western New Hampshire.

◆ **Womanship,** Newport, RI (tel. 800/342-9295). Women teach women in this sailing school in Newport, Rhode Island.

◆ **Women's Sailing Adventures,** 39 Woodside Avenue, Westport, CT 06880 (tel. 203/227-7413 or 800/328-8053). Teaches women how to sail on Con-necticut's Long Island Sound.

◆ **Zoar Outdoor,** Mohawk Trail, Charlemont, MA 01339 (tel. 800/532-7483). White-water kayaking instruction on the Deerfield River in Massachusetts.

Maps

It has been my intention throughout this book to guide you along trails and roads via words, without maps. However, if you're a map lover like me, many of you will still want to know exactly where you started and where you're going. For that reason, I have listed under each featured trip how to locate maps. Many hikes simply have maps at the trailhead. Other times, I have mentioned the respective United States Geological Survey (USGS) maps—topographical maps designed by the U.S. government. Many of these maps can be found at local bookstores or retail sporting goods stores like **The Globe Corner Bookstores** in Boston and Cambridge (call 617/523-6658 or 617/859-8008 in Boston, 617/497-6277 in Harvard Square). If you can't locate the map for a particular section, go to the source, **U.S. Geological Survey,** Federal Center, Building 810, P.O. Box 25286, Denver, CO 80225.

Many of my biking routes in Maine, Vermont, and New Hampshire were found by using the Atlas and Gazetteer published by **DeLorme Mapping Company.** These large-scale maps are excellent for biking and driving to hiking trailheads, especially *The Maine Atlas,* which has topographical maps and local logging roads. By the time this book is published, the Vermont and New Hampshire publications should also have topo maps. Contact DeLorme Mapping, P.O. Box 298, Freeport, ME 04032 (tel. 207/865-4171 or 800/452-5931).

If you plan on doing any hiking or cross-country skiing in the Mount Mansfield region of Vermont, the maps published by Jared Grange, owner of **Huntington Graphics,** are indispensable. The maps depict all the hiking and backcountry ski trails centered around Mount Mansfield. Huntington Graphics, P.O. Box 163, Huntington, VT 05462 (tel. 802/434-2555).

Books

During the course of my research, many books have proved helpful, including guidebooks on specific sports in one region, nonfiction on a host of subjects ranging from ecology to geology to history to anecdotal New England stories, and fiction from the likes of Nathaniel Hawthorne, Herman Melville, and Sarah Orne Jewett. Let's start with sporting guides that I found useful.

Single-Sport Guides. *Classic Backcountry Skiing* by David Goodman (AMC Books), *25 Ski Tours in Vermont* by Stan Wass (Backcountry), *The Mountain Biker's Guide to Southern New England* by Paul Angiolillo (Menasha), *The Mountain Biker's Guide to Northern New England* by Paul Angiolillo (Menasha), *The Best Bike Rides in New England* by Paul Thomas (Globe Pequot), *25 Bicycle Tours in Vermont* by John S. Freiden (Backcountry), *25 Bicycle Tours in Maine* by Howard Stone (Backcountry), *Touring New England by Bicycle* by Peter Powers (Terragraphics), *Quiet Water Canoe Guide, New Hampshire, Vermont* by Alex Wilson (AMC Books), *Quiet Water Canoe Guide, Massachusetts, Connecticut, Rhode Island* by Alex Wilson (AMC Books), *Connecticut Walk Book* (Connecticut Forest and Park Association), *Fifty Hikes in Vermont* by the Green Mountain Club (Backcountry), *Guide Book of the Long Trail* (Green Mountain Club), *Hiker's Guide to the Mountains of Vermont* by Jared Grange (Huntington Graphics), *Fifty Hikes in Northern Maine* by Cloe Caputo (Backcountry), *Maine Geographic Hiking,* Volumes 2 and 3 (DeLorme), *Fifty Hikes in the White Mountains* by Daniel Doan (Backcountry), *Fifty More Hikes in New Hampshire* by Daniel Doan (Backcountry), *AMC White Mountain Guide* (AMC), *Walks & Rambles on Cape Cod and the Islands* by Glenda Bendure and Ned Friary (Backcountry), and *A Cruising Guide to the New England Coast* by Roger F. Duncan and John P. Ware (Putnam), the invaluable guide for sailors.

General Travel Guides. The Explorer's Guide Series published by Countryman Press are the most comprehensive and fact-filled guides on specific New England states. They include *Vermont* by Christina Tree and Peter Jennison, *New Hampshire* by Christina Tree and Peter Randall, *Maine* by Christina Tree and Elizabeth Roundy, *Massachusetts* by Christina Tree and William Davis, *Rhode Island* by Phyllis Meras and Tom Gannon, and *Connecticut* by Barnett Laschever and Barbara Beeching.

Aside from small-press one-state books like those Countryman publishes,

Frommer's New England and *Frommer's Northern New England* are probably the best general guides to New England, giving you all the lodging, dining, and sightseeing info you'll need. And they're getting better with each edition.

Literary Non-Fiction, Natural History, Ecology & Geology. *Walden* by Henry David Thoreau, *Cape Cod* by Henry David Thoreau, *The Maine Woods* by Henry David Thoreau, *A Week on the Concord and Merrimack Rivers* by Henry David Thoreau, *Essays on Nature* by Ralph Waldo Emerson, *The Outermost House* by Henry Beston, *Northern Farm, A Chronicle of Maine* by Henry Beston, *The Survival of the Bark Canoe* by John McPhee, *A Year in the Maine Woods* by Bernd Heinrich, *Changes in the Land* by William Cronon, *Hope, Human, and Wild* by Bill McKibben, *The Changing Faces of New England* by Betty Flanders Thomson, *The Sierra Club Guide to the Natural Areas of New England* by John Perry and Jane Greverus Perry, *A Guide to New England's Landscape* by Neil Jorgensen, and *Ecology of Eastern Forests* by John Kricher and Gordon Morrison.

New England History. The Pulitzer prize-winning *The Flowering of New England* by Van Wyck Brooks; *Inside New England* by Judson Hale, a witty combination of anecdotes, history, and highly opinionated satire; *Maine: A Bicentennial History* by Charles E. Clark; *The Coast of Maine: An Informal History* by Louise Dickenson Rich; *New Hampshire: A Bicentennial History* by Elizabeth Forbes Morison and Elting Morison; *Massachusetts: A Bicentennial History* by Richard D. Brown; *Vermont: A Bicentennial History* by Charles T. Morrissey; the best of the group, *Connecticut: A Bicentennial History* by David M. Roth; and *Literary New England* by William Corbett, a guidebook to the historical literary sites of New England.

Fiction. *Moby Dick* by Herman Melville, *Mosses from an Old Manse* and *The Great Stone Face* by Nathaniel Hawthorne, *The Country of the Pointed Firs* by Sarah Orne Jewett, *The Beans of Egypt, Maine* and *Merry Men* by Carolyn Chute.

Spas

New England's spas are more than mere retreats to rejuvenate your weary body or instill a healthy lifestyle. More and more spas are taking advantage of their bucolic surroundings, whisking guests outdoors to breathe in the clean, crisp air, before returning them to the invigorating massage and aromatherapy rooms indoors. Considering that many of New England's spas are located in the mountains, on lakes, or near the ocean, it's a shrewd move.

Canyon Ranch, in the heart of Massachusetts' Berkshire Mountains, was one of the first to venture off-premises. The resort's Outdoor Sports Department takes their clientele on the best hikes, bike rides, canoe jaunts, and cross-country skiing trails the Berkshires have to offer. Elsewhere, the elegant **Norwich Inn and Spa** in eastern Connecticut sponsors an "Outdoor Adventure Week" where guides bring visitors on ocean walks and boating trips. **Northern Pines** in Maine arranges canoe, sailing, and cross-country skiing trips on its lake-front property. And Killington's **New Life** brings guests on hikes through the Green Mountains for exquisite views of Vermont's rolling green farmland. Obviously, aerobic classes, weight rooms, and other indoor services are still in place, but New England spas are finally realizing that you don't have to be in southern California to savor spectacular surroundings year-round.

Many of these spas are listed in the regional chapters:

◆ **Canyon Ranch in the Berkshires,** 165 Kemble Street, Lenox, MA 01240 (tel. 800/742-9000). With 40 aerobic classes, wholesome food, and an incredible list of services including seven types of massage and hydrotherapy, Canyon Ranch is arguably the finest spa in New England. Week-long packages range from $2,280 to $3,190 per person, including all meals, facilities, five personal services (for the week), and outdoor recreation.

◆ **The Equinox,** Route 7A, Manchester Village, VT 05254 (tel.800/362-4747). Body scrubs, therapeutic herbal wraps, and massages are just a few of the services offered at this prestigious 225-year-old resort. Rates per person, including all meals, facilities, one herbal wrap, one loofah salt glow scrub, and a daily short massage cost $2,170 for a seven-night package.

◆ **Kripalu Center for Yoga and Health,** P.O. Box 793, Lenox, MA 01240 (tel. 800/967-3577). Kripalu follows a spiritual path to health, featuring yoga and meditation courses. Rates per person, including all meals, facilities, and basic services range from $471 to $535 for a seven-night stay.

◆ **New Life,** The Inn of the Six Mountains, Killington Road, Killington, VT 05751 (tel. 800/545-9407). Like the name implies, New Life specializes in changing poor health habits through yoga, smart eating, and hiking. Rates per person, including all meals, facilities, and two one-hour massages range from $899 to $999 for a five-night package.

◆ **Northern Pines Health Resort,** 559 State Route 85, Raymond, ME 04071 (tel. 207/655-7624). Located 40 minutes west of Portland, this rustic resort emphasizes a holistic approach to stress control and weight loss. Rates per person, including all vegetarian meals, spa facilities, and basic services range

from $780 to $1,170 for a seven-night stay.

◆ **Norwich Inn & Spa,** 607 W. Thames Street, Route 32, Norwich, CT 06369 (tel. 800/ASK-4-SPA). The long list of services at this intimate retreat includes invigorating loofah scrubs, clay wraps, and thalassotherapy, a sea water–based treatment. Rates per person, including all meals, spa facilities, and two personal services daily range from $2,170 to $3,185 for a seven-night stay.

◆ **Spa at Grand Lake,** Route 207, Lebanon, CT 06249 (tel. 203/642-4306). Set in a grove of old evergreens, this spa is known for its no-frills, casual atmosphere. Rates per person, including all meals, facilities, and six half-hour massages range from $799 to $899 per week.

◆ **Topnotch at Stowe,** Mountain Road, Stowe, VT 05672 (tel. 800/451-8686). Catering to sports enthusiasts, Topnotch gives every client a "Fitness Profile" for planning a customized exercise regimen. Rates per person, including all meals, facilities, and one daily personal service of your choice range from $1,505 to $2,247 for a seven-night package.

Campgrounds & Other Accommodations

Names of the top public campgrounds, inns, and resorts have been provided at the end of each regional chapter. In the Maine Woods chapter, I also featured sporting camps as a sidebar. I have personally stayed at many of these places and can attest to their high quality. Others were recommended by rangers, locals, or friends. The inns and resorts all feature outdoor activities or are situated near recreational areas.

2

The Litchfield Hills and Western Connecticut

ITH A POPULATION EXCEEDING THREE MILLION, Connecticut is often pegged as a small industrialized state with sprawling suburbs—a nice place to raise kids, but not much to visit. This is especially true of the southwest corner, a combination of small cities like Stamford and Bridgeport and wealthy communities like Greenwich and Westport, where men and women line up every morning to catch the Metro North train to New York City. However, there is another Connecticut that rarely anybody except New Englanders knows about. A Connecticut with 52 state parks and 9 state forests, a Connecticut with mountains, 200-year-old white clapboard houses, village greens, and long, narrow rivers that weave through the rural countryside.

This Connecticut is best exemplified by the Litchfield Hills region in the northwest corner of the state. The Litchfield Hills are, in actuality, the foothills of the Taconic and Berkshire Mountains. They are the start of a long mountainous corridor that stretches north through eastern New York and western Massachusetts to the southern end of Vermont and the Green Mountains. New Yorkers have cherished this region for some time. Indeed, many people like myself feel that this is where authentic New England begins. The heavily traveled routes in the southern part of the state are replaced by country roads that lead through covered bridges to pre-Revolutionary War towns. New Yorkers have been taking the two- to three-hour train ride to this rural region since the 1920s, when they would pack their steamer trunks with a wardrobe suited for summer in the countryside. Lately, the Litchfield Hills have served as a refuge for famous actors, authors, tennis players, and a former Secretary of State.

Thankfully, New Yorkers have taken a hands-off approach to the region, leaving the landscape intact. More than 56 miles of the Appalachian Trail meander through the forest. The Housatonic River runs the length of the state, attracting flatwater and whitewater canoeists, kayakers, and rafters. Bikers can roll through the hills past streams from village steeple to village steeple. The state forests are a haven to mountain bikers and cross-country skiers. And the hills are home to four family-oriented downhill ski slopes.

Even the southwestern part of the state entices visitors. Sherwood Island State Park provides a long stretch of beach, and the islands off Norwalk are scenic anchorages for sailors and sea kayakers. Connecticut is often overlooked by outdoorsmen in favor of its more obviously rustic neighbors farther north. If you haven't been here recently, it deserves a second look.

The Lay of the Land

With the exception of Sherwood Island State Park and the Norwalk Islands, the western coast of Connecticut is far less impressive than the eastern half of the state or the rest of the New England shoreline. Western Connecticut has its share of beaches, bays, and rocky coves, but its proximity to New York City and the surrounding suburbs has lessened its allure.

The landscape is far more intriguing in the northwest corner of the state. North of New Milford, the southern tail of the Taconic Mountains start to appear. Forests of oaks, hickories, and thickets of hemlocks, chestnut, and white pines blanket the region known as the Litchfield Hills. Remarkably, some of this forest is as old as the clapboard houses that line the small village greens. In Cornwall, the towering Cathedral Pines are over 200 years old. Believed to be second-growth forest, these 150-foot-tall trees suggest what the New England forest might have looked like when settlers arrived here. Century-old chestnut trees can be found at higher altitudes, as on Bear Mountain. Nestled within this historic forest are lakes, ponds, and winding rivers like the Housatonic, which runs from the Massachusetts border to Long Island Sound. Unlike the Massachusetts stretch of the Housatonic, where the river flows gently through a broad, soft limestone valley, the Housatonic in Connecticut has carved a niche through much harder and more resistant rock. The result is a more volatile and quicker river which is often carried by a series of rapids over large boulders and through narrow gorges.

The climate in western Connecticut is typical of southern New England. On the average, the temperature goes above 90° fewer than twenty times per year, and below zero fewer than seven times per year. In Hartford, average highs range from 84° in July to 35° in January. Temperatures in the mountains of the Litchfield Hills area can sometimes be ten degrees below Hartford's temperature. Away from the coast, most of the state has some snow cover between late December and early March. Peak season for fall foliage is usually around

Columbus Day Weekend. Call 800/CT-BOUND for the latest updates.

The highlight of western Connecticut birding are the bald eagles spotted in the waters of the Housatonic River near Shepaug Dam in Southbury. The eagles start migrating to the Housatonic in late December. Wild turkeys are frequently observed in the Litchfield Hills, especially since they are breeding at an exponential rate. On the coast, migrating shorebirds include herons, egrets, and osprey. Deer, raccoons, woodchucks, cottontail rabbits, and the occasional bobcat and bear have been spotted in this region.

Orientation

Interstate 91, which splits the state in two, is my boundary line for the western and eastern Connecticut chapters. **Interstate 95** will bring you to the Connecticut coast. North of **Interstate 84, U.S. 7** and **State Route 8** head to the Litchfield Hills region. **State Route 4** and **U.S. 44** are two of the numerous roads that venture east to west through the northwest corner of the state. **State Route 128** through the covered bridge in West Cornwall is one of the more scenic drives. **State Route 63,** south of Goshen, and **State Route 45,** north of New Preston, are also picturesque roads.

The Litchfield Hills area is made up of historic hamlets, covered bridges, short sloping mountains, and crystalline bodies of water. You get the gist. There are small villages where antique shops, bookstores, cozy restaurants, and century-old inns predominate; Washington, Kent, Litchfield, Cornwall, West Cornwall, Salisbury, and Colebrook are excellent examples. For more information, contact the **Litchfield Hills Travel Council,** P.O. Box 968, Litchfield, CT 06759 (tel. 203/567-4506).

Southwestern Connecticut is also known as the Gold Coast, probably due to the million-dollar estates that line the Long Island Sound. The area is split between affluent New York suburbs and small industrialized cities. Not surprisingly, the Gold Coast is best seen from the shores or islands of the Sound.

Parks & Other Hot Spots

THE LITCHFIELD HILLS

The Housatonic River

This turbulent river, accessible via U.S. 7, runs the length of the state, providing one of the best waterways for canoeists and kayakers in Connecticut. The river is also known for its trout fishing.

The Farmington River

Another popular river, especially for tubing.

The State Parks

Mohawk Mountain, Macedonia Brook, Housatonic Meadows, Peoples, American Legion, and Nepaug are home to hundreds of trails, ideal for the hiker, mountain biker, and cross-country skier.

The Appalachian Trail

The AT enters Connecticut just south of Kent before hugging the Housatonic

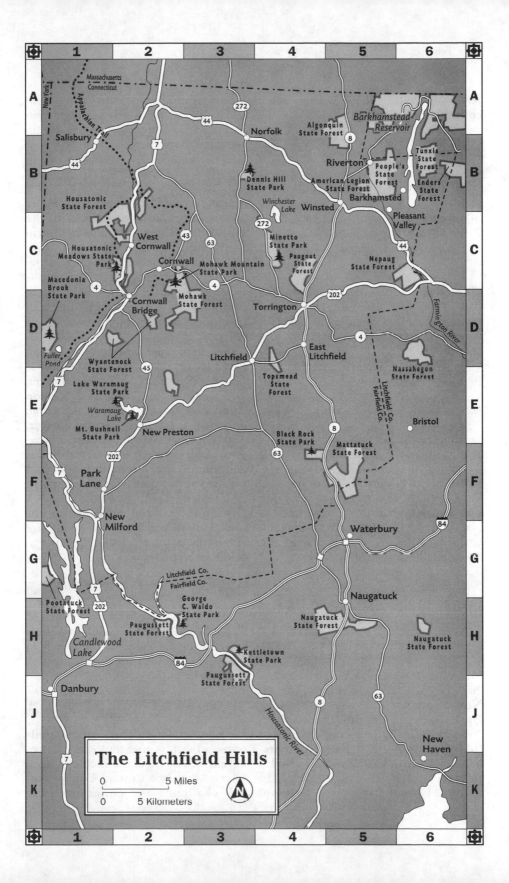

The Litchfield Hills

0   5 Miles

0   5 Kilometers

River and heading north to the Massachusetts border.

Sherwood Island State Park

Situated off I-95, Exit 18. Tel. 203/226-6983.

The closest of Connecticut's public beaches to New York City, this 2-mile stretch of sand in Westport is covered with beach towels and families on warm summer days.

Norwalk Islands

Accessible via Norwalk by boat.

A favorite haunt for sailors and sea kayakers, the Norwalk Islands have been home to dairy farms, mansions, and now large populations of waterfowl. A National Wildlife Preserve resides on Chimon Island, while Sheffield Island houses an historic lighthouse.

What to Do & Where to Do It

Watershed Balloons in Watertown (tel. 203/274-2010), **Balloon Hollow, Inc.** in Newtown (tel. 203/426-4250), **Steppin' Up Balloons** in Southbury (tel. 203/264-0013), **Kat Balloons** in Farmington (tel. 203/678-7921), **A Balloon Squire** in Farmington (tel. 203/521-7208), **Berkshire Balloons** in Southington (tel. 203/250-8441), and **Livingston Balloon**

Company in Simsbury (tel. 203/651-1110) are just a few of the companies that run hot-air balloon flights in western Connecticut.

Starting in late December, **bald eagles** are seen feeding in the waters of the **Housatonic River** near Shepaug Dam in Southbury. This hydroelectric facility has set aside a special eagle observation area staffed by naturalists. The area is free to the public, but reservations are essential since space is limited. Call 800/368-8954 for more information and to reserve a space.

Other popular birding areas in the Litchfield Hills are the **White Memorial Foundation & Conservation Center,** U.S. 202, Litchfield; the **Sharon Audubon Center,** State Route 4, Sharon; and the **Flanders Nature Center,** Flanders Road, Woodbury. **Scarlet tanagers, purple finches, orioles, grosbeaks, wild turkeys, herons, terns, hawks,** and **owls** have been spotted at these centers.

Chimon Island, one of the Norwalk Islands, and the **Nature Center for Environmental Activities** in Westport are two of the better places on the coast to watch migrating shorebirds.

On the coast, **Gone With the Wind** (tel. 203/852-1857) rents sailboards and offers instruction on **Calf Pasture Beach** in Norwalk. Inland, windsurfers head to **Bantam Lake.**

Whether you crave plummeting rapids or placid waters, and travel in a canoe, kayak, raft, or tube, the medley of waterways that lace western Connecticut will challenge and entice paddling aficionados. Numerous spring-fed mountain lakes and serpentine rivers are nestled within the hills. First and foremost are the **Housatonic** and **Farmington Rivers.** From the ridges of Mount Greylock in Massachusetts, the **Housatonic** flows 150 miles through the Berkshire and Taconic ranges before entering Long Island Sound. The Litchfield Hills are home to one of the most pristine stretches of the river. Quiet country villages and forests of maples, oaks, and ashes line the banks of the Housatonic as it snakes over rocky gorges and under century-old covered bridges. **Flatwater canoeists** can put-in above Falls Village and canoe more than 14 miles north to Ashley Falls, Massachusetts, and Bartholemew's Cobble (see "Walks & Rambles" in the Berkshires chapter). In Falls Village, take State Route 126 to Main Street, continuing on Water Street past the power station. Cross the river and turn right on Housatonic River Road. The put-in is situated just above the power dam.

Whitewater canoeists can put-in at Power Plant Park, just below Great Falls in Falls Village. From here you can travel 10 to 12 miles south on the Housatonic, cruising under the West Cornwall covered bridge on the way to Housatonic Meadows State Park. Along the way, you'll encounter a series of Class I, II, and III rapids. The take-out is the Housatonic Meadows State Park picnic area off U.S. 7.

The majority of the **Farmington River** caters to **white-water enthusiasts.** Arguably, the finest strip of water is the 11- or 12-mile run between Riverton and New Hartford. Class I to III rapids glide through American Legion and Peoples State Forests, passing the small villages of Riverton, Pleasant Valley, Pine Meadow, and New Hartford along the way. The put-in is the state picnic area

in Riverton on State Route 20, across from the Hitchcock Chair Factory Store. The take-out is Satan's Kingdom Access Area, before the U.S. 44 bridge on the right. If you want to go south of Satan's Kingdom, you had better be a skilled canoeist to maneuver through Satan's Kingdom Gorge. You will also have to contend with a popular tubing run. The waters on the **Lower Farmington River** off State Route 4 in Farmington are more tranquil, and ideal for inexperienced paddlers. For information regarding the water conditions on the Housatonic, contact **Northeast Utilities** (tel. 860/824-7861) or the **Housatonic Valley Association** (tel. 860/672-6678). For water conditions on the Farmington River, contact the **Farmington River Watershed Association** (tel. 860/658-4442).

In addition to these two cherished rivers, consider canoeing on **Lake Waramaug, Burr Pond,** and **Winchester Lake.**

OUTFITTERS, RENTALS & INSTRUCTION

◆ **Clarke Outdoors,** 163 U.S. 7, West Cornwall, CT 06796 (tel. 860/672-6365), provides canoes, kayaks, and rafts for guided and self-guided trips on the Housatonic River. Owner Mark Clarke also offers kayak instruction. He's a nine-time National Canoe Champion.

◆ **Riverrunning Expeditions,** 85 Main Street, Falls Village, CT 06031 (tel. 860/824-5579), offers self-guided canoe, kayak, and raft trips on the Housatonic. They will shuttle you and your means of transportation to the put-in. You do the rest.

◆ **Main Stream,** U.S. 44, New Hartford, CT 06057 (tel. 860/693-6791 or 860/379-6657), provides canoe rentals and shuttles paddlers to the Upper and Lower Farmington River. They also offer moonlight canoe trips and instruction.

◆ **North American Canoe Tours,** 65 Black Point Road, Niantic, CT 06357 (tel. 860/739-0791), rents canoes on Lake Waramaug, Burr Pond, Squantz Pond, and Mount Tom State Park.

CROSS-COUNTRY SKIING

Challenging backcountry ski runs are not nearly as prevalent in Connecticut as in the network of trails further north that weave through the Berkshires or Vermont. That's not to say that decent cross-country skiing is nowhere to be found. You just have to search a little harder. The best variety of trails in Connecticut is in the northwest corner of the state in the Litchfield Hills region. For a complete listing of state parks that offer backcountry skiing, contact the **Department of Environmental Protection,** Office of State Parks and Recreation, 79 Elm Street, Hartford, CT 06106-5127 (tel. 860/424-3200).

BACKCOUNTRY

The White Memorial Foundation

Allow 2–2.5 hours. Easy to moderate. Access: From Litchfield, take U.S. 202 West towards Bantam. You'll see a big sign for White Memorial on the left-hand side. Make a left turn on Bissell Road, a right turn onto White Woods Road and then another left onto Webster Road. Parking is located on the left-hand side next to Catlin Woods. Map: Available at visitor center.

The old adage that the best restaurant in a town is the one with the most people has always proved to be true in my travels. This does not apply to cross-country skiing. Usually people flock to a place for convenience's sake—the trails are easily marked, the location nearby—rather than roughing it in the woods to find a serene path. But on occasion, I find a popular place whose selection of trails is so spectacular that it's worth mentioning. This is the case with White Memorial, or White Woods as the locals call it. There were ski tracks everywhere I looked, from the main parking lot to the most remote trail. But it was such a pleasure to glide over the gently rolling hills that it didn't really matter how many skiers or big dogs I said hello to. One Saint Bernard puppy named Billy couldn't wait to greet me. He jumped up and practically pinned me to the ground.

The trail I chose was a little less populated. I parked the car next to Catlin Woods and did a quick 10-minute warm-up in the forest of oaks, maples, and white pines. Then I crossed Webster Road and started cruising on the blue rectangle-blazed Mattatuck Trail. The trail is relatively flat, passing cattails, sedges, and other marsh vegetation alongside Cranberry Pond. Bearing left, I stayed on Mattatuck until I hit State Route 63. Here, I had to take off my skis to cross the road, but that's where the fun began.

Mattatuck curves down to Heron Pond and then begins to turn gradually uphill. At the top, I stuck with the blue rectangles and swept downhill past Plunge Pool, turning right to avoid plunging into this small body of water. This is supposedly one of Alain White's favorite spots to bird watch. An avid naturalist, White bought most of these defunct farmlands between 1908 and 1912. Since he was paralyzed from the waist down, White created horse-and-buggy paths to go on his bird-watching expeditions. I'm sure he didn't realize how well these paths are suited for cross-country skiing.

I stayed on Mattatuck until I veered right onto Beaver Pond Trail, following the white rectangles. Crossing Route 63 again, I took a quick right turn onto Big

Cathedral Trail and continued with the orange rectangles. This is a swift downhill run through shrubs and maples on a narrow trail, which was obviously not created in Alain White's day. Big Cathedral connects with Mattatuck at the bottom of the slope. A right turn and then a left at the fork brought me back to Catlin Woods.

Fuller Pond

Allow 1.5–2 hours. Moderate. Access: From Kent, take State Route 341 West to Macedonia Brook Road. Take a right on Macedonia and then another right on Fuller Mountain Road. The parking lot and sign are on the right-hand side. Map: Available at the trailhead.

I was told that the Appalachian Trail from Kent to Cornwall was a nice flat path along the Housatonic River. However, the man who mentioned this neglected to tell me that the trailhead was located on River Road, a road that's inaccessible to all cars except four-wheel-drive vehicles in the winter months. Gliding along on skis is fine, but skidding on snow in my Mercury Lynx is terrifying. I might overestimate my capabilities, but wisely, not my car's. After a mile of swerving along River Road only feet from the icy Housatonic, I turned around. The AT didn't entice me enough to risk turning my car into a boat.

I drove to Backcountry Outfitters in Kent where owner Dave Fairty found a map and showed me one of the local treasures, the loop around Fuller Pond. A little over 2 miles long, the trail weaves in and out of barren forest and wide-open fields, all centered around the spring-fed glacial lake known as Fuller Pond.

I signed in and then headed up the Entry Trail. At the top of the hill, the path descends sharply down to the pond—it would probably make a good bunny hill if it was located on a ski slope. I stayed on Entry until I saw the white-frosted pond glowing under the sun's rays like a diamond in the rough. I took a right on Pond Trail, winding along the water's embankment, then another right on Red Gate, and a left onto Saturday Afternoon Trail. Disregard the name; Saturday Afternoon is a great trail anytime there's snow on the ground. The path climbs sharply to an 1,130-foot lookout over the park, then winds downhill through an expansive field. Don't make the mistake I made by turning right at the end of the field and ending up at Fuller Mountain Road. Bear left on Saturday Afternoon along a creek and through the woods, and you'll eventually hook up with Fuller Pond again. Another right and I was heading back up the bunny hill and down to my safe-and-sound car.

Mohawk State Forest Loop

1.5–2 mile loop. Allow 1 hour. Easy to moderate. Access: From Goshen, take State Route 4 West 4 miles to the large Mohawk State Forest sign at Toumey Road. Go about a mile, until you see a log gate with a Closed at Sunset sign. There's a small turn off to the right. Map: Contact the Department of Environmental Protection, Office of State Parks and Recreation, 79 Elm Street, Hartford, CT 06106-5127 (tel. 203/424-3200).

I didn't have much time before sunset, but I needed a quick fix. That's when I got lucky, and haphazardly came upon the Mohawk State Forest Trail. The hardest part about this 1¹/₂- to 2-mile loop is finding the trailhead (don't bother visiting the forest headquarters in winter—there's rarely anyone there). But once you arrive, you're in for a treat.

Squeeze between the log and the adjacent rock and make your way to the left of the lean-to up the short hill. When you reach the top, it's smooth gliding all the way. This is Connecticut bog country, where berries from mountain holly and leaves from pitcher plants drop to the trail. Low-hung branches from the white pines will help improve your diagonal stride and duck routine. The trail is relatively straight until it bends toward the left near Mohawk Mountain Road—a small sign confirms that this is, indeed, a cross-country trail. Then the trail curves left again, descending back towards Toumey Road. At Toumey, I had a small problem. My car wasn't parked at campsite number 12, it was parked 0.3 mile up the road, to the left. Since there was very little snow on the plowed pavement, I had to do a drop-and-carry. Oh well, life is full of imperfections, like loops that don't loop. At least the walk back to my car gave me a great view of the Litchfield Hills and the skiers slaloming down Mohawk Mountain.

Steep Rock Loop, Steep Rock Reservation

Allow 1.5 hours. Moderate to strenuous. Access: From Washington, take State Route 47 North just past the Shepaug River bridge. There's parking on the right-hand side. Map: Available from the Wilderness Shop, U.S. 202, in Litchfield.

Steep Rock is an apt name for the loop I took in the Hidden Valley region of this reservation. I parked my car north of the bridge, climbed up the short hill, stayed to my right, and cruised down the other side of the slope. As it curves along the pristine S-shaped Shepaug River, the trail is flooded with the soothing sound of water rushing over ice-covered rocks. I glided past fireplace number 4 and a footbridge, in my usual deep-in-the-forest meditative trance, when the trail started to switchback up the side of the hill. I should have taken the footbridge that led to the other side of the river and more trails.

Yet, against better judgment, I chose to take this punishing, unrelenting—all the grueling adjectives you could possibly think of, thrown into a pot and boiled—climb. Two treacherous zigs and two treacherous zags traversing the side of the hill and I finally reached the top. And don't think I was the only sucker who skied up this hill. There were numerous V-shaped wedges along the way. Thighs burning, I stopped and waited for someone to pin a button to my lapel that reads, "I Conquered Steep Rock." Instead, a couple birds twittered and I was on my way.

Take a quick right turn on top of the hill and bear right every time to complete the loop. The narrow trail slices between coniferous hardwoods the whole way down, almost justifying the uphill battle. You'll be back at the beginning in no time, ready to try it again.

SKI TOURING

If there's snow anywhere in Connecticut, you can usually find it at the 1,391-foot peak of Pine Mountain. Fifteen miles of groomed trails weave through the woods and open meadows of the **Pine Mountain Ski Touring Center,** State Route 179, East Hartland, CT 06027 (tel. 860/653-4279). The center also connects with a challenging backcountry run, the 5.9-mile (one-way) Tunxis Trail to State Route 219.

East of Pine Mountain, **Cedar Brook Cross Country Ski Center,** 1481 Ratley Road, West Suffield, CT 06093 (tel. 860/668-5026), offers 10 km of groomed trails on their 200-acre working horse farm.

Twenty kilometers of rolling groomed trails are provided by the **Winding Trails Cross Country Ski Center,** 50 Winding Trails Drive, Farmington, CT 06032 (tel. 860/678-9582). They also offer instruction and moonlight tours.

DOWNHILL SKIING

With the longest vertical drop at 660 feet, don't expect Connecticut ski areas to rival the heavyweights in northern New England. They're better known as family resorts, places to learn how to ski before you tackle tougher terrain, resorts where you sit down and have a hot chocolate at the lodge after a long day of cruising on forest trails that are scenic but not difficult.

Mohawk Moutain

46 Great Hollow Road, Cornwall, CT 06753. Tel. 860/672-6100; 860/672-6464 for snow conditions. 23 trails (20% beginner, 60% intermediate, 20% expert); 5 lifts including 1 triple and 4 doubles; 660-foot vertical drop. Full day tickets are $25 all week.

Mohawk Mountain is where artificial snowmaking technology evolved. In the winter of 1949, owner Walt Schoenknecht was desperate for snowfall. When February arrived and there was no white wet stuff on the mountain, Schoenknecht bought an ice pulverizer and all the ice within a 50-mile radius. He proceeded to produce a powdery ice that was barely skiable. Years later, Schoenknecht was one of the first to create snow from water and compressed air. The slopes here are mostly gentle, though there are exceptions, like steep and bumpy Wildwood.

Ski Sundown

State Route 219, New Hartford, CT 06057. Tel. 860/379-9851; 860/379-SNOW for snow conditions. 15 trails (8 beginner, 4 intermediate, 3 expert); 4 lifts including 3 triples and 1 double; 625-foot vertical drop. Full day tickets are $30 all week.

Covering 65 acres, Ski Sundown is the second-largest ski resort in the state, though it is arguably first in scenery. Sundown's Gunbarrel is one of the state's most advanced runs.

Woodbury Ski Area

State Route 47, Woodbury, CT 06798. Tel. 203/263-2203. 14 trails (4 beginner, 5 intermediate, 5 expert); 1 double lift; 300-foot vertical drop. Full day tickets are $20 all week.

Experts will get bored here, but there are several decent runs for intermediates. Snowboarders have three half-pipes and their own run complete with jumps to choose between.

Mount Southington Ski Area

396 Mount Vernon Road, Southington, CT 06489. Tel. 860/628-0954; 800/982-6828 for a snow report from within CT. 14 trails (5 beginner, 5 intermediate, 4 expert), 2 lifts including 1 triple and 1 double; 425-foot vertical drop. Full day tickets are $28 weekends, $26 weekdays.

Young families crowd the slopes of Mount Southington Ski Area. There's also a half-pipe for snowboarders.

FISHING

The stretch of the **Housatonic River** near Housatonic Meadows State Park is a nine-mile trout management area, with three miles reserved for **fly-fishing.** It is one of the premier **trout** fishing rivers in the state. **Browns** and **rainbows** are plentiful. In the warmer months, you might hook a **smallmouth bass.** There's a catch-and-release policy in effect since PCB's dumped by the General Electric plant in Pittsfield, Massachusetts, from 1940 to 1967 have collected in the sediment. Anglers also congregate on the banks of the **Farmington River** where **brown, brook,** and **rainbow trout,** smallmouth bass, yellow perch, and **pickerel** have been caught. An inland fishing license is required for anyone 16 or older. They can be purchased from any town clerk. For more information, contact the **Fisheries Division,** DEP, 79 Elm Street, Hartford, CT 06106 (tel. 203/424-FISH), and ask them for their "Connecticut Angler's Guide."

If you're in need of a guide in the Litchfield Hills area, contact **Rob Nicholas,** P.O. Box 282, West Cornwall, CT 06796 (tel. 203/672-4457). **O'Hara's Landing Marina,** Twin Lakes Road (tel. 860/824-7583), rents 16-foot aluminum boats with 10 horsepower engines on Twin Lakes. The lake is known for its **brown trout** fishing.

On the coast, **Sometime Charters** in Bridgeport (tel. 203/438-5838), **My Fair Lady** in Stamford (tel. 203/853-6465), **Reel Thing** in Stratford (tel. 203/375-8263), and **Stacy Ann** in South Norwalk (tel. 203/866-9671) take anglers out on one- to six-passenger boats in search of **stripers, blues, cod, pollock, flukes, porgies,** and **flounder. Fisherman's World** in Norwalk (tel. 203/866-1075) rents fishing supplies and guides. For a complete listing of fishing charters, contact the **Connecticut State Tourism Office** (tel. 800/CT-BOUND) and ask for their Connecticut Vacation Guide. If you want to head out on your own, **Overton's Boat Livery,** 80 Seaview Avenue, Norwalk (tel. 203/838-2031), rents 16-foot dories with 6 horsepower motors. For larger boats, contact **Jubilee Yacht Charters** (tel. 800/922-4871).

GOLF

Golf Digest ranks the par-72 **Richter Park** (Aunt Hack Road, Danbury; tel. 203/792-2552) first in Connecticut and among the top 25 public golf courses in the country. If you can't get a tee time here, try two other favorite courses in the area: **Ridgefield Golf Course** in Ridgefield (tel. 203/748-7008) and **Tashua Knolls Golf** course in Trumbull (tel. 203/261-5989).

HIKING & BACKPACKING

DAY HIKES

The hikers who cut the Appalachian Trail didn't just connect Georgia to Maine in a straight line from Point A to Point B; they created a path through the finest forest and mountains on the East Coast. Thus, it's not surprising that the AT in Connecticut provides some of the premier trails in the state; 56 miles of the Appalachian Trail weave through the western corner of Connecticut. This might seem like a small amount compared to the trails total length of 2,144 miles, but it provides numerous opportunities for the average day hiker. All three of the following hikes were on sections of the AT.

Ten Mile Hill

4 miles round trip. Allow 2–2.5 hours. Easy to moderate. Access: From the junction of State Route 341 and U.S. 7 in Kent, head 3 miles south on U.S. 7 and turn right onto Bull's Bridge Road. Go through the covered bridge, passing the parking lot on your right, and continue across the second bridge; there's a small parking area on your left.

This hike combines two river walks with a hike up to the summit of Ten Mile Hill. If you're not interested in climbing, you should at least stroll along the rivers to the point where the path makes its ascent. You'll be following the white blazes that mark Connecticut's contribution to the Appalachian Trail.

Before tackling the Ten Mile Hill hike, walk back to Bull's Bridge, one of two operating covered bridges in the state. (The other is in West Cornwall.) Spanning the Housatonic River, Bull's

Bridge was originally built in 1842. To the left of the bridge is the Bull's Bridge Scenic Trail Loop. This short path will guide you to the bank of the river, where you can watch and hear the rapids swirling around the massive boulders. According to local lore, the Housatonic was a raging river long before hydroelectric dams. This area of Kent played a strategic role in the Revolutionary War. It was located on the marching road between Lebanon, site of the Continental supply depot, and George Washington's New York headquarters. Evidently, Washington himself passed through these woods once. According to his own expense account, on March 3, 1781, our illustrious general, first president, and national icon, might have taken a nasty spill on his horse. His travel expense reads, "getting a horse out of Bull's Bridge Falls, $215.00." That was an incredible amount of money in those days to spend on saving an animal, so we can only assume that it was Washington's mount.

Once you've observed the falls, return to the Appalachian Trail to begin your walk. The rushing waters of the Housatonic are to your left as you meander along the wide path. When the trail forks, bear left, following the white blazes on the far more narrow path. The trail starts to rise above the water, before descending to Ten Mile Gorge. This is where the waters of the Housatonic and Ten Mile rivers merge. Cross the bridge and turn right through the camping area. The trail hugs the shores of Ten Mile River for a short time before veering left into a forest of maples, oaks, and hemlocks. Here the walk ends and the hike starts. A series of switchbacks climb steadily to the crest of Ten Mile Hill. When you reach a set of blue blazes, continue to climb until you notice blue blazes again. Walk several yards to your right for a wide-open vista of this sylvan landscape. The westward view overlooks the Taconic Mountains, with the Catskills in the distance and rolling farms in between. To return to the trailhead, simply retrace your steps.

Bear Mountain

6.7-mile loop. Allow 5 hours. Moderate to strenuous. Access: From the junction of U.S. 44 and State Route 41 in Salisbury, follow Route 41 north for 3.2 miles. The parking area is on your left. Map: USGS 7.5 minute Bash-Bish Falls Topo.

Connecticut's most strenuous hike reaches the highest peak in the state, Bear Mountain. Oddly enough, it's not the highest point. That honor goes to the south shoulder of Mount Frissel, which rises to 2,380 feet on the Connecticut-Massachusetts border. This 6.7-mile loop to the summit starts on the blue-blazed Undermountain Trail. The narrow path is gentle at first, but soon widens to a dirt road as it climbs steadily through the hardwood and pine forest. At the 1.1-mile mark, turn right on Paradise Lane for an uphill climb past a spruce bog, mountain laurel and huckleberry bushes, thick American chestnut trees, and a copse of hemlocks that sits atop the steep south bank of Sages Ravine. The white blazes denoting the Appalachian Trail appear shortly thereafter. Turn left on the AT for a strenuous ascent up Bear Mountain's rock face. At several sharp ledges, you'll have to use both hands and feet to propel yourself upward. Eventually, you'll reach the 2,316-foot open summit. Beyond the wind-stunted scrub pines are panoramic views of mountains and lakes. The Catskills and Mount Frissel are to the west, tower-topped Mount Everett and Race Mountain lie to the north, Twin Lakes and Cannan Mountain are eastward, and Mohawk and Haystack Mountains can be seen to the south.

To start your descent, follow the AT south along a rocky trail which offers more stunning views to the southwest; 0.6 mile from the summit, a tote road merges from the right. Bear left on the AT and in another 0.2 mile, you'll be at a T-intersection known as Riga Junction. This is where the Appalachian Trail connects with the Undermountain Trail. Turn left on this blue-blazed trail for a 1.9-mile descent through the deep forest back to your car.

Pine Knob Loop

2.5-mile loop. Allow 1.5–2 hours. Moderate. Access: From the junction of State Route 4 and U.S. 7 in Cornwall Bridge, head 1.7 miles north on U.S. 7 to a parking lot on the left-hand side of the road. You'll see the oval blue sign for the Pine Knob Loop Trail. Map: USGS 7.5 minute Ellsworth Topo.

This 2.5-mile loop is an excellent introduction to the peaks of the Litchfield Hills. From the parking lot, cross Hatch Brook, and continue walking parallel to U.S. 7 past the first trail junction. The sound of cars fades away as you begin your ascent to the first knob through a forest of oaks, ashes, maples, and hickories. Follow the blue blazes up the steep rocky slopes to your first lookout. Row after row of rounded hilltops stand to the east. The blue blazes continue to climb to the first summit before descending precipitously into a col. Here, you meet up with the Appalachian Trail and veer left back into the forest. Soon, you're atop the second knob, which provides you with the best views on the hike. The waters of the Housatonic River wind through the valley, while the ski trails of Mohawk Mountain can be seen to the left in the distance. The Pine Knob Trail and the AT eventually split when you reach Hatch Brook. Veer left and venture downhill, accompanied by the sounds of rushing water. When you reach the loop junction, turn right to return to your car.

BACKPACKING

There are 56 miles of the **Appalachian Trail** that weave through the northwestern corner of Connecticut from Kent north to Cornwall, Salisbury, and the summit of Bear Mountain, before reaching the Massachusetts border. All three climbs detailed in the "Day Hikes" section are on segments of the AT. If you'd like to do some backpacking, the Connecticut segment is one of the easiest stretches of the 2,144-mile trail. It includes a level 7.8-mile walk along the Housatonic River, the longest river walk on the trail.

There are also the 500-plus miles of the **Blue-Blazed System** which branch out across Connecticut in every direction. Many of these trails run for 30 to 40 miles, ideal for extended overnight hikes. For further information, contact the **Connecticut Forest and Park Association,** 16 Meriden Road, Rockfall, CT 06481-2691 (tel. 860/346-TREE).

GUIDES

Michael Cavallaro, owner of **Pathfinders,** 181 Indian Trail Road, New Milford, CT 06776 (tel. 860/354-1824), takes groups of eight or more walkers on customized day hikes through the region. Michael infuses his talks with local Indian tales and natural history as he guides you on remote trails to archaeological sites and scenic overlooks. The price is $25 per person.

Wild Earth Adventures, P.O. Box 655, Pomona, NY 10970 (tel. 914/354-3717), offers a one-day guided hike around Steep Rock Reservation (see "Cross-Country Skiing").

HORSEBACK RIDING

Lee's Riding Stable (tel. 860/567-0785) in Litchfield offers scenic rides through the forests of the Litchfield Hills region. In Falls Village, **Rustling Wind Stables** (tel. 860/824-7634) offers both Western and English-style riding. Closer to the coast, **Chance Hill Equestrian Center** (tel. 203/762-3234) and **Stonyside Farms** (tel. 203/762-7984) both offer trail rides in Wilton.

MOUNTAIN BIKING

Western Connecticut has its own share of state forests and parks, replete with hundreds of miles of challenging terrain to lure mountain bikers. That's one of the nicest things about mountain biking in Connecticut: simply pick a state forest and you're bound to find decent double- and single-track riding.

Chestnut Hill

Allow 2–3 hours. Moderate. Access: From the center of Litchfield, take State Route 63 South to the junction with State Route 61. There will be a small parking area on your left. Map: The White Memorial trails can be found on a map available at the Foundation's headquarters on U.S. 202.

The network of trails that exist in the outlying areas of Litchfield are praised by cross-country skiers in the winter (see "White Memorial" under "Cross-Country Skiing") and mountain bikers in the summer. Former carriage-path trails, hard-packed dirt roads, and the legendary "Ho Chi Minh Trail" challenge fat-wheelers of all levels. Start your ride on the wide Beaver Pond Trail. This carriage-path trail is just one of many bike routes found at White Memorial. Be considerate of walkers by paying attention to signs that prohibit bikers and horseback riders on certain paths. The white rectangles of the Beaver Pond Trail sweep down to the pond, circle the eastern shores, and eventually stop at a dirt road. Turn right and veer

right again when Chestnut Hill Road merges to reach a large reservoir. Do not bear left along the embankment, but continue uphill. Halfway into your climb, you'll find a blue-blazed trail rambling off to your left. This is the Ho Chi Minh, a technical single-track that weaves up and down the hillside like the Great Wall of China. Get ready for a rock-hopping, log-jumping, root-studded ride that's guaranteed to test your skills. The blue blazes will lead you up and down the hills until you arrive at a dirt road. Here, you have three choices. You can turn left and continue to follow the blue blazes over a hill and somehow make your way back to East Chestnut Hill Road; return the way you came; or you can turn right on a dirt road past several farms onto Farnham Road, veer right at State Route 109 West, and right again on State Route 63 North. The latter is the quickest way back to your car.

Nepaug State Forest

Ride as long as your legs will hold out. Moderate. Access: From the junction of U.S. Routes 44 and 202, just west of Canton, head west on U.S. 202 for approximately 2.8 miles. Look for a small, hidden Nepaug State Forest sign where you turn right on a dirt road. Park at any of the turnoffs. Map: Contact the Department of Environmental Protection, Office of State Parks and Recreation, 79 Elm Street, Hartford, CT 06106-5127 (tel. 860/424-3200).

The finest web of trails in the western half of the state are at Nepaug and Nassahegon State Forests. Nepaug has more than 1,100 acres of secluded single-tracks, double-tracks and dirt roads to play on. Park your car anywhere and then head toward the power lines that forge up the hillside. Parallel to the sandy road, there's a grassy double-track. Take this up to your first dirt road, where you bear right. A network of single- and double-track trails branch off in every direction. Simply take one and see where it leads you. If you somehow manage to get lost in this small forest, find the power lines which will guide you back down again.

ROAD BIKING

Finding "the road less traveled" in western Connecticut is not as hard as you might expect. To escape car traffic, get as far away from I-95 as possible and head to the northern fringes of the state. Unfortunately, as the name Litchfield Hills implies, the rural roads here are not flat. Short hills roll past dairy farms, bodies of water, and rarely visited villages. The rewards far outweigh the effort.

THE RIDES

Farmington River Ride

Allow 2–3 hours. Moderate. Access: Colebrook is located on State Route 183 north of Winsted. You can park behind the town hall. Map: Any good state road map.

You're never far from water on this 24-mile loop through the northern reaches of the Litchfield Hills region. The ride starts in Colebrook, a picturesque village where colonial clapboard homes and Connecticut's oldest general store line the well-kept village green. From the town hall, bear left on Smith Hill Road to begin a gradual ascent. The road starts to rise and fall as you pass horse farms, secluded houses, and rows of forest. After two miles, turn left on Smith Hill Road and left again almost immediately at the fork, onto unmarked Deer Grass Road. This is an exhilarating $1^1/_2$-mile downhill run through the woods. When you reach State Route 8, bear left and then right after the bridge onto Riverton Road. The Farmington River appears on

your right. You'll be following the waters of this winding river for the next 13 miles. At the stop sign in Riverton, continue straight over the bridge, and take your first right onto East River Road. This narrow road weaves with the waterway through the maples, oaks, and evergreens of Peoples State Forest. When East River Road reaches the junction of State Routes 181 and 318, bear right across the bridge. Another right turn onto West River Road will loop you back to Riverton via the American Legion State Forest. At the stop sign in town, turn left to ride on Riverton Road again. Bear right onto Route 8, and less than a mile later, bear left onto Sandy Brook Road. For the next 4 miles you will be biking steadily uphill along the brook, until you reach the junction of State Route 183. Turn left to return to the village of Colebrook.

Salisbury

Allow 2–2.5 hours. Moderate; rolling hills. Access: Salisbury is located in the northwestern corner of the state at the junction of U.S. 44 and State Route 41. Park your car anywhere along Main Street. Map: Any good state road map.

Tucked snugly within the undulating terrain of the Litchfield Hills are small New England communities replete with church steeples, town greens, and antique shops that beckon urbanites from along the Eastern seaboard. Jumping from village to village on the main arteries, most visitors miss the real beauty of the Litchfield Hills, the pastoral countryside. This 21-mile loop leads you away from the villages on quiet backcountry roads to the rolling mountains, lakes, farmland, and forest that make up the region.

Park your car on Main Street in Salisbury and continue on U.S. 44 West past the village green and the White Hart Inn's long front porch. A little more than a mile later, turn left at the blinking light onto Taconic Road, and watch out for deer—the last time I biked here, I had to swerve off the road to avoid hitting a large buck. A red barn on the left has the perfect vantage point atop a small hill. The Taconic Mountains rise to the west; the shores of Twin Lakes can be seen to the east. At the bottom of the hill, veer right onto Twin Lakes Road. More than a mile later, veer right again as Twin Lakes Road curves around the shores of this secluded lake. A right turn onto Weatogue Road will bring you past green pastures back to U.S. 44. Turn left and then right onto State Route 126 South. The road climbs sharply at first but soon levels off.

A little more than 3.5 miles from the junction of U.S. 44, turn right onto Point of Rocks Road and veer right again onto Water Street. You'll cruise under a railroad bridge and across a blue iron trestle bridge before taking an immediate left onto Dugway Street. For the next several miles, the waters of the Housatonic River will be your companion. When Dugway Road ends, turn right onto State Route 112. Directly across the street is the Lime Rock Park motor speedway, Paul Newman's favorite racing track. Turn right on Salmon Kill Road. Dairy farms and palatial estates stand side by side, living up to Litchfield's reputation as a getaway for the rich and famous. Henry Kissenger, Whoopi Goldberg, Meryl Streep, Dustin Hoffman, and Walter Matthau all own property here. At the end of Salmon Kill Road, turn right onto U.S. 44 to reach Salisbury and complete the loop.

RENTALS

Mountain bikes and road bikes for the above rides can be rented at **Cycle Loft,** 25 Litchfield Commons, Litchfield, CT 06759 (tel. 860/567-1713).

SAILING

With relatively little surf and numerous island anchorages, the Long Island shore is an excellent place to rent a boat or learn how to sail. **Off-Shore Yachts** in South Norwalk (tel. 203/853-2031) rents sailboats. The **Norwalk Sailing School,** Calf Pasture Beach, Norwalk (tel. 203/852-1857), rents sailboats and offers instruction. **Russell Yacht Charters,** 404 Hulls Highway, Fairfield (tel. 203/255-2783) can arrange bareboat charters.

Tired of the male-dominated sailing world? In 1989 Sherry Jagerson founded **Women's Sailing Adventures** (39 Woodside Avenue, Westport, CT 06880; tel. 203/227-7413 or 800/328-8053) to teach women the fine art of sailing. An inveterate sailor and impassioned instructor, Jagerson is the perfect person to learn from. She offers two-, three-, and seven-day courses out of Westport on 37- to 44-foot boats. She also arranges a four-hour beginner's course on J/24s. More than three-quarters of the class is taught under sail, and the student-to-instructor ratio is 2 or 3 to 1.

Longshore Sailing School (Longshore Club Park, 260 South Compo Rd., Westport, CT 06880; tel. 203/226-1646) is one of the most popular day-sailing schools in the country. Twelve hours of instruction in four sessions over two weekends are provided for all levels and ages. You sail at the mouth of the salt water Saugatuck River on boats under 16 feet long. How to rig a boat, start, stop, trim your sail, jibe, and tack are just some of the essential skills taught in the course.

SEA KAYAKING

The **Small Boat Shop,** located at 144 Water Street, South Norwalk, CT 06854 (tel. 203/854-5223), offers one-day guided sea kayaking tours of the

Norwalk Islands. Starting at their dock on the Norwalk River, you paddle past Manresa Point and across the channel to Sheffield Island to see its historic lighthouse. After lunch at Shea Island, the journey continues to Chimon Island, where a National Wildlife Preserve is located. A variety of herons, snowy egrets, American oystercatchers, and ospreys have been spotted on the shores. Cost of the trip including guide and rentals is $80. They also offer instructional tours for $95. Call for specific dates.

SNOWMOBILING

Peoples, Housatonic, Mohawk, Naugatuck, and **Pootatuck** all have extensive trail systems for the snowmobiler. For additional information, contact the **Department of Environmental Protection,** Office of State Parks and Recreation, 79 Elm Street, Hartford, CT 06106-5127 (tel. 860/424-3200), and ask for their "Snowmobiling in Connecticut" brochure and state forest maps.

SWIMMING

On the Gold Coast, access to the shoreline is limited. Most of the **beaches** are town-owned and available to local residents only. The major exception is **Sherwood Island State Park** in Westport, the closest of Connecticut's beach parks to New York. The two-mile stretch of sand is wide and flat, and ideal for children. To reach Sherwood Island, take I-95 North to Exit 18 and then turn right onto the Sherwood Island Connector.

In the Litchfield Hills area, the popular **swimming holes** are **Lake Waramaug State Park; Sandy Beach,** on the western end of Bantam Lake; **Northfield Dam Recreation Area,** south of Litchfield; **Mount Tom State Park, Burr Pond**

State Park, and **Park Pond,** near Winchester Center.

TUBING

The Class I, II, and III rapids on the **Farmington River** are perfectly suited for tubing. **Farmington River Tubing,** Satan's Kingdom State Recreation Area, located on U.S. 44, New Hartford (tel. 860/693-6465 or 860/739-0791), supplies guests with comfortable inner tubes for their 2.5-hour spine-tingling journey down the river. No, the tubes are not bald tires, but big yellow-and-green river tubes with two separate air chambers just in case one of the chambers goes flat. The highlight of the trip is **Satan's Kingdom Gorge,** a series of rapids that propel you quickly through a narrow chasm. Children must be at least 10 years old and stand 4 feet, 5 inches tall. The cost of the trip is only $9.

WALKS & RAMBLES

Connecticut's web of **Blue-Blazed hiking trails** is one of the finest trail networks in the Northeast. The paths weave inland, through forests of maples, oaks, and birches. **Connecticut Forest and Park Association** (16 Meriden Road, Rockfall, CT 06481-2691; tel. 203/346-TREE) has information on all the blue-blazed trails and hosts a "Trails Day" in early summer to introduce more walkers to the system. They also publish the *Connecticut Walk Book,* which details all blue-blazed trails.

WHITEWATER KAYAKING

The **Housatonic and Farmington Rivers** are two of the top waterways in the Northeast for whitewater kayaking. For more information, look under "Canoeing."

Campgrounds & Other Accommodations

CAMPING

Many of Connecticut's state parks and forests have campgrounds. For reservations and a listing of all camping facilities, Contact the **Office of State Parks and Recreation,** 79 Elm Street, Hartford, CT 06106-5127 (tel. 860/424-3200).

Housatonic Meadows State Park

From the junction of State Route 4 and U.S. 7 in Cornwall Bridge, head north on U.S. 7 for several miles. Tel. 860/672-6772. 97 sites, no hookups. Sewage disposal, public phone, tables, and fire rings.

Twenty-two of the sites are located on the Housatonic River, so you'll need to book far in advance to compete with the fly-fishermen and canoeists. This is not a swimming river.

Lake Waramaug State Park

From New Preston, head north on Lake Waramaug Road. Tel. 860/868-2592. 88 sites, no hookups. Sewage disposal, public phone, tables, and fire rings.

One of the most scenic campgrounds in the state, the sites are spread out along the shores of this majestic lake. Swimming, fishing, and canoeing are popular.

White Memorial Family Campground

From the junction of Route 63 and U.S. 202 in Litchfield, go 2.5 miles southwest on U.S. 202 and 1 mile south on North Shore Road. Tel. 860/567-0089. 68 sites, no hookups, sewage disposal, public phone, tables, fire rings, grocery store, ice, and wood.

Situated on the grounds of the White Memorial Foundation, the sites are near the walking and biking trails.

Macedonia Brook State Park

From the junction of State Route 341 and U.S. 7 in Kent, head 3 miles northwest on Route 341 and then 2 miles north on Macedonia Brook Road. Tel. 860/927-4100. 84 sites, no hookups. Pit toilets, public phone, tables, and fire rings.

The sites are positioned along the hillside near the brook.

Burr Pond State Park

From the junction of State Routes 4 and 8, head 6 miles north on Route 8 to Exit 46. Take West Highland Lake Road to Burr Mountain Road. Tel. 860/379-0172. 40 sites, no hookups. Sewage disposal, public phone, tables, fire rings.

The park is best known for its public beach and fishing. Most of the campsites are in the dense forest.

INNS & RESORTS

Boulders Inn

East Shore Road (State Route 45), New Preston, CT 06777. Tel. 860/868-0541. Rooms start at $150 per night, but there are many packages that include dinner at their reputable restaurant, so call for prices.

Located on the shores of Lake Waramaug, this country inn is surrounded by eight secluded cottages that hug the hillside. Many of the rooms have lake views and fireplaces. The inn offers boating on the lake and provides tennis courts, a private beach, and a hiking trail.

The White Hart

The Village Green, P.O. Box 385, Salisbury, CT 06068. Tel. 203/435-0030. Double rooms start at $75 a night.

The wide porch of this recently renovated inn overlooks the village green in Salisbury. Rooms are sumptuous and the historic tavern downstairs is a good place to cool off after you complete the Salisbury bike loop.

Hilltop Haven B&B

175 Dibble Hill Road, West Cornwall, CT 06796. Tel. 860/672-6871. Double rooms cost $112 per night and include breakfast.

You can thank Everett Van Dorn for opening up his family's summer home to the public, and you can thank me for telling you about it. Hilltop Haven is one of those accommodations that is almost impossible to find on your own. The intimate inn is perched high above the Housatonic River in the forest of West Cornwall. It is an ideal location for canoeing or fly-fishing in the Housatonic or for hiking the Pine Knob Loop. Unfortunately, Everett only has two rooms available, so you'll need to reserve far in advance.

Old Riverton Inn

State Route 20, Riverton, CT 06065. Tel. 860/379-8678. Rooms start at $75 and include breakfast.

The Old Riverton Inn has been providing comforts for the weary traveler since 1796, when this historic tavern was on the post route between Hartford and Albany. The 12-room inn is situated on the shores of the Farmington River, close to Main Stream canoe rentals, Farmington River Tubing, and Pine Mountain cross-country ski center.

Interlaken Inn

74 Interlaken Road, State Route 112, Lakeville, CT 06039. Tel. 203/435-9878. Rooms start at $85.

Situated on 26 acres near the New York border, the Interlaken is one of the largest resorts in the Litchfield Hills. The facility is perfect for families. Activities include sailing, canoeing, and fishing on Lake Wononskopomuc, and practicing your serve on two tennis courts. Or you can simply lounge in the outdoor pool.

The Inn at Longshore

260 South Compo Road, Westport, CT 06880. Tel. 203/226-3316. Double rooms cost $130.

This small cozy inn is conveniently located near the beach of Sherwood Island State Park and the sailing schools of Westport. Ask for a room that overlooks Long Island Sound.

3

Eastern Connecticut

N THE WHOLE, CONNECTICUT IS A RELATIVELY COMPACT STATE with many cosmopolitan areas and few undiscovered natural landmarks. In contrast to areas like Bar Harbor in Maine and Crawford Notch in New Hampshire, there has never been any great surge of tourism here to once-remote areas. Instead, visitors have been trickling in over the last century to fish pristine rivers, sail on Long Island Sound, hike the short hills and explore the villages along the coast and Connecticut River—to travel where early settlers and whalers once trod.

When the first wave of immigrants arrived in the New World, they searched for a land that was both fertile and accessible. Heading southwest by boat from Massachusetts, they arrived at the Connecticut coast, excited at the potential prospects of the terrain. The settlers found the mouth of the Connecticut River and immediately headed inland, where large tracts of rich soil were waiting at the bottom of the valley. Farmers began to grow corn, rye, oats, barley, and the vegetables that became an important part of the Colonial diet: beans, peas, squash, turnips, onions, and pumpkins. They also learned to cultivate tobacco. European traders successfully established fur posts in the towns of Hartford, Windsor, and Wethersfield.

It was too good to be true. By 1700, there were eighty thousand people living in the low-lying areas along the coast and up the central valley. By

1776, writer Thomas Pownall stated that the land between New Haven and Hartford was "a rich, well cultivated Vale thickly settled and swarming with people. . . . It is as though you were still traveling along one continued town for 70 or 80 miles on end." Large families, not new immigrants, made up the bulk of this population explosion. In a pamphlet entitled simply *Population in Eighteenth Century Connecticut*, Albert Laverne Olson wrote, "travelers passing houses frequently noticed ten or twelve little heads peeping out of doors and windows. . . . Eight to twenty children to a family were not uncommon."

The increase in population threatened the thriving economy. A new generation of farmers tried to expand outside the central lowland but instead found a range of hills, rising from 1,300 feet in northeastern Connecticut to 2,380 feet in northwestern Connecticut. This heavily forested highland was strewn with boulders and stones and proved futile for tillage. The land's wealth resided in its stands of oak, pine, and spruce. Farming subsided and shipbuilding emerged in the latter half of the 18th century. Hartford, Middletown, New Haven, and the small coastal town of Mystic flourished as they produced ships for all purposes. Trading vessels were built for the expanding commerce between the small Connecticut River villages and the West Indies. Whaling fleets were constructed for the town of New London, the third-largest whaling port in America behind Nantucket and New Bedford, Massachusetts. During the Civil War, Mystic builders launched more than 30,000 tons of shipping for the Union Navy, including over 50 steamers.

The centuries of farming and shipbuilding took its toll on the land. In 1860, 73 percent of the entire state had been deforested—enormous expanses of wilderness had been razed to produce

timber and farmland. When farming and whaling went into a serious state of decline in the latter half of the 19th century, much of the land was abandoned. Magically, as in the other states of southern New England, a new forest sprouted. By 1910, the woods had expanded to cover 45 percent of the state. Today, more than 60 percent of the land is covered by trees.

The Lay of the Land

The mighty glacier that formed notches in the granite in the White Mountains and thousands of islands, coves, and rocky promontories along the Maine coast did relatively little damage to eastern Connecticut. There's the occasional detritus, like the large boulders found at Glacial Park near Groton, but relatively speaking, this half of Connecticut is like most areas of the Atlantic seaboard—a combination of soft sand and gently rolling hills. Beaches, bays, salt marshes, and rocky headlands form the shoreline, which is protected from the open sea by Long Island and the Sound. Heading inland, forests of red cedars, oaks and hickories, and bogs of rhododendrons and white cedar are evident. As you approach the northeastern corner of the state, sugar maples, birches, and beeches become abundant atop the hills of the sylvan countryside.

The most interesting aspect of the Connecticut terrain is the Connecticut Valley Lowland, which was created when a major fault occurred along the eastern side of the valley some 200 million years ago. As the earth's crust cracked, the land around the fault slowly rose into a range of mountains. The lowland is several hundred feet lower than the surrounding hillside. A huge wedge, this corridor stretches from the Connecticut coast through the central part of the state to a point near the

Massachusetts-New Hampshire border. The lowlands' most distinctive feature is the reddish color of its soil, which stems from the color of the underlying bedrock. This sediment is, in actuality, layers of dried lava, created when the volcanic layer of the earth's crust was severed in the fault.

Compared to the rest of New England, Connecticut's climate is relatively mild. On the average, the temperature rises above 90° fewer than 20 times per year, and sinks below zero fewer than seven times per year. In Hartford, average highs range from 84° in July to 35° in January. Away from the coast, most of the state has some snow cover between late December and early March. Temperatures in the northeastern hills can sometimes be 10° below Hartford's temperature. Peak season for fall foliage is usually around Columbus Day Weekend. Call 800/CT-BOUND for the latest updates.

Not unlike the rest of the Atlantic coast, migrating shorebirds can be found along Connecticut's saltwater marshes and estuaries. Bald eagles can be seen on the Connecticut River from January to mid-March. Ospreys, snowy egrets, and marsh hawks are a few of the birds observed. Wildlife includes deer, raccoons, woodchucks, and cottontail rabbits.

Orientation

This chapter includes all the sporting activities east of **Interstate 91,** the highway that splits Connecticut in two from New Haven through Hartford to Springfield, Massachusetts. There are numerous highways that criss-cross this section of Connecticut. **Interstate 95** covers 69 miles along the coastline from New Haven to Westerly, Rhode Island. On Sunday nights in summer, the lanes of I-95 heading towards New York City are transformed into a parking lot with cars

lining up from the Connecticut coast, Newport, Cape Cod, and all other points along the eastern coast. **Interstate 395** heads north parallel to the easternmost border of the state from New London to Worcester, Massachusetts. **State Route 9** connects the small villages of the Connecticut River as it meanders from Old Saybrook to Hartford. **Interstate 84** connects Hartford with Boston via the Mass Pike. With all these highways, you'll be surprised at how many rural routes there are in this part of the state, especially in the northeast corner between I-84 and I-395. **State Route 169** from Canterbury to Woodstock is a scenic roadway lined with acres of unspoiled countryside and historic villages flanked by Federal-style homes. **U.S. 1** from Mystic to Westerly, Rhode Island, is crowded in the summertime, but there are many side roads leading to lonely bluffs.

Once you've visited **Mystic Seaport,** a "living museum" that features a restored 19th-century village, several authentic whaling and fishing vessels, and working craftspeople, hit the soft sand and the warm waters of the shore or go biking inland. Mystic is reached by taking Exit 90 from I-95.

Important note: Connecticut is in the process of changing its area code from 203 to 860. By the time this book is published, the change might have already taken place.

Parks & Other Hot Spots

THE CONNECTICUT COAST

The Connecticut coast needs no introduction. Once home to large whaling vessels and the captains who ran them, Mystic, New London, Stonington and the other coastal ports now play host to the thousands of tourists who swarm the beaches in the warm weather. Walkers can stroll along the bluffs, and sailors and fisherman can rent boats to venture out on the Long Island Sound. Bikers should head inland to escape the traffic on U.S. 1. For more information, contact the **Southeastern Connecticut Tourism District,** P.O. Box 89, New London, CT 06320 (tel. 203/444-2206 or 800/863-6569).

Bluff Point Coastal Reserve

From I-95, take Exit 88 and head south on U.S. 117. Take a right on U.S. 1 and drive 0.3 miles to Depot Road. Turn left until you see the sign for Bluff Point. Headquarters: Department of Environmental Protection, Office of State Parks and Recreation, 79 Elm Street, Hartford, CT 06106-5127 (tel. 203/424-3200).

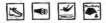

One of the last sections of undeveloped Connecticut shoreline, this reserve is known for its popular walking trail that weaves through the beach vegetation to a bluff overlooking Long Island Sound. This is one of the premier bird-watching spots on the shore.

Hammonasset Beach State Park

From I-95, take Exit 62, then head 1 mile south. Headquarters: Department of Environmental Protection, Office of State Parks and Recreation, 79 Elm Street, Hartford, CT 06106-5127 (tel. 203/424-3200).

Sun worshipers cover this 2-mile stretch of beach in the summer; birders enjoy viewing grackles and warblers feeding off the marshes in spring and fall. Connecticut's largest state campground is found here, with 558 sites overall.

Rocky Neck State Park

Exit 72 off I-95, in Niantic. Headquarters: Department of Environmental Protection, Office of State Parks and Recreation, 79 Elm Street, Hartford, CT 06106-5127 (tel. 203/424-3200).

One of Connecticut's few state beaches, this mile-long crescent of sand slopes gently down to the surf. Not surprisingly, the beach is extremely crowded in summer. 169 campsites are available.

THE CONNECTICUT RIVER & INLAND

Two hours east of New York City, the sprawling coastal Connecticut suburbs and cites subside, giving way to the splendor of New England. Small hamlets, forests, and large state parks replace urban congestion just about the time the Connecticut River comes into view. Stretching 410 miles to the Canadian border, the Connecticut is New England's longest river. One of the most serene portions is the stretch of river from the mouth to Middletown, once home to more than 50 shipyards in the mid-1800s. Sea captains who made their living from the West Indian, Chinese, and African trade lived in clapboard houses on the river's banks. The village of Deep River was once known as Ivorytown, because its major industry was the manufacture of piano keys from tons of elephant tusks.

However, by the latter half of the 19th century, the region was in a sad state of decline. The river was dammed and polluted, earning its reputation as the country's "best-landscaped sewer." Spring runs of salmon and shad disappeared, and people turned their backs on the water. We can thank the Connecticut River Watershed Council for restoring water quality to the river and its tributaries. Shad and salmon have started to return in the last decade, and wetlands and estuaries necessary for wildlife habitat have also reappeared. Fishermen, canoeists, sailors, bird-watchers, and bikers have followed the wildlife back to the river. For more information, contact the **Connecticut River Valley & Shoreline Visitors Council,** 393 Main Street, Middletown, CT 06457 (tel. 203/347-0028 or 800/486-3346).

Cockaponset State Forest

From State Route 9, take Exit 6 and U.S. 148 West. Approximately 1.5 miles later, turn right after a large lake onto Cedar Lake Road. Take a left at the Pattaconk Lake sign 1.5 miles later, and continue past the lake until you reach a large parking lot on the right. Headquarters: Department of Environmental Protection, Office of State Parks and Recreation, 79 Elm Street, Hartford, CT 06106-5127 (tel. 203/424-3200).

Second in size to Pachaug, Cockaponset is a 15,652-acre forest of oaks, hickory, maples, beeches, and birches. There are 25 campsites available.

Devil's Hopyard State Park

Located 3 miles north of the junction of State Routes 82 and 156 in East Haddam. Headquarters: Department of Environmental Protection, Office of State Parks and Recreation, 79 Elm Street, Hartford, CT 06106-5127 (tel. 203/424-3200).

The main attraction at Devil's Hopyard is Chapman Falls, where Eight Mile River plunges down a 60-foot escarpment. A dense hemlock forest surrounds the river, providing ideal company for hikers. There are 20 campsites available here.

Salmon River State Forest

Take State Route 2 to Exit 16 and turn onto U.S. 149 South. You'll see signs for the Day Pond State Park. There are numerous other spur roads west of Colchester that approach the river. Headquarters: Department of Environmental Protection, Office of State Parks and Recreation, 79 Elm Street, Hartford, CT 06106-5127 (tel. 203/424-3200).

Known for its excellent trout fishing and canoeing, the once-polluted Salmon River may one day reclaim its name. Salmon have been seen spawning in the river in the last decade. Two walking trails lead from Day Pond into the adjacent forest, eventually reaching the bluffs over the river.

THE QUIET CORNER

Unless you attended the University of Connecticut in Storrs, you probably have never heard of "Quiet Corner," the northeast section of the state. Connecticut has done very well publicizing the coast and Litchfield Hills, but ignores this region. If you were like me, you simply drove through this part of Connecticut on the way to Boston or New York. Well, you're in for a pleasant surprise. The "Quiet Corner" is a pastoral blend of historic mills, attractive villages, charming B&Bs, and a seemingly endless array of country roads that lead to winding rivers. Canoeists, fishermen, mountain bikers, road bikers, and hikers will savor this "off-the-beaten-track" destination. For more information, contact the **Northeast Connecticut Visitors District,** P.O. Box 598, Putnam, CT 06260 (tel. 203/928-1228).

Pachaug State Forest

The main entrance is off State Route 49, north of Voluntown. Headquarters: Department of Environmental Protection, Office of State Parks and Recreation, 79 Elm Street, Hartford, CT 06106-5127 (tel. 203/424-3200).

With 22,398 acres, Connecticut's largest state forest is home to numerous streams, seven lakes, white-cedar swamps, and 35 miles of hiking trails. The Rhododendron Sanctuary and Mt. Misery overlook are a few of the highlights (see "Walks & Rambles"). There are 40 sites available at two campgrounds.

Mansfield Hollow State Park

One mile east of Mansfield Center off State Route 89. Headquarters: Department of Environmental Protection, Office of State Parks and Recreation, 79 Elm Street, Hartford, CT 06106-5127 (tel. 203/424-3200).

Known for its exemplary trout and smallmouth bass fishing, Mansfield Hollow Lake is the centerpiece of this 2,500-acre park. The adjacent forest is popular with hikers and mountain bikers.

What to Do & Where to Do It

BACKPACKING

Known as the Blue-Blazed system, more than 500 miles of trails criss-cross the state. Many of these trails run for 30 to 40 miles, ideal for extended overnight stays. Recommended trails include the **Nipmuck Trail** from Puddin' Lane to north of U.S. 171, the **Mattabesett Trail** from the Connecticut River to U.S. 15, the **Metacomet Trail** from U.S. 15 to the Mass border, the **Natchaug Trail** from U.S. 6 to Westford, the **Shenipsit Trail** from Great Hill Road to Valley Falls Park, the **Salmon River Trail,** and the **Pachaug Trail.** For further information, contact the **Connecticut Forest and Park Association,** 16 Meriden Road, Rockfall, CT 06481-2691 (tel. 203/346-TREE).

BALLOONING

Mystic River Balloon Adventures, 17 Carriage Drive, Stonington (tel. 203/535-0283) takes people on hot air balloon rides over the Mystic and Stonington coastline. **Mystical Balloon Flights,** 40 Forest Drive, Salem (tel. 203/537-0025) offers champagne brunches and hot air balloon bungee jumping for the intrepid. **Brighter Skies Balloon Company** (tel. 203/963-0600 or 800/677-5114) in Woodstock features ballooning in the Quiet Corner.

BIRD WATCHING

Migrating shore birds are prevalent along the Connecticut shoreline in late spring and fall. **Green backed herons, yellow warblers, snowy egrets, swallows, ospreys, doves,** and **Canada geese** are just some of the birds sighted along the tidal pools and beaches of the coast. Jerry Connolly, president of the

Menunkatuck Audubon Society in Madison, conducts bird walks at **Hammonasset Beach State Park** every Saturday in May, June, September, October, and November. The tours leave at 7:50 A.M. from the **Audubon Shop,** 871 Boston Post Road, Madison (tel. 203/245-9056). Cost is $2.

Captain John Wadsworth takes bird lovers aboard the heated *Sunbeam Express* in January and February to view **bald eagles.** These majestic birds can be found hovering above the Yankee atomic power plant on the Connecticut River. For information, contact **Captain John's Sport Fishing Center,** 15 First Street, Waterford, CT 06385 (tel. 203/443-7259).

A vast assortment of birds also congregate at **Bluff Point** (see "Walks & Rambles") and **Barn Island State Management Wildlife Area** in Stonington. The most surprising place to spot a **hawk** is the lighthouse in **East Haven,** just outside the city of New Haven.

CANOEING

Remarkably undiscovered, the rivers of northeastern Connecticut offer flatwater and whitewater canoeists several good day runs. **Quincbaug's** smooth waters are ideal in late spring, before the river gets too shallow. An 11- or 12-mile journey from State Route 205 to Butts Bridge Road takes four to five hours to complete. To find the put-in, drive east on U.S. 14 into Central Village, bearing left onto U.S. 12 North. Once in Wauregan, veer left on Route 205 for views of the river. The parking and launch area is located on a dirt road on the left, just before the bridge. Leave your second car at the Butts Bridge Road. Drive west on U.S. 14 through Central Village to U.S. 169 South. Turn left and go approximately 4 miles to Butts Bridge Road. Turn left again and cross the bridge. The take-out is located on the left bank where there is ample parking space.

The 14½-mile stretch of the **Willimantic River** from State Route 32 to Eagleville Dam is easy whitewater, perfect for paddlers who want to move on to faster waters without having to face the fury of New England's more tumultuous rivers. The put-in is located on Route 32, 2½ miles north of the I-84 overpass. A small side-road goes downhill from the bridge to the river. Place your second car at Eagleville Dam. Take Route 32 six miles north of Willimantic to Eagleville. Turn left onto State Route 275 to find the dam and parking spaces.

North American Canoe Tours, 65 Black Point Road, Niantic, CT 06357 (tel. 203/739-0791), rents canoes at **Hopeville Pond State Park** near Pachaug State Forest, **Quaddick Pond State Park** in the northeastern corner of the state, and on the **Connecticut River** near the Gillette Castle in Hadlyme. Advance reservations are necessary for the Connecticut River. Cost is $10 per hour, or $30 per day.

Down River Canoes, State Route 154, Haddam, CT 06438 (tel. 203/345-8355) offers one- to three-day outings on the Connecticut River.

CROSS-COUNTRY SKIING

The 4½-mile loop around the reservoir in **Mansfield Hollow State Park** (tel. 203/455-9057) is popular with local hikers, bikers, and cross-country skiers (see "Mountain Biking"). **Gay City State Park** in Hebron (tel. 203/295-9523) has 12 miles of trails through rolling hardwood hills. There is a warming hut staffed by the Nordic Ski Patrol on weekends. They also offer moonlight tours. There are 7½ miles of trails in **Wadsworth Falls State Park** in Middlefield (tel. 203/344-2950). For a free "Ski Touring" brochure, contact the

Office of State Parks and Recreation, 165 Capitol Avenue, Hartford, CT 06106 (tel. 203/566-2304).

Ski touring is available at **Quinebaug Valley Ski Touring Center,** Roosevelt Avenue, Preston (tel. 203/886-2284).

DOWNHILL SKIING

Powder Ridge in Middlefield (tel. 203/ 349-3454), conveniently located between Hartford and New Haven, is where many Connecticuters learn to ski. The ski area has 14 trails and 5 lifts. They offer a Snow Guarantee and time tickets that let skiers choose how much skiing they want to do. Call 800/CT-BOUND for downhill ski conditions.

FISHING

Whether you surfcast or fly, crave the lakes, ponds, rivers, or ocean, the abundance of fish found in eastern Connecticut waters is guaranteed to keep you busy. **Natchaug, Fenton,** and **Mount Hope rivers** in the northeast corner of the state are known for their **trout.** The once-polluted **Salmon River** is now home to numerous **trout,** and, as the name implies, landlocked **salmon.** However, taking home salmon is currently prohibited. **Northern pike** can be found just after ice-out on the **Connecticut River. Largemouth bass** and **pickerel** are prevalent in numerous lakes and ponds including **Mansfield Hollow** and **Hopeville Pond.** For more information, contact the **Fisheries Division, DEP,** 79 Elm Street, Hartford, CT 06106 (tel. 203/424-FISH).

As on the rest of the Atlantic coast, **stripers** and **blues** can be hooked in late spring and summer months. They can be found anywhere from the base of the Holyoke Dam on the Connecticut River to Bluff Point. **Captain John Wadsworth** takes anglers out on party boats in search of **stripers, blues, cod, pollock, flukes,** **porgies,** and **flounder.** He also offers longer trips for **albacore, yellowfin tuna,** and **sharks.** Prices start at \$40 per person. For information, contact **Captain John's Sport Fishing Center,** 15 First Street, Waterford, CT 06385 (tel. 203/ 443-7259). *Magic* (tel. 203/429-9276) and *Lorna Anne* (tel. 203/429-5242) are two of the charter boats (taking six people or fewer) found at **Shaffer's Marina** on Mason's Island Road in Mystic. At the same location, **Shaffer's Boat Livery** (tel. 203/536-8713) rents 16-foot skiffs so you can play the role of captain. For a complete listing of captains and their boats, contact the **Connecticut State Tourism Office** (tel. 800/CT-BOUND) and ask for their *Connecticut Vacation Guide.*

GOLF

Lyman Orchards Golf Club, U.S. 157, Middlefield, CT 06455 (tel. 203/ 349-8055), in Middlefield is home to two highly regarded courses, one designed by Robert Trent Jones, and the other, opened in 1994, by Gary Player. Take time out to go apple picking in the orchards between playing both courses. Dick Bierkan, golf pro at Lyman Orchards, gave me his list of other favorite courses in the area. He recommended **Elmridge Golf Course** in Pawcatuck (tel. 203/599-2248), the **Norwich Municipal Golf Course** (tel. 203/889-6973), and **Shennecosset Golf Course** in Groton (tel. 203/445-0262). A local favorite in the northeast corner is the historic **Woodstock Golf Course** (tel. 203/928-4130) in the village of the same name.

HORSEBACK RIDING

Excellent horseback-riding trails can be found on the hills outside of Woodstock. Contact the **Woodstock Acres Riding Stable** (tel. 203/974-1224) and **Trapalanda Stables** (tel. 203/974-1064) for instruction and guided rides. Other stables offering scenic rides in the Quiet Corner are **Coventry Meadows,** Coventry (tel. 203/642-6563), **Coventry Riding Stables,** Coventry (tel.203/742-7576), **Woodcock Hill Riding Academy,** Willington (tel. 203/487-1686) and **Hawthorne Farm,** Willington (tel. 203/684-5487). **Greystone Farms** in North Stonington (tel. 203/535-3696) offers rides and lessons in the southern part of the state.

MOUNTAIN BIKING

Open up a Connecticut map and you'll notice the numerous green circles across the state, indicating state forests and parks. A web of trails weave through more than 160,000 acres of unspoiled hardwood forest. Simply head out the front door. There's bound to be a little green circle somewhere near you.

Pachaug State Forest

Various trails. Spend as long as you want. Easy to moderate; relatively flat terrain. Access: From I-395, take Exit 85 to U.S. 138 East. Turn left at State Route 49. The headquarters and parking sign are on the left-hand side of the road. Drive past the office sign, and at the first fork, take a right and park. Map: Contact the Department of Environmental Protection, Office of State Parks and Recreation, 79 Elm Street, Hartford, CT 06106-5127 (tel. 203/424-3200).

Pachaug State Forest's 23,000 acres of land make it Connecticut's largest public space. What does this mean to us mountain bikers? Virtually unlimited single- and double-track trails to get lost on. It's no wonder Theo Stein, Connecticut Coordinator of the International Mountain Bikers Association, named Pachaug one of his favorites, if not the best spot in Connecticut to go

fat wheeling. Just pick a trail, bring a compass, and bike to your adventurous soul's delight. I usually ride past the H.H. Chapman and Mount Misery Camping Area signs, turning left at the small Mount Misery sign. I cruise up and down the small hill, then choose one of the numerous double-tracks that fork off. Make your own loop, have fun, and go early so that you can make it out of this seemingly endless forest by sunset.

Mansfield Hollow State Park

Various trails. Allow 1 hour. Easy; several small hills. Access: From I-84, take Exit 68 to U.S. 195 South past the University of Connecticut and Mansfield Center. Turn left at Bassett Bridge Road and park at the boat launch, just before a bridge. Map: Contact the Department of Environmental Protection, Office of State Parks and Recreation, 79 Elm Street, Hartford, CT 06106-5127 (tel. 203/424-3200).

Seven o'clock on a cold and rainy Sunday morning, I drove over to Mansfield Hollow State Park expecting to be alone, but I was wrong. The parking lot was full of jeeps and trailers owned by fisherman who were already out casting for bass on the waters of Naubesatuck Lake. This manmade lake was created by the Mansfield Hollow Dam to capture flood waters before they swamped southeastern Connecticut. Five miles of single-track hiking and cross-country skiing trails circle the body of water, creating an ideal loop. The anglers crowded the waters, but the hikers and bikers left this trail to me. I headed uphill from the parking lot, veering right on a wider path along a rocky dike. This led to a ballfield, where I biked around the backstop to State Route 89. To extend the ride, you can take several trails across the road, but I turned right on Route 89 and right again across Mansfield Hollow Road to a trail that leads down to the water. A left turn onto a paved path and a right turn onto a single-track brought me to my favorite part of the loop, a cross-country ski trail that weaves up and down the rocky terrain on a narrow path. Heavy branches wet with water whipped my legs, arms, and face to give me an early morning wake-up call. I turned right across the paved bridge into someone's driveway, following the blue blazes along the eastern side of the lake. This part of the trail is much gentler—pine needles strewn by the dense forest pad the path. A right turn across another bridge brought me back to the boat launch.

Cockaponset State Forest

Various trails. Ride as long as your legs can stand it. Easy to moderate; hilly. Access: From State Route 9, take Exit 6 and U.S. 148 West. Approximately 1.5 miles later, turn right after a large lake onto Cedar Lake Road. Take a left at the Pattaconk Lake sign 1.5 miles later, and continue past the lake until you reach a large parking lot on the right. Map: Contact the Department of Environmental Protection, Office of State Parks and Recreation, 79 Elm Street, Hartford, CT 06106-5127 (tel. 203/424-3200).

Cockaponset is Pachaug's smaller brother, Connecticut's second-largest state park. There's only a mere 15,652 acres to play in here. Numerous double- and single-tracks abound. Simply turn right out of the parking lot and take your first double-track. This will eventually loop around the lake if you bear right on the correct paths. If you get lost like I do almost every time I venture here, have fun and let the trail play itself out. Just make sure to bring a bag of bread crumbs to find your way back. You'll want to go swimming in the lake's crisp water after a long day of hopping rocks.

ROAD BIKING

Traffic on Connecticut roadways can be heavy, but the state is big enough for bikers to leave the city and highways behind and find their own stretch of country road. Although Connecticut is not usually thought of as a good road-biking state, the following three rides were some of the best biking I did in New England.

Connecticut River, Essex

Allow 3 hours. Moderate; several short hills. Access: Exit 3 on Route 9 will bring you to Essex Center. Map: Any good state road map of Connecticut.

In the mid-1800s, the Connecticut River was home to more than 50 shipyards. Sea captains sailed up the river carrying spices from the West Indies and crates of ivory tusks from Zanzibar, soon to be turned into piano keys. Today, very few of the shipyards or the small clapboard houses that lined the river banks remain, but this 22-mile ride along New England's longest river is still a favorite for bikers.

The tour starts in the center of Essex, where you take a right on North Main Street and continue on River Road. Captains' houses have been replaced by stately Colonial, Victorian, and Federal-style homes whose manicured lawns slope to the lazy river's edge. The road turns inland at Essex Street, crossing marshes inundated with migrating birds. At U.S. 154, turn right and continue on this fairly congested road through the towns of Deep River and Chester. Take another right on State Route 82 and cross the river on what was, when it was built in 1913, one of the largest drawbridges in the world. Sitting on the eastern bank of the Connecticut in East Haddam is the four-story gingerbread

Goodspeed Opera House. Opened in 1876 to present vaudeville acts and minstrel shows, the theater was restored in the 1960s and now stages revivals of Gershwin, Porter, and Rogers & Hammerstein musicals.

After a strenuous uphill climb, Route 82 levels off and veers right. Turn right at the sign for the Gillette Castle State Park and you'll eventually see a field-stone citadel that looks like a poor Medieval prop for one of Goodspeed's plays. The actor William Gillette, who amassed millions playing Sherlock Holmes, had this castle built in 1917. Venture inside to learn a lesson or two on inferior interior decorating before strolling through the grounds (which Gillette thankfully left unscathed). A right turn on U.S. 148 will have you gliding downhill past the quaint village of Hadlyme to the dock of the ferry. Pay the 75 cents and climb aboard with your bike to cross the Connecticut River. Continue straight until you reach U.S. 154, where you take a left and return to Essex.

Sew 'N So Shop, 21 Main Street, Essex (tel. 203/767-8188), rents bicycles in the summer months.

Northeast Corner

Allow 3–4 hours. Moderate to strenuous; rolling hills. Access: From Boston, take the Mass Pike to I-395 South. Take Exit 97 or Route 44 West to U.S. 169 North. Park anywhere in Woodstock. Map: Any good state road map of Connecticut.

To most people, the northeast corner of Connecticut is little more than a passing thought on the road from Boston to New York or Hartford. Speeding by on I-84, drivers have no idea that this part of the state is home to historic villages dating back to the late 17th century, several of the country's first mills, and rolling farmland sprinkled with Federal-style houses and century-old barns. Called the "Quiet Corner," this part of Connecticut is all Yankee, a preserved slice of Americana that is best seen on two wheels on the backroads.

This 36-mile ride is a slight variation of the Roseland Trail, one of the three bike loops that the local chamber of commerce publishes in a pamphlet. Start the loop in Woodstock, a small village that is just as quaint as the other "Woodstocks" in New York and across New England. The ride begins at the Bowen House, also known as the Roseland Cottage, a blinding pink gothic house built in 1846 that is better suited for the Broadway stage. Cruise downhill on U.S. 169, veering left after the ice cream stand onto Joy Road. Apple orchards soon appear on your right, and fields of corn to your left. Watch out for the flock of swallows that swoop down in front of you near the pasture. A left on County Road, a quick right on Center School Road, and a left on Center Road will bring you to a sheep farm and emerald green hills that look strikingly similar to a Grant Wood painting.

Bear left on U.S. 197 and left again onto a dirt road called Old Turnpike. The hard gravel is relatively easy to ride on, but still, be cautious of rocks and bumps. Cross U.S. 198 for more views of farms and pastures before veering left onto Bigelow Hollow Road (U.S. 171). Ride downhill, veering right on Crystal Pond Road and, at the fork, bear right again onto Ashford Road. You'll pass more apples and corn stalks before pedaling uphill to the end of the road. Beyond the pond on your left, turn left onto North Road and right onto U.S. 44. Shocked to see cars again, you'll soon leave the hum of engines behind by veering left onto Pumpkin Hill Road. Another left onto Kennerson Reservoir

Road will bring you to the shores of this pristine pond. Continue past U.S. 198 onto Morey Road, which soon turns into Station Road. This long stretch rolls up and down hills through the Natchaug State Forest, becoming a dirt road before reaching the junction of State Route 97. Here, you have the option of bearing right for a slight detour into the small village of Hampton, or turning left for an 8-mile run on Route 97. The road takes you on a rollercoaster ride through the genteel landscape. Cross U.S. 44 and turn left onto U.S. 169 North past Pomfret's historic homes, inns, and private academies. A good place to stop for lunch is the Vanilla Bean. U.S. 169 North will bring you back to Woodstock and the bizarre, pink-colored house.

Mystic

21 miles. Allow 2–3 hours. Moderate; hilly. Access: I-95 Exit 90 will bring you to the town of Mystic. Map: Any good state road map.

Connecticut's coastal segment of U.S. 1 from Mystic to Stonington is one large parking lot in the summer time. Avoid the traffic and head to the hills on this 21-mile trail that hugs the Mystic harbor before traveling through rarely seen Connecticut pastures. Start in the center of Mystic, cross the drawbridge by foot, and take your first right on Gravel Street. Another left on Eldredge and a right on Pearl will take you through Mystic's historic housing district, dating from the 1850s, the height of the whaling industry. Across the harbor is a lighthouse where a schooner is usually docked. Head right on River Road where you'll find ospreys nesting atop poles and numerous geese, ducks, and swans lounging in the Mystic River. You'll glide along the river, coasting under I-95 and crossing State Route 27, before going straight on North

Stonington Road. Veer left on Lantern Hill Road to swing past expansive farmland dotted with secluded ponds. A right on State Route 214 will bring you straight to the Foxwoods Casino. I bet you've never biked to a casino before, but if you're dreaming of that new $3,700 Trek Y-33 with Fox air/oil rear shock and Rockshox Judy SL suspension forks, then lock up and run to the blackjack tables screaming, "Hit me!"

Take a right on State Route 2, which is heavily congested but has a large shoulder. You'll soon turn right on State Route 201 South past silos and the wholesome smell of manure. The briny sea air will seem like a distant memory with every whiff. At U.S. 184 go straight onto North Stonington Road past the Old Mystic Fire Station (don't turn left onto Route 27). This will get you back safe and sound to River Road and the fried clam rolls of Mystic.

A good place to rent bikes in Mystic is the **Mystic Cycle Center** on U.S. 1 (tel. 203/572-7433), just outside of Mystic toward Stonington.

SAILING

Sterling Yacht Charters, 44 Water Street, Mystic, CT 06355 (tel. 203/572-1111) offers customized bareboat and skippered charters along the Connecticut coast. Rental times range from an afternoon to a month, depending on the size of boat and number of passengers.

For instruction, contact **Coastline Sailing School,** 8 Marsh Road, Eldridge Yard, Noank, CT 06340 (tel. 203/536-2689). Lessons are available for all levels of experience.

SEA KAYAKING

If you own a sea kayak, the trip from Old Lyme to Great Island is, arguably, the best paddle on the Connecticut coast. Starting at the mouth of the

Yankee Doodle Dandy

According to Judson Hale, editor of *Yankee* magazine since 1970, there are many differing opinions on how the term "Yankee" originated. One theory suggests that the word derived from Dutch settlers. When English settlers starting selling cheese, the Dutch began calling the English "John Cheese" or "Jan Kass" in their native tongue. Over the years, the word Yankee evolved. Other linguists believe the Indians coined the phrase. In a footnote from *The Deerslayer* (1841), James Fenimore Cooper stated, "All the old writers who speak of the Indians say the Indians pronounce "English" as "Yengeese."

Regardless of the word's origin, the term Yankee seems to suit the people of Connecticut best. Mark Twain emphasized this point by writing *A Connecticut Yankee in King Arthur's Court*. Natives of Connecticut seem to have acquired all of the necessary Yankee traits—pride, good ole' Yankee ingenuity, and a strong desire for privacy. Joe McCarthy, author of *New England*, states that the Connecticuter's pride stems from his ability to withstand the worst of weather: "The Yankee's survival in his isolated war against the elements has . . . given him his special tight-lipped and proud aloofness; he feels slightly superior to people who have not been toughened by such a rigorous exposure."

Connecticut inventiveness is much easier to prove. Since the United States Patent Office opened in 1790, Connecticut has averaged more patents per capita than any other state in the nation. We can thank Connecticut for the lollipop, shaving cream, combination locks, submarines, anesthesia, and hundreds of other inventions. In *The Yankee of Connecticut*, W. Storrs Lee states that Connecticut's ingenuity results from the people's lack of patience. In an attempt to escape the tediousness of life, inventors would come up with "some clever contrivance that would do a distasteful chore quicker and better than the old method—shaping a lighter cradle for mowing wheat, making a gadget for paring apples, cracking nuts, or shelling corn, devising a pump to make water-drawing easier."

The third characteristic, desire for privacy, is best understood by a story Spencer Tracy told Garson Kanin, author of *Tracy and Hepburn*. One Sunday evening Tracy was having dinner with Katherine Hepburn and her family at their beach house in Old Saybrook. They were in the midst of a heated discussion about the "rights of the common man" when Dr. Hepburn spotted someone walking along the beach in front of the house. The whole family jumped up and started yelling, "Hey, this is private property! Get off the beach immediately!" When the trespasser ran off, the family proceeded to sit back down and, once again, defend the rights of the common man.

Privacy, ingenuity, and pride. It's too bad George Steinbrenner, owner of the Yankees ball club, possesses only the latter trait.

Connecticut River, you wind through a small channel on the eastern side of the island, before retracing your strokes back to the put-in. There are no sea-kayak rentals in Eastern Connecticut. **H2Outfitters** gives kayaking lessons at **North Cove Outfitters,** 75 Main Street, Old Saybrook, CT 06378 (tel. 203/388-6585).

SNOWMOBILING

Pachaug, Cockaponset, Natchaug, Nipmuck, and **Shenipsit State Forests** all have extensive trail systems for the snowmobiler. Contact the **Department of Environmental Protection,** Office of State Parks and Recreation, 79 Elm Street, Hartford, CT 06106-5127 (tel. 203/424-3200), for additional information.

SWIMMING

The three finest beaches on the eastern Connecticut shore are **Hammonasset Beach** in Madison, mile-long **Rocky Neck State Park** in Niantic, and **Ocean Beach,** just beyond Monte Christo College in New London. Singles tend to cross the border into Rhode Island for fun in the sun.

Inland, check out **Alexander Lake,** off U.S. 101 in the Quiet Corner. Farther west, both **Day Pond State Park,** off U.S. 149, and **Wadsworth Falls State Park,** off U.S. 157, are popular swimming holes.

WALKS & RAMBLES

Connecticut's extensive network of blue-blazed hiking trails weave across relatively flat terrain, creating one of the best walking systems in the Northeast. The trails are all inland, through forests of maples, oaks, and birches. However, there are several coastal walks not associated with the blue-blazes that are worthy of a visit. **Connecticut Forest and Park Association,** at 16 Meriden Road, Rockfall, CT 06481-2691 (tel. 203/346-TREE), has information on all the blue-blazed trails, and hosts a "Trails Day" in early summer to introduce more walkers to the system. The **Northeast Connecticut Visitors Bureau,** P.O. Box 598, Putnam, CT 06260 (tel. 203/928-1228), sponsors "Walks, Talks, & More" every Columbus Day Weekend for visitors interested in taking guided walks of this historic region.

Salmon River

4 miles round trip. Allow 2–3 hours. Easy. Access: Take State Route 2 to Exit 16 and turn onto U.S. 149 South. You'll see signs for the Day Pond State Park. Drive around the swimming area, across the bridge to the far side of the park. The trailhead is located behind the parking area near two outhouses. Map: Contact the Department of Environmental Protection, Office of State Parks and Recreation, 79 Elm Street, Hartford, CT 06106-5127 (tel. 203/424-3200).

It had just rained the day I took the Day Pond Trail to the Salmon River. All the leaves on this early spring day were wet, green, and alive after the long dismal winter. I walked on the southern part of the Day Pond Loop, deep into a dark forest of oaks, cedars, and maples. At the second clearing (the first opening is close to the entrance), I turned left at the fork and continued toward the Salmon River. After approximately 45 minutes, the winding trail led me out of the darkness to a bank high above the rushing waters. The sun was now shining and my eyes had to readjust to the brightness. I walked along the embankment into the forest again until I reached a street. Just to my right stood the Old Comstock Bridge.

Comstock is only one of three covered bridges remaining in Connecticut. Inside, the bridge was vandalized by modern-day graffiti, but still smelled of old wood. I peered through one of the windows overlooking the river and watched an older man in waders fish for bass, walleye, and trout. Anglers have also caught salmon here recently, which is miraculous when you consider that the Salmon River was once a polluted tributary of the Connecticut River, and all the river's namesake were killed. Now the waters are pristine and the bridge is the perfect place to ruminate. After eating lunch on the river's edge, I returned to Day Pond via the same trail.

Bluff Point

4.5 miles round trip. Allow 2 hours. Easy. Access: From I-95, take Exit 88 and head south on U.S. 117. Take a right on U.S. 1 and drive 0.3 miles to Depot Road. Turn left until you see the sign for Bluff Point. Map: Available at the trailhead.

Bluff Point is one of Connecticut's few coastal walks. Far from campsites and crowded beaches, this 778-acre state park in Groton is one of the most undeveloped areas of the Connecticut coastline. You only have to contend with horseback riders and mountain bikers, but they usually stay off the main trail. Keep to the wide dirt path or you might end up on one of those bike trails. Stay to the right and the trail winds along the Poquonock River, before heading inland and reaching the bluffs. From here one can see directly across the Long Island Sound to New York's Fisher's Island. To the left is Rhode Island's Watch Hill. If time allows, meander among Bluff Point's beach plums, beach peas, and white shore roses to Bushy Point. Then turn around and follow the main trail as it curves inland. You'll pass the site of Governor Fitz-John Winthrop's farmhouse, built in the early 1700s. Evidently, the governor had a brick chimney the size of a bedroom in his basement to hide in from Indian attacks. When the inland trail ends, head right to return to the parking lot.

Rhododendron Sanctuary and Mount Misery

Allow 1 hour. Easy. Access: From I-395, take Exit 85 to U.S. 138 East. Turn left onto State Route 49 North. The sign for Pachaug State Forest is located on the left side of the road. Drive past the office and turn right into the parking lot. Map: Contact the Department of Environmental Protection, Office of State Parks and Recreation, 79 Elm Street, Hartford, CT 06106-5127 (tel. 203/424-3200).

The path to Rhododendron Sanctuary and Mount Misery is on the combined Pachaug-Nehantic trail, two of the numerous blue-blazed hiking routes. From the parking lot, head back to the main road, cutting through the forest for five seconds before turning right. (Why did they bother cutting a path through this small portion of woods?) Past the H.H. Chapman sign, you'll see a clearly marked sign for the Rhododendron Sanctuary. Turn right and follow the blue blazes to a moss-covered swamp filled with towering rhododendrons. These fibrous, evergreen shrubs line the trail, creating a Brobdingnagian effect. Come in early July when the blossoms are in peak and you'll be treated to an exhilarating pink-and-white light show.

The trail veers to the right, past the swamp and out to the main road again. Head right and look for the blue blazes on the left-hand side of the road. This is the trail to Mount Misery, which is far from miserable when you consider that its peak is only 441 feet. The path climbs gently through oaks and cedars to a rocky summit. An ideal picnic spot, the flat ledge offers clear views of the surrounding forest. To head back to the car, simply retrace your steps. The trail can be extended by descending the west base of the mountain or by continuing on the Pachaug Trail past the parking lot to Lowden Brook.

Glacial Park

Allow 45 minutes. Easy to moderate. Access: From Groton, take U.S. 117 North to Sandy Hollow Road. Take a left and then another left onto Whalehead Road. The sign for Glacial Park Boulder Train Site will be on your right-hand side. There is a small parking spot across the street.

Unless you enjoy boulder hopping, Glacial Park is a walk that you'll probably try just once. However, the terrain here is so bizarre that I want to include it in this book as a curiosity. Cross the street and enter the forest under the power lines. About 300 yards later, the trail splits. The main trail veers left while the alternate trail forks to the right. If you are in any condition to rock jump, I highly suggest the main trail. The path proceeds up a small hill, where you suddenly see hundreds of boulders in a ravine to your right. Your first thought is that some construction worker has played a practical joke on you with his lift. The truth is that these boulders are the remains of a moraine from the 12,000-year-old Wisconsin glacier. This huge rock formation is a result of glacial melting. In a few moments, you'll be clambering over these massive stones trying to find the blotches of blue paint that somehow denote a trail. Don't worry, the torture will end in about fifteen minutes when the main trail catches up with the alternate trail and loops back to your car. Try to keep a sense of direction, because the path has arrows pointed every which way but the exit. I wouldn't want you to slander my good name while you crawl on boulders eternally.

Nipmuck Trail

Allow 1 hour. Easy. Access: From Mansfield Center, take U.S. 195 North to Clovermill Road. Look for the signs on the right for the Schoolhouse Brook Park and the Nipmuck Trail. Map: Contact the Connecticut Forest and Park Association, 16 Meriden Road, Rockfall, CT 06481-2691 (tel. 203/346-TREE).

Tony Holt, who with his wife, Kay, owns the Fitch House in Mansfield Center, is an avid hiker who has ventured to Europe on numerous occasions to hike the continent's best trails. However, one of his favorite hikes, the Nipmuck Trail, lies practically in his backyard. The well-blazed, 39-mile Nipmuck Trail runs from Mansfield Center to the Nipmuck State Forest on the Massachusetts border. The name comes from an Indian tribe that lived in central Massachusetts.

Tony brought my wife and me on a mile-long section of the trail that meanders from Clovermill Road to Spring Hill Isolation Farm. We crossed Schoolhouse Brook, hugging the far side of the rushing stream for most of our walk. Ferns lined the trail approaching Bicentennial Pond, a small swimming hole in the 500-acre Schoolhouse Brook Park. We soon reached a clearing and turned right on Spring Hill Road. The Spring Hill Isolation Farm stood across U.S. 195. Tony's wife and kids claim to have seen a cow with a glass stomach here, a result of research done by the University of Connecticut's School of Agriculture. We only saw cows with intestines intact. However, the view of the surrounding countryside made up for the lack of bovine oddities.

Since this part of the trail is relatively short, Tony recommends two other portions of the Nipmuck—the section that hugs the Fenton River from Gurleyville Road to U.S. 44, and the northern part of the trail that meanders through Yale Forest from Boston Hollow Road to Bigelow Brook.

Devil's Hopyard State Park

Allow 1.5 hours. Easy. Access: From the junction of State Routes 82 and 156 in East Haddam, take Route 82 East for 0.1 miles to Hopyard Road. Turn left and follow the road for about 3 miles to the park entrance. Map: Contact the Department of Environmental Protection, Office of State Parks and Recreation, 79 Elm Street, Hartford, CT 06106-5127 (tel. 203/424-3200).

The orange-blazed Vista Trail at Devil's Hopyard State Park is never far from the sounds of rushing water. Stroll under the covered bridge, bearing right at the sign for the Vista Trail. Shaded by sturdy, umbrageous hemlocks, the path leads to a vista where rolling hills and farms stand before you. Follow the loop in a counterclockwise fashion and you'll arrive at a brook. Its trickling water is soon replaced by the surging deluge of Chapman Falls. Waves of cascading water crash to the rocks 60 feet below. Follow the Vista Trail back to the covered bridge to complete the loop. Families with small children should consider doing the shorter blue loop trail.

Campgrounds & Other Accommodations

CAMPGROUNDS

Several of the state parks and forests have campgrounds. Call 203/566-2304 for reservations and a listing of all camping facilities.

Rocky Neck State Park

From the junction of State Routes 161 and 156 in Niantic, head 3 miles west on Route 156. Tel. 203/739-5471. 169 sites, no hookups. Sewage disposal, public phone, tables, and fire rings.

Situated next to the mile-long Rocky Neck Beach.

Hammonasset Beach State Park

From the junction of Routes 79 and U.S. 1 in Madison, head 3 miles east on U.S. 1. Tel. 203/245-1817. 558 sites, no hookups, flush toilets, showers, public phone, tables, and fire rings.

This is the largest camping facility in Connecticut. The beach says it all. Often crowded and noisy.

Pachaug State Park

From the junction of State Routes 138E and 49N in Voluntown, head one mile north on Route 49 N. Tel. 203/376-4075. 40 sites, no hookups. Pit toilets, tables, and fire rings.

Green Falls Campground has 18 wooded sites near a pond. Mount Misery Campground has 22 wooded sites near a stream.

Devil's Hopyard State Park

From East Haddam, head 1 mile east on State Route 82, then continue 8 miles east on Hopyard Road. Tel. 203/873-8566. 21 sites, no hookups. Pit toilets, public phone, tables, and grills.

Only 21 sites. Perhaps the most peaceful campground in the state park system.

INNS & RESORTS

Norwich Inn & Spa

607 W. Thames Street, Route 32, Norwich, CT 06369. Tel. 800/ASK-4-SPA. Rooms start at $115 per night, but there are many packages that include meals at their restaurant and spa facilities, so call for a brochure.

Conveniently located near the coast, the Quiet Corner, and Pachaug State Forest, this elegant spa is the perfect retreat for people who play hard and then want to be pampered. The long list of spa services includes massages, mud and herbal wraps, facials, and aromatherapy. The inn overlooks the Norwich Municipal Golf Course. Every October, they sponsor an "Outdoor Adventure Week" in which guides bring guests on hikes walks, and fishing trips.

The Fitch House

563 Storrs Road, U.S. 195, Mansfield Center, CT 06250. Tel. 203/456-0922. Rooms range from $75 to $119 and include a breakfast that will force you to loosen your belt buckle.

You can thank Kay and Tony Holt for selling their plastic business, retiring, and opening up their exquisite home to visitors. The Fitch House is located in the quaint village of Mansfield Center in the heart of the "Quiet Corner." The house was constructed in 1836 by Colonel Edwin Fitch in order to impress his future father-in-law and to launch his architectural career. Built in the Greek Revival, the Ionic columns of the front facade not only impressed his in-laws 150 years ago, but will turn everyone's head who rides down Storrs Road today. Kay has

lived in the house since 1935, and her husband Tony is so rooted in this area that there's a book on his family called the *Three Generations of the Holt Family*. Their 70-acre backyard borders Schoolhouse Brook Park and the blue-blazed Nipmuck Trail. Unfortunately, the Holts only have three rooms, so book well in advance.

Lighthouse Inn

Lower Boulevard, New London, CT 06320. Tel. 203/443-8411. Rooms start at $110 and include breakfast.

Situated at the mouth of the Thames River, this restored mansion dates from 1902 (no, it's not a lighthouse). The inn's private beach is only a few blocks from Ocean Beach Park.

The Inn at Mystic

U.S. 1, Mystic, CT 06355. Tel. 203/536-9604 or 800/237-2415. Rooms start at $195 for the estate, $185 for the Gatehouse rooms, and $135 at the motor inn.

Set on a 15-acre plateau overlooking the Mystic River and the harbor, this former estate is now a mishmash of accommodations. The estate offers five suites, the adjacent Gatehouse has five rooms with fireplace, and the upscale motor inn features 47 rooms, 5 suites, and 4 efficiencies. The inn is also known for its highly regarded restaurant, Flood Tide.

Randall's Ordinary

P.O. Box 243, North Stonington, CT 06359. Tel. 203/599-4540.

This extraordinary 17th century farm has three spacious rooms over the dining room in the old farmhouse and nine more rooms in the barn. Some of the rooms have fireplaces and whirlpools. Don't overlook the $30 prix fixe dinner, cooked in an old fireplace over an open hearth. The farm is listed on the National Register of Historic Places.

Spa at Grand Lake

State Route 207, Lebanon, CT 06249. Tel. 203/642-4306. Rooms start at $120.

This 51-room spa is known for its individualized attention. Reduce your stress level with a variety of activities such as swimnastics, yoga, and tennis.

Griswold Inn

36 Main Street, Essex, CT 06426. Tel. 203/767-1776. Rooms range from $90 to $175.

Standing at the foot of Main Street in Essex, the Griswold Inn is a three-story clapboard Colonial house dating from the late 18th century. The inn is conveniently located near the Connecticut River (see "Road Biking").

4

Coastal Rhode Island, Block Island & Beyond

NFORTUNATELY FOR RHODE ISLAND, AMERICA'S SMALLEST state is used as a measuring stick. Texans love to say that several of their ranches are larger than Rhode Island. Journalists exacerbate the small-state image by comparing such events as the *Exxon Valdez* oil spill to an area "the size of Rhode Island." Yes, there are seven counties in Maine larger than Rhode Island, but there are at least 25 countries still smaller than the state.

With a width less than 40 miles, most people underestimate Rhode Island's more than 400 miles of coastline. The southern coast of the "Ocean State" is a complex combination of bays, estuaries, islands, sounds, and vast beaches. Salt marshes and tall, coarse reeds guard the entrance to long crescents of sand, dunes rise and fall, rocky promontories coated with lichen form an impenetrable barrier, and bluffs plunge to the waters below.

This is the scenery that has enchanted travelers for centuries. Most people associate Rhode Island with the palatial estates that sit on the southern end of Aquidneck Island in the town of Newport. Yet visitors were venturing to these shores long before the Gilded Age. In the late 1700s, Newport was a summer resort for wealthy planters fleeing the humidity of South Carolina, Jamaica, and Antigua. In 1783, George Washington sent his ailing nephew here to regain his strength. During the summers of the mid-1800s,

Rhode Island was home to a long list of luminaries including Edgar Allan Poe, Henry Wadsworth Longfellow, George Bancroft, Robert Louis Stevenson, and John Singer Sargent.

Then came the arrival of "The Four Hundred." Samuel Ward McAllister, friend and confidant to Mrs. William Astor, coined this phrase in reference to the 400 wealthiest families in New York worth knowing. McAllister had just bought a summer home in Newport and successfully persuaded Mrs. Astor to build a summer "cottage" there as well. The others soon followed. These so-called cottages were no rustic cabins. They were 50- to 70-room mansions with large stables, spacious lawns, gardens, and greenhouses—immense palaces of marble, limestone, and granite. Some of these lofty establishments, like Cornelius Vanderbilt's "Breakers," built between 1892 and 1895, and Oliver Hazard Perry Belmont's "Belcourt," constructed in 1894, cost well over five million dollars. Most of these homes lacked taste and originality, styled after their European counterparts. The Belcourt was fashioned after a hunting lodge owned by Louis XIII of France. William Vanderbilt's "Marble House" was based on the Grand Trianon at Versailles.

At the turn of the century, Newport's social scene was in full swing. Wives of these rich men were given budgets of $100,000 to $300,000 to administer their estates, and, most importantly, throw a damn good party. Fifty to one hundred employees were hired for each house—butlers, maids, stablehands, grounds-keepers, and caterers. When an elaborate dinner or ball was thrown, twice as many employees were necessary.

This excessive show of wealth had its share of detractors. More reserved members of the upper class spent their summers on Block Island, Jamestown, and Watch Hill. Many of the Washington socialites preferred Narragansett to Newport. However, the affluent were not the only ones arriving on the shores of Rhode Island. The middle class stayed at large hotels or rows of cottages that were beginning to open up on the coast. Those who could not afford a night's accommodation spent the day at one of the numerous amusement parks.

Alas, all good things must come to an end. When the stock market crashed in 1929, many of Newport's mansions were boarded up, torn down, sold for taxes, or destroyed by vandals and fire. The resorts were vacant and the amusement parks closed. This lasted for a very short time. Sailors, saltwater fishermen, walkers, bikers, and hordes of other travelers soon came back. Like the waves that continuously crash the shores only to fall gently back into sea, people who have the good fortune to visit Rhode Island return with regularity.

The Lay of the Land

Look at a map of southern New England and you'll notice the large indentation known as Narragansett Bay. The same ice sheet that Cape Cod owes its existence to formed the jagged shoreline of Rhode Island. Rock debris accumulated at the melting ice front to form a terminal moraine, an irregularly shaped ridge that fringed the lobes of ice. Over the years, the bedrock eroded. The sea stretched far north into the lowlands, creating Narragansett Basin and long, narrow Prudence and Conanicut Islands. Geologists have found that the soft bedrock forming the ridge of the basin is the same age as the Pennsylvania coal formations, and, indeed, coal has been found at several spots within the bay.

Other areas of the coastline were created when the ice retreated. Rocks were carried hundreds of miles, only to be discarded at random as "glacial erratics." This is how Watch Hill, Rhode Island's westernmost point, was formed. Called a "glacial dumping ground," Watch Hill is a mass of large boulders, knobs, and vertiginous ridges. Proceeding inland from the sea, outwash plains and salt ponds replace long strips of sand. Farther north, Rhode Island begins to look like the other regions of southern New England. Forests of oaks, maples, beeches, and hickories surround bogs of white cedar and small bodies of water.

Climate varies drastically between the coast and interior. The snow that usually covers the western interior of the state from late December to mid-March quickly changes to rain along the shore. During summer, the beaches are cooled by ocean breezes. The average temperature in July is 72°; in January, 30°. Temperatures rarely exceed 90° or drop below zero. The western part of the state undergoes fall foliage changes in late September and early October.

With more than 300 recorded species of birds, Rhode Island's birding is first-rate. This is especially true of Block Island, located on the Atlantic Flyway. A colorful variety of warblers are seen on the island in early October. Other species found on the mainland shores and salt ponds include ospreys, American oystercatchers, red-tailed hawks, and sandpipers. Deer, beaver, snowshoe hares, foxes, and the occasional otter are some of the animals reportedly sighted in the interior forest.

Orientation

Although it stretches less than 40 miles from east to west and 50 miles from north to south, distances between points within Rhode Island are a lot longer than you would expect. This is due to the bizarre shape of the shoreline. Providence to Westerly, Rhode Island, is only 53 miles on **Interstate 95,** but to reach the central shoreline and islands is more complicated. Newport is reached via **State Routes 24** and **114** from the northeast, across **Newport Bridge** and **State Route 138** from the west. From Providence to Narragansett, take I-95 south and switch to **State Route 4** and **U.S. 1**.

The closest ferry to **Block Island** departs from Galilee, just south of Narragansett. **State Route 1A** from Narragansett north to Wickford is a scenic drive that hugs the western shores of the bay. **State Route 138** over the Jamestown Bridge to Conanicut Island is another picturesque journey.

Newport, a city that has attracted the upper crust of society since the late 1700s, now entices visitors of all economic backgrounds. The sea, beaches, and bluffs are still the main attractions, followed closely by the extravagant mansions and some of the older Colonial buildings. Sailors come here to attend renowned schools, while everyone else absorbs the city's beauty and opulence on bikes or on foot. For more information, contact the **Newport Visitor's Center,** 23 America's Cup Avenue, Newport, RI 02840 (tel. 401/849-8048 or 800/326-6030).

Once a prosperous shipping port and center for boat building, the village of **Bristol** still reeks of history. Federal and Greek-revival houses dating from as far back as 1634 line the red, white, and blue sidewalks. Bristol can be reached via State Route 114 from the north or the south.

A flourishing ocean resort in the late 1800s, **Narragansett** changed drastically in 1900 when a devastating fire burned down much of the ocean district. Today, the town is undergoing a resurgence, with new stores, resorts, and of course, the spectacular beach. Narrangansett can be reached via U.S. 1. For more information, contact the South County Tourism Council, 4808 Tower Hill Road, Wakefield, RI 02879 (tel. 401/789-4422 or 800/548-4662).

Jamestown (Conanicut Island), Newport's neighbor to the east on State Route 138, has its own share of history, as evidenced by the older buildings that line Jamestown harbor. **Beavertail State Park** occupies the southern end of the island, offering some of the finest ocean views. The island can be reached from the east by crossing the Newport Bridge.

Prudence Island is a 20-minute ferry ride from Church Street Wharf in Bristol, and a trip into another century. Dotted with the occasional farm, most of this pastoral terrain is public land. The **Narragansett Bay National Estuarine Sanctuary** is located in the northern half of the island; South Prudence State Park is situated on the opposite end. With miles of dirt roads, trails, and a dense population of deer, the island is ideal for biking or walking. Call 401/253-9808 for ferry times.

Sakonnet, the southeasternmost part of Rhode Island, is New England at its finest—an exquisite combination of small village greens, rolling farmland, the ocean, rocky shores, and high headlands. On hot summer weekends, when Newport and Narragansett are in bumper-to-bumper traffic, this part of the state is still a placid retreat. Sakonnet can be reached by taking State Route 24 to State Route 77 South.

Only 7 miles long and 3 miles wide, lamb chop–shaped **Block Island** offers a remarkable variety of outdoor activities. The low hills, rocky bluffs, moors, and valleys are ideal for hiking and biking; the surrounding sea is a magnet for sailors, fishermen, and kayakers. Block Island is accessible only by ferry. Several leave the mainland, but the 70-minute ride from Galilee is the shortest. Call 401/783-4613 for times.

Parks & Other Hot Spots

The Coastline

People invariably come to Rhode Island for the sea. The 420-mile coastline beckons far more boaters and saltwater fishermen than hikers and mountain bikers. Highlights include **Newport,** "the yachting capital of the world" (before the U.S. lost the so-called America's Cup), **Narragansett Bay** and her many islands, the **Sakonnet River,** and the swells of white sand and pink hedgerows that blanket the beaches.

Arcadia Management Area

Take I-95 to Exit 5A onto State Route 102 South. Turn right onto State Route 3 South and right again at the blinking light, onto State Route 165 West. Tel. 401/789-3094.

Rhode Island's largest public land is an oasis for the state's hikers, mountain bikers, and cross-country skiers. The densely wooded forest of evergreens contain streams, ponds, marshes, and wetlands.

Great Swamp

Take Exit 3A off I-95 onto State Route 138 East toward Kingston and Newport. Just before the junction of State Route 110, turn right on Liberty Lane. Tel. 401/789-0281.

This 2,895-acre swamp of red maple, white cedar, holly, and rhododendrons is a popular spot for birders and fishermen. Ospreys, herons, and snowy egrets are just a small sampling of the birds observed here.

George Washington Management Area

From the junction of U.S. 44 and State Route 102, head 5 miles west on U.S. 44. Tel. 401/568-2013.

Located several miles east of the Connecticut line in northwestern Rhode Island, this 3,489-acre oak and maple forest is home to Bowdish Reservoir, a good swimming and fishing hole. The majority of people who venture to this remote park are locals.

What to Do & Where to Do It

BALLOONING

Stumpf Balloons, P.O. Box 1143, Providence (tel. 401/253-0111), arranges champagne and foliage flights for private parties. For balloon flights in southern New England, contact **Kingston Balloon Company** (tel. 401/783-9386).

BIRD WATCHING

The same migrating shorebirds that flock to other areas of the Atlantic coast can be found in the coastal marshes of Rhode Island. **Warblers, goldfinches,** and **marsh hawks** congregate on Block Island (see "Walks & Rambles"). **Ospreys, herons,** and **Canada geese** can be seen at Great Swamp (see "Mountain Biking"). And **snowy egrets** are often found feeding in the Narrow River (see "Canoeing").

BOARDSAILING

Ninigret Pond and **Narragansett Town Beach** are the two best places on the coast to boardsail. **Sail Newport,** 53 America's Cup Avenue, Newport, RI 02840 (tel. 401/849-8385), offers eight one-week boardsailing classes to youths during the summer. Cost is $170 per week. **Island Windsurfing,** 86 Aquidneck Avenue, Newport (tel. 401/846-4421), offers rentals and lessons for all levels. Sailboards and instruction are also available from **Windsurfing of Watch Hill,** 3 Bay Street, Watch Hill (tel. 401/596-0079).

CANOEING

The numerous ponds that dot Rhode Island are havens for canoeists and fishermen. The state's largest coastal pond, **Ninigret** in Charleston, nearby **Worden Pond** in South Kingston, and **Bowdish Reservoir** in Glocester are three of the perennial favorites. If you don't own your own canoe, you can paddle the Narrow River with **Narrow River Kayaks,** 95 Middlebridge Road, Narragansett, RI 02882 (tel. 401/789-0334). The river is an inlet on the western side of Narragansett Bay. Canoeists and kayakers can paddle upstream to Lower and Upper Pond or downstream around a small island to Pettaquamscutt Cove.

Baer's River Workshop, 222 Water Street, Providence (tel. 401/453-1633) offers canoeing trips on the Woonasquatucket and Blackstone rivers.

Oceans & Ponds (tel. 401/466-5131) rents canoes on Block Island. A complete list of canoeing routes and facilities is available from the **Rhode Island Canoe Association** (tel. 401/725-3344).

CROSS-COUNTRY SKIING

Pulaski Memorial Park in Burrillville has four loops with a total of 10 miles that start from Peck Pond. From Providence, take I-295 North to U.S. 44 West. The parking lot is located on the right-hand side of the road close to the Connecticut border.

Arcadia Management Area's 4-mile Tripp Trail hugs the eastern portion of Breakheart Pond, venturing up Breakheart Hill before returning on the Bliven Trail. For directions, see "Mountain Biking." The trailhead is located 0.2 mile west of the church. For information call 401/789-3094.

Norman Bird Sanctuary (tel. 401/846-2577) in Middletown, **Slater Memorial Park** in Pawtucket, and **Goddard State Park** (tel. 401/884-2010) in Warwick are three other areas that feature backcountry skiing.

DOWNHILL SKIING/ SNOWBOARDING

Considering Rhode Island's highest point is only 812 feet, you might be somewhat shocked to learn that this relatively flat state has a downhill ski area. **Yawgoo Valley Ski Area** (tel. 401/295-5366) in Exeter has 12 trails, 2 double chairlifts, and night skiing. The longest trail is 2,300 feet, with a whopping vertical drop of 245 feet.

FISHING

Whether you crave freshwater or saltwater fish, there's no lack of choice in this state. Surfcast anywhere along the coastline for stripers and blues. The rocks of **Sakonnet Point, Brenton Point** in Newport, **Beavertail State Park** in Jamestown, the inlet to **Ninigret Pond,** and **Point Judith** are some of the more popular places. Point Judith is also the best place to find party boats and charters. **Captain Frank Blount** (tel. 401/783-4988) has three boats taking anglers out on half-day, full-day, and night trips for **cod, blues, porgies, blackfish,** and **fluke.** He also has overnight trips on which you can reel in **pollack, tuna, bonita,** and **shark.** Prices start at $20.

There are more than 40 charter boats for six or fewer people serving the Point Judith area. Call the **Rhode Island Party & Charterboat Association** (tel. 401/737-5812) for prices and reservations. On Block Island, **Captain Bill Gould** (tel. 401/466-5151) takes six people or fewer aboard the *G. Willis Makit* for inshore and offshore fishing trips. **Captain Jack Cagnon** (tel. 401/423-1556) takes fishermen out on a 38-foot Harris from Jamestown. **Captain Bud Phillips** (tel. 401/635-4292) of Sakonnet Point Marina will bring parties of up to six on his 38-foot Oceans. In Newport, contact **Captain Jim Korney** (tel. 401/849-9642), skipper of *Fishin' Off,* for full- or half-day charters.

Freshwater game fish include **largemouth bass, chain pickerel, yellow perch, northern pike,** and **crappies. Brook, brown,** and **rainbow trout** and **landlocked salmon** are also stocked in many of the rivers and ponds. Also known for their fishing are: **Clear River** in Burrillville; the **Pawcatuck** and **Wood rivers** in southern Rhode Island; and a number of ponds, such as **Breakneck** in Arcadia Management Area, **Worden Pond** near Kenyon, and **Bowdish Reservoir** in Glocester. For more information, contact the **Rhode Island Department of Economic Development** (tel. 401/277-2601). For license information, call 401/277-3756.

GOLF

Several locals highly recommended **Green Valley Country Club,** 371 Union Street, Portsmouth (tel. 401/847-9543). Green Valley's pro, Gary Dorsi, also suggested two other courses: **Triggs Memorial Golf Course,** 1533 Chalkstone Avenue, Providence (tel. 401/272-4653), and **Exeter Country Club,** Victory Highway, Exeter (tel. 401/295-8212).

HORSEBACK RIDING

Newport Equestrian Center, 287 Third Beach Road, Middletown (tel. 401/848-5440), **Roseland Acres Equestrian Center,** 594 East Road, Tiverton (tel. 401/624-8866), and **Rustic Rides Farm,** West Side Road, Block Island (tel. 401/466-5060) all offer instruction and trail rides, including paths along the beach.

In the western part of the state, contact **Stepping Stone Ranch** in West Greenwich (tel. 401/397-3725).

MOUNTAIN BIKING

Not especially known for its off-road trails, Rhode Island does have three spots that are highly recommended.

Arcadia Management Area

Allow 2–3 hours. Easy to moderate; several hills. Access: Take I-95 to Exit 5A onto State Route 102 South. Turn right onto State Route 3 South and right again, at the blinking light, onto State Route 165 West; 2.5 miles later, you will see a small white church on the right where you can park. Map: Contact the Department of Environmental Management, Division of Parks and

Recreation (tel. 401/539-2356) or the Rhode Island Fat Tire Club (tel. 401/364-0786).

Rhode Island's largest public land, the 13,817-acre Arcadia Management Area is a mecca for the state's mountain bikers. Over 30-plus miles of single-track trails and less technical double-tracks and dirt roads weave through the woods. I turned left from the church and headed uphill for 0.3 mile on State Route 165. Two more lefts at a dirt road and a fork brought me to a rocky single-track that tested my skills almost immediately. When I reached my first set of double-tracks, I was content to turn right under a forest of oaks and hickories. A sharp left and I was at the shores of Breakheart Pond. After crossing a small bridge and bearing right, I noticed numerous single-tracks to my left. I took one of these trails, zipping through the trees, to reach Frosty Hollow Road. A left turn on this gravel road brought me directly back to my car. What a stroke of luck.

Prudence Island

8 miles. Allow 2 hours. Easy; flat terrain. Access: 20-minute ferry ride from Church Street Wharf in Bristol. Call 401/253-9808 for times. Map: Available from the Division of Parks and Recreation (tel. 401/277-2635).

Until a few years ago, Prudence Island was one of the state's top walking destinations. Miles of trails snaked through the undeveloped landscape, interrupted only by the occasional deer grazing by an old vineyard or apple orchard. However, with the deer came the dreaded Lyme disease. Several people were infected, the media brought it to the public's attention (but exaggerated), and Dear Prudence, no one came out to play. Hikers have avoided the trails and the meddlesome tick ever since.

Mountain biking is a completely different scenario. We can cruise on the dirt and gravel roads without having to venture too deep into the woods, and we're obviously going at a much faster pace. No nasty bug is going to attach itself to your body when you're cruising 15 to 20 miles per hour. Take advantage of the empty roads. Without restaurants, hotels, or camping sites, very few tourists outside of sailors venture here. Traveling to Prudence is like visiting the Rhode Island of the 1850s—a combination of farmland, small villages, and spectacular ocean views around every bend.

This 8-mile jaunt circles the southern end of the island, within South Prudence State Park. From the ferry landing in Homestead, turn left onto Narragansett Avenue past the small lighthouse at Sandy Point. The road soon veers uphill, away from the village and the sea. When Narragansett turns right, go straight ahead on the secondary road and turn left at the T-intersection. This narrow path cruises down to the water along an old fence. The fence was put up during World War II for coastal defense purposes. Narragansett Bay was thought to be one of the first places our adversaries would target if the United States were attacked. Follow the gravel lane as it laces the shores of the island. Through the brush, you can see Newport Bridge to the right and Mount Hope Bridge to the left. You'll soon pass the first of many underground ammunition bunkers. At the next junction, veer left and follow the road to a long fishing pier. Continue to the right along the narrow trail until it intersects with a concrete road near another bunker. When the road veers right, bear to your left on a gravel path that hugs the shoreline.

Wide-open vistas of the ocean soon appear. Turn right at a large garage and continue on the paved road, which soon becomes a gravel lane. When you reach the T-intersection you saw earlier, veer left to get back to Narragansett Avenue and Homestead.

Great Swamp Management Area

5.5-mile loop. 1 hour. Easy; flat. Access: Take Exit 3A off I-95 onto State Route 138 East toward Kingston and Newport. Just before the junction of State Route 110, turn right on Liberty Lane. Follow the road past the park buildings to the end where there's a small parking lot and barred gateway. Map: Available at the park headquarters.

Who says you can't go mountain biking and bird watching at the same time? Certainly not the folks who run the Great Swamp Management Area. An easy 5.5-mile loop on grassy roads and double-tracks surrounds a wetland that is teeming with incredible bird life.

Binoculars dangling from neck, I turned left twice through the holly trees, soon arriving at a popular fishing spot, Worden Pond. Backtracking, I turned left on the main trail to a large dike and marsh. An ibis foraged on vegetation to my right, forcing me to slow down. Families of ducks followed their parents, while a turtle sunned itself on a tree limb. Yet, nothing prepared me for the four large nests that were perched atop consecutive power-line poles. Four osprey peered down at me from their lofty positions as I cruised underneath the wires. As I circled around the far side of the swamp, one of these huge birds circled overhead squawking loudly. I suddenly had a vision of a prehistoric bird swooping down upon Jonny Quest and clutching him with its claws. "Haji, help me, help!" Needless to say, I heeded the bird's warning, bearing left out of the swamp back to the safety of my car. Fortunately, I didn't need Race Bannion's assistance this time.

Adventure Sports, 2 Bowen's Landing, Newport, RI 02840 (tel. 401/849-4820) rents Boston Whalers—18-foot boats with 90 HP, and 22-foot boats with 150 HP. Prices for the boats start at $55 per hour. They also rent Waverunners, which are similar to Jet Skis except that you sit down, for $65 to $75 per hour.

Rhode Island has one of the highest population densities in the nation, second only to New Jersey. Thus, the roads can be extremely congested. The following rides are fun in the summer, but far less crowded in the spring or fall. There's also the 14$\frac{1}{2}$-mile **East Bay Bicycle Path.** Starting at India Point Park, the path crosses rivers, weaves through woods, and hugs Narragansett Bay as it makes its way from Providence to Warren to Bristol. Contact the Rhode Island Tourism Department for a map of the path (tel. 800/556-2484).

THE RIDES

Newport

10 miles. Allow 2–3 hours. Easy; several hills. Access: From points east, follow State Route 138 to State Route 138A to Memorial Boulevard. Turn left on Bellevue Street. Parking is across the street from the International Tennis Hall of Fame. From Newport Harbor, look for the signs to Bellevue Mansions. Map: Any good state road map.

Nowhere else on the Atlantic seaboard is opulence taken to the extravagant heights of the Newport mansions. Built in the mid to late 1800s and early 1900s, these lavish stone palaces and marble chateaux were once summer playgrounds for the heads of American finance. The Vanderbilits, Astors, and Belmonts of the world would descend upon their 50- to 70-room summer " cottages" to rest, relax, and of course, entertain.

This short 10-mile ride takes you on a road to riches (albeit, not yours) before hugging the shoreline to Newport harbor. Park your car and bear right down Bellevue Avenue. Kingscote, an 1839 Victorian mansion with Tiffany glass windows, is the first "cottage" to appear on this broad, tree-lined street. The home was owned by George Noble Jones, one of the southerners who summered in Newport. A left turn onto Ruggles will bring you to Newport's most elaborate summer home, The Breakers, constructed in 1895 for Cornelius Vanderbilt. It took more than two years and a hundred workers to complete the building. Unfortunately for Vanderbilt, he died three years after his dream house was finished. Back on Bellevue, you'll pass Chateau-sur-Mer, built for William Wetmore who amassed a fortune in the China trade, William Vanderbilt's sumptuous Marble House, and Rosecliff, the famed mansion designed by the illustrious architect Stanford White in 1900 and seen in the film, *The Great Gatsby.* At the Astors' Beechwood, actors portray servants and high-society guests in a lively re-enactment of Newport's Gilded Age.

Follow Bellevue to the end, where there's a small turnaround at Bailey's Beach. Here you can see the magnificent backyards of these mansions, the size of football fields, on the 3-mile-long Cliff Walk (see "Walks & Rambles"). Back on two wheels, veer left onto

Ocean Avenue past the perfect crescent of sand known as Gooseberry Beach. Further along is King's Beach and the rocky shoreline of Brenton Point State Park. Cattle grazing on manicured lawns signal your arrival at Hammersmith Farm. Jacqueline and John F. Kennedy held their wedding reception on these grounds, and returned for numerous summer vacations. During the summer of 1995, the farm was up for sale for a measly $9.5 million. Go straight on Brenton Road to Halidon Street, which will you give you an unobstructed view of the yachts anchored in Newport Harbor. A right turn on Thames and two left turns onto Narragansett and Bellevue will bring you back to the parking lot.

Tiverton-Little Compton

29 miles. Allow 3–4 hours. Easy to moderate; rolling hills. Access: Park at The Stone Ridge Inn, located on State Route 77 in Tiverton, south of State Route 24. Map: Any good state road map.

While the crowds flock to Newport, the small stretch of land across the Sakonnet River is popular with Providencers and Bostonians who would prefer to keep Rhode Island's southeastern corner a coveted secret. Quintessential New England villages, more evocative of Vermont than Rhode Island, lie several miles inland from the harbors of the Sound and the coastal marshes of the river.

I took this 29-mile ride with my wife Lisa on a cloudless Saturday morning. After parking our car at the Stone Ridge Inn in Tiverton, we took a left onto State Route 77 for our first views of sailboats gliding along the harbor. A right turn across a small bridge onto Nannaquaket Road brought us past our dream houses, spacious dwellings with manicured yards sloping down to the river or woods. The road merges back with Route 77, where we turned right for a short run before veering right again onto Seapowet Road. On the right-hand side of Seapowet is the Emilie Ruecker Wildlife Refuge. Fiddler crabs and a vast assortment of sea birds were found on a quick walk along the salt marshes, rocky outcroppings, and uplands. Seapowet Road turns into Neck Road, which is lined on both sides by potato farms and small tidal pools. Before making a left turn onto Pond Bridge Road, we saw a snowy egret fly overhead. Surprisingly, llamas were grazing at the first farm to our left.

Pond Bridge Road ventures downhill to Route 77, where we turned right and continued south. We found homemade salsa, chips, fresh fruit, and hot baked bread at the stands that line Route 77. Weighted down with our goodies, we pedaled to Sakonnet Point at the end of Route 77 and picnicked on the rocks overlooking this working harbor. Anglers fished off the large boulders and sailboats tacked around a lighthouse that overlooks the Rhode Island Sound. After a quick energy boost, we ventured back on Route 77 North turning right on Swamp Road. Our first left brought us to a white steeple that towered over a perfectly designed village green. This is the town of Little Compton. We continued past farmland to the road's end, where we turned left, climbing uphill to Route 77. Veering right, we cruised on the shoulder of Route 77 all the way back to the Stone Ridge Inn.

Block Island

12–13 miles. Allow a full day. Easy; rolling hills. Access: Catch the ferry from Galilee, Rhode Island, for the shortest ferry ride to Block Island. Call 401/783-4613 for updated times and costs. Ferries also leave from Newport and New London, Connecticut. Map: Any decent map of Block Island.

Weathered houses bravely face the ocean's wrath atop small hillsides that are more reminiscent of Scotland than Rhode Island. Bluffs plummet to the water's edge and moors line the long stretch of beach. Inland, century-old stone walls and small blue-green ponds speckle the rolling terrain. This is Block Island, a small sliver of land 12 miles south of the town of Galilee. The ferry ride takes a little more than an hour, leaving you the rest of the day to roam on two wheels, stop, and see all of the island's wondrous sights.

This 12- to 13-mile ride is more a tour of the island than a strenuous workout. After disembarking in Old Harbor, turn left past the Victorian motels, continuing straight around the statue. You will bear left in a counterclockwise manner for most of the trip. Almost immediately after leaving the town, small fields cropped with cedar-shingle houses appear on the right, the vast ocean to the left. Cruising uphill, the redbrick Southeast Lighthouse stands tall over the sea. You can stop to walk around the lighthouse, but I would continue a little further to the Mohegan Bluffs parking lot. A small trail lined with raspberry bushes and rose hips (when the rose hips turn red, people use them to make tea) leads to a majestic overlook where Mohegan's 200-foot cliffs fall to the sea. Another trail leads down to a beach—the massive sheets of rock towering above you will make you feel inconsequential.

Back on the bikes, turn left through a series of small ponds covered with lily pads, frogs, and turtles. Ride past Center Road to Cooneymus Road. At the intersection you can usually find one of the numerous lemonade stands that appear on the island during the hot summer months. Bring lots of change to support the local adolescent population. On Cooneymus, look for a sign for Rodman's

Hollow. Here, you can give your bikes a rest and walk on one of the Greenway trails through this forested glacial ravine to Black Rock Beach (see "Walks & Rambles"). When you return to the bikes, continue around the southwestern part of the island, turning left at the sign for Chaplin's Marina. Situated on Great Salt Pond's New Harbor, this is a good place to have lunch and watch the sailboats glide in and out of their slips. When you reach Corn Neck Road, turn left to ride along the moors that line Crescent Beach, Block Island's most popular shore. Just north of the beach, Clay Head Nature Trail meanders along red clay cliffs to a network of intricate hiking trails called "The Maze." The road ends at Settler's Rock, where you can walk over the sand to the granite North Lighthouse, built in 1867. Return on Corn Neck Road to Old Harbor for the 7PM ferry back to the real world.

RENTALS

Ten Speed Spokes rents bikes in Newport at 18 Elm Street (tel. 401/847-5609). On Block Island, rent bikes from **Esta's Bike Shop,** 53 Water Street (tel. 401/466-2651).

SAILING

Narragansett Bay's deep natural harbor is regarded as one of the finest cruising grounds in the Northeast. On any sunny afternoon, you're bound to see hundreds of full sails coasting up and down the bay. Marked by Newport at its southern tip, the bay is an estuary, in which saltwater arms are fed by freshwater streams and rivers. Come summer, the prevailing wind is the "smoky sou'wester," the same breeze that drew the America's Cup races to Rhode Island for more than 50 years, until America's defeat by Australia in 1983. Almost without exception,

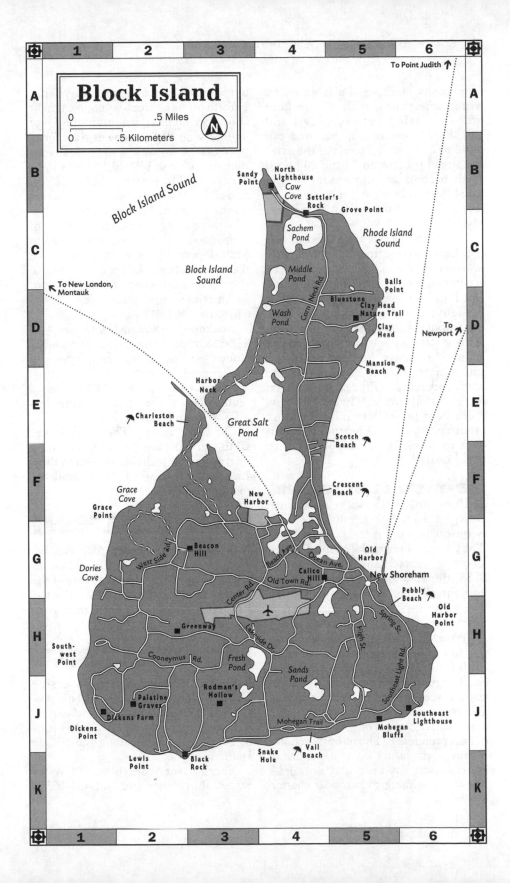

Block Island

0   .5 Miles

0   .5 Kilometers

To Point Judith ↑

Block Island Sound

Sandy Point

North Lighthouse

Cow Cove

Settler's Rock

Grove Point

Rhode Island Sound

Sachem Pond

Middle Pond

Block Island Sound

Corn Neck Rd.

Balls Point

Bluestone

Clay Head Nature Trail

To New London, Montauk

Wash Pond

Clay Head

To Newport

Mansion Beach

Harbor Neck

Charleston Beach

Great Salt Pond

Scotch Beach

Grace Cove

Crescent Beach

Grace Point

New Harbor

Beacon Hill

Dories Cove

West Side Rd.

Beach Ave.

Ocean Ave.

Old Harbor

New Shoreham

Calico Hill

Old Town Rd.

Pebbly Beach

Center Rd.

Old Harbor Point

Southwest Point

Greenway

Cooneymus Rd.

Lakeside Dr.

Fresh Pond

Sands Pond

High St.

Spring St.

Southeast Light Rd.

Palatine Graves

Rodman's Hollow

Dickens Farm

Mohegan Trail

Mohegan Bluffs

Southeast Lighthouse

Dickens Point

Lewis Point

Black Rock

Snake Hole

Vail Beach

calm sunny mornings are followed by windy afternoons, with the onshore breeze arriving between 12PM and 1PM. By mid-afternoon, the wind can build to 25 knots or more, but the average speed is between 10 and 20 knots. "Fair breezes and clear skies" is the usual forecast in the summer, and fog is less prevalent here than in coastal Maine.

To escape Newport's crowds, cross the East Passage to find two largely undiscovered anchorages: Jamestown Harbor on the island of the same name and Potter's Cove at the north end of Prudence Island. Jamestown's historic waterfront is a great place to find a meal. With a state park at the south end, a Wildlife Heritage Foundation in the center, and an Estuarine Sanctuary at the north end, much of Prudence Island has remained wilderness. The island boasts more deer per square mile than any other spot in New England. The sail over to Block Island is popular with larger boats.

CHARTERS & INSTRUCTION

Sail Newport, 53 America's Cup Avenue, Newport, RI 02840 (tel. 401/849-8385) is based in Fort Adams State Park. They have 14 boats, J/22s and Rhodes 19s, with rentals ranging from $35 to $153, depending on the day and the amount of time you plan on sailing. They rent their boats for three, six, or nine hours.

J World is consistently rated one of the top sailing schools in the country. With facilities in Key West, Annapolis, San Diego, and Newport, J World offers two-, three-, and five-day courses that guarantee to improve your performance as a sailor, regardless of your experience or boat preference. The intensive course features six hours on the waters of Narragansett Bay every day on a J/24. For those wishing to bareboat charter,

but who don't have the necessary skills, J World offers a three-day course taught aboard an auxiliary sailboat in the 35- to 45-foot range. Depending on the course, prices range from $295 to $825. For information contact J World, P.O. Box 1509, Newport, RI 02840 (tel. 800/343-2255).

Sail Newport also offers instruction on their fleet of J/22s and Rhodes 19s. The three-day course offers six hours of instruction. Prices range from $109 to $129 depending on whether you take the course on weekdays or weekends. For information contact Sail Newport, 53 America's Cup Avenue, Newport, RI 02840 (tel. 401/849-8385).

Shake-a-Leg Sailing Center (tel. 410/847-3630) has specially designed 20-foot sloops equipped for the physically challenged.

Womanship (tel. 800/342-9295) is a sailing school where, as the name implies, women teach women.

On Block Island, **The Block Island Club** (tel. 401/466-5939) offers sailing instruction to individuals or families. Lasers, Sunfish, and JY1s are available to members.

SCUBA DIVING

Newport Diving Center, 550 Thames Street, Newport (tel. 401/847-9293), arranges two-tank charters to many of the wrecks found on the ocean floor of the bay. The dives usually range from 70 to 120 feet.

SEA KAYAKING

Sakonnet Boathouse, 169 Riverside Drive, Tiverton (tel. 401/624-1440), provides rentals, guided tours, and clinics. They also have three-day guided trips to Block Island and along the Rhode Island coast.

Baer's River Workshop, 222 Water Street, Providence (tel. 401/453-1633), offers sea kayaking trips off India Point and on the Seekonk River.

Oceans & Ponds (tel. 401/466-5131) rents kayaks in Block Island.

Kayakers can also rent at **Narrow River Kayaks,** 95 Middlebridge Road, Narragansett, RI 02882 (tel. 401/789-0334), to venture through The Narrows around Narragansett Town Beach to the wide open sea. Strong paddlers can make it to Beaver Tail State Park at the southern tip of Jamestown Island in less than an hour.

SNOWMOBILING

Like many of the sports listed here, the state's best snowmobiling is also at **Arcadia Management Area** (tel. 401/789-3094). For directions, look under "Mountain Biking." The snowmobile parking lot is 0.9 miles west of the church. Other state parks that allow snowmobiling are **Pulaski State Park** in Burrillville, **Colt State Park** in Bristol, **Lincoln Woods State Park** in Lincoln, and **Burlingame State Park** in Charlestown. Call the Division of Parks and Recreation (tel. 401/277-2632) for more information.

SURFING

Narragansett Town Beach and Second Beach in Middletown are two of the best spots in Rhode Island to catch waves. **The Watershed,** 409 Main St., Wakefield (tel. 401/789-1954), rents boards for Narragansett Town Beach and teaches free lessons every Wednesday at noon from June 15 through Labor Day. **Rodney's Surf & Turf,** 89 Aquidneck Ave., Middletown (tel. 401/846-2280), rents boards for Second Beach.

SWIMMING

The white sand beaches and grassy dunes of Rhode Island entice visitors who want to bask in the sun and swim in the warm surf. Yes, I said warm surf. While the waters of Maine, New Hampshire, and Cape Cod remain frigid in August, the waters of Rhode Island can be a balmy 65° to 70°. Families venture to **Easton Beach** in Newport, **Roger Wheeler State Beach** in Galilee, **Gaspee Point** in Warwick, and **East Beach** in Charlestown. Singles check out **Gooseberry** or **Bailey's** in Newport, **East Matunuck State Beach** in South Kingstown, **Second Beach** in Middletown, **Narragansett Town Beach, Grinnell's Beach** in Sakonnet, and **Crescent Beach** on Block Island.

WALKS & RAMBLES

I took numerous walks in Rhode Island, but, unfortunately, only a few impressed me. Coastal walkers should venture to Cape Cod; inland hikers should check out the blue-blazed trails of neighboring Connecticut. The following two walks are on par with the rest of New England:

THE WALKS

The Greenway Trail, Block Island

Allow 3 hours. Easy. Access: From Old Harbor, take Old Town Road and turn left onto Center Road. The small parking lot is located on the right side of the road across from the airport at Nathan Mott Park. Map: Available from the Block Island Nature Conservancy (tel. 401/466-2129).

Remarkable as it might seem, tiny Block Island has some of the finest walks in the state. Called the Greenway, rarely another human is found (even in the hectic summer months) on these Conservancy-maintained trails that wind from mid-island to the southeast coast.

Park your bike and ramble away from the ruckus on a green, spongy carpet that leads straight through a four-way junction to the Enchanted Forest. Appropriately named, this deep, dark forest of red pines, spruces, and maples takes you back to the Block Island of yore. Bear right to circle around Turnip Farm, a wide-open field of BushyRockrose, Northern Blazing Star, and other, more prosaic wildflowers. Bear right again to cross the unpaved Old Mill Road. Bright yellow goldfinches, graceful marsh hawks,and brown-and-yellow butterflies, distinctive to Block Island, can sometimes be seen along this stretch of the trail. Before crossing Cooneymus Road and continuing to Rodman's Hollow, you'll spot a small house that mysteriously looks like a bookend.

Rodman's Hollow is a glacial cleft that is actually a sandy depression in the land. Take the short loop atop a knoll for panoramic vistas of the surrounding hills, ocean, and old stone walls. From this vantage point, it seems you could easily be in the English countryside. When you reach the Black Rock Trail, turn left to reach Black Rock Beach, a remote cove dwarfed by high bluffs. Then simply turn around and start walking back.

Cliff Walk

Allow 2–3 hours. Easy. Access: Take State Route 138 South to State Route 138A South. Turn right on Memorial Boulevard and park at Easton Beach. The walk starts behind nearby Cliff Walk Manor. Map and tours are offered by the Cliff Walk Society (tel. 401/ 849-7110).

Rhode Island's most popular stroll is the Cliff Walk, a 3³/₄-mile walkway that follows the rugged Newport shoreline on one side, the backyards of the massive Bellevue Avenue mansions on the other. Start on the sidewalk behind Cliff Walk Manor and continue uphill above the ocean. Fences and hedges soon appear on the right, guarding the privacy of these summer "cottages." However, many of the backyards remain open to the sea—and we voyeurs. Most impressive is the sight of The Breakers, the Italian-style villa commissioned by Cornelius Vanderbilt in 1895. The manicured lawns of the mansion slope down toan open iron gate on the Cliff Walk. Another highlight is the Chinese-style teahouse at the Marble House. You'll see the red-and-gold lacquered pagoda just before you walk through the first tunnel. When Alva Vanderbilt realized there was no means to boil tea inside the pagoda, she ordered a small railroad to be built from the main house so that her servants could quickly transport the tea before it got cold. Only God knows what happened to the poor servant who brought Alva a tepid pot of tea!

A second tunnel leads you to an area called Rough Point, where the ocean surf batters the boulders below. I usually turn around here, but you can continue along the rocky trail (which has replaced the sidewalk) to Ledge Road and return via shady Bellevue Avenue. This way, you can see both sides of the mansions.

OUTFITTERS
Walking the World 50 Plus, P.O. Box 1186, Fort Collins, CO 80522 (tel. 303/ 225-0500 or 800/340-9255), offers an

eight-day walking and canoeing tour on the Rhode Island coast and Block Island. Walks average 5 to 8 miles per day.

Campgrounds & Other Accommodations

CAMPGROUNDS

Fishermen's Memorial State Park

From Narragansett, head south on Point Judith Road, near Galilee. Tel. 401/789-8374. 182 sites, 40 full hookups, 35 no hookups.

Conveniently located near Narragansett Town Beach and the ferry to Block Island.

Melville Ponds Campground

Located at 181 Bradford Avenue in Portsmouth, off State Route 114. Tel. 401/849-8212. 123 sites, 33 hookups, 57 no hookups. Handicapped restroom facilities, sewage disposal, public phone, ice, tables, fire rings, and wood.

This is the closest campground to Newport.

Burlingame State Park

Located on Route 1, 4 miles west of Charlestown. Tel. 401/322-7994. 755 sites, no hookups. Sewage disposal, showers, public phone, grocery store, ice, tables grills, wood. $8 resident, $12 non-resident.

Most of this park's 755 sites are situated on the shores of Watchaug Pond. The

Atlantic is only a few miles away. The gigantic complex, also open to trailers, is always crowded due to its proximity to the ocean.

Charlestown Breachway (State Camping Area)

From Charlestown, head south on Charlestown Beach Road. Tel. 401/364-7000. 75 sites for self-contained trailer units, no hookups.

Close to Burlingame State Park, this camping area is much smaller, but just as close to the Atlantic and Ninigret Pond.

George Washington Management Area

Located in Glocester, on Route 44, 5 miles west of Route 102. Tel. 401/568-2013. 45 sites, no hookups. Tables.

Located in the northwestern part of the state near the Connecticut and Massachusetts borders, this 3,200-acre park is known primarily by locals. The 45 sites are housed in a wooded area overlooking Bowdish Reservoir.

INNS & RESORTS

Doubletree Islander Hostel

Goat Island. Tel. 401/849-2600 or 800/222-8733. Double rooms start at $149.

Located in a private setting on a small island in Newport Harbor, The Doubletree Islander Hotel is only a short walk from the restaurants and stores of Newport. The hotel is one of the few accommodations on the coast of Rhode Island that has tennis courts.

Inn at Castle Hill

Ocean Drive, Newport. Tel. 401/849-3800. Double rooms range from $115–$325.

Looking for the perfect place for his marine laboratory, zoologist Alexander Agassiz chose this plot of land on Newport's western shores. Built in 1877, the small mansion sits on a 30-acre bluff separating Newport Harbor from the open ocean. Describing the view from his room, Thornton Wilder wrote, "I could see at night the beacons of six lighthouses and hear the booming and chiming of as many sea buoys." Seven of the ten rooms in the main house have private baths and ocean views.

Rockwell House Inn

610 Hope Street, Bristol. Tel. 401/253-0040. Rates start at $85.

Located on historic Hope Street in Bristol, this Federal-style building was originally built in 1809. If you can somehow manage to pull the quilts off your body and slip out of the comfortable bed, you'll be treated to a gluttonous breakfast of homemade muffins, homemade granola, and a hot course of Dutch puffed pancakes, stuffed breakfast pudding, or sticky French toast. Sit near the "courting fireplace," built in 1910 for the then-owner's daughter, who later became engaged beside it. The inn is close to the East Bay Bike Path and the ferry to Prudence Island.

Hotel Manisses, Block Island

Spring Street, Old Harbor. Tel. 401/466-2063. Double rooms start at $78 in the low season, with breakfast.

This 125-year-old inn is known for its gourmet cuisine. The inn's garden produces much of the vegetables on the menu. Enjoy breakfast and dinner on the outdoor deck overlooking the sea or in the enclosed garden terrace.

Bay Voyage Hotel

150 Conanicus Avenue, Jamestown. Tel. 401/423-2100. Rooms start at $95 during the summer, $65 the rest of the year.

Jamestown's premier accommodation is the Bay Voyage Hotel, the last of the island's grand fin-de-siecle hotels. A converted beach cottage, the hotel was transported across the bay by barge in 1899. Get a room with a balcony overlooking the harbor.

Shelter Harbor Inn, Westerly

10 Wagner Road, Westerly. Tel. 401/322-8883. Double rooms range from $96–$120 in the summer.

Locals venture to this graciously refurbished 18th-century farmhouse, barn, and carriage house for its gastronomic delights. Out-of-staters stay here for the private 2-mile-long beach. Most of the 23 rooms have fireplaces.

5

The Berkshires

PLEASE DEPOSIT YOUR RUGBY SHIRTS IN A BIN ON THE Connecticut side before entering Massachusetts. You are now entering the Berkshires. Plaid flannel replaces Ralph Lauren, public schools are more popular than prep schools, and sprawling acreage surrounding summer estates has been cut into smaller lots to make room for the middle-class. It's not that the affluent aren't welcome. On the contrary, no one is excluded. No other region in New England is more multidimensional. Rich/poor, black/white, Catholic/Jew, urban/rural, art/nature—Yin embraces Yang in the Berkshires. Indeed, a Martian could feel comfortable here.

Towns like West Stockbridge and Egremont to the south and Williamstown to the north resemble the pastoral setting of Vermont. Other parts of the region, like Lenox and Stockbridge, become bustling metropolises in the summer when carloads of New Yorkers and Bostonians flock here for culture. Then there's Adams' redbrick rowhouses on State Route 8, and communities in Pittsfield that look more like mill towns in Pennsylvania. The Berkshires area doesn't hide its eyesores, nor does it alter its image to lure tourists. There's no need.

Classical music, theater, and art have been the attraction of late. Yet, few of the cultural elite fail to walk away without being enamored of the scenery. Long before Tanglewood and Norman Rockwell, the likes of Thoreau,

Emerson, Hawthorne, and Melville were frolicking on mountain trails and loving every minute of it. Legendary Mount Greylock found its way into many novels and short stories. Melville said the shape of the mountain reminded him of a whale, thus inspiring him to write Moby Dick at his Pittsfield home. Greylock's open summit and majestic views remain the centerpiece of the Berkshires, but there are many lesser-known mountains, lakes, and rivers to tempt you. Mount Everett and Mount Washington in the south offer excellent trails through dense forests. The Housatonic, which flows from Greylock all the way south to the Long Island Sound, is known for its quietwater canoeing. Perhaps the best kept secrets are the state parks and forests. Bird-watchers, bikers, cross-country skiers, canoeists, and fishermen will cherish the woods and ponds of October Mountain, Beartown, and Savoy Mountain.

It was not always so easy to get here. For centuries, the mass of mountains and uncut valleys proved to be an impediment to travel and a serious hindrance to pioneer settlement. So much, in fact, that the region was once called the "Berkshire Barrier." The first white man who managed to cross the mountains in 1694 reported that the "greatest part of our road this day was a hideous howling wilderness beset with hideous high mountains." Settlers finally managed to venture into the Berkshires in the 1720s via a trail from Westfield to Great Barrington. Eventually, a stagecoach would bring guests to Stockbridge on the Boston-Albany line.

However, the northern half of the range was only traversed by intrepid travelers until the latter part of the 19th century. A trickle of visitors would cross Hoosac Mountain into North Adams on a bridle path called the Indian Trail.

Bands of Canadian Mohawks had filed along this path on hunting and war expeditions for centuries. Minutemen took the trail on the morning of August 16, 1777, to reinforce the troops in the Battle of Bennington. Even Nathaniel Hawthorne, in 1850, attempted to ride over the range. In his *American Note-Books*, Hawthorne wrote, "I have never driven through such romantic scenery, where there was such a variety and boldness of mountain shapes." Nonetheless, the route from Greenfield to North Adams remained impervious to most travelers until February 9, 1875, when the Greenfield Railroad Company finished boring a 4 3/4-mile tunnel through Hoosac Mountain. The Hoosac Tunnel was the second-longest in the world at the time, but it came with a hefty price tag. Over a span of 24 years, 195 men were killed and 15 million dollars were spent to build this massive cavern. Less than 40 years later, the tunnel became obsolete when the Mohawk Trail was paved in 1914. Now known as State Route 2, the road weaves along the old Indian Trail.

Other industries soon followed the railroads and early farmers into the Berkshires. The world's first commercial electric system was built along the main street of Great Barrington, prompting General Electric to set up factories in Pittsfield. Paper mills pioneered the manufacture of wood-pulp newsprint and textile mills utilized the wool from sheep that grazed on the hillsides. Ironically, the same scenery that first enticed visitors to the region was drastically changed to create railroad ties, paper, and crops. By the end of the 19th century, 80 percent of the land was cleared and the rivers were polluted.

Less than one hundred years later, one of the most remarkable environmental turnarounds has occurred. The decline of heavy industry has led to reforestation of oaks, maples, and other young hardwoods, and 75 percent of the land has been restored to its original stature, with 100,000 acres set aside as state forests and nature preserves. Wild turkeys, beavers, moose, even black bears have returned to the now verdant habitat.

Travelers have taken their cue. They come searching for solace in the "hideous high mountains" and tranquility in the rivers and ponds. At night, after a complete day of outdoor activity, hikers, bikers, and canoeists can relax under the stars and listen to the sounds of classical music being performed by the Boston Symphony Orchestra on the lawns of Tanglewood. You can also watch actors recreate legendary roles at the Berkshire Theater Festival. Ethel Barrymore, Katharine Hepburn, and Paul Newman are just a few of the well-known thespians who have worked here. Together with a panoply of other musical and theatrical activities—plays staged at Edith Wharton's former estate, The Mount, the Williamstown Theater, and contemporary dance choreographed at Jacob's Pillow—the Berkshires offer the best of both worlds to the cultured outdoorsperson.

The Lay of the Land

The Berkshires constitute one of the oldest continuously surviving lands on earth. Some geologists have suggested that the Berkshires and neighboring Green Mountains emerged from the waters of an ancient inland sea in Cambrian times, more than half a billion years ago. With the exception of Greylock, the mountains (officially called the Berkshire Hills) at first glance are not nearly as impressive as other ranges in New England. Rising from the east to an extensive upland plateau, they seldom make pronounced individual summits.

Venture from your car, however, and you'll stumble onto a second-growth forest with many hidden treasures. Mountain brooks break into waterfalls which tumble over rocks dripping green with moss and maidenhair. Hobblebush and laurel line forests of yellow birch, red oak, maple, and hemlock. At higher altitudes, the woods take on the appearance of a northern New England forest, with the occasional spruce and fir popping up among the alpine vegetation. Rivers have carved the valley floor into steep and narrow gorges of bedrock. There are even cobbles, knobs of quartzite and limestone blanketed by gardens of ferns—walking ferns, purple cliff brakes, and ebony spleenwort.

Typical of southern New England, the mean temperature in January in the Berkshires is approximately 26°Fahrenheit. During the height of the summer, the mean temperature is closer to 77°. Obviously, conditions in the uplands vary considerably from weather in the valley. In April, for example, when tree buds and crocuses are slowly coming to life in the valley, the hills are still locked in a wintry tundra.

With more than 100,000 acres of state forest and nature preserves, the Berkshires contain a wealth of wildlife, including many animals that have recently returned to the hills. Black bears have been spotted, as well as bobcats, deer, coyotes, red foxes, cottontail rabbits, and perhaps the Berkshire's best loved inhabitant, the beaver. Wild turkeys, hawks, great horned owls, and blue herons are among the 200 species of birds found in the forests.

Orientation

This small mountainous plateau is a clearly bounded entity: the northern

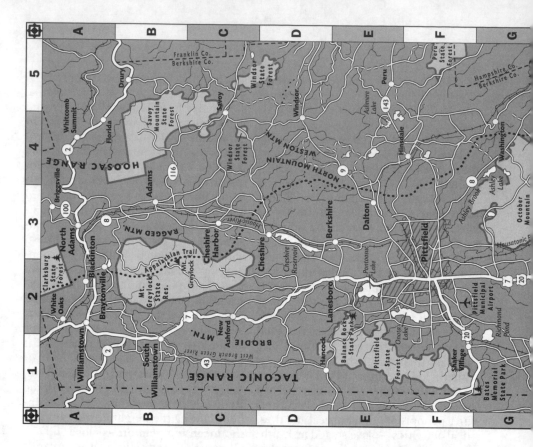

section of the Berkshires is bordered by the southern end of Vermont's Green Mountains; to the south are Connecticut's Litchfield Hills; to the west is the Taconic Range and the Housatonic Valley; and to the east lies the Connecticut Valley. For centuries, until the Hoosac Tunnel was created, traveling from east to west was a formidable task. Now you can travel on either the **Mass Pike** or **State Route 2.** Route 2, formerly the **Mohawk Trail,** is by far the better choice. Crossing and, at times, bordering the old Indian Trail, the Mohawk Trail is a serpentine road that weaves up and down the Hoosac Range, offering stunning overviews of the countryside. In the background to the west stands Mount Greylock. **U.S. 7** travels south to north the length of the state. The highway rides alongside the Berkshires from Great Barrington to Pittsfield all the

way north to Williamstown. Congestion can be overwhelming between Lenox and Stockbridge during the Tanglewood season and fall foliage period.

The towns in the Berkshires vary greatly in size and style, from rural hideaways to countrified villages to blue-collar cities. Starting in the south, antique shops and cozy B&Bs line the streets of **Egremont, Sheffield,** and **Ashley Falls. Great Barrington** is more city than village, but offers a great selection of restaurants. Continuing north, **Stockbridge** and **Lenox** are my favorite places to stay in the southern half of the Berkshires. Both towns are conveniently located near the state forests, parks, Tanglewood, and the theaters. For a more rural feeling, consider staying in **West Stockbridge,** where farmland branches out in every direction. **Pittsfield** is the urban center of the Berkshires, where most locals live and

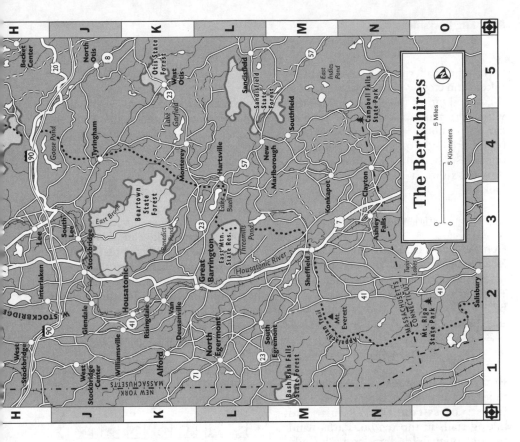

work. If you plan to climb Greylock, ski Brodie, or bike Savoy Mountain State Forest, **Williamstown** is the finest place to stay in the northern region. The sloping lawns and ivy-covered buildings of Williams College are the perfect backdrop for a peaceful vacation. **North Adams** and **Adams** are far more industrial.

Parks & Other Hot Spots

The parks below are listed in a north to south order, roughly following U.S. 7.

Savoy Mountain State Forest

From North Adams, take State Route 2 East to Florida, Massachusetts. Turn right on Central Shaft Road to reach the forest headquarters. Headquarters: North Adams (tel. 413/663-8469).

Adjacent to the Mohawk Trail State Forest, this is one of the largest tracts of undeveloped land in Massachusetts. The forest has an extensive trail system, ideal for hiking, mountain biking, and cross-country skiing.

Mount Greylock State Reservation

From Pittsfield, head 5 miles north on U.S. 7, and then follow the signs. Headquarters: Lanesboro (tel. 413/499-4262).

Standing 3,491 feet, Mount Greylock is the state's highest and most accessible mountain. Besides the numerous hiking trails that weave through the maples, beeches, yellow birches, and spruces and pass over swift mountain brooks on the way to the peak, there's a paved road for bikers and cross-country skiers to get to the top. During the summer months, when the mountain is crowded, you can still choose from a wide variety of trails to find a quiet spot. Hawthorne once described the view from the 360-degree summit as "a daydream to look at."

Notchview Reservation

From Pittsfield, take State Route 9 East and look for signs just past Windsor. There's a small visitor center at the reservation. Trustees of Reservations headquarters: 572 Essex Street, Beverly (tel. 508/921-1944).

Run by the Trustees of Reservations, this 3,000-acre retreat offers some of the finest cross-country skiing and hiking trails in the region. Paths wind through open fields, farmland, a heavily wooded forest, and up 2,297-foot Judges Hill.

Pleasant Valley Wildlife Sanctuary

From the junction of U.S. 7 and U.S. 20 in Lenox, drive 3 miles north on U.S. 7 and then west on W. Dugway Road. Turn left on West Mountain Road to come to the entrance.

Operated by the Massachusetts Audubon Society, this 1,100 acre preserve is known for its beaver ponds and wide selection of birds. The tract of land was originally donated by a group of Lenox residents in 1929. Here, 2,124-foot Lenox Mountain towers over a forest of northern hardwoods, hemlock, and white pine.

Housatonic River

Accessible via U.S. 7 at many points. For more information, contact the Southern Berkshire Chamber of Commerce, 362 Main Street, Great Barrington, MA 02130 (tel. 413/528-4006).

From its northernmost source at the base of Mount Greylock, the Housatonic flows 150 miles south through the Berkshire and Taconic ranges to the mouth of the Long Island Sound. The river ranks high on the list for quiet-water canoeing and bird watching.

October Mountain State Forest

Head east on U.S. 20 to the forest entrance. Headquarters: Woodlawn Road, Lee (tel. 413/243-1778).

Formerly a privately owned game preserve, mountain bikers, hikers, and cross-country skiers now take advantage of this 15,710-acre forest. Within the dense woods, several bodies of water are found, including Finerty Pond and Lake Felton. Elevations range from 1,800 to 2,000 feet.

Beartown State Forest

From Great Barrington, head east on State Route 23 to Blue Hill Road. The headquarters is located 0.5 miles north. In Monterey (tel. 413/528-0904).

Beartown is October's smaller brother (only 10,852 acres). It is 90 percent forested with mixed hardwoods and lined with laurels and azalea.

The numerous streams and ponds, including Benedict, are ideal for fishing or cooling off after a long day of heated activity.

Mount Washington State Forest

From South Egremont and State Route 41, travel south on Mount Washington Road. Headquarters: Mount Washington (tel. 413/528-0330).

Straddling the New York and Connecticut borders, the hills of Mount Washington offer views of all three states. On the Mass. side are some of the state's highest mountains, including Mount Everett (2,623 feet). One of the highlights of the park is Bash-Bish Falls, which makes a drop of 200 feet to the narrow gorge below.

Bartholemew's Cobble

Situated west of U.S. 7 in Ashley Falls, close to the Connecticut border. Take Rannapo Road south to Weatogue Road to the entrance. Headquarters: Ashley Falls (tel. 413/298-8600).

A National Natural Landmark, the cobble is a limestone formation rising in sharp little cliffs from a bend in the Housatonic River. The extraordinary variety of plants includes over 40 species of ferns and 500 types of wildflowers.

Appalachian Trail

Accessible throughout the Berkshires. For more information, contact the Berkshires chapter of the AMC located at the Mount Greylock Visitor's Center (tel. 413/443-0011).

The AT rambles 87 miles from Mount Washington and the Connecticut border through the Berkshires to the Vermont state line. In between lie some of the region's best day hikes, like the ridge walk atop Mount Race and the climb to Mount Greylock. Overnight hikers should know that shelters are sparse—every 18 to 22 miles. Low-impact shelters are located along the trail at 7 to 8 mile intervals.

What To Do & Where To Do It

BIRD WATCHING

There are more than 200 species of birds in the Berkshires. **Finches, robins, bobolinks, phoebes,** and **cedar waxwings** are commonly found in the fields. Climbing into the woods, you might hear **yellow-bellied sapsuckers, red-eyed vireos, orioles, scarlet tanagers,** and **American kingbirds.** At the highest elevations, expect to find **warblers, white-throated sparrows,** and **juncos.** There's also a good chance you'll spot a **wild turkey** scurrying through the forest. They were reintroduced to the region several decades ago and are thriving. The southern Vermont birding section in chapter 8 more thoroughly describes the environments and kinds of birds you're likely to see in the New England woods.

Pleasant Valley Wildlife Sanctuary, Canoe Meadows Wildlife Sanctuary, Bartholemew's Cobble, and the **Housatonic River** are four of the best places to bird watch in the region (See the "Hiking & Backpacking," "Walks & Rambles," and "Canoeing" sections, respectively). For additional information regarding bird watching, contact the **Berkshire Sanctuaries,** a division of the

Massachusetts Audubon Society. They are located at Pleasant Valley, 472 West Mountain Road, Lenox, MA 01240 (tel. 413/637-0320).

BOARDSAILING

Boardsailors catch the breeze at Pontoosuc Lake in Pittsfield and Stockbridge Bowl.

CANOEING

Searching for a long stretch of river to forget your troubles for a week? Sorry, you're in the wrong section. The Berkshires are better known for day paddles on ponds and lakes—placid bodies of water where you bring lunch, drop a fishing line, relax. However, there is one river worth mentioning.

QUIET WATER

Housatonic River

Allow 2–3 hours. Easy. Access: From Lenox, head north on U.S. 7 and turn right onto New Lenox Road. You'll see a small Canoe Access sign. The take-out is located in Lenoxdale at the end of Crystal Street.

If you yearn for a slice of tranquility and solitude far away from the culture-hungry crowds of Stockbridge, Lenox, and Williamstown, step into a canoe. The only sign of civilization is a large dairy farm at the put-in. The hills on the eastern shores of the river are part of the October Mountain State Forest. Here, the Tory Caves were supposedly located—shelters where several hundred British troops hid during the Revolutionary War. Unfortunately, these caves disappeared long ago.

It was impossible to get lost the day my friend Kenny and I paddled 7 miles

downstream on the Housatonic. Every 500 yards or so, two great blue herons would gracefully fly away until we caught up to them again, continuing this game of hide-and-seek all the way to the end of our journey in Woods Pond. Families of Canada geese and the gnawed wooden remnants left by beavers' teeth lined the banks of the river. Two hours later, we returned to our car in Lenoxdale, as relaxed as monks after meditation.

Benedict Pond

Monterey. Access: From Great Barrington, take State Route 23 approximately 5 miles to Blue Hill Road. Take a right. The parking lot is located past the headquarters, about 2 miles down the road. Camping is available year-round, although there are only 12 campsites.

Nestled within Beartown State Forest, this 35-acre pond is the perfect retreat on a hot summer's day. The still waters are shaded by a dense forest of conifer trees, hemlocks, and mountain laurel. In late May, you're in for a special treat when the azaleas bloom. A web of trails cover the large park, including the AT, which runs past the southern tip of the pond. Thus, you can turn your canoeing trip into a combination hiking and mountain-biking trip as well.

Buckley Dunton Lake

Becket. Access: From Lee, take U.S. 20 East for 4 miles and turn left onto Becket Road. After 2.5 miles, you'll notice the southern tip of the lake. Turn left on a road just before a large garage marked by a sign that reads "Buckley Dunton Reservoir—Day Use Only"; 0.5 mile later, you'll arrive at the boat access. Camping is permitted at the state forest campground.

Much larger than Benedict, Buckley Dunton is also part of a state forest—October Mountain. This 195-acre lake can be fairly crowded on weekends when the waters are populated by fishermen. Bass, pickerel, perch, and bullhead have been hooked here. The shores of the lake are heavily forested with a mixture of white pines, hemlocks, spruces, red maple, sugar maples, ashes, and yellow birches. Come in here July and August and you'll be picking blueberries on the shores.

RENTALS & A GUIDE/ SHUTTLE SERVICE

Main Street Sports & Leisure, 48 Main Street, State Route 7A, Lenox, MA 01240 (tel. 413/637-4407) will shuttle you and a rental canoe to New Lenox for the abovementioned 7-mile ride down the Housatonic River. Trips for two start at $40. Guided trips are also available.

YMCA Marina (tel. 413/499-0694), in Pittsfield, rents canoes on Pontoosuc Lake.

CROSS-COUNTRY SKIING

The only reason New Yorkers should venture farther north than the Berkshires is to find better snow or more challenging terrain. The beginner to intermediate trails here are just as good as Vermont. Main Street Sports & Leisure rents skis and has a cross-country snow phone which offers up-to-date skiing conditions on the best trails around. They also offer free clinics; located at 48 Main Street, P.O. Box 2164, Lenox, MA 01240 (tel. 413/637-4407).

IN THE BACKCOUNTRY

Beartown State Forest

Allow 1.5–2 hours. Moderate; relatively flat. Access: From Great Barrington, take State Route 23 approximately 5 miles to Blue Hill Road. Take a right. The parking lot is located past the headquarters, about 2 miles down the road. Map: Contact the Massachusetts Division of Forest and Parks, 100 Cambridge Street, Boston, MA 02202 (tel. 617/727-3180).

It was a perfect day for cross-country skiing: 20° to 25°, blue skies, sun beating down, and best of all, there was snow on the ground. I was with George Roberson, owner of a sporting goods store in Lenox and the cross-country skiing guru of the Berkshires. George coaches the region's best high school aged cross-country skiers for the AAU's and Junior Olympics. Needless to say, he knows every backcountry trail in the Berkshires. The trail George chose for us is a place where he loves to bring his students.

As soon as we parked the car at the entrance of Beartown State Forest, I understood why. Livermore Peak and Mount Wilcox, 1,863 and 2,155 feet tall, respectively, tower over Benedict Pond. Beartown's grand mixture of pine greens and cerulean waters stood before us. From the name, you may be inclined to think that bears run rampant in these parts, but, in actuality, black bears are a rare find. You're more likely to see red and gray squirrels, snowshoe hares, cottontails, and deer.

The $2^1/2$-mile trail loops around Benedict Pond, every angle offering a magnificent vista. There are four downhill portions of the trail that can be tricky to maneuver. I wiped out on the second one as George smiled. Soothing my ego, he told me a story about the time he was skiing in Putney, Vermont, and a man fell with a thud in front of him. When the man got up, he brushed himself off and said to George, "Nobody's perfect." It was the legendary cross-country skier, Bill Koch.

At the northern part of the trail, take a left under the gate and continue around the loop. Die-hards can opt for the 8-mile Ski Trail which can be found at the western end of the pond. The trail climbs the side of Beartown Mountain rather steeply before meeting up with Beartown Road and circling back to the pond trail. If conditions are favorable, you might be able to ski the last portion of this loop on the pond itself. But make sure there is a significant amount of snow before attempting this. The water is beautiful to look at from a distance, not eye-to-eye.

October Mountain State Forest

Allow 2–6 hours. Easy to moderate; relatively flat. Access: From Lenox, take U.S. 20 East past Lee to Becket Road. Take a left on Becket Road and proceed for five minutes to County Road. There is a two-story white clapboard house on the left, just in case the road sign is missing (which it was when I last came here). Make a sharp left and go until the road is unplowed. Map: Contact the Massachusetts Division of Forest and Parks, 100 Cambridge Street, Boston, MA 02202 (tel. 617/727-3180).

With close to 16,000 acres, October Mountain is Massachusetts' largest state forest. There are a host of unplowed roads and skiable passes to choose from. Thus, picking one route is almost like choosing a movie at a video store with a large group of friends. My favorite trail is County Road. Simply park your car when the paved road suddenly becomes white—unplowed. Throw on your skis and continue for as long as your thighs and calves can endure. This is high plateau region, with elevations ranging from 1,800 to 2,000 feet. Hemlocks, spruces, birches, oaks, and flowering shrubs line the road like spectators at a marathon to cheer you on.

Since the trail is a road, it's extremely wide. For one cross-country skier, it can be lonely gliding along the middle lane. For a large group of people, the road can't be beat. Huddle together on the relatively flat terrain, passing the lucky guy who lives in a small wooden cabin at 1811, until you encounter a V in the road about 1^1/$_2$ miles further. Here's your first option. Take County Road to the left for ^{3}/$_4$ mile and you hit lovely Schoolhouse Reservoir. Continue on Lenox-Whitney Place to the right for another 1^1/$_4$ miles and you'll run into an intersection known as Four Corners. If you take a left on West Branch Road for half a mile, you can picnic at the enchanting Washington Mountain Lake; 2 miles to the right on West Branch Road will lead you out of the forest to the doorstep of Bucksteep Manor. Or you can continue on Lenox-Whitney Place for another 3^1/$_2$ miles. The choice is for your legs and your Rolex to decide.

Ashley Hill

Allow 1.5–2 hours. Moderate; hilly. Access: From South Egremont, take State Route 41 South and turn right on Mount Washington Road where there's a big sign to Mount Washington. Continue for 8 miles past the Mount Everett State Reservation until you reach the Mount Washington State Forest Headquarters. Park here. Map: Contact the Massachusetts Division of Forest and Parks, 100 Cambridge Street, Boston, MA 02202 (tel. 617/727-3180).

Try not to break your pole when you go cross-country skiing. It's almost like losing a limb, especially on tough uphill climbs. That's what I learned at Ashley Hill. Trying to locate a bird squawking loudly overhead, I suddenly went flying downhill, slipped, and landed on my left pole. When I wiped the snow off my glasses and raised myself up, I realized

October Mountain or Kilimanjaro?

Wildlife in the Berkshires is prevalent. Chances are you'll see a deer, maybe even a bald eagle or a moose. But here in the October Mountain region, you have the chance of spotting animals not usually found in this type of habitat. At the turn of the century, William C. Whitney, Secretary of the Navy under President Grover Cleveland, purchased about 11,000 acres of land as a gift to his son. He proceeded to build a 15-foot fence and started importing moose, elk, and a herd of eight Wyoming buffalo, one of which was supposedly the largest buffalo in the world at the time. Other areas were devoted to sheep, goats, and Belgian hares. An aviary was stocked with approximately 2,000 pheasants. There were 55 game wardens and workmen on Whitney's payroll to preserve the grounds. Yes, dear old dad had bought his son a New England safari. However, young Whitney wasn't much of a Hemingway-type hunter and rarely ventured into the forest. The animals were eventually sold to the Bronx Zoo or shot to place above the mantelpiece . . . or were they? As local legend has it, there have been some bizarre sightings of animals in this neck of the woods. So don't be surprised if that deer you supposedly spotted is really a gazelle or an impala.

my pole was shattered. Fortunately, I was at the end of Ashley and the walk back to my car wasn't that bad.

Ashley Hill is strictly reserved for people who prefer not to see other people. Tucked neatly away in the southwest corner of the Berkshires on Mount Washington, this is an ideal trail for skiers yearning for solitude. In other words, Ashley is a clandestine destination known only to a handful of local outdoorsmen . . . so don't tell anybody, okay?

I started on the Alander Trail, gliding across an expansive field, before being protected from the wind by a cluster of oaks and maples. A quick downhill stint on another open field and I crossed the bridge over Bash-Bish Brook. Stay to the right and you'll pass a sign for the Charcoal Pit Trail. Unless you like swimming in snow, keep on moving. After crossing another bridge, I saw the sign for the Ashley Hill Trail and began my ascent up the challenging hill.

Two hundred feet later, the trail leveled off, and I had a picturesque view of the ravine to my right sharply sloping down to the Ashley Hill Brook.

The trail is relatively wide, so don't worry about disappearing down the hillside. The day I went, I followed a packed snowmobile trail the entire way. Several more short hills and I came upon the Alander Trail again. The Ashley Hill trail continues, eventually making its way into New York and Connecticut. You can do the three-state loop, but I turned around at the next Ashley Hill sign, which had two arrows pointing in opposite directions. The trail back down is exhilarating. Just don't look for loud birds in trees.

Becket Road

Allow 1.5–2 hours. Easy to moderate; sloping hill. Access: From Lenox, take U.S. 20 East past Lee towards Becket. Just before you reach Belden Tavern, take a left onto Becket Road and go up two hills. At the end of the second rise, you'll see a small Appalachian Trail sign. The path is located $1/2$ mile past the sign on the left-hand side. There will be a small turn-off with a yellow triangular snowmobile sign hanging from a tree.

If you're desperate for snow, try this remote trail that rolls along a hilltop in Becket. I didn't think I would have the opportunity to ski the day I ventured here. All I thought about as I drove from upstate New York to the Berkshires was a photograph in a recent *New York Times* that showed Martin Dearborn of Tilton, New Hampshire, cleaning the street with a broom instead of a shovel. It was the first day of February in one of the mildest winters in recent memory. Patches of snow were mixed with dirt on the side of the highway, and the dirt was winning by a margin of two to one. I called a ranger at nearby October Mountain State Forest to find out the trail conditions. He happened to see several skiers that morning on a snowmobile path just past the Appalachian Trail on Becket Road. Bingo! If Groucho was alive, the duck would drop with the magic word, SNOW.

For some reason, El Nino forgot about Becket Road. The glorious white stuff was almost a foot deep on the trail. Yet, El Nino wasn't the only one who forgot about this exquisite path the day I went. There were no snowmobilers, cross-country skiers, or any other type of Homo sapiens. Just me, gliding along on a 4-foot-wide path, hedged in on both side by a dense birch, maple, and oak forest. The only sounds heard were my skis swooshing effortlessly along someone else's tracks, and the occasional peep-peep-peeping of a bird.

Since the trail was designed with the snowmobiler in mind, it's simple to follow. The terrain is relatively flat, passing under fallen branches and over icy streams. I descended down a short hill under a tunnel of overhanging white pine trees before stopping at a cemetery of dead limbs, trunks, and roots jutting up from the track. You can easily take your skis off, walk through the maze of extended branches, and continue on to Finerty Pond in October Mountain State Forest. However, I was content to simply sit down on a fallen trunk, grab my raisins and water, and listen to the sounds of silence.

Notchview Reservation

Allow 2–3 hours. Easy to strenuous; rolling hills. Access: From Pittsfield, take U.S. 7 North to State Route 9 East or Tyler Street. Notchview is located on State Route 9, 1 mile east of the State Routes 8A and 9 intersection in Windsor. Map: Available at visitor center.

There were seven cars in Notchview's parking lot by the time I arrived noon Monday. The temperature was a balmy 4°Fahrenheit with a windchill factor of −26°. As soon as I walked out of my car, the blustery wind kissed my cheeks with its arctic lips. But in New England, this type of weather is expected and ignored. This is the land where bare-handed gas station attendants stand outside all day to fill up your tank; where you crank your heater to full blast and suddenly turn around to see a motorcyclist driving next to you, oblivious to the harsh conditions. All we care about is snow, and thankfully, there was plenty of it. A recent snowstorm had dumped over a foot of fine white powder on the Berkshire Hills.

Notchview is a splendid 3,000-acre property owned by the environmentally sensitive Trustees of Reservations. It costs $6 to enter the densely forested grounds, but it's worth every penny: 30 km of trails weave in and out of the reservation and its fields, specifically designed for cross-country skiers of all levels.

By the time I got my skis on outside the visitor center and took a left onto the Circuit Trail, my face was numb and the tips of my fingers were freezing. That quickly changed as soon as I took my right at Ant Hill Loop. Oaks and white pines, limbs heavy with snow, provided the perfect protection against the chilly winds. The half-mile trail is a gradual climb, guaranteed to leave you cozy by the time it drops you back off at the Circuit Trail. I took a quick right and then a left onto the Whitestone Trail, arguably the most scenic trail in the Berkshires. Especially on such a day, when the horizontal branches of the hemlocks held three inches of snow, creating Mondrian-like right angles with the trunks, and a spectacular mesh of Malevich white-on-white wherever I looked. It had a dizzying kaleidoscopic effect.

Wind whistled, limbs moaned, there was even a completely uprooted tree, but I was as warm as a baby's bottle of milk. The 1½-mile, pine-needle-strewn path was a favorite for animals as well, since I followed raccoon tracks the whole length of the way.

I was quite content when I made my left onto the Mixed Wood Trail, avoiding the snow dunes and wind of the Sawmill Field. A mile later I left the Mixed Wood Trail disheartened and exhausted. Due to the recent snowfall, this untried trail was better suited for snowshoes than cross-country skis. My legs were practically paralyzed in knee-deep snow, each step becoming a monumental effort. If I were wise, I would have made an about-face and returned back to the visitor's center the same way I came. However, I foolishly continued on, praying that there would be a break in the heavy snow. There wasn't. I somehow managed to finish the "Legs-Like-Wood" trail and returned to the starting point via the Circuit Trail. It was certainly a full day of skiing.

Rockwell Road

Allow 3–4 hours. Strenuous!; mountainous. Access: From Pittsfield, take U.S. 7 North through Lanesborough Village. Watch for Greylock Reservation signs on the right as you head north out of Lanesborough. Turn right and follow the signs for 2 miles to the visitors center. Map: Available at the visitor center.

So you've done every trail in October, Beartown, and Notchview, and you're yearning for more. Your adrenaline is in overdrive and you won't be satisfied until you've conquered the Berkshires' greatest triumph. Then it's time for the Rockwell Road challenge. But you better be an expert nordic skier and a damn good alpine skier as well. Rockwell Road is an 8-mile uphill climb to the peak of 3,491-foot Mount Greylock, the tallest mountain in southern New England. Ralph Waldo Emerson called it "a serious mountain."

Since the road is open to snowmobilers, come on a weekday to avoid the noise and traffic. The first mile is a grueling, steep uphill climb on which you're more inclined to look at your skis than the birches, beeches, and maples surrounding you. Don't worry. The road levels off somewhat, becoming a gradual climb the rest of the way. On the northern slopes, you'll pass a yellow birch forest, bogs, and stunted firs—the result of heavy squalls that could stunt you if you're not prepared for its angry torrent.

Finally you reach the top. Your reward is a stunning view of the Berkshires, the Taconic Mountains to the west, and the Green Mountains to the north. Closer by, there's great sights of the majestic Hopper, a V-shaped snow slide down the mountain, and the aptly named cliff, Stony Ledge. To get back to the visitor center, put your skis back on and let gravity pull you.

NORDIC SKIING CENTERS

Located just west of the Berkshires, the 23 km of trails at the **Swift River Inn,** 151 South Street, Cummington, MA 01026 (tel. 413/634-5751), are some of the best in Massachusetts—especially the 4.5 km Beaver Pond Loop which circles the grounds. The well-marked and groomed trail system takes skiers over 560 acres of rolling hills.

If there's snow anywhere in the Berkshires, then you're bound to see it at the **Bucksteep Manor Cross-Country Ski Center,** Washington Mountain Road, Washington, MA 01223 (tel. 413/623-5535). Bordering October Mountain State Forest, Bucksteep Manor's trails snake through forests of fir and open meadows at an elevation of 1,900 feet. Accommodations are available at the inn and surrounding cottages.

Better known for its downhill skiing, **Brodie Mountain Cross-Country Touring,** U.S. 7, New Ashford, MA (tel. 413/443-4752) has 25 km of track-set trails and another 40 km of backcountry skiing. The variety of terrain includes undulating pastures, dirt roads, and short steep hills.

DOWNHILL SKIING/ SNOWBOARDING

The Berkshire runs might not be as challenging as those in Vermont, but the lack of lines, easy rentals, and affordable accommodations more than make up for it. Most of the downhill areas have at least 90 percent snowmaking capability. Jiminy Peak, Brodie, and Bousquet ski areas are north, near Greylock's peak. Further south are Catamount, Butternut, and Otis Ridge.

Jiminy Peak

Corey Road, Hancock, MA 01237. Tel. 413/738-5500; snow report, tel. 413/738-PEAK. 28 trails (21% easy, 50% intermediate, 29% expert), 5 lifts including a quad, a triple, and 3 doubles; 1,140-foot vertical drop. Full day tickets $37 weekend, $30 weekday, $20 nights.

Jiminy Peak is a popular learn-to-ski and family resort. Jericho, one of the toughest trails, has an average pitch of more than 32 percent; Whitetail, passing underneath the quad, is the mountain's see-and-be-seen bump run. Boarders will find a half-pipe and terrain park.

Brodie Mountain Ski Resort

U.S. 7, New Ashford, MA 01237. Tel. 413/443-4752; snow report, tel. 413/443-4751. 28 trails (11 beginner, 9 intermediate, 9 expert), 4 double chair lifts; 1,250-foot vertical drop. Full day tickets $35 weekend, $30 weekday.

Just down the road from Jiminy, Brodie offers skiing with an Irish flair—somehow it picked up the moniker, "Kelley's Irish Alps," and the shamrock-and-Blarney-stone theme is carried through the resort. There's a lot of fun après-ski around here, and Brodie draws a lot of young singles. Experts shouldn't miss Danny Boy's Trail or Shamrock.

Bousquet Ski Area

Dan Fox Drive, Pittsfield, MA 01201. Tel. 413/442-8316. 21 trails evenly split between novice, intermediate, and expert; 2 double chairs; 750-foot vertical drop. Tickets $15.

Bousquet manages some good, scenic beginner and intermediate skiing on its smallish hill, but the best part about this place is the price. Go ahead—try and find another lift-serviced alpine area where $15 will get you up the hill all day and night.

Catamount

State Route 23, South Egremont, MA 01230. Tel. 413/528-1262; snow report, tel. 800/342-1840. 24 trails (30% easy, 40% intermediate, 30% expert); 5 lifts, 1,000-foot vertical drop. Full day tickets $37 weekend, $25 weekday.

In the far southwest corner of Massachusetts, Catamount is a good place for learners to sharpen their skills on wide-open terrain. The area recently added a solid bump run cut down a 35 percent pitch.

Butternut Basin

State Road, Great Barrington, MA 01230. Tel. 413/528-2000; snow report, tel. 800/438-SNOW. 22 trails (20% easy, 60% intermediate, 20% expert); 6 lifts including a quad, a triple, and four doubles; 1,000-foot vertical drop. Full day tickets $38 weekend, $30 weekday.

Set amid beautiful scenery near one of the Berkshires' classic towns, Butternut has a good ski school, lots of gentle, narrow New England-style trails, and a warm ambience. It's definitely the place to go for families and beginners.

Otis Ridge Ski Area

State Route 23, Otis, MA 01253. Tel. 413/269-4444. 11 trails (3 easy, 4 intermediate, 3 expert); 1 double chair; 400-foot vertical drop. Full day tickets $22 weekend, $15 weekday; night skiing $8.

Otis Ridge is known for its ski camp, which has taught numerous beginners the essentials of alpine skills: how to snow plow, slalom, and stop.

FISHING

Many Berkshire waterways are popular fishing spots year-round. The Housatonic and Deerfield Rivers are the best streams for trophy-caliber **trout** fishing. The Deerfield from Buckland to Shelburne is a good stretch for **brookies**. Buckley Dunton Lake (see "Canoeing"), Benedict Pond (see "Canoeing"), the boat ramp on Laurel Lake, Stockbridge Bowl's causeway, and Goose Pond in Lee are all good locales for catching **bass**, **pickerel**, and **perch.**

Get the updated scoop on where to fish from the local bait and tackle shops: **Norm's Bait & Tackle** in Great Barrington (tel. 413/528-6628) and **Nota Boat Livery** in Pittsfield (tel. 413/442-1724).

If you're looking for a guide who knows the area inside and out, contact Rick Moon at **Moon Sporting Goods** in Pittsfield (tel. 413/442-8281). He'll take you trout fishing in remote spots on the Housatonic and Deerfield Rivers that would take years to find. **Points North Outfitters** in Adams offers guides and lessons for **fly-fishing** (tel. 413/743-4030).

GOLF

Cranwell Resort's 360-acre golf course, built in the 1920s, is considered one of the premier courses in the Berkshires. The eighth tee, situated in front of the century-old mansion, has expansive views of the Berkshires. The Cranwell Resort is located on Lee Road, Lenox (tel. 413/637-0441). Cranwell's pro, David Strawn, recommends two other golf courses he enjoys—The **Taconic Golf Club** on Meacham Street in Williamstown (tel. 413/458-3997) and the **Wahconah Country Club** on Orchard Road in Dalton (tel. 413/684-1333).

HIKING & BACKPACKING

This is the Berkshires' forte. No one should walk away from the Berkshires without first walking up one of its mountains. All of these climbs leave you with vast views of the valley below and an invigorating feeling of accomplishment.

DAY HIKES

The Appalachian Trail to Mount Greylock

Allow 3–4 hours one way, 6–8 hours round trip. Moderate to strenuous. Access: From Pittsfield, take State Route 8 North to Cheshire. Turn left on West Mountain Road and right on Outlook Avenue. Look for the small triangular signs designating the AT. Map: Available from Greylock visitor center.

The stretch of the Appalachian Trail from Outlook Avenue in Cheshire to the summit of southern New England's highest peak, Mount Greylock, is undoubtedly a challenge. It is also one of the most remote and scenic approaches to this popular peak. The trail up is almost 7 miles long, which is why I usually go with a friend, take two cars, and leave one at the summit. If you want to do the 14-mile round-trip, give yourself at least seven hours, bring lots of water, and be in good shape.

Look for the small triangular AT signs on Outlook Avenue and park your car off to the right. The trail begins in a birch grove, following the white blazes of the AT through a meadow. In less than a quarter of a mile, you begin your ascent through a sheltered forest of maples and oaks. For approximately 2 miles, the trail winds upward through the deep forest, occasionally giving you glimpses of the valley below. You'll pass thickets of hemlocks and red spruces before approaching the Old Adams Road junction. Here, you can significantly shorten your hike by turning left for 1.2 miles to the Jones Nose parking lot, or continue on the AT past the Mark Noepel Shelter for another 3.1 miles to Greylock's Bascom

Lodge. For the next several miles, the trail is level as you stroll through the spruces atop Saddleball Mountain. At Rockwell Road, you merge with the Chelshire Harbor trail for your final ascent to the 100-foot-high War Memorial Tower resting on the peak of Greylock. The views from the summit on a clear day are stunning—the Green Mountains are to the north, the Adirondacks are off in the distance to the west, and the smaller Berkshire Mountains pop up nearby.

People with dry T-shirts and clean socks congregate atop Greylock in the summer months, having driven up Rockwell Road from the Visitor Center. Paved roads to mountain summits should be outlawed unless you're a weary hiker who needs to drive back to his second car at the bottom of the hill.

Monument Mountain

2.7 miles (round trip). 1.5–2 hours. Easy. Access: The parking lot is located on the left side of U.S. 7, 3.6 miles north of the State Route 23 junction in Great Barrington. Map: Available from the Trustees of Reservations headquarters, 572 Essex Street, Beverly (tel. 508/921-1944).

Rich Woller is not content with simply pointing out natural highlights of a hike. As owner of Berkshire Hiking Holidays, Rich has an insatiable passion for history, which adds flavor to any outdoor activity—thus, the reason why he insisted on escorting me up Monument Mountain, a hike rich with legendary anecdotes. We parked our car in the Trustees of Reservations parking lot and strolled for several minutes on a trail along U.S. 7. The sound of traffic quickly vanished when we veered right onto a carriage path trail up the mountain. This is where Oliver Wendell Holmes, Nathaniel Hawthorne, and

Herman Melville started their ascent up the mountain on August 5, 1850. Melville and Hawthorne had never met before and they brought a wagon loaded with picnic food and champagne to keep the conversation lively. There are many accounts of the story, but the one Rich told me is that it rained that day. After reaching the peak, the literary party took to shelter and champagne in a recess on the west side of the mountain. The Trustees of Reservations re-enact the climb every year, but I'm not sure who brings the Dom Perignon.

The hike up, less than 45 minutes, is one of the easiest hikes in the Berkshires—a gradual climb on a well-trodden path through mixed woods of hemlocks, oaks, beech, white pines, red maples, and birches. At a fork, we veered left up to a large boulder, which commemorates the donation of the park to the Trustees of Reservations in 1899. Here, the trail crawls over rocky ledges to the peak. Hawthorne said that Monument's summit resembled "a headless sphinx wrapped in a Persian shawl." Views of Mount Everett, the Catamount ski area, and the Catskills stood before us. Time for another Rich Woller history lesson. The summit is known as Squaw Peak because, as the legend goes, a young female Indian plunged to her death from the rocky pinnacle to appease the gods. Fortunately, Rich was not interested in re-enactment.

Race Brook Trail

Allow 5 hours. Strenuous. Access: From Great Barrington, take State Route 23 South to Egremont. From the junction of State Routes 23 and 41, take State Route 41 South for 5 miles. A small parking lot is located on the right hand side of the road. Map: USGS Bash-Bish Falls.

The Race Brook Trail is one of the most strenuous climbs in the Berkshires, but your efforts are rewarded when you reach the Appalachian Trail up top. You have the opportunity to climb two of Massachusetts' highest mountains and, for an encore, take a spectacular ridge walk where the entire southern Berkshire valley lies beneath your feet.

Start your climb on State Route 41 along Race Brook. You'll start climbing higher and higher above the brook until you cross Race Brook Falls. The trail continues upwards unrelentingly, finally reaching a level area where you veer to the left. The blue blazes that line the trail become much harder to spot at this point, but the path catches up to Race Brook, where you stay to the right. When you see a bridge made from two tree trunks, cross over the stream and continue on the trail to a sign that marks the Appalachian Trail. You are at the 2-mile mark. Turn right, and for the next 0.7 mile you'll be clambering up the steep rocky ledges that lead to the peak of Mount Everett. Exquisite views of New York, Connecticut, and Massachusetts open up as you reach the lookout tower. This is the perfect place to have lunch and re-energize before climbing down the rocks and attempting your second ascent.

Retrace your steps back to the Race Brook Trail and continue on the AT up to the summit of Mount Race. This ascent is much easier than the climb to Everett. From atop Mount Race, you have great views of the Housatonic Valley 1,500 feet below, the Catskills, and the Litchfield Hills. It would be a mistake to turn around here. Continue south on the AT toward Bear Rock Falls for an exhilarating walk on a bare ledge. Walk for as long as you like before turning back to the Race Brook Trail and heading downhill to State Route 41. The total distance is 8 or 9 miles depending on how long you walk on the ridge.

Herman, I'd Like to Introduce You to Nathaniel

The intense bond that Herman Melville and Nathaniel Hawthorne formed on the fateful walk up Monument Mountain would last a little more than a year. In November 1851, the Hawthornes moved from Lenox to West Newton. Melville and Hawthorne would meet only once more, in 1856, in Liverpool, England, where Hawthorne was working as consul for his friend, President Franklin Pierce. However, the friendship they developed in this short amount of time would become one of the most significant relationships in American literature.

A few days after the hike, Melville stopped by Hawthorne's red shanty at Lenox (which still stands on the grounds of Tanglewood) for more champagne, heated discussions, and a walk around Stockbridge Bowl. They became fast friends. Every time Melville came to the red shanty, someone in the Hawthorne family shouted, "Here comes Typee!" This pet name refers to Melville's first novel, an autobiographical story about the four months he spent with cannibals in the Marquesas Islands of the South Pacific. Melville would often tell the Hawthorne children hair-raising tales of his adventures there. Several months later, Melville moved into Arrowhead, a house in Pittsfield that looks out onto Mount Greylock. Melville came to Pittsfield to work on a farm so he could support himself while he wrote. The huge barn in the back often sheltered the two men, who reclined on the hay, deep in conversation. Inspired by his continuous talks with Hawthorne and the view of Greylock in winter, which reminded him of a whale, Melville completed the 600-plus pages of *Moby Dick* in less than a year. For his part, Hawthorne wrote and published another classic work, *The House of Seven Gables*. That's quite a productive year.

Pleasant Valley Wildlife Sanctuary

Allow 2 hours. Easy to moderate. Access: From Pittsfield, take U.S. 7 South, turning right onto West Dugway Road. If you reach the junction of U.S. 7 and State Route 7A, you've gone too far. The parking area for the sanctuary is located 1.5 miles down West Dugway Road. Map: Available at the visitor center.

The Pleasant Valley Wildlife Sanctuary in Lenox features 7 miles of trails that weave through 1,500 acres of Berkshire uplands. Part of the Mass Audubon Society, Pleasant Valley is known for its exemplary bird watching. The swamps here are also home to beavers, which is one of the reasons why Jude McCarthy took me to this wildlife sanctuary. Jude is the Director of Outdoor Sports at the Canyon Ranch Resort in Lenox. He has a wealth of environmental knowledge, ranging from horticulture to ornithology, but his favorite subject is the beaver.

"It takes the average beaver an hour to gnaw down a 4-inch sapling," Jude informed me on the Pike's Pond Trail. We saw several frogs and a garden snake, but no beaver. From Pike's Pond, we quickly switched to the Yokun Trail to the Beaver Trail to the Overbrook Trail. This last path climbs through forests of maples, oaks, beeches, and birches before reaching the peak of Lenox Mountain. Here, we had views of Richmond Pond and Bartlett's Apple Orchards in front of us, Mount Greylock, Mount

Everett, and the Catskills in the distance. A turkey vulture flew gracefully overhead. Part of the condor family, the bird has no feathers from his breast to his head and is guaranteed to scare you close-up. We took the much rockier Trail of the Ledges back down. Rounding Pike's Pond, we saw a furry head break the surface of the water. Jude smiled as he pointed towards the beaver. Both excited and exhausted, I thought I saw Jude's front teeth grow much larger.

If you don't feel like climbing a mountain, you should still make an effort to walk around Pleasant Valley's beaver ponds.

Roaring Brook/Stony Ledge Loop

Allow 3 hours. Moderate to strenuous. Access: From Williamstown, follow U.S. 7 South past the State Route 43 junction. Look for a small wooden sign at the left-hand side of U.S. 7 indicating the Roaring Brook Trail. This is Roaring Brook Road. Turn left, and you'll soon approach a small parking lot on the left-hand side of the road. Map: Available at the Greylock visitor center.

The Stony Ledge and Roaring Brook Trails both lead to Stony Ledge, a group of rocky cliffs that offer magnificent views of Mount Greylock's summit. Perhaps even more stunning is the V-shaped wedge of trees that forms a valley between the peaks, known as The Hopper. From the parking lot on Roaring Brook Road, follow the path along the right side of the brook. Cross the stream three times, until you see the two trails split. Both trails are strenuous uphill climbs, but the Roaring Brook Trail is somewhat less precipitous than Stony Ledge, a former ski trail. Climbing more than a 1,000 feet through forests of hemlocks, spruces, yellow birches, and beeches, the Roaring Brook Trail passes the Deer Hill and Circular Trails, finally reaching Sperry Road. Turn left on the gravel road through the campground to the end of Sperry Road at Stony Ledge. From the rocks you can see the War Memorial atop Mount Greylock, Mount Prospect, Mount Williams, and The Hopper's velvety carpet of trees lying between them. To get back to your car, go through the Stony Ledge Group Campsite to the Stony Ledge Ski Trail. The upper part of this trail is steep, gradually leveling off, then becoming steep again before it merges with the Roaring Brook Trail. Turn right at the bottom and retrace your steps back to the car.

OVERNIGHTS & LONG-DISTANCE HIKES

Several of the climbs in the "Hikes & Backpacking" section of this chapter describe portions of the Appalachian Trail. The AT meanders 87 miles from the southwest corner of the state over Mount Everett, through the valley of the Berkshires, to the top of Mount Greylock, and eventually making its way to Vermont's Green Mountains. Combine several day hikes along the trail and you have an overnight trip that can last as long as 10 days. Many backpackers simply drive to the top of Greylock and start walking north or south. To avoid backtracking, leave a second car at your final destination and drive back to Greylock or vice versa. The Berkshires chapter of the AMC (tel. 413/443-0011), located at Mount Greylock visitor's center, will help you plan a route depending on how many days you want to spend in the woods. The Greylock portion of the AT combines mountain climbs in heavily wooded forests with level walks through expansive farmland.

In the southern part of the state near Connecticut, the ridge walk south of Mount Race is one of the most exhilarating stretches of the trail (see above). There are far fewer people on

Leave It to Beaver

Perhaps no other animal symbolizes the re-emergence of wildlife in New England better than the beaver. Prior to the white man's arrival, beaver ponds numbered as many as 300 to the mile and populations swelled to over 100 million in North America. But with colonization came the fur trade. The settlers persuaded the Indians to use beaver pelts as wampum in exchange for basic European goods, firearms, and alcohol. This worked well with the colonists, who William Wood noted were ineffective hunters anyway. Wood, English traveler and author of *New England's Prospect* (published in 1633) noted that "these beasts [beavers] are too cunning for the English, who seldom or never catch any of them; therefore we leave them to those skillful hunters [Indians] whose time was not so precious." Precious or not, the fact is that the Indians hunted far more efficiently than the English. Once the skins were in the hands of the settlers, they shipped the prized commodity back to Europe in exchange for a huge profit.

The decimation of beavers lasted for several hundred years, until the New England species had vanished. By the time Henry David Thoreau wrote in his journal in 1855, the long list of animals absent from the New England forest included "bear, moose, deer, porcupines, and beaver." Fortunately, with the advent of second-growth forest, the furry critter has returned with his friends. According to wildlife experts, there are now more than 60,000 beavers in New England, and the number is increasing rapidly. The trappers are even returning, but with the purchasing of fur products at an all-time low, beavers need not worry.

On the contrary, beavers are exercising their freedom as the newest members of America's oldest colonies. They are flooding scores of public roads, backing pond water into private wells, and may even be the cause of illness. In December 1985, an outbreak of giardiasis affected 686 people in Pittsfield, Massachusetts, the Berkshire's largest town. Giardiasis is an intestinal parasite that produces severe dysentery. An old reservoir had recently been tapped while work proceeded on a new filtration system for the city's water supply. The tap was immediately shut off and nine beavers were trapped in the reservoir by the state Department of Health. Lo and behold, one beaver tested positive for giardia. So the next time your boss asks you why you were out yesterday, just tell them that you had beaver fever.

this section. One note of caution: Full-fledged shelters are few and far between, situated at 18 to 22 mile intervals. However, you can camp at primitive low-impact shelters, stationed every 7 to 8 miles.

OUTFITTERS

The three- to six-day packages offered by **Berkshire Hiking Holidays,** P.O. Box 2231, Lenox, MA 01240 (tel. 800/877-9656), are more than mere walks up mountains. They are hikes and canoe rides with an historical or cultural edge that befits the owner, Rich Woller. An anecdotal hike up a mountain with a naturalist might be followed with a trip to the **Clark Art Institute** to view the vast selection of Renoirs, Homers, and Cezannes, or a canoe ride down a portion of the Housatonic.

It all depends on what the group wants. Rich is a local who knows the area and its many attractions intimately, and saves the best for his small groups.

New England Hiking Holidays, P.O. Box 1648, North Conway, NH 03860 (tel. 800/869-0949), offers three-day weekends to the Berkshires in May, July, and October.

Hiking Holidays, P.O. Box 750, Bristol, VT 05443 (tel. 802/453-4816), has five-day trips to the Berkshires during spring, summer, and fall.

Backroads, 1516 Fifth Street, Berkeley, CA 94710-1740 (tel. 800/ GO-ACTIVE), has just started a walking trip to the Berkshires.

Wild Earth Adventures, P.O. Box 655, Pomona, NY 10970 (tel. 914/ 354-3717), offers one-day trips to Mount Everett and Bash-Bish Falls.

HORSEBACK RIDING

Undermountain Farm, 252 Undermountain Road, Lenox, MA 01240 (tel. 413/637-3365), located in a genteel setting close to Lenox, offers all levels of instruction and guided trail rides catered to your party. Trails are open year-round.

Eastover Resort, 430 East Street, Lenox, MA 01240 (tel. 413/637-0613), has a large network of trails open to the public. You don't have to stay overnight there to ride.

In the northern Berkshires, **Twin Ponds Farm** in Stephentown, New York, offers trail rides and lessons. They are located three miles from the Mass state line, near Hancock (tel. 518/733-6793).

MOUNTAIN BIKING

The same State Forest trails that cross-country skiers enjoy in the winter are exciting summer rides. Check out October and Beartown State Forests under the "Cross-Country Skiing" section for two of the better locales. **Pittsfield State**

Forest also has good trails with maps. However, my favorite forest ride is the **Savoy Mountain** ride, described below.

RIDES

Savoy Mountain State Forest

Allow 2–3 hours. Moderate to strenuous; hilly. Access: Take State Route 2 East from North Adams to Florida, Massachusetts. Turn right on Central Shaft Road, continuing past the forest headquarters to the second parking lot, where the campground is located. Pick up a trail map and then continue driving on Florida Road, turning left on Burnett Road and right on New State Road. There's a small parking lot on the right-hand side of the road near Burnett Pond. Map: Available at the park ranger station.

Starting at an elevation over 2,000 feet, Savoy Mountain State Park puts the mountain back into Massachusetts mountain biking. Follow the Burnett Pond Trail across New State Road for a sweeping rollercoaster ride through the deep woods. The challenging trail rolls up and down the hillside, connecting with Kammick Road and leading to the fire tower atop Border Mountain. This is a good place to rejuvenate and take in the vast countryside before cruising back down to Burnett Pond.

John Drummond Kennedy Park

Allow 1–2 hours. Easy to moderate; short hills. Access: The park is west of Main Street or State Route 7A in Lenox. Map: Available at Main Street Sports & Leisure.

Kennedy Park in downtown Lenox is another example of a place crowded with cross-country skiers in the winter and mountain bikers in the summer. I had the good fortune to ride with George Roberson, cross-country skiing coach and owner of Main Street Sports & Lei-sure, who ventures to these 12 miles of trails year-round. Kennedy Park was once a grand 500-room resort that burned down in the 1930s. Local leg-end has it that the owner wanted the insurance money since he was making very little income in post-Depression times.

We cruised from George's store up Main Street, veering left into Kennedy Park. We took the Main Trail, a double-track, all the way past Dead Horse Pond to a single-track trail called Balance Rock. This sloping path through maples and birches was a warm-up for the invigorating single-track Summit Trail, which rolled high over the hillside. Eventually, we made it down to a picnic area where views of Catamount, Monument, and Rattlesnake Mountains loom on the horizon.

RENTALS

For Savoy Mountain, you can rent hy-brids at the **Mountain Goat,** 130 Water Street, Williamstown (tel. 413/ 458-8445). Bikes for the Kennedy Park ride can be rented at **Main Street Sports & Leisure,** 102 Main Street, Lenox (tel. 413/637-4407).

ROAD BIKING

This is one sport where the Berkshires' neighbor to the north excels. The Berk-shires area is such a condensed region of the state that the roads tend to be con-gested, especially during the height of the summer. As a rule of thumb, the closer you get to Vermont, the better the biking.

RIDES

The Williamstown Loop

Allow 3 hours. Moderate; rolling. Access: From Pittsfield, take U.S. 7 North to Brodie

Mountain Road, where you turn left. The Jiminy Peak Mountain parking lot will be on the left-hand side of the road before the junction of State Route 43.

The northeast corner of Massachusetts looks very much like Vermont. Rolling hills and large tracts of farmland blanket the valleys between moun-tain ranges. This 28-mile loop around Williamstown takes you through the heart of the countryside, where moun-tains shade you from the hot sun.

Turn right out of the Jiminy Peak parking lot for a long uphill climb be-fore sweeping downhill to U.S. 7. Turn left onto U.S. 7's broad shoulder head-ing north. You will soon pass Brodie Mountain's ski trails on the left and Mount Greylock State Reservation on the right. The War Memorial atop Greylock's peak can be seen in the distance. Turn right on State Route 43 for a relatively flat ride through farmland, which gives way to bookstores and cafes as you approach Main Street in Williamstown. A left turn on Main Street (or State Route 2 West) will bring you past the baroque and ivy-covered buildings that are home to Williams College. Veer left on Spring Street for a quick detour through Williamstown's main thoroughfare—a good place to find lunch—then return to State Route 2 West, pedaling around the rotaryto U.S. 7 South. When State Route 2 and U.S. 7 split at the Taconic Inn, continue on U.S. 7 for a downhill run that will bring you back to State Route 43. Turn right on State Route 43 for my favorite stretch of the trip. The Taconic Mountain range in New York looms to the right while the Berkshires appear to the left. Roll up and down the valley hills, passing the occasional dairy farm. Eventually, you'll see the large Brodie sign where you turn left on Brodie Mountain Road to return to the Jiminy Peak parking lot.

Lenox-Stockbridge Loop

Allow 2–5 hours depending on how many sites you want to visit. Moderate; hilly. Access: From U.S. 7, take State Route 7A to Main Street, Lenox. Main Street Sports & Leisure is located at 102 Main Street.

This 17-mile ride, designed by George Roberson of Main Street Sports & Leisure, hits several of the major sightseeing destinations without making you fight your way through the summer traffic. From George's shop in Lenox, bear right on Main Street, left on Cliffwood Street, and veer left at the fork onto Undermountain Road. Climb up this street past several horse stables for sweeping views of the pastoral panorama. Then cruise downhill all the way to the gate of Tanglewood, where the Boston Symphony Orchestra has the good fortune to play in July and August. Turn right on State Route 183. On the left, you'll soon pass Stockbridge Bowl, the largest lake in the area. Bear left at the boat launch to rent sculls on the lake (see "Sculling").

Continue on State Route 183 and you'll see a large sign for the Norman Rockwell Museum on the left. This is the new home for the largest collection of Rockwell originals. My favorite work is "Triple Self-Portrait," in which an older Norman Rockwell looks in the mirror only to paint a much younger-looking version of himself. Less than a half-mile later, you can turn right on Mohawk Lake Road to visit Chesterwood. This is the former home of Daniel Chester French, the sculptor who created the Lincoln Memorial and the Minuteman statue in Concord. Venture back on State Route 183 and turn left on Glendale Middle Road. Veer left over the next two bridges and merge right onto State Route 102 past the Stockbridge Town Hall. You'll soon be in the center of Stockbridge, a charming village for antique-shop strolling. For lunch, try the Daily Bread for fresh baked goods. Turn left onto Pine Street across from the Red Lion Inn, and bear left at the fork up Prospect Hill Road. You'll climb past some of the more exclusive homes in the area before crossing over the Mass Pike and reaching the far shores of Stockbridge Bowl. Another uphill pedal will bring you to Hawthorne Street, where you turn right. At the end of Hawthorne, you need to take a left onto Stockbridge Road, a grueling uphill climb that will bring you back to Main Street, Lenox. Feel free to get off your bike and walk up the hill. I won't tell anybody (snicker, snicker).

RENTALS, REPAIRS

You can rent bikes for the Williamstown loop at **The Spoke,** 618 Main Street, Williamstown (tel. 413/458-3456), or the **Mountain Goat,** 130 Water Street, Williamstown (tel. 413/458-8445). Bikes for the Lenox/Stockbridge ride can be rented at **Main Street Sports & Leisure,** 102 Main Street, Lenox (tel. 413/637-4407).

OUTFITTERS

Vermont Bicycle Touring, P.O. Box 711, Bristol, VT 05445 (tel. 800/245-3868), offers five-day tours of the Berkshires during the spring, summer, and fall.

ROCK CLIMBING

To find the rock climbing scene in the Berkshires, head down East Street in Great Barrington. The dirt road will bring you to a glacial deposit where you can scramble over large boulders or climb moderate-sized walls of rock. The premier source for equipment and information is **Appalachian Mountain Gear,** 777 South Main Street, Great Barrington, MA 01230 (tel. 413/528-8811).

If you're interested in technical rock climbing, ice climbing, or general mountaineering, Stephen Lewanick, owner of **Ascents of Adventure,** is one of the most respected guides in New England. He recently returned from Mount Kilimanjaro, having climbed Africa's highest peak with a group of blind hikers. The age range of his clientele is 6–74. Contact Stephen at P.O. Box 6568, Albany, NY 12206 (tel. 518/475-7519).

SAILING & POWERBOATING

YMCA Marina (tel. 413/499-0694), on the shores of Pontoosuc Lake, rents Sunfish for $15 per hour. Also on Pontoosuc is **U-Drive Boat Rentals,** 1651 North Street, Pittsfield, MA, 01201 (tel. 413/447-7512); it rents two 100-horsepower boats for water skiing, fishing, or simply cruising. They also rent Jet Skis.

SCULLING

Contact **Lewis Cuyler** (tel. 413/496-9160) a day in advance and he will bring a scull to Stockbridge Bowl, Goose Pond in Lee, or any other convenient location. Rentals cost $15 an hour, $60 for three lessons.

SNOWMOBILING

Cruising up Rockwell Road to Mount Greylock's summit in the winter is a great thrill. October Mountain, Beartown, and Pittsfield State Forests also have decent trails. For more information, contact **Region 5 Headquarters,** P.O. Box 1433, Pittsfield, MA 01202 (tel. 413/442-8928).

SNOWSHOEING

Several trails in Mount Washington State Park and Mount Greylock State Reservation are good for snowshoeing.

Acadian Sporting Goods Store, on U.S. 7, in Lenox, rents snowshoes and provides information (tel. 413/637-3010).

SWIMMING

Head south on State Route 23 towards Egremont on a sweltering summer day and you'll spot a bridge where cars are parked on the side of the road. The locals come here to cool off in the refreshing waters of Green River. Another popular swimming hole is pristine Upper Goose Pond. You'll earn this dip by hiking 1.7 miles south on the AT. The trailhead is located on U.S. 20, due west of Lee. Finerty Pond in Becket, Stockbridge Bowl, Laurel Lake in Lee, and Pontoosuc Lake in Pittsfield are the other local favorites.

WALKS & RAMBLES

Bartholemew's Cobble

Allow 2 hours. Easy. Access: From Great Barrington, take U.S. 7 South through Sheffield to State Route 7A. Turn right on Rannapo Road and left onto Weatogue Road to reach the parking lot. There will be clearly marked signs. Map: Available at site.

A mysterious mist shrouded Bartholemew's Cobble the day my friend Dan and I ventured here, enhancing the eerie feeling already created by a forest of umbrageous hemlocks and cavernous rock. Dan requested a leisurely stroll, so we chose this Trustees of Reservations locale situated near the Connecticut border. We paid the $3 and started walking on the Ledges Trail. The Housatonic River snaked through dairy farms on the left, while eroding limestone and quartzite rocks formed the cobble to our right. We took a slight detour at Corbin's Neck to get a closer view of the river and the cows resting on the banks. Continuing along the waterway on the Bailey Trail, Dan found a small frog to hold and harass. However, he soon put the terrified amphibian down, concentrating his energies on the Tulip Tree Trail. This trail leads uphill through a forest of tall hemlocks before reaching a clearing. We followed the sign to the summit for a short walk through an open field covered with wildflowers and playful monarch butterflies. There was a small bench to sit on while we watched the bright monarchs float above our heads and the hazy views of Mount Everett and Mount Race rising in the background.

Skipping down the field, we went straight on the Cobble Trail, taking a slight detour on the Borman Trail to visit the Ashley House. Built by Colonel John Ashley in 1735, this is the oldest dwelling in Berkshire County. Colonel Ashley was a pioneer, lawyer, judge, and patriot who furnished iron and other supplies for the Revolutionary War effort. We retraced our steps on the Borman Trail, turning left at the Cobble Trail to return to our car.

Canoe Meadows Wildlife Sanctuary

2.5 miles round-trip. Allow 2 hours. Easy; rolling meadows and forest trails. Access: From Lenox, head north on U.S. 7 and turn right on Holmes Road. You'll see a sign for the sanctuary approximately three miles down the road. Map: Available at the visitor center.

Belonging to the Mass Audubon Society, Canoe Meadows was once home to the Native American Housatonic tribe. Thus, the reason your first trail is named Sacred Way. Turn right past the entrance and loop around a meadow that overlooks a beaver pond and the Housatonic River. When you return to the road, turn right through a thicket of pines. Grouses, finches, phoebes, orioles, and cedar waxwings are often found in the wetlands

to your left. A right turn onto Wolf Pine Trail will lead you to a massive white pine tree that dates back to the early 1800s. A hemlock forest soon follows. To return to the entrance, simply turn left onto the road.

Bullock Woods

2.5 miles round-trip. Allow 2 hours. An easy stroll through ancient woodlands to the shores of Stockbridge Bowl. Access: From Lenox, head south on State Route 183 past Tanglewood. Turn left on Hawthorne Road for 0.75 miles, where you reach a junction with Prospect Hill Road. You can park your car at the junction. The trailhead starts at the chained opening across from the junction. Map: USGS Lenox.

The Bullock Woods walk is a favorite among Tanglewood concertgoers. This 50-acre preserve is one of the oldest growths of forest in Berkshire county. Cross a meadow and continue on an old logging road into a thicket of large oaks mixed with conifers—some approaching 18 feet in diameter. The road veers right near a private beach club to the shores of Stockbridge Bowl, a lake known for its fine fishing and swimming. Turn right across another meadow and then left back to the waters of the pond. Monument Mountain can be seen on the far shores. You can retrace your steps to return to the trailhead or turn right from Stockbridge Bowl through Gould Meadows and right again anywhere before Hawthorne Road.

WHITEWATER KAYAKING & RAFTING

If you spend any amount of time in Williamstown or North Adams during the summertime, you'll notice the influx of cars crossing the New York border with kayaks tied to their roofs. They're all headed on State Route 2 East, along the Mohawk Trail, to the surging Deerfield River in Charlemont. Dam releases by the New England Power Company cause rapids to tumble down two stretches of the river—the exhilarating Class IV rapids in the Dryway and the Class II–III rapids farther south in the deep pools of Zoar Gap.

OUTFITTERS

To kayak or raft, that is the question? If you want to rent a kayak, contact **Wildwater Outfitters,** 451 Russell Street, State Route 9, Hadley, MA 01035 (tel. 413/253-5500). They charge $25 for the day to experienced whitewater kayakers. **Zoar Outdoor** offers daily rafting trips on the Deerfield. Cost is $80 on the Dryway (minimum age 14), $61 on the Zoar Gap weekdays, $65 weekends (minimum age seven years). Owner Bruce Lessels, a former World Whitewater Champion and author of the *Whitewater Handbook*, also offers whitewater kayaking instruction. Contact Zoar Outdoor, Mohawk Trail, Charlemont, MA 01339 (tel. 800/532-7483).

Campgrounds & Other Accommodations

CAMPGROUNDS

The Berkshires' numerous State Forests provide an abundance of camping opportunities:

Sperry Campground

From Pittsfield, head 5 miles north on U.S. 7, then follow signs. 47 sites, no hookups, pit toilets, handicapped rest room facilities, tables, and grills. Tel. 413/499-4262.

Located in the Mount Greylock State Reservation, this is perhaps the best camping facility in the region; 35 of the sites sit on Sperry Road in a dense forest near scenic Stony Ledge (see "Hiking & Backpacking").

October Mountain State Forest

From U.S. 20 in Lenox, head east to the forest entrance. 50 sites, no hookups, handicapped rest room facilities, sewage disposal, public phone, tables, grills, and wood. Tel. 413/243-1778.

Convenient for fishing, mountain biking, snowmobiling, and cross-country skiing.

Savoy Mountain

From North Adams, head 5 miles east on State Route 2, turning right onto Central Shaft Road. 45 sites, no hookups, handicapped rest room facilities, public phones, tables, and grills. Tel. 413/663-8469.

The 45 campsites are situated near South Pond.

Beartown State Forest

From Great Barrington, head east on State Route 23 to Blue Hill Road. The headquarters are located 0.5 mile north. Tel. 413/528-0904. 12 sites, no hookups, public phones, tables, and grills.

Strangely enough, Beartown State Forest, which is larger than Savoy Mountain, has only 12 campsites. However, RVs have trouble getting up the winding road, so most sites are rented by backpackers. Get there early if you expect to grab a spot. The sites overlook Benedict Pond (see "Canoeing").

INNS & RESORTS

Canyon Ranch

165 Kemble Street, Lenox, MA 01240. (tel. 800/742-9000). 3-night weekday packages start at $760 per person, including all meals, facilities, and outdoor recreation.

Canyon Ranch is more than a spa with 40 daily fitness classes and wholesome food. Set on 120 acres, the resort has an excellent Outdoor Sports Department, whose sole function is to take the clientele off the grounds on the best hikes, bike rides, canoe jaunts, and cross-country skiing trails the Berkshires have to offer. Director Jude McCarthy has implemented a program that caters to all levels of experience and tastes, from an early morning Tai Chi walk to a strenuous mountain-bike ride up fire roads to Lenox Mountain.

Cranwell Resort

U.S. 20, Lenox, MA 01240. Tel. 800/272-6935. Rooms start at $99 in the winter and spring, $199 summer and fall.

Cranwell's magnificent brick Tudor mansion is hard to miss from the road. Over a hundred years old, the property sits on a hill with a commanding view of the surrounding Berkshires. The 18-hole PGA championship golf course is one of the best in the region. Other facilities include groomed cross-country ski trails, hiking trails, an indoor driving range, and two Har-tru tennis courts.

The Williamsville Inn

State Route 41, West Stockbridge, MA 01266. Tel. 413/274-6118. Rooms range $120–$185.

Ask owner Gail Ryan about the secret cross-country and hiking trail that weaves along a creek near her inn. The trail starts across the street behind several houses, before leaving civilization for good. Work up an appetite for your return for one of the best dinners in the Berkshires.

Race Brook Lodge

684 Undermountain Road, Sheffield, MA 01230. Tel. 413/229-2916. Rooms range from $65–$125.

This former barn's backyard is Race Brook and Mount Race (see "Hiking & Backpacking"). If you can somehow manage to tear yourself away from the trails on summer Sundays, you're in for a musical treat: the lodge sponsors a series of jazz concerts.

Swift River Inn

151 South Street, Cummington, MA 01026. Tel. 413/634-5751. Rooms range from $89–$199, depending on season and suite.

Not only does the Swift River Inn have some of the finest cross-country trails in Massachusetts, but the accommodations and adjoining fire-lit restaurant will keep you cozy in the evenings. Come summer, the property is swarming with mountain bikers, fly-fishermen, and hikers.

6

Greater Boston, Cape Ann & the South Shore

REMARKABLY, BOSTON NEVER BECAME A SPRAWLING METRO-
polis like its neighbors to the south. Today, you can drive
20 minutes from the city center and be in Concord or at
Walden Pond. A 30-minute drive will take you to Carlisle
and the rural communities northwest of Boston. An hour north, and you'll
be on the soft sands of Cape Ann or Plum Island. An hour from the center
of Manhattan still leaves you in the suburbs, or perhaps battling traffic in
the Holland Tunnel. That's not to say Boston doesn't have its share of traffic problems. Traveling south on I-93 from the city on "The Artery" is a
nightmare, especially during rush hour. Now that construction is going on
to expand the number of lanes (the operation's called the "Big Dig"), you
can expect delays southbound until the year 2004. Regardless, Boston is
the hub of New England and the usual starting point for a vacation in the
region.

Head outdoors here and you'll almost always be met with the origins
of American history. Bike around Cape Ann through Gloucester, the
oldest fishing community in the nation, and Rocky Neck, the oldest still
active art colony in the country. Canoe on the Concord River under Old
North Bridge to see the spot where the first battle of the Revolutionary
War took place. Walk on World's End, one of the last remaining drumlins in

Massachusetts Bay. And then there's the sea that brought the Pilgrims here. The North and South Shores offer a variety of beaching opportunities, from mile-long stretches of sand to intimate coves. There are also several outfitters that arrange sea-kayaking trips, one of which visits the humpback whales at Stellwagen Bank. Run into one of these massive mammals in a small plastic boat and you might just get a sense of how it felt to be on the *Mayflower* for its perilous nine-week journey across the Atlantic.

Look carefully at this region and you'll realize that the history of colonial America runs concurrently with the history of American sports. The first sailors were the Pilgrims who, on December 8, 1620, sailed into Plymouth Bay in a snowstorm. They soon became the first European walkers on the new land when on December 11, William Bradford reported that a small party of Pilgrims "marched into the land and found diverse cornfields and little running brooks, a place fit for the situation." Unfortunately for them, these hardcore adventurers were also the nation's first campers. Living in lean-tos they dug in the ground, less than half the Pilgrims survived their first winter.

In time, the Pilgrims prospered and communities spread north to Boston, Salem, and the fishing towns of Gloucester and Marblehead. By the mid-1630s, immigrants, chiefly Puritans, were coming to the coast of Massachusetts at a rate of 2,000 a year. They entered a land devoid of trees. As William Cronon noted in his book *Changes in the Land*, "Boston was nearly barren and colonists were forced to seek wood from nearby islands." It became the perfect place for urban development. By 1700, the population of Massachusetts Bay had swelled to over 100,000.

The Lay of the Land

Drumlins and boulder trains predominate in the 30 to 50-mile wide coastal plains of eastern Massachusetts. Drumlins are smooth, gentle hills no more than 200 feet high, and which are essentially piles of glacial till—an infertile mixture of clay, gravel, and sand. They have no core of bedrock. At one time, more than fifty of these oval-shaped mounds were located in or around low-lying Massachusetts Bay. The best known example of a drumlin is Bunker Hill, the site of the Revolutionary War battle. Over the years, however, the number of drumlins has diminished due to the continuous battering of waves and ongoing urban development. Waters from the Atlantic have washed away many of the islands in the Boston Basin, including 12-acre Nixes Island, which was granted to John Galop in 1636. All that remains of this drumlin is a small shoal. Real estate development has camouflaged other hills, making it hard to recognize the shape under sprawling highways and houses. One of the finest examples of a drumlin today is World's End, just north of Hingham (see "Walks & Rambles").

Similar to Narragansett Basin in Rhode Island, the low relief of Boston Basin is known for its soft clay and coal deposits. Bedrock is much more evident in the Cape Ann area. The retreating ice cap split the bedrock into large boulders which are now strewn along the rugged shores. This is best seen on the coast of Halibut Point State Park (see "Walks & Rambles"). Inland, eastern Massachusetts has many state forests and reservations where oaks, hickories, and maples thrive.

Be prepared for all types of weather. One summer day in Boston can be hot and humid with highs in the 80s and 90s, and the next day can be perfect—

mid-70s with a cool breeze. The average high in July is 74°, and 30° in January. June and September are two of the nicest times to visit the region. Temperatures range in the upper 60s.

Bird watching in the Greater Boston area is on par with the rest of the Atlantic coast. Piping plovers are seen on Plum Island, herons and warblers are commonly observed searching for food at Great Meadows National Wildlife Refuge in Concord, and Eastern kingbirds and snowy egrets can be found at the Ipswich River Sanctuary. Snowshoe hares, foxes, raccoons, and deer are several of the wildlife species observed in the state forests.

Orientation

Heading north from Boston are **I-95** and **U.S. 1,** with **State Route 128** veering off I-95 east toward Cape Ann. State Route 128 and I-95 also form a beltway around the suburbs of Boston.

To head toward the South Shore, take **State Route 3** from Boston, which eventually reaches Cape Cod.

Cruising around a rotary without cutting off too many cars is Boston's version of a scenic drive. Outside the city, **State Route 114** to Marblehead, **Plum Island Road,** and **State Route 127** around Cape Ann are picturesque drives. In October, the bogs that line **State Route 58** in Plympton are red with cranberries.

Fishermen with wizened faces sew their nets in the early hours of the morning on a harsh, rocky coastline. Several hundred yards away, broad, sandy beaches gently fade into the ocean. Welcome to Massachusetts' lesser known Cape—**Cape Ann.** Forty miles north of Boston, Cape Ann beckons sun worshipers to its long stretches of sand, and hikers and bikers are lured to its

state parks and ocean-lined roads. A fleet of fishermen still leave **Gloucester's** harbor every morning, continuing the tradition of America's oldest fishing port. **Rockport** is a small village known for the shops, galleries, and restaurants that line Bearskin Neck. **Halibut Point State Park** is a naturalist's highlight (detailed below). For additional information, contact the **Cape Ann Chamber of Commerce,** 33 Commercial Street, Gloucester, MA 01930 (tel. 508/283-1601).

Parks & Other Hot Spots

Obviously the main attraction of this region, the **Atlantic Ocean,** makes many appearances in this chapter; its many beaches are discussed in the "Swimming" section, below.

Eastern Mass has a slew of state forests with extensive networks of hiking and biking trails. They also offer the best camping in the region. The list of state forests includes 14,651-acre **Myles Standish State Forest,** home to the state's largest public campground (tel. 508/866-2526); 3,014-acre **Harold Parker State Forest** (tel. 508/686-3391); 2,400-acre **Willowdale State Forest** (tel. 508/887-5931); and 1,112-acre **Georgetown Rowley State Forest** (tel. 508/887-5931).

Maudslay State Park

Take I-95 to State Route 113 East and turn left onto Noble Street. At the stop sign turn left onto Ferry Road and follow signs. Tel. 508/465-7223.

Located on the banks of the Merrimack River, this small, 476-acre park has a good network of walking and mountain biking trails.

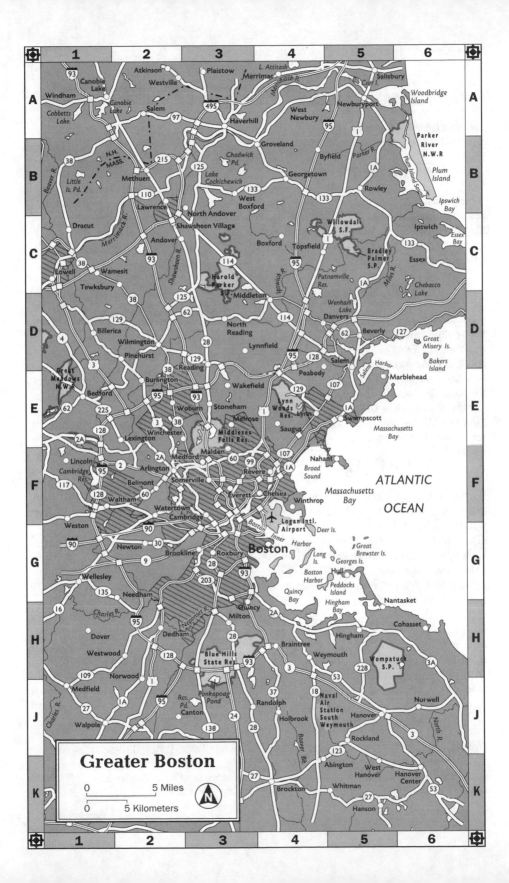

Greater Boston

0   5 Miles

0   5 Kilometers

Parker River National Wildlife Refuge

Located on Plum Island, 4 miles from U.S. 1, near Newburyport. Tel. 508/465-5753.

The premier bird-watching locale in the region, Parker River and Plum Island also feature 6 miles of beaches, walking and biking trails, and surfcasting sites for blues and stripers.

Essex Marsh and Hog Island

From Exit 14 on State Route 128, take State Route 133 West in the direction of the town of Essex. About 3 miles along, you'll see Woodman's Restaurant on your left; boat access to Essex River is across the road. Contact Trustees of Reservations, Northeast Regional Office, P.O. Box 563, Ipswich, MA 01938 (tel. 508/356-4351), for more information.

Salt marshes are among the most productive natural environments in the world—the salt-meadow grass and cordgrass of a marsh hide an amazing variety of creatures, from crabs and mussels to a wide array of birdlife. This marsh, less than an hour from Boston in the splintered shoreline between Cape Ann and Plum Island, offers protected paddling through hundreds of creeks and streams, exceptional birding, and trails on Hog Island. Come as the tide is coming in, because much of the marsh is left high and dry at low tide.

Halibut Point State Park

From downtown Rockport, take State Route 127 North past Pigeon Cove to a small green sign that says State Park. This is Gott Avenue. Turn right and you'll see the much larger Halibut Point State Park sign and parking lot. Tel. 508/546-2997.

Walk around one of the last remaining quarries on the coast and then rock-hop on the huge boulders that slide down to the ocean.

Ipswich River Sanctuary

Located 20 miles north of Boston in Topsfield. From U.S. 1, head east on State Route 97; turn left on Perkins Row and head 1 mile to the entrance. Tel. 508/887-9264.

This 2,217-acre sanctuary is maintained by the Mass Audubon Society. Perhaps the best way to see the wide variety of birds is from a canoe (see "Canoeing").

Great Meadows National Wildlife Refuge

From the center of Concord, follow State Route 62 East for 1.8 miles to Monsen Road. Turn left and look for the clearly marked signs to the refuge. Tel. 508/443-4661.

Bordering the Concord and Sudbury Rivers, this 2,883-acre refuge of river bottomland and marshes is an oasis for migrating birds. More than 200 species have been recorded here recently, including spotted and least sandpipers, black-crowned night herons, great blue herons, many species of ducks, and Canada geese. There are canoeing and fishing along the rivers as well.

Walden Pond State Reservation

Located on State Route 126, off State Route 2 in Concord.

Thoreau's cabin is gone and the woods are no longer secluded, but one can still find solitude on the trails that weave through the forest, which you can take on foot or on Nordic skis in winter. Just don't venture here on a hot summer day when swimmers lounge in the pond.

Blue Hills State Reservation

From the junction of I-93 and State Route 28 (Exit 5), drive 1.4 miles north on State Route 28 and turn right onto Chickatawbut Road. There's a small gravel lot on your right. Tel. 617/727-5114.

Granite is the number one component of this 6,000-acre reservation. The rugged trails up and down hills are popular with mountain bikers and walkers—and with cross-country skiers in winter.

What to Do & Where to Do It

BIRD WATCHING

You don't have to travel far from Boston to find excellent birding. **Great Meadows National Wildlife Refuge** is only twenty minutes away in Concord. Located on the shores of the Concord River, this 3,000-acre freshwater wetland is home to a large number of migratory birds. **Glossy ibises, snowy egrets, great blue herons,** and **yellow warblers** are some of the more than 200 species that have been recorded here in the past 10 years (see "Walks & Rambles," below). **Halibut Point State Park** on Cape Ann is another top bird watching location.

Arguably the finest viewing in the region can be had at the **Parker River National Wildlife Refuge** on Plum Island. Of the 300 bird species found at Parker River National Wildlife Refuge, the **piping plover** earns the most respect. Most areas of the refuge, including the beach, are closed during the prime suntanning months of June, July, and August so that these short, stocky endangered birds can nest undisturbed. Although the beach is off limits at these times, the marsh is still an excellent area to spot migrating shore birds like **black-bellied plovers, short-billed dowitchers, sandpipers,** and **godwits.** The boardwalk on the Hellcat Swamp Trail circles around the murky grasses to an observation tower and blind. Park at Parking Lot 4 to start the trail. Plum Island is located on the North Shore, 4 miles from U.S. 1, near Newburyport.

BOARDSAILING

Strong winds are commonly found off the shores of **Plum** and **Nahant islands.** On the South Shore, boardsailers head to **Duxbury Bay.** The bay is good for shortboarding since it's protected by Duxbury Beach.

CANOEING

Four rivers in the Greater Boston area attract canoeists. On the South Shore, the **North River** meanders more than 20 miles from the sparsely populated headwaters of Hanson and Hanover to the ocean just south of Scituate. It's not uncommon to find herons, warblers, terns, and red-winged blackbirds flying over the waters. Most people paddle west of the Union Street Bridge, avoiding the deadly riptide where the North and South Rivers meet.

In Boston and the northern suburbs, canoeing is popular on the 80-mile long **Charles River** (see "Sculling" section, below). North of Boston, the **Concord**

River has changed little since Thoreau ventured here and wrote *A Week on the Concord and Merrimack Rivers.* Rent a canoe from the South Bridge Boat House and paddle under Old North Bridge and Minute Man National Historical Park, following the migrating birds to Great Meadows National Wildlife Refuge. The round trip on this silver maple, birch, and oak-lined river is about four hours. **Essex Marsh,** between Cape Ann and Plum Island, is also a great place to paddle—try early morning at high tide; you can park at Woodman's Restaurant on State Route 133 and portage across the road to the put-in.

Finally, there's this popular canoe route on the North Shore:

Ipswich River, Topsfield

Allow 4 hours. Access: Foote Brothers is located on Ipswich Road, 3 miles from U.S. 1. Take U.S. 1 North past the Topsfield Fairgrounds and turn right at the second light. This is Ipswich Road.

The first day of summer was a perfect afternoon to paddle down the Ipswich River. Woody from Foote Brothers Canoe Rentals drove 10 other canoeists and me to the Salem Road put-in, where we began our 7.25-mile jaunt back to the rental outpost. The Ipswich is one of those narrow, serpentine rivers that was designed for canoeists. The glassy waters of the river were only interrupted by the occasional tree limb jutting up into the air that we had to go under or over. We paddled under three bridges, veering left at the last bridge. If we had veered right, Woody would have to pick us up that evening at the end of the canal. The river winds through the largest wildlife sanctuary operating under the jurisdiction of the Mass Audubon Society. Needless to say, great bird watching abounds. Snowy egrets stood

tall in the marsh, Eastern kingbirds nested on overhanging branches, and the iridescent blue-green head of the common grackle was seen eagerly searching for food on the banks of the river. There was also "Mother Mallard" followed by her row of fuzzy chicks, large turtles resting on rotted-out logs, and the call of the bullfrog, which sounded like a broken guitar string, emanating from the ever-present lily pad.

I stopped for lunch on the shores of Perkins Island to re-energize for the remainder of the trip. The river continued to curve through fields of unadulterated forest, slowly starting to widen as it approached Foote Canoes. A whole school bus of boys were jumping from bridges and ropes into the waters a mile before the put-out. Their shouts of elation as they hit the river were the perfect celebration to start the beginning of summer.

RENTALS

The Salem Run costs $25 per canoe. You can also rent canoes at the outpost and paddle upstream for $18 a canoe, or take the 9.75-mile Thunder Bridge Run for $28. Call **Foote Brothers Canoe Rentals** at 508/356-9771 for more information.

For the Concord River, canoes can be rented at the **South Bridge Boat House,** 496-502 Main Street, Concord (tel. 508/369-9438).

On the Charles, canoes can be rented from the **Charles River Canoe and Kayak Center** in Newton and Boston (tel. 617/965-5110). **King's Landing Marina,** off State Route 123 in Norwell, rents canoes for the North River (tel. 617/659-7273).

CROSS-COUNTRY SKIING

More than 20 km of backcountry trails leave from the backdoor of **Lincoln Guide Service,** 152 Lincoln Road, Lincoln (tel. 617/259-1111), through

Thoreau country. Indeed, one of the trails leads to Walden Pond. Rentals and guided tours are also available.

A favorite for local high school and college teams is the **Weston Ski Track,** which has 15 km of groomed trails spread across the Leo J. Martin Golf Course. They are located on Park Road, Weston (tel. 617/891-6575).

If you want a quick workout, try the 5 km of trails at the **Rolling Green Ski Touring Center.** 311 Lowell Road, Andover (tel. 508/475-4066).

Great Brook Farm Ski Touring Center provides 15 km of groomed trails over farm meadows and through woods. They also feature snowmaking and night skiing; 1018 Lowell Street, Carlisle (tel. 508/369-7486).

Pro-motions in Bedford rents cross-country skis for the Minute Man Bike Trail; 111 South Street, Bedford (tel. 617/275-1113).

DOWNHILL SKIING

There are several small hills near Boston that feature downhill skiing. **Nashoba Valley Ski Area,** Power Road, Westford (tel. 508/692-3033), has 15 trails, 3 triple chairlifts, 1 double chairlift, and night skiing. The longest trail is 1/2 mile with a vertical drop of 240 feet. Prices for adults are $27 weekends, $20 weekdays.

Blue Hills, 4001 Washington Street, Canton (tel. 617/828-5090), has 7 trails, 1 double chairlift, and night skiing. The longest trail is 3/4 mile with a vertical drop of 350 feet. Prices for adults are $20 weekends, $15 weekdays.

Bradford Ski Area, South Cross Road, Haverhill (tel. 508/373-0071), has 10 trails, 2 triple chairlifts, and night skiing. The longest trail is 1,200 feet with a vertical drop of 250 feet. Prices for adults are $25 weekends, $18 weekdays.

It might be worth the extra effort to go to **Wachusett Mountain** ski area, just west of I-190 at 499 Mountain Road, Princetown (tel. 508/464-2300). Wachusett has 18 trails (30 percent beginner, 45 percent intermediate, 25 percent expert), one quad chairlift, one triple, one double, and night skiing. The longest trail is 1 1/2 miles with a vertical drop of 1,000 feet. Prices for adults are $34 weekends, $28 weekdays.

FISHING

Considering that Gloucester is the oldest fishing port in America, how can you go wrong with saltwater fishing in this region? Surfcast for **blues** between late July and October and **stripers** starting in late May. On the North Shore, schools of fishermen congregate on the beaches of **Plum Island** at the mouth of the Merrimack and Parker Rivers. On the South Shore, anglers head to **Humarock Beach** to fish at the mouths of both the North and South rivers. Other popular locales include the end of **Fourth Cliff** in Scituate and **Third Cliff Beach** on the seawall. Just find the seagulls swarming and diving into the water and you'll find the blues. The gulls are looking for leftover pieces of fish flesh, the result of a bluefish feeding frenzy. For bait, use poppers during the day and sand eels at night for the blues; use sand eels during the day and live eels at night for stripers.

Scup, tautog, fluke, sea bass and other bottom fish are found when you venture offshore. There's also the chance you'll catch **cod, pollock, haddock, mackerel, flounder,** and **tuna.** In the North Shore, contact the **Yankee Fishing Fleet** (tel. 508/283-0313 or 800/942-5464) and **Captain Bill's** (tel. 508/283-6995) in Gloucester. **Andy Lynn Boats** (tel. 508/746-7776), **Captain John Boats** (tel. 508/746-2643), and **Captain Tim Brady & Sons** (tel. 508/746-4809) all arrange deep-sea fishing trips from Plymouth, on the south shore.

GOLF

The best golf in eastern Massachusetts is found 20 to 30 miles outside Boston. **The North Course** at Stow Acres Country Club in Stow (tel. 508/568-8690), **Shaker Hills Golf Club** in Harvard (tel. 508/772-2227), the **Tara Ferncroft Country Club** in Danvers (tel. 508/777-5614), and the **Trull Brook Golf Course** in North Tewksbury are all popular with Bostonians.

HORSEBACK RIDING

On the South Shore, **Briggs Riding Stables,** in Hanover on Hanover Street (tel. 617/826-3191), offers private and group lessons as well as trail rides. **Bobby's Ranch** in Acton, 6 Durkee Lane (tel. 508/263-7165) offers guided rides on the North Shore.

MOUNTAIN BIKING

Head to any of eastern Massachusetts' state forests, parks, and reservations and you'll find a vast web of trails to get lost on. These are my favorites:

Maudslay State Park

Allow 1 hour. Easy; relatively flat terrain. Access: From Boston and all other points south, take Exit 57 off I-95 towards Newburyport and turn right on State Route 113. After 0.4 mile, turn left onto Noble Street. When the road ends, veer left and look for signs to the park. Map: Trail maps are usually located at the parking area.

Purchased by the state in 1985, Maudslay State Park is a former estate where annual literary festivals were held in the 1850s and 1860s. Ralph Waldo Emerson, John Greenleaf Whittier, and William Lloyd Garrison were just a few of the noted writers who gathered on a 20-acre stretch of the Merrimack River

to compete in one of the country's first poetry slams. I wonder what the response would be if this limpid poem by Whittier was heard today in a Lower East Side coffee house:

Sing soft, sing low, our lowland river,
Under thy banks of laurel bloom,
Softly and sweet as the hour becometh,
Sing us the songs of peace and home.

Mountain laurel, azaleas, rhododendrons, and flowering dogwood still line the carriage-path trails that loop around the property. For the budding biker who doesn't have time to venture to Acadia National Park, this easy 6- or 7-mile loop is an excellent alternative. From the parking lot, cross the large field and continue to bear right on the pine needle and cone-strewn paths the entire way. The single-track hiking trails are strictly off-limits to bikes. After a short cruise in the woods, you'll soon hug the shores of the mighty Merrimack. The trail cruises up a short hill to the remains of the estate's formal gardens, before veering right to the parking lot. On the drive home, don't forget to sing sweet nothings about flowering dogwood into your buddy's ear.

Willowdale State Forest

Time: your call. Easy to moderate; relatively flat terrain. Access: From Ipswich, take State Route 133 West, turning turn left onto Linebrook Road. Take another left onto Old Right Road and you'll see a small pullover on the left just before the road turns to gravel. Map: Contact the Bradley-Palmer State Park (tel. 508/887-5931).

If you want to go mountain biking on the North Shore, Willowdale State Forest is the locals' number one choice. Former logging roads, double-tracks and single-tracks snake through the deep, dark oak and pine forest. Cruise toward the unpaved road and take a left past the gate 100 yards later. The road curves around a farm for a quick dose of sunshine before heading back into the forest. Here, a single-track led me into the heart of darkness. The only sounds heard were the ruffling of chipmunks scurrying through the leaves. An hour later, I made it back to the pavement of Linebrook Road. I haven't the slightest idea how I got there—probably the same way a mouse goes through a maze.

Blue Hills State Reservation

Time: your call. Moderate. Access: From the junction of I-93 and State Route 28 (Exit 5), drive 1.4 miles north on State Route 28 and turn right onto Chickatawbut Road. There's a small gravel lot on your right.

Boston's favorite place to mountain bike is this 6,000-acre reservation, located just south of the city. Park your car in the lot and cruise up the dirt road known as the Braintree Pass Path. Branching off the road are numerous single and double-tracks routes including the "Skyline." Blue-blazed, rock-littered Skyline cruises up Chickatawbut Hill, rising up and down, before descending past Blue Hills Reservoir. The major drawback of this challenging ride is that traffic from I-93 can often be heard. When you reach the layers of granite known as "The Crags," you can attempt to take the Crags Foot Path or simply retrace your steps on the Skyline back to the parking lot.

POWERBOATING

Sunsplash Boat Rentals in Gloucester rents boats on the North Shore (tel. 508/283-4722). **Mary's Boat Rentals** in Marshfield (tel. 617/837-2322) and **Plymouth Parasail** (tel. 508/746-1415) rent motor boats on the South Shore. Plymouth Parasail also rents Jet Skis.

ROAD BIKING

Boston takes its biking very seriously. When I lived in Cambridge, there were four bike shops within a three-block radius of my apartment. Just on Mass Avenue, I saw bikers with suits going to work, bikers with backpacks heading to school, and crazed riders who just seemed to enjoy weaving in and out of the car traffic. Needless to say, road biking is more than just a sport in this town, it's a mode of travel. Boston has two bike paths where you can escape the traffic and get a workout. The 10.5-mile **Minute Man Bikeway** starts in Somerville and swings by a football field, the Alewife MBTA Red Line Station, and the white swans of Spy Pond, before connecting with the Arlington portion of the ride. From here, the paved trail follows a former Boston and Maine railroad line behind homes, factories, and warehouses. When you get closer to Lexington, fields of wildflowers and small playgrounds replace the real estate. The trail ends in the small village of Bedford. All along the path, there are places to rent and repair bikes and get cold drinks.

The 17.1-mile **Charles River Bike Path** runs from the Museum of Science along the Boston side of the Charles through the Esplanade to Watertown Square. The trail then crosses the river to the Cambridge side on its way back to the Museum of Science. The problem with this bike path is that it's hard to enjoy the scenery when cars are zooming next to you. There are very few places on the trail to escape the noise.

On the South Shore, the **Myles Standish State Forest** has 16 miles of bike trails. There's also a 7.2-mile bike path along the **Cape Cod Canal** which runs under the Sagamore and Bourne Bridges. If you are searching for two of the better bike loops in New England, try these:

Lincoln/Concord/Carlisle Loop

26 miles. Allow 3 hours to all day, depending on how many sights you want to see. Moderate ride over terrain with several short hills. Access: From Boston or Cambridge, take State Route 2 to State Route 126 South. Turn left at Codman Road and left at Lincoln Road. Park on the left-hand side at the Mall at Lincoln Square. Map: any good Greater Boston road map will do.

This 26-mile ride will satiate all history buffs, whether your specialty is art, architecture, literarature, or American history. Stops on the loop include the sculpture garden at DeCordova Museum, the Gropius House (built by the founder of the Bauhaus Movement), Thoreau's Walden Pond, the Old Manse (the former home of Ralph Waldo Emerson and Nathaniel Hawthorne), and the Minute Man National Historical Park, site of the first battle of the Revolutionary War. To top it off, you ride through miles of pastoral backcountry roads in the town of Carlisle.

From the mall parking lot, turn left onto the bike path that hugs Lincoln Road. Another left onto Sandy Pond Road and you'll see the sign for the DeCordova Museum on the right-hand side. Set on a hill overlooking Sandy Pond, the grounds of this intimate museum are blanketed by large contemporary sculptures. Once you've had your fill of art, continue on Sandy Pond Road and turn left onto Baker Bridge Road. At 68 Baker Bridge Road stands the Gropius House. Walter Gropius, founder of the Bauhaus Movement in Germany, was a leading proponent of modern architecture. Gropius built this house for himself in 1938 after accepting a position at Harvard's Graduate School of Design. He combined traditional elements of New England architecture—brick, fieldstone, and clapboard—with innovative materials rarely seen in

houses, such as welded steel, chrome banisters, and glass blocks.

Tour the structure and then head back to Baker Bridge Road, which soon connects with State Route 126. Veer right and on the left-hand side of the road Walden Pond soon appears. On July 4, 1845, 28-year-old Henry David Thoreau moved into a spare cabin he had built on the side of Walden Pond. For two years, two months, and two days, the naturalist and philosopher retreated from society and roughed it in the woods. He recounted every experience in his journal, and seven years later published the legendary book, *Walden*. Today, the beaches of Walden Pond are lined with towels and suntanners in the summertime. It is one of Boston's favorite swimming holes. Stone posts mark the site of Thoreau's cabin, which was later used as a pig shed before being dismantled for lumber. Lock your bike and wander into Walden Woods, the 2,680-acre area that encompasses the pond; 65 percent of the woods is protected from development, including a parcel bought by the Walden Woods Project, a land trust formed in 1990.

Back on State Route 126, cross State Route 2 and be wary of traffic. State Route 126 turns into Walden Street as you approach the historic hamlet of Concord. Turn right on Main Street and go halfway around the rotary, veering right again onto Monument Street. Your next stop is the Old Manse, a three-story house on the left-hand side of the road. Built in 1770 for the Reverend William Emerson, the Old Manse is best known as the place where grandson Ralph Waldo Emerson wrote his book, *Nature*, and as the home of Nathaniel Hawthorne and his new bride, Sophia. The Hawthornes rented the home for three years (1842–45) for an annual rent of $100. Nathaniel's desk was placed facing a wall on the second floor to help him concentrate on his writing. It obviously worked, for at the young age of 22, he wrote the short story, *Mosses from an Old Manse*. Sophia, an artist, etched statements with her wedding ring on glass windows around the house. Comments regarding her children and the weather can still be seen on several panes. Outside, Thoreau planted a garden as a wedding gift to the Hawthornes. The grounds are a good place to picnic before walking to the Minute Man National Historical Park next door.

On the morning of April 19, 1775, a small group of minutemen met the British soldiers (called "Redcoats") at this same spot. The British had been dispatched from Concord to seize arms and supplies that the provincials had hidden at Barrett Farm on the other side of the Concord River. Before they could cross North Bridge, the minutemen fired shots. The Redcoats fired back before retreating, and thus, the first Revolutionary War battle occurred. On the near side of the Old North Bridge (a reproduction), you can see Daniel Chester French's sculpture, *Minuteman*, which he created in 1836 to commemorate the battle. Ralph Waldo Emerson's famous lines, spoken at the same ceremony, are found at the base of the sculpture:

By the rude bridge that arched the flood
Their flag to April's breeze unfurled,
Here once the embattled farmers stood
And fired the shot heard round the world.

American history soon gives way to a century-old rural landscape when you leave Concord and head into Carlisle. Go straight on Monument Street to River Road, lined on both sides by horse farms. Turn left onto State Route 225, where you can stop for a scoop of homemade ice cream and pet the goats at Kimball's. Continuing on State Route 225, take a sharp left onto Cross Street while you're heading downhill. Here, the ride gets tricky as you start to meander on country roads lined with barns, farmland, and recently built mansions. Next, 0.9 mile from the junction of State Route 225, turn right at a stop sign onto unmarked South Street. A mile later, you're going to take a left onto West Street and a quick right onto Pope Road. Your next left will be onto Strawberry Hill Road, 1.2 miles away. Former farms have been replaced by large estates that sit on the hillside above. Two miles later, veer left onto Barrett's Mill Road and then right onto Lowell Road. This will bring you back to the rotary in Concord, where you turn right on Main Street and make a quick left on Walden Street to reach Walden Pond once again. You've now earned a dip in the pond's waters.

After cooling off, proceed on State Route 126 to Codman Road. Turn left, veering left once more on Lincoln Road to return to the Mall at Lincoln Square. You've successfully completed your history course for today.

Cape Ann Loop

Allow 3 hours. Easy; relatively flat terrain. Access: From State Route 128 North, take a right onto State Route 133 East and turn right again onto State Route 127. The Stage Fort Park is located on the left-hand side of the road. Drive up the hill to find the large parking lot. Map: any road map of eastern Massachusetts will do.

Put blinders on and you can complete the 26-mile loop around Cape Ann in less than three hours. The rest of us will need twice that amount of time to stop at the many scenic, artistic, and historic offerings. Cruise downhill from Stage Fort Park and turn right where "The Man At The Wheel" statue faces the Atlantic Ocean on Pavilion Beach. Created in 1920, this sculpture is a memorial to fisherman who lost their lives at sea. It's a fitting tribute to Gloucester, one of the largest fishing communities

Walden Pond

"I went to the woods because I wished to live deliberately, to front only the essential facts of life, and see if I could not learn what it had to teach, and not, when I came to die, discover that I had not lived," wrote Henry David Thoreau in his best known work, *Walden*. Thoreau ventured to the woods with axe in hand in March 1845 to build his historic hut. Never would this modest writer imagine what an impact his philosophical musings would have on the world more than 150 years after he cut down his first tall pine. For two years, two months, and two days, Thoreau lived alone in the woods, a mile from any neighbor, in his rustic abode built near the shores of Walden Pond. All of the thoughts collected in his journal relate to how Thoreau survived in the woods independently.

Contrary to what most people think, Thoreau did not want to be a hermit, nor did he live an existence entirely on his own. He simply enjoyed the chance to mull over his ideas in quietude, and, as Van Wyck Brooks noted in *The Flowering of New England*, "he had long cherished the notion of a forest-life." "I never found the companion that was so companionable as solitude," Thoreau wrote in *Walden*, perhaps as a backlash against the hordes of curious onlookers and voyeurs who arrived unexpectedly at his house. Most of these uninvited drop-ins were schoolchildren, family, friends, and other philosophers from Concord and Lincoln. The more intriguing guests were a runaway slave, a French Canadian woodchopper who was learned in Greek mythology, and the newly arrived Irish immigrants who worked on the railroad.

Almost daily, Thoreau walked to Concord to exchange beans for rice and collect news of his family. The townspeople would frequently ask him if he was lonely. To this he replied, "I am no more lonely than a single mullein or dandelion in a pasture, or a bean leaf, or sorrel, or a horse-fly, or a bumble-bee. I am no more lonely than the Mill Brook, or a weathercock, or the north star, or the south wind, or an April shower, or a January thaw, or the first spider in a new home." Another favorite topic on which he liked to vent his enmity was materialism. "I would rather sit on a pumpkin and have it all to myself, than be crowded on a velvet cushion. I would rather ride in an ox cart with a free circulation, than go to heaven in the fancy car of an excursion train and breathe a *malaria* all the way."

If it wasn't for his friend, Ralph Waldo Emerson, Thoreau could have easily lived out his life in this 10-by-15-foot log cabin. Emerson was going abroad for a year and he needed Thoreau to be in Concord to look after his wife and two children. Thoreau would eventually live with his parents and three unmarried sisters until he died of tuberculosis at the age of 45.

on the Atlantic seaboard. If you ride along the harbor in the morning hours, you have a very good chance of spotting a commercial trawler unloading its day's catch on the docks.

Stay on State Route 127 as it curves downhill to Gloucester's Inner Harbor, and be cautious of the heavy traffic. A granite building sits atop the hill on Harbor Loop. Home to the noted marine artist Fitz Hugh Lane in the mid-19th century, the building was later converted to a prison. Gloucester must have been a relatively safe city in those days, since the house is not much larger than a cottage. Turn right at the light onto E. Main Street, passing the small village of East Gloucester, and bear right again onto Rocky Neck Avenue. You are now entering the oldest working art colony in the country. Winslow Homer, Maurice Prendergast, Childe Hassam, and John Frederick Kensett are just a few of the renowned artists who have been lured to Rocky Neck's rugged shores over the last two centuries. A quick loop around Rocky Neck's wharf will bring you to a slew of galleries featuring the region's more contemporary talents.

Continue on East Main Street past Niles Beach, turning right between two stone pillars onto Eastern Point Boulevard. Mansions line both sides of the road all the way to Eastern Point lighthouse. You can tour all 45 rooms at one of the houses, Beauport, in the summer months. From the lighthouse, join the fishermen on the stone jetty that stretches a half-mile across the mouth of the harbor. Back on your bike, turn around and veer right onto Farrington Avenue, which soon becomes Atlantic Road. Sweeping vistas of Cape Ann's rocky coastline come into view as you ride along the ocean, while the twin lighthouses of Thacher Island hover in the distance. A right turn onto State Route 127A or Thacher Road will bring you to the quaint town of Rockport, passing Cape Ann's finest beaches along the way. The strip of stores and restaurants on Bearskin Neck is a great place to find lunch before continuing to the northern part of Cape Ann.

. Go straight onto Main Street and veer right onto Beach Street, looking for signs to Pigeon Cove. This will bring you to State Route 127 North. Turn right and in 1 or 2 miles you'll see a small State Park sign. The Halibut Point parking lot is less than 100 yards to your right. Lock up your bike and cross the street to find the huge rainwater-filled granite quarry

(a longer walk to the ocean is described under the "Walks & Rambles" section). After your stroll, continue on State Route 127 to the Annisquam Village Church, where you turn right and then bear left twice to get to the small fishing village of Annisquam. Two artists were painting the serene harbor when I crossed the footbridge to return to State Route 127. Bear right and 3 miles later you'll enter a rotary. Be careful of the oncoming traffic and go halfway around, continuing on State Route 127. Turn right on Centennial Avenue for an invigorating downhill run back to State Route 127, where you bear right to get back to Stage Fort Park.

RENTALS

Across the street from the Mall at Lincoln Square, **Lincoln Guide Service** rents bikes and supplies maps for a variety of routes. They are located at 152 Lincoln Road (tel. 617/259-1111). **Seaside Cycle** in Manchester rents bikes for the Cape Ann loop (23 Elm Street; tel. 508/526-1200).

SAILING

You don't have to venture to Cape Cod to rent boats. On the South Shore, **Plymouth Bristol Charters** rents a 41-foot yacht for day or overnight trips (P.O. Box 903, Plymouth, MA 02362; tel. 508/746-3688). Contact **Sunsplash Boat Rentals** on the North Shore (tel. 508/283-4722).

There are several renowned sailing schools in and around Boston, including the **Boston Harbor Sailing School** on India Row (tel. 617/523-2619), the **Boston Sailing Center** on Lewis Wharf (tel. 617/227-4198), and the **Courageous Sailing Center** in Charlestown (tel. 617/725-3263). On the North Shore, contact Bert Williams, owner and director of the **Coastal Sailing School** in Marblehead (tel. 617/639-0553). Burt uses a 30-foot boat for his 20-hour course.

SCUBA DIVING

Why pay $15 for a lobster at a restaurant when you can find your own crustacean on the floor of the ocean? Whether you dive from a boat or simply walk in from the beach, the Atlantic offers an unlimited amount of diving opportunities. Divers on the South Shore head to **Brant Rock Public Beach** in Marshfield and the **wrecks** off of Scituate. **North Atlantic Scuba** in Marshfield rents all the necessary equipment (tel. 617/834-4087). Charters are offered by **Andy Lynn** in Plymouth (tel. 508/746-7776).

Charters off Cape Ann are provided by **Cape Ann Divers**, tel. 508/281-8082.

SCULLING

The Charles River is home to the Harvard crew team and hundreds of other rowers who yearn to be on the Harvard crew team. On a warm day in summer, there are probably more sculls on the Charles than on the Thames in Oxford, especially between the Science Museum and the B.U. Bridge. From the B.U. Bridge, the river snakes through Allston and Brighton to Watertown. The **Charles River Canoe and Kayak Center** rents sculls and provides lessons. They have locations in Newton and in Boston (tel. 617/965-5110). The **Globe Corner Bookstores** in Boston and Cambridge publish a small Charles River distance map. They can be reached in Boston at 617/523-6658 or 617/859-8008. In Harvard Square, call 617/497-6277.

SEA KAYAKING

Want to get a close-up photo of Moby Dick without using a long zoom lens?

Try sea kayaking with whales. **Adventure Learning,** on the North Shore, will transport you and five other kayakers to Stellwagen Bank or Jeffrey's Ledge on the *Rainbow Chaser*, a large motorboat. Once at the bank, you have the rare and exhilarating opportunity to glide eye-to-eye with humpback and minke whales. Since there is always the possibility of rough weather, kayakers should be experienced. The cost of the one day outing is $130. Adventure Learning also leads guided day-trips to Plum Island, Thacher Island, Cape Ann, and Marble-head Harbor, and offers sea-kayaking clinics. They are located at 67 Bear Hill, Merrimack, MA 01860 (tel. 508/346-9728 or 800/649-9728).

Essex River Basin Adventures offers three- to six-hour tours from the estuaries of the Essex River to Plum Island, Thacher Island, Hog Island, or over to Crane Beach (Main Street, Essex, MA 01929; tel. 508/768-ERBA or 800/KAYAK-04).

On the South Shore, **Billington Sea Watercraft** arranges two-hour tours of historic Plymouth Harbor (tel. 508/746-5444).

SNOWMOBILING

Most of the trails in the state forests and parks are open to snowmobiles. Contact the **Division of Forests and Parks,** 100 Cambridge Street, Boston, MA 02202 (tel. 617/727-3180), for maps and a list of public lands.

SURFING

On the North Shore, surfers hone their skills at **Long Beach** in Rockport, **Good Harbor Beach** in Gloucester, and **Plum Island** in Newburyport. On the South Shore, check out **Nantasket Beach** in Hull.

SWIMMING

On hot summer days, Bostonians don't need to travel far to find a long stretch of sand. Not surprisingly, the waters of the Atlantic are just as frigid here as they are in Cape Cod. Let's start with the white sands of 4¹/₂-mile **Crane Beach.** Located on the North Shore, east of Ipswich, Crane's smooth, shallow surf and dunes are popular with families. Watch out for those nasty greenhead flies that invade the beach in mid-July. **Plum Island** and **Salisbury Beach** are two more large strips of sand that attract families. Federally protected piping plovers nest on Plum Island, closing the beach for most of the summer. Call the **Parker River National Wildlife Refuge** at 508/465-5753 for current information regarding Plum Island. Rockport and Gloucester have a number of small beaches—you'll need to arrive early if you want to find a parking spot and a place on the sand. They include **Back, Front,** and **Long Beaches** in Rockport and **Wingaersheek** Beach in Gloucester. Singles head to **Long Beach** and **Good Harbor Beach** in Gloucester.

Heading south, Manchester's **Singing Beach** is a picturesque crescent of sand, and Marblehead's **Devereux Beach** has a playground that's fun for children. If you have a boat, head to the beach on **Great Misery Island,** about a half-mile out to sea from Manchester. On the South Shore, families crowd **Duxbury** and **Plymouth**'s long narrow beaches. More secluded beaches include **Onset** in Wareham and **Rexhame** and **Humarock** in Marshfield.

WALKS & RAMBLES

In addition to these three strolls, check out **Arnold Arboretum,** just outside of Boston in Jamaica Plain, and **Great**

Misery Island. Located approximately a half mile from the shores of Manchester, Great Misery is only accessible by boat. The 82-acre island was once home to a large resort, but is now maintained by the Trustees of Reservation. They have cleared trails and cleaned beaches, making the *misery* far more pleasant.

Any time of year, go stroll around the campus at **Wellesley College,** west of center city—in F.L. Olmstead's words, "It is a landscape not merely beautiful but with a marked individual character not represented so far as I know on the ground of any other college in the country." The campus buildings have lovely old architecture. There's a large lake suitable for swimming for both humans and canines—all the local people take their dogs there. Around the lake is a nice trail about 2 miles long. According to Wellesley tradition, the first guy you manage the entire circuit with, you'll marry.

Halibut Point State Park

Allow 1 hour. Access: From downtown Rockport, take State Route 127 North past Pigeon Cove to a small green sign that says State Park. This is Gott Avenue. Turn right and you'll see the much larger Halibut Point State Park sign and parking lot. Map: Available at the trailhead.

At Halibut Point State Park and Reservation, you have the unique opportunity to visit a huge quarry once used by the Rockport Granite Company, and a boulder train that slopes down to the ocean. The park did not get its name from the fish but from sailors who tacked around Cape Ann at this point and yelled, "Haul about." Cross Gott Avenue and continue on the woodchip-lined path to the small roundabout. Just before you turn right, you'll notice the large oval slab of granite which was used as a mooring for a fishing boat's anchorage. The mooring was one of the many chunks of rock ripped out of the earth to form the large quarry. The hole is now filled with 60-plus years of blackened rainwater, providing a mirror-like reflection of the clouds and granite walls.

Several hundred yards past the overlook, you'll find a narrow trail off to the right that leads through the brush to two iron staples. Turn right through the scrub oak, shadbush, and greenbrier and you'll soon come to a wide gravel path. At the next juncture, turn left to continue through the brush to the large rock pile, or go straight over the boulders that line the shore. Veer left at the large gravel path that leads to an overlook atop the heaping rock pile. Plum Island and the shores of New Hampshire can be seen to your left on a clear day. Returning to the main trail, veer right and turn right again at the two black cherry trees to reach the Bayview Trail. This path is a quick loop along the ocean, where black cormorants and other marine birds sit atop the rocky perches. A left turn at the headquarters will give you one last glance at the quarry before retracing your steps on the trail back to Gott Avenue and the parking area.

Great Meadows National Wildlife Refuge

Allow 1 hour. Access: From the center of Concord, follow State Route 62 East for 1.8 miles to Monsen Road. Turn left and look for the clearly marked signs to the refuge. Map: Available at the trailhead.

A chorus of birds greeted my wife Lisa and me upon our arrival at the Great Meadows National Wildlife Refuge. Bright goldfinches and common yellowthroats flew from red maple to red maple at the beginning of the Dike Trail. They were a good omen. As we crossed the open-water marsh and uplands, Lisa spotted a black-crowned night heron dipping his beak into the waters like a mechanical oil well. Nearby, 10 great blue herons and a family of Canada geese were spotted searching for food. We walked straight to the Concord River and then retraced our steps, taking a left and continuing in a clockwise fashion around the swamp. Red-winged blackbirds flashed their brilliant streak of color, more vibrant than a Matisse painting, as they flew over the cattails and shrubs. A right turn on the Edge Trail brought us through the woods back to our parking lot. Who would have thought that one of New England's best bird-watching spots is less than a 30-minute drive from Boston?

World's End

4 miles. Allow 2 hours. Access: Take Exit 14 off State Route 3 and follow State Route 228 north for 6.7 miles. Go left on State Route 3A for 0.9 miles to Summer Street, where you turn right for another 0.3 miles. Cross Rockland Street to Martin's Lane and go 0.7 miles to the end. Map: Available at the tollhouse.

South of Boston, World's End juts out of Hingham Harbor like a rooster at daybreak. In 1890, noted landscape architect Frederick Law Olmstead was hired to transform World's End into a "planned community" of 150 homes. Thankfully, this never came to fruition. The 251-acre estate was farmed and owned by one family until the Trustees of Reservation purchased the property with the help of the public in 1967. The Trustees of Reservation is a nonprofit organization that maintains over 75 preserves in the state.

To start your walk (jogging is also popular here), head to the end of the parking lot and proceed past the chain onto a wide path bordered by white pines, hickories, oaks, and bracken ferns. Continue along the trail in a counterclockwise fashion, starting with the rooster's tail first. A right turn through a row of sugar maples will bring you to the rocky outcroppings that form the shoreline of the Weir River. The path narrows as it hugs the rocky shores and clambers over boulders, before reaching the broad main trail again. Turn right and head across the manmade sand spit to World's End proper. Another right will lead you around the perimeter of this drumlin. Bumkin Island obstructs the views of Boston Harbor and the city's skyline. However, this problem is quickly alleviated once you turn right, cross the sand bar again, and head up Planter's Hill. From atop the small hill, you can see across Hingham Bay to Boston and the islands of the harbor. Head straight down the hill to return to the parking lot.

WHALE WATCHING

You don't have to go all the way to Provincetown to catch a whale-watching cruise to Stellwagen Bank. Seven miles north of Provincetown, Stellwagen is 25 miles east of Boston and 12 miles southeast of Gloucester. Stellwagen is an 18-mile long crescent-shaped underwater mesa. The bank ranges from 80-500 feet below the surface. Currents slam into the bank, bringing nutrient rich cold water to the surface. This attracts fish, which in turn attracts numerous species of whales from April to November, including **humpbacks,** the larger **finbacks,** and smaller **minkes** (for more information, see the "Whale Watching" section in chapter 7).

Yankee Whale Watching runs four-to-five-hour trips from Gloucester. They are located at State Route 133, Gloucester (tel. 508/283-0313 or 800/942-5464). In Boston, contact the

New England Aquarium (tel. 617/973-5277). On the South Shore, in Plymouth you can take a four-hour cruise with **Captain John Boats** (Town Wharf, tel. 800/242-AHOY).

Campgrounds & Other Accommodations

CAMPGROUNDS

Salisbury Beach State Reservation

From Salisbury, head 2 miles east on State Route 1A. Tel. 508/462-4481. 483 sites, 159 no hookups, handicap restroom facilities, sewage disposal, public phone, tables, and grills.

Located near the shores of the beach, these sites are always crowded in the summertime.

Harold Parker State Forest

From the junction of I-495 and State Route 114, head 9 miles south on State Route 114. Tel. 508/686-3391. 130 sites, no hookups, sewage disposal, public phone, ice, tables, and fire ring.

A good spot to camp for mountain bikers.

Winter Island Park

From the junction of Derby Street and Fort Avenue in Salem, head northeast on Winter Island Road. Tel. 508/745-9430. 41 sites (31 no hookups), handicapped rest room facilities, sewage disposal, public phone, ice, tables, grills, and wood.

Conveniently located in the historic town of Salem near the beaches of Marblehead.

Boston Harbor Islands State Park

The ferry to the islands is located in Hingham at 349 Lincoln Street (State Route 3A). Tel. 617/740-1605. 29 sites, pit toilets, handicapped rest room facilities.

The campgrounds are spread over four islands situated in Boston Harbor.

Myles Standish State Forest

From Federal Furnace Road in South Carver, head 3 miles west on Cranberry Road. Tel. 508/866-2526. 475 sites, no hookups, handicapped rest room facilities, sewage disposal, public phone, ice, tables, and grills.

The largest camping facility in any Massachusetts state forest or park, this large state forest is only several miles from the shores of Plymouth.

INNS & RESORTS

Ralph Waldo Emerson Inn

Phillips Avenue, Pigeon Cove, MA 01966. Tel. 508/546-6321. Double rooms are $85–$130, $149.50–$184.50 MAP.

Located in Pigeon Cove, just outside of Rockport on Cape Ann, most of the 36 rooms in this rambling inn have views of the ocean. Swim in the outdoor pool or wander to Cathedral Rocks, large boulders that form the shoreline.

Yankee Clipper Inn

96 Granite Street, State Route 127, Rockport, MA 01966. Tel. 508/546-3407 or 800/545-3699. Double rooms range $99–$239 in the summer months.

Situated at the opposite end of Pigeon Cove from the Ralph Waldo Emerson, the elegant Yankee Clipper is surrounded by green lawns that slope down to the sea. Many of the 27 rooms have glass-enclosed porches or sundecks overlooking the water.

Governor Bradford Motor Inn

98 Water Street, Plymouth, MA 02360. Tel. 508/746-6200 or 800/332-1620. Double rooms range $89–$119 during the summer months.

Only one block from Plymouth Rock, this inn is set right on the waterfront. All 94 rooms have air-conditioning and refrigerators. There is also a heated outdoor pool.

Central Branch YMCA

316 Huntington Avenue, Boston, MA 02115. Tel. 617/536-7800. Double rooms cost $55.

For the budget-oriented in Boston, you can't go wrong with the Central Branch Y, situated near the Boston Museum of Fine Arts. Each room has maid service and television, and rates include use of the pool, gym, and fitness center.

7

Cape Cod, Nantucket & Martha's Vineyard

Far below us was the beach, with a long line of breakers rushing to the strand. The sea was exceedingly dark and stormy, and the wind seemed to blow not so much as the exciting cause, as from sympathy with the already agitated ocean. The waves broke on the bars at some distance from the shore, ten or twelve feet high, like a thousand waterfalls, then rolled in foam to the sand. There was nothing but that savage ocean between us and Europe.

—Henry David Thoreau, *Cape Cod*

AND AND SEA, THESE ARE THE IMAGES THAT APPEAR WHEN WE THINK of Cape Cod and the Islands. Undulating dunes and long stretches of fine white beach serve as soft welcome mats for the angry surf that rolls ashore. Multicolored clay cliffs plummet to the waves below and sweeping inlets form natural harbors. Yet, as locals will attest, the Cape and the Islands are more than the National Seashore and Gay Head Cliffs. Sandwiched between the seas are heavily forested state parks criss-crossed with hiking trails and bike paths, cranberry bogs that turn deep reddish-blue in October, and moors that fade to the ocean's edge. It's a region that's small enough to entice, large enough to explore. Indeed, I love getting lost on the Cape—finding another beach where the only footprints in the sand are mine, another marsh or pond that the native birds know best.

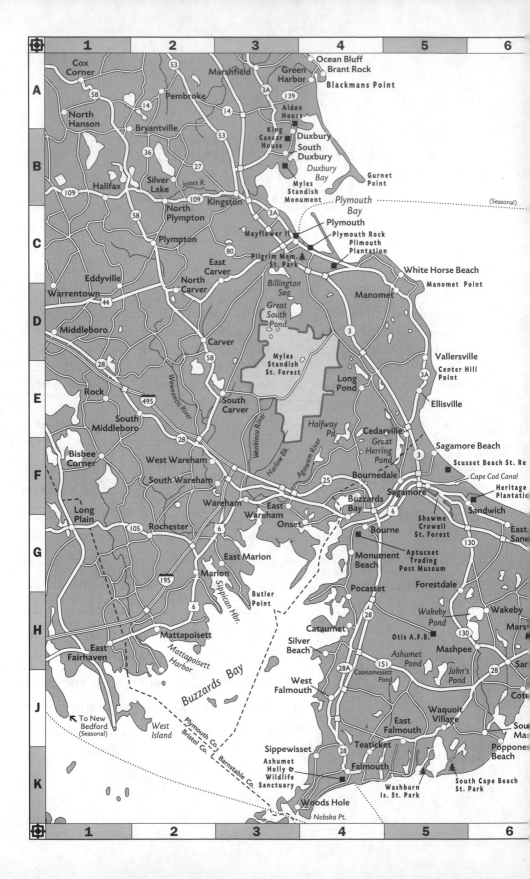

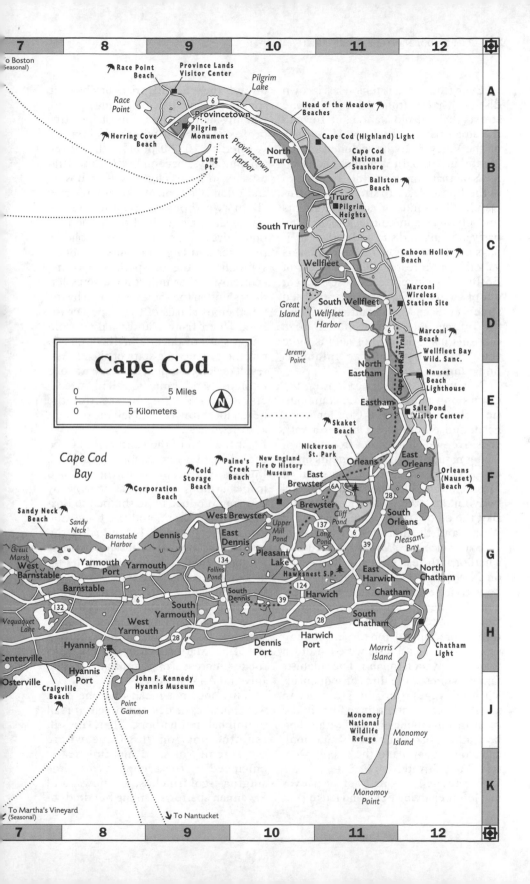

Every town in this region has its own distinct charm, from the cobblestone streets that line old Nantucket Town to the small fishing shacks of Menemsha on the Vineyard to the secluded stretch of sand in Truro. In Wellfleet, the Wildlife Sanctuary and Fort Hill Trail are two of the finest places to stroll in New England. Thousands of college students find jobs in Hyannis during the summer, party at night, and sun and surf on their days off. Provincetown is known for its galleries, fine restaurants, and host of B&Bs. Tiny gingerbread houses straight out of a fairy tale line the rose-trellised streets of 'Sconset on Nantucket. Wildlife refuges on Chappaquidick prove that this majestic strip of land is more than just the site of an infamous drowning.

Not unlike steamers or lobster, the Cape's prevalent and prized commodities, the typical Cape Codder has a hardened exterior that masks a soft, sensitive side. This comes from years of facing nature's harshest elements on an exposed strip of land that juts out of Massachusetts like the flexed arm of a bodybuilder—the shoulder at Buzzard's Bay, the elbow at Chatham, the wrist at Truro, and the fist at Provincetown.

Ever since the *Mayflower* sailed into a harbor at the eastern end of Cape Cod on November 11, 1620, settlers have been trying to subsist on the land's meager offerings. The pitch pine forests were exploited for their wood and resin, trees were tapped for turpentine and sap, and the oak forests were cut down to make way for farmland. The colonists failed to foresee the dire consequences. Without vegetation, blustery ocean squalls forced sand drifts to form in the most inconvenient places—within harbors, atop cobblestone streets, and, ironically, on the farmland the people were trying to cultivate.

By the late 1700s, many of the natives had left their dying fields and looked out towards the sea. With prices of whale oil, spermaceti, and baleen surging upward, whaling had become a most lucrative profession. Nantucket's population swelled to 10,000 people during the whaling days, becoming the third largest city in Massachusetts after Boston and Salem. Cod and mackerel supported about two thousand families on the Cape, almost one third of the population. Successful captains brought home treasures and large amounts of money, symbolizing the prosperous maritime economy. Other unfortunate souls left their ships on the shores, wrecked by the treacherous shoals of the Cape's coastline. When fishing and whaling went into a state of decline in 1860, people returned home in a state of shock. As a result of deforestation, the Cape was one immense sand dune. So-called "wreckers" earned a living by scouring the beach for shipwrecks to sell the remains as driftwood.

At the turn of the century, the Cape experienced a remarkable turnaround. Forests were replanted, the railroad made farming economically viable by allowing produce to be shipped to Boston and New York, and the Cape Cod Canal opened in 1914, reducing the number of shipwrecks because boats no longer needed to travel around the tip of Provincetown. The most significant factor, however, was tourism. Visitors started arriving in the 1920s and have ceased to stop. With the construction of summer homes, the populations on the Cape, Martha's Vineyard, and Nantucket increase exponentially during July and August.

This does not mean that one can't walk for miles on desolate beaches or sail to uninhabited harbors. There are still remote spots on the Cape where the serenity of sand meeting sea is enhanced by the cacophony of birds singing—goldfinches, swallows, and Savannah sparrows, among hundreds of others species. The mesmerizing force of nature is interrupted only by the occasional greeting from a clamdigger or fisherman who leaves his cedar-shingled house to probe his vast front yard—his face wizened, his hands calloused, and his eyes watery, pale blue, like the ocean he knows so well.

On the Vineyard and Nantucket, it's more of a challenge to find your own stretch of shoreline, but peruse these pages and ye shall find privacy, even in summer. Whatever season or sport you choose, the salty sea will never be far away, pervading your senses and leaving a feeling of tranquillity in its wake.

The Lay of the Land

The Cape's unique formation, along with Nantucket and Martha's Vineyard, owe their existence to a melting ice front. When the ice moved, rock debris of all kinds was released to form a terminal moraine—a high pile of sand, clay, and boulders. Bordering the moraines on the ocean side were gently sloping outwash plains and small, irregular depressions in the land called kettleholes.

Over thousands of years, the constant battering of the surf created long sandy beaches, soft cliffs, and bluffs. Today, the beaches are an extensive network of dunes, barrier beaches and islands, and long sand spits. Salt marshes and tidal estuaries have appeared, protected from the impact of ocean currents by the sand. Inland, the kettleholes have been filled with rainwater to create ponds; surprisingly, woodlands have grown from the poor sandy soil. When Captain John Smith published *A Description of New England* in 1616, he portrayed the interior of Cape Cod as "onely a headland of high hils of sand overgrowne with shrubby pines, hurts [huckleberries], and such trash." Not much has changed. Scrub forests of oaks and pitch pine

cover the hillside. In areas where the soil receives more moisture, thickets of red maples and hickories are found. Yet, the beeches, birches, and maples that form dense forests throughout most of New England are few and far between here.

Plants and shrub life are also scarce, with heaths being the most notable exception. Blueberries, huckleberries, and sheep laurel grow in the dry woodlands, while cranberries and azaleas thrive in the wet, boggy sections of the countryside. The cranberries have adapted so well to Cape Cod's acrid soil that they have become one of the region's few lucrative crops and a multimillion dollar industry. On the island of Nantucket, Scotch heather and heath were introduced to the moorland in the mid-19th century and now grow naturally all over the island. American holly, popular for Christmas decorations, can be found at two preserves on Cape Cod.

The mean temperature on Cape Cod and the islands is 32° in the winter, 70° during the warmest month, July. Warm and sunny days on the Cape can quickly turn damp and chilly when the fog rolls in with the ocean breeze. This happens when warm, moist air moving north with the Gulf Stream hovers over the cold ocean and condenses into a cloud of droplets. The thick haze rises gently above the sea, enshrouding everything in its path as it proceeds to land. If you're fortunate enough to be caught in this mysterious mist, give your eyes a rest and listen to the meditative sounds of mooing foghorns and clanking bellbuoys.

Thoreau once stated that the best time to visit Cape Cod is during "a storm in the fall or winter." This is true only if you enjoy seeing an enraged Mother Nature. I like to stroll along the Cape in the springtime, when land and sea stretch their arms and waken from their long slumber. Fall is my favorite time on the islands—Nantucket's cranberry bogs are rich with redness, and the Vineyard's Gay Head Cliffs turn the colors of a rainbow.

The wildlife on the Cape can't possibly compete with the 300 or more species of migrating shorebirds that are funnelled along by the Atlantic Flyway. The most exciting mammals are found in the ocean—humpback and minke whales, harbor seals, and porpoises. On land, cottontail rabbits and their predators, the red fox, are prevalent. Raccoons, woodchucks, and deer can also be found.

Orientation

Access to the 70-mile-long arm of the Cape is accomplished via two bridges that span the Cape Cod Canal. The **Bourne Bridge,** which New Yorkers and other travelers from the south take, connects with State Route 28 south to Falmouth. The **Sagamore Bridge** is to the north and connects with U.S. 6, the Cape's main thoroughfare.

Sooner or later, you will have to contend with the traffic on **U.S. 6,** which travels the entire length of the Cape from Sandwich to P-town. During Friday and Sunday evenings in the summer, U.S. 6 and the rotaries leading to the bridges are heavily congested. I would avoid these times at all costs. If Provincetown is your destination, consider taking the ferry direct from Boston. **Bay State Cruises** (tel. 617/723-7800) runs the *MV Provincetown II* daily from late June through Labor Day.

The other two roads that run roughly parallel with U.S. 6 are State Route 6A, which runs north of U.S. 6 from Sagamore to Brewster, and State Route 28, which dips down to Falmouth before turning east and heading through Hyannis, Yarmouth, and on to Chatham. Route 6A, decidely the scenic route, is bordered by quaint old villages and

clogged with slow-moving rubber-neckers. Much of Route 28, on the other hand, is the commercial strip that's tarnished the image of the Cape—ticky-tacky souvenir shops, lobster joints, motels, malls, and factory outlet stores. Put it this way: It will take you a while to get there, but you'll breathe a lot easier once you get to the more charming destinations on the Cape—Brewster, Chatham, and on up the Outer Cape toward P-town.

The best place to catch a ferry to Martha's Vineyard is Woods Hole, off State Route 28 on the Cape. From Hyannis, off U.S. 6, you can fly or take a ferry to Nantucket. The island of Nantucket is small enough that a car is not necessary. However, if you're planning to spend more than a day on the Vineyard, a car is advisable to get to the more remote areas of the island like Chappaquiddick and Gay Head.

Parks & Other Hot Spots

CAPE COD

Sandy Neck & the Great Marsh

Main access from State Route 6A. 2 miles west of junction of Route 6A and State Route 149 in Barnstable, turn north at the sign for Sandy Neck Beach. Rest rooms, changing rooms, snack bar, foot trails, fishing, and public beach. Boat access possible from Barnstable Harbor. Day use fee. Tel. 508/790-6200 for more information.

Sandy Neck is a long spit of barrier beach that faces north into the wide expanse of Cape Cod Bay. Winds and tides have built 100-foot dunes onto the 6-mile-long beach—you'll think you're in North Africa. Inland of the dunes closest to the beach are yet more rolling sand hillocks, most of these covered with wild cranberries, beach grass, bayberry, and even gnarled coastal hardwoods such as American holly. The dunes are an important habitat for threatened species such as piping plovers and diamondback terrapins. The seemingly endless beach has the warmer waters of the bay to swim in, and surfcasters are a common sight here.

Even more remarkable than the dune environment is the Great Marsh. Protected by Sandy Neck, the salt marsh here is the largest (about 4,000 acres) and oldest (it's been carbon-dated back nearly 4,000 years) living salt marsh in New England. The peat deposits are as much as 40 feet deep. The trails here offer expansive views of the marsh, and you'll likely see herons, marsh hawks, and maybe even osprey. Close inspection of the salt creeks will show you fiddler crabs, snails, hermit crabs, and huge schools of minnows. If you're willing to front a little labor, carry a canoe to the first creeks along the marsh trail and you'll be rewarded by some wonderful exploring.

Cape Cod National Seashore

Access points along U.S. 6. Headquarters: South Wellfleet, MA 02663. Tel. 508/349-3785.

Forty miles of rolling, windswept sand dunes, kettlehole ponds, bogs, plains, scrub forest, and marshes combine to form this serene, protected land. Like most of Cape Cod, the land was coveted by developers until Congress intervened and purchased the region in 1961. Also known as the Outer Cape, this fragile,

barrier spit stretches from the southern tip of Nauset Beach to Race Point Lighthouse outside of Provincetown. In between lie some of the finest beach walks on the East Coast, including Nauset Light, Marconi, Head of the Meadow, and Province Lands.

Nauset Beach

From U.S. 6, take Exit 12. Follow State Route 6A to Orleans; turn right onto Main Street. Continue through intersection with State Route 28 and drive several miles, veering left at the sign for Beach Road. Continue on Beach Road, following signs to parking lot. Rest rooms, changing facilities, and snack bar. Tel. 508/240-3700 for more information.

Run by the town of Orleans and not by the national seashore, Nauset Beach is without question *the* big beach scene on the Cape. A long, wide swath of perfect sandy beach, Nauset is packed solid with sun worshipers for hundreds of yards during the summer, making for one giant beach party. The clam shack at the head of the boardwalk from the parking lot down to the beach has been feeding generations of beach-goers. The north end of the beach is set aside for surfers.

Coast Guard Beach & Nauset Marsh

East off U.S. 6 in Eastham. Park at Salt Pond Visitor Center of Cape Cod National Seashore (tel. 508/255-3421) for nature trails, at beach parking area at end of Doane Road for beach use.

A major gathering place for waterfowl and shorebirds, this long barrier beach shelters the extensive Nauset Marsh. Herons, snowy egrets, and marsh hawks are just some of the birds spotted here. There are three nature trails, including the highly recommended Fort Hill (see "Walks & Rambles").

Province Lands

At the tip of the Cape, off U.S. 6 in P-town. Visitor center, rest rooms, and changing rooms. Foot and bike paths, beaches, extensive naturalist programs, birding. Contact the visitor center at tel. 508/487-1256.

This is the Cape Cod you dreamed of—rolling sand dunes, open ocean, and seemingly endless shoreline. Most of this area was heavily forested until European settlers cleared the land in the mid-1600s for farming and homes. This wasn't a wise idea. Once the vegetation vanished, there was nothing to hold the sand in place. Storms and gale-force winds brewed by the ocean blew sand everywhere, forming dunes. Mounds of sand eventually clogged the harbor, buried the P-town streets, and turned Province Lands into the windblown sand spit it is today—covered with bayberry, wild cranberry, and beach grass. There are still a few small stands of the beech trees that once covered the entire area.

The huge dunes of the Province Lands (which you'll usually find trying to cover U.S. 6 in the North Truro area) make for fascinating, if grueling, walking. Race Point Beach, at the northernmost tip, is perhaps the Cape's most beautiful.

Great Island

From U.S. 6, head west into Wellfleet Center, taking a left on East Commercial Street and a right at the marina onto Chequessett Neck Road. There's a sign for Great Island several miles down the road on the left side. Foot trails and birding.

Once an island off the southwest tip of Wellfleet, Great Island is now a peninsula jutting south into Cape Cod Bay. In the 1700s, the island was a lively center for whalers. Today, it is an uninhabited wilderness area containing the longest trail in the National Seashore (see "Hikes & Rambles").

Wellfleet Bay Wildlife Sanctuary

Located on the western side of U.S. 6 just north of the Wellfleet-Eastham line. Naturalist programs, foot trails, and birding. Day use fee. Tel. 508/349-2615.

One of the prime-bird watching areas on the Cape, this 700-acre sanctuary is operated by the Massachusetts Audubon Society. The unspoiled area includes 430 acres of salt marsh, freshwater ponds, pine forests, and moors overlooking the bay.

Nickerson State Park

Entrance off State Route 6A in Brewster, near Orleans town line. Rest rooms, picnic areas, 420 campsites, foot and bike trails, quietwater canoeing, birding, and fishing. Tel. 508/896-3491.

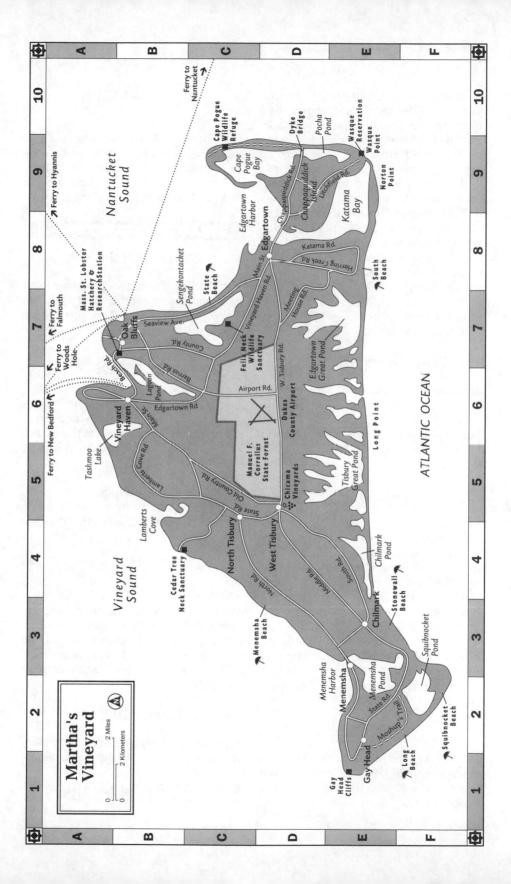

Canoeing, hiking, and biking abound at this 1,779-acre forest, which has more than a dozen kettlehole ponds left over from the last ice age. Songbirds and waterfowl are abundant in the park, and deer, red-tailed foxes, and other woodland animals make their homes here.

Nickerson is regarded as the best camping spot on the Cape. Consider yourself fortunate to get one of the 420 capacious sites—they are let on a first-come, first-served basis, and the park is packed to capacity throughout the summer. The park is located inland, only minutes from the ocean and Cape Cod National Seashore.

Monomoy National Wildlife Refuge

Accessible only by private or chartered boat, Monomoy is made up of two islands due south of Chatham, at the Cape's elbow. Foot trails and birding. Headquarters: Morris Island, MA 02633 (tel. 508/945-0594).

Take a guided trip with Wellfleet Bay Wildlife Sanctuary or The Cape Cod Museum of Natural History to Monomoy and you're in for a special bird-watching treat. Sandpipers, terns, and black-bellied plovers are just some of the more than 250 species reportedly seen on the undeveloped shores of North and South Monomoy Island. Just as exciting is the school of harbor seals that play offshore (see the "Bird Watching" section.

Cape Cod Rail Trail

Runs through the middle of the Cape from South Dennis to South Wellfleet. You can begin and end your ride at numerous access points.

This former railroad bed is now one of New England's longest bike paths. Off-limits to motorized vehicles, the 25-mile trail passes four ponds, Nickerson State Park, and cranberry bogs along the way.

MARTHA'S VINEYARD

Martha's Vineyard State Forest

From Vineyard Haven, take Edgartown Road south and go right at the blinking light. This is Airport Road. The park headquarters are located on the left-hand side.

The premier spot on the Vineyard for mountain biking, this 4,000-acre forest is smack dab in the center of the island. The forest is a great retreat to escape the summer crowds.

Gay Head Cliffs

The southwestern-most point on the Vineyard.

The most famous natural landmark on Martha's Vineyard, the mile-long expanse of the Gay Head Cliffs provides a melange of brilliant colors comparable to a Monet painting. For the best views, walk on the narrow strip of sand between the cliffs and the ocean.

Chappaquiddick Island

A one-minute ferry ride from Edgartown. Foot and bike trails, fishing, and birding.

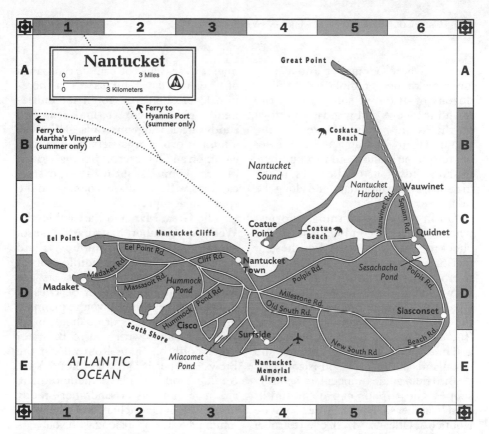

Nantucket

Best known for Ted Kennedy's mishap, "Chappy" is also home to the Cape Poge Wildlife Refuge, Wasque Reservation, and Mytoi. Cape Poge's six miles of barrier beach lead south to Wasque Reservation. Both regions are known for their bird watching and fishing. Oystercatchers, black-crowned night-herons, and least terns have been observed nesting here. Mytoi is a 14-acre Japanese garden that lies just inland from the beach. The Trustees of Reservation run all three sites, 572 Essex St., Beverly, MA 01915 (tel. 508/921-1944).

NANTUCKET

Sanford Farm, Ram Pasture, and The Woods

From Nantucket Town, take Madaket Road 2 miles west.

Purchased by the Nantucket Conservation Foundation in 1971 and later extended in the mid-1980s, this is Nantucket's premier walking destination. Sanford Farm was the site of Nantucket's original colonial settlement, while Ram Pasture and The Woods were used as pasture. Moors, freshwater ponds, and ocean beaches are found on the property.

What to Do & Where to Do It

BIRD WATCHING

Cape Cod, Martha's Vineyard, and Nantucket offer some of the best birding on the East Coast, certainly as good as any area covered in this book. They are important rest stops for migratory birds traveling the Atlantic Flyway, and more than 300 species of birds have been recorded here. Compact and varied lands make for incredibly rich birding: dozens of different songbirds in the inland meadows and woods; waterfowl on the kettle ponds—gouged by the hundreds into the Cape, and to a lesser degree on the islands; and vast numbers of shorebirds along the beaches, in the marshes, on the mud flats, and along the tidal creeks.

Go in the early morning, and just when the tide's coming in if you're checking out tidal flats, beaches, or marshes. In winter, look for seabirds on the beaches and in the harbors, and snowy owls in the dunes. Wear a hat and a pair of shoes that can get wet (which they will!), and long pants and bug dope (there's a profusion of both poison ivy and mosquitoes in the marshy areas and woodlands of the Cape and islands).

Bird field guides, binoculars, spotting scopes and tripods can be found at **Bird Watcher's General Store,** 36 State Route 6A, Orleans, MA 02653 (tel. 508/255-6974).

CAPE COD

On the Cape, the diverse range of land birds includes **orioles, catbirds, grackles, red-winged blackbirds, yellow-rumped warblers, downy woodpeckers** and **flickers, cardinals, scarlet tanagers, saw-whet, short-eared,** and **great horned owls, sharp-skinned** and **red-tailed hawks, kingbirds,** and **kingfishers,** just for starters. The **Beech Forest Trail** at the Province Lands center of the Cape Cod National Seashore is one great spot, **Nickerson State Park** in Brewster is another. Really, the woods around any of the kettle ponds in the lower and mid-Cape are apt to offer exceptional birding.

Many people, myself included, have a particular fascination with shorebirds and waterfowl—for one thing, there are many species, such as terns, that congregate in giant rookeries, and during migratory seasons you can see thousands of birds in a day. The Cape is a shorebird-lover's bonanza. You'll see **buffleheads, eiders, scoters, mallards** and **ruddy ducks, widgeons, rails, gallinules,** a **loon** or two, **mergansers, cormorants, common** and **least terns, herons, egrets, plover, skimmers, shearwaters, oystercatchers, willets, gulls,** of course, and the spectacular **osprey.**

The **Great Marsh** in Barnstable, the **Wellfleet Audubon Sanctuary, Nauset Marsh,** and **North Monomoy Island** (listed below) are all incredible spots to see water- and shorebirds, as are **Marconi** and **Nauset Light Beaches** on the national seashore. If you're planning to clam for steamers or quahogs, bring your binoculars with you to **Brewster Flats,** north off State Route 6A at the Brewster General Store, when the tide's just coming in off low tide. Sometimes there are huge numbers of sandpipers, ruddy turnstones, oystercatchers, and other birds mining the area right along with you.

Monomoy National Wildlife Refuge

Accessible only by charter or private boat. Headquarters: Morris Island, MA 02633 (tel. 508/945-0594). Access contacts: The Wellfleet Bay Wildlife Sanctuary, P.O. Box 236, 291 State Highway U.S. 6, South Wellfleet, MA 02663 (tel. 508/349-2615); Cape Cod Museum of Natural History, P.O. Box 1710, State Route 6A, Brewster, MA 02631 (tel. 508/896-3867). Tours through both cost $30.

Both the Cape Cod Museum of Natural History and the Wellfleet chapter of the Massachusetts Audubon Society offer trips to North Monomoy Island in the summer. This three-hour guided tour is highly recommended for anyone with an appreciation of nature, not just the avid bird-watcher. I was fortunate enough to venture to the island with Rich Blake of the Audubon Society. A recent graduate of Brown University, Rich had spent the last two summers giving tours of the island, and thus has a thorough knowledge of all its inhabitants. He also had a boyish fascination with Monomoy which rubbed off on us. Take, for example, the small little bug that jumps on the sand, known as the beach hopper. Rich couldn't wait to pick up one of these minuscule creatures to show us that the bug's eyes were cross-eyed. Only a naturalist with a feverish curiosity could detect the facial features of a beach hopper.

The seven-minute boat ride from Chatham dropped us off on the shores of the island. Back in 1959, Monomoy was still part of the Cape, but a tumultuous storm and the constant battering of the waves severed this barrier beach from the mainland. Years later, more inclement weather split the island in two. We disembarked and slowly made our way around the island. Herring gulls occupy most of the island's interior, but fortunately they made room for other species like the American oystercatcher. This bird's orange beak makes him look like he has a carrot sticking out of his mouth. We also spotted several species of the sandpiper (Rich has seen 12 different types of sandpiper in late August, the best time for viewing Monomoy's migrating birds) and the black-bellied plover. Then there were the swift willets, a V-shaped flock of black cormorants, and the graceful northern harrier or marsh hawks, who seem to fly on autocruise. One of the most exciting viewings was not on land, but sea. Fifteen to twenty harbor seals were playing with two kayakers who were circumnavigating the island. The animals' playful heads bobbed up and down like lobster buoys.

MARTHA'S VINEYARD

Good inland places for birding on the Vineyard include **Cedar Trees Neck**

Sanctuary, facing Vineyard Sound in North Tisbury off Indian Hill Road, and **Long Point Refuge** off West Tisbury Road.

The Vineyard's marshes and sandy headlands are prime habitats for the endangered piping plover as well as trumpeter swans, red-tailed hawks, sandpipers, and even bald eagles. The **Wasque Reservation** and **Cape Pogue** on Chappaquiddick are excellent spots. Look for terns nesting on the Vineyard's Atlantic beaches (and watch out for their dive-bomber attacks!).

NANTUCKET

Piping plovers can also be found at **Great Point** on Nantucket amongst numerous least and common terns, marsh hawks, and American oystercatchers. **Sanford Farm** is a good place to spot ospreys and red-tailed hawks. And **Madaket**'s harbor and beaches and **Siasconet**'s cranberry bogs, meadows, and beaches are also birding hot spots.

BOARDSAILING

The same prevailing winds and protected coves that are good for sailing are excellent for boardsailing. The strongest and most consistent winds are at **Kalmus Beach** in Hyannis. Unfortunately, every boardsailer on the Cape knows this, so the waters are usually covered with sails. Try the cove at the end of **Forest Beach Road** off State Route 2, in Chatham, or the **public beach** on Pleasant Bay on State Route 28 if the crowds get to you. Phil Clark, owner of Nauset Sports, is an avid windsurfer. He rents sailboards, gives instruction, and tends to give away his secret spots when coaxed. **Nauset Sports**, State Route 6A, Orleans (tel. 508/255-4742).

Boardsailers sail to Pocomo Heads on Nantucket. Rentals and instruction are available from **Force 5** on Jetties Beach (tel. 508/228-0700). Rentals and lessons are available from **Wind's Up on the Vineyard,** 95 Beach Road, Vineyard Haven (tel. 508/693-4252). You can sail behind the shop on Lagoon Pond or try the long stretch of beach between Oak Bluffs and Edgartown.

CANOEING & KAYAKING

The 300-plus kettle ponds found on the Cape and Islands are entirely dependent on groundwater and precipitation. There are no rivers or streams feeding these ponds. These ponds and the tributaries that run to the harbors are ideal flatwater canoeing and kayaking locales. If you want to rent canoes, check out **Cape Cod Waterways** in Dennisport (tel. 508/398-0080). They're located on the shores of **Swan Pond**. Another local favorite is **Flax Pond** in Nickerson State Park. Call **Jack's Boat Rentals** at Nickerson State Park (tel. 508/ 896-8556). **Goose Hummock** rents canoes in Orleans, State Route 6A (tel. 508/255-2620).

If you own your own canoe or kayak, **Barnstable Harbor** is a fun place to spend several hours gliding through the **Great Marsh**. This is especially true on Wednesdays or weekends, when clammers are digging for their weekly bucket of steamers or raking for littlenecks. The harbor is a long inlet located on the southern shores of Sandy Neck Beach. The best time to paddle is high tide, before the water level drops dramatically. From Yarmouth, take State Route 6A West past Barnstable. Take a right on Scudder Lane. There's parking at the end of the road.

The Vineyard's abundance of ponds, lagoons, and coastline are ideal for flatwater kayaking or canoeing. Most noted are **Edgartown Great Pond, Lake Tashmoo, Pocha Pond** in Chappaquiddick, **Squibnocket Pond** in Gay Head, and this trip:

Tisbury Great Pond

Access: From West Tisbury, take West Tisbury Road toward Edgartown. Turn right at Tiah's Cove Road and make another right on Clam Point Road. The parking is located on the right-hand side. Maps: Contact the Vineyard Land Bank Commission. It is part of the Sepiessa Point Reservation on the land bank maps.

On a breezy Sunday in late spring, I went kayaking with a passionate local paddler named Ed Pierce, his five-year-old Portuguese waterdog, Zach, and my brother, Jim. Ed had a special kayak designed so that 50-pound Zach can sit in the back. Like his owner, Zach was alert and attentive during the trip. They took us to their favorite spot, Tiah's Cove, one of the fingers that form inlets to Tisbury Great Pond. The cove is part of the Vineyard's land bank—conserved lands that were bought by the island after a 2 percent "land bank" tax was added to all real estate transactions in 1986. The rest of America should take heed of this law, which has already preserved thousands of acres of environmentally sensitive habitat.

The put-in was located at the northeastern part of the cove near a small parking lot. There was a strong southerly wind that day, but we managed to paddle the whole length of the cove into Great Pond before we turned back and faced the elements. On a clear day, you can paddle to Quansoo and continue on to Black Point Pond. Bring your shucking knife, because the pond is known for its delicious oysters. Simply reach down to pick up one of the shells on the pond floor, open it up, and you'll have one of the most succulent oysters on the half shell you've ever tasted. On the way back, we tried to avoid the wind by staying close to the shore. We saw several sandpipers on the beach, an osprey hovering above, and a large trumpeter swan. Zach was quite content.

Kayaks and canoes can be rented at **Wind's Up,** 95 Beach Road, Vineyard Haven (tel. 508/693-4252). The **Trustees of Reservation** are offering natural history canoe tours on Pocha Pond and Cape Pogue. The tours last two hours and cost $30 ($27 for members); tel. 508/627-3599.

CROSS-COUNTRY SKIING

When the Cape gets snow, which is about as common as a Republican mayor in Boston, the locals ski **Nickerson State Park**'s Middle Trail. The ponds in the park are also popular for ice skating and ice fishing, but I'm not so sure I'd go skating on a pond where fishermen are hovering near large holes in the ice.

FISHING

Cape Cod and the Islands are to blues and stripers what Montana is to trout—a fishing frenzy. Between late July and October, the **bluefish** are abundant, striking hard and fighting tirelessly. Every time you throw your line out, you'll get a bite from these insatiable eaters. **Striped bass** are a bit more elusive, but still very catchable. Locals start hooking "keepers" in late May and continue throughout the summer. The best surfcasting is on the **Outer Cape,** from Nauset to Race Point. Favorite beaches include **Coast Guard Beach** in Eastham and **Race Point Beach** in P-town. The fish will move farther north as the summer wears on. In July and August, crowds of suntanners scare off the fish, thus the night or early morning hours are the best time to be out there. For bait, use poppers during the day and sand eels at night for the blues; use sand eels

Creature of Habit

President Clinton's trips to Martha's Vineyard in the summers of 1993 and 1994 spawned a slew of stories. In one instance, the president's staff set up a meeting with an 87-year-old fisherman to get photographs of the president with some local color. The staff set up a time of 9:30 AM, but mentioned that the president might be late for he had lots of other appointments that morning.

"Well, I always meet my friend for donuts at 9:45," said Mr. Fisherman.

"We understand that, but the president is a very busy man," reiterated a staff person. The fisherman agreed.

The day of the photo shoot, the president was running late. He arrived at the fisherman's house a little past 10, but the man was nowhere to be found. One member of the staff eventually found him eating donuts with his friend.

during the day and live eels at night for stripers. All the Cape's bait and tackle shops sell them.

In **Nantucket,** surfcast off **Great Point** or **Sankaty Head.** Paul Doyle is an excellent guide and instructor for surfcasting and fly-fishing. He can be reached at P.O. Box 2331, Nantucket, MA 02584 (tel. 508/228-7660).

As for the **Vineyard,** wherever there's water is conceivably a good place to cast. However, some of the highly recommended spots are the rip off of **Wasque Point** in Chappaquidick, **Town Beach** in Gay Head, and the beach south of the Edgartown Great Pond.

I promised Cooper Gilkes not to reveal the spot on the Vineyard he showed us after my brother Jim and I both caught a fish for the first time in a decade. Coop's a third-generation islander who has the patience and skill to deal with two blundering fools. My brother and I had our lines tangled together several times before Coop showed us how to cast straight and reel the line in. He bet us a dollar that we would each catch a striper and I was getting ready to collect. Suddenly, I looked to my right and Jim's pole was arched with the line pulled tight. "I think I got something!" he said, more shocked than I was. Coop ran over to give Jim more of his much-needed advice, and several minutes later my brother reeled in a 15-pound striper. I hooked a small striper just before we left. The feel of pulling that fish in was well worth the two bucks I owed Coop. Coop's guided trips last four to five hours and he offers fly fishing and deep-sea fishing as well as surfcasting. **Coop's Bait and Tackle,** 147 West Tisbury Road, near Edgartown (tel. 508/627-3909).

There's **elephant tuna, blue tuna,** and **bonita** to be had when you venture offshore, but most likely you'll catch **scup, tautog, fluke, sea bass** and other bottom fish. On the **Cape,** *Hy-line* and the 65-foot *Navigator* both operate out of Hyannis' Ocean Street Docks. Call 508/790-0696 for *Hy-line,* 508/771-9500 for the *Navigator.* The *Bluefin* operates out of East Dennis (tel. 508/697-2093). In Harwichport, the *Pauly V* comes highly recommended; call Saquatucket Harbor (tel. 508/430-0053).

In **Nantucket,** try the *Albacore,* located on Slip 17, Straight Wharf (tel. 508/228-5074) and **Just Do It Too,** Slip 13, Straight Wharf (tel. 508/228-7448).

Besides Coop, **North Shore Charters** (tel. 508/645-2993) operates out of Menemsha on the **Vineyard.**

GOLF

There are more than 45 golf courses on the **Cape** and approximately 20 are open to the public. Arguably, the best public course is the **Ocean Edge Resort** course in Brewster. The par-four second hole is a 425-yard, uphill approach to a small green. Beware of the grass-lined pot bunkers protecting the green, which have steep sides and treacherous lies. Ron Hallett, pro at Ocean Edge, gave me a short list of his favorite courses to play on the Cape: **Cape Cod Country Club,** State Route 151, North Falmouth, MA 02556 (tel. 508/563-9842); the fairly new **Olde Barnstable Fairgrounds Golf Course,** 1460 Route 149, Marston Mills, MA 02648 (tel. 508/420-1142); and one of the oldest on the Cape, the **Cranberry Valley Golf Course,** 183 Oak Street, Harwich, MA 02645 (tel. 508/430-7560). Close to the Ocean Edge and designed by the same person is the **Captains Golf Course,** 1000 Freeman's Way, Brewster, MA 02631 (tel. 508/896-5100). Finally, there's the nine-hole **Highland Links Golf Club,** Highland Road, North Truro, MA 02652 (tel. 508/487-9201).

On the **Vineyard, Farm Neck Golf Club** (tel. 508/693-3057) in Oak Bluffs is highly regarded.

HIKING

Great Island Trail, Wellfleet

Allow 3–4 hours. Moderate. Access: From U.S. 6, head into Wellfleet Center, taking a left on East Commercial Street and a right at the marina onto Chequessett Neck Road. There will be a sign for Great Island several miles down the road on the left-hand side. Map: Available from Cape Cod National Seashore Headquarters, South Wellfleet, MA 02663 (tel. 508/349-3785).

The Cape Cod National Seashore's longest trail, the 7-mile (round trip) Great Island Trail is worthy of being designated a hike, not a walk. This three-hour plus trail through marsh, woods, and soft sand is a strenuous thigh-burner. The trail follows the circumference of Great Island, a former whaling port and now one of the most secluded areas in Cape Cod. For the serious walker who yearns to get away from the summer crowds, this path should not be missed. Simply bring several bottles of water, a hat, sunscreen, and perhaps, a picnic lunch, and you're on your way.

Stroll down the short hill from the parking lot and take a right, continuing around the marsh the entire distance. This small strip of sand is called The Gut—the other side being Great Island. At the fork, take a left toward Smith Tavern. Just prior to reaching the easternmost tip of the island, where people often fish for stripers and blues, you'll see another sign directing you over the dunes through the woods. The trail winds through the pine forest to the site of an original whaling tavern. However, you'll have to use your imagination, since there is only a small plaque now. Just picture ole' Pegleg banging his way to the bar, smelling god-awful from bathing in baleen and whale oil. "Give me another whiskey," he says to the bartender, just itching to get back to sea to find himself another Moby Dick. If this image doesn't work, look for red fox (not the actor). When I was here last, I saw this golden sheen of fur whisk by me with something in his mouth—most likely a jackrabbit.

The Tavern trail catches up with the main trail, where you take a left. Continue out of the woods to a marsh where sand dunes tower on your right and Wellfleet Harbor can be seen to your left. This soft, sandy path leads up to Great Beach Hill. Five minutes later, you'll reach another marsh and a sand spit known as Jeremy Flats. At low tide, you can walk out to the tip, but I'd save your energy. You have a 2.2-mile walk down the beach of Cape Cod Bay to reach The Gut. I have rarely seen another person on this desolate strip of sand, just large scallop shells and tiny fiddler crabs—funny-looking critters who have one oversized claw bigger than their entire body. (Only the males have the monster claw, which they wave before the females during mating season and brandish threateningly against rival males invading their territory. I see now that bodybuilding must be an instinctual urge.) If you start to feel like Lawrence of Arabia lost in the desert, look out at 10 o'clock and you'll see Provincetown's Pilgrim Monument—a symbol of civilization. Thankfully, you won't have to walk that far. Just take a right at the first staircase over the dunes and take a left back to the parking lot. Don't forget to stretch.

HORSEBACK RIDING

Nelson's Riding Stable, 43 Race Point Road, Provincetown, MA 02657 (tel. 508/487-1112) offers two-hour guided rides on the National Seashore's sand dunes and forest.

MOUNTAIN BIKING

In addition to the three rides below on the Cape, **Nickerson State Park,** off State Route 6A between Brewster and Orleans, has dirt roads and forest paths that make for fun, if easy, mountain biking. Look out for the sand traps, though.

Trail of Tears, Barnstable

Allow 1–2 hours. Overly strenuous; steep hills. Access: Take U.S. 6 to Exit 5. Take Route 149 South for a few seconds before you take a quick right on the Service Road. Parking is located on the left under the huge power lines.

So you think Cape Cod is flat, without benefit of any good hills to rock your mountain bike. Hah! You have yet to try the aptly named Trail of Tears. Located on Barnstable Conservation Lands, this hellish trail was devised by motorcross motorcyclists before they were booted off the grounds. But the trail remains to test the skills of so-called expert mountain bikers. Go for it!

Start riding under the power lines and then take your second left. Within moments, you're huffing and puffing up a steep hill, before cruising down single-tracks with very little leeway to maneuver. You're looking at another hill as soon as you touch bottom, and before you know it, you're coasting down again. The cycle is unrelenting—up, down, up, down, until you make it out of this area 30 to 45 minutes later, sweating like a sprinkler system.

If your legs feel like Jell-O, take a right on the double-track path and head back to the parking lot. If you still want more, take a left and cross under the power lines twice before ending up where you started from. If you get lost, simply follow the power lines back to the parking lot or ask any of the other masochists for directions.

Mashpee River Woodlands

Allow 1 hour. Easy to moderate; rolling hills. Access: From Falmouth, take State Route 28 towards Hyannis; 1.5 miles after the rotary, take a sharp right onto Quinaquisset Avenue. Pass the sign on the right for the Mashpee River Woodlands/North Parking Lot and continue until you reach Mashpee Neck Road. Turn right and look for a small parking lot and another Mashpee River Woodlands sign.

The single-track trail through the Mashpee River Woodlands is a good hour-long ride for any mountain biker, regardless of skill level. The path loops along the Chickadee Trail before joining the main trail that borders the Mashpee River. Only the occasional fallen branch breaks up the flow of this rolling forest. Don't veer left on the main trail unless you want to stop at several overlooks. At the northern end, the trail loops around the Partridge Trail, before meeting up with the main trail for the return-trip back to the parking lot. This five-mile route is a great workout to start or end your day.

Punkhorn Parklands, Brewster

Allow 1–2 hours. Easy to moderate; low hills. Access: From Brewster, follow State Route 6A East towards Dennis. Take a left at Stony Brook Road (a blinking light) and another left onto Run Hill Road. The sign and makeshift parking lot are located on the left-hand side of the road.

The maze of hiking trails that weave in and out of the 1,000-acre Punkhorn Parklands are challenging trails for bikers as well. Go early or late in the day, though, to avoid flattening hikers or being flattened by horseback riders. The Punkhorns were once sheep-grazing land and an active cranberry-producing area, before the town of Brewster purchased the land and turned it over to the public.

From the so-called parking lot, I followed the double-track main trail into the woods, making a right turn at the blue hiking sign. This trail rolls down into a bowl of mixed hardwoods and then curves back uphill to the main double-track. To the left of the main trail are single-tracks that lead down to a small pond. I cruised down to the water and around the pond, ending up under the power lines, which led me back to my car. Take any trail you want and have fun, because it's almost impossible to get lost in this small thicket of trees.

Martha's Vineyard State Forest

Time: Up to you. Easy; relatively flat terrain. Access: From Vineyard Haven, take Edgartown Road south and go right at the blinking light. This is Airport Road. The park headquarters are located on the left-hand side.

The most exciting part of mountain biking is creating your own trail. There's an incredible degree of freedom in any sport in which you can get lost in the woods and then find your way back. Thus, there's a certain challenge in writing about mountain biking. I could describe in detail the route I took, but then you would stop every five minutes to follow my directions and get lost the same way I did. That's no fun. Find your own trail and keep the spontaneity in the sport. This is especially true of a place like Martha's Vineyard State Park (also called Manuel F. Correlius State Park), 4,000-plus acres of pines, oaks, and low-lying scrub which are criss-crossed by miles of fire roads, double-track, and single-track trails. The fire roads follow a strict north-south and east-west pattern, so it's relatively easy to find your way back to the parking lot. I stayed on the eastern part of the park, following deer tracks on the sandy roads. Except for several small hills at the northeastern corner, the ride is relatively flat, but watch out for heavy sand drifts that will cause you to fishtail. From the parking lot, you can ride across Airport Road to play in the western part of the forest. You can ride for as long and as hard as you like. Just don't try to explain your route to anybody else.

The **Vineyard Off-Road Biking Association** meets every Sunday at 9:00 A.M. at W. Tisbury's old Agricultural Hall. The three or four hour ride, open to the public, cruises on Land Bank and Ancient Way trails that only locals could know about. Call David Whitmon at 508/693-4905 to check it out. There's also a women's off-road ride starting at 5 PM every Wednesday. Meet at **Cycle Works,** 105 State Road, Vineyard Haven, or call Lisa Rogers for more information (tel. 508/693-1148).

Note: You need to bring your own mountain bike over from the Cape. I didn't find any bike rental places that would let you go off-road riding with their bikes.

POWERBOATING

Flyer's in Provincetown rent 16-foot skiffs built by the original owner, Boston Whalers, speedboats designed for water skiing, and a 24-foot party boat; 131A, Commercial Street, tel. 508/487-0898.

Motorboats can be rented in Nantucket at **Nantucket Boat Rental,** Slip 1, Boat Basin at the end of Main Street (tel. 508/325-1001).

ROAD BIKING

The Cape Cod Rail Trail is one of the most popular bike paths in New England. However, it's the islands that I love to cruise upon. Biking is the best way to see Nantucket and the Vineyard. You can explore the less-traveled side roads before resting on a stretch of sand only the natives know about.

CAPE COD

Idle Times Bike Shop, U.S. 6, North Eastham (tel. 508/255-8281); **Rail Trail Bike Rentals,** 302 Underpass Road, Brewster, (tel. 508/896-8200); and the **Goose Hummock Shop,** State Route 6A

(508/255-2620), are three of the many bike rental shops that line the Rail Trail.

Here are a few places to rent bikes in Provincetown: **The Cycle Shop,** 306 Commercial St. (tel. 508-487-6628); **Galeforce Bike Rentals,** 144 Bradford St. Ext. (tel. 508/487-4849); and **P'town Bikes,** 42 Bradford St. (tel. 508/487-8735).

Province Lands, Provincetown

Allow 1 hour; ideal during sunset. Moderate; hilly terrain. Access: Take U.S. 6 North to the end. Look for signs for Herring Cove Beach. Park at the end of the lot.

If I lived in Provincetown, my daily workout would be a ride on the Province Lands Bike Path. Only 8 miles long, the trail is anything but flat. Rollercoaster hills dip in and out of sand dunes, weaving through scrub-pine forests and beaches; it is one of the most unique bike paths I've ever been on. Park at the back of Herring Cove Beach and start pedaling. At the fork, take a left and head around Great Pond to Beech Forest (Cape Codders and the Islanders tend to use the word *Great* far too often in naming locations; what's wrong with other superlatives, like spectacular, superb, or, in keeping with New England understatement, "Fine Pond"?). The 1-mile Beech Forest trail is a worthwhile walk. Lock up your bikes and stroll among the beeches and birds around a small pond. The best part of the bike trail awaits you. Before you sweep downhill to the Province Lands visitors center, stop and look at the mounds of sand as they fade into the ocean. Continue on to Race Point Beach, which is the only spot in New England where you can watch the sun set over the Atlantic. The path continues around the loop and catches up with the main trail on the way back to Herring Cove Beach.

Cape Cod Rail Trail

50 miles round-trip. Allow 3–6 hours. Easy, but long; flat. Access: Take U.S. 6 North to South Wellfleet. Turn right on Lecount Hollow Road. The trail begins behind the general store. In South Dennis, take U.S. 6 to State Route 134 South until you see signs for the trail and parking lot. There are also numerous places to start along the trail.

The 25-mile Cape Cod Rail Trail is one of New England's longest and most popular bike paths. Once a bed of the Penn Central Railroad, the trail is relatively flat and straight. On weekends in summer months, you have to contend with dogs, clumsy rollerbladers, young families, and bikers who whip by you on their way to becoming the next Greg Lemond. Yet, if you want to venture away from the coast and see some of the Cape's countryside without having to deal with motorized traffic, this is one of the only ways to do it.

The trail starts in South Wellfleet on Lecount Hollow Road or in South Dennis on State Route 134, depending on which way you want to ride. Beginning in South Wellfleet, the path cruises by purple wildflowers, flowering dogwood, and small maples, where red-winged blackbirds and goldfinches nest. In Orleans, you have to ride on Rock Harbor and West Roads until the City Council decides to complete the trail. At least, you get a good view of the boats lining Rock Harbor. Clearly marked signs lead back to the Rail Trail, on which you'll soon enter Nickerson State Park. Here, you can give your legs a rest and go canoeing on Flax Pond, veer off onto 8 miles of old Nickerson State Park bike trails, or continue straight through Brewster to a series of swimming holes—Seymour, Long, and Hinckleys Ponds. A favorite picnic spot is the Pleasant Lake General Store in Harwich. Shortly afterwards, you cross over U.S.

6 on State Route 124 before veering right through farmland, soon ending in South Dennis.

THE ISLANDS

You can rent bikes on Martha's Vineyard in Vineyard Haven right off the ferry. One of the better places is **Martha's,** 4 Lagoon Pond Road (tel. 508/ 693-6593). In Nantucket, rentals are available from **Young's Bicycle Shop** (tel. 508/228-1151), just off the ferry on Steamboat Wharf.

East Island Route, Martha's Vineyard

Allow 3–5 hours. Easy to moderate; very low hills. Start from ferry dock in Vineyard Haven.

Martha's Vineyard's short hills, limited car traffic, and bike trails attract a growing number of bikers each year. If you only have a short amount of time but want to test your legs, try the East Island Route. This 20-mile ride is a great workout, yet far less challenging than the ride to Gay Head. The route takes you through the historic towns of Oak Bluffs and Edgartown before reaching the nature preserves of Chappaquiddick Island.

Once you disembark the ferry at Vineyard Haven, go left onto Beach Road and head toward Oak Bluffs. A mile into the journey, take a left at the sign for East Chop and follow the road past the million-dollar homes and the picture-perfect East Chop lighthouse, and then cruise down to Oak Bluffs. Pedal through town to the coastline and turn right. You'll soon approach a bike path that winds through Joseph Sylvia State Beach. Bike traffic here can be heavy in the summer months and the sea breeze can be fierce, so be aware.

Eventually you'll reach Edgartown, which is a fine place to stop for lunch and wander around. The charming one-

minute ferry ride to Chappy leaves from the edge of town. Continue on Chappaquiddick Road for 2.7 miles and you'll reach a dirt trail called Dyke Road. The road passes a Japanese-style garden called Mytoi, which is worth a stop. Azaleas, daffodils, dogwoods, and rhododendrons line the fresh-water creeks in this 3-acre garden. The dirt road continues over the bridge that Ted Kennedy made infamous, before stopping at East Beach. Lock up your bikes and walk over the dunes to see one of the most pristine stretches of beach on the Atlantic coastline. Part of the Cape Poge Wildlife Refuge, this barrier beach is perhaps the best place to birdwatch on the Vineyard. Ospreys, oystercatchers, piping plovers, terns, and the occasional bald eagle nest, feed, and rest here.

Return to Edgartown on the same road and short ferry ride. You'll pass through town again before veering left on the Vineyard Haven–Edgartown Road. This bike path is less scenic than the Oak Bluffs beach path, yet far more direct. There's a short hill on the way into Vineyard Haven just in case you've felt this loop was an underachievement.

Gay Head Ride, Martha's Vineyard

Allow 3–5 hours. Moderate to strenuous; hilly terrain. Start from ferry dock in Vineyard Haven.

The ride from Vineyard Haven to Gay Head Cliffs is not for casual bikers. It's for biking aficionados who want the challenge of a hilly ride close to 40 miles long.

Pedal up South Main Street and continue on the equally crowded State Street. Take a left onto Old County Road for one of the most pleasant rides in the Vineyard. Farms line the right side of the road while the State Forest sits on the left. Take a right onto Edgartown Road, past the tranquil town of West

Tisbury, before making another right onto Music Street. Your first left will be Middle Road, a rolling road with little traffic that passes through farmlands and green pastures. Eventually, you'll end up in the small town of Chilmark, where we stopped at the community center to check out a flea market and came upon the best chowder I've ever tasted— meaty chunks of clams, and chockfull of potatoes in a light cream broth. I've learned a valuable lesson traveling through New England—to always check the local papers for flea markets and fairs. You never know what you might find. Whether it's the most authentic chowder you've ever tried, grandma's toffee brownies, or a priceless antique, these local get-togethers are always worthy of a stopover.

Continue on South Road, stopping at the lookout over Menemsha Pond and the fishing village of the same name. Shift to low gears up the hill and then turn left at the Moshup Trail, which will take you all the way to Gay Head Cliffs. You can walk up the hill to the lighthouse for a spectacular vista of the rainbow-colored clay, or head down to the beach for a refreshing swim and hike (see "Walks & Rambles" section, below).

To return to Vineyard Haven, take a left onto Lighthouse Road and another left onto West Basin Road. Here, wait for Hughie Taylor and his boat to pick you up and bring you on a one-minute voyage to Menemsha. The price is $2. (*Note:* This is only possible during the peak summer months. If you are biking at any other time, you will have to backtrack to Chilmark and go left on Menemsha Cross Road to get to this pristine village.) If you're still hungry, stop in Menemsha at Poole's or Larsens' fish markets for incredibly fresh steamers, oysters on the half shell, or fish cakes. The route continues on North Road, which connects with State Road and leads you back to the starting point. For those of you whose legs are not yet weary, take a left at Lambert's Cove Road, off of State Road. This scenic trail loops around several ponds before returning to State Road.

Nantucket

Allow 3 hours. Easy to moderate; relatively flat terrain. Start ride at Steamboat Wharf in Nantucket town.

Nantucket's fairly flat terrain is ideal for road biking. Indeed, traveling on two wheels is the best way to get around and see the island's well-known cranberry bogs, moors, and beaches. Two bike paths lead to the eastern and western points on the island. I prefer the longer loop (23 miles) which goes past the cranberry bogs and moors to the charming town of 'Sconset.

From Steamboat Wharf in Nantucket town, turn left on S. Water Street and right on Main Street. You'll have to walk your bike here since the roads are old cobblestone. A left onto Orange Street will bring you to a rotary. Take another left around the circle onto the Milestone Road bike path. This 6-mile trail is a straight line through the heart and heath of the island to the town of 'Sconset. Quaint rose-trellised cottages with names like "The Snuggery" and "Very Snug" line the small streets. These former fishing shacks (with low ceilings that look snug) are still used as summer homes by residents who live year-round in Nantucket town. After the bike path ends, the road continues to a rotary, where you can take a right onto Ocean Beach for views of the Atlantic or lock up your bikes and head down to the beach. The route continues on Broadway to Sankaty Avenue. A left at the next main intersection and a right on Wauwinet Road will bring you to my favorite village on the island, Wauwinet. I usually splurge for lunch at the **Wauwinet Inn** ($20 to $25 per person, but I figure it's my reward for getting here). The innovative cuisine and the intimate setting overlooking the manicured lawns and harbor make it hard to get back on the bike. But now you'll have the energy to head back down Wauwinet Road and take a right onto Polpis; 4 ½ miles later, take a right onto Milestone Road and another right at the rotary to Orange Street. This will bring you back to the cobblestone streets of Nantucket town.

OUTFITTERS

Vermont Bicycle Touring, P.O. Box 711, Bristol, VT 05433 (tel. 800/245-3868) and **Backroads,** 1516 Fifth Street, Berkeley, CA 94710-1740 (tel. 800/GO-ACTIVE), offer five-day guided bike trips to Martha's Vineyard and Nantucket.

SAILING

Numerous coves and protected harbors, a strong southwesterly wind blowing 15 to 20 knots almost every afternoon, and the Elizabeth Islands are the reasons why Cape sailing is considered some of the finest on the East coast. The waters are inundated with yachts, Hobie cats, Sunfish, schooners—even the 6' 2"-long dinghy known as the *Cape Cod Frosty.*

The **Elizabeth Islands** are a string of islands that begin off Woods Hole and run to the south. The only ones that are public are Cuttyhunk, the outermost island, and Penikese, a former leper colony that is now a state-owned bird refuge and site of a school for troubled boys (maybe Hollywood will someday make a movie entitled *The Birdboy of Penikese*). The two most popular anchorages, however, are **Hadley Harbor** and **Tarpaulin Cove** on the north and south sides of **Naushon Island.** Tarpaulin is a half-mile long cove with small oak trees lining the beach. The owners of the

island, the Forbes family, allow sailors on the beach, but not inland.

Other favorite sailing destinations include **Monomoy Island** at the Cape's elbow and **Buzzard's Bay** near the Cape Cod Canal.

Flyer's in P-town rents a 27-foot Irwin, a 67-year-old 20-foot wooden sloop, 19-foot Rhodes, 19-foot lightnings, lasers, javelins, Sunfish, and Hobies (131A Commercial Street, tel. 508/487-0898).

On the **Vineyard**, **Spindrift Charters** rents 40- to 72-foot crewed sailboats by the day or week (Vineyard Haven, tel. 508/693-4658). **Wind's Up** rents Sunfish and catamarans at 95 Beach Road, Vineyard Haven (tel. 508/693-4252).

Nantucket Harbor Sail offers 19-foot Rhodes for the half-day or day ($85–170) at Swains Wharf, Nantucket (tel. 508/228-0424). **Force 5 Watersports** rents Sunfish from Jetties Beach (tel. 508/228-0700).

SCUBA DIVING

Cape Cod Divers takes people wreck diving near Monomoy and Provincetown. A two-tank dive costs $59. Contact them at State Route 28, Harwich (tel. 508/432-9035).

In Nantucket, divers meet in front of **Sunken Ship** every Sunday morning at 8 AM to scuba dive off Jetties Beach; $25 with equipment, $50 without. Contact them at 12 Broad Street, Nantucket (tel. 508/228-9226).

SEA KAYAKING

As on the rest of the Atlantic coast, sea kayaking is also growing in popularity on the Cape and Islands. Sea kayak rentals and instruction are available at **Wind's Up on the Vineyard,** 95 Beach Road, Vineyard Haven (tel. 508/693-4252). Stronger sea kayakers can paddle a little over an hour to reach

Naushon Island and the docking point of Tarpaulin Cove. Naushon is one of the Elizabeth Islands, which lie across the Vineyard Sound. People have also kayaked to Nantucket, but you had better be an expert to attempt this. In Nantucket, rent sea kayaks from **Force 5** at Jetties Beach (tel. 508/228-0700) for trips within the protected harbor to Pocomo Head or Polpus Harbor.

And on the mainland . . .

Hyannis Harbor

Allow 2–3 hours. Access: From downtown Hyannis, head east on Main Street and take a right on Lewis Bay Road. Another right on Bayview Road will bring you to the Inner Harbor parking lot. Map: Available at Eastern Mountain Sports.

Don't miss the opportunity to sea kayak on Cape Cod's shores. When the sun's shining and the surf's relatively calm, the sport's sublime. These ideal conditions prevailed the day I went kayaking with Eric Johnson, manager of the Eastern Mountain Sports store in Hyannis. Eric's an avid kayaker who had just recently completed a month-long sea kayaking jaunt on the Maine Island Trail. He brought me to one of his favorite sightseeing spots, the Hyannis Harbor.

The put-in was at the Hyannis Inner Harbor. We slipped into our 14-foot wardrobe, threw on our sea skirts and off we went. Coasting along the Inner Harbor shoreline, we glided by the John F. Kennedy Memorial before passing the jetty which leads to the wide-open Nantucket Sound. Most sailboats, fishing, and tour boats will give you the right-of-way through this narrow passage, but be cautious nonetheless. We turned right, zig-zagging by the numerous windsurfers off Kalmus Park Beach before continuing on to Hyannisport. This is where the famous Kennedy compound is located—John, Robert, and Ted Kennedy's summer homes are all located here. Not to be overlooked is talk-show host Morton Downey's house, just to the left of those of the famous brothers. Depending on your arm strength, you can keep on paddling around the breakwater and lighthouse to Craigville Beach or head back.

For more experienced kayakers, Eric recommends the loop from Harding Beach around **North Monomoy Island**. This national wildlife refuge is known for its incredible birdlife and the schools of harbor and gray seals waiting for your arrival (see the "Bird Watching" section above).

OUTFITTERS & RENTALS

Eastern Mountain Sports, located at 233 Stevens Street, Hyannis (tel. 508/775-1072), has kayak demonstrations every Saturday morning in the summer months. They also host guided kayak tour and hikes. Rentals for flatwater kayaks start at $25, sea kayaks at $35.

Eric Gustafson of **Fun Seekers Inc.,** P.O. Box 1143, Wellfleet, MA 02667 (tel. 508/349-1429), will take kayakers on guided tours of Monomoy and through the tidal rivers of Wellfleet and Truro. **Nauset Sports** (tel. 508/255-4742) and **Goose Hummock** (tel. 508/255-0455), both in Orleans on State Route 6A, also rent sea kayaks and offer instruction.

SURFING

The stormy weather of spring and fall is the best time to hit the waves. In June, July, and August, the Atlantic can look like a lake. But, hey, that's no reason to stay inside watching reruns of *The Simpsons*. Check out the beaches of the Outer Cape, especially **White Crest Beach** in South Wellfleet, **Ballston Beach** in Truro, and sections of **Nauset Beach** in Orleans. You can rent boards from **Nauset Sports,** State Route 6A in Orleans and U.S. 6 in North Eastham (tel. 508/255-4742 for the Orleans store, and 508/255-2219 for the North Eastham location).

Jonny D., my bustin' wave buddy on the Vineyard, says you can sometimes catch double waves at **Squibnocket Beach** and **Bell's Beach.** Both are private, so if you get booted, go to nearby **Moshup Beach** in Gay Head. Rent boards from **Wind's Up,** 95 Beach Road, Vineyard Haven (tel. 508/693-4252).

Surfers in Nantucket flock to **Cisco** and **Madaket Beach.**

SWIMMING

The category you've been patiently waiting for. The envelope please. . . .

From Memorial Day to the end of June, you might as well consider yourself an honorary member of some Polar Bear Swimming Club if you think swimming in the Atlantic off the Cape is a swell idea; water temperatures are usually in the mid-50s. But on hot days in mid- to late summer, nothing on the Cape can beat the **Cape Cod National Seashore. Marconi, Newcomb Hollow,** and **Cahoon Hollow** in Wellfleet are all incredibly scenic, with huge sandstone cliffs rising behind the white-sand beaches; Marconi's my favorite. **Race Point** in P-town is exquisite. **Flyer's** in P-town (tel. 508/487-0518) will shuttle you to **Long Point Beach,** the finger at the end of the Cape that curls back in toward town; the only other way to get there is an hour-long walk. The round-trip price is $10.

The biggest, brawlingest beach scene of them all on the Cape is **Nauset Beach,** at the end of Beach Road in East Orleans. It's a surfer, family, collegiate, and singles beach all rolled into one, and has the size to accommodate everyone nicely. It's good sometimes to have some

peace and quiet on the beach—there are many places on the Cape for that—but sometimes you just want to immerse yourself in good old American beach culture, with loud radios, sand-kickers, and all. Good onion rings and fried clams can be had at the clam shack. Get here early or you'll spend an hour in your car waiting to park. **Craigville Beach** in Centerville and **Cahoon Hollow** can have a similar vibe.

The Bay-side beaches are a good alternative to the ocean when you're on the Cape before the water's warm, and are primarily family scenes. **Skaket Beach** in Orleans on the Bay side (no stairs), **Corporation Beach** in Dennis, **Cold Storage Beach** on the border between East Dennis and Brewster, and **Paine's Creek** in Brewster just east of the Cape Cod Museum of Natural History are all great beaches; kids will particularly love Paine's Creek if you time your visit with the beginning of the incoming tide—a fast-flowing tidal creek gives your air mattress quite a ride.

One last Cape swimming tip: If what you want is just a nice refreshing dip, don't forget those myriad kettlehole ponds. For years I made the bike trek from a relative's house up to **Slough Pond,** at the intersection of Slough and Red Top Roads off Satucket Road, and I'd feel guilty if I didn't tell you how fondly I remember those clean, cool waters.

On the Vineyard, you won't go wrong with **East Beach** in Chappy, **Moshup** or **Lobsterville Beach** in Gay Head. Families head to **State Beach** between Oak Bluffs and Edgartown and **Menemsha Beach. Katama Beach,** near Edgartown, is a serious college scene.

In Nantucket, head to **'Sconset Beach.** The best family beaches in Nantucket are **Fisherman's** and **Jetties. Surfside Beach** is Nantucket's equivalent to Craigville or Nauset.

Nude suntanning is illegal and I wouldn't want to be arrested as an accomplice, but you might try **Lucy Vincent Beach** in Gay Head on the Vineyard, **Miacomet Beach** in Nantucket, and the remote corners of **Longnook Beach** in Truro.

WALKS & RAMBLES

One of the highlights of New England is strolling on Cape Cod. Forest and moors combine with coastal marsh and sands to create the best of both worlds. The splendid bird watching on all of these walks is a bonus.

CAPE COD

Fort Hill Trail

2 miles (round trip). Allow 1 hour. Access: Take U.S. 6 North 1.5 miles past the Eastham-Orleans rotary. A small red sign will tell you where to take a right turn. Park at the lower lot. Map: Available from Cape Cod National Seashore Headquarters, South Wellfleet, MA 02663 (tel. 508/349-3785).

Marshes, forests, and swamps merge with deep-rooted history and outlandish architecture to make the Fort Hill trail one of the most magical walks on the Cape. From the parking lot, walk under the whalebone gateway to get a good look at Captain Edward Penniman's dream home. In the mid-19th century, Penniman climbed the whaling ranks, from harpooner to captain, amassing a fortune in the process. He circled the globe seven times, scouring the ocean for its most lucrative products— whale oil, spermaceti, baleen, and ivory. He returned home in 1867 and proceeded to build this house in the French Second Empire Style.

The walk continues around the back of the house, where I saw a fox jump into his hole (a tree stump), and several jackrabbits. Ascending a short hill to the second parking lot, sweeping views of Nauset Marsh and the long stretches of sand known as Nauset and Coast Guard Beaches opened up. This is all part of the vast Cape Cod National Seashore. In 1605, the great explorer Samuel de Champlain arrived on a tiny vessel to chart this area for a new French settlement. However, the shallowness of the harbor and the less-than-amicable welcome by the Nauset Indians forced Champlain to look elsewhere, and it wasn't until 1644 that the first colonists settled here.

The trail continues through a section of red cedar trees before arriving at an overlook called Skiff Hill. This is a prime location for birdwatchers to spot the great blue, green, and black-crowned night herons feasting on the marsh. Several hundred yards later, I took a left at the Red Maple Swamp Trail onto a winding boardwalk through a murky swamp of tall red maples. A right turn at the end of the swamp brought me back to my car.

Wellfleet Bay Wildlife Sanctuary

1.5 miles (round trip). Allow 1–2 hours. Access: Heading north on U.S. 6, the clearly marked sign is located 0.3 mile past the Eastham/Wellfleet town line, at the southern end of Wellfleet. Map: Available at the sanctuary.

A chorus of chirping birds greeted me at the entrance to the Wellfleet Bay Wildlife Sanctuary. There were white-crowned sparrows with a white adornment to their heads, red-winged blackbirds, and two rare orange and brown rufous-sided towhees. Yet this is only a small fraction of the bird life found on the sanctuary's splendid trails. The Massachusetts Audubon Society, who own and maintain the property, have

Noted Naturalists of Cape Cod

"Wishing to get a better view than I had yet had of the ocean, . . . I made a visit to Cape Cod in October, 1849." Thus, began the account of Henry Thoreau's adventures in the book *Cape Cod*. Better known for the two years he spent at Walden Pond and his essay, "Civil Disobedience," Thoreau walked the coastline from Eastham to Provincetown three times: in 1849, 1850, and 1855. He compared crossing the barren and desolate landscape to "traveling a desert." Indeed, the Cape in the mid-1800s was one massive sand dune due to deforestation. In his dissertations on the Cape, Thoreau was particularly fascinated with oystermen and wreckers, people who searched the beach for driftwood and fragments of wrecked vessels. He writes about the interaction of these people with a "nature that was hostile and indifferent to human life," one that forced Cape Codders to eke out a living from the barren shores and stormy seas.

Henry Beston followed Thoreau's path to Cape Cod. In *The Outermost House*, Beston describes his experience of living in a house on the dunes of Eastham between 1926 and 1927. Beston lived alone, 2 miles from his nearest neighbor, so he could "observe carefully, brood long, and write slowly." Hmmm, I guess deadlines weren't much of an issue back then. Beston explored the "relation of nature to the human spirit." Contrary to Thoreau, he was only interested in his own isolated spirit and the consequences the ocean would have for him. His book has more of a naturalistic tone, explicitly describing the way sea and beach change during the different seasons. By the 1920s, trees were reappearing on the Cape, people no longer needed to scour the beach for firewood, and tourists were starting to arrive by train and automobile. Thoreau's statement that "the time will come when this coast will be a resort" was an astute prophecy.

claimed to have seen over 250 different species.

The Goose Pond Trail is a leisurely ramble through marsh, forest, ponds, and fields. At low tide, take a right at the cabin and continue on the Try Island Trail to a boardwalk that leads to Cape Cod Bay. On the marshes and beaches surrounding the trails, I saw green herons and large gooselike brants. Retrace your steps back to the cabin and continue on the Goose Pond Trail through a field to Goose Pond. The first bench overlooking the pond is one of the most serene spots on the Cape. Northern hummingbirds fly in and out of the branches overhead, forming a choir whose voices will soothe any man's soul.

John Wing Trail/South Trail

2.25 miles (round trip). Allow 1.5–2 hours. Access: From Brewster, follow State Route 6A East towards Dennis. The Cape Cod Museum of Natural History is located on the right-hand side, 1.6 miles from the Dennis/Brewster line. Park in the museum's parking lots. Map: Available at the Cape Cod Museum of Natural History.

These two relatively flat trails, which start from the Cape Cod Museum of Natural History in Brewster, are ideal for young families and avid bird-watchers.

The South Trail is a three-quarter-mile-long path that passes through marshes and over a creek before looping around a small beech forest back to the main trail. Two young osprey were nesting in the power-line poles when I came here in the spring.

Across the street, in the back of the museum, the longer John Wing Trail winds through more marshlands to the beaches of Cape Cod Bay. Once you cross over the dunes, take a right and walk along the sand until you see another trail leading back to a forest of oaks and pines. A right turn at the John Wing Memorial sign leads you past the site where this European settler built a house in 1656. Take a left to reach the main trail that goes back to the museum.

Pamet Cranberry Bog Trail

1 mile. Allow 1 hour. Access: Take U.S. 6 to North Pamet Road, Truro, and park at the Environmental Education Center (a youth hostel in the summer) at the end of the road. Map: Available from Cape Cod National Seashore Headquarters, South Wellfleet, MA 02663 (tel. 508/349-3785).

The Pamet Cranberry Bog Trail is a short hike around a pond to an abandoned bog house that was once used to cultivate cranberries. Take the dirt path to the right of the house, and the bucolic Cape countryside quickly gives way to some of the most majestic and secluded beach scenery on the Cape. The path leads to the edge of the moors overlooking Truro's Ballston Beach. On a clear summer's day, you'll find an occasional surfer battling the waves. Continue along the main trail to the left for even better views and the freshest sea air your deprived lungs can handle. If I was an artist and I wanted to paint the Cape Cod coast, this is the spot I'd choose.

MARTHA'S VINEYARD

Cedar Tree Neck Sanctuary

2.5 miles (round trip). Allow 1–2 hours. Access: From Vineyard Haven, take State Road south towards West Tisbury. At Indian Hill Road, take a right and follow the signs to the sanctuary. Take a right at the dirt road known as Obed Daggett and watch out for large potholes. Map: Available at the trailhead.

I never realized how varied the Vineyard's landscape was until I took a ramble through Cedar Tree Neck Sanctuary. Forest of oaks, beeches, and sassafras trees led to serene ponds, swampy bogs, and the rocky coastline, before combining all three elements in a scenic overlook. Start at the white trail just to the left of the trail map signboard and continue through this forest of oaks and sassafras until you reach the second branch of the Yellow Trail. Take a right and pass under the maples and yellow beeches before stopping at peaceful Ames Pond. It was spring and birds sang overhead, a butterfly played hide-and-seek with my brother and me, and frogs trilled from sunken logs. Walk along the edge of the pond and you'll meet up with the white trail again, which leads to a swampy area known as a sphagnum bog where tree roots jut out from carpets of velvety green moss. Soon you'll reach the white sands of the seashore with views of the Elizabeth Islands across the Vineyard Sound. This beach lies on the western part of the Vineyard, ideal for a sunset stroll, except for one problem: for some reason, the sanctuary closes at 5:30 PM, not dusk. Take a right between two rows of roped fences where dune restoration work is being done and you'll skirt Cedar Tree Neck Pond, once an operating cranberry bog. When the red trail forks, go left for a great vista of all the diverse terrain you've just encountered—forest, ponds, beach, and ocean. This is the perfect ending to an enchanting loop.

Gay Head Cliffs

1–3 miles (round trip). Allow 2 hours. Access: The Gay Head Cliffs are at the southwestern corner of the island. Simply take State Road all the way south to where it ends at a parking loop. Parking is at the town-owned lot at the corner of State and the Moshup Trail. The fee is $10 in the summer, and the trail starts directly behind the lot.

Gay Head Cliffs is justifiably one of the most popular spots on the island. Layers of clay create varying degrees of vivid color depending on the sedimentary deposit. The result is a dramatic backdrop of rose-colored reds, frog greens, van Gogh yellows, and whites along the faces of the jagged cliffs. Come summer, the shores below the cliffs known as Gay Head Beach are swarming with suntanners. So come early, or even better, during sunset, when the sun's rays create a spectacular light show across the clay. You might even find several seashells in mint condition to add to your growing collection.

The trail starts from the parking lot, winding through the brush alongside the Moshup Trail before ending at the beach. Turn right and you'll notice that the rounded cliffs become more jagged as they gain in height. You can walk along the beach as far as the surf lets you, but the closer you get to the taller cliffs, the more striking the clay becomes. For the past 20 years, nude bathers covered themselves in red clay before jumping in the ocean, to get soft, smooth skin. Sunbathing *au natural* remains, but any use of the clay is now prohibited, so we'll

have to resort to spending hundreds of dollars for mud baths at overpriced spas.

NANTUCKET

Sanford Farm and The Woods

4 miles (round trip). Allow 1.5–2 hours. Access: From Nantucket Town, take Madaket Road 2 miles west. The parking lot is clearly marked on the left-hand side of the road. Map: Available at trailhead.

Sanford Farm's pastoral setting is well worth the detour from the beach. This is the Nantucket of yore, far away from the million-dollar mansions of today. Indeed, Sanford Farm was Nantucket's first settlement—colonists who were happy just to have a roof over their heads and enough sustenance to survive. I entered through a turnstile onto a dirt road, passing fields of wildflowers and a freshwater marsh, Trots Swamp. The trail continues past two wooden posts which once were the boundary line of an area called The Woods. Winterberry, blackberry, and bayberry shrubs line both sides of the path and are home to white-tailed deer and cottontail rabbits (which you'll undoubtedly see). Another 15 minutes, and I ended up at a vacated barn, which sits in the center of a large clearing. With views of Hummock Pond to the left and the town of Madaket to the right, the Atlantic Ocean stood before me. The trail continues to the ocean and an area called Ram's Pasture. However, I usually sit on the bench, take in the countryside, and then retrace my steps back to plaque 7. A right turn here takes you on a quick loop around a small pond which offers some of the best bird watching on the island. A red-tailed hawk and several osprey hovered above on my last trip here Take a right at the end of the loop to return to the lot.

WHALE WATCHING

There was a steady drizzle coming down the Saturday morning I chose to board the **Dolphin Fleet Whale Watching** cruise out of Provincetown Harbor. Still half asleep when I stepped aboard the boat, I didn't realize that stormy weather on land might mean high seas on the Atlantic—until I spotted a bowl of Dramamine on the back counter.

"It could be pretty rough out there today," said the food server, wearing a sadistic smile. I popped a couple pills in my mouth even though I have never gotten seasick (that includes a short stint in the Marines on an oiler and a 16-day freighter cruise in the South Pacific). Close to an hour later, the boat was riding the 10-foot ocean swells like a see-saw; 80 percent of the Chicago Zoological Society and the freshmen biology class from the University of Rochester were clinging to the railing of the boat, feeding the fish orally. I was outdoors, sucking in large breaths of salt-water, getting soaked from the rain, and clutching a plastic seasickness bag tightly. Were it not for the fact that I woke up too late for breakfast, I would have joined the ranks. Instead, I made it back to the docks an hour later, green but intact. We never did find any whales, and frankly, most of the people on board didn't really care. We were just happy to be back on *terra firma*. As we disembarked, we were given a small card that entitled us to a free trip on the *Dolphin Princess* whenever we desired. We were now members of the One Percent Club, the 1 percent who never saw a whale.

Were it not for this book, I would have been happy to be a member of the One Percent Club eternally. Yet, how could I possibly write about whale watching when I had yet to see one? So there I was the next morning, apprehensively aboard the Dolphin Princess once again.

This time, the sky was blue and the sea was like a mirror. Less than 45 minutes into our ride, someone shouted on the starboard side of the boat. Everyone ran over to find a huge shadow rising from the water only 15 feet away. A small geyser shot from his back as the sounds of clicking cameras reverberated around the deck. Several minutes later, the same whale's tailfin or fluke surfaced. Wow! What a difference a day makes. Instead of feeling nauseous, I was exhilarated.

According to naturalist Phil Trell from the Center for Coastal Studies, we had just spotted a humpback whale. Phil had given us an extensive introduction to the whales of the northeast on the ride over to Stellwagen Bank. Located about 7 miles north of Provincetown, 25 miles east of Boston, and 12 miles southeast of Gloucester on Cape Ann, Stellwagen is an 18-mile-long crescent-shaped underwater mesa. The bank ranges from 80 to 500 feet below the surface. Currents slam into the bank, bringing nutrient-rich cold water to the surface. This attracts fish, which in turn attract numerous species of whales between April and November—humpbacks, the larger fins, and smaller minkes. One gulp from a hungry humpback whale can take in a ton of fish.

We followed the humpback for a good hour, saw him playing with a buddy, and then returned to Provincetown. The entire trip took four hours, yet this time I wasn't so eager to kiss the ground. I learned an important lesson: Always check the weather before going whale watching.

The **Dolphin Fleet Boats** leave from Provincetown Harbor daily in the morning, afternoon, and at 5:00 PM for a sunset cruise. The cost is $17.50. Their office is located in the Chamber of Commerce building at the head of the pier. Call 800/826-9300 for more information.

Campgrounds & Other Accommodations

CAMPGROUNDS

Unfortunately, Nantucket has no camping facilities.

Nickerson State Park, Cape Cod

From the junction of U.S. 6 and State Route 6A in Brewster, head 3 miles west on State Route 6A. 420 sites, no hookups, handicap rest room facilities, sewage disposal, public phone, tables, and grills. Park offices: 3488 Main Street, Brewster, MA 02631-1521 (tel. 508/896-3491).

The 420 well-spaced camping sites at Nickerson State Park are in extremely high demand during the summer. If you're one of the fortunate few to grab one, have fun exploring the hiking and biking trails that weave through its ponds and woods.

Shawne Crowell State Forest, Cape Cod

From Sandwich, head 1.5 miles north on State Route 6A and then 1.5 miles on State Route 130. Tel. 508/888-0351. 280 sites, no hookups, handicap rest room facilities, sewage disposal, public phones, table, and grills.

If Nickerson is booked, this is the second-best choice. The campgrounds are located near the historic village of Sandwich.

Webb's Camping Area, Martha's Vineyard

Barnes Road, Oak Bluffs. Tel. 508/693-0233. From the Oak Bluff ferry, go 0.25 miles west on Oak Bluff Road, 0.5 mile southwest on Circuit Road, and 1.5 miles southwest on Barnes Road. 166 sites, 140 no hookups, 26 water and electricity, group sites for tents, sewage disposal, laundry, public phone, grocery store, ice, tables, fire rings, grills, and wood. No pets. $24–$26 per two people. Reservations recommended in the summer.

Friends who live on Martha's Vineyard rated the two private campgrounds on the island poor, but if you're desperate for a spot to sleep, this is the more peaceful of the two.

INNS & RESORTS

Ocean Edge, Cape Cod

State Route 6A, Brewster, MA 02631. Tel. 508/896-9000. Rooms range from $90–$350.

One of the Cape's best golf courses is at this resort in Brewster. They also have tennis courts, a basketball court, and four outdoor swimming pools.

Ship's Knees Inn, Cape Cod

186 Beach Road, East Orleans, MA 02643. Tel. 508/255-1312. Double rooms with bath start at $88 in the off-season, shared bath ranges from $45–$70.

A five-minute stroll from Nauset Beach, the Ship's Knees Inn in East Orleans is a restored sea captain's home. The 19 rooms are all decorated in a distinctly nautical style. Breakfast is served outside, where birds are often seen nesting in nearby trees or under the patio roof.

Ship's Bell Inn, Cape Cod

586 Commercial Street, Provincetown, MA 02657. Tel. 508/487-1675. Rates start at $86 per night.

Conveniently located near the heart of P-town, Ship's Bell Inn offers a wide range of accommodations: three-room apartments, studios, and motel rooms with views of Cape Cod Bay. Province Lands is a short ride by bicycle. The owner often has discounts for the whale-watching cruises.

The Wauwinet, Nantucket

P.O. Box 2580, Wauwinet Road, Nantucket, MA 02584-2580. Tel. 800/426-8718. Prices range from $190–$690 depending on the time of year and the amount of luxury.

Flanked by Nantucket Bay and the Atlantic Ocean, the Wauwinet is not only the best resort for outdoor recreation on Nantucket, but the entire Cape Cod region. Boardsailing, rowboats, Sunfishes, mountain bikes, and tennis facilities, including two clay courts, are all complimentary to guests. Managing Director Russ Cleveland takes visitors on daily bird-watching tours to Great Point. Here, rare piping plovers, hundreds of least and common terns, northern harrier or marsh hawks, ospreys, and Russ's favorite, the American oyster-catchers, are seen. The tastefully decorated 30 rooms all have spacious decks overlooking the water. The resort is only open May 12 to October 30.

White Elephant, Nantucket

Tel. 508/228-2500. Double rooms start at $215.

Sprawling alongside the harbor, this exclusive hotel combines historical charm with the natural seascape of Melville's favorite island. The most luxurious rooms are on the third floor of the Breakers. King-size canopy beds, wall-to-wall carpeting, and refrigerators stocked with champagne furnish the bright rooms. Open the French doors to your balcony, breathe in the salt-filled air, and view the landscaped gardens. A couple bottles of bubbly, and you just might think you saw Moby Dick bobbing with the boats in the harbor.

Aldworth Manor, Martha's Vineyard

26 Mt. Aldworth Road, PO Box 4058, Vineyard Haven, MA 02568. Tel. 508/693-3203. Rates are $109–$219, depending on the room and season.

Minutes from the Vineyard Haven ferry, the smoke-free rooms at Aldworth Manor overlook two secluded acres. Innkeeper Lynne Nippes cooks one of the best breakfasts on the island, guaranteed to keep you biking or hiking the rest of the day. She also is extremely knowledgeable about the sporting facilities on the island.

8

Southern & Central Vermont

NYONE WHO'S DRIVEN THE STRETCH OF INTERSTATE 91 FROM Bernardston, Massachusetts, north across the state line more than once or twice, takes it as an article of faith that an ineffable change occurs when the WELCOME TO VERMONT sign slides by on the roadside. The landscape sweetens, somehow. It's not just the absence of billboards, which Vermonters outlawed long ago. Hills rise higher, and undulate away toward the horizon. The green that clothes them becomes greener by the mile. The hayfields seem more golden; Holstein cows seem to increase on the pastures; and the very air seems fresher. And in winter, when it seems that every other northbound car is topped with a loaded ski rack, the snow cover rapidly gets deeper the farther north you go. The snowbanks mount and the branches of roadside evergreens droop under their wintry burden. Travelers from other places realize they've arrived, and Vermonters know they are home.

In contrast to almost any other place I can think of in the United States, Vermont's three centuries of settlement seem actually to have *enhanced* the land's appeal. The no-billboards law is only one of the ways Vermonters have defended their sense of what their home should look like. The hundreds of tiny historic villages that dot the state look like they did a century ago, complete with white-painted Victorian homes and church steeples reaching toward the sky. At last count, there were still more than 100 covered bridges intact along lonely country roads. All in all, you'd be hard put to find another place where people and all their works seem to fit so harmoniously with the natural features of the land; so many generations have lived here in balance with the land that it's hard to say whether the land has shaped the people or the people have shaped the land.

I'd say that the reason Vermonters have behaved so well is that the hand of nature always was and always will be very insistent up here, both in its harsh, exacting demands on humans and in its willingness to reward them with both livelihoods and any number of simple pleasures, from the quiet beauty of the country to delicacies like wild trout, game, and strawberries. Each of Vermont's seasons is forceful enough to define completely what life is like for the people who live here, from summer's alternating sultry days, wild thunderstorms, and crystal-clear sunshine, to fall's brisk snap and explosion of foliage; from winter's blankets of snow and frigid −30° mornings that make your throat catch when you leave the house to the monochromatic drear of mud season, which is followed by fast and brilliant springtime.

Vermont's pastoral dairy-farm and corn-field look is kept intact by its tiny population. Although about the same size as New Hampshire, its inverted neighbor to the east, Vermont has only a little more than half that state's population; whereas southern New Hampshire is more or less a suburb of Boston, all of Vermont north of U.S. 4 is far enough away from the urban centers of the Northeast to hold most of the hordes at arm's length. Less than 9,000 people live in Montpelier, the nation's smallest state capital, and only a third of the state's total population lives in anything like an urban area. Add the state's strict environmental statutes and the result is a state overrun with small villages and their signature white steeples, backcountry roads, and more farmland than you could possibly imagine.

The countrified feeling of Vermont's valleys, along with its wilder, mountainous areas, has been attracting visitors for almost 200 years. George Round opened the Clarendon Mineral Springs in 1798; his hotel soon was bringing carriageloads of "flatlanders" north to breathe the crisp fresh air and indulge in the invigorating, supposedly therapeutic waters of his spring. In many other Vermont towns, other entrepreneurial types followed suit. The most famous of these "water-cures" was created in 1845 in Brattleboro; the spring became a rural retreat for some of the most distinguished figures among New England's literati—Harriet Beecher Stowe, Henry Wadsworth Longfellow, James Russell Lowell, and William Dean Howells. These salubrious retreats soon declined in popularity, and their patrons were replaced by pleasure-seeking summer vacationers. Mary Todd Lincoln and her son Robert first visited Manchester during Abe's presidency in 1863. Robert would later build an estate called Hildene, where he summered ever year until he died in 1925.

These summer visitors weren't always appreciated by the locals. Vermonters, understandably proud of their state and their way of life, have a longstanding reputation for being prickly, laconic, and sometimes downright cranky toward their southern countrymen. A fellow named Matthew Buckham, who would later reign as president of the University of Vermont, provided an early record of the mischievous nature of the Vermont yank when he unleashed this long-winded article in an 1867 issue of the *Vermont Historical Gazetteer.*

Let us do all we can to keep up the notion among our city cousins, that to live "away up in Vermont," is the American equivalent for being exiled to Siberia.

Not that we do not think very highly of our city cousins, especially *when we see them in the city*. But when they come with their long baggage-train of trunks and band-boxes, and take possession of a country village, bringing their livery and their minister with them, occupying all the finest building sites, ordering all their groceries and toggery from the city, and importing into industrious communities the seductive fashion of doing nothing and doing it elegantly, they turn the heads of the young, demoralize the whole tone of society, convert respectable villages into the likeness of suburban Connecticut and New Jersey, and for all these losses do not compensate by adding any appreciable amount to the circulating capital or to public improvement.

Vermonters soon learned to live with the increasing numbers of tourists, however; there was room enough for all in the green hills. The locals confined their jibes against New Hampshirites and the cityfolk to the occasional dig, and turned their wit to appreciating all that Vermont had given them. In a 1905 *Chicago Tribune* article, a reporter asked a Vermont politico how he got his start in life. "I was born on a hillside farm in Vermont," said the statesman with a twinkle, "and at an early age I rolled down."

The state government did its best to encourage tourism. In 1891, it established the first state publicity service in the nation. Fishermen flocked to the rivers and hunters took to the forests, where they were soon joined by hikers and skiers. In 1930, the Green Mountain Club cleared the last stretches of the Long Trail, which runs continuously along the ridges of the Green Mountains from the Massachusetts border all the way to Canada. Five years later, a Ford Model T engine in Clinton Gilbert's pasture in Woodstock powered the first alpine-skiing rope tow in America. By 1975, the state had 78 downhill and cross-country ski areas; the latter boomed in the 1970s. Legions of vacationers took up biking as well, and the gently undulating roads that follow the contours of the Vermont countryside have earned a reputation as some of the finest road-biking terrain in the nation. The hundreds of trails that entice hikers in the summer are transformed in wintertime into easy woodland Nordic-skiing trails and major backcountry-skiing challenges. In short, there is far more to this small state than the annual leaf-peeping auto caravan that clogs its roadways every October. There's just no excuse for restricting your experience of the Vermont outdoors to a view through the glass windowpanes of your car.

The Lay of the Land

One reason why the southern and central Vermont countryside is so pleasing to the eye is that the scale of the landscape neither overwhelms nor is overwhelmed by the farms, roads, and communities scattered across it. The Green Mountains are imposing, but not to the point that they render the villages in the valleys at their feet ant-sized by comparison. The valleys are commonly just wide enough to support an operation like a small family farm, and the homes you see on individual hillsides east of the mountains seem to complement the view, rather than put a blemish on it. Everything seems to fit into its place.

Drive east to west in Vermont and you'll inevitably run into the high barrier of rising ridges called the **Green Mountains.** This sturdy backbone marches the whole length of the state and on into Canada, and varies from 20 to 36 miles in width. In southern Vermont they roll along in one distinct ridge, whereas at Sherburne Pass, the border between southern and central Vermont (for the purposes of this chapter) they split into three ridges: the Hogback Range, which runs north from Brandon; the Main Range, which continues on and is the route of the Long Trail; and in the east, the Lowell Mountains, starting at Stockbridge and running on up toward Morrisville.

As suggested by their fairly gentle contours, these are old mountains, created 450 millions years ago by a running fold in the earth's crust. They contain rock among the oldest on the continent, more than a billion years old. The official state rock, green metamorphic schist, is the building block of the Green Mountains; its brilliant green coloring reflects the presence of the mineral chlorite.

In some spots, the continental folding was so strong that huge slabs of rock toppled from the heights of the Green Mountains to create other mountain ranges, such as the **Taconic Mountains** in Vermont's southwestern corner. Mount Equinox, standing just west of Manchester, is the highest peak in the Taconics at 3,816 feet.

The remoter parts of the Green Mountain National Forest are the best places in southern and central Vermont to gain a fleeting encounter with Vermont's abundant wildlife; moose, black bears, beavers, gray foxes, and otters all do quite well in the backcountry, and white-tailed deer are so common everywhere that they rival snow and ice as the state's chief driving hazards. Maybe you'll be the lucky one to catch the definitive glance of the fabled

catamount; pessimists think the species long since extirpated from the Northeast, but the faithful continue to see the golden, long-tailed big cat out of the corner of their eye (or, at least, imagine they do). Birds are everywhere as well, including such marquee species as wild turkeys, great horned owls, yellow-bellied sapsuckers, peregrine falcons and numerous kinds of hawks, eastern kingbirds, huge flocks of snow geese and Canada geese, great blue herons, and snowy egrets. There are also warblers, thrushes, and many other species of waterfowl and songbirds too numerous to mention.

Between the southern Green Mountains and the Taconics on the border with New York State is the **Valley of Vermont,** the narrow southern extension of the broad Champlain Valley. It's only a mile wide in places, and is the corridor along which the picturesque villages of southwestern Vermont— Bennington, Arlington, Manchester, Dorset, and Danby, beehives of tourism all—are located.

There are plenty of streams, rivers, ponds, and lakes in southwestern Vermont and the Green Mountain National Forest, from the Hoosic River in the far southwestern corner, to Somerset and Harriman reservoirs just east of the Green Mountains, to the famed Batten Kill River and Otter Creek, which runs north into Lake Champlain. East of the mountains, narrow streams tumble down hillsides into ponds, rivers, and lakes, eventually draining into the Connecticut River on Vermont's eastern border. The part of Vermont's Connecticut River watershed that begins on the eastern slope of the Green Mountains and extends from Brattleboro in the south all the way up to the Northeast Kingdom (see chapter 9) is called the **Vermont Piedmont.** The Piedmont is among the prettiest areas of the state, still given over to dairying for the most part, and consisting of an endless succession of modest rolling hills, narrow settled valleys, a spider web of dirt and frost-heaved paved roads, and villages that greet the world with signs like EAST RANDOLPH, POP. 216.

Although skiers and road bikers make their presence loudly felt in the state, let's face it: the big hoo-hah, which every town uses as its pitch to tourists, is the fall foliage season. In September and October, the leaves transform the landscape into a vibrant, ever-changing kaleidoscope of color. The leaves on the white birches turn yellow; aspens are transformed into a copper-coin color; sugar maples produce a combination of yellow, green, orange, and red (depending on how much sugar is trapped in the leaf); white ashes change to the color of a ripe plum; and oak leaves turn to a warm, dark brown. This is not news to most of us. Indeed, "Autumn in Vermont" has become a cliché.

In southern Vermont, peak season usually occurs during the last week in September and the first two weeks in October. Columbus Day Weekend is absolute madness. It seems like the entire population of New York and Boston is behind the wheels of rental cars, congesting New England's roadways with Jersey-Turnpike traffic. There's a basic problem with the usual Autumn driving trip—one of you has to drive. Prime leaf-watching soon becomes tiresome road-watching. Your significant other keeps prodding you to look, but you barely get a glimpse of the purple-leafed tree, suffering severe neck strain in the process. Thus, the reason I have written this book. Hike away from the crowds on trails where you can slow down, stop easily, and appreciate Mother Nature wearing her most flamboyant dress. The Department of Travel in Vermont maintains a foliage hotline (tel. 800/ VERMONT) updating the conditions of the leaves.

As for the rest of the year, summer days can be hot and humid, cooler at night. January temperatures are below freezing most of the time, with snowfall averaging 55 inches in the valleys to over 120 inches on high elevations. Call 802/ 464-2111 or 802/773-8056 for current weather conditions in southern Vermont.

Orientation

This chapter covers all of the southern as well as the eastern central part of the state of Vermont. West of the ridge of the Green Mountains, the northern limit of the chapter's coverage extends to just south of the town of Brandon, on U.S. 7. From the Green Mountains east to the Connecticut River, coverage runs as far north as the Moretown/Middlesex exit off Interstate 89, includes the Barre/ Montpelier area, and employs U.S. 302 from Barre to Wells River on the Connecticut as its northern border. For coverage of the Champlain Valley, the Green Mountains north of Interstate 89, and the Northeast Kingdom, turn to chapter 9.

This chapter is further split into two sections: one on southern Vermont and the other on central Vermont. It took some hard thinking to decide where to draw the line between southern and central Vermont, mainly because no one can seem to agree on where the one ends and the other begins. Vermont's state tourism office breaks things down according to county lines, calling southern Vermont everything in Bennington and Windham counties, and central Vermont everything in Rutland, Windsor, Orange, Addison, and Washington counties. I've gone a very different route, trying to balance the natural topographic divisions between Vermont's areas with the way visitors and residents tend to travel through and use the land. Roughly speaking, I've decided to define southern Vermont as everything from the Massachusetts border north to the area immediately surrounding U.S. 4. Central Vermont is the area north of U.S. 4 (including Woodstock) up to U.S. 302, bordered on the west by the Green Mountains (including all of the mountains' highlights that are easily accessible from State Route 100) and on the east by the Connecticut River. See the locator map for the precise boundaries.

To me the border between southern and central Vermont is drawn more by the much greater numbers of visitors in the south than by any feature of the landscape. From the Massachusetts border north through all of the areas covered here, both east and west of the ridge of the Green Mountains, southern Vermont is by and large the stuff of postcards and *Yankee* magazine covers— long-settled rolling hills and valleys, with the soft, green, but massive contours of the mountains looming up wherever you look. The forest-and-farmland countryside is broken up frequently by the historic small towns, lonely farmhouses, and covered bridges that give Vermont that harmonious rural feel for which it is justly famous.

The combination of a still-unruly natural beauty with this rustic, well-lived-in quality makes Vermont an awfully appealing place to visit, and southern Vermont has been drawing tourists in droves for over a century. It's not that there aren't other parts of the state with this kind of appeal—the Northeast Kingdom is an incredibly lovely place, for example—but that the other parts of the state are just that much farther away from the big cities. Looking at a difference of several hours of tedious driving between central Vermont and southern Vermont, most "flatlanders" happily settle for a southern destination like Manchester, Bennington, or even the area up around Killington, rather than waste more of their precious weekend time going all the way to areas such as central Vermont's Mad River Valley.

This gives the two regions a subtle difference in character. Southern Vermont still has the little white villages with the ubiquitous church steeple, but it's more aggressively "open for business" than central Vermont. Look closely under the rustic veneer of places like Brattleboro, Bennington, and especially Manchester, and you'll find all the hallmarks of the affluent, sophisticated communities around Boston or New York. In Manchester, for example, there are as many Mercedes sedans in town as there are pickup trucks, and for every old-time general store (not too many of the authentic kind are left around here), there's an Armani or Anne Klein outlet store. Southern Vermont has simply been cashing in on its old-time New England character for more years and with more efficiency than has central Vermont.

Southern Vermont's primary north-south corridor on the western side, **U.S. 7,** passes through **Bennington, Arlington, Manchester,** and eventually **Rutland,** and is more commercially developed than any route east of the Green Mountains, with the possible exception of **State Route 100,** which might simply be called Ski Country Road. Running just east of the main ridge of the Green Mountains, Route 100 is rural—there's nothing remotely like a city along its entire length from the Massachusetts border nearly to Canada—but all the state's major ski resorts are either right on it or within a few miles of it. From south to north, you'll pass the signs for **Mount Snow/Haystack, Stratton Mountain, Bromley, Okemo,** and the

Killington/Pico area. Passing through fairly narrow valleys between the green-swathed mountains, Route 100 is thick with the cozy inns and B&Bs, beautiful small towns, antique shops, small lakes and rivers, and "gulfs"—wild, forested, steep-walled gorges that twist through mountainous areas—that are the very picture of Vermont's lure for tourists.

Along the Connecticut River runs **I-91,** the fast lane for travel from the south or east to any part of the state east of the main mountain chain. If you're coming from New York and are bound for a town along U.S. 7, you're probably better off taking the Adirondack Northway, Interstate 87, instead; for Bennington/Manchester, change to U.S. 7 in Albany and follow it into Vermont; and for the Rutland/Killington area, take the Northway to Glens Falls, New York, change to U.S. 4, and follow it on up into the Vermont mountains. If you're coming from the Boston area to any point in Vermont, you'll be taking I-91 up from the Mass Pike to whatever point in Vermont at which you need to turn west again.

The east and west sides of the Green Mountains offer distinctly different recreational menus: on the east, between the mountains and I-91, is a seemingly endless amount of hilly, rural country and lonely road that's perfect for both road and mountain biking as well as cross-country skiing. All the feeder streams of the Connecticut River offer good trout fishing, and some of them have runable whitewater, notably the West River. West of the mountains, the heavier traffic of U.S. 7 and State Route 7A make road biking a little bit less inviting, but then again you've got world-class trout fishing on the Batten Kill, bass and perch fishing and boating on nice big lakes like Bomoseen and St. Catherine, and an easygoing canoeing river in Otter Creek.

In either case, you're never more than a short drive from the main attraction, the Green Mountains. If I-91 and slow-moving U.S. 7 are the sidepieces to a ladder running north up the length of southern Vermont, it's the Green Mountain **gaps** that are the crosspieces. Cut through natural breaks and gorges in the otherwise impassable ridge of the mountains, these are usually the most beautiful, and hairy, roads in the state. Narrow, steep, and replete with hairpin turns around blind curves, they can pose a considerable challenge to even four-wheel-drive vehicles in snowy weather, and some are closed in winter. All of them provide access to the Green Mountain backcountry, the best place in southern Vermont to do many of the things you'll want to do in the outdoors. The least precipitous is the southernmost, **State Route 9,** which connects Brattleboro and Bennington. From south to north, the others are **Kelley Stand Road,** between West Wardsboro and Arlington, which provides access to some of southern Vermont's most pristine country and is closed in winter; **State Route 11,** which runs from Manchester to Londonderry and on to Springfield; **Green Mountain National Forest Road No. 10,** another remote dirt road closed in winter, which connects North Landgrove with Danby; **State Route 140,** the Wallingford Gulf Road; **State Route 103,** the Rutland–Bellows Falls Highway; and **U.S. 4,** which connects Glens Falls, New York, and Rutland with Woodstock and I-89, and which is also the access road for the Pico Peak and Killington Ski Areas, near Sherburne Pass.

Whatever the season, Killington siphons off so much of the tourist traffic that it makes U.S. 4 the natural boundary between southern and central Vermont. North of here and east of the mountains, especially off the ski country corridor of Route 100, the landscape and atmosphere are different than in southern Vermont. Tourist-related businesses are scarce (excepting Woodstock), and there are far fewer B&Bs and inns. All the recreational areas, including the ski areas (**Sugarbush, Mad River,** the **Middlebury College Snow Bowl**), have a stronger local flavor. The outdoors people around here tend to be Vermonters or those who have had a long association with the state. Places like Mad River and Camel's Hump are only a short shot away from Burlington, Vermont's one true city. And aside from the area right around the Green Mountains, central Vermont really remains cow country. Dairy farming and other agricultural enterprises such as maple sugaring are in evidence everywhere, and the tiny towns, like **Bethel, Randolph, Chelsea,** and **Thetford,** still have a genuine rural-crossroads feel.

I-91 continues on up the eastern border of the state toward the Northeast Kingdom, but the main thoroughfare of central Vermont is **I-89.** It cuts northwest up the White River Valley, straight through the heart of central Vermont, and is one of the few interstate highways I know of that truly qualifies as the scenic route. Rolling farmland is all around, granite bluffs poke out of the divider between the north- and southbound lanes, and occasionally you'll be stunned by the sight of the distinctive rocky summit of Camel's Hump peeking out above the surrounding mountains. The three branches of the White River all have swimming holes and crafty trout galore; if you can't find what you're looking for here, ask at the local general store. To the east and west of the interstate are beautiful country roads like **State Routes 110, 14, 12,** and **12A.** All but Route 14 are nearly desolate, though it would seem odd to me to say that Route 14 has much traffic—it really doesn't. These roads all seem tailor-made for a road-biking trip.

In winter, there are usually snowmachine trails everywhere around, which constitute the locals' Nordic-skiing centers—who really needs groomed trails that you have to pay for when it's this good right outside your back door?

At the northerly end of central Vermont is the **Barre-Montpelier area,** the only thing like a urban zone in central Vermont (hah!). Montpelier is a pretty town that's gained an arty/intellectual gloss in the last decade or so. In Onion River Sports, it's got a good outdoor-sports shop; in the Inn, a truly fine New England hostelry; and in Bear Pond Books, a truly great bookstore strong on nature writing and local writers, among other things. Barre is the more workman-like town of the pair, famous for its granite quarries. It's not much to look at, but go to a bar here and you're guaranteed to hear a real Vermont accent in all its glorious oddness.

As in southern Vermont, the gaps through the mountains are the most beautiful drives of all, and offer access to what's probably my favorite stretch of Green Mountain backcountry (not an easy thing to settle on). The first of these drives north of Sherburne Pass is **Brandon Gap,** State Route 73, connecting Rochester and Brandon. Next up are the three must-sees—three roads that have more of a high-country feel than anyplace else in Vermont: **Middlebury Gap** (State Route 125, connecting Ripton and Hancock); **Lincoln Gap** (Lincoln-Warren Highway, closed winter); and **Appalachian Gap** (State Route 17). The forested Lincoln Gap is gorgeous and offers access to a prime stretch of the Long Trail, and the view west from Appalachian Gap is unforgettable.

Parks & Other Hot Spots

I've tried to round up the places in southern and central Vermont that come up again and again in the sports section as great spots for different kinds of outdoor recreation.

Connecticut River

Along all 235 miles of the Vermont–New Hampshire border. Access: state-owned public boating access sites in southern Vermont include Old Ferry Road Access Area (Brattleboro, off U.S. 5); Putney Landing Area (Putney-Dummerston town line, off U.S. 5); Hoyt Landing Access Area (Springfield, off Interstate 91); and Hammond Cove Access Area (Hartland, off U.S. 5).

The lower half of Vermont's Connecticut River is not nearly as pristine as the northern half, but it's still a decent place to fish—for trout, walleye, pike, bass, and shad—or canoe. In fact, you can make a small-scale Huck Finn journey on the Connecticut, canoe camping at points along its shores. There are, however, a few unrunnable sections of the river, near Bellows Falls being one example. If you're interested in more than a day trip on the Connecticut, you'll need a river guide such as the *AMC River Guide: New Hampshire/Vermont* (AMC Books, 1989), or the *Connecticut River Guide* (available from Connecticut River Watershed Council, 125 Combs Rd., Easthampton, MA 01027).

The Connecticut is also a good spot for birding and wildlife watching, with river otters, muskrats, beavers, bitterns, bank swallows, and various accidental shorebirds.

Vernon Black Gum Swamp

Contact Vernon Town Clerk for more information, P.O. Box 116, Vernon, VT 05354-0116 (tel. 802/257-0292). Picnic area, no developed facilities. Access: 4 miles south of Brattleboro on State Route 142; turn east onto Pond Road about 1.25 miles south of Vernon; proceed 1.2 miles then turn right onto Huckle Hill Road; proceed 1.3 miles then turn right onto Basin Road, following it to parking lot at road's end. Map: USGS 7.5 x 15 minute Brattleboro; 7.5 minute Bernardston.

The Vernon Black Gum Swamp is an unusual place to find as far north as Vermont—its namesake trees are far more common a considerable distance to the south, as are the mountain laurel and Virginia chain fern that also grow here. Marked trails in the swamp take you past gnarled, weirdly shaped 400-year-old black gums, and offer good birding—flickers, thrushes, cedar waxwings, wood ducks, and other species frequent the swamp.

Molly Stark State Park

On State Route 9 in Wilmington, 3 miles east of junction with State Route 100. Tel. 802/464-5460. 34 campsites, lean-tos, wheelchair accessible rest rooms, picnic area.

A 158-acre preserve, with hiking trails that include one to the expansive views from the fire tower atop 2,145-foot Mount Olga. The park also offers cold-water fishing on Beaver Brook and good camping.

Harriman Reservoir

Public boating access from State Route 9 west of Wilmington; access also from Whitingham at southern end of reservoir, off State Route 100. For information, contact the Green Mountain National Forest, 231 N. Main St., Rutland, VT 05701, tel. 802/747-6700, or the New England

Power Company, P.O. Box 218, Harriman Station, Readsboro, VT 05350 (tel. 802/ 423-7700). Picnic areas; marked trails for biking, hiking, cross-country skiing. Contact Vermont Department of Forests, Parks, and Recreation, RR 1, P.O. Box 33, North Springfield, VT 05150 (tel. 802/ 886-2215), for more information on Atherton Meadow Wildlife Management Area, at southern end of reservoir. Map: USGS 7.5 minute Readsboro.

One look at a map will show you that this huge reservoir is situated in the closest thing to truly remote country you'll find in southern Vermont. The place is teeming with wildlife—there are bears, loons, moose, and other icons of the northern wilds around here, and deer and wild turkeys are abundant. Harriman is prime fishing, cross-country skiing, mountain biking, canoeing, and even sailing country; there are swimming beaches off Castle Hill Road a mile from Wilmington Village and off State Route 100 near Flame Stables; and the Harriman Trail, following the west shore of the lake from State Route 9 to Harriman Dam, passes numerous relics of abandoned settlements along the shore—old stone walls and ruined foundations.

The reservoir is owned by the New England Power Company, which permits day use only. However, at the Whitingham end of the lake is the Atherton Meadow Wildlife Management Area; it has a large and lively marsh and primitive camping is permitted.

The Green Mountain National Forest/South Half

For more information contact U.S. Forest Service, Green Mountain and Finger Lakes National Forest, 231 N. Main St., Rutland, VT 05701 (tel. 802/747-6700). Map: USGS Green Mountain National Forest/ South Half.

Since the outer boundaries of the Green Mountain National Forest's southern half contain within them at least half of the best spots to get outside in southern Vermont, this is necessarily a kind of umbrella listing. Within its boundaries are cold streams and beaver ponds famous for brook and rainbow trout fishing; the Long Trail, a tramper's treasure; a latticework of remote forest roads and old logging roads, all perfect for mountain biking, cross-country skiing, or simple scenic drives; and the major ski areas of southern Vermont— Mount Snow, Stratton, Bromley, Okemo, Killington, and Pico.

With a total of 325,534 acres, the Green Mountain National Forest occupies half of all the publicly owned land in Vermont. The boundaries of the southern half of the forest encircle the entire southwestern corner of the state. From around U.S. 7 to the western border it's settled, if clearly rural, country, characterized by small picturesque hamlets like Danby, larger towns such as Bennington and Manchester, and dairy farms and hay fields everywhere in between. Most of this land is in private hands. The quintessential experience of the Green Mountain National Forest, however, begins when you leave settled areas along U.S. 7 or State Route 100 and begin winding up one of the "gaps" into the rugged spine of the Green Mountains. Your car labors up ever-steeper grades and around ever-tighter hairpin curves; your ears pop; the scenery outside the window changes from settled farmland to hardwood forest to high-country spruce and fir; the air temperature drops 10°. And then you see the sign, gold paint on brown wood, that says NOW ENTERING THE GREEN MOUNTAIN NATIONAL FOREST. You've entered the wild side of Vermont, a place very different from the sweet, rolling countryside of the valleys; here you see MOOSE CROSSING signs, it snows three times as much in the winter, and you can really imagine that wild catamounts still roam unseen. And it never fails to set the pulse racing.

The forest-service headquarters functions as a clearinghouse of recreational information, and publishes the most useful maps. The South Half map is a perfectly good overall topo map, and if you want more detailed small-scale topos to specific areas of the forest you can write or call for an index. The service's Winter Recreation map is a few years out of date but remains an indispensible guide to ferreting out the best cross-country and backcountry skiing.

The Long Trail

For information and maps, contact the Green Mountain Club, State Route 100, P.O. Box 650, Waterbury Center, VT 05677 (tel. 802/244-7037).

The Long Trail, Vermont's long-distance, high-country hiking trail, is the oldest such trail in the nation. And it's still as its founders intended it to be—a narrow, unforgivingly rugged "footpath in the wilderness" that winds through all the best parts of Vermont's unassumingly rich and beautiful country. By all means, go whole hog and devote the four weeks or so necessary for an end-to-end hike; it will be an unforgettable experience. I once met a man on the trail who'd walked from Massachusetts to Canada, found himself so loathe to leave the trail that

he retraced his steps to Massachusetts, and was on his third rebound when we shared a lean-to for a night. Maybe he was a little crazy, but I can understand the impulse.

If, however, you can't afford to drop out of the world for that long, the many roads that carve through the mountains make perfect trailheads for day hikes or overnights to the parts of the mountains you most want to see. The "Long Trail" box later in this chapter fills in the details on using the trail.

Woodford State Park

On State Route 9, 10 miles east of Bennington. Tel. 802/447-7169. 103 campsites, public phone, picnic area. Map: USGS 7.5 minute Woodford.

Note: This 400-acre area is centered around Adams Reservoir, a good swimming hole. Rowboats and canoes are available. There's a great network of backcountry cross-country ski trails here, too. Near Harriman and Somerset reservoirs, a Long Trail access point (see southern Vermont's hiking section, below, for details on the climb to Harmon Hill), and Bennington.

Shaftsbury State Park

On State Route 7A, 10.5 miles north of Bennington. Tel. 802/375-9978. Day use only, wheelchair accessible rest rooms, picnic area.

The lake here is a good spot to cool off on a hot afternoon or explore lazily in a canoe. Shaftsbury has one outstanding feature—its nature trail. It's a short jaunt around the 26-acre lake, but the trail passes through a lot of different little "natural zones"; there's a swampy area with cottonwood trees, a diverse hardwood forest (oaks, hornbeams, maples), and great birdwatching. The trail also passes atop a glacial esker—a weird, narrow ridge in the middle of an otherwise fairly flat area. Check in at the park entrance for a good nature guide to the trail.

Somerset Reservoir

Vehicle access: from State Route 9, 6 miles west of Wilmington, turn north onto Somerset Road; drive 9 miles. For information and maps, contact the Green Mountain National Forest, 231 N. Main St., Rutland, VT 05701, tel. 802/747-6700, or the New England Power Company, P.O. Box 218, Harriman Station, Readsboro, VT 05350 (tel. 802/423-7700). Picnic areas; boat ramp; marked trails for biking, hiking, cross-country skiing.

Like Harriman Reservoir, this large lake is a great place to fish or canoe. It's a popular ice-fishing spot in wintertime, although you might need a snowmachine to get here. Trails at the south end, where the direct road access is, are a little scant, but Somerset is also accessible off Kelley Stand Road, the access point for a mother lode of trails, backwoods ponds, and old logging roads. It's a walk of a little under a mile from the Grout Pond parking lot to the reservoir. As at Harriman, you can't camp on land right near the lake (the power company forbids it), but the forest service can give you a map showing where the public lands are, on which primitive camping is permitted.

Grout Pond Recreation Area

South off Kelley Stand Road (Arlington–West Wardsboro Road), 8 miles from Arlington, 7 miles from West Wardsboro. For information and maps, contact U.S. Forest Service, Manchester Ranger District, RR 1, P.O. Box 1940, Manchester Center, VT 05255 (tel. 802-362-2307). Boat ramp, picnic area, campsites, lean-tos, rest rooms, marked trails for mountain biking, hiking, and cross-country skiing. Map: USGS 7.5 minute Stratton Mountain.

This might be my choice of venues if I just wanted to spend a week in the woods doing a variety of different things—and be a long way away from people while I was at it. Kelley Stand Road cuts right through the Green Mountains at one of their more intractable points, meaning that there's a lot of land here that will never see development. A slew of nearby trails (including the good old Long Trail) make all sorts of multi-day loop hikes an option; my suggestion for a three- or four-day ramble would be a Stratton Mountain–Stratton Pond–Bourn Pond–Branch Pond loop, beginning and ending right here at Grout Pond. A wonderful spot for canoeing and cross-country skiing as well.

Batten Kill River

Accessible at various points, especially all the bridges, from State Routes 7A or 313 in Manchester or Arlington. For information, contact Manchester and the Mountains Chamber of Commerce, RR 2, P.O. Box 3451, Manchester Center, VT 05255 (tel. 802/362-2100).

Hallowed ground among fly-fishers, the upper Batten Kill is considered Vermont's best wild trout stream. Both Orvis, one of the top fly-fishing schools in the country (see Fishing section, below), and Manchester Village's

American Museum of Fly-Fishing (tel. 802/362-3300) are located nearby. The Batten Kill is also one of the best rivers in southern Vermont for canoeing, swimming, tubing, etc.

West River/Jamaica State Park

From Jamaica, head a half-mile north on the town road. Tel. 802/874-4600. 59 campsites, lean-tos, wheelchair accessible rest rooms, public phone, picnic area, canoe/kayak access.

The West River has what's arguably Vermont's best whitewater, after water releases from Ball Mountain Dam; the river used to host national kayaking championship races. The upper reaches of the stream are runnable only by experts, while further down toward the Connecticut River the stream widens and slows. Good swimming holes and fishing are found at various points all along the West. Jamaica State Park offers campsites right on the river, a classic Vermont swimming hole, and a network of hiking/cross-country skiing trails.

Hapgood Pond Recreation Area

From Peru, head 1.75 miles northeast on Hapgood Pond Road. Tel. 802/824-6456. 28 campsites, picnic area, rest rooms.

The campsites are slightly removed from the pond, but the pond itself is a blessed place to take the kids swimming on a hot day. Good fishing for brookies and rainbows, nearby access to a rough but beautiful section of the Long Trail, and a lot of dirt roads and faded old logging roads that beckon mountain bikers.

Emerald Lake State Park

Off U.S. 7 near North Dorset. Tel. 802/362-1655. Campsites, lean-tos, picnic area, wheelchair accessible rest rooms, canoe/boat access, marked trails.

This state park lies deep in the narrowest part of the Valley of Vermont, which separates the Taconics from the Green Mountains. Emerald Lake makes for serene canoeing, and Otter Creek picks up at the south end of the lake. Good birding on the open water, in the marshes, and on the woodland trails, which lead through a beautiful ash and hickory forest.

Lake St. Catherine State Park

Located 3 miles south of Poultney on State Route 30. Tel. 802/287-9158. 61 campsites, lean-tos, public phone, wheelchair accessible rest rooms, picnic area, canoe/boating access, marked trails.

The campsites are ideally located on the shores of this 7-mile long lake. Sandy beaches make for good swimming, and there's good small- and largemouth bass, perch, pike, and walleye fishing in the lake. Big Trees nature trail rambles through meadows and woodlands that sport some true giants of the woods—maples, eastern white pines, several enormous red oaks.

Bomoseen State Park

Follow U.S. 4 west from Rutland to State Route 30/Castleton Corners Exit. South on State Route 30 to State Route 4A, then west on State Route 4A, right (north) onto road to West Castleton/west shore of Lake

Bomoseen. Tel. 802/265-4242. 66 camp-sites, public phone, wheelchair accessible rest rooms, picnic area, large boat access, marked trails.

Lake Bomoseen is a large, very long body of water ringed by summer houses and cabins. It gets heavy recreational use—lots of powerboaters and waterskiers rip to and fro across its surface. If it's lakeside camping and waterborne recreation you're looking for, however, Bomoseen is a good place for it. There's excellent fishing on the lake, and the Slate History Trail meanders through the leftovers of the 19th century's booming slate quarries and mills. The campsites are set slightly back from the shores of the lake in a wooded refuge.

Half Moon Pond State Park

Follow U.S. 4 west from Rutland to State Route 30/Castleton Corners Exit. South on State Route 30 to State Route 4A, then west on State Route 4A, right (north) onto road to West Castleton/west shore of Lake Bomoseen. Continue for about 7 miles on this road to Half Moon State Park. Tel. 802/273-2848. Campsites, wheelchair accessible rest rooms, picnic area, canoe access, marked trails.

A small pond with a pretty state park that gets fairly crowded on summer week-ends, Half Moon's facilities make it a good place to take young children. This is wild turkey country—you're as likely to encounter a gobbler on the nearby nature trail (see "Bird Watching" below) as anywhere in southern Vermont. The pond has good trout, bass, and pike fish-ing; a good swimming beach; and some beaver activity.

Chittenden Reservoir

Follow U.S. 4 east of Rutland to Mendon, then turn north on East Pittsford/Chittendon Road; keep right and road will end at boating ac-cess. For information, contact the Green Mountain National Forest, 231 N. Main St., Rutland, VT 05701 (tel. 802/747-6700).

Stocked with trout, bass, perch, and salmon, Chittendon Reservoir is a little like the Somerset and Harriman reser-voirs to the south—remote, but crowded with fishermen year-round who are in on the secret. In the winter, you'll see the snowmobiles and the large holes drilled in the ice. Come summer, the waters are filled with drifting boats.

Calvin Coolidge State Park

From the junction of State Routes 100 and 100A in Plymouth, head 2 miles north on State Route 100A. Tel. 802/672-3612. 60 campsites, lean-tos, public phone, wheelchair accessible rest rooms, picnic area, marked trails.

A network of hiking trails traverses this large 16,165-acre preserve, and not too far away is the trail up Shrewsbury Peak, one of the few lofty Green Mountain peaks the makers of the Long Trail didn't feel compelled to include on their route.

Ascutney State Park

From U.S. 5 between Windsor and Ascutney, take State Route 44A north 1 mile to Mount Ascutney Road; the park is about a mile up this road to the left. Tel. 802/674-2060. Campsites, lean-tos, public phone, wheelchair accessible rest rooms, picnic area, marked trails.

Near the base of knoblike Mount Ascutney, this park has excellent camping. A day hike up Ascutney is a popular outing, offering expansive views from the summit and good hawk-watching.

Silver Lake State Park

From Barnard, head 0.25 miles north on Town Road. Tel. 802/234-9451. 47 sites, no hookups, public phone, wheelchair accessible rest rooms, sewage disposal, tables, fire rings, grills, wood.

Located on the eastern side of the state, the park is known for its swimming.

Camel's Hump Forest Preserve

Contact the Department of Forests, Parks, and Recreation, 108 South Main Street, Waterbury, VT 05676 (tel. 802/241-3655).

One of Vermont's most popular day hikes is the climb up Camel's Hump. The distinctive 4,083-foot bare rock summit can be seen from almost the entire western part of the state.

Southern Vermont ◆ What to Do & Where to Do It

BIRD WATCHING

Old, clunky, and more than a little heavy, my trusty pair of binoculars can seem less and less essential when I'm stuffing my pack for a backcountry trip. But I can't bear to leave them behind when I head for the Green Mountains: more than 270 species of birds have been documented in the state, and I never know when I'll be graced by the sight of a golden eagle or peregrine falcon wheeling above the crag ahead, an egret or heron stoically picking through a marsh, or the silent shadow of a great horned owl blacking out the moon on a frosty night.

I won't have space here to do much more than run through the kinds of birds you're likely to see through the seasons in the wetland areas, northern hardwood and boreal forests, and alpine summits of Southern and Central Vermont—these are the "life zones," as biologists like to say, that make up the great part of Vermont's lands.

Up in the hills or down in the valleys, you'll find spring and fall the richest seasons for birding. The two lowland corridors that bracket the state—in the east the Connecticut River Valley, and in the west the Valley of Vermont (between the Taconics and the southern Green Mountains) and the broad Champlain Valley—are major conduits of the Atlantic Flyway, the aerial superhighway along which migratory birds pass on their way between southern wintering grounds and breeding grounds in the Arctic.

Marshes, fens, bogs, and calm inshore waters draw abundant **waterfowl,** including mallards, black ducks, wood ducks, huge numbers of ring-billed gulls, Canada and snow geese, blue- and green-winged teal, great blue herons, black-crowned night herons, and many other birds. New England's bogs and swamps also are popular with birders for the many **songbirds** that nest in them almost exclusively, including Nashville warblers, black-backed woodpeckers, and olive-sided flycatchers. Two places in southern Vermont to check out are the

West Rutland Marsh, off State Route 4A (you can walk the gravel roads or canoe through the marsh; go to the West Rutland Town Hall, at Marble and Main streets, tel. 802/438-2263, for more information) and the fascinating pitcher-plant, sphagnum moss, and black spruce environment of the **North Springfield Bog** (State Route 11 west from Springfield; first right onto Fairground Road; park at the sand pit next to the town garage; contact the Ascutney Mountain Audubon Society, P.O. Box 191, Springfield, VT 05156, tel. 802/674-5510, for more information). The marshes at the junction of many feeder streams and rivers and the **Connecticut River** are also prime birding spots; you might see great blue herons, bitterns, and spotted sandpipers. And the **Black Gum Swamp,** in the town of Vernon in the far southeast corner of the state, with its rare stands of centuries-old black gum trees, is a spot for varied forest- and wetlands-dwelling birds (right onto Pond Road about a mile south of Vernon off State Route 142; 1 mile, then right onto Huckle Hill Road; 1 mile, then right onto Basin Road and park at road's end; call Vernon's town clerk, tel. 802/257-0292, for more information).

The open waters draw diving species like buffleheads, goldeneyes, and ring-necked ducks. And though loons are much more common in northern Vermont, New Hampshire, and especially Maine, pairs of these birds—whose maniacal laughing call is one of the most unforgettable sounds of a summer night in the wilderness—nest as far south as the **Somerset Reservoir**.

An event to plan around is the migration in March and October of tens of thousands of **snow geese**—sometimes as many as 20,000 in a flock. The Champlain Valley is the best place to watch this spectacle, but you'll have plenty of opportunity around the lakes of southwest Vermont.

Hardwood forests—the mix of maples, beeches, birches, aspen, and occasional stands of softwood white pine and hemlock that dominate the wooded landscape of Vermont—are infiltrated more and more by seed- and nut-bearing hickories, various species of oaks, and hop hornbeams in southern Vermont, particularly in the Taconics. One of the more spectacular bonuses of this forestry pattern is the population of **wild turkeys** in the south. You might find them gobbling away in the oak-hickory forest of the **Glen Lake Trail** where it passes through **Half Moon State Park.** (Directions: from intersection with State Route 30, west on State Route 4A 1.3 miles and make right turn at sign for Lake Bomoseen, West Shore. After about 5 miles, near the entrance to Lake Bomoseen State Park, turn where you see the sign for Half Moon State Park and follow Moscow Road 3 miles. Park on the shoulder at the first open meadow; across the road from the meadow look for the trail heading off into the woods.) Here and throughout the forested areas of southern Vermont, you might see yellow-bellied sapsuckers, more than a dozen species of warblers, flycatchers, hermit thrushes—Vermont's state bird—and year-round residents such as black-capped chickadees, blue jays, ruffed grouse, white-breasted nuthatches, and woodpeckers, along with turkeys.

Other good hardwood-forest birding spots in the area include the nature and hiking trails in **Lake St. Catherine State Park** (see "Road Biking," below); the trails around **Big Equinox** and **Equinox Pond** (a map is available at the Equinox Hotel on State Route 7A in Manchester); the **Healing Springs Nature Trail** at **Shaftsbury State Park** (a mix of oak forest and marsh—watch for herons and cedar waxwings; located on State Route 7A, 4 miles south of Arlington; pick up a trail guide at the park concession); the

Wantastiquet Mountain hike that leads to an overlook of Brattleboro (trailhead off Bridge Street just across the Connecticut River in New Hampshire); and the **Springweather Nature Area,** a really fine and varied birding area (State Route 106 north from Springfield; right on Reservoir Road at 2.5 miles; nature area will be on your left).

Up above 3,000 feet in the Green Mountains, in the spruce and fir **boreal forests,** spring and summer bring great numbers of warblers, Swainson's and other thrushes, spruce grouse, scarlet tanagers, sapsuckers, flycatchers, and rose-breasted grosbeaks, among others. And on Vermont's highest peaks, those nearing or exceeding 4,000 feet, the last tortured-looking stunted balsam firs (called "krummholz") give way to an **arctic/alpine region** of bare rock, lichens and mosses, and low shrubs (only Camel's Hump and Mount Mansfield further north support true "alpine tundra" plant communities). This is a very difficult environment for life to maintain a foothold in, but it is still home to nesting ravens and dark-eyed juncos, gray-cheeked thrushes, and blackpoll warblers. Hike up into the boreal forest on any of the biggest peaks of the southern Greens, such as **Pico Peak Killington Peak, Shrewsbury Peak, Bromley Mountain,** and **Stratton Mountain** (all accessible from the Long Trail), as well as **Mount Equinox** near Manchester (accessible either by the Sky Line Drive toll road, off State Route 7A about 6 miles south of Manchester, or by a strenuous day hike from Burr & Burton Seminary, just off State Route 7A in Manchester Village via Seminary Avenue). You can get up into the mountains by chairlift in summertime and during foliage season at **Mount Snow,** Stratton, and Killington, as well as under your own steam.

Any open summit is also, of course, a good place to station yourself for fall hawk migrations. Sharp-shinned, broad-winged, Cooper's, red-winged, and red-shouldered hawks, goshawks, osprey, and the occasional golden eagle, bald eagle, or peregrine falcon (master of the 175-mph bullet dive) are all seen aloft from early September to the end of November. The best spots in Vermont are the isolated peaks, such as **Mount Ascutney** in the Connecticut River valley—they create an updraft that makes flying easy for the birds. (A paved road and hiking trail ascend to the summit from Ascutney State Park; left off U.S. 5, north of Ascutney.) Peregrines, once nearly extirpated from New England, are nesting again in a few of the steep crags they've historically occupied in Vermont, including **Hawk Ledge** (also great for watching its namesake) on Birdseye Mountain near West Rutland (2¹/₂ miles west of town in Birdseye Mountain Park on the south side of State Route 4A; North Peak Trail 1¹/₂ miles to Castle Peak Trail, Castle Peak Trail just under 1 mile to Hawk Ledge; contact Bird Mountain WMA at tel. 802/483-2314 for closings to protect birds).

My personal favorites among New England's avians are **owls.** Great horned owls are all over the woods, while screech owls are found in hardwood forests and aren't uncommon in residential parts of towns. Saw-whet owls live in stands of coniferous woods (especially pine and eastern hemlock), and snowy owls are particularly fond of wide, open fields. The amazing thing about owls is their responsiveness to calls; you can go out with a flashlight and either a tape player and a recording of owl calls (make an edited recording of the owl calls from Roger Tory Peterson's *Field Guide to Bird Songs of Eastern and Central North America,* Cornell University, 1983) or nothing but your own imitations of owl hoots. If you're game for the latter, try *hoo-hoo-hoo, hoooo-hoooo*—the call of the great horned owl—with the last two hoots

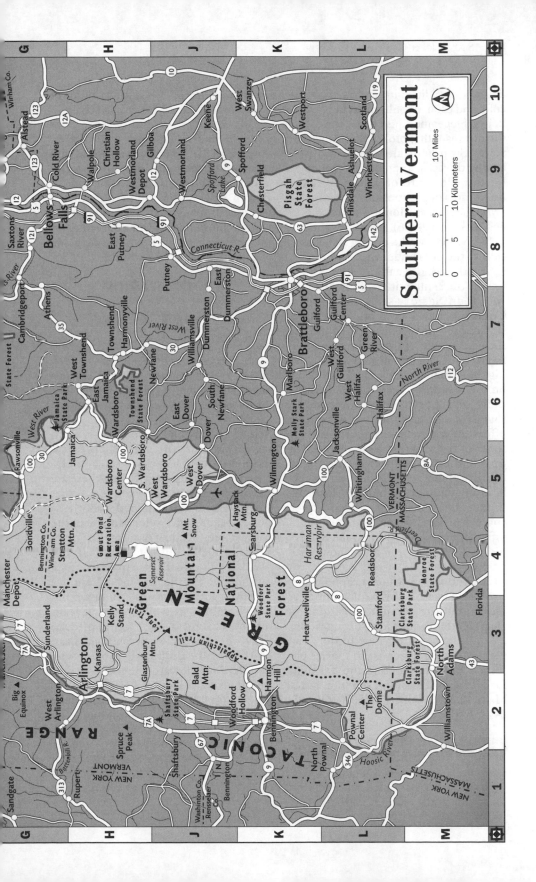

Southern Vermont

descending a little in pitch. On a clear, cold, and calm moonlit night in November or December, just drive out one of the dirt roads that proliferate all over the state. Stop here and there and play or sing the calls, keeping an eye peeled for the silhouette of your owl. It can be an amazing experience. Naturalist Lynn Levine, at Mount Snow (tel. 802/ 464-3333, ext. 4356), offers a nighttime "Owl Moon" walk, during which she calls to the owls under the bright moon.

Another cold-weather birding highlight is the annual ritual of the National Audubon Society's **Christmas Bird Counts.** Within a week or two on either side of the holiday, local chapters of the society venture out into the frigid Vermont winter for an entire day of counting the different species and individual numbers of birds they can find within their area. I've never done it, but it sounds like one of those activities that offers an esprit-de-corps and unique sense of the wild that more than makes up for the hardship of dealing with the elements. CBCs are currently held in southern Vermont in Rutland, Bennington, Brattleboro, Saxton's River, and Springfield; contact the Vermont office of the National Audubon Society (tel. 802/496-5727) for info on how to get involved.

See the other Vermont chapter in this book for more nearby birding opportunities, and the section on birding in chapter 1 for various local organizations and guidebooks. Serious birders can get a complete checklist of species observed in Vermont from the **Vermont Department of Fish and Wildlife,** 103 S. Main St., Waterbury, VT 05676 (tel. 802/ 241-3700).

CANOEING

Vermont's three great canoeing waterways—the Missisquoi, Lamoille, and Winooski rivers—are up north, but the southern third of the state has a lot of good paddling. The **West River** in springtime is probably the best whitewater run Vermont has to offer. There's good, and fairly long, novice and intermediate paddling runs on the **Connecticut River, Otter Creek,** and the **Batten Kill.** And I found a couple of unspoiled ponds that offer interesting, varied shorelines and perfect spots for primitive camping—the locals are going to kill me for revealing these!

QUIET WATER

Grout Pond

West of Stratton. Access: Take Grout Pond Road 1 mile south off Kelley Stand Road (Arlington–West Wardsboro Road); 12 miles east of Arlington, 7 miles west of West Wardsboro. Primitive camping permitted.

Seeing ghostly mists over glass-smooth water become suffused with early-morning sun, or listening to an amphibian choir warm up at twilight—these are the serene and magical experiences that you find at an undeveloped backwoods pond. Grout Pond is deep in one of the wildest and loveliest parts of the Green Mountain National Forest; though small, it's a perfect place to retreat for a day or two in the woods. There are tentsites with fire rings strung around the shoreline, as well as several lean-tos and a cabin. It's a beautiful place to fish—sunnies, yellow perch, some bass; on the small side but all good eating. Paddle down toward the south end of the pond for a look at a beaver lodge. There are lots of good hiking trails around, too, including a loop around the pond, a walk south from the pond to the north end of Somerset Reservoir, a precipitous climb up Stratton Mountain, and the Long Trail, accessible a couple miles west along Kelley Stand Road.

Branch Pond

East of Arlington. Access: Take Branch Pond Road 2 miles north off Kelley Stand Road (Arlington–West Wardsboro Road); 8 miles east of Arlington, 13 miles west of West Wardsboro. 0.25-mile carry to pond from parking area. Primitive camping permitted.

Much the same kind of place as Grout Pond (see above), but even more remote. There are some really nice tent sites here, but you'll be happier in late summer or early fall if you're camping— I was eaten alive by mosquitoes here in June. The general bogginess of the pond, which makes paddling the shoreline so interesting, probably has a lot to do with the bug situation.

Half Moon Pond

Hubbardton County, north of West Castleton. Access: Take U.S. 4 west from Rutland to State Route 30/Castleton Corners Exit. South on State Route 30 to State Route 4A, then west on State Route 4A, right (north) onto road to West Castleton/ west shore of Lake Bomoseen. Continue for about 7 miles on this road to Half Moon State Park.

A small pond with a pretty state park that gets fairly crowded on summer weekends, Half Moon's facilities make it an easier place to take young children than the two ponds above. There's a good nature trail (see "Bird Watching," above), good trout, bass, and pike fishing, and some beaver activity on the pond.

QUICKWATER

Otter Creek, North Dorset to Rutland

31 miles, mostly quickwater; portages at South Wallingford (Class III ledges) and Wallingford (dams, Class II rapids). Best put-ins at North Dorset, east off U.S. 7;

1 mile north of Emerald Lake onto dirt road; and at northmost bridge in Wallingford. Last take-out in Rutland, River Street Bridge— dam is not far beyond. Maps: USGS 15 minute Wallingford, 7.5 minute Rutland.

Otter Creek's best paddling sections are a bit further north, but even here, close to the creek's source, you can have yourself a fine afternoon's run. It's really only runnable in late spring, and then it's still quite narrow, with an occasional fallen log to contend with. Probably the most consistently runnable section (and the way to avoid any portages) is from just north of Wallingford where Otter Creek is joined by the Mill River, and Rutland.

Batten Kill River, Manchester to New York State Line

10.5 miles. Mostly flat- and quickwater, with some undaunting rapids. No portages, but very possibly fallen trees you'll need to carry or line your canoe around, and a washed-out dam at second bridge in Arlington. Put-in: east on Union Street from town square in Manchester about 0.75 miles; enter water below bridge. Take-outs: State Route 313 bridge in Arlington; any of the bridges from Arlington to state line. Maps: USGS 7.5 minute Manchester, Sunderland, Arlington.

The Batten Kill comes close to exemplifying every pastoral stereotype people have about Vermont: swimmin' holes and cold waters ("invigorating," for the hardy) that are heaven-sent when the mercury climbs in August; wild, wise old brown trout and brookies, and the requisite fly fishermen hellbent on landing them; silos and Holsteins seemingly everywhere you look; and, when it's really hot, a lot of unusual watercraft competing for current with you—enormous innertubes, rafts, floating chaise longues and the like.

The Manchester–Arlington section of the Batten Kill is fairly narrow for the most part, and you may have to line around fallen trees here and there; there are also some Class II rapids at the mouth of Roaring Branch which you can carry on the right bank if you want. The river widens out some as it departs Arlington, and from then on it's smooth, fast sailing all the way to the border.

Connecticut River, Bellows Falls to Brattleboro

17 miles. Easy; flat- and quickwater. No portages. Put-in: below dam at Bellows Falls. Take-out: Route 9 bridge to Keene, N.H., just above Brattleboro. Maps: USGS 15 minute Bellows Falls, Keene, Brattleboro.

An effortless paddle through Hallmark-perfect farming country. Good bass and pike fishing. Bring along some floatin' music—Hoagy Carmichael is just about the right speed. You could continue on, through deadwater for the most part, to Vernon Dam, but then you'll have to take out within sight of Vermont Yankee, a nuke plant that I've been terrified of since I was a kid.

WHITEWATER

The few good whitewater runs in southern Vermont are on tributaries of the Connecticut River; among them are the **Black River** near Cavendish, the **Williams River** from Chester to Brockways Mills, **Saxton's River** from Grafton to Saxton's River Village, and the **Winhall River** and **Wardsboro Brook,** two tributaries to the West River. All of these are runnable for just a few weeks in spring, and can be sufficiently treacherous that only truly competent paddlers and those under a guide's supervision should attempt them. See "Outfitters," below, if you're looking for a guide.

The **West River** is the most consistently navigable and most famous of southern Vermont's whitewater streams—it's well known for the races it hosts on dam-release weekends in spring and fall. The lower sections are fairly safe for intermediate paddlers.

West River, Townshend Dam to Connecticut River

19 miles. Quickwater, and Class I–II rapids (mostly the former). No portages. Put-in: below the dam on east (town) side of river, between dam and covered bridge. Take-out: under Interstate 91 bridge, at State Route 30. Maps: USGS 15 minute Brattleboro.

I'll leave the pulse-raising upper reaches of the West—where lurk ornery Class III–IV rapids such as the Londonderry Ledges and the Dumplings below Ball Mountain Dam—to the experts, who already know about this place, and to those of you who want to take on whitewater challenges under the watchful eye of outfitters and instructors. The lower section of this river is neither as scenic nor as daunting, but it is an excellent place to practice technique in fast currents and moderate rapids. Water levels are optimal during the Ball Mountain Dam releases and fairly rainy periods. The rapids that take the most concentration here are those right underneath the West Dummerston covered bridge—stay to the right.

The spring and fall releases from the Ball Mountain Dam, just upstream from Jamaica, usually occur during the last weekends of April and September. Call the **Department of Forests, Parks & Recreation** in North Springfield for more information, tel. 802/886-2215.

OUTFITTERS

Battenkill Canoe, Ltd. (U.S. 7A, Arlington, VT 05250; tel. 802/362-2800), located on the river, offers daily rentals.

They also feature two-, three-, and five-day inn-to-inn trips on Vermont's finest waterways.

Canoe the lower Connecticut with **North Star Canoes** (N.H. 12A, Cornish, N.H.; tel. 603/542-5802), situated just across the river from Windsor, VT. The check-in desk is the owner's barn. They offer full- and half-day trips.

Connecticut River Safari (P.O. Box 3A, Putney Road, Brattleboro, VT 05301; tel. 802/254-3908) also rents canoes and has guided tours on the Connecticut.

CROSS-COUNTRY SKIING

Vermont, of course, goes way back with cross-country skiing—Nordic skiing first took hold in the United States on trails through the valleys and woods of the Green Mountain State, and legends such as the Von Trapp family and Olympic medalist Bill Koch made their names here.

But let's cut to the chase: Vermont has an unbelievable wealth of cross-country opportunities, including dozens of Nordic skiing centers offering traditional striding tracks and groomed skating trails; lift-serviced areas where numerous telemarkers make their elegant lunges amid all the Lycra-clad mogul-bashers; limitless challenge and variety on snow-covered trails and unplowed forest roads criss-crossing the Green Mountains; the Catamount Trail, a long-distance trail that will soon stretch continuously from Canada to Massachusetts (see chapter 9 for details); and finally, a huge network of marked trails overseen by VAST (the Vermont Association of Snow Travelers). The latter are primarily for snowmobiles (one of which every self-respecting Vermont teenager simply must own), but they're great for skiing, too. Sure, Vermonters go to the ski-touring centers, but sometimes

picking out your own route among the "snowmachine" tracks and bushwhacks available just beyond your back yard is the most satisfying thing you can do on skis.

IN THE BACKCOUNTRY

The network of trails that guide hikers through the Green Mountain National Forest in the summer entice backcountry skiers come snow time. Miles and miles of trails leave you at serene ponds or atop small summits rarely visited in the winter. Backcountry skiing is a chance to soothe your soul on skis in a pastoral setting far away from the crowds who cruise downhill or venture to Nordic skiing centers. A helpful guide is the **"Winter Recreation Map"** of the **Green Mountain National Forest** (231 N. Main Street, Rutland, VT 05701; tel. 802/747-6700). There is also a **cross-country ski report** available by phone, recorded every Thursday (tel. 802/828-3239). Contact the **Catamount Trail Association** (P.O. Box 1235, Burlington, VT 05402; tel. 802/864-5794) for a map of the 200-mile Catamount Trail (see Northern Vermont section for more information). For trail and membership information about 3,500 miles of groomed snowmobile trails, contact the **Vermont Association of Snow Travelers** (P.O. Box 839, Montpelier, VT 05601; tel. 802/229-0005).

Worth a special mention here is the **Merck Forest & Farmland Center,** located in Rupert, not far from the New York border, between Rutland and Manchester. The miles of rolling farmland and stands of sugar maples are home to a slew of ungroomed XC trails. There's a trail map available at the parking area. This is a great place to try your hand at winter camping. To get here from the junction of State Route 30 and State Route 315 in East Rupert, take State Route 315 West for 2.6 miles. Turn left and drive a half mile to the parking lot and visitor center. (for more information on the Merck Forest see "Hiking & Backpacking," below.)

The four tours below are all on or near the spine of the Green Mountains, and are listed from south to north.

Harriman Reservoir

Allow 2–4 hours. Moderate; logging road with gradual ascent. Access: From Wilmington, take State Route 9 west for 3 miles until you spot a bridge on the left-hand side. Cross over, take another left, and drive for 0.2 mile. You'll see a blue Catamount X-C Skiing diamond hanging from a tree. Parallel park on the left-hand side of the road. Map: GMNF Winter Recreation map.

This old logging road owned by the New England Power Company is the southernmost portion of the Catamount Trail. The trail runs alongside the Deerfield River before swerving right and going uphill, providing vistas high above the Harriman Reservoir. You can continue on this trail the whole length of the reservoir to Readsboro if you like.

On the cold day I set forth on this trail, the Deerfield River looked positively arctic. Steam rose from the rushing rapids as the dark blue waters carved through a torpid mix of ice and hard snow. I glided alongside the river, taking in the arresting sight before the trail took a sharp right and headed uphill. Ascending gradually past several dilapidated houses and old logging operations, I started to think that the trail was turning into a dud. But soon the path leveled off and the rusted RVs were replaced by magnificent views of the reservoir. Through the barren maples, oaks, and birches, I could see ice fishermen standing on the frozen lake.

I turned around at the point where a spit of land juts out east, but you might feel like going considerably farther, which is certainly possible. If not, it's an easy downhill glide back to the Deerfield River and your car.

Woodford State Park

Loop trail; allow 1.5 hours. Easy to moderate; rolling terrain. Access: From Wilmington, take State Route 9 West for 9.6 miles. Parking is located on a side road 0.2 mile past the country store on the right-hand side of State Route 9. Parallel park on the side-road. Carefully walk across Route 9. The trail starts behind a gate on the left-hand side of the road. Map: GMNF Winter Recreation map.

The Vermont license plates on cars parked across State Route 9 from Woodford State Park say it all—this is a trail that only locals know about and one I'm sure they would prefer to keep to themselves. It's a loop through beautiful winter scenery—over frosted ponds and under dense evergreens. If you're in southern Vermont for only a day or two, this is a good trail to take.

One bit of winter magic that every Vermonter is aware of is the way snow levels seem to rise the minute you begin ascending into the Green Mountain National Forest. There certainly was more than enough accumulation on the paths of Woodford State Park on the day my wife and I tried the trail. We began by cruising down a short hill before crossing iced-over Adams Reservoir. At Campsite 23, we veered right and started our loop around the park. It was early morning; sunlight glistened off branches heavy with snow. The only sound we heard was the rapid patter of a woodpecker overhead. You'll have a lot of options for mini-loops as you glide along, and the main trail coasts up and down short hills and over rushing brooks before returning you back to the starting point.

Somerset Reservoir

4 miles round-trip; allow 2–3 hours. Easy; evergreen/hardwood forest and open meadows; mild rolls in pitch. Access: from West Wardsboro on State Route 100, turn west at the West Wardsboro Store and continue for 7 miles on Kelly Stand Road (Arlington–West Wardsboro Road). There's a parking area at the end of the plowed section. Map: GMNF Winter Recreation map.

In a region of the Green Mountain National Forest known for its wealth of cross-country skiing trails, Somerset Reservoir is one of the finest. The 4-mile round-trip trail straddles a brook before crossing an open meadow that leads to the large body of water. Vistas of Mount Snow's North Face ski trails carved into the mountain can be seen on the far shores.

When I pulled into the parking lot here early on a Saturday morning, there was already a buzz in the air. Unfortunately, the noise came from numerous snowmobilers whipping down Kelly Stand Road. It sounded like the Indianapolis 500. I quickly threw on my skis and headed across the street to the start of the trail, hurrying toward peace and quiet. Several vigorous strides later, I began to breathe fresh air instead of fumes. The noise faded, replaced by the singing of birds. It seems few snowmobilers use this choppy but relatively flat trail, even on busy weekends.

The trail winds along a small brook known as the East Branch of the Deerfield River. The creek was barely visible beneath its blanket of snow, except for several holes where I could see water rushing by. Mountain ash and snow-laden evergreens lined the trail, with branches so burdened I had to duck

many times to avoid being decapitated—remember to watch your head out there.

As I reached the point where the East Branch opens into the Somerset Reservoir, I found to some dismay that the buzz was back. Groups of snowmobilers were cruising on the iced-over waters, but the view was so majestic that I didn't care. You can follow the snowmobilers and ski on Somerset to get a closer view of Mount Snow—I skied over to where the stone levees stood before turning around.

If you want to extend the trip, go back to where you veered right onto Somerset, then simply continue straight ahead. This 2.8-mile loop leads you to Grout Pond—one of the more serene and unspoiled little lakes I know of—and then back to the middle of the Somerset trail.

Mount Tabor Road Trail

Loop trail; allow 2.5–3 hours. Moderate to strenuous; narrow, occasionally steep trails through deep woods. Access: From Manchester, take State Route 11 East. Keep left through the village of Peru and continue 4.5 miles until you reach the Landgrove Town Hall. Turn left and drive for 0.7 mile before you take another left where the road forks. Cross a brook and take your first right onto Forest Road 10. Parallel park at the right-hand side of the road, avoiding the plowed turnaround area. Map: GMNF Winter Recreation map.

The Mount Tabor Road Trail has a misleading name: you only ski on this unplowed road for five minutes before veering left onto a winding narrow path that sweeps up and down short hills. Once you get the hang of this roller-coaster ride, the trail suddenly climbs steeply up the side of a mountain ridge, leaving you high atop the Green

Mountain National Forest. Several logging roads intersect the trails, making an already complicated route even more so—you'll do well to get the map. The trail is a good workout through pretty wild country.

The day I set out on this trail was accompanied by steady snowfall. By the time I parked my car in this remote region of southern Vermont, 6 inches of powder covered the ground, with the flakes still coming down. My diagonal stride felt as smooth and effortless as a Fred Astaire dance. I took Mount Tabor Road (Forest Road 10) for less than 0.2 mile and then made a left onto the Utley Brook Trail, marked with the diamond for "most dangerous." A better name would have been the Hallucinogen Trail, because whoever designed this path must have been on some serious drugs. The trail weaves up and down slopes, and turns sharply left or right without warning. It's also extremely narrow—only wide enough, mostly, for one svelte skier. Don't daydream or you might end up impaled on the trunk of an evergreen.

I was dizzy by the time I found myself looking up at the ridge of Pete Parent Peak. Instead of following the trail's blue diamonds and attacking the uphill climb, I took a left and followed another skier's tracks rapidly disappearing under the new snow. They brought me straight to the backdoor of his farmhouse. I guess I was destined to climb the 400 feet up Utley Brook Trail. I learned a valuable lesson—stick to the blue diamonds.

I climbed past a family of yellow birches and numerous uprooted oaks before reaching the top of the ridge, where a pair of black-capped chickadees congratulated me. A left onto Little Michigan Trail and another quick left brought me to the Stone Place Trail. Speeding downhill, I heard rustling in an evergreen's branches and suddenly two wild turkeys appeared, flying to the lead.

From here the trail is quite an orienteering challenge: continuing on Stone Place Trail, I veered right at a road and left across Griffith Brook. A mile later, the trail curves left onto Jones Brook Trail, a sweeping path that gently slopes downhill across fields of short brush and dense forests of hardwoods. I was just beginning to have fun when Jones Brook Trail abruptly ended at another logging road. A left turn brought me to a steep downhill, at which point I had to take off my skis and walk through a gracious farmer's backyard. A left and a quick right back to Forest Road 10 brought me to my snowed-in car.

NORDIC SKIING CENTERS
In Vermont, it seems like every inn has its own network of Nordic trails. There are literally thousands of miles of trails criss-crossing the state, and the **Catamount Trail** (see chapter 9 for more information) has taken advantage of it, weaving trails from many Nordic skiing centers into the state-long run.

The task of choosing one Nordic skiing center above the rest can be daunting given the limitless array of choices. However, you won't go wrong with any of the centers listed below, in south-to-north order.

The **White House Touring Center** (State Route 9, P.O. Box 757, Wilmington, VT 05363; tel. 802/464-2136), located in the foothills of Mount Snow and Haystack Mountain, offers 45 km of trail and a base elevation of 1,573 feet (high enough to mean fairly reliable snow). The White House is a turn-of-the-century classical mansion that is now a bed-and-breakfast (see "Inns & Resorts," below, for more information). Trails tend to cater to intermediates.

Prospect Ski Mountain (State Route 9, Woodford, VT 05201; tel. 802/

442-2575), on the Bennington side of State Route 9, is an old ski hill that now offers 50 km of scenic and well-maintained groomed trails, with an emphasis on wide skating lanes. It also is a jumping-off point for a nearly unlimited number of backcountry ski trails.

If you're lucky enough to be staying in the Old Tavern in Grafton (see "Inns & Resorts," below), don't miss the opportunity to cross-country ski at **Grafton Ponds Cross-Country Ski Center** (Grafton, VT 05146; tel. 802/843-2231), just down the road. A 30 km trail system starts from the center's log cabin, winding through the forested hillside and over long meadows.

Situated on the outskirts of the Green Mountains' Lye Brook Wilderness Area, **Viking Center** (Little Pond Road, RR Box 70, Londonderry, VT 05148; tel. 802/824-3933) is one of the oldest New England Nordic skiing centers. The 40 km of trails (30 km of which are groomed) have been challenging all levels of skiers for over 25 years.

Located in a remote part of the Green Mountain National Forest, the elegant **Village Inn** (Landgrove, VT 05148; tel. 802/824-6673 or 800/669-8466) is better known for its food and lodging than skiing. The 15 miles of groomed trails can often feel like a maze, but it really doesn't matter once you get back to that fireplace in your room. (See "Inns & Resorts," below, for more information on the inn.)

Close by, **Wild Wings Ski Touring Center** (Peru, VT 05152; tel. 802/824-6793) offers 20 km of groomed trails in the Green Mountain National Forest. There's usually snow here when there isn't much elsewhere—elevations are up around 2,000 feet.

Mountain Meadows (P.O. Box 2080, Killington, VT 05751; tel. 802/775-7077) is the cross-country equivalent of Killington, only 5 miles down the road.

Serious skiers tackle the 40 km of groomed trail that sit at 1,500 to 1,800 feet elevation. There's also an extensive network of backcountry skiing available.

If you can't find a trail that suits you at **Mountain Top Ski Touring Center** (Chittenden, VT 05737; tel. 802/483-6089), then you're hopeless. 70 km of groomed trails snake through forests and open fields, offering fine views of the Green Mountain National Forest.

OUTFITTERS

Nordic Adventures (P.O. Box 155, RD 1, Rochester, VT 05767; tel. 802/767-3996) offers guided inn-to-inn tours. **North Wind Touring** (P.O. Box 46, Waitsfield, VT 05673; tel. 802/496-5771) leads weekend to five-day ski tours in central Vermont.

DOWNHILL SKIING/ SNOWBOARDING

Alpine skiing is right up there with leaf-peeping as one of the pursuits that put Vermont on the tourism map. Vermont's been synonymous with skiing since 1934, when a Ford Model T engine was installed on a hill near Woodstock to power the nation's first rope tow (little Suicide Six now occupies the spot). As recently as 10 years ago, there were still rope tows around here and there, along with other stone-age relics such as J-bars, poma lifts, all-natural snow—and grizzled, flannel-clad mountain men on skis. But two decades of frantic work to keep pace with Rocky Mountain skiing have changed the face of Vermont skiing. Now we have trams and detachable quads, 100 percent snowmaking coverage, grooming on even the steepest of steeps, and, ripping around everywhere, grizzled, flannel-clad snowboarders. Every year there are more trails, more lifts, more lines, more condos, more people. What keeps 'em coming? And what has all this development meant to the quality of the skiing?

Well, the big draw is Vermont's mountains: they're BIG mountains by almost anyone's standards—there are 10 ski areas here with vertical drops of 2,000 feet or more, second only to Colorado's 16. The mountains themselves may not be the 12,000-footers you'd find in the Rockies or the Alps, but ski areas here take full advantage of what they've got. This means long runs and an amazing diversity of terrain, from windblown summits offering huge views and steep drops through gnarled fir trees, to glade skiing through spruce or hardwood forest, to wide-open cruising boulevards and bump runs that always have snow and can seem like a fashion runway, to alarmingly narrow, unpredictable trails that rarely have adequate cover and bristle with hazards like tree stumps, ledges, and frozen waterfalls even after a big dump, and seem to roll and fall down the mountain as naturally as a mountain stream would.

The big drawback of all the development, as far as I'm concerned, is the slow disappearance of the last mentioned type of trail—the classic stuff of New England skiing—as ski areas widen and groom more and more trails. You'll still find plenty of these narrow, quirky trails further north, at places like Stowe, Sugarbush, and Mad River.

Another reason the skiers keep coming is that Vermont's ski area operators become ever more wily in their annual battle against the elements, maintaining good machine-made snow cover on a variety of terrain through the most depressing of January thaws. Of course, there's nothing like natural snow; the excitement a big snowstorm sparks in eastern skiers is something to behold. The rare big powder day brings out hot skiers from all over the hills, and when you head up the mountain in the morning the whoops and hollers you hear from people making first tracks below remind you how much fun skiing can be.

Southern Vermont, relatively so close to Boston and New York, has ski hills that are very different from those you'll find in central and northern Vermont. The big areas here—Mount Snow, Stratton, Okemo, and Killington—are now thoroughly built up; there are scores of restaurants, bars, condos, and other resort stand-bys clustered round the base lodges. The skiing itself has been tailored to give huge numbers of intermediate skiers as much cruising satisfaction as they could ask for, with much wider trails and more snowmaking than you'll find farther north, intense grooming that leaves trails buffed to a sheen every morning, generally gentler pitch on the slopes, and both high lift capacity and a lot of skier traffic.

SKI AREAS

The ski areas below are listed south to north, starting from the bottom of the state and driving straight up State Route 100—the carotid artery of Vermont ski area access, which runs east of the ridge of the Green Mountains.

Mount Snow/Haystack

West Dover, VT 05356. Tel. 802/ 464-3333, ext. 371; snow report, tel. 802/ 464-2151. 130 trails (21% beginner, 61% intermediate, 17% expert); 24 lifts including 2 quads, 9 triples, and 10 doubles; 1,700-foot vertical drop. Full day tickets $47 weekends, $42 weekdays.

For years Mount Snow has had a rep as a sort of magnet for singles from the cities; these days it's trying to attract more families. If you want a day of effortless high-speed cruising—whether on skis or on a snowboard—this is the place for you: Nearly the whole front face of the mountain is one broad, groomed, and well-covered boulevard after another, none of which will trouble you with difficulties beyond the optional jump or two. (I've never seen so many people seemingly obsessed with getting air— sometimes Mount Snow can look as if a huge herd of jackrabbits is hopping its way down the mountain.)

Mount Snow has an entire area reserved for neophytes, and anyone with a few days' confidence can comfortably handle all those extra-wide intermediate trails. Experts will find some genuinely steep pitches on the North Face, but in my opinion all the grooming and snowmaking does an injustice to them— manmade snow on steep slopes seems to inevitably establish a base of rock-like hardpack, and on the steeps I'd rather pick my way down a nice, well-established line through big moguls than scrape and rattle across concrete. A large glade-skiing area was due to open in 1995–96, which could up the interest level for good skiers.

Stratton

Stratton Mountain, VT 05155. Tel. 802/ 297-2200; snow report, tel. 802/297-4211. 92 trails (34% beginner, 38% intermediate, 28% expert); 12 lifts including 4 quads, a 12-passenger gondola, 1 triple, and 3 doubles; 2,003-foot vertical drop. Full day tickets $46 weekends, $40 weekdays.

Get those spanking new outfits ready for Stratton, a mountain known for its Day-Glo dress code. It's also a groomed, cruiser's mountain, but with a little more variety than Mount Snow. It's also the birthplace of snowboarding—Jake Burton, founder of Burton Boards, did his experimenting here, and is still king of the East as far as snowboarding is concerned. The half pipe is perfectly maintained, and carving through Stratton's long boulevards is as good as it gets.

Stratton has a new 10-trail "Learning Park" that's perfect for both first-timers and intermediates looking to bone up on the finer points of carved turns and bump skiing. And there's easy skiing from the summit at Stratton, a rare commodity that lets novices get the good snow and big-mountain views that they otherwise might have to write off with a rueful "Wait 'til next year." (No Red Sox pun intended, really.) Intermediates will like Supertrail, a wide avenue that has more going on than meets the eye. And yes, there are good moguls at Stratton— try Upper Middlebrook, Upper Spruce, and Free Fall.

Bromley

P.O. Box 1130, Manchester Center, VT 05255. Tel. 802/824-5522. 39 trails (35% beginner, 34% intermediate, 31% expert); 9 lifts including 1 quad and 6 doubles; 1,334-foot vertical drop. Full day tickets $39 weekends, $25 weekdays.

Not nearly as overwhelming as the other Vermont ski resorts, Bromley is one of the oldest in the country. Lift lines are shorter and people are more down-to-earth. Don't let that seemingly even distribution of terrain across the skill levels fool you—this is a novice and intermediate area with a good ski school and plenty of slowpoke and cruising terrain, but not much to keep the ambitious challenged. One secret about Bromley: If you've rolled all the way up from the city to find your family ski weekend caught in the deep freeze of a Vermont cold snap, this is the place—it faces *south*, and a little sun on such days really is the difference between misery and a good time.

Okemo

RFD 1, Ludlow, VT 05149. Tel. 802/ 228-4041; snow report, tel. 802/228-5222.

Southern Vermont Ski & Winter Sport Shops				
City	**Shop**	**Location**	**Telephone**	**Additional Services**
Brattleboro	Burrows Sports Shop	97 Main Street	802/254-9430	repairs; alpine ski rentals (monthly or seasonal rentals only); rollerblade rentals
Mt. Snow	Bonkers Board Room	Dover Retail Center, Rt. 100, West Dover	802/464-2536	repairs; alpine ski and snowboard rentals; snowboard demos
	World Class Ski Experts	Rt. 100, Brookhouse Complex, West Dover	802/464-8852	alpine ski rentals and demos
	The Cupola	Rt. 100, West Dover,	802/464-8010 or 800/535-5013	repairs; alpine ski rentals and demos
	Frasers' Mountain Shop	Mt. Snow Access Road, West Dover,	802/464-2222	repairs; alpine ski, snowboard, snowshoe rentals; alpine ski demos
Manchester	Manchester Sports	Rt. 7A	802/362-2569	repairs; xc ski rentals
	Great Outdoors Trading Co.	Rts. 11 & 30, Manchester Depot Station	802/362-0410	repairs only
Stratton/ Winhall	Equipe Sport	Junction 30 & 100, Rawsonville	802/297-2847	repairs; alpine ski, xc ski, snowboard, and snowshoe rentals; alpine ski demos
	North House	Rt. 30, Bondville	802/297-1755	repairs; alpine ski, xc ski, ice skate, snowshoe, and snowboard rentals; alpine ski demos
	Purple Alpine Outfitters	Rt. 30 (across from Stratton Access Road), Bondville	802/297-3475	repairs; alpine ski, snowboard, and ski rack rentals; alpine ski and snowboard demos
Okemo/ Ludlow	Sports Odyssey	Okemo Market Place	802/228-2001	repairs; alpine ski, snowboard, and snowshoe rentals
	Totem Pole	16 $\frac{1}{2}$ Pond Street	802/228-8447	repairs; alpine ski, snowboard, and snowshoe rentals; alpine ski demos

(continued)

City	Shop	Location	Telephone	Additional Services
Okemo/ Ludlow (cont.)	Northern Ski Works	10 Main Street	802/228-3344	repairs; alpine ski, snowboard, bike, and rollerblade rentals; alpine ski and snowboard demos
Killington/ Pico	Ski Shack	Rts. 4 & 100 North	802/775-2821	repairs; alpine ski and snowboard rentals; alpine ski and snowboard demos
	Dark Side Snow Board Shop	Killington Road	802/422-8600	repairs; snowboard rentals and demos
	Peak Performance	Killington Road	802/422-9447	repairs; alpine ski rentals and demos
Rutland	The Great Outdoors Trading Company	219 Woodstock Avenue	802/775-9989	repairs; alpine ski rentals and demos

83 trails (30% beginner, 50% intermediate, 20% expert); 11 lifts including 7 quads and 3 triples; 2,150-foot vertical drop. Full day tickets $46 weekends, $43 weekdays.

On a day when you had to look *really* hard to find a dirty patch of snow on a Vermont hill, I went skiing at Okemo and finally learned that machine-made snow really could be a godsend. The snowmaking and grooming are so good here I'm half-surprised they don't stay open year-round. Intermediates always have and will continue to love Okemo; it's got tons of good cruising terrain, and the area will let moguls form from time to time on runs down the main face of the mountain that are pitched just right to give a learner a little bit of slack. Until recently, the black-diamond skiing was a little disappointing, but word is that the new South Face area has some honest-to-god white-knuckle trails. Still, if it's terror you want, Killington is more inspiring.

Ascutney Mountain

State Route 44, Brownsville, VT 05037. Tel. 802/484-7000. 31 trails (26% beginner, 39% intermediate, 35% expert); 4 lifts including 3 triples, and 1 double; 1,530-foot vertical drop. Full day tickets $36 weekends, $32 weekdays.

Like nearby Bromley and Suicide Six, Ascutney Mountain is a great place to ski with the kids for a day or a week. This monadnock has plenty of easy skiing on which first-timers can get their footing, and there are meandering intermediate runs and a few shortish mogul trails to challenge the upwardly mobile.

Killington

Killington Road, Killington, VT 05751. Tel. 802/422-3333; snow report, tel. 802/422-3261. 165 trails (49% beginner, 20% intermediate, 31% expert); 20 lifts including 7 quads, an 8-passenger gondola, 4 triples, and 5 doubles; 3,150-foot vertical drop. Full day tickets $42 all week.

With six interconnected mountains and six base lodges, Killington isn't just big, it's massive. Maybe that's why you find so many New Yorkers here. After a week of skiing far more trail than you can keep track of, you still find yourself saying "Oh yeah, I forgot all about *that* chairlift."

This can be both good and bad. You can get lost at Killington as easily as you might on the tangle of freeways through the slag heaps of eastern New Jersey; the trail map might qualify as a one-volume encyclopedia; and when you do screw up, you may be looking at a skate over a quarter-mile flat to the nearest lift. Even with all those lifts and trails, you'll still run into some godawful lift lines and bottlenecks on the hill. And watch out for the teenybopper hotdoggers who think they own the mountain. In short, this is just not the place to go if you're looking for skiing that has that sense (like all the best of Vermont) of the hand of man working in wholesome concert with the hand of nature.

Now for the good news: You'll simply never run out of skiing here, no matter what your level. Beginners and novices should take advantage of one of the best ski schools anywhere, a landmark learning hill in Snowshed, and good novice cruising runs in the Rams Head and Snowdon areas. Rams Head is relatively serene for Killington, and has excellent intermediate cruisers as well—and check out Swirl if you're feeling particularly strong. Skye Peak has an avalanche of moderate to strong intermediate terrain—and even more skier traffic. The Glades and South Ridge chairs also have lots of intermediate cruisers. And speaking of glades, Killington, like several other eastern areas, is trying to take better advantage of the one thing the East has that the treeline-and-up areas of the Rockies and Sierra Nevada don't always have—trees. About 100 acres of tree-skiing—they're calling it "fusion zones"—should open during the 1996 season.

Onward to the steeps. Bear Mountain was probably the most-hyped ski-area improvement in Vermont history, and Outer Limits indeed has the buffalo-sized moguls and gut-wrenching pitch every Type-A bump freak dreams of. Hundreds of thoughtless onlookers on the chair and sidelines are dying to see you eat it—go ahead, prove 'em wrong. Me, I'm happier on the Killington Peak black diamonds like Cascade and Down Draft, the lesser lights on Bear Mountain, and East Fall and Royal Flush near the Snowdon area, all of which will tax you plenty.

The Skye Peak trails, Snowdon, and Glades—Killington abounds in good snowboarding possibilities. The only thing to be extra careful to avoid is those damn flats. Read those trail maps. And one last tip: if you're here on one of the busy weekends, park at the Sunrise Mountain Base Lodge off State Route 100, not the main Killington Base Lodge; you'll save yourself a little time, as well as the sensation of being in a herd of neon-clad cattle.

Pico

Sherburne Pass, Rutland, VT 05701. Tel. 802/775-4346; snow report, tel. 802/775-4345. 42 trails across 4 peaks (9 beginner, 20 intermediate, 13 expert); 10 lifts including 2 quads, 2 triples, and 3 doubles; 2,000-foot vertical drop. Full day tickets $41 weekends, $37 weekdays.

Next door to Killington, Pico is much more low-key than its gargantuan neighbor. It offers a good breather and then some from wrestling that monster, especially on a powder day. The resort, opened way back in 1938, is a little short on true beginning terrain, but has lots of fairly easy and interesting cruisers, peaking in difficulty with Pike and Forty-Niner. There's some tricky terrain at Pico, including bump runs like Summit Glade, Upper Giant Killer, and Sunset '71. Pico was one of the first Vermont hills to go snowboard-friendly, and still draws a lot of stick-riders.

FISHING

Southern Vermont's waters harbor all the major sport fish you'll find elsewhere in the state. Wild coldwater species such as brook and rainbow trout are found in the upper watersheds of most of the big rivers (with "brookies" or "square-tails," as everyone calls them, particularly common in the purest, coldest streams and mountain ponds, and rainbows in whitewater). The notoriously finicky brown trout is found (along with rainbows) in the middle part of these rivers and sometimes in the warmer waters downstream. Warmwater lakes and big rivers are rich fisheries for large- and smallmouth bass, landlocked salmon, lake trout, walleye, northern pike, yellow perch, sunfish, and smelt.

The 27-mile-long **Batten Kill River** is famous for its wild trout fishing. It runs from Manchester village south to Arlington, and then west into New York. In Vermont, its clear, cold waters harbor brown and brook trout. The trout are known for their elusiveness, perhaps due to the large population of fishermen and the abundance of natural food. Most of the fly-fishing situations can be handled with a fly rod that takes a 6-weight line. However, if you have a rod that will take a 5- or 4-weight line, you have an even better chance of hooking a fish. The fishing season on the river extends from the second Saturday in April to the last

Sunday in October. The fall months can provide some of the best fishing of the year—trout feed heavily as they sense the lean times of winter coming on. Other southern Vermont streams with wild trout include the tributaries and mid- to upper sections of the **Hoosic, Walloomsac, Green, Mettawee, Poultney, Mill,** and **Castleton Rivers,** all west of the Green Mountains, and the **Deerfield, West, Saxtons,** and **Williams Rivers** east of the mountains.

The **Connecticut River's** fishing gets short shrift, considering the variety and health of its recreational fishery. Anglers try to hook yellow perch, walleye, smallmouth bass, pike, and pickerel—as well as shad, which are beginning to re-establish themselves after a long absence from the Connecticut, with more and more fish using the Vernon and Bellows Falls fish ladder every year. An Atlantic salmon run may not be far behind.

North of the Batten Kill, **Lakes Bomoseen** and **St. Catherine** are replete with bass, lake trout, northern pike, and perch. **Otter Creek** is a warmwater stream good for northern pike and smallmouth bass. In the large, still-unspoiled wild areas of the Green Mountain National Forest in the central south, the **Somerset** and **Harriman Reservoirs** offer exemplary trout, bass, pike, and perch fishing year-round.

If you're looking for more specific information about where to position yourself on these waters for specific kinds of fishing, the **Vermont Fish and Wildlife Department,** 103 South Main Street, Waterbury, VT 05671-0501 (tel. 802/241-3700), provides an excellent combination map and fishing guide that shows where the dozens of state-owned fishing access sites are on the map. **DeLorme Mapping Company,** P.O. Box 298, Freeport, ME 04032 (207/865-4171 or 800/452-5931), publishes the *Vermont Atlas & Gazetteer,* which has a profusion of detail on fishing, in both text and maps. Finally, the guides and bait-and-tackle stores listed below will provide the most up-to-date handle of all on stream and river conditions and what the fish are hitting.

INSTRUCTION, BAIT-AND-TACKLE SHOPS & RIVER GUIDES

Manchester and the Batten Kill River are home to one of the top fly fishing schools in the country, **Orvis,** Manchester, VT 05254 (tel. 800/235-9763). The 2 to 2 ¹/₂-day courses are taught on the river and on Orvis' own casting ponds. The classes run twice a week from early April to mid-July, then on weekends only through August. They also offer parent/child and women-only weekends. The **Battenkill Anglers,** P.O. Box 2303, Route 7A, Manchester Center, VT 05255 (tel. 802/362-3184), provides private instruction or tours for one or two people. Also in the Battenkill Region, the **Brookside Angler,** State Route 7A, Manchester Village (tel. 802/362-3538), arranges 3 to 8-hour on-stream fly-fishing tutorials, guided float trips, and equipment rental.

The **Tangled Line,** on U.S. 4 near Killington (tel. 802/773-0736), is a good source of information in the area. They provide guided trips and rent fishing gear.

In the eastern part of the state, **Strictly Trout** in Westminster West (tel. 802/869-3116) offers guided service as well as overnight trips on the Connecticut River and its tributaries. **River Excitement,** Hartland Four Corners (tel. 802/457-4021), also offers drift trips on the Connecticut for trout fishing.

Larry Leonard sells fishing equipment near the Harriman Reservoir. He can be reached at Delar Depot, tel. 802/464-5391.

GOLF

Consistently rated one of the top golf courses in the state, the **Gleneagles Golf Course** is located on the historic grounds of the Equinox Resort in Manchester Village, State Route 7A, Manchester Village, VT 05254 (tel. 802/362-4700 or 800/362-4747). Avoid the loathsome "Snake Pit," a gaping hole of sand and scrub carved out of the hilltop green at the 13th hole. There's also a fair number of watery ditches bisecting the fairways. Other noted courses in southern Vermont include the venerable **Woodstock Country Club** (tel. 802/457-2114), a Robert Trent Jones redesign of a course founded in 1895; **Basin Harbor Golf Club** (tel. 802/475-2309), the 700-acre resort in Vergennes on Lake Champlain; challenging **Mount Snow Golf Club** in West Dover (tel. 802/464-5642); **Stratton Mountain's** 27-hole course composed of the 9-hole Lake, Mountain, and Forest courses (tel. 802/297-4114); **Rutland Country Club** (tel. 802/773-3254); and the **Sugarbush Golf Course** in Warren (tel. 802/583-2722).

For **golf instruction,** your best bets are the **Stratton Golf School** (tel. 802/297-4114), which offers one- to four-day sessions on its 22-acre training facility, ranked as one of the best in New England; and the **Golf School at Mount Snow** (tel. 800/240-2555), which offers two-day weekend or midweek courses, starting at $439 per person, including accommodations.

HIKING & BACKPACKING

Trying to pick a mere handful of trails from the vast web of footpaths that criss-cross southern Vermont borders on the absurd. In addition to the many unforgettable stretches of the Long Trail that are perfect for an afternoon walk or a three-day section hike, there are dozens of summits (in the Taconics, west of the Greens, as well as east of the main ridge of the Green Mountains) that have well-marked and maintained day-hiking trails. There are trails rolling through the foothills to back-country beaver ponds, and trails to low summits offering views of the Green Mountains and New Hampshire's White Mountains, with verdant farmland spread out in between. The sound of the wind, smells of evergreen and sweet air, and all the other subtle intricacies of Vermont's wilder lands were meant to be experienced at a hiker's pace.

Vermont's mountains can seem unrelenting. Very few of the hikes here are slow and steady. You start climbing from the trailhead and don't stop till you reach the summit. The soft-soil trails are usually hidden within a deep forest, the perfect place to lose yourself and others for a few hours.

A helpful overall guide is the USGS Green Mountain National Forest/ South Half map, available from the **Green Mountain National Forest** (231 N. Main St., Rutland, VT 05701; tel. 802/747-6700). If your jones for tramping in the Vermont hills is only whetted by what space allows me to list here, I suggest first of all that you buy the *Guidebook of the Long Trail* (Green Mountain Club, 1993), a model of what a trail guide should be; it includes a lot of side trails connecting to the LT. *50 Hikes in Vermont* (Backcountry) is selective and thus has good armchair trip-planning value, and the *Day Hiker's Guide to Vermont* (Green Mountain Club, 1993) has more hikes *off* the Long Trail than 10 people could walk in a lifetime.

DAY HIKES

Harmon Hill

3.4 miles round-trip. Allow 4 hours. Very steep, difficult climb from State Route 9, then a rambling lark on a high meadow. Access: On the Long Trail near Bennington; take Route 9 5.2 miles west, take the LT

south. Map: USGS 7.5 minute Woodford, Stamford.

It's an arduous trip up, but come at the right time of year and a big payoff awaits you. Harmon Hill's open summit is the result of an old burn that's maintained by the forest service to keep the views intact—and what views they are: to the west, Bennington spreads out below, along with the Bennington Battle Monument, with Mount Anthony rising on the far side. To the north, you can spy Glastenbury and Bald mountains. I once snuck a night's camp in up here (although Harmon Hill is within national forest boundaries, camping is officially *verboten;* it must lie on private land), and was treated to a long evening watching the sun sink and the lights of Bennington beginning to twinkle.

But for my money, the real treat here is the berry picking. An absolute mother lode of wild strawberries, blueberries, raspberries, and blackberries come to fruition up here every year in their respective seasons. The latter two, my favorites, ripen in mid- to late summer. Happy eating! And when it's time to go back down, maybe you'll have the chance, as I did, to tell a troop of miserable-looking boy scouts being forced up that hill that there really is a reason to get to the top.

Merck Forest & Farmland Center

Over 26 miles of forest trails, including this dirt road. Allow as much time as you want; you can camp here if you like. Easy, rolling farmland and forest trails. Access: from the junction of State Routes 30 and 315 in East Rupert, take State Route 315 west for 2.6 miles. Turn left and go a 0.5-mile to the parking lot and visitor center. Map: Available at the visitor center.

It was New Year's Day in Vermont and there was less than an inch of snow

The Long Trail

Vermont's crowning achievement for hikers is the Long Trail, a 265-mile-long footpath that runs the rugged length of the Green Mountains from Massachusetts to Canada. It was the country's first long-distance hiking trail, and Vermonters take great pride in both its claim to precedence and the endless variety of hiking along its narrow, rough, unspoiled route. All the special backcountry places you can find elsewhere in the state—high-country boreal bogs; many different kinds of hardwood and evergreen forests; rocky, windblown summits; ice-cold streams and beaver ponds; mountain meadows covered with wild strawberries and blueberries; and so on—you'll also happen on during a traverse of the Long Trail. And there are places on the Long Trail's route that are unique in Vermont: in particular, the tufts of Alpine/Arctic tundra and top-of-the-world feeling of Camel's Hump and Mount Mansfield.

The founders of the Green Mountain Club began cutting their "path through the wilderness" along the ridge of the Green Mountains in 1910, and by 1931 the trail ran continuously along the ridge of the Green Mountains from border to border. Even during these early years, the GMC had committed itself to providing primitive shelters along the trail. Today, the GMC has approximately 6,200 members who maintain the trail system, which is 440 miles in total if you include the 175 miles of side-trails. A little less than half of the trail is located in the two sections of the Green Mountain National Forest, in southern and central Vermont; the rest of the trail is on either state- or privately-owned land.

From the Massachusetts border, the trail heads north and joins the **Appalachian National Scenic Trail** for more than 100 miles. The trail gets much heavier use on this stretch, with both AT through-hikers and the generally greater numbers of people in southern Vermont (locals and tourists alike) getting out on the trail. The trail thus tends to be a little

on the ground; instead of going skiing, my friends T-Bone and Patti D. and I opted for a walk in the Merck Forest & Farmland Center, located northwest of Manchester near the state line. Former home of George Merck, president of Merck Pharmaceuticals, the 2,800-acre farm is now run by a nonprofit organization dedicated to education and preservation. We parked our car at the visitor center, grabbed a map, and walked through the gate onto Old Town Road. Our first stop was an old red barn where horses grazed on leftovers from summer, which seemed a long time ago on that frigid day. Bearing right and heading uphill, Old Town Road eventually reached Spruce Lodge, a picnic spot overlooking Mount Antone and the other mountains of the Taconic Range (trails run up both Mount Antone and Spruce Peak, offering some grand pastoral vistas). We skirted Birch Pond and found numerous yellow sugar ties in the woods, signaling our arrival at the sugar house. Climbing a ladder, we poked our heads inside the old wooden structure. During early spring, the sugar house is in full operation, and manufactures over 200 gallons of syrup a year. The syrup can be purchased at the visitor center. Once our curiosity was satisfied, we returned to the parking lot via the same route. We all slipped and wider and less wild, and you'll definitely run into more hikers than you would up north. And though this seems like splitting hairs to me, the south is a little flatter than northern sections—like the absolutely brutal sections fore and aft of Camel's Hump and Mansfield. But there are still climbs up 3,000-foot-plus peaks like Glastenbury Mountain (unrelentingly steep), Bromley, and the mighty Killington Peak, along with steep dips down into the gulfs that occasionally pierce the ridge. Make no mistake: There are certainly sections of the LT easygoing enough to be suitable for a family out on a day hike, but any multiday hike on this trail will take you over terrain that will challenge anyone's endurance. The 265 miles of the Long Trail are very long indeed. The trail climbs up a peak and descends steeply into a gap before ascending another mountain, which is the reason why many Vermonters call the Long Trail the "Up-and-Down" Trail.

At Sherburne Pass (U.S. 4) the AT veers east toward New Hampshire, while the Long Trail winds north into one of its most pleasurable sections. The Green Mountains from Sherburne Pass all the way through Appalachian Gap consist primarily of a narrow ridge that falls off sharply toward the Champlain Valley on the west, and a little less regularly toward the White River and Mad River valleys on the east. The ridge walking of this section, rising up to and descending down from greater and lesser summits, is wonderful high-altitude hiking. The forests range from mixed hardwood and evergreen transition forest to gnarled balsam-fir "krummholtz" on the high peaks. The trees give way to grand views of the valleys, and on overcast days you hike through clouds that lend everything an ominous gloom—and always, the wind rushes through the trees. The ridge is narrowest—and steadiest—on the Lincoln Gap to Appalachian Gap stretch,

continued

fell on our butts when we tried to walk down icy Old Town Road. Who said walking in the wintertime isn't as challenging as skiing?

White Rocks Trail

1.6 miles round-trip. Allow 1–1.5 hours. Easy; short switchbacking ascent to summit. Access: From the junction of State Routes 7 and 140 in Wallingford, follow State Route 140 east for 2.1 miles. Turn right and less than 0.1 mile later veer right again. You'll see a clearly marked sign for the White Rocks Picnic Area. 0.4 mile later, you'll reach the parking lot. Map: GMNF Summer Recreation map.

A short drive south of Rutland, the hike to White Rocks Cliff and the Ice Beds is a geologist's dream come true. Rocks of every size and shape blanket the hillside, the result of an ancient retreating ice cap. From the parking lot, follow the blue blazes along the pine-strewn Ice Beds Trail. The springy path is soon replaced by moss-covered rocks as you ascend a hogback. At impressive White Rocks Cliff, look out across Otter Creek Valley where a slope of white rocks careens down to the forest floor. Peregrine falcons and red-tailed hawks are often observed hovering in the skies above. From here, the blue-blazed trail is hard to follow as you walk through the dark one of my favorite walks anywhere. The views from Mount Abraham, Lincoln Peak, and Mount Ellen are unforgettable.

With Camel's Hump, Mount Mansfield, and Smuggler's Notch on the itinerary, the next section of the trail is spectacular—and is also the most popular day hiking trail in the state. After the Appalachian Gap, the LT descends gradually to its lowest elevation (on the Winooski River), before beginning its sternest test, the Bolton Mountain–Mount Mansfield/ Whiteface Mountain stretch. This is just unrelentingly steep, up-and-down hiking on rocky terrain, but hikers are rewarded with fantastic views and a rarified feeling of having spent a number of days up where the eagles live.

From State Route 15, near Johnson, the LT begins its last push, to Canada. This is by far the most remote, least traveled section of the trail, which passes through a great variety of interesting terrain. Meandering through quiet forests of firs and spruce, many through-hikers find this section a fitting finale to the trail.

For shelter, the Green Mountain Club maintains more than 60 lodges, camps, and lean-tos—this is one of the really special aspects of the trail. Hikers can easily walk from one shelter to the next in a day as they're set at 5- to 7-mile intervals. The shelters are generally warmer and drier than tents, and you'll make fast friends with the other hikers who share your shelter. Many LT end-to-enders—including myself— actually omit a tent from their pack, although it's not necessarily advisable to do so. You might be that one unfortunate who arrives late to a shelter, only to find it full, in which case you'll be glad if you do have a tent. The lodges are usually built of logs and hold up to 32 bunks. The camps are cabins with bunks and sleep 8 to 12 people. Both the lodges and camps can be almost luxurious, with indoor tables, windows, and even woodstoves. The lean-tos are the most common and the simplest accommodation, sleeping 6 to 8 people.

My favorite time to walk the Long Trail is mid-summer to early fall, when the bugs are gone (they can be murder in early summer), the berries are ripe (I

forest down to a brook. Cross the creek several times to get a close-up view of the Ice Beds, a boulder slide where shattered quartzite rock flows like a river down the hill. If you mistakenly lose the blue-blazed trail on the return trip, don't worry. Veer right on the dirt road and right again on the paved road to reach the parking lot.

OVERNIGHTS

Stratton Pond

7.8 miles round-trip. Allow 4–5 hours. Easy to moderate ascent on wide, fairly smooth trail. Access: From State Route 100 in West Wardsboro, take the Arlington–West Wardsboro road west for 8.2 miles, until you reach the intersection of Forest Road 71. There's a small parking lot due south of the intersection. A wooden sign marks the trailhead. Map: GMNF Summer Recreation map.

Stratton Pond is the largest body of water on the Long Trail. According to the *Guide Book of the Long Trail* published by the Green Mountain Club, "the pond receives the heaviest overnight use of any location on the trail, accommodating over 2,000 hikers between Memorial Day and Columbus Day." You'll easily understand why once you've must have consumed a ton of heavenly black- and raspberries on my hikes), and the trails are generally drier. Keep in mind that nights on the mountains, even in August, can be *really* cold; pack appropriately. Good rain gear and a reliable backpacking stove are always essential. It will take three to four weeks to cover the entirety of the LT, and you'll need to spend at least that much time planning your trip. If you're planning to spend more than three or four days on the trail, and especially if you want to go whole hog and do an end-to-end trip, the GMC's *Guide Book of the Long Trail* is indispensable. Also recommended is the *Long Trail End-to-Ender's Guide* (also published by the GMC), which is packed with nitty-gritty details on equipment sales and repairs, mail drops, and B&Bs that provide trailhead shuttle services. Two well-known food drops are the Inn at Long Trail, between Rutland and Killington on Route 4, and the Jonesville Post Office, east of Burlington on Route 2.

Many of the day hikes I've described in the hiking sections of the Vermont chapters are on the Long Trail. And in truth, it's in day hikes and weekend trips that most of us will get to sample the LT. The passes that cut through the Green Mountains make convenient trailheads; for day hikes all you'll need for an up-and-back jaunt is a jug of water, binoculars, and a really sturdy pair of boots. For section hikes it's ideal to go with another person and take two cars—you can drop one at the endpoint you've chosen for the hike and park the other at your starting point, thus leaving yourself a ride when you finish. Vermont is also one of the few places in the country where hitchhiking hasn't become an impossibility—there are plenty of people who know that the unkempt backpacker near a Long Trail access point isn't likely to be a scary drifter type, and will stop and gladly drive you all the way back to wherever your car is parked. All they'll ask in return is that you tell them some good trail stories.

For more information, contact the **Green Mountain Club,** State Route 100, P.O. Box 650, Waterbury Center, VT 05677 (tel. 802/244-7037).

hiked to this hidden gem in the wilderness: It's an idyllic dream of a backwoods beaver pond, with pure waters, lush forest on its shores, water lilies dotting its surface, and an abundance of wildlife—birds, deer, frogs and salamanders, perch, sunnies, and brookies in the water, and so forth.

The 3.9-mile (one-way) Stratton Pond Trail meanders through a young forest of beeches and ferns, before descending slightly into a thicket of white birches. At the 2.3-mile mark, you cross an old road and begin a gradual climb through the dense woods. A mile and a half later, hop from stone to stone over the small brook and then turn left on an old logging road to reach the junction of the Long Trail. Most of the LT through-hikers have just arrived from Stratton Mountain, 2.6 miles away. The pristine shores of Stratton Pond soon come into view. If you feel like adding another 1.4 miles to your hike, you can continue around the perimeter of the pond; it's beautiful if somewhat difficult walking, all green moss and slippery tree roots, with the brackish shallows of the pond alongside. I've spent some memorable nights here, listening to the chorus of peepers and waking to the sight of a ghostly mist spread across the pond. If you want to do the same, tent at one of the designated sites and pay the

Green Mountain Club caretaker-in-residence the overnight fee, which is just a few dollars. Otherwise, enjoy the picnic spot and then retrace your steps back to the trailhead.

OUTFITTERS & INN-TO-INN TOURS

Hiking Holidays, P.O. Box 750, Bristol, VT 05443 (tel. 802/453-4816) offers five-day trips around Manchester, Camel's Hump, and the historic villages of Woodstock and Grafton. **Walking Tours of Southern Vermont,** RR2, P.O. Box 622, Arlington, VT 05250 (tel. 802/375-1141), offers five-day, seven-day, and weekend inn-to-inn trips to some of my favorite spots in the region, including Merck Forest, Goshen, and Manchester Village. They also offer tours strictly for women. **Berkshire Hiking Holidays,** P.O. Box 2231, Lenox, MA 01240 (tel. 800/877-9656), offers five-day tours through the Green Mountains. **4 Seasons Touring,** P.O. Box 132, Townshend, VT 05353 (tel. 802/365-7937), offers inn-to-inn tours with an historical bent. **Merrell Hiking Center,** Killington Resort, Killington, VT 05751 (tel. 802/422-6708), provides information about hiking on Killington's five peaks. **Country Walkers,** P.O. Box 180, Waterbury, VT 05676 (tel. 802/244-1387), offers inn-to-inn tours, some led by natural history grad students at the University of Vermont. **Walking-Inn-Vermont,** P.O. Box 243, Ludlow, VT 05149 (tel. 802/228-8799), specializes in self-guided inn-to-inn tours where they shuttle your luggage to the next accommodation. **North Wind Touring** in Waitsfield offers inn-to-inn and nature trail tours (P.O. Box 46, Waitsfield, VT 05673, tel. 802/466-5771). Last but not least, **Country Inns Along the Trail,** RR3, P.O. Box 3115, Brandon, VT 05773 (tel. 802/247-3300), custom designs self-guided hiking trips where you can walk inn-to-inn.

HORSEBACK RIDING

Horseback riding in Vermont isn't confined to an hour-long ride around a farmer's backyard. The state has an extensive network of trails weaving through the forests and meadows, and —much as you can on foot, skis, or bicycle—you can actually go on four-day inn-to-inn riding tours.

On the eastern side of the Green Mountains, perhaps the best-established of all Vermont's stables is **Kedron Valley Stables,** State Route 106, South Woodstock (tel. 802/457-1480). Owner Paul Kendall will guide you through secluded woods and historic villages like South Woodstock, Grafton, and Proctorsville. Get used to your saddle because you'll be on it for five to six hours at a stretch during a four-day inn-to-inn jaunt. The horses average 15 miles a day. Kedron Valley offers riding lessons and short trail rides as well.

Close to the Bromley and Stratton areas, **Horses for Hire** (tel. 802/824-3750) is on South Road in Peru, just east of the ridge of the Green Mountains. Owner Debra Hodis accompanies all levels of riders on scenic trails in the Green Mountain National Forest. She also offers winter riding.

A little farther south and not too far from Putney, the **West River Lodge and Stable,** on Hill Road in Brookline (tel. 802/365-7745) has been offering guided rides and instruction since 1930. Trail rides commonly last the entire day. In nearby Newfane are the **West River Stables** (tel. 802/365-7745), offering riding instruction and trails.

West of Brattleboro you'll find **Flame Stables,** State Route 100, Wilmington (tel. 802/464-8329), offering Western saddle trail rides.

In the southwest corner of the state are **Valley View Horses & Tack Shop** (tel.

802/823-4649), located on Northwest Hill Road in Pownal and offering trail rides and lessons, and **Kimberly Farms** (tel. 802/442-4354), on Myers Road in Shaftsbury, about 10 miles north of Bennington, known for their sunset trail rides and cookouts.

If you're in the Killington/Rutland area, **Mountain Top Stables** in Chittenden (tel. 802/483-2311) offers guided trail and pony rides. Castleton's **Pond Hill Ranch** (tel. 802/468-2449) has lessons and trail rides.

ICE FISHING

Judging by the increasing number of snowmobiles on southern Vermont's largest lakes, ice fishing is becoming nearly as popular as fishing in summer. **Harriman** and **Somerset Reservoirs** are popular smelt and perch ponds. Smelt, northern pike, and perch are found in the waters of the western lakes— **Dunmore, St. Catherine,** and **Bomoseen.** For maps and additional information, contact the **Vermont Fish and Wildlife Department,** 103 South Main Street, Waterbury, VT 05671-0501 (tel. 802/ 241-3700).

LLAMA TREKS

Many of the five-day, seven-day, and weekend inn-to-inn trips offered by **Walking Tours of Southern Vermont** are accompanied by lunch-carrying llamas (RR2, P.O. Box 622, Arlington, VT 05250 tel. 802/375-1141).

MOUNTAIN BIKING

There's just no end to the old logging roads, primitive dirt roads, and even cowpaths that lace through southern Vermont. Your best source for up-to-the-minute local finds is going to be the area's bike shops (see below); an invaluable resource will be USGS 7.5-minute and 15-minute map series to the area (see chapter 1 for information on acquiring these maps).

BACKROADS RIDES

Bennington-Pownal Loop

14 miles. Moderate climbing; stretches of pavement fore and aft with a lot of dirt road in between. Access: Park at the Bennington Museum, on State Route 9 in Old Bennington, west of Bennington Village. Map: USGS 7.5-minute Bennington, Pownal, North Pownal.

This ride is like Bucolic Vermont Scenery 101—it's got the hay fields, the century-old roadside maples, apple orchards, old Victorian farmhouses, and an honest-to-god Revolutionary War battle site, marked by the Bennington Battle Monument, which commemorates the battle fought on August 16, 1777. Follow State Route 9 west for about 2 miles, then turn left onto Mount Anthony Road—there's a dairy farm right across from this intersection. After a half mile of gradual climbing, the pavement gives way to dirt. A flat stretch is followed by the major climb of the route as the road slowly and obliquely skirts the western slope of Mount Anthony, which rises to your left. There are classic rural views to your right and, shortly after you begin rolling downhill again, long views to the south toward Massachusetts. From here on, all you need to remember is to keep left; the mound of Mount Anthony is the hub around which these back roads revolve. Right where the road becomes paved again is the aforementioned monument, all of 306 feet high. When you hit U.S. 7, dodge back into the quiet again by taking a sharp left; this road will take you all the way back to State Route 9 and your starting point, located a half-mile to the east.

Green Mountain National Forest Road No. 10

10 miles (20 miles round-trip). Moderate; gradual elevation gain over dirt and gravel road. Access: Since the roads around Landgrove get a bit complex, come at this one from the west end; turn east off U.S. 7 at Danby and drive the short way to the village of Mount Tabor. In Mount Tabor, just after you enter the Green Mountain National Forest, you'll see a parking lot on the right. Map: USGS 7.5-minute Mount Tabor.

Impassable in winter, this little-traveled forest-service road rolls along above 2,000 feet through archetypal Green Mountain scenery, connecting the hamlets of Mount Tabor and North Landgrove. Brooks babble alongside for nearly its entire length, and you'll have an opportunity to make this a sort of backwoods triathlon—maybe 1½ miles east of the village of Mount Tabor is a Long Trail access point, and a 2-mile walk north will bring you to Little Rock Pond, a fine cold swimming hole if ever there was one. If you want to add some serious technical single-track to this otherwise undaunting ride, see the Mount Tabor Road Trail under "Cross-Country Skiing," above; the complex network of logging roads and narrow track here is equally inviting in warm weather.

MOUNTAIN BIKING CENTERS

Downhill ski areas are perfectly set up to provide a taste of mountain biking; they've got a pre-established trail network, of course, as well as lifts—which means you can take the laborious climbing out of the picture if you want. The **Killington Mountain Bike Center** (tel. 802/422-6232), **Pico Resort** (tel. 802/775-4346), and **Stratton Mountain Resort** (tel. 802/297-2200) all rent bikes and

have knowledgeable staffs that can set you up with everything from easy rides through meadows to very technical single-track. Mount Snow, however, was the first ski area to cater to fat-tire enthusiasts, and it still reigns supreme.

Mount Snow Resort Mountain Biking Center

Mountain Road, just off State Route 100 in West Dover. Tel. 802/464-3333. There is a $5 fee for trail access; $15 for chairlift ticket.

If you decide to venture to a ski resort to bike, Mount Snow is by far the best in the state. It was the first large ski resort to devote itself to mountain biking and now has 140 miles of rides to challenge everyone from first-timers to world champions. This number doesn't even take into account the miles of rides in the outlying country. Maps of the entire network are available in the base lodge. Grueling uphill single- and double-tracks climbs suddenly start their descent for mile-long exhilarating runs through secluded woods and bare mountain ski trails. If you want downhill thrills without lung-busting climbs, ride the chairlift to the 3,556-foot summit. Mount Snow also has numerous dirt roads to challenge mountain bikers who are new to the sport.

RENTALS, SCHOOLS, OUTFITTERS & INN-TO-INN TOURS

Mount Snow (tel. 802/464-3333) rents bikes, gives two-, four-, and seven-hour tours, and runs one of the top mountain biking schools in the northeast. The two-day program is offered every weekend from June 20 through October 4. The $132 price includes 12 hours of instruction, guided tours, unlimited lift access, and lunch both days.

Matt Moses and Greg Rosenthal have a large network of trails branching out from their 1,500-acre base camp at the foot of Bear Mountain. They also offer canoeing, hiking, and spelunking. Contact **Green Mountain Adventures,** P.O. Box 1711, Manchester Center, VT 05255 (tel. 802/375-2448). And **Viking Biking** (tel. 802/824-3933), on Little Pond Road in Londonderry, runs both mountain-biking day trips and inn-to-inn tours.

In the Lower Connecticut River Valley, the **Brattleboro Bike Shop** (802/254-8644) and Putney's **West Hill Shop** (tel. 802/387-5718) rent fat-tire bikes and are the nexus of local biking information.

Ludlow's **Cycle-Inn-Vermont,** P.O. Box 243, Ludlow, VT 05149-0243 (tel. 802/228-8799) rents bikes and sets up inn-to-inn tours.

In Bennington, you can rent mountain bikes from **Cutting Edge North,** 160 Benmont Ave. (tel. 802/442-8664).

POWERBOATING

Fishing boats and motorboats can be rented at **Lake Bomoseen** (tel. 802/265-4242) and **Lake St. Catherine State Parks** (tel. 802/287-9185); on Harriman Reservoir from **Lake Front Restaurant** (tel. 802/464-5363); on the lower Connecticut River from **Green Mountain Marine,** Rockingham (tel. 802/463-4973); and on Lake Dunmore from **Waterhomes** (tel. 802/252-4422) and **Lake Dunmore Kamperville** (tel. 802/352-4501). For a complete listing of all motorboat, sailboat, and canoe rentals, contact the **Vermont Department of Travel,** 134 State Street, Montpelier, VT 05602 (tel. 800/VERMONT) for their "Vermont Boating, Rentals & Marinas" publication.

ROAD BIKING

There are four reasons why Vermont biking is the best in the East and possibly the finest in the country. First, though the state is mostly rural and has a relatively small population, it's thoroughly settled country. The dozens of backcountry roads connecting scenic little hamlets make for a web of ideal road-biking terrain, all with very little traffic. Second, the state is compact enough to create hundreds of 20-, 30-, 40-, 50-, and 100-mile loops. Third, the landscape is neither flat nor dauntingly vertiginous. Rolling hills challenge the experts, but also allow the novice to feel a sense of accomplishment.

It's really the scenery that makes a bike trip in Vermont so appealing. Around every bend, there's another meadow greener than the last, another freshly painted white steeple piercing the clouds overhead, and another Green Mountain standing tall in the distance. This state was meant to be seen at a slow pace.

LOOP RIDES

Grafton Loop

A 25-mile loop. Allow 3 hours. Moderate; one steep hill, otherwise rolling terrain. Access: Start and finish in Grafton, south of Chester via State Route 35 or west of Interstate 91 via State Route 121. Map: USGS 7.5 x 15-minute Saxton's River, but most any state map will do.

Very few places in New England epitomize small-town charm better than the historic village of Grafton. It is the ideal starting and ending point for a number of different bike trips; this loop ties together a wealth of rural scenery and the equally picturesque little towns of Chester, Rockingham, Saxton's River, and Cambridgeport.

The well-appointed old houses and churches in Grafton testify to a prosperous past. Indeed, Grafton's history is pretty characteristic for Vermont: in the mid-1800s, Grafton was populated by 1,500 people—and 10,000 sheep. The woolen textile industry was supplemented by active soapstone quarries, and mills that turned the quarries' output into stoves, sinks, and foot warmers. (Foot warmers?) By the end of the century, Grafton's historic Old Tavern (see "Inns" under "Camping & Other Accommodations," below), had hosted such luminaries as Emerson, Thoreau, Rudyard Kipling, Ulysses S. Grant, and Teddy Roosevelt.

However, the village soon took a turn for the worse. Sheep farmers moved west to find new land, and the mills shut down as the owners left in search of cheaper labor farther south. By the end of the Depression, the population had shrunk to less than 100 and most of the houses were up for sale. If it wasn't for the generosity of Pauline Dean Fiske, and the foresight of her nephews, Dean Mathey and Matthew Hall, the exquisite homes would have been torn down and turned to pasture. With their aunt's money, the two nephews founded the Windham Foundation in 1963 and proceeded to restore the entire town, including the Old Tavern. The turnaround was dramatic. The village now looks as it did a century and a half ago, replete with white steeple, sparkling white clapboard homes, and a country store.

Start this 25-mile loop at the Old Tavern and proceed over the bridge, turning left (north) immediately onto Chester Road (State Route 35). For the first half mile, the tree-lined road rises sharply before leveling off. For the next 5 or 6 miles, the road cruises downhill, finally arriving at the houses and inns of Chester. Veer right onto State Route 11 East and continue straight onto State Route 103 South. There's a large shoulder, but be wary of traffic as you roll up and down the hills through town; 6.4 miles from the junction of State Route 35, leave modernity behind as you bear right onto Pleasant Valley Road. You'll pass grazing horses and dilapidated barns. When the road ends, turn right onto State Route 121 West. Saxtons River soon appears on your left as you follow the winding road by the ever-present cow pastures and cornfields. The pastoral landscape never leaves your side as you pedal through Cambridgeport all the way back to Grafton.

Lake St. Catherine

A 24-mile loop. Allow 2–3 hours. Moderate; rolling terrain. Access: From Rutland, take Route 7 to State Route 140 West. Nine miles later, you'll reach the Middletown Springs Village Green. Park anywhere. Map: USGS 7.5-minute Wells and Poultney, but most any state map will do.

Verdant Vermont meets Victorian Vermont on this loop through a rarely visited portion of the state. The ride starts in Middletown Springs, known in the early 19th century as a resort town because of its iron and sulfur springs. From the village green, proceed on State Route 133 South beyond the Victorian homes and wraparound verandas. The road heads straight into a lush green valley. Mountains fringe the pastures on the left. Bear right at the 4.9-mile mark toward Wells, passing numerous dairy farms along the way. The road becomes dirt for a half mile, but soon turns to pavement as you cruise downhill. Wave after wave of gently undulating hills fade into the horizon, as green as the Irish countryside. In the village of Wells, turn right at the library onto State Route 30 North and follow the road as it rolls alongside a forest. Fewer than 3 miles later, the waters of Lake St. Catherine come into view, with New York's Taconic Range standing on the far shores. You'll soon pass the Lake St. Catherine State Park on the left, a good place to stop and picnic. At the 15.9-mile mark, turn right at the fork and head uphill toward East

Poultney. A tall white steeple welcomes you to the town square. Just past a country store, turn right on State Route 140 East and bike along a stream; you'll re-enter Middletown Springs 6.6 miles later.

RENTALS, OUTFITTERS & INN-TO-INN TOURS

Bikes for the Grafton loop can be rented at the **Old Tavern** (tel. 802-843-2231). For the Lake St. Catherine Loop, you can rent bikes in Manchester at **Battenkill Sports Bicycle Shop** (tel. 802/362-2734).

In Bennington, you can rent road bikes from **Cutting Edge North,** 160 Benmont Ave. (tel. 802/442-8664).

John Friedin, author of *25 Bicycle Tours in Vermont* (Backcountry) and founder of **Vermont Bicycle Touring,** P.O. Box 711, Bristol, VT 05443 (tel. 802/453-4811 or 800/245-3868), knows every country road in the state. His knowlege shows in his catalog and in the success of his company. VBT now runs bike tours through 14 states in nearly every region of the country, and has teamed up with Travent International to guide Americans abroad in places like New Zealand, Switzerland, and Italy. In the southern part of the Green Mountain State, he takes bikers on weekend jaunts to Randolph, Plymouth, and Okemo. Five-day inn-to-inn trips are available to Grafton and the Saxtons River Valley, the Champlain Valley, and the Mad River Valley.

Bike Vermont, P.O. Box 207, Woodstock, VT 05091 (tel. 800/257-2226), operates exclusively within the borders of the state. They are celebrating their 20th anniversary this year. Two-, three-, five-, and six-day guided tours are offered all over the southern part of Vermont, from Lake St. Catherine to the Connecticut River Valley to the outskirts of Robert Frost's Breadloaf Wilderness.

Backroads, 1516 Fifth Street, Berkeley, CA 94710-1740 (tel. 800/GO-ACTIVE), features a five-day inn-to-inn tour through Woodstock, Weathersfield, and Grafton.

SAILING

Sailboats can be rented on the Harriman Reservoir from **Lake Front Restaurant** (tel. 802/464-5363) and on Lake Dunmore from **Lake Dunmore Kamperville** (tel. 802/352-4501) and **Waterhomes** (tel. 802/252-4422). For a complete listing of all sailboats, motorboats, and canoe rentals, contact the **Vermont Department of Travel,** 134 State Street, Montpelier, VT 05602 (tel. 800/VERMONT), for their "Vermont Boating, Rentals & Marinas" publication.

SNOWMOBILING

The **Vermont Association of Snow Travelers** (VAST) is a group of more than 200 local snowmobile clubs that maintain over 3,000 miles of groomed trails. The trails extend from the Massachusetts border to Canada, and from the Connecticut River to Lake Champlain. Eighty-five percent of the land is located on private property, and without the work of volunteers, the use of this land would not be possible. For detailed maps, route suggestions, and information about guided tours, contact VAST at P.O. Box 839, Montpelier, VT 05602 (tel. 802/229-0005). A "Winter Recreation Map" is also available from the **Green Mountain National Forest,** 231 N. Main St., Rutland, VT 05701 (tel. 802/747-6700).

Guided Snowmobile Tours (tel. 802/362-0552 for reservations) provides rides through the Green Mountain National Forest from Manchester.

In Wilmington, **High Country** and **Greenduck Snowmobile Tours** arrange guided hourly, half-day, full-day, and overnight trips into the national forest. Contact High Country at tel. 800/627-7533 or tel. 802/464-2108. Greenduck can be reached at tel. 800/479-3284 or tel. 802/464-3284. In Wilmington, snowmobiles can be rented at the **Sitzmark Lodge** (tel. 802/464-5504).

Marina St. Catherine (tel. 802/645-0410), on the shores of Lake St. Catherine, offers snowmobile rentals.

For a complete list of snowmobile tours and rentals in the state, get a copy of the "Vermont Winter Guide" from the **Vermont Department of Travel**, 134 State Street, Montpelier, VT 05602 (tel. 800/VERMONT).

SNOWSHOEING

Naturalist Lynn Levine takes guests on two-and-a-half hour snowshoeing adventures from the base of Mount Snow (tel. 802/464-3333, ext. 4356) into the heart of the Green Mountain National Forest. Types of walks include a daytime animal tracking tour and a nighttime "Owl Moon" walk, during which Lynn calls to the owls under the bright moon.

SPELUNKING

Matt Moses and Greg Rosenthal take guests spelunking in New England's longest cave. Located at the foot of Dorset Mountain in East Dorset, the cave was discovered in 1967. Much of the interior is marble. Contact **Green Mountain Adventures**, P.O. Box 1711, Manchester Center, VT 05255 (tel. 802/375-2448).

SWIMMING

With hundreds of lakes, rivers, and ponds in southern Vermont, you'll never be far from a cool, refreshing body of water. The most obvious choices are the

parks on **Emerald Lake, Lake St. Catherine, Lake Bomoseen, Half Moon Pond,** and at **Jamaica State Park.** However, locals tend to keep their precious swimming holes a clandestine destination. Crash the party at the following places:

◆ The section of the **West River** under the covered bridge on State Route 30 in West Dummerston;

◆ The **Rock River** about a mile north on State Route 30;

◆ The **Dorset Quarry** off State Route 30 on Kelly Road between Dorset and Manchester;

◆ **Grout Pond** (see "Quiet Water Canoeing," above);

◆ **Hapgood Pond** in Peru;

◆ **Buttermilk Falls,** on State Route 103 north of its junction with State Route 100 in Ludlow.

TENNIS

The highly regarded **Killington School for Tennis** (tel. 800/343-0762) offers two-, three-, and five-day programs on their eight outdoor courts.

WALKS & RAMBLES

You don't have to kill yourself to get a taste of the Green Mountain outback, or some such. Many of the parks listed above under "Parks & Other Hot Spots" have wonderful nature trails, often with interpretive signs. The **Healing Springs Nature Trail** at Shaftsbury State Park north of Bennington, the **Emerald Lake Nature Trail,** and the **Big Trees Nature Trail** at Lake St. Catherine State Parks are all excellent. **Merck Forest & Farmland Center** (see "Hiking & Backpacking," above) has an endless variety of walking over archetypical Vermont countryside. See "Birdwatching," above, for more walks and easy hikes through very interesting country.

Hamilton Falls

5 miles round-trip. Allow 3 hours. Easy walking alongside the whitewater of the West River. Access: In Jamaica State Park, off State Route 30.

Very few things are as crowd-pleasing as a big waterfall. This one, on the West River, tumbles and pools spectacularly down 125 feet of granite ledges, making it Vermont's highest waterfall. The riverbank trail follows an old railroad bed that was built in 1881 and long ago lapsed into decay. If you come here during spring or fall, when water is being released from the Ball Mountain Dam upriver, the park is likely to be crowded; however, you'll get to see whitewater paddlers take on the challenge of The Dumplings, a set of enormous boulders about a mile up the trail that were left in the river when the glaciers of the last ice age retreated. And if it's a warm afternoon, back down by the parking lot you can take a dip in Salmon Hole, a perfect example of a Vermont swimmin' hole.

Central Vermont ◆ What to Do & Where to Do It

BALLOONING

Boland Balloon offers early morning, sunset, and champagne flights over Lake Fairlee, the Connecticut River valley, and the foothills of the Green Mountains. Brian Boland can be reached at the Post Mills Airport (tel. 802/333-9254).

In conjunction with Boland Balloon, the **Silver Maple Lodge,** P.O. Box 8,

Fairlee, VT 05045 (tel. 800/666-1946 or 802/333-4326), offers Balloon Inn Vermont. The package includes one to three nights at the Silver Maple Lodge and a one-hour champagne balloon ride. Purchase that engagement ring and propose to her up in the clouds.

Stoweflake Resort (tel. 802/253-7355) offers hot-air balloon rides in the Mount Mansfield area.

BIRD WATCHING

The habitats in central Vermont are not so different from those you'd find in southern Vermont—take a look at the southern Vermont "Bird Watching" section, above, for lots of general information on what kinds of birds you should expect to see and where. **Hawks** above the Green Mountains and Connecticut River Valley monadnocks; **vireos, thrushes, owls, ruby-throated hummingbirds,** and **wild turkeys** through the hardwood forests; **bitterns, egrets,** and **bank swallows** on the Connecticut; and high up on the hillsides of the Green Mountains in the red spruce/balsam fir boreal forest, **spruce grouse, black-capped** and **boreal chickadees, Swainson's thrushes,** and numerous vernal **warblers.** High-country beaver ponds are always a likely spot for birding; there's usually activity around them, and keep an ear open for a **loon**'s whinnying call.

The **Vermont Institute of Natural Science & Raptor Center,** Church Hill Road, Woodstock, VT 05091 (tel. 802/457-2779), is a fascinating place for birders to visit. Bald eagles, peregrine falcons, owls, and hawks are four of the more than 25 species seen in the outdoor flight cages.

A "Check List for Birds of Vermont" is available from the **Green Mountain Audubon Society,** P.O. Box 33, Burlington, VT 05401. A similar checklist that

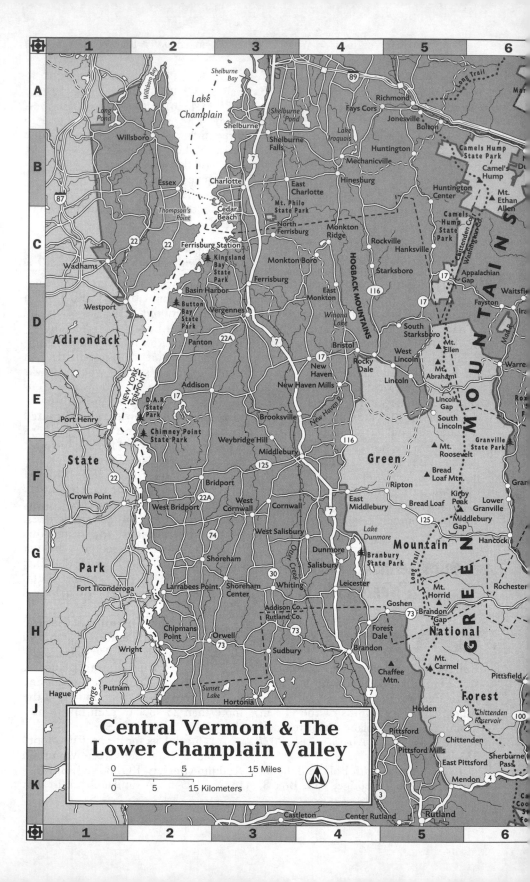

Central Vermont & The Lower Champlain Valley

| 0 | | 5 | | 15 Miles |
| 0 | 5 | | 15 Kilometers |

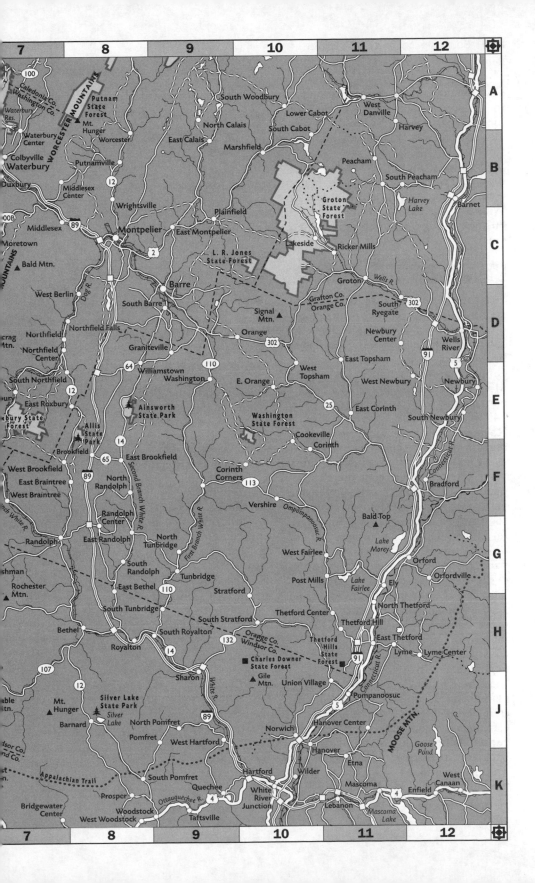

also covers all manner of fauna observed in Vermont is available from the **Vermont Department of Fish and Wildlife,** 103 S. Main St., Waterbury, VT 05676 (tel. 802/241-3700).

It's a little out of the way, but if you drop your binoculars off Camel's Hump (ouch), the **Wild Bird Center,** on Williston Road east of Burlington (tel. 802/878-4400), ought to be able to help you out.

CROSS-COUNTRY SKIING

What a bonanza! Every one of the cross-country centers listed here has a tremendous variety of skiing and charming settings. There are well-established backcountry skiing trails throughout central Vermont's half of the Green Mountain National Forest; for a map, contact the forest service at tel. 802/ 747-6700 and ask for their Winter Recreation Map, or failing that, their regular map to the north half of the forest. Finally, almost anywhere you find yourself in central Vermont, there's spectacular backcountry skiing right outside your door. The intricate network of snowmobile trails are crucial thoroughfares but also a tremendous aid for do-it-yourself Nordic touring—they wind through every cow pasture, up every hill, and through sugarbushes. The cross-country crowd may dislike a snowmachine's noise, but I've never met the skier who wasn't grateful for the machine's trailbreaking power on days when the snow isn't that easy to negotiate.

Although the **Catamount Trail**—the planned border-to-border cross-country trail network from Massachusetts to Canada—is overall still a little spotty, central Vermont has some of its best backcountry skiing. The **Catamount Trail Association,** 1 Main St., Burlington, VT 05401-5291 (tel. 802/864-5794),

publishes a comprehensive guidebook to the trail.

IN THE BACKCOUNTRY

Chittenden Brook

5.5 miles. Allow 3–4 hours. Moderate; some steep climbs and downhills. Access: 12.5 miles east of Brandon on State Route 73; 8 miles west of Rochester on State Route 73. The parking lot and large sign is located on the south side of the highway. Map: USGS 7.5 minute Rochester, Mount Carmel.

It was St. Patrick's Day and the terrain of central Vermont dressed up for the occasion—the ground was green wherever you looked. Not to fear, I was at Blueberry Hill, one of the most respected cross-country skiing centers in New England. Owner Tony Clark, an inveterate cross-country skier, knows this neck of the forest like a bee knows honey. He directed me to one of his favorite spots, an area of the Green Mountain National Forest called Chittenden Brook.

Chittenden has a northeast exposure, which keeps the trail white long after the rest of central Vermont started to thaw. I parked my car, walked through the gate, and skied uphill to the start of the trail, 0.6 mile away. At trail intersection number 2, the path bordered a rushing brook. The early warm spell created high, raging waters which I continued to hear throughout the day. Three bridges and numerous birches and white pines later, I arrived at intersection 3. The trail started to climb steeply into the rolling hills of the forest. By the time I reached intersection 4, I was high above the brook. A short 0.1 mile detour brought me to Beaver Pond, where locals often find an occasional moose slurping water by the shore.

From intersections 4 to 7 to the campground is the exciting part of the loop. The trail narrows as it sweeps downhill back to the brook. This part is only recommended for skiers who can turn on a dime while cruising downhill. Otherwise, you might end up in the brook and have to water ski back to your car. I had lunch at the campground before taking a left onto unplowed Forest Road 45. A quick 2.3 miles down the curving road and I was back at Route 73 faster than you can say, "Let it snow, let it snow, let it snow!"

Texas Falls/Hancock Branch Brook

3 miles round-trip. Allow 3–4 hours. Moderate to difficult; backcountry trails that may or may not have defined tracks, and your choice as far as taking on steep parts. Access: From State Route 100 in Hancock, west on State Route 125 for 1.2 miles; turn north (right) onto Texas Falls forest-service road. Park where the plowed road ends. Map: USGS 7.5 minute Hancock.

Texas Falls and its sylvan surroundings, which by virtue of its photogenic qualities and roadside access can be a mob scene in summertime, might actually be a better place to visit in the dead of winter. With maybe 4 inches of new snow the falls and the trails upstream along Hancock Branch Brook took on an otherworldly look; the water was mostly frozen over, and where it wasn't there was still rimey, blue-green snow and ice choking it. From the car park, follow the forest road until you reach a fork; to the right is the Texas Gap Trail, and to the left is the Hancock Branch Brook Trail. I took a left and began a moderate climb up the forest road, which follows and repeatedly crosses the brook. You'll face several more directional choices as you go; take what looks most inviting and you can't really seem to go wrong here.

Down the road apiece is the **Robert Frost Wayside Trail**; these trails also suit skiers, and will hook you to the Catamount Trail as well. To get there, just continue west on State Route 125 about 2 miles past the Middlebury Snow Bowl, and look for the signs on your right.

NORDIC SKIING CENTERS

Located at the Woodstock Country Club, the **Woodstock Ski Touring Center,** State Route 106, Woodstock, VT 05091 (tel. 802/457-2114), has 58 km of groomed trails that ring the base and then climb Mount Tom and Mount Peg—don't miss the classic woodland trails of the former. The base lodge is well-equipped with rentals, rooms, showers, a restaurant, and a lounge with fireplace. The touring center also has maps for the 6.3-mile Skyline Trail, which goes from the Suicide Six downhill skiing area to Amity Pond. This is a great backcountry route.

The Three Stallion Inn, on Stock Farm Road, left off State Route 66 just before Randolph Village, is home to the **Green Mountain Touring Center,** Randolph, VT 05060 (tel. 802/728-5575). Thirty-five kilometers of groomed trails branch out from the Victorian farmhouse to the fields and forests below.

There could hardly be a more picturesque site for a ski center than that enjoyed by the **Green Trails Inn** in Brookfield (tel. 802/276-3412). Hard by the Floating Bridge, Green Trails has 35 km of groomed trails through Brookfield's wooded high country.

The **Inn at Round Barn,** East Warren Road, Waitsfield (tel. 802/496-2276), features 23 km of track-set trails that weave through the 85 acres of meadows on Mad River Valley. Good views of Sugarbush and Mount Abraham can be seen to the west.

Also in the Mad River Valley is **Ole's Cross-Country Center** (tel. 802/496-3430). Ole Moseson, the Norwegian owner, lays out a network of 47 km of skating and traditional diagonal-stride trails on the snowed-under Warren Airport and the surrounding woods.

DOWNHILL SKIING

I was actually at Killington, in what I've called southern Vermont, when I first guessed that certain Vermont skiers constitute their own unique breed. It was a mediocre day for skiing, not long after the snowpack had hardened to a brick-like consistency after a January thaw; we decided to go where the snowmaking was, and so the five of us—four native Vermonters and lifelong skiers and one New Yorker—piled into a van for the trip south to Killington.

All was fine at first. We got the blood moving with some warm-up runs on manicured intermediate trails, all of us cutting a fine, fast figure as we carved our way down the hill. All met the suggestion that we hit the hard stuff with hearty assent—and thus I found myself, on the kind of day that separates the proverbial men from the boys, about 30 yards below the topmost lip of Cascade, with one ski loose above me and the other skidding away below. A patch of blue ice had made short work of me; I could see a lot more like it ahead and knew it was going to be a long goddamn way down. Resigning myself, I trudged about fetching my equipment, waved off my friends' inquiries, and watched them pick their way down the trail nimbly, without major mishap, like mountain goats.

My bump technique, like most people's these days, was high-energy, rubber-legged, and on the edge of control—and absolutely useless on snow like this. Vermonters, however, have a long tradition of never skiing as if the snow's going to be easy and forgiving; on the contrary, they make it look like it is, where they come from: hard, unpredictable, to be warily respected. The way they ski makes you understand what *knowing the mountain* really means. It's knowing everything about how a particular trail is skiing on a particular day—what the workable lines are, where the hazards are, and so forth. It's interacting with the mountain and taking what it gives you, rather than forcing your style on it.

The central Green Mountains are the breadbasket to this kind of skier. All the areas here—from south to north, the Snow Bowl, Sugarbush, Mad River Glen, on up to Stowe and Smuggler's Notch— are diehard bastions of the narrow, erratic, traditional New England ski trail. And skiing well on these kinds of trails is simply more of a head game than blasting down a wide boulevard, be it groomed or moguled. If you've skied here before you'll know what I mean; if you haven't, your first ride up the Castlerock Chair at Sugarbush or the Single Chair at Mad River on a powder day will show you examples. Look for the bearded, unfashionably clad gent linking turn after perfect turn down the hill without once pulling up, utterly in control, and maybe taking some air from time to time with an unselfconscious holler.

Reverting to the practical, there are simpler reasons to ski in central Vermont, not least among them the generally less-crowded, lower-key atmosphere on the slopes and in the lodges. Many ski shops in the area, notably the Downhill Edge in Waitsfield, have knowledgeable staffs and lots of good deals on both sales and rentals. But it's really the overall quality of the skiing that keeps me coming back—great terrain, good skiers, and more natural snow, for some reason, than most places within a few hundred miles.

SKI AREAS

Suicide Six

Woodstock, VT 05091. Tel. 802/457-1666; snow report, tel. 802/457-1666. 19 trails (30% beginner, 40% intermediate, 30% expert); 2 double chairs; 633-foot vertical drop. Full day tickets $29.50 weekends, $16 weekdays.

The tiny hill where Vermont skiing was born over 60 years ago, Suicide Six is now part of the Woodstock Inn and Resort. It's cheap, is a great place to take the kids or learn to ski, and has some genuinely difficult runs in The Face and the runs to its left—though the name is a lot more frightening than the skiing in general. You won't find the fluff you get at upper elevations on the bigger mountains because the summit here is a modest 1,200 feet high. Suicide Six built a halfpipe for snowboarders for the 1996 season.

Middlebury College Snow Bowl

State Route 125 between Hancock and Ripton (mail: Middlebury, VT 05753). Tel. 802/388-4356. 14 trails (33% beginner, 34% intermediate, 33% expert); 3 double chairs; 1,020-foot vertical drop. Full day tickets $26 weekends, $20 weekdays.

A small, unassuming place that can't help but get lost in the shadows of its much more ambitious neighbors to the north and south, the Snow Bowl has charms that sneak up on you. Its trails are short and there are hellishly long flats here and there, but everything—the skiing included—has an unhurried, old-time New England glow. The summit chair passes over a forested crag I never tire of looking at, then finishes with a painfully long haul over a flat that's invariably blasted by arctic winds. Warm

up by skating down the flat to the left of the chair, and you'll be ready for the classic multiple fall-line steeps of Ross and Allen. Or wind down the backside of the mountain on Youngman, my personal favorite. There's a snowboard park here now as well.

The Snow Bowl has beefed up its snowmaking, but anytime machine-made snow is the surface you don't want to be here. The time to come to the Snow Bowl is within a few days of a snowstorm—I don't know why, but when 10 inches fall elsewhere, this place will get a legit 14 inches. *A tip:* State Route 125 is *really* steep and you'll be blessing your four-wheel drive if you have it. Lastly, the Snow Bowl is the only place I know of with a *morning* half-day ticket—$15 weekdays and $20 weekends to ski from 9 AM to 12:30 PM.

Sugarbush

Sugarbush South access road runs west off State Route 100 south of Waitsfield; Sugarbush North access via State Route 17, which runs west off State Route 100 in Waitsfield (mail: Warren, VT 05674). Tel. 802/583-2381; snow report, tel. 802/583-SNOW. 111 trails (23% beginner, 48% intermediate, 29% expert), 18 lifts including 7 quads, 3 triples, and 4 doubles; 2,600-foot vertical drop. Full day tickets $42 all week.

I've been skiing in the Mad River Valley since back in the days when Sugarbush North was known as Glen Ellen, and to my mind Sugarbush has always been at or near the top of Vermont's ski areas. It begins with two beautiful, rugged, and huge mountains—3,975-foot Lincoln Peak to the south and 4,135-foot Mount Ellen to the north. I'll always remember riding the Castlerock chair on an early spring day when the mountain was beginning to wake up from winter's sleep—a warm wind hissing through the waving evergreens, the brown-green skin of mud and underbrush peeking through the dirt-streaked moguls, and the air filled with the piney, raw-earth smell of a mountain thaw.

The North and South ski areas—finally united in 1995 by a superfast high-speed quad that gets you from one mountain to the next in minutes—are both totally satisfying places for any skier at the intermediate level or higher. There are dozens of perfectly pitched cruisers that always seem to have great snow, and bump trails that range from ideal mogul-skiing practice runs to hair-raising steeps. It also has more of those true challenges of New England skiing—narrow, rock-and-tree-root strewn, variably pitched tumblers that demand utter control of your planks—than any other area with the possible exception of Mad River.

Sugarbush is also a great place to learn to ski; they've got one of the older, more respected ski schools in Vermont, and both mountains have beginner and novice terrain that's honest-to-god interesting skiing, instead of the bland bunny slopes you find most places.

Here's the skinny for the more advanced, beginning with Sugarbush South: there's more intermediate skiing at the other hill, but Murphy's Glades/Lower Organgrinder, Moonshine, and Domino (a favorite that gets overlooked by most skiers) are all terrific strong-intermediate trails. The Snowball/Spring Fling combo is an ultrawide cruiser made to be taken at a rocket-like pace, but it's also one of the most congested parts of the mountain. Stay away on crowded weekends, unless it's either frigid out or there's not much snow—always plenty of snowmaking and sunshine here.

Strong skiers won't find a better array anywhere in the Northeast. Moguls, moguls, and more moguls: Stein's Run, The Mall, and Twist (often forgotten) off the Gate House Chair; Upper Organgrinder and Spillsville (best lines) off Heaven's Gate; Castlerock Run and Middle Earth off the Castlerock Chair. (Stay off Ripcord; except on the very edges, it's usually a horrifically broad sheet of ice.) Then there's the luminous trio at the very top: Paradise off Heaven's Gate; Lift Line off Castlerock; and sliver-thin Rumble. Don't even look for this last one unless you can confidently say you've had your way with the rest of the mountain; I made this mistake once and had a painfully close encounter with a spruce tree. I think it's the toughest trail in New England.

Over at North, perfect intermediate trails abound, with Rim Run and especially Elbow being my favorites. The truly tough skiing is a little thinner, but still very good: Black Diamond and Bravo are splendid bump runs (though I hear they're making snow on the former now); Exterminator is a nice trail with a skewed fall line, but no double-black diamond by this mountain's otherwise-lofty standards; and Tumbler, the most fun of all when there's lots of snow. As for the much-talked about F.I.S., it's a shorter version of Killington's Outer Limits—very steep and hillocky, to be sure, but nary a good line to be found in the whole wide swath.

North is the place to go after a thaw, as the layout there doesn't bottleneck skier traffic too badly when the mountain's only partly open; South, on the other hand, is the ticket when the wind's up and after a big snowstorm, when Stein's, Paradise, and the Castlerock trails can be truly sublime.

Mad River Glen

State Route 17, Waitsfield, VT 05673. Tel. 802/496-3551; snow report, tel. 802/

Central Vermont Ski & Winter Sport Shops				
City	Shop	Location	Telephone	Additional Services
Sugarbush/ Mad River Area	Vermont North	Sugarbush Access Rd., Warren	802/583-2511	repairs; alpine/xc ski rentals, snowshoe rentals; alpine-ski demos
	Downhill Edge	Sugarbush Access Rd., Warren	802/583-3887	repairs; alpine ski, snowboard rentals and demos
	Downhill Edge	Rt. 17, Waitsfield	802/496-3887	repairs; alpine ski, snowboard rentals and demos
Montpelier	Onion River Sports	20 Langdon St.	802/229-9409	xc ski/snowshoes sales/rentals
Suicide Six/ Ascutney Area	Sitzmark Ski Shop	Rt. 44, Windsor	802/674-6930	alpine ski, xc ski, snowboard rentals
	The Dartmouth Co-Op	25 S. Main St., Hanover, N.H.	603/643-3100	xc/alpine skis
	Omer & Bob's Sport Shop	7 Allen St., Hanover, N.H.	603/643-3525	xc/alpine skis, snowboards
	Wilderness Trails, Inc.	Clubhouse Rd., Quechee	802/295-7620	xc ski, snowshoe, ice-skate rentals

496-2001. 33 trails (25% beginner, 40% intermediate, 35% expert) 4 lifts, including 3 doubles and the country's only surviving single chairlift (riding this is even scarier than skiing the trails); 2,000-foot vertical drop. Full day tickets $26 all week.

Rustbucket Subaru wagons with Vermont license plates often have a bumper sticker offering the following dare: "Mad River Glen, Ski It If You Can." No lie. Mad River Glen is the nastiest lift-served ski area in the East, a combination of rocks, ice, trees—and snow, of course. It's truly a place where skiing seems little removed from a mountain's gnarled, primal state.

Think you're tough enough? Start with Grand Canyon, a steep mogul trail where the bumps are perfectly spaced. Next up are Fall-Line and Chute from the summit, two of the most precipitous, obstacle-strewn, yet perfect mogul runs you'll ever find. And for the finale—drum roll please—a trail that's not even on the map, Paradise. Don't let the name fool you—it should be called Hell. Barely a trail, Paradise stumbles over rocky ledges and an enormous frozen waterfall to reach the bottom. Have fun trying to hold an edge.

Mad River pales against Sugarbush as far as easy skiing, snowmaking, and lift capacity are concerned. (Its sole summit lift remains the venerable Single Chair.) Save Mad River for a day when there's deep, fresh powder, and you're feeling feisty. That way you'll give yourself a chance to experience the place at its best. You'll feel privileged to be among so many world-class skiers, all feeling as if they're in heaven's playground.

FISHING

Trouters will find some of Vermont's best fishing—spooky rainbows, brookies, and browns—on the watersheds and feeder streams of the White and Winooski Rivers. Wait for one of those characteristic central Vermont flash rainstorms, and the fish seem to drop their objections to just about anything.

In the lower part of the region, the **Ottauquechee** along U.S. 4, the **Ompompanoosuc River** around Thetford, and the First, Second, Third, and Main Branches of the **White River** are the hot spots. One of the best spots on the White is in Stockbridge, near the intersection of State Routes 100 and 107; rainbows and browns can also be hauled in along the reach from Bethel to Royalton.

A little further north, check out the **Mad River** in the Warren-Waitsfield area, the **Dog River** along State Route 12A from Roxbury to Northfield, where rainbows 10 inches and up, along with trophy-class brookies, are not uncommon; and the **Winooski** itself, especially around its confluence with the **Little River** near Waterbury—huge browns can be had here, if you're lucky.

One of the best things about the Winooski is its recreational versatility—in addition to fly-fishing for brown trout, the river's great in summertime for smallmouth bass, from around Middlesex all the way to Lake Champlain. The big-water Winooski is also one of Vermont's three great canoeing waterways, navigable for 78 miles. And central Vermont is home to most of the best of the **Connecticut River's** warm-water fishing—smallmouth and largemouth bass, pickerel, walleye, and bullhead are everywhere. See the "Canoeing" section, above, for good access points along both the Connecticut and the Winooski.

There aren't very many lakes or ponds along the I-89 corridor, but one very good spot to take the kids out fishing for sunnies and pumpkinseeds is **Silver Lake State Park,** off State Route 12 in Barnard. It's a beautiful spot, with rowboat and canoe rentals (see "Parks & Other Hot Spots," above). To the northeast, closer to the Connecticut River and I-91 and between the villages of Fairlee and Thetford, are lakes **Fairlee** and **Morey;** these are sizable bodies of water with good bass, pike, and panfish angling.

GUIDES & BAIT-&-TACKLE SHOPS

In Woodstock, the **Vermont Fly Fishing School,** situated at the Quechee Inn (tel. 802/295-3131), offers guided trips and fishing gear.

Northland Trout Tours (tel. 802/496-6572), located in North Fayston in the Mad River Valley, offers instruction and guided trips on the Mad and Dog Rivers. Peter Cammann at **Steamline** (tel. 802/496-5463) also offers fly-fishing instruction in the area.

In Northfield, where the Dog River flows, **Goodwin's Guide Service,** 2 Pinehill Dr., Box 2120, Northfield, VT 05663 (tel. 802/485-6185) will help you find the best trout holes. The Paiges of **Green Mountain Outdoor Adventures,** HCR 32 Box 90, Montpelier, VT 05602 (tel. 802/229-4246) should be able to do the same for you on the Winooski.

The following places, all on or a little outside the borders of the area covered in this section, either sell fishing tackle or offer guide service on central Vermont rivers: **Briggs Ltd,** 12 N. Main St., White River Junction (tel. 802/295-7100); **The Brookside Angler,** U.S. 7, Manchester (tel. 802/362-3538); **Classic Fly Fishing Shop,** 166 S. Main St., Stowe (tel. 802/253-3963); **Classic Outfitters,** Champlain Mall #66, Winooski (tel. 802/655-7999); and **Vermont Bound,** Killington (tel. 802/773-0736).

GOLF

Two Robert Trent Jones courses, the **Woodstock Country Club** (tel. 802/457-2112) and the **Sugarbush Golf Club** (tel. 802/583-2722) in the Mad River Valley, are the long-established class operations of central Vermont golf. The verdant Woodstock course, through which a brook rushes, is probably the nicer, while the arduous Sugarbush course not only plays hard but might qualify as a "hike," considering all the elevation changes.

I've never been much for the more genteel aspects of the golf scene, and so my local favorite is Randolph's almost-earthy **Montague Golf Course** (tel. 802/728-3806). It's old, cheap, and doesn't truck with putting on airs. Plus, there's just something unusual about carrying on the standard waiting-for-tee-time small talk about the evil golf god with the guys scheduled to follow you—and hearing them speaking in an untamed Vermont accent. *Aah-yaaup.* (The *p* is silent, by the way; say the word as if you were going to speak it, then cut your voice dead just before.)

HIKING & BACKPACKING

I just can't say enough about hiking in the central Green Mountains. Maybe the White Mountains are higher and more spectacular, but there's something about the way things are knit together on the ridge of the Greens. Rising and descending along the Long Trail, you pass through richly varied ecologies, from the hardwood trees and ferny understory of the lower reaches, to transitional forests mixing conifers, aspen, and birches, to upcountry meadows overrun by blackberry and raspberry thickets, and finally up toward the treeline, where things start to look as though they came out of C. S. Lewis's *Chronicles of Narnia.* One of the day hikes

follows a stretch of the LT from Lincoln Gap to Appalachian Gap that's as magical as any trail I know of, anywhere. Nearly its whole length is atop a ridge so narrow you feel a slight vertigo; both sides fall away steeply not 20 feet from the trail. The Sunset Ridge walk is less popular but is nonetheless a magnificent hike. And hiking Camel's Hump—one of the two mountains in Vermont that supports patches of genuine alpine/arctic tundra on its summit, holdovers from the last ice age—is a rite of passage for Vermonters. It's not so much that it's unusually difficult but that it's hard to feel like a "real" Vermonter without having stood upon that odd hummock in the clouds, surveying your land.

It's with great relief that I report that Montpelier's **Onion River Sports** (tel. 802/229-9409) is now selling top-rung hiking and camping gear—I used to have to drive into the traffic of Burlington or all the way to North Conway, New Hampshire, to reach an Eastern Mountain Sports store.

Sunset Ledge

2.2 miles (round-trip). Allow 1–2 hours. Easy to moderate hiking without too much abrupt elevation gain; ideal for young children. From either Lincoln to the west or Warren to the east, follow Lincoln Gap Road up into the mountains until you see a parking lot on the left-hand side of the road. Map: USGS 7.5 minute Lincoln.

My car had a far more rigorous workout getting to the trailhead than I did walking the Sunset Ledge path. Lincoln Gap Road is a mountainous pass that climbs steeply into the heart of the Green Mountains. I parked high atop the hill and continued on foot, south on the Long Trail toward the Middlebury Gap; 0.4 mile later, the leaf-littered trail turned rocky as the eastern slopes of the mountains came into view. The trail continued steadily uphill for another 0.7 mile until I reached Sunset Ledge. It was late September and the rocky promontory overlooked a forest of fall foliage in orange and red. Views of the Adirondacks could be seen to the west, far beyond the meadows and farms of Vermont. To the north, a turkey vulture hovered over Mount Abraham. For such a small amount of effort, the rewards were great.

Mount Abraham

5.2 miles round-trip. Allow 4 hours. Moderate to difficult. Access: From either Lincoln to the west or Warren to the east, follow Lincoln Gap Road up into the mountains until you see a parking lot on the left-hand side of the road. Map: USGS 7.5 minute Lincoln.

South of Camel's Hump and Mount Mansfield, Mount Abraham is another one of Vermont's popular 4,000-plus foot ascents. Since you begin high atop Lincoln Gap on the Long Trail, the actual climb is only 1,700 feet. The 2.6-mile (one way) trail starts gradually across the parking lot, weaving its way over tree roots and small rocks. Bring all your belongings with you; this parking lot is a notorious hunting ground for thieves. At 1.2 miles, you pass The Carpenters, two large boulders named after stalwart trail workers, not the singing group. A little more than a half-mile later, the path passes the Battell Trail and a small shelter of the same name—a GMC lean-to that sleeps six to eight people. This hike gets such heavy use that the GMC keeps a caretaker here, something they do for only a very few of their shelters and lodges; I pity this individual in comparison to the plush natural spots caretakers at Sterling Pond or Stratton Pond have as their lookout.

From here, the going gets rough, often scrambling over large, slippery slabs of rock until you reach the open summit. The views are supposedly stunning from the top, though I wouldn't know, the mountain having been socked in by clouds both times I took this hike. Watching the clouds roil around, and literally walking right through them, was an experience worth the loss of the vista. All I could see on the bare rock summit were red squirrels scurrying through the krummholz, Labrador tea, and other high-altitude vegetation. Be cautious of slipping on the smooth rocks on the way down, especially if they're wet.

Camel's Hump

7.2 miles. Allow 5–6 hours. Moderate to difficult. Access: From the junction of U.S. 2 and State Route 100, east of Waterbury (across from the Feed Bag), take State Route 100 south for 0.2 mile. Turn right on Main Street for 0.1 mile and veer right again onto River Road for 4.9 miles. Turn left on Camel's Hump Road and continue 3.1 miles to a fork where you bear right. The last 0.3 mile to the parking lot is on a horrible dirt road. Be very careful. There are several approaches to Camel's Hump; this one is via the Forestry, Dean, and Long Trails. Map: USGS 7.5 minute Waterbury.

On every Vermonter's list of favorite hikes is the climb up the distinctive mass of rock known as Camel's Hump. Standing 4,083 feet tall, the summit can be seen from Burlington all the way to Jay Peak and Mount Pisgah across the state. My wife Lisa and I decided to make our ascent from the eastern slopes of the mountain on a relatively clear and crisp autumn day. By the time we arrived in the late morning, the parking lot was already full.

We began our walk on the Forestry Trail. Lined with ferns and strewn with yellow leaves, the soil was soft to the sole as we wandered deeper and deeper into the dark forest. At 1.3 miles, we veered left onto the Dean Trail, crossing over Hump Creek, where there is a small campground. The trail climbed ever so gradually to a boreal forest where the air became cooler and resonant with the sweet smell of firs. Sun started to seep into the woods when we approached a small, stunning pond. Trees with leaves the shade of Van Gogh's yellow fringed the shores. In the background stood our ultimate destination, the Hump, towering over a ridge of rock.

One mile from the intersection of the Forestry Trail, we turned right on the Long Trail for a rigorous 1.7-mile climb. The narrow trail winds steeply up a face of rock before leveling off at an overlook. Below us was the pond surrounded by a sea of orange, red, and yellow leaves. We climbed through a glacial morass, following the rocky trail upward. The large boulders would be a good hideout for people on the lam. Every so often, views of the Hump would tease us—for, as we continued forward, it felt like we weren't making any ground. Finally, we descended into a col where the massive peak stood directly above us. We proceeded to hike slowly up the sharply rising trail, stopping to look at the hundreds of hilltops that encircled us under a layer of marshmallow clouds. At the bare summit, the wind was howling, but that didn't deter us from having lunch and taking in the views of Lake Champlain, Mount Mansfield, the White Mountains, and the Adirondacks.

We chose the Alpine Trail for the first 0.7 mile of our descent. Halfway down the path, a wing from an airplane can be seen. It was here on October 16, 1944, that a B-24J bomber crashed and nine crew members died. The Alpine Trail eventually connects with the Forestry Trail. We veered right and continued for

2.5 miles to the trailhead and parking lot, weary yet invigorated by our day's accomplishment.

HORSEBACK RIDING

A jaunt into central Vermont will take you to Waitsfield's **Vermont Icelandic Horse Farm** (tel. 802/496-7141). In a state known for the imposing Morgan horse, these small pony-size horses are a special treat. Icelandics move at a very steady pace without much rocking—it's like driving a car with good shock absorbers. Owner Christina Calabrese offers half- to three-day rides. Also in the Mad River Valley is Moretown's **Navajo Farm** (tel. 802/496-3656), which offers lessons and trail rides. And in the White River Valley is Brookfield's **Birch Meadow Trail Rides** (tel. 802/276-3156).

ICE SKATING

Snow is cleared from Silver Lake for ice skating; this is an almost laughably Norman Rockwell–like setting for skating. In Barnard off State Route 12.

MOUNTAIN BIKING

Trying to locate the best mountain biking trails in Vermont was turning into a grueling exercise in futility. I knew, looking round the forested rolling hills, that there were riches out there, but no one was giving up their secrets. Many of the rides are on private lands owned by farmers who only let the local contingent bike there. Downhill and cross-country ski resorts have taken up the slack, especially in northern Vermont, but riding on numbered trails will never provide the thrill that biking out in the wild does. On the verge of giving up, I did what every good writer does who has a book to finish—I groveled like an idiot and begged a local for his coveted knowledge.

Waitsfield

Allow 2–3 hours. Moderate; technical single-track riding. Access: Park at John Egan's Big World, located on State Route 100, between Waitsfield and Warren. Map: Dream on!

The daunting task of finding good mountain biking in Vermont finally came to an end when I was taken to an incredible network of single-track trails weaving through the hills north of Rolston Road to the Waitsfield covered bridge. Having been told by bikers in Burlington, Stowe, and Jeffersonville in northern Vermont that the best riding is on private lands, cross-country ski centers, or large dirt roads, I was extremely frustrated by the time I sat down and had dinner with John Egan at his Big World restaurant in the Sugarbush area. No worries. By the time my "Extreme" beer was finished, John had told me about the extensive riding possibilities in the Waitsfield-Warren area and introduced me to his chef and co-owner, Jerry, an avid biker. Chef Jerry invited me to go biking with him the following morning and I accepted.

It wasn't until the next morning, when the alcohol rubbed off, that I realized who I was riding with—friends of John Egan, the crazed skier seen in many of Warren Miller's ski films skillfully maneuvering down the bumpy slopes of an incredibly steep mountain. Maniacal John Egan, whose hobby is collecting rocks from volcanoes that have never been skied on before. Indeed, Egan has skied on nine virgin slopes and is aiming for his tenth (somewhere in Peru). My fears were exacerbated when I finally saw Jerry without his chef's smock. His legs were the size of a professional running back's. However, it was too late to turn back; plus, I had this bloody book to write. We were accompanied by a third biker, Chris, known as the "Cowboy."

We pedaled from the Big World parking lot over a wooden bridge, past a barn, and veered right on Rolston Road. The single-track trailhead was located on the left-hand side of the dirt road, 0.4 mile uphill from the junction of State Route 100, just past the houses and a large meadow on the left. From here, we zipped along the narrow trail as it went up and down the hills over soil, grass, rocks, and roots. Numerous trails veered off in every direction, each route as exciting as the last. Not surprisingly, I had trouble keeping up with Chef Jerry and especially Cowboy Chris, whose nickname was starting to become clear to me. He cruised up the sinuous rock- and root-studded hills like John Wayne on a horse. They were patient, however, and waited for me as I pedaled through "Maple Syrup" country, under sugar lines, and past dilapidated sugar shacks. Eventually we stopped at a ledge overlooking the small town of Irasville. The panorama of Mount Abraham, the slopes of Sugarbush, and State Route 100 running through the valley lay before us. The ride back down was exhilarating, ending at the covered bridge in Waitsfield. We turned left onto State Route 100 to cruise back to the Big World parking lot, but first we made one important stop. Cowboy Chris is co-owner of American Flatbread, which makes thin pizza cooked in a wood-fired oven which is shipped frozen everywhere, from the Boston Garden to supermarkets in Chicago. Chris offered us a Revolution Flatbread fresh from the oven, covered with mushrooms, tomato sauce, onions, and cheese. It was the perfect ending to the perfect ride.

Ask Mad River Bike Shop about other great trails in the area, including "The G.S." and the killer ride known as "The Clinic."

Maple Ridge Sheep Farm

Allow 2 hours. Moderate; hilly terrain. Access: From Slab City, bear left and follow State Route 12 North through East Braintree. At 5.2 miles from Slab City, you'll see a cemetery on the left-hand side of the road and a sign pointing towards West Brookfield. Turn left and go up the dirt road until you reach the West Brookfield Community Church. Park here. Map: Available from Slab City Bike & Sports.

Don't know any locals who will show you the secret trails of the state or farmers who will let you ride on their land? Fret not. Head to Randolph and its environs for the best selection of public trails Vermont has to offer. Slab City Bike & Sports offers more than ten maps with in-depth directions to the serious fat-wheeler. Bike treks include the outrageous 44.9-mile double-track Circus Ride (it can be considerably extended), used in the late 1800s to bring the circus into town, as well as the 9.8-mile Maple Ridge Sheep Farm Loop. Once you've parked your car at the church, veer left around the building and then bear right to ride next to the river. Disregard the BRIDGE CLOSED sign and head to the right of the bridge to cross the river. Veer left at the Y intersection and continue on the double tracks, crossing the river a second time. When you come to a three-way intersection, go straight on the dirt road until you reach a four-way intersection. A left-turn will bring you out of the woods past several run-down buses at the bottom of the hill. When you hit a road, continue straight, veering left at the next three-way intersection. You'll cruise up and down the hills, eventually passing the Maple Ridge Sheep Farm and an old red school house on the left. Turn left just past the school house and start climbing on the single tracks before

coasting downhill to a T-intersection. Veer left toward the white house called Davis Acres. Once in West Brookfield, take a sharp right turn to reach the church again. (If you understood those directions, your navigational skills are better than Captain Cook's. Get the map from Slab City!)

RENTALS, SCHOOLS, OUTFITTERS

Mad River Bike Shop, on State Route 100 in Waitsfield, rents bikes and provides guided tours and instruction, including a five-day bike camp for teenagers. Tel. 802/496-9500.

Slab City rents bikes and offers guided half-day and full-day tours. Junction of State Routes 12 and 12A, Randolph, tel. 802/728-5747.

Montpelier's **Onion River Sports** (tel. 802/229-9409) is another good all-around outdoor shop that carries mountain bikes.

ROAD BIKING

Upper Connecticut River

Allow 3 hours. Moderate; rolling hills with one steep climb. Access: Fairlee is located off Exit 15 on I-91. Take U.S. 5 North to the junction of State Routes 5 and 25A. Park at the Cumberland Farms. Map: Any good state road map will do.

New England's longest river, the Connecticut, is perhaps most scenic at the Vermont-New Hampshire border, north of White River Junction and Hanover. Here, the river snakes though the rural landscape, looking like it has for the past hundred years. This 28.4-mile loop brings you to both states, riding though small historic villages that sit above the winding waters. Start your trip in Fairlee at the junction of State Route 25A and U.S. 5, continuing on Route 25A East across the river into another state and another era. You have entered Orford, New Hampshire, a small village listed in the National Register of Historic Places. Bear left on State Route 10 North to view the seven Federal-style buildings, known as the Orford Ridge houses, constructed between 1773 and 1840. Continuing on the rising and falling road, the Connecticut River is seen to your left, hemmed in by farmland on either side. Patches of pumpkins, zucchini, and butternut squash line the route prior to entering the handsome village of Haverhill and its double Commons. Historic 18th- and 19th-century houses are gathered about the Village Green. Just past the town, the Indian Corn Mill is a great place to stop for apple cider and doughnuts.

Take the next left, crossing the river once again into Vermont, and veer left onto U.S. 5 South. Fields of corn soon vanish, replaced by Bradford's stores. Eight miles from the junction of U.S. 5 and the bridge, veer right onto unmarked Maurice Robert Memorial Highway. The road goes slightly upwards, under two bridges, before venturing up and down a steep hill. Another right on Lake Morey West Road brings you to a lake. The lake is named after native Samuel Morey, an inventor that some locals credit with designing and operating the world's first steamboat. Ten years before Robert Fulton launched *Clermont,* Samuel Morey was supposedly seen cruising down the Connecticut on a homemade boat that housed a steam boiler. Ride around the perimeter of the lake which is bordered by numerous summer camps. The road swings by a golf course and under I-91, before veering left onto U.S. 5 North back to the starting point.

Silver Maple Lodge in Fairlee offers bikes to their guests for the Upper Connecticut River ride (see "Campgrounds & Other Accommodations").

Randolph

Allow 3–4 hours. Easy to moderate; relatively flat terrain. Access: Park at Slab City Bike & Sports, at the junction of State Routes 12 and 12A in Randolph.

In an area of Vermont renowned for its road and off-road biking, this 36.5-mile loop is easily one of the best in the state. From the Slab City parking lot, turn left onto State Route 12A North through Randolph and the outskirts of Braintree. Civilization soon fades away as the ride becomes a mix of green meadows, corn pastures, and farms nestled at the foothills of the Green Mountains. Come late September, the trees' leaves all display a different hue—burnt red, bright orange, and a yellow like the yolk of an egg. It's like biking into an impressionist painting. The road is soon hidden by hills on both sides as you ride along a railroad bed and small stream. You'll pass Roxbury, with its requisite white steeple, and Northfield Country Club, whose putting greens are camouflaged by the surrounding hillside. At 20.6 miles, prior to entering the town of Northfield, turn right on State Route 12 South to pedal by apple orchards, a small pond, and more farmland. Gradually, you go uphill on the State Route's only ascent, before zipping downhill on a serpentine road past a flash of forest color. Don't blink or you might miss the small town of East Braintree.

The final 6 miles are a special treat— acre upon acre of uninterrupted land so rich and green you'll consider quitting your job and becoming the next Johnny Appleseed. Riding through this fertile farmland on a rolling country road with just a trace of traffic, it's easy to understand why Vermont is rated one of the best places to bike in the country. At the junction of State Routes 12 and 12A, bear left and then make an immediate right to return to your car.

Waitsfield-Warren Loop

Allow 2 hours. Easy to moderate; one short hill. Access: Mad River Bike Shop is at the junction of State Route 100 and State Route 17 between Waitsfield and Warren.

The Waitsfield-Warren area is home to Sugarbush and Mad River, two of the best-loved ski resorts in the Northeast. This short, 15-mile loop skirts the mountains and enters these two small villages via covered bridges. Start your ride from the parking lot of the Mad River Bike Shop at the junctions of State Route 100 and State Route 17, turning right on State Route 100 South. Considering the high peaks of Lincoln, Ellen, and Abraham to your right, the road is remarkably flat. When I took this ride in early autumn, the maples on the hillside to my left were as red as a newly painted barn. At 5.4 miles, take a sharp left onto Covered Bridge Road. Constructed in 1880, the wooden bridge spans the Mad River. Turn left and ride through the village of Warren, making a point to stop at the Warren Store for lunch. Dagwoodesque sandwiches on thick French bread can be savored at the picnic tables overlooking Mad River. Try to save room for the home-made peanut butter, oatmeal raisin, and chocolate chip cookies. You'll easily burn off the calories when you take your next right onto Brook Road and climb into Lincoln Valley. Dairy farms, green meadows, and fields of corn, typical of Vermont's bucolia, stand at the side of the road. The slopes of Sugarbush appear to your left and a rare round barn can be seen to your right. Built in 1910, the barn is now part of the Inn of the Round Barn. From here, you cruise downhill all the way to the

covered bridge in Waitsfield, built in 1833. Pedal through town and turn left onto State Route 100 South, being cautious of traffic.

RENTALS, OUTFITTERS & INN-TO-INN TOURS

For Randolph, rent bikes from **Slab City Bike & Sports,** tel. 802/728-5747. In Waitsfield, bikes can be rented at **Mad River Bikes,** tel. 802/496-9500. In Montpelier, check out **Onion River Sports** (tel. 802/229-9409).

ROCK CLIMBING

Vermont's rock-climbing scene isn't what you might think it would be judging from all those mountains and cliffs. Problem is, the flakey metamorphic schist that is the most common foundation of the Green Mountains is about the worst climbing rock imaginable.

There are a few moderate-sized walls of good rock around the state that have kept the locals happy. Most of them are still relatively undiscovered. Probably the three best walls in the middle part of the state are **Deer Leap Mountain,** off U.S. 4 at Shelburne Pass, right behind the Long Trail Inn (a half-dozen climbs on good rock, in the 5.8 to 5.10 range); the **Bolton Valley Walls,** north off U.S. 2, not far west of the Bolton Valley Ski Area access road (rumored to be as good as it gets in the Green Mountains but difficult to find); and the rock at **Lake Dunmore** just across from the entrance to Branbury State Park (looks like about eight climbs, 5.5 to 5.6 or so, developed climbs).

The one-stop-shopping source for equipment and all sorts of information about Vermont rock climbing is **Climb High,** 1861 Shelburne Rd., Shelburne, VT 05482 (tel. 802/985-5056, or 802/985-9141).

SNOWMOBILING

There are literally thousands of miles of nonpareil snowmobile trails all over Vermont. Contact the **Vermont Association of Snow Travelers,** P.O. Box 839, Montpelier, VT 05601 (802/229-0005) for information and maps.

If you just want to take a casual stab at "snowmachinin'," there are a few places in the area that rent snowmobiles, maintain networks of safe trails, and lead guided tours. In north-central Vermont, try **Ride Snowmobile Tours,** P.O. Box 416, Williamstown, VT 05679 (tel. 802/433-1208). Killington's **Cortina Inn** (tel. 802/773-3333) also has rentals and trails. Off the Waterbury exit of I-89 toward Stowe is **Nichols Snowmobile Rentals** (tel. 802/253-7239), which has a fleet available to take out on its vast pastures.

SWIMMING

No, they're not mirages; they're authentic Vermont swimming holes:

◆ **Quechee Gorge,** U.S. 4, Quechee. An easy trail from the highway leads down to this genuine geological phenomenon; at its north end is an excellent swimming hole.

◆ **Silver Lake State Park,** State Route 12, Barnard. A scenic lake with a diving board, large grass beach, and changing facilities; a good place to take the kids.

◆ **White River,** off State Route 14 in the South Royalton–Sharon area. The joining of the four branches of this river just upstream creates big enough water for some great swimming holes. Keep your eyes peeled for cars parked at pull-overs.

◆ **White River,** near intersection of State Routes 100 and 73, Rochester.

◆ **The Floating Bridge,** State Route 65, Brookfield. Where all the locals go— a genuine scene.

◆ **Osgood Brook Culvert,** Tunbridge Road, East Randolph. The real thing— an icy, crystal-clear swimming hole known to only a few— and so small you couldn't fit more than two or three people in it—about a half-mile up this dirt road that heads east off State Route 14.

◆ **Mad River,** off State Route 100 immediately after Lincoln Gap Road; park at the gravel pit.

◆ **Mad River,** off State Route 100 between Moretown and Waitsfield; look for the parking lot and picnic area on the riverbank. Large, very popular, and graced with more skipping-stones than any 12-year-old boy could throw.

◆ **Beaver ponds, Winooski feeder streams, Winooski River,** in the North Calais–Kents Corner area, off U.S. 2 east of Montpelier. Boundless swimmin' options in a little area that seriously contends to be Vermont's prettiest.

Campgrounds & Other Accommodations

If you find yourself without something like, oh, a tent, proceed to Montpelier's **Onion River Sports** (tel. 802/229-9409), which is now stocking excellent camping gear.

CAMPING

There are 94 campsites scattered across the **Green Mountain National Forest,** available on a first-come, first-served basis for a small fee. Free camping is also permitted anywhere on national forest land. For more information, contact the Green Mountain National Forest, 231 N. Main St., Rutland, VT 05701 (tel. 802/747-6700).

The **Department of Forests, Parks, and Recreation** maintains 35 campgrounds in the state. For a brochure, contact The Department of Forests, Parks, and Recreation, 108 South Main Street, Waterbury, VT 05676 (tel. 802/241-3655).

SOUTHERN VERMONT

Molly Stark State Park

From the junction of State Routes 100 and 9 in Wilmington, head east on State Route 9 for 3 miles. Tel. 802/464-5460. 34 sites, no hookups, wheelchair accessible rest rooms, sewage disposal, tables, fire rings, wood.

The sites here are located in a 158-acre preserve with hiking trails leading to the summit of 2,145-foot Mount Olga.

Woodford State Park

From Bennington, head 10 miles east on State Route 9. Tel. 802/447-7169. 102 sites, no hookups, public phone, sewage disposal, tables, fire rings, wood.

This 400-acre area is centered around Adams Reservoir, a good swimming hole.

Jamaica State Park

From Jamaica, head 0.5 mile north on the town road. Tel. 802/874-4600. 59 sites, no hookups, public phone, sewage disposal, tables, fire rings, grills, wood.

Camp by the West River in this densely forested park.

Hapgood Pond Recreation Area

From Peru, head 1.75 miles northeast on Hapgood Pond Road. Tel. 802/824-6456. 28 sites, no hookups, tables, fire rings, grills, wood.

Set in the Green Mountain National Forest, the campsites are slightly removed from the pond.

Lake St. Catherine State Park

Located 3 miles south of Poultney on State Route 30. Tel. 802/287-9158. 61 sites, no hookups, public phone, wheelchair accessible rest rooms, sewage disposal, limited grocery store, tables, fire rings, wood.

The campsites are ideally located on the shores of this 7-mile-long lake.

Bomoseen State Park

Follow U.S. 4 west of Rutland and take Exit 3. The park is located 5 miles north on West Shore Road. Tel. 802/265-4242. 66 sites, no hookups, public phone, wheelchair accessible rest rooms, limited grocery store, tables, fire rings, wood.

The campsites are set slightly back from the shores of the lake in a wooded refuge.

Calvin Coolidge State Park

From the junction of State Routes 100 and 100A in Plymouth, head 2 miles north on State Route 100A. Tel. 802/672-3612. 60 sites, no hookups, public phone, wheelchair accessible rest rooms, sewage disposal, ice, tables, fire rings, wood.

A network of hiking trails traverse this large 16,165-acre preserve.

CENTRAL VERMONT

Silver Lake State Park

From Barnard, head 0.25 mile north on Town Road. Tel. 802/234-9451. 47 sites, no hookups, public phone, wheelchair accessible rest rooms, sewage disposal, tables, fire rings, grills, wood.

Located on the eastern side of the state, the park is known for its swimming and nice, relaxed perch fishing.

INNS & RESORTS

It's almost an absurd proposition to list the best inns in southern Vermont. The competition is fierce, forcing many inn-keepers to cut cross-country ski trails, shuttle hikers or canoeists, or be affiliated with a golf course if they want to survive. You rarely come across an accommodation that doesn't feature some sporting activity. These are simply my own personal favorites.

SOUTHERN VERMONT

The White House

Off State Route 9, Wilmington, VT 05363. Tel. 802/464-2135 or 800/541-2135. Rates start at $55 per person, including breakfast.

Set on a hill overlooking the town of Wilmington, the stately White House is a sight that's hard to miss from State Route 9. Built as a summer home for a wealthy lumber baron in 1915, white pillars, two-storied terraces and French doors form the facade of this Colonial Revival mansion. The inn is known for its continental cuisine and 45 km of groomed cross-country ski trails that start from the back porch. It is also located near Mount Snow.

West Mountain Inn

State Route 313, Arlington, VT 05250. Tel. 802/375-6516. Rooms start at $152, double occupancy, including breakfast and dinner; $102 for breakfast-only accommodation.

If you hook old tires instead of trout on the Battenkill, the West Mountain Inn will undoubtedly cheer you up. The inn is set high in the valley overlooking the mountains of the Taconic range. There are 5 miles of hiking and cross-country trails leading from the back porch.

The Equinox

State Route 7A, Manchester Village, 05254. Tel. 802/362-4700 or 800/362-4747. Rates for double rooms start at $119.

Woodstock's top-notch counterpart on the western side of Vermont is this 225-year-old inn. Once a fashionable summer retreat for rich northeasterners and presidents in the late 1800s, The Equinox continues to captivate guests who yearn for the elegance of yesteryear coupled with today's finest amenities. Step out of modernity onto the marble sidewalks of 19th-century Manchester Village, and enter through the Equinox's stately columns and rambling white verandah. Inside the lobby, velvet chairs and marble tables are set around a Federal-style fireplace. The inn sits at the foot of 3,816-foot Mount Equinox. Go golfing on one of the finest courses in the state, cross-country skiing on 20 km of groomed trails, alpine skiing at nearby Bromley or Stratton, or simply take a stroll through the Inn's backyard gardens of tulips and azaleas. You'll feel like you just stepped out of an Edith Wharton novel.

The Old Tavern

Grafton, VT 05146. Tel. 802/843-2231 or 800/843-1801. Rooms start at $115 and include breakfast.

Renting a room at the Old Tavern in Grafton is like renting a historic hamlet for the weekend. This former stage-coach stop has 66 rooms, cottages, and guest houses scattered about the quaint village. All have been meticulously restored to their 19th-century splendor. The Old Tavern's tennis courts and 40 km cross-country trail system are just down the road. This is also the start of the Grafton Bike Loop (see "Road Biking").

The Village Inn

P.O. Box 215, Landgrove, VT 05148. Tel. 802/824-6673 or 800/669-8466. Rates start at $68 per person MAP in the fall and winter, $65 per couple B&B during the summer.

A toss-up with Blueberry Hill for the most remote inn in southern Vermont, the cozy Village Inn is set in the small village of Landgrove on the outskirts of the Green Mountain National Forest. The 18 rooms branch out from the original 1820 house. The inn is within close proximity to Bromley and Stratton, and offers 15 miles of groomed cross-country trails. They also are known for their romantic sleigh rides.

Lake St. Catherine Inn

P.O. Box 129, Poultney, VT 05764. Tel. 802/287-9347 or 800/626-LSCI. Prices are $74–$88 per person including dinner and breakfast.

Located on the shores of seven-mile-long Lake St. Catherine, the rustic Lake St. Catherine Inn in Poultney is the perfect place for water-sports enthusiasts who enjoy being pampered without all the formalities. It's the type of inn where children feel comfortable. During the day, rent a canoe, sailboat, or paddleboat and fish for small- or large-mouth bass. At night, indulge in a gourmet five-course meal.

Inn at Windsor

106 Main Street, Windsor, VT 05089. Tel. 802/674-5670 or 800/754-8668.

Prices for rooms start at $85 and include breakfast.

Passion and history seep from the walls of this new inn, opened just last summer. The passion stems from the owners, Larry Bowser and his wife, Holly Taylor, who have spent the last 12 years painstakingly restoring this Georgian-style house. Built in 1791 for apothecarian Dr. Issac Green, the gracious house remained in the family until being sold to the Knights of Columbus in 1963. The new owners have carefully peeled away the 20th-century facade to recreate the historic charm of yesteryear. The three-room inn is located near the banks of the Connecticut River and the slopes of Mount Ascutney. Larry and Holly's exuberance over their inn is contagious. Catch it while you can.

CENTRAL VERMONT

Woodstock Inn & Resort

Fourteen the Green, Woodstock, VT 05091. Tel. 802/457-1100 or 800/448-7900. Double room rates start at $139.

Once the Richardson Tavern in 1793, the Woodstock Inn is now one of the two premier resorts in southern Vermont. Rooms are sumptuous, service is impeccable, and the sporting facilities are unparalleled. The 136 rooms and 7 suites are located in the heart of the picturesque village of Woodstock. The vast range of sporting options include an 18-hole golf course designed by Robert Trent Jones, Sr., more than 60 km of groomed Nordic skiing trails at the base of Mount Tom and Mount Peg, downhill skiing at one of the oldest ski resorts in the country (Suicide Six), and guided hiking tours to the peak of Mount Tom.

You can't do much better than this in Vermont.

Silver Maple Lodge

RR 1 Box 8, Fairlee, VT 05045. Tel. 802/333-4326 or 800/666-1946. Double rooms start at a remarkably low $49 double occupancy, including breakfast.

In addition to their hot-air balloon package (see "Ballooning"), the Silver Maple Lodge arranges self-guided biking, canoeing, and walking inn-to-inn tours. The inn is located near the banks of the Connecticut River, north of Hanover, NH. First opened to guests in the 1920s, the lodge's antique farmhouse dates from the late 1700s.

Three Stallion Inn

Randolph, VT 05060. Tel. 802/728-5575 or 800/424-5575. Rates start at $65 double occupancy.

Set on 1,300 acres of pasture, this former farm caters to outdoor enthusiasts. The affordable inn features 50 km of groomed cross-country skiing trails, two tennis courts, an adjoining golf course, and, of course, horseback riding. The inn is also situated in Randolph, one of the top biking locales in the state (see "Road Biking," above).

The Inn at Round Barn Farm

P.O. Box 247, East Warren Road, Waitsfield, VT 05673. Tel. 802/496-2276. The 11 rooms start at $100 and include a gluttonous breakfast.

There's always some special event happening at the Round Barn. When I was there last, they were hosting two weddings in the same week. People were more sociable than relatives at a family reunion. The inn gets its name from the adjacent round barn built in 1910, one of the few round barns that remain in Vermont. The lower level of the barn now has a 60-foot lap pool, and 23 km of groomed cross-country trail snake through the outlying farmland and forests. If you feel like going downhill skiing, you're close to Sugarbush and Mad River. The woods across East Warren Road are known for their mountain biking trails (see "Mountain Biking," above).

9

Lake Champlain, the Northern Green Mountains & the Northeast Kingdom

IT'S NOT FOR NOTHING THAT THE HUB OF NORTHERN VERMONT, Burlington, is Vermont's biggest city. Straddling the line between friendly, medium-size town and burgeoning metropolis, Burlington has an attractive waterfront and the vigorous cultural life that comes with playing host to five colleges. The Champlain Valley also has a milder climate than most of Vermont—if the difference between –10° and –25° on a January morning means something more to you than "head south."

But the lure of Burlington for its young, active population is the diversity of outdoor playgrounds within shooting range. Sailing and deep-water fishing on Lake Champlain; the mix of open water, freshwater marsh, and farmland you see from almost any vantage on the roads of Grand Isle County; miles upon miles of quiet two-lane roads through the rolling, wide-open farmland of the Champlain Valley; Vermont's highest peaks and best ski areas in the northern Green Mountains; and the rugged and remote reaches of the Northeast Kingdom—all of these are within a short drive of Burlington. People who live in central Vermont or the Northeast Kingdom— and especially Montpelier, Burlington's chief rival as a sort of center of the intelligentsia—like to disdainfully portray Burlington as an unwanted beachhead in their state of the kind of overcommercialized, overdeveloped landscape you find almost anywhere else in the country. But if you want to live within reach of the best skiing, birding, canoeing, road and mountain biking, sailing—really, any outdoor pursuit you can think of—and be able to eat in a good restaurant and catch a first-run movie of your choice, there's no place in the state like the "Queen City."

The outdoor playgrounds of northern Vermont, most of them a whopping seven-hour drive or so from New York, are more for the locals than they are for tourists. Towns up here (with the notable exception of Stowe) don't have the overmanicured charm of places like Manchester and Woodstock to the south. Yet they're just as beautiful—take a look at the perfect little villages of Craftsbury and Cabot and see what you think. The Northeast Kingdom is completely unabashed cow country, still characterized by working family farms and small-time timbering operations. What's all this mean for the sportsperson who ventures this far north? You're entering the *real* Vermont with *real* people. The rolling green farmland and high peaks are here, perhaps even more spectacular than farther south, but the majority of people do not have jobs that cater to tourists, and the majority of farms have not been refurbished as country inns.

This is especially true of the Northeast Kingdom, the large chunk of land bordering Quebec and New Hamsphire in the northeast corner of the state. Ride a bike on one of the country roads here and you'll find hills and farms branching out in every direction. Come winter, the Nordic and Alpine ski areas have much more snow than in the south and there are far fewer people on the trails.

Located south of the Northeast Kingdom, Stowe began as a resort after the Civil War, when travelers would take the train to Waterbury, ride the trolley to Stowe, and then hire a horse-drawn carriage to bring them to the Mount Mansfield House. Atop the barren summit of Vermont's highest peak, urbanites could enjoy the views and fill their lungs with the crisp mountain air. Over a century later, the trails are still filled with hikers who yearn for the same pleasures. Then there's Lake Champlain and its many tributaries. Canoeists head towards the lake via Vermont's three great canoe-camping rivers, the Winooski, the Lamoille, and the Missisquoi, while sailors, fishermen, kayakers, and scuba divers stake out their spots on Champlain itself. Head to this part of the state and you'll soon understand why it's worth the extra one- to two-hour drive.

The Lay of the Land

North of Bolton Gorge, the notch cut by the Winooski River through the ridge of the **Green Mountains,** the summits loom up again and eventually climb to the 4,393-foot Mount Mansfield, the state's highest point. From here, the Greens pass the baton to the **Cold Hollow Mountains,** which extend close to the Canadian border. The range includes Belvidere Mountain and Jay Peak. Paralleling the main ridge 10 to 20 miles to the east is the **Worcester Range,** which boasts peaks such as Mount Hunger, near Stowe.

To the east of Jay Peak is the **Northeast Kingdom,** a sparsely populated, very hilly land of farms and lakes. A fine example of glacial scouring is evident at Lake Willoughby, north of St. Johnsbury. The indigenous granite has been carved into a deep trough lined by dramatic cliffs on either side of the water.

West of the mountains is 120-mile-long **Lake Champlain** and the outlying land known as the Champlain Valley. The massive lake was formed when an ice cap retreated to the St. Lawrence Seaway and the ocean. Close to 1,500 feet lower than the mountains, the lake's islands and outlying valley contain prodigious amounts of marble. In fact, Vermont is the second-largest marble producer in the nation. Isle La Motte, an island in Lake Champlain, was once home to a black marble quarry; in the southern part of the state, quarries still yield marble in West Rutland, Danby, and Proctor.

Fall foliage usually peaks in late September in northern Vermont. The Department of Travel in Vermont maintains a foliage hotline, updating the conditions of the leaves (tel. 800/VERMONT). The rest of the year, summer days are usually in the high 70s, cooler at night. In the Northeast Kingdom, it is not uncommon to find frost on your window in early September. January temperatures are below freezing most of the time (especially near the Canadian border), with snowfall averaging 55 inches in the valleys to over 120 inches on high elevations. Call 802/862-2475 or 802/476-4101 for current weather conditions in northern Vermont.

The chances of finding moose in the northern fringes of Vermont are becoming better and better. Last summer, a local told me she spotted a moose every time she took the trail up to summit of Mount Hor on Lake Willoughby. Sightings of black bear and otters are far less common. Beavers, gray foxes, and white-tailed deer are frequently observed on the shores and waters of Vermont's northern lakes. (Speaking of deer, the Northeast Kingdom is definitely the kind of place where hunting is such an obsession that high schools closed down for deer season, at least until fairly recently.) The state's numerous wildlife management areas and preserves are prime birding territory. Wood ducks, herons, mallards, and green-winged teals are prevalent.

Orientation

This chapter covers all of Lake Champlain and the Champlain Valley south to Brandon and east to just below the ridge of the Green Mountains (ski areas and other spots right on the ridge are covered in the central Vermont section in chapter 8). It also covers the entirety of the Green Mountain chain above Bolton Gorge (I-89), and all of the Northeast Kingdom above the Barre-Montpelier area and U.S. 302. (This is a broader definition than most people give the Kingdom, but this whole area really is of a piece, and it works for my purposes.)

I-89 connects Montpelier, Waterbury, and the Mount Mansfield area with Burlington. North of Burlington, **U.S. 2** takes you to the Lake Champlain islands. When you get within a half hour or so of Burlington, **State Route 15** becomes one of the ugliest and most congested routes in the state.

North of Waterbury, **State Route 100**—the Ski Country corridor all the way up and down the state—continues to Stowe and Jay Peak. The village of **Stowe** and the roads within 5 miles of town are really the only clearly touristy area in northern Vermont—but nevertheless, this is definitely one of Vermont's most beautiful places, well deserving all the attention. **State Route 108** through Smuggler's Notch is one of the most majestic drives in New England.

The **Northeast Kingdom** got its name when Senator George Aiken, speaking to a small group of his constituents in Lyndonville in 1949, noted that "this is such beautiful country up here. It ought to be called the Northeast Kingdom of

Vermont." The Northeast Kingdom now consists of Essex, Orleans, and Caledonia counties, a large tract of land wedged between the Quebec and New Hampshire borders. To get to the gems of the Northeast Kingdom—**Craftsbury, Greensboro,** and **Lake Willoughby**—you have to earn it. A combination of smaller byways like State Routes 14, 16 and 5A will eventually guide you there. There are numerous scenic drives to and through the Kingdom: **State Route 5A,** skirting the shores of Lake Willoughby; **State Route 58** from Montgomery Center to Lowell through Hazen's Notch; **State Route 14** from Irasburg to Craftsbury Common; and—my favorite—**State Route 12** from Montpelier to Morrisville.

Even Vermonters speak of the Kingdom as the Boonies, or the Sticks. Wave after wave of unspoiled hillside form a vast sea of green. No slick resorts, just a few inconspicuous inns and lots of Holsteins. **St. Johnsbury** and **Lyndonville** are its business centers, workmanlike towns with nary a fancy carved-wood roadside sign between them. Around them for many miles are spread small villages and farms, a few high mountains, and a lot of abruptly hilly countryside. Some of these villages, like Craftsbury and Greensboro, are iconic in their appeal. You haven't seen a New England village green until you've visited Craftsbury Common. Founded in 1789, Craftsbury Common is an incredibly peaceful village where white clapboard houses embrace the perimeter of the town square. And the small community of Greensboro, located on the shores of Caspian Lake, is vintage Vermont. Sitting in the center of the village is Willey's, one of Vermont's largest country stores, selling everything from apple cider to rubber barn boots. Other villages up here are plagued by an all-too-apparent rural poverty. For more information, contact the **Northeast**

Kingdom Chamber of Commerce, 30 Western Avenue, St. Johnsbury, VT 05819 (tel. 802/748-3678).

Parks & Other Hot Spots

Lake Champlain

Accessible from the east off State Route 22A, U.S. 7, and U.S. 2; from New York, off State Route 22, U.S. 9, and I-87. For information, contact the Vermont Department of Travel, 134 State Street, Montpelier, VT 05602 (tel. 800/VERMONT).

Forming the western boundary of Vermont with New York, this 120-mile-long lake swells with boaters in the summer. Sailboats jibe along the shore, powerboats cruise through the center of the lake with water skiers in tow, and kayakers head north to the islands. Burlington, the largest city in Vermont with close to 125,000 people, sits on the eastern shores of the lake overlooking New York's Adirondack Mountains.

Lake Champlain Islands

Accessible via U.S. 2. For information, contact the Lake Champlain Islands Chamber of Commerce, South Hero, VT 05486 (tel. 802/372-5683).

With the Green Mountains to the east and the Adirondacks to the west, the islands of Lake Champlain have the perfect vantage point. The three islands, Grand Isle, North Hero, and Isle La Motte, are located at the northern end of the lake, just south of the Quebec

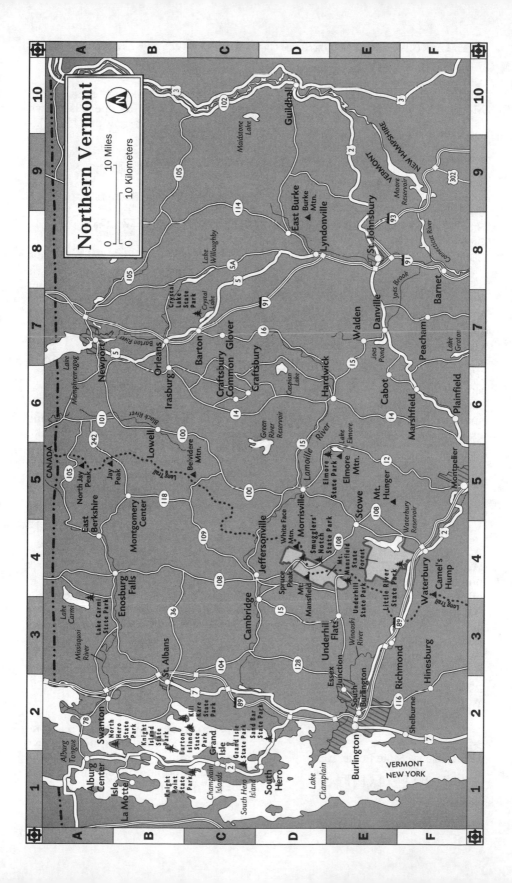

Northern Vermont

10 Miles

10 Kilometers

0

0

border. State Route 129 and Isle La Motte are popular bike routes.

Mount Mansfield

Accessible via State Route 108 from Stowe or Jeffersonville in the summertime. State Route 108 is closed from Jeffersonville in the winter. For information, contact The Stowe Area Association, P.O. Box 1320, Stowe, VT 05672 (tel. 802/253-7321 or 800/24-STOWE).

Vermont's tallest mountain is the most popular hiking destination in Vermont and the premier cross-country skiing area in New England. Home to Stowe, it could arguably be the finest downhill ski area in the state as well. Needless to say, it is the cornerstone for outdoor sports in Vermont and well worth the extra effort to get here.

Smuggler's Notch

Accessible via State Route 108 in summer only.

Who said New Hampshire has all the notches in New England? This is one of the most spectacular passes in the Northeast, one that I would definitely go out of my way to drive through. Large slabs of rock force State Route 108 to twist and turn as it narrowly coasts through the mountainous gap. Not surprisingly, the road is closed to cars in the winter (but open to snowshoers).

Jay Peak

Accessible via State Route 105.

The northernmost skiing destination in the state. The 3,861-foot peak is known for its abundance of snow and long skiing season.

Lake Willoughby

Accessible via State Route 5A.

One of the most striking sights in New England, the 5-mile long Willoughby is sandwiched between the cliffs of Mount Pisgah and Mount Hor.

Northern Lakes

Accessible via I-91 or State Route 114.

Some of the best fishing and boating spots in the state are north of Lake Willoughby. They include Seymour Lake, the Averills, Norton Pond, and 32-mile-long Lake Memphremagog.

Burke Mountain

Accessible via State Route 114.

Virtually unknown to most skiers outside the state, Burke has uncrowded yet challenging trails. The mountain towers over the small village of East Burke.

Lamoille, Winooski, and Missisquoi Rivers

These three tributaries of Lake Champlain are the finest long distance canoeing routes in Vermont. For more detailed information, consult the "Canoeing" section.

Connecticut River

Accessible via I-91.

North of White River Junction, New England's longest river looks more like its old self—an unspoiled and undeveloped waterway fringed by farmland. This is especially true of the Connecticut Lakes region at the Quebec border and the section of the river just north of Fairlee. Blue-ribbon trout are found in the waterway between the Connecticut Lakes and Bloomfield.

What to Do & Where to Do It

BIRD WATCHING

The northern part of Vermont offers exceptional birding, with far more opportunities than you'll find in southern and central Vermont. This is largely due to the presence of an immense number of wetland areas, from the huge bird sanctuary of Lake Champlain's open waters and freshwater marshes to the myriad fens, marshy ponds, and kettlehole bogs of the Northeast Kingdom.

I'm going to concentrate on wetlands birding here, although of course there's also plenty of hardwood- and boreal-forest birding in the piedmont and mountains of Northern Vermont, just as there is in the state's southern reaches. Expect to find **broad-winged hawks, grouse, barred owls, kingfishers, woodpeckers,** and many other birds; see the southern Vermont "Bird Watching" section in chapter 8 for more information on the kinds of uplands birding habitat and species you find in the New England woods.

Lake Champlain and the **Champlain Valley** are a crucial rest stop for migratory birds traveling the Atlantic Flyway. Out on the open water of the lake, you may see **buffleheads, ring-necked ducks, canvasbacks, ruddy ducks,** and **mergansers,** along with the occasional sea duck, such as a **scoter** or **eider.** The huge freshwater marshes on the Vermont side of the lake are even richer. Waterfowl and shorebirds like the **pied-billed grebes, Canada geese, black-crowned night herons,** and **green herons** top the long list of native birds.

One of the most remarkable birding events in the Champlain Valley is the spring and fall stopovers of tens of thousands of migratory **snow geese** in the area. **Missisquoi National Wildlife Refuge** (tel. 802/868-4781), in Swanton near the Canadian border, is one hot spot; **Dead Creek Wildlife Management Area** (tel. 802/878-1564) is another. Seeing 20,000 large, shrieking white birds take to the air is a natural spectacle of a rare order. Dead Creek is an excellent spot for birding year-round; in warm weather you can canoe its calm marshes, where you'll see all variety of migratory waterfowl, including **great blue herons.** And in winter it's one of the best places in New England to seek out a **snowy owl.** Drive around for a while and you're nearly guaranteed to spot one, stoically posed on a fence post or some such perch.

Elsewhere in northern Vermont, the **South Bay Wildlife Management Area** on the southern end of Lake Memphremagog is good for the same kind of birding.

The Northeast Kingdom has a number of large kettlehole bogs; amid the pitcher plants, sundews, orchids, and sphagnum moss of the bog environment are a lot of birds—songbirds, primarily, such as **olive-sided flycatchers, black-backed woodpeckers, Nashville, black-throated blue,** and **blackburnian warblers.** Three such places are: **Victory**

Bog in the 4,970-acre Victory Basin Wildlife Management Area, just east of St. Johnsbury; **Moose Bog** in the Wenlock Wildlife Management Area, 9.7 miles east of Island Pond off State Route 105; and **Yellow Bog.** This last one's about 5 miles east of Island Pond on State Route 105. The second real road you'll see to the left of Route 105 after Island Pond is Lewis Pond Road, where you turn left; follow the road for a few miles, then veer right at the fork. You'll then be in this huge bog; you can backtrack out of it or follow a counterclockwise loop through the bog area that will eventually bring you back to State Route 105.

Watch yourself in a bog—there may be quicksand-like areas you'll have trouble extricating yourself from if you're alone, and it's easy to get lost. Bring a good map; the USGS 7.5-minute quadrangles for the above areas are: the Concord map for Victory Bog; the Bloomfield map for Moose Bog; and the Spectacle Pond map for Yellow Bog; On the plus side, these northern bogs are also moose country—there's a decent chance of seeing one of the huge, ungainly animals here. Just keep your distance.

BOARDSAILING

After becoming a member at **The International Sailing School and Club,** you are entitled to unlimited use of the sailboards. 253 Lakeshore Drive, Colchester, north of Burlington (tel. 802/864-9065).

Great Outdoors Trading Company offers rentals and lessons in the South Bay area of Lake Memphremagog. Located at 73 Main Street, Newport (tel. 802/334-2831).

CANOEING

Most of the longer river journeys in the state are located in the north. The **Winooski, Lamoille,** and **Missisquoi Rivers** are all tributaries of Lake Champlain. For the Winooski, canoeists usually put in at Montpelier and head west to the lake. The Lamoille is popular from Johnson to the lake, and the Missisquoi is canoeable from Richford to the lake. If you plan on canoeing the Winooski, the **Winooski Valley Park District,** Ethan Allen Homestead, Burlington, VT 05401 (tel. 802/863-5744), publishes the *Winooski River Canoe Guide,* a 33-page book with maps that costs $4.

In addition to these three rivers, there's also the Upper Connecticut River, which runs with mild riffles and flatwater through an endless succession of dairy farms. The 24.5-mile stretch between Canaan and Bloomfield, about as far as you can go for a little recreation in Vermont, is a scenic (but not wilderness), nicely paced paddle. About 2 miles before you reach Bloomfield are the remains of an old dam, which should be portaged by all but the experts, and scouted by anyone.

Green River Reservoir

Northeast of Morrisville. Access: From the junction of State Route 15 and State Route 15A, head east on State Route 15 for several hundred yards and turn left onto a paved road (Garfield Road); 3.1 miles from State Route 15, turn right at the T-intersection in Garfield, and then immediately left up a hill. 1.3 miles later, bear left on the gravel road and head downhill for 0.2 mile to a large parking lot. The road is in poor condition, so be careful. Map: USGS 7.5 minute Morrisville, Eden.

A light frost covered the ground and a heavy fog hung low in the air the morning Vermont Waterways invited me to come along on one of their canoe tours. Owned by Mark and Hope McAndrew, two avid canoeists who have competed professionally, Vermont Waterways is an outfitter that specializes in canoeing the rivers and lakes in the state. Paddling down the Connecticut, Lamoille, and White Rivers and kayaking through the Lake Champlain islands are several of the jaunts featured in their weekend or five-day tours. Today we were headed for a hidden gem known as the Green River Reservoir.

I met the other canoeists (four couples from the West Coast who have traveled together for the past 35 years) at the Fitch Hill Inn tucked neatly away in Hyde Park, Vermont. From here we crawled into a van and drove off to the lake, canoe trailer in tow. By the time we reached our destination, the fog was replaced by a hazy mist that skimmed over the waters as if something was brewing under the surface. Within moments, the mist vanished and the sun took its rightful place atop the cloudless skies, and the blue-green waters of Green River Reservoir shone like it was just washed with Windex. Our guides were Ed, a prosecuting attorney from Montpelier who took a year off to battle the elements instead of sparring with defense lawyers, and Liz, who runs a dogsledding business in Bethel, Maine, during the winter.

We slid the canoes into the water and paddled to our right around a large island that sat in the center of the reservoir. It was early autumn and the red maples, yellow birches, and beeches were slowly starting to put on their coats of vibrant colors. Thankfully, the absence of farmland and all other forms of real estate have left these shores undeveloped and heavily forested. We paddled around a bend where two mating loons called to one another between dunks in the water. The Green River Reservoir is one of the few places in Vermont where nesting loons are found.

Mark McAndrew has also spotted otters, beavers, moose, and bear in the northern reaches of the lake, where it turns into a narrow stream. However, today we would have to be content with the loons, the cedar waxwings, and the pictures of moose on Liz's shirt. By the end of the morning I was convinced that the only way to truly enjoy the splendors of fall foliage is not from behind the glass window of a large automobile, but inside the wooden frame of a canoe.

Morrisville has seen fit to allow camping along the shores of this reservoir, and this place is thus one of the treasured secrets of Vermont's canoeists. Even when there are a lot of cars in the lot, you should still be able to find a peaceful site a long way away from anyone else, and spend the night with no company but the loons.

Lamoille River

Runs from Horse Pond north of Greensboro down to Hardwick, following State Route 15 to Lake Champlain. Below Johnson, mostly quickwater and flatwater, navigable at most water levels; put-ins at Johnson Bridge, Fairfax Falls, and Milton; portages at ledge under State Route 15 bridge and Ithiel falls (a few miles below Johnson), dam at Fairfax Falls, two dams in Milton, and Peterson Dam 1.75 miles beyond I-89. Above Johnson, a number of portages and Class II-III rapids, navigable at high and medium water.

It was while I was canoeing the Lamoille River, paddling through the sylvan splendor of this rural state, that it finally dawned on me how incredibly tranquil and private this sport really is. Biking inevitably shares the road with car traffic, and the best hiking trails are popular. Mountain biking and backcountry skiing give you the same sense of solitude, but are far more strenuous.

Canoeing is a sport where the workout is small and the rewards are great. Paddling down a river where no motorboats are allowed ultimately leaves me in a state of solace.

This was certainly the case with the Lamoille. Smuggler's Notch Canoe Touring, run by the Mannsview Inn, helped transfer my car to the put-out and shuttled me to the put-in, just off Hogback Road between Jeffersonville and Johnson. They offer two trips on the Lamoille, either 6 or 9 miles. I chose the former due to time constraints, and off I went down the narrow curving river. For the next two hours, I did not see or hear another human being. Instead, I saw numerous cows grazing at the river's edge and large families of ducks. The cows tended to pick their heads up and stare at me in bewilderment, perhaps astonished at my presence. Tall fields of corn fringed the river, surrounded by the foothills of the Green Mountains. Everywhere was farmland; the smell of manure permeating the air served as a remembrance just in case I dropped my head to look at my stroke. Mount Mansfield, shrouded in clouds, came into view upon the end of the trip. The trip went far too quickly. I tied my canoe to a tree and drove my car back to the Mannsview Inn, in a relaxed, almost catatonic state.

OUTFITTERS

In addition to the Green River Reservoir, **Vermont Waterways,** RR 1, P.O. Box 322, East Hardwick, VT 05836-9707 (tel. 800/492-8271), also visits the White, Winooski, Connecticut, and Lamoille rivers on their weekend or five-day tours. Prices start at $350 per person, including accommodations and all meals.

Smuggler's Notch Canoe Touring and Mannsville Inn are located on State Route 108 just south of Jeffersonville (tel. 800/937-6266). Canoe rentals,

including shuttle, are $40, and tours leave at 9:30 AM, 11:30 AM, and 1:30 PM. Mannsville Inn also offers a two-night, two-day canoe package for $199 double occupancy.

Umiak Outdoor Outfitters, 849 South Main Street, Stowe, VT 05672 (tel. 802/253-2317), offer rentals and guided trips on the Lamoille, Winooski, White, and Mad rivers. They also provide private guides and instruction.

Clearwater Sports, State Route 100, Waitsfield, VT 05673 (tel. 802/496-2708), offers day and overnight trips on the Winooski, Mad, and White rivers.

Vermont Voyager Expedition, Montgomery Center, VT 95471 (tel. 802/326-4789), in the Northeast Kingdom, offers guided canoe trips on the Missisquoi River.

Dartmouth's **Ledyard Canoe Club** (tel. 603/643-6709) in Hanover, NH, rents canoes on the Connecticut but no longer operates a shuttle service.

CROSS-COUNTRY SKIING

IN THE BACKCOUNTRY

With more than 400 km of interconnected ski trails, the area around Mount Mansfield is the premier cross-country skiing destination in the Northeast. Five of the top ski touring centers in New England, including the oldest in the nation, connect via some of the most challenging backcountry ski runs available. These backcountry trails are not simple loops around ponds, but grueling uphill and exhilarating downhill runs for skilled skiers only. They include the **Bruce** and **Teardrop Trails,** two of the earliest downhill trails in the country, cut by the Civilian Conservation Corps in the early 1930s. Maintained cooperatively by the Mount Mansfield and Trapp Family Ski Touring centers, the Bruce Trail drops 2,600 feet as it plummets down the slopes of Mount

Mansfield. The trails starts from the Octagon, reached by Stowe's Forerunner Quad chairlift, and ends 6 km later at the Mount Mansfield Touring Center ski shop. Also starting at the Octagon, but even steeper, is the Teardrop Trail. The 1.2-mile trail starts south of Mansfield's Nose and swoops down the backside of the mountain for 1,700 feet.

Much easier backcountry trails are the **Nebraska Notch** and the **Skytop.** The Nebraska Notch trail starts from the Underhill side of Mount Mansfield and gently climbs close to 600 feet to Nebraska Notch. The round-trip is 6 km and you can add an extra 2 km to reach Taylor Lodge, a spacious wooden shelter built by the Green Mountain Club. Known for its impressive views of Mansfield, the Skytop Trail is one of Vermont's most popular backcountry routes. Reached from Topnotch, Trapp Family, or Mount Mansfield Ski Touring centers, the 4.5 km trail ascends the Skytop Ridge and then drops steeply into Dewey's Saddle.

If you want to ski one of the nicest parts of the 280-mile long Catamount Trail (see the box below), try the **Bolton-Trapp Trail.** Created in 1972, the 20 km route connects the Bolton Valley Ski Touring Center with Trapp Family Ski Lodge. Starting in Bolton, the path weaves through the hardwoods, plunging almost 2,000 feet to Nebraska Valley before heading on to Trapp's. An easy side-trail from Nebraska Valley Road is the Lake Mansfield Trail, which skirts the lake on its way to Taylor Lodge.

Besides these routes, three other CCC trails have recently been restored— The Houston, The Steeple, and The Dewey. For information regarding these three trails, contact John Higgins at the Stowe Mountain Resort (tel. 802/253-3000)

If you're serious about backcountry skiing in the Mount Mansfield area, consider purchasing two indispensable guides. One is a book called *Classic Backcountry Skiing*, written by David Goodman and published by the Appalachian Mountain Club. Goodman, who lives in nearby Waterbury, Vermont, details the most challenging, yet thrilling backcountry and telemark skiing in the Northeast, including the treacherous trails listed above. The second important purchase is the "Ski Touring Guide to the Mount Mansfield Region," published by Jared Grange, owner of Huntington Graphics. The map depicts all the backcountry trails and ski-touring centers around Mount Mansfield. Contact **Huntington Graphics,** P.O. Box 163, Huntington, VT 05462 (tel. 802/434-2555). A replica of the 1943 Stowe Trail map is available from the Cottonbrook Gallery on Mountain Road (tel. 802/253-8121).

For additional information, get a copy of the "Winter Recreation Map" from the **Green Mountain National Forest,** 231 N. Main St., Rutland, VT 05701 (tel. 802/747-6700). There is also a cross-country ski report recorded every Thursday (tel. 802/828-3239). Contact the Catamount Trail Association for a map of the 200-mile **Catamount Trail,** the cross-country trail that runs the length of the state (P.O. Box 1235, Burlington, VT 05402; tel. 802/864-5794).

CHAMPLAIN VALLEY NORDIC SKI CENTERS

Located in a small family farm outside of Burlington, **Catamount Family Center** offers 40 km of trails over their gently rolling fields and woods. There are good views of Mount Mansfield and Camel's Hump to the east. Contact Catamount Family Center, 421 Governor Chittendon Road, Williston, VT 05495 (tel. 802/879-6001).

The western flank of Camel's Hump is the stunning site of the **Camels' Hump Nordic Center,** where 60 km of groomed trails, ranging from 1,100 to 2,300 feet, weave through the woods, challenging all levels. The renowned 7.5-mile Honey Hollow Ski Trail climbs to 1,900 feet and then plummets 1,500 feet for an exhilarating 9 km downhill run to the shores of the Winooski River. P.O. Box 422, Huntington, VT 05462, tel. 802/434-2704.

The **Carroll and Jane Rickert Ski Touring Center** is located at the Breadloaf Campus of Middlebury College. Fifty kilometers of trails weave through the forest made famous by Robert Frost's poems. Trails actually skirt his farm. Contact Middlebury College, Middlebury, VT 05073 (tel. 802/388-2579).

With a remote locale and an abundance of trails, **Blueberry Hill** easily deserves its reputation as one of Vermont's finest ski-touring centers. Its 50 to 75 km of groomed trails are nestled in the Green Mountain Forest, offering unparalleled tranquility. The eight-room inn is known for its gourmet cooking and delectable chocolate chip cookies. Located in Goshen, VT 05733 (tel. 802/247-6735 or 800/274-6535).

MANSFIELD/STOWE AREA NORDIC SKI CENTERS

Thanks to **Trapp Family Lodge,** ski touring in northern Vermont is legendary. The lodge, made famous by Maria von Trapp, whose flight from the Nazis was immortalized in *The Sound of Music*, is one of the oldest ski-touring centers in the nation. It is also one of the finest. The ski touring center is one of the few places in the East that take their back-country skiing as seriously as their track-set skiing; 60 km of groomed trails, 95 km total, weave through the 1,700 acres of forest and open fields. Elevations range from 1,100 to 3,000 feet. Contact Trapp Family Lodge, Stowe, VT 05672 (tel. 802/253-8511).

Located on Mountain Road 6 miles from the center of Stowe, the **Mount Mansfield Cross Country Ski Center** is neatly tucked in between the slopes of Mount Mansfield and Skytop Ridge. Its 50 km of trails, 30 km groomed (over 100 km more if you consider the backcountry connections to other ski touring centers), line the slopes of Ranch Valley. Intermediates love the 9-km Timber Lane/Bear Run/Burt Trail loop, while beginners enjoy the Peavey Trail. Mount Mansfield Ski Touring Center is also known as the Stowe Mountain Resort Touring Center, Mountain Road, Stowe, VT 05672 (tel. 802/253-7311).

When Trapp and Mansfield are packed on winter weekends, **Edson Hill** gets remarkably little traffic. Skiers don't realize that the 50 km here are just as fun as at the other two centers. Intermediates enjoy the West Hill Trail while beginners are content with the 1-mile Center Loop. Contact Edson Hill Nordic Center, Edson Hill Road, Stowe, VT 05672 (tel. 802/253-8954).

Just down the road from Mount Mansfield, the 25 km of trails at **Topnotch Touring Center** cater to intermediates and beginners. Try the 3.5-km Deer Run Loop or the Lower Meadow Loop. Topnotch is also linked with the other ski touring centers. Mountain Road, Stowe, VT 05672 (tel. 802/253-8585).

Only 30 to 40 km of **Bolton Valley Ski Area** are groomed daily. The rest is sheer wilderness skiing, rising from 1,600 to 3,200 feet and ideal for telemarking. Cross-country skiers enjoy Broadway and the trip up to Bryant Lodge, while telemarkers tempt fate with the Cliffhanger. Bolton Valley Ski Resort, Bolton, VT 05477 (tel. 802/434-2131).

NORTHEAST KINGDOM NORDIC SKI CENTERS

It was late March 1995 and, surprisingly, there was no snow anywhere in Vermont.

I had just left Trapp Family Lodge in Stowe because the trails were only open to walkers that day. Desperate to ski, I called one last place, the **Craftsbury Nordic Ski Center** in Craftsbury Common. "Yeah, come on up," the voice on the other end said, "we just had a race this morning." Needless to say, the season at Craftsbury lasts far longer than in the rest of Vermont. The 130 km of trails, (80 km groomed) are impressive. They rise and dip over meadows and through forest of maples and firs, ideal for all levels. The ski center is located on a hill overlooking the picturesque Northeast Kingdom; Craftsbury Nordic Ski Center, P.O. Box 31, Craftsbury Common, VT 05827 (tel. 802/586-7767).

Just down the road in Greensboro, **Highland Lodge**'s 65 km of trails connects to Craftsbury. Many of the trails weave through the evergreens down to the shores of Caspian Lake. The lodge itself is one of the most comfortable places to stay in the Northeast Kingdom (see "Campgrounds & Other Accommodations"); Highland Lodge, Caspian Lake, Greensboro, VT 05841 (tel. 802/533-2647).

You're bound to find snow at **Hazen's Notch Ski Touring Center,** situated near Jay Peak in the town of Montgomery Center. Connected with the Catamount Trail, 45 km of trails sweep through this remote forest to clearings that offer good views of Jay Peak. Located on State Route 58, Montgomery Center, VT 05471 (tel. 802/326-4708).

OUTFITTERS, RENTALS & INFORMATION

Umiak Outdoor Outfitters in Stowe offers guided cross-country ski tours and rentals; 849 South Main Street, Stowe, VT 05672 (tel. 802/253-2317).

Outdoor Bound of Vermont arranges four-day cross-country and telemark ski trips to Bolton Valley and Stowe.

RR#5-2147, Bear Swamp Road, Montpelier, VT 05602 (tel. 802/223-4172 or 800/639-9208).

In the Northeast Kingdom, **Vermont Voyageur Expeditions** offers guided tours on the Catamount and provides telemark instruction. Montgomery Center, VT 95471 (tel. 802/326-4789).

Also in the Northeast Kingdom, Bruce Aschenbach, history teacher on weekdays and telemarker on weekends, owns **Kingdom Tele Boys** (tel. 802/472-6128). He takes backcountry skiers on three- to six-hour tours to Woodbury Mountain, Stannard, Mount Mansfield, and Mount Hunger. They also offer full-moon skiing.

For a real treat, **Backroads** will take skiers on a six-day, inn-to-inn trip through the Mount Mansfield/Craftsbury Region. The tours are offered in February and March. Contact them at 1516 Fifth Street, Berkeley, CA 94710-1740 (tel. 800/GO-ACTIVE).

DOWNHILL SKIING

Stowe

5781 Mountain Road, Stowe, VT 05672. Tel. 802/253-3000; snow report, tel. 802/253-2222. 46 trails (16% beginner, 59% intermediate, 25% expert), 11 lifts including an 8-passenger gondola, 1 quad, 1 triple, and 6 doubles; 2,360-foot vertical drop. Full-day tickets $43 all week.

Every year I see them. Cocky adolescents who run roughshod over my skis as they cruise down the black diamonds of Stratton, Mount Snow, or Okemo. Down at the bottom, I smile, coat their ego, and tell them that they're pretty good. "Have you skied Stowe yet . . . the Front Four. Oh no. Well, I think you guys would love that." Then I walk away and giggle maliciously at the

The Catamount Trail

If you have not yet heard of the 280-mile cross-country ski trail known as the Catamount, you soon will. Ben Rose and Steve Bushey's dream to build a state-long trail is almost on the verge of being completed. Rose and Bushey conceived of the idea during the summer of 1981 on a bike ride from British Columbia to Vermont. Joined by a third skier, Paul Jarris, the threesome started mapping the Catamount in March of 1984. They stayed as close to the central corridor of the state as possible, running along the ridge of the Green Mountains. At the completion of their expedition, they were determined to make their dream a reality. They founded the Catamount Trail Association and solicited memberships. Today, the CTA has over 1,000 members and, more importantly, the trail is almost 90 percent completed.

Starting in Readsboro, just north of the Massachusetts border, you ski down from town along an old railroad bed to the border and then retrace your tracks north to the town of Wilmington. The trail follows a brook, skirts the Harriman Reservoir, and then enters the trail system of the White House Ski Touring Center. From here you follow the black pawprint signs, the symbol for the Catamount, on remote wilderness trails, groomed ski center tracks, and old logging roads. You pass by Stratton Pond, Stratton Mountain, through Killington to Waitsfield to Camel's Hump, Mount Mansfield, Craftsbury, Jay, all the way to North Troy on the Canadian border. Along the way, you ski through the top ski touring centers in the state, like Mountain Top, Mountain Meadows, The Village Inn, Blueberry Hill, Camel's Hump, Bolton Valley, Trapp Family, Craftsbury, and Hazen's Notch. You also ski on some of the finest backcountry trails in New England, like the Bolton-Trapp trail in Mount Mansfield and the route from Waitsfield to Camel's Hump. And with average elevations above 1,500 feet, you can almost guarantee that there's white fluffy stuff on the ground from late December to late March.

Over 250 miles of the trail are now in use. The Catamount Trail Association publishes a guide book with up-to-date maps and route descriptions. For more information, contact the **Catamount Trail Association,** P.O. Box 1235, Burlington VT 05402 (tel. 802/864-5794).

thought of these young hotdoggers hurling themselves down the face of 4,393-foot Mount Mansfield. The Front Four teaches the brazen the meaning of respect. There's Starr, with a 37° pitch, the Lift Line, Goat, and National. The latter two separate the men from the boys and the women from the girls. Goat is a narrow serpentine trail that weaves down Mansfield. National is a little bit wider than Goat, but it's still one of those trails where you stand at the edge and look way down. Don't worry. Many people before you have stood there, statuesque, whimpering statements like, "I don't know. I think I'm gonna try to take another trail." Smart idea.

One of the oldest ski resorts in New England, Stowe deserves its reputation as one of the best. The ski area also caters to beginners and intermediates at neighboring Spruce Peak, and is known for its snowboarding.

Northern Vermont Ski & Winter Sports Shops				
City	**Shop**	**Location**	**Telephone**	**Additional Services**
Burlington	**Alpine Shop**	1184 Williston Rd., S. Burlington	802/862-2714	repairs; alpine ski, xc ski, snowboard, snowshoe rentals
	The Downhill Edge	65 Main St.	802/862-2282	repairs
Stowe	**Action Outfitters**	216 Mountain Rd.	802/253-7975	repairs; alpine ski, xc ski, telemark, snowshoe, bike, canoe rentals; alpine ski and boot demos
	AJ's	Mountain Rd.	802/253-4593	repairs; alpine ski, xc ski, snowboard, snowshoe, ice skate, ski rack, and bibs/parkas rentals; alpine ski and boot demos
	Boots & Boards	430 Mountain Rd.	802/253-4225	repairs; alpine ski, xc ski, snowboard rentals
	Pinnacle Ski & Sports	Mountain Rd.	800/458-9996	repairs; alpine ski, snowboard rentals; alpine ski and boot demos
Middlebury	**Skihaus of Vermont**	Merchants Row	802/388-6762	repairs; apparel
	Bike and Ski Center	74 Main St.	802/388-6666	repairs of wood skis; xc ski and bike rentals
Jay Peak	**The Snow Job**	State Route 242	802/988-4464	repairs; alpine ski rentals and demos

Smuggler's Notch

State Route 108, Smuggler's Notch, VT 05464. Tel. 802/644-1156; snow report, tel. 802/644-8851. 58 trails (16% beginner, 50% intermediate, 34% expert), 5 double chairlifts; 2,610-foot vertical drop. Full day tickets $39 weekends, $36 weekdays.

Smuggler's Notch is much more of a family resort. The three-mountain ski area caters to all levels. Morse is gentle, Sterling's trails are good for intermediates, while Madonna Mountain is for experts only (Madonna's always had a complex personality). The view of Mount Mansfield atop Madonna is staggering.

Experts take note: A good deep dump of snow brings Smuggler's right to the top of the heap, especially midweek when there are no lift lines. Narrow Robin's Run, Upper Lift Line, and FIS soften up their bad attitude just enough with a fresh coat of powder to make them as good as any steeps in Vermont.

Bolton Valley

Bolton Access Road, Bolton Valley, VT 05477. Tel. 802/434-2131; snow report, tel. 802/434-4443. 48 trails (28% beginner, 49% intermediate, 23% expert); 6 lifts including 1 quad, 4 double chairlifts; 1,625-foot vertical drop. Full day tickets $37 weekends, $32 weekdays.

Bolton Valley is also family oriented, and equipped with a condominium complex and sports center. Most of the trails on this family-owned resort are on moderate terrain. If you're with someone who's a cross-country fanatic, Bolton's also got an excellent network of Nordic trails.

Jay Peak

State Route 242, Jay, VT 05859. Tel. 802/988-2611; snow report, tel. 800/451-4449.

65 trails (20% beginner, 55% intermediate, 25% expert); 6 lifts including a 60-passenger tram, 1 quad, 1 triple, and 2 doubles; 2,153-foot vertical drop. Full day tickets $38 all week.

If only it weren't so far away from most of us. Whenever Killington, Sugarbush, or Stowe get three inches of snow, Jay Peak gets eight. In fact, Jay supposedly gets more snow than any other mountain in New England. Close to the Quebec border, the ski area also has a distinctly French flavor. Experts will enjoy the steeper runs off the tram, while neophytes find the trails in Bonaventure Basin to their liking.

Burke

P.O. Box 247, E. Burke, VT 05832. Tel. 802/626-3305; snow report, tel. 800/922-BURK. 30 trails (30% beginner, 40% intermediate, 30% expert); 4 lifts including 1 quad and 1 double; 2,000-foot vertical drop. Full day tickets $29 weekends, $25 weekdays.

Considering that some of Burke Mountain's trails were cut in the 1930s, it's surprising that this Northeast Kingdom ski area is still relatively unknown. Unknown, that is, outside of Vermont. Locals love the challenging trails and the lack of lift lines.

FISHING

An abundance of **trout** and **landlocked salmon** are found in the deep cold-water lakes and long streams in the Northeast Kingdom. Most notable are **Willoughby, Caspian, Seymour, Memphremagog,** and **Big Averill lakes.** Stream fishing for **trout** is prevalent on the **Black, Barton, Willoughby,** and **Clyde rivers.** Runs of spawning **rainbow trout** occur around opening day in April on the Willoughby. The Black features runs of spawning **browns** during the fall. **Brown** and **rainbow trout** are caught in the upper Connecticut River.

Heading west, **smallmouth bass** and **brown** and **rainbow trout** are commonly hooked on the **Missisquoi, Lamoille,** and **Winooski rivers. Lake Champlain** has a wealth of fish, including **lake trout, landlocked salmon, steelhead, smelt, sauger, walleye, large** and **smallmouth bass, northern pike, pickerel, yellow perch,** and **channel catfish.**

Down in the Champlain Valley near Middlebury is **Lake Dunmore,** stocked with **bass, northern pike,** and **perch.**

For maps and additional information, contact the **Vermont Fish and Wildlife Department,** 103 South Main Street, Waterbury, VT 05671-0501 (tel. 802/ 241-3700).

INSTRUCTION, GUIDES & BAIT-AND-TACKLE SHOPS

Fly Fish Vermont in Stowe arranges half and full-day trips to Stowe's tributaries and the upper Connecticut River. They also provide instruction and own a stocked retail store. 804 S. Main St., Unit 4, Stowe, tel. 802/253-3964. Just north of Stowe, the **Pleasant Valley Trout Farm** is a two-acre pond stocked with rainbows. They rent tackle. Pleasant Valley Road, Underhill Center, (tel. 802/899-2435).

On Lake Champlain, **Sure Strike Charters** offers half- and full-day tours from Perkins Pier. 218 River Road, Essex Junction (tel. 802/878-5074). A good retail shop is **Schirmer's Fly Shop,** 34 Mills Avenue, South Burlington; tel. 802/863-6105.

Charlie North is the fishing guru in the islands. He can be found at **Charlie's Northland Lodge** in North Hero (tel. 802/372-8822). Charlie rents boats and operates a retail store.

Two sporting camps in the northern lakes area cater to fishermen. **Seymour**

Lake Lodge is open year-round for landlocked salmon, brown, lake, and brook trout fishing. Owner Dave Benware is a fly-fishing guide who will steer you in the right direction. Located on State Route 11 in Morgan, VT 05853 (tel. 802/895-2752). **Quimby County's** 19th-century lodge and 20 cabins are spread out on the shores of 70-acre Forest Lake. If the fish aren't biting at Forest, the lodge is in close proximity to Little and Big Averill Lakes. Contact them in Averill, VT 05901 (tel. 802/822-5533 or 717/733-2234).

GOLF

Golfing in northern Vermont is not nearly as good as in the southern part of the state, but **Stowe's** hilly par-72 course is certainly a challenge (tel. 802/ 253-4893). Also recommended was the **Country Club of Barre** (tel. 802/ 476-7658).

HIKING & BACKPACKING

North of I-89, the 265-mile **Long Trail** heads straight over 4,393-foot Mount Mansfield, through breathtaking Smuggler's Notch to the top of Jay Peak, and finally reaches the Canadian border. Unlike the ridge walks of, say, the Lincoln Gap area, this part of the Long Trail is rarely flat. It's up and down all the way, but your rewards are vast—stunning vistas atop barren summits overlook miles of undeveloped landscape. This is especially true of the last 29 miles from State Route 118 to the summit of Belvidere Mountain, through Hazen's Notch to the top of Jay Peak, and ending at the Canadian border. If you don't have time to do the whole trail, these last 29 miles are a good three- to four-day run.

For more information regarding time, access, shelters, useful guides, and the history of the nation's oldest long-distance trail, see the "Long Trail" box in chapter 8. The **Green Mountain Club,** which maintains the Long Trail, can be reached at State Route 100, P.O. Box 650, Waterbury Center, VT 05677 (tel. 802/244-7037).

Northern Vermont's best hiking is centered around Mount Mansfield and the Long Trail. As in the southern part of the state, the trails tend to be steady uphill climbs. In the eastern part of the state, I found one incredible trail:

Mount Pisgah

3.4 miles (round trip). Allow 3 hours. Moderate to strenuous. Access: From West Burke, take State Route 5A North for 6 miles to a parking area on the left-hand side, just south of Lake Willoughby. The South Trail begins across the highway. Map: USGS 7.5 minute Sutton.

Nothing prepared me for the striking beauty of Lake Willoughby, not even the earnest recommendation from my sister-in-law, a UVM graduate. As I approached the lake from the north, the dark blue waters came into view, dwarfed by faces of rock that stand directly across from each other—Mount Hor and Mount Pisgah. Cliffs plummet over 1,000 feet to the glacial waters below, creating, in essence, a land-locked fjord. The scenery became even more enchanting as I made my way up to the 2,751-foot summit of Mount Pisgah.

Several bridges crossed ponds inundated with twisted white pines, the result of forceful gales or hard-working beavers. The trail started gradually on switchbacks, but soon took a much more precipitous course. More than halfway up the peak, the trail leveled off as I walked along a ridge. Before the path curved to the right and began its rigorous uphill climb once again, a small detour to the left brought me to aptly named Pulpit Rock. This small,

semi-oval rock juts out of Mount Pisgah's sheer cliff like a box seat at a Broadway play. Looking down at Lake Willoughby in its entirety and across at Mount Hor, a mountain that's been sliced in half, I felt like I was trespassing on sacred ground. This small platform should be reserved for the likes of Vergil, Lincoln, Churchill, and other noted orators who could engage the masses below.

The strenuous trail continues upward, proceeding in a spiral fashion as it climbs to the summit. Just prior to reaching the peak, I had excellent views to the east—the ski slopes of Burke Mountain, the Connecticut River, and the White Mountains forming a ridge line in the horizon. Since the peak was not above tree-line, I had to continue down a side trail to a level rock which provided vistas to the west. Now I could see beyond Mount Hor to Mount Hunger, Mansfield, Camel's Hump, and all the other mountains that stood in between. Why visit nearby St. Johnsbury's Athaeneum and view Albert Bierstadt's famous painting, *Domes of Yosemite,* when I can see such beauty come to life less than an hour north?

Mount Mansfield, via Laura Cowles and Sunset Ridge Trails

6.5 miles (round trip). Allow 4–5 hours. Moderate to strenuous. Access: From Jeffersonville, take Upper Valley Road toward Underhill Center for approximately 7 miles, until you see a sign for Underhill State Park. Turn left for 3 miles on the dirt road and park in the lot. Map: Available from the Park Ranger Station. However, the best map of the area is in "Twenty Day Hikes in the Mount Mansfield Region" published by Jared Grange, owner of Huntington Graphics. The map depicts all the trails around Mount Mansfield. Huntington Graphics, P.O. Box 163, Huntington, VT 05462; tel. 802/434-2555. The GMC's Long Trail guide also includes a map of all the Mansfield side trails.

There are numerous approaches up Mount Mansfield. The Long Trail meanders southwest from State Route 108 to Taft Lodge and the summit. A toll road leaves you at the Nose of the mountain (4,062 feet) where you can then take a 1.4-mile walk on the Long Trail heading east to the Chin or summit (4,393 feet). A gondola ride leaves you even closer to the summit on the same stretch of the Long Trail. You can also take the Haselton/Nose Dive trail from Smuggler's Notch State Park Campground to the Nose and continue onward to the Chin. However, my favorite hike up the mountain is from the south, up the Laura Cowles Trail and down the Sunset Ridge Trail.

The hike starts at the Underhill State Park Ranger Station, where you pay a small fee and continue walking uphill on the gravel road for about a mile to the trailhead; 0.1 mile later, the Sunset Ridge and the Laura Cowles trails split. Veer to the right on the Laura Cowles trail for a steep 1.7-mile ascent. (For a more moderate hike, continue on the Sunset Ridge Trail) The trail climbs on rocks along trickling water in the beginning, before sharply rising halfway up. Several times you have to walk in the shallow water as you grab tree roots and rocky grips to pull yourself upward. Close to the summit, views of Lake Champlain open up to the west. When you reach the Long Trail, veer left to reach the Chin. The path on the right called Profanity leads to Taft Lodge. Be prepared for strong winds as you make your final ascent. From atop the summit, Lake Champlain can be seen in its entirety, as well as the northern islands, Burlington, and the Adirondacks on the far shores. Look to the north to see Jay Peak and Canada, to the east to see the White Mountains. Everywhere

you turn your head, you see more hills and mountains. I hate to inform you bikers, but Vermont ain't flat.

To reach the Sunset Ridge Trail and the descent, backtrack past the Laura Cowles trail and continue right along the ridge. Sweeping views of Lake Champlain and points west are seen as you walk along the open ridge for the next mile. A little more than halfway down, where hardwood forests have replaced bare rocks, veer right for a 0.1-mile detour to Cantilever Rock. This axe-like rock juts precariously out of the ridge like a guillotine ready to sever the head of anyone who dares to look up. The trail becomes more gradual as you continue to the trailhead and the dirt road back to the State Park.

Mount Hunger, via Waterbury Trail

3.8 miles. Allow 4 hours. Moderate. Access: From Waterbury, follow State Route 100 North to Waterbury Center. Turn right on Barnes Hill Road, left onto Maple Street, and right onto Loomis Hill Road. Bear left atop the hill as the road turns to dirt. Park 3.7 miles from the junction of Maple Street on the right-hand side of the road. Map: USGS 7.5 minute Stowe.

Judging from the three cars parked at the trailhead, all with Vermont license plates, the climb up Mount Hunger is a trail treasured by locals only. Once my brother Jim and I made it to the 3,538-foot peak, we easily understood why. From the barren summit, we could see every mountain that forms the backbone of the Greens, from Killington to Camel's Hump to Mount Mansfield. First we had to hike up the Waterbury Trail. Like most of Vermont's trails, the climb started from the first step, a steady uphill walk that became steep at some stretches. Since this was Jim's first ascent up a mountain in over a decade, we took numerous stops along the way so he could catch his breath, the first clean air my citified brother had inhaled in a long time. Eventually the beeches, yellow birches, and maples gave way to white birches, spruces, and balsam firs. Then, 0.2 mile from the top, the trail meandered over large boulders bordered by scrub brush. The bare rocks atop the summit offer commanding views of the entire state. Burke and Bald Mountains are seen guarding the entranceway to the Northeast Kingdom; Mount Mansfield's chin, nose, and other facial features are visible to the east, with the Camel's Hump trails are close behind. Waterbury Reservoir sits in the valley below, fringed by White Rock, Hunger's next door neighbor. Unlike Camel's Hump, Mount Mansfield, and the other popular peaks of the Green Mountains, here atop Hunger, you can relish the view in relative solitude before making the descent back down.

Sterling Pond

2.6 miles (round trip). Allow 2 hours. Moderate. Access: Park at Smuggler's Notch, situated on State Route 108, 10 miles north of Stowe and 8 miles south of Jeffersonville. Map: USGS 7.5 minute Mount Mansfield, or LT guidebook.

The 1.3-mile hike on the Long Trail to the Sterling Pond shelter starts from Smuggler's Notch, one of the most majestic sights in all of New England. From the mountainous cliffs above, sheer walls of quartzite and mica drop down to the large boulders resting on the floor below. The result is a mountainous pass or notch formed by a glacial retreat over 10,000 years ago. The notch's name comes from the Vermont smugglers who ventured north to illegally trade with Canada after Thomas Jefferson declared an embargo in 1807. The route was also used by

fugitive slaves to find freedom in Canada, and by Vermonters in the 1920s to sneak liquor into America during Prohibition.

Cross State Route 108 and continue on the rock steps up the side of the ridge. The views of the notch and surrounding Green Mountains get better with every steep step. At the top of the slope sits Sterling Pond, which was engulfed in a cloud upon my last ascent. The water could barely be seen under a layer of white mist, providing an ominous setting ideal for a Stephen King novel. Veer left around the pond to reach one of Smuggler's Notch's ski trails, offering impressive views to the north and west. Follow the white blazes to reach the Sterling Pond shelter, a small lean-to at the edge of the pond maintained by the Green Mountain Club for backpackers. From here, you can continue on Long Trail for another mile to reach Madonna Peak, skirt the pond to find the Elephants Head Trail, or backtrack to your car. The Elephants Head Trail leads to a massive ledge approximately 1,000 feet above the notch.

Prospect Rock (Johnson)

Allow 1–1.5 hours. Easy to moderate. Access: From Johnson, drive west on State Route 15 for 1.5 miles and turn right before the bridge onto Hogback Road. You can park on the right-hand side across from Ithiel Camp 2.3 miles later, or on the left-hand side in a small parking lot at 2.2 miles. The hike starts from the driveway on the right-hand side. Map: USGS 7.5 minute Johnson or LT guidebook.

Prospect Rock is an ideal picnic spot, so don't forget to bring lunch. The climb is one of the easiest hikes on the Long Trail. Believe it or not, this part of the Long Trail actually has switchbacks instead of the typical Vermont hike—straight up a mountain. Start on the driveway and then veer left following the white blazes up the soft, spongy trail. The hike becomes more strenuous as you approach the switchbacks. In less than 45 minutes, you'll be on top of Prospect Rock staring across at Vermont's Whiteface Mountain and down at the Lamoille River as it snakes through the sylvan landscape. To extend the hike, continue north on the Long Trail for as long as your legs desire.

Jay Peak

3.4 miles (round trip). Allow 2.5–3 hours. Moderate. Access: From Montgomery Center, drive 6.8 miles on State Route 242 North and park in the lot on the right-hand side. The trailhead is across the street. If you want to take the gondola down the mountain, park a second car at Jay Peak, 1.4 miles north on Route 242. Map: USGS 15 minute Jay Peak or LT guidebook.

One of the most picturesque stretches of the Long Trail is from State Route 242 up to the summit of Jay Peak. Starting at an elevation over 2,000 feet, the trail climbs steadily through a forest of birches and spruces until you reach one of Jay Peak's ski trails. Continue straight, following the white blazes over the rocky bare ledges to the 3,861-foot peak. The summit is legendary for its blustery winds, where twisted branches creak with each successive gale. The mountain is also known for its snowfall: it has the most accumulation of any ski area in the Northeast. If you can somehow stand in the unmerciful winds, you can spot Mount Washington to the east, Lake Memphremagog to the northeast, Montreal to the northwest, Mount Mansfield to the south, and all the small farms and rural communities that exist in between. Less ambitious hikers can park one car at State Route 242 and one car at the bottom of Jay Peak and simply take

the tram down. You also have the option of walking down one of the ski trails.

OUTFITTERS & GEAR

Hiking Holidays offers five-day trips around the Northeast Kingdom and Mount Mansfield; P.O. Box 750, Bristol, VT 05443 (tel. 802/453-4816).

New England Hiking Holidays has a five-day tour to the Northeast Kingdom that includes stops at Trapp Family Lodge in Stowe and Highland Lodge in the heart of the region. Contact them at P.O. Box 1648, North Conway, NH 03860 (tel. 800/869-0949).

Backroads has an excellent six-day tour through Northern Vermont that also includes Trapp, Highland Lodge, and a night at the Inn on the Common in Craftsbury Common; 1516 Fifth Street, Berkeley, CA 94710-1740 (tel. 800/ GO-ACTIVE).

Wild Earth Adventures offers an eight-day guided backpacking trip through Mount Mansfield and the other Green Mountains. For more information, contact Wild Earth Adventure, P.O. Box 655, Pomona, NY 10970 (tel. 914/354-3717).

Vermont Walking Tours in Craftsbury Common (P.O. Box 31, Craftsbury Common, VT 05827; tel. 800/729-7751) offers luggage transport for self-guided hikes in the Northeast Kingdom.

In the Lake Champlain region, **American Expeditions,** located at 86 Lake Street, Burlington, VT 05401 (tel. 802/864-7600), helps walkers with luggage transport on self-guided inn-to-inn tours.

Umiak Outdoor Outfitters (1880 Mountain Road, Stowe, VT 05672; tel. 802/253-2317) offers guided tours for groups and maps for self-guided hikes.

Country Inns Along the Trail custom designs self-guided hiking trips where you can walk inn-to-inn. Contact them at RR3, P.O. Box 3115, Brandon, VT 05773 (tel. 802/247-3300).

HORSEBACK RIDING

Numerous stables scattered across the northern part of the state offer trail riding and lessons. They include **Topnotch Stables** in Stowe (tel. 802/253-8585), **Circle K Ranch** in Bolton just outside of Burlington (tel. 802/878-0170), **Rohan Farm** in East Burke (tel. 802/467-3701), **Jay Mountain Trail Rides** in Westfield (tel. 802/744-8271), and **Mountain Ridge Ranch,** just south of Island Pond on State Route 114 (tel. 802/723-6153).

In addition to guided trail rides, **Cambridge Stables** (tel. 802/644-5568) and **Vermont Horse Park** (tel. 802/644-5347), just north of Smuggler's Notch, feature overnight trips.

ICE FISHING

Considering ice fishing's brief, two-month season, you might find it surprising that almost three-quarters of the state's trophy fish are caught during this time. Larger fish spend most of the year cruising the deep waters. But when the ice starts to form, these prize-winners head to shallow waters, closer to the schools of smaller fish . . . and our lines. So start drilling.

Lake trout are caught in the Northeast Kingdom, at **Caspian, Willoughby, Echo, Crystal, Maidstone, Seymour,** and **Averill lakes**. Northern pike and walleye can be found in **Lake Champlain**. Anglers have also been known to hook smelt and perch at Lake Champlain, **Lake Memphremagog, Fairlee** and Echo lakes.

For maps and additional information, contact the **Vermont Fish and Wildlife Department**, 103 South Main Street, Waterbury, VT 05671 (tel. 802/241-3700).

LLAMA TREKS

If you want to go llama trekking, but can't afford that $1,000 to $2,000 flight to the Andes Mountains in South America, head to northern Vermont. Gale and John Birutta, owners of **Northeast Kingdom Llama Expeditions** (RR 2 Box 71-A, Groton, VT 05046; tel. 802/584-3198), arranges half- and full-day trips into the 26,000-acre Groton State Forest. They also offer short walks around their farm and fall foliage and sunset hikes. Llamas carry gear and equipment, never people. Book well in advance, especially during fall foliage season, since these trips are extremely popular.

Near Stowe, **Northern Vermont Llama Treks** guides hikers into the Mount Mansfield State Forest. They're located in Waterville (tel. 802/644-2257).

MOUNTAIN BIKING

You would think that rural northern Vermont would be home to some great mountain biking. That's true, but unfortunately, the trails are not out in the wild unknown. The best routes are located at cross-country ski centers like Catamount, Smuggler's Notch, Mount Mansfield, and Craftsbury Nordic Center (see "Cross-Country Skiing" section, above, for details). This brings up the philosophical mountain biking question of fate versus predestination. I tend to agree with that well-known mountain biker Immanuel Kant, who firmly believes that bikers can only experience the ecstatic feeling of freedom when routes lead to nowhere in particular (fate). When trails are numbered or proceed in a circular fashion back to the starting point (predestined), mountain-biking bliss is considerably lessened. The following two trails were exciting to ride, but I'm not sure they fall under the category of mountain biking.

Burke Mountain

Allow 1–2 hours. Moderate to strenuous; every type of terrain imaginable. Access: From the village of East Burke, bear right at the sign for Burke Mountain and right again at the Sherburne Base Lodge. Map: Available from East Burke Sports (tel. 802/626-3215).

I was fortunate that the people of East Burke were setting up a professional mountain-biking course the few days I stayed at Burke Mountain. The race was scheduled for the following Sunday, but I had the 6-mile loop to myself the weekday I rode it. All the arrows showing direction were in place, and, according to the guys at East Burke Sports, will remain in place for the mountain-biking season. East Burke Sports can also suggest trails at the mountain's cross-country ski center, which is free to the public.

The ride begins to the left of Sherburne Base Lodge, where I cruised up the grassy double tracks to a dirt road. To my left, Mount Pisgah and Mount Hor stood like bookends on opposite sides of Lake Willoughby. I continued up the dirt road, venturing on grass across a paved road to reach the mid Burke section of the mountain. The ski slopes stood straight ahead. Narrow single-tracks soon appeared as I veered left on the grassy double-tracks for the last time. A grueling hill stood before me, but once I made it up, the single-tracks swept down through the forest, soon becoming level again. Eventually, the course turns into a dirt road that goes right down the ski slopes of the mountain. Another left turn, and I was pedaling up and down the mountain on single-tracks, double-tracks, dirt roads, and grassy ski slopes as the ride became an exhilarating blur. I thought I was finally down at the bottom when the course took one more uphill turn

and then cruised downhill on technical single-tracks back to the lodge.

Craftsbury Common

Allow 1.5–2 hours. Easy to moderate, on hilly dirt road. Access: From Craftsbury Common, follow the white signs to Craftsbury Center. You can park in their parking lot.

I'm still not sure whether riding on a dirt road is mountain biking or road biking with fat tires. Regardless of category, biking through the Northeast Kingdom is like biking though the Vermont of your imagination, a bucolic landscape replete with grazing horses and cows, bright white steeples, decrepit barns, and layer after layer of mountainous hillside. This secluded 11-mile loop on a hard-packed dirt road is a good warm-up to more technical riding at Craftsbury Center. However, here you'll have the trails to yourself, give or take a couple cows. From the parking lot, cruise up and down the short hills. At 2.3 miles, take a sharp right turn past a young balsam tree farm and the stubby headstones of an old cemetery. A little more than a mile later, after biking uphill, you'll get exquisite views of Vermont's countryside. I was momentarily delayed by a dairy farmer who was herding his cows from the meadows back to the barn. At 7.7 miles, take another sharp right and continue straight on TH 28 (do not make a right turn 0.4 mile later onto TH 32). Views of Great Hosmer Pond soon appear. Bear right around this blue-green body of water to return to Craftsbury Center.

RENTALS & OUTFITTERS

East Burke Sports is located on State Route 114 in the center of East Burke Village (tel. 802/626-3215).

In Craftsbury, you can rent bikes at the **Craftsbury Center,** Craftsbury

Common (tel. 800/729-7751). They also offer three- and six-day guided mountain-biking tours.

POWERBOATING

Fishing boats and motorboats can be rented at **McKibben Sailing Vacations,** 176 Battery Street, Burlington (tel. 802/864-7733 or 800/522-0028); **Charlie's Northland Lodge** in North Hero (tel. 802/372-8822); and **Newport Marina** in the northern lakes area (tel. 802/334-5911).

For a complete listing of all motorboats, sailboats, and canoe rentals, contact the **Vermont Department of Travel** for their "Vermont Boating, Rentals & Marinas" publication, at 134 State Street, Montpelier, VT 05602 (tel. 800/VERMONT).

ROAD BIKING

The same rolling terrain and small villages that entice bikers in the south can be found in the north. However, some of the pavement turns to gravel for brief stints, so it might be wise to ride with hybrid tires.

Lake Champlain

Allow 3 hours. Easy to moderate; relatively flat farmland. Access: From Burlington, take U.S. 7 South to State Route 22A South. Park around the town square in Vergennes. Map: Any good state road map will do.

South of Burlington, fertile farmlands and desolate country roads replace the strip malls and steady flow of traffic on U.S. 7. Lake Champlain's 12-mile girth narrows to bring into view a dramatic backdrop of the Adirondacks and the New York shore. This 27-mile ride takes you on relatively flat roads along the waters of this immense and historic lake, on a route where silos and cows outnumber cars. Start your ride from the town square in Vergennes and go south on State Route 22A. A half-mile later, turn right onto Panton Road for a steady downhill run. The Adirondacks appear directly in front of you while carpets of green blanket both sides of the road, so rich that you'll want to stop the bike and dig your hands into the soil. A right turn onto Basin Harbor Road will bring you past numerous dairy farms along the shores of Otter Creek. Continue biking on this road as it curves right to Basin Harbor. You'll pass the Lake Champlain Maritime Museum and its large collection of wooden watercraft built around the shores of the lake in the past 150 years. Veer left by the boats anchored in Basin Harbor for your first views of the lake. Basin Harbor Club's main house and golf course are located a few hundred yards further on the right.

Backtrack less than a mile on Basin Harbor Road to Button Bay Road. Turn right on this unmarked street, following the signs for Button Bay State Park for one of the most majestic sights in all of Vermont. Lake Champlain and the Adirondacks are to your right; cornfields and dairy farms lead up to the Green Mountains on your left. The wedge of rock above, aptly named Camel's Hump, is seen in the distance. Turn right on Arnold's Bay Road, which soon turns to gravel. Watch out for large bumps and potholes as you ride through the dense woods. A mile later, the road becomes paved again as Arnold's Bay comes into view. Here, in October 1776, Benedict Arnold and his small band of boats successfully thwarted the attempts of the British flotilla to sail south toward Fort Ticonderoga. Arnold's fleet was decimated, but won nonetheless. Before the British could return south, the lake was frozen over.

Veer right at the stop sign onto Pease Road as you continue to hug the shores of the lake. Apple orchards appear on both sides of the hilly road. Soon you'll see the Yankee Kingdom Country Store and Orchards. This is a good place to stop, have lunch, go apple-picking, taste homemade cider moments after it's made, or simply pet the rabbits in the small petting zoo. This is also the spot where I usually turn around and retrace my tire treads back to Vergennes (excluding the Basin Harbor detour). However, if you're a loop lover, continue on Pease Road (now called Lake Road) and turn left on State Route 17. This will bring you to State Route 22A North back to Vergennes. Be forewarned: State Route 22A is hilly and can be congested since it's a main thoroughfare. The loop is a little over 30 miles long.

Isle La Motte

Allow 1–2 hours. Easy; relatively flat terrain. Access: From Burlington, take I-89 North to U.S. 2 North, bearing left at State Route 129. Follow the signs to Isle La Motte and cross over the bridge. Park your car on the left-hand side of the road at the small monument. Map: Any good state road map will do.

Venture off U.S. 2 in the Lake Champlain islands and the sound of cars fades away, replaced by the quietude of backcountry roads and the seemingly endless expanse of water. This 12.6-mile loop around Isle La Motte is the finest ride in the region. I parked my car just across the bridge at the small monument. Happily on two wheels, I noticed a great blue heron and a family of ducks lounging on Blanchard Bay. A half-mile later, I turned right toward St. Anne's Shrine, passing small stone houses rich with history, dilapidated barns, and rolled hay on large tracts of the greenest

grass I've ever laid eyes on. St. Anne's Shrine is an open-sided Victorian chapel that marks the site of Vermont's first French settlement, founded in 1666. Today, more than 50 boats dock in the harbor each Sunday to attend mass in the church. Across the road there's a statue of Samuel de Champlain, created for Montreal's Expo of 1967.

I continued along the shores of the lake, passing long barns that would seem more at home in the hills of Provence than Vermont. A right turn at the sign for Terry Lodge brought me to a vast wilderness—sweeping vistas of rolling forests to my left and broad views of the lake to my right. Half-way into the ride, I spotted a deer grazing in the meadows on the outskirts of the forest. The road then becomes hard gravel, switching back to pavement a mile and a half later. Apple orchards and another stone house, home of the Isle La Motte Historical Society, came into view. A right-hand turn here brought me to the Ruthcliffe Lodge, irrefutably the best restaurant in the Lake Champlain island region. After making reservations for that evening, I backtracked to the main road, veered right, and turned right again at the nine-mile mark. A stone Methodist church built in 1893 appeared on the left, followed by more farmlands and the bright yellow patch of a mustard field. At 10.7 miles, I turned left, avoiding the dead-end road and pedaled uphill. A right-turn on State Route 129 brought me back to the monument and my car.

Note: You can easily extend this route by crossing the bridge and veering left, following the road along the water, and then taking any number of right-hand turns into the countryside.

Jeffersonville Loop

Allow 1–2 hours. Moderate; hilly terrain. Access: From Stowe or Smuggler's Notch, take State Route 108 North to Jeffersonville. Park anywhere on the main street. Map: Any good state road map will do.

This spectacular 14.6-mile jaunt through the backroads of Smuggler's Notch and Jeffersonville was a tip from a local, Barbara Thompke. Once you've taken this route, you'll feel indebted to her as well. Some of the roads are hard-packed gravel, so a hybrid or mountain bike will survive better than a road bike. Park the car in Jeffersonville, veering right onto State Route 108 North and making a quick left onto Upper Valley Road near the Smuggler's Notch Inn. The road gradually goes uphill, bordered by mountain ridges on your right. Just when your legs start to burn from the steady uphill run, the road veers left, sweeping downhill as Vermont's highest peak appears directly in front of you. The sight of massive Mount Mansfield towering over you is breathtaking. At 3.7 miles, continue straight on Westman Road. A little more than a mile later, turn left onto Andrews Road and then left again onto Iron Gate Road. These are country roads that only locals who have lived here for years know about. Iron Gate goes up a short hill and then rolls down a narrow road past apple orchards, sheep farms, and a dark, deep forest. The road can be somewhat bumpy, so use caution. Turn right on Stebbins Road for views of Smuggler's Notch Ski Area. At the stop sign, turn left for 0.1 mile and then veer right onto paved State Route 108 South.

Here's where this route gets a little tricky. You need to turn left onto Edwards Road, but skip the *first* Edwards Road sign, turning left over a mile later at the second Edwards Road sign. The paved road goes steadily uphill before cruising down through fields of wildflowers and tall-tasseled corn. The peaks of Vermont's mountains stand before you, as compact as skyscrapers on the Manhattan skyline. Turn right at Junction Hill Road, rolling up and down with the farmland; 1.8 miles later, veer left past an old barn onto Canyon Road. This road sweeps downhill through a narrow canyon and a dark-ribbed covered bridge, before bearing right on State Route 108 North back to Jeffersonville.

RENTALS & OUTFITTERS

Both the **Thomas Mott Homestead** and **Ruthcliffe Lodge** furnish bikes and maps to their guests for the Isle La Motte Loop (see "Campgrounds & Other Accommodations").

Foot of the Notch Bicycles rents bikes for the Jeffersonville ride at State Route 108, Church Street, Jeffersonville, VT 05464 (tel. 802/644-8182).

In the northern part of the state, **Vermont Bicycle Touring** takes bikers on five-day inn-to-inn trips to the Mount Mansfield Region and the Northeast Kingdom. Contact Vermont Bicycle Touring, P.O. Box 711, Bristol, VT 05443 (tel. 802/453-4811 or 800/245-3868).

Bike Vermont (P.O. Box 207, Woodstock, VT 05091; tel. 800/257-2226) features five- and six-day guided tours to the Northeast Kingdom and the upper Connecticut River Valley.

Backroads offers a five-day inn-to-inn tour through Craftsbury Common, Greensboro, Stowe, and Montpelier. Contact them at 1516 Fifth Street, Berkeley, CA 94710-1740 (tel. 800/GO-ACTIVE).

SAILING

Lake Champlain

Access: Winds of Ireland is located at Burlington's Community Boathouse on Lower College Street.

Approximately 120 miles long and 12 miles wide, Lake Champlain is the largest freshwater lake in the country after the Great Lakes. Consistently good wind, sheltered bays, hundreds of islands, and scenic anchorages combine to make this immense body of water one of the top cruising grounds in the Northeast. One overcast day last summer, my family decided to charter a Hunter 35 from Winds of Ireland, located at the edge of Burlington Bay. When we heard the forecast for the day on my father's weather radio (a new toy which my dad couldn't bear to turn off even after we heard the weather report for the umpteenth time), we decided to hire a captain. "Lake Champlain, 25 to 35 knot winds with 3 foot swells. A wind advisory is in effect," said the monotone voice over and over again.

Winds of Ireland provided us with a captain named Mikey who lives on the bay during the summer on a 30-foot Yankee built in 1938. We were surprised that anyone would take us out in these ominous conditions. Whitecaps were thrashing against the breakwater and the haunting sky was steel gray, but Mikey was as cool as a chunk of chocolate in a pint of Ben & Jerry's New York Super Fudge Chunk. He loaded us into the spacious boat and off we went into the wild blue yonder. Outside the bay, we turned off the motor and put up the jib, and already, we were sailing across the lake at six or seven knots. There was no need to put up the mainsail. Even in this wild weather, the Hunter was as smooth as the bark on a birch tree. We each took turns at the helm (no tiller on this big boy), guiding the boat along the eastern shores of the lake. Black cormorants flew over our heads as we cruised by a privately owned island called Juniper, the luxurious houses of South Cove, and Shelbourne Point peninsula, and on into sheltered Shelbourne Bay. Hundreds of sailboats were wisely docked at the Lake Champlain Yacht Club, their bare masts bobbing from side to side. Indeed, we were the only boat on the lake, except for the ferry going back and forth to the New York side. However, the sun was starting to peek through the layers of clouds and we felt confident in Mikey's sailing ability.

Views of Shelbourne Farm and other fertile fields appeared on the eastern shores before we left the bay and ventured toward the Adirondack Mountains on the other side of the lake. Once in the open water, we asked Mikey if he ever saw "Champ," Lake Champlain's version of the Loch Ness Monster. Fortunately, he didn't, but some of his friends have sworn they have seen this sea monster lurking from the depths. We headed for Four Brothers, four small islands that were not very inviting. Stunted and gnarled trees stood atop rocky cliffs, wet with the continuous bombardment of waves. A more appropriate name would have been Four Ex-Cons. From here we returned to Burlington and the dock, knowing that we'd be back on this lake for a longer sail on sunnier days.

OUTFITTERS, RENTALS & INSTRUCTION

Winds of Ireland charters five Hunters, from 30 to 40 feet, on a day or weekly rate. Prices start at $145 per day. A captain costs extra. Winds of Ireland also offers two-hour daysails and sunset sails. Contact Winds of Ireland, P.O. Box 2286, S. Burlington, VT 05407 (tel. 802/863-5090).

McKibben Sailing Vacations also offers bareboat and crewed charters on the lake. Located at 176 Battery Street, Burlington, VT 05407 (tel. 802/864-7733 or 800/522-0028).

The **Burlington Community Boathouse,** at the foot of College Street, offers daily Rhodes and Laser rentals and lessons; tel. 802/865-3377.

The **International Sailing School and Club** charges a membership fee which entitles you to sailing workshops, clinics, and unlimited use of their sailboats and sailboards. Contact them at 253 Lakeshore Drive, Colchester, VT 05446 (tel. 802/864-9065).

Tudhope Sailing Center and Marina, at the foot of the Grand Isle Bridge in the Lake Champlain islands, provides instruction and charters; tel. 802/372-5320.

In the northern lakes region of the Northeast Kingdom, sailboats can be rented at the **Newport Marina;** tel. 802/334-5911.

SCUBA DIVING

Who needs the Caymans when you have Champlain!

Lake Champlain

Access: Waterfront Diving Center is located on 214 Battery Street in Burlington, right next to the lake. Divers must be certified.

Lake Champlain has always been a major thoroughfare from the St. Lawrence Seaway to Champlain Canal and the Hudson River. Numerous historic battles were fought on the lake during the French and Indian War, Revolutionary War, and War of 1812 to control this navigational stronghold. In the mid to late 19th century, commercial vessels replaced gunboats. Many of the military and merchant ships never made it out of the water, sinking to the deep, dark bottom from the power of the cannonball or temperamental weather. In fact, the cool waters of the lake contain one of the finest collections of wooden shipwrecks in North America. The 54-foot Revolutionary War boat *Philadelphia* was pulled from the waters in 1935 and now stands in the Smithsonian. The *Eagle, Allen,* and *Linnet,* three naval craft that participated in the War of 1812, were recently located in Plattsburgh Bay,

adding to the growing list of wrecks that lie on the lake's floor. These vessels' misfortunes are good luck to the scuba diver.

Late last summer, Jonathan Eddy, owner of the Waterfront Diving Center in Burlington, brought me to see the *General Butler.* Located near the southern end of the Burlington Breakwater, this 88-foot commercial vessel is one of five boats preserved by the state of Vermont as an underwater historical site. On December 9, 1876, this schooner-rigged ship set sail for Burlington from Isle La Motte with a cargo of marble blocks. The boat was almost in the bay when a powerful gale broke the steering mechanism. The Captain put a chain around the tiller to try to steer the boat, but to no avail. The *General Butler* continued to thrash about on the rocks of the breakwater, before submerging 40 feet below, where she now rests. Fortunately, the five people aboard the ship were saved.

Jonathan tied up to one of the large yellow buoys provided by the state and we soon made our descent. The water was a frigid 65° on the surface, and 10° lower by the wreck. Needless to say, we wore wet suits from the top of our heads to the bottoms of our feet. Several minutes later, we were staring at the long length of the wooden boat. Visibility, normally 15 feet, was lower than average. Nevertheless, we could still see everything on the boat, including the jury-rigged chain still wrapped around the tiller, the cargo of marble blocks, and cleats used for lowering and raising the anchors. Unfortunately, her masts are no longer there. We swam around the boat several times, followed by rock and smallmouth bass. Small, snail-like zebra mussels had attached themselves all over the wood. These mussels are causing an alarming epidemic in the northern lakes. They clog boat engines and can cause irreversible damage to these historic ships. Since there is no remedy in sight,

I would advise seeing the wrecks soon, before they're all covered in green slime.

Waterfront Diving Center offers rental, charters, and instruction. They can be found at 214 Battery Street, Burlington (tel. 802/865-2771).

SNOWMOBILING

The **Vermont Association of Snow Travelers** (VAST) is a group of more than 200 local snowmobile clubs that maintain over 3,000 miles of groomed trails. The trails extend from the Mass border to Canada, from the Connecticut River to Lake Champlain. Eighty-five percent of the land is located on private property, and without the work of volunteers, the use of this land would not be possible. For detailed maps, route suggestions, and information about guided tours, contact the Vermont Association of Snow Travelers, P.O. Box 839, Montpelier, VT 05602 (tel. 802/229-0005). A "Winter Recreation Map" is also available from the **Green Mountain National Forest,** 231 N. Main St., Rutland, VT 05701 (tel. 802/747-6700).

In Stowe, **Nichols Snowmobile Rentals** offers daily rentals; (tel. 802/253-7239). In the northern lakes region, **Seymour Lake Lodge** is a good base for snow-mobilers. Located at State Route 11, Morgan, VT 05853 (tel. 802/895-2752).

For a complete list of snowmobile tours and rentals in the state, get a copy of the "Vermont Winter Guide" from the **Vermont Department of Travel,** 134 State Street, Montpelier, VT 05602 (tel. 800/VERMONT).

SNOWSHOEING

Snowshoeing expeditions can be arranged through **Umiak Outdoor Outfitters,** State Route 100, Stowe, VT 05672 (tel. 802/253-2317). They offer rentals, lessons, and guided snowshoeing tours through Smuggler's Notch on unplowed State Route 108.

SWIMMING

With **Lake Champlain** to the west, the **Connecticut River** to the east, and hundreds of lakes, rivers, and ponds in between, choices of swimming holes in northern Vermont are virtually unlimited. **North Beach Park** is a crowded beach on Lake Champlain. Just outside of Burlington, **Bristol Falls** in Richmond attracts the UVM crowd. In Stowe, check out **Sterling Falls** and the other small ponds in Ranch Valley. **Brewster River Gorge** is located north of Smuggler's Notch outside of Jeffersonville. On the west side of the mountains, check out **Bartlett's Falls** in Lincoln two miles east of Bristol and the **Middlebury Gorge** off State Route 125 in East Middlebury.

In the Northeast Kingdom, swimming options increase exponentially. There's **Shadow Lake Beach** in Glover, **Lake Groton** just outside of Rickers Mills, **Harvey's Lake** in West Barnet, **Miles Pond** in Concord, **Crystal Lake State Beach** in Barton, and **Prouty Beach** in Newport.

WALKS & RAMBLES

The 3-mile-long **Stowe Recreation Path** starts behind the Stowe Community Church on Main Street and weaves back and forth over the Little River to the foothills of Mount Mansfield. The 8-foot-wide paved trail is never far from the restaurants on Mountain Road, so you can have lunch and then make your way back to town. Then there's this lyrical trail:

Robert Frost Interpretive Trail

Allow 1 hour. Access: From Ripton, take State Route 125 East (Robert Frost

Memorial Highway) for 2 miles. A sign indicating the small parking area is located on the right-hand side of the road. Map: Available at the trailhead.

In 1920, 44-year-old Robert Frost moved from New Hamsphire to Vermont. For the next 39 years, he would summer in a scanty log cabin standing on the crest of a hillside in Ripton, Vermont. The state adopted Frost as their native son, designating him their official poet laureate in 1961, and in 1983 bestowing the name "Robert Frost Country" to this section of the Green Mountain National Forest. Robert Frost Country includes the farm where he lived, the Robert Frost Wayside Picnic area, the Robert Frost Memorial Drive, Middlebury's Bread Loaf School of English (which Frost co-founded), and the Robert Frost Interpretive Trail.

This mile-long level dirt path weaves through a forest setting where seven Frost poems are posted at regular intervals. I took the trail in late winter, an ideal time since many of the mounted poems are set in this season, like "Stopping By Woods on a Snowy Evening" and "A Winter Eden." I crossed over Beaver Pond into a forest of birches, beeches, and spruce. Frost's words, like his 1946 poem, "A Young Birch," perfectly complement the scenery:

> *It will stand forth, entirely white in*
> *bark,*
> *And nothing but the top a leafy green—*
> *The only native tree that dares to lean,*
> *Relying on its beauty, to the air.*
> *(Less brave perhaps than trusting are*
> *the fair.)*

The trail seems far too short, leaving the forest and entering a field of blueberries and huckleberries, before arriving back at the parking lot. To continue the Frost tour, I drove to the dirt road just east of the Robert Frost Wayside picnic area. In typical Vermont fashion, the road is unmarked. I followed the dirt road for approximately a half-mile and parked near a white house. A hundred yard walk past this house brought me to a clearing on my left. The rustic cabin where Frost lived for two months every summer was situated here. Middlebury College now owns the grounds and keeps the door to the interior of the cabin locked.

Campgrounds & Other Accommodations

CAMPGROUNDS

The **Department of Forests, Parks, and Recreation** (108 South Main Street, Waterbury, VT 05676; tel. 802/241-3655) maintains 35 campgrounds in the state. Contact them for a brochure.

Button Bay State Park

Located on Panton Road, just south of Basin Harbor. 72 sites, no hookups, public phone, wheelchair-accessible rest rooms, sewage disposal, tables, fire rings, and wood. Tel. 802/475-2377.

Located on the southern shores of Lake Champlain, all of the sites have exceptional views of the Adirondacks across the lake.

Underhill State Park

From Underhill Center, off State Route 15, go 4 miles east on paved Town Road, then head 4 miles east on gravel Town Road. Tel. 802/899-3022. 25 sites, no hookups, handicapped rest room facilities, flush toilets, hot showers, public phone, tables, fire rings, and wood.

The campground is scattered around the base of Mount Mansfield, near the Laura Cowles and Sunset Ridge trailheads. The limited sites are extremely popular during the summer months.

Smuggler's Notch State Park

Located on State Route 108, 10 miles west of Stowe. Tel. 802/253-4014. 38 sites, no hookups, handicapped rest room facilities, flush toilets, hot showers, public phone, tables, fire rings, and wood.

Located just beyond the notch. Can be extremely windy at times.

Little River State Park

From the junction of State Route 100 and U.S. 2, go 1.5 miles west on U.S. 2 and 3.5 miles north on Little River Road. Tel. 802/244-7013. 101 sites, no hookups, handicapped rest room facilities, flush toilets, hot showers, public phone, tables, fire rings, and wood.

Located on the shores of Waterbury Reservoir, close to the Mount Hunger hike.

North Hero State Park

From North Hero, go 4 miles north on Route 2, then 4 miles northeast on Town Road. Tel. 802/372-8727. 117 sites, no hookups, handicap rest room facilities, flush toilets, hot showers, public phone, tables, fire rings, and wood.

The sites are located in three loops in a lowland forest, accessible to a beach on Lake Champlain.

Knight's Island State Park

Accessible only by boat. Larry Tudholpe offers a Knight Islander Taxi service from North Hero; tel. 802/372-6104. Tel. 802/

524-6353. 7 sites, no hookups, fire rings, and wood.

Located on Lake Champlain 2 miles east of North Hero, these seven sites are stricly reserved for those who yearn for privacy.

Grand Isle State Park

Situated on U.S. 2, 1 mile south of Grand Isle. Tel. 802/372-4300. 155 sites, no hookups, handicapped rest room facilities, flush toilets, hot showers, public phone, tables, fire rings, and wood.

Nature trails and the beach arc close to the sites at this 226-acre park.

Brighton State Park

From Island Pond, go 2 miles east on State Route 105, then 0.75 mile south on local road. Tel. 802/723-4360. 84 sites, no hookups, handicapped rest room facilities, flush toilets, hot showers, public phone, tables, fire rings, and wood.

The sites are on the shores of a well-known fishing hole near Lake Willoughby.

Stillwater Campground

From Groton, head 2 miles west on State Route 302, 6 miles north on State Route 232, and then 0.5-mile east on Boulder Beach Road. Tel. 802/584-3822. 79 sites, no hookups, flush toilets, hot showers, public phone, tables, fire rings, and wood.

Located on the northwest side of Lake Groton, a favorite swimming spot.

Ricker Pond Campground

From Groton, go 2 miles west on State Route 84, then 2.5 miles north on State Route 232. Tel. 802/584-3821. 55 sites, no hookups, flush toilets, hot showers, public phone, tables, fire rings, and wood.

Located on the south side of Ricker Pond, near larger Lake Groton.

INNS & RESORTS

Thomas Mott Homestead

P.O. Box 149B, Alburg, VT 05440-9629. Tel. 802/796-3736. Rooms from $59 a night, including breakfast.

1987 was a busy year for Pat Schallert. He retired from the wine-exporting business, moved from Los Angeles to Alburg, Vermont, and completely refurbished an 1838 farmhouse into one of the nicest inns on the Lake Champlain islands. Years of selecting the finest wines in the world seems to be the perfect training ground for becoming a competent innkeeper. Pat has an impeccable eye for detail that makes guests feel right at home. Little touches, like keeping a freezer full of free Ben & Jerry's ice cream, showing visitors where the ripe raspberries are on the property, and selecting the finest restaurants in the region for his guests are the reasons why people return year after year. The inn is located on the northern shores of Lake Champlain. Pat also provides canoes and bicycles.

Ruthcliffe Lodge

P.O. Box 32, Isle La Motte, VT 05463. Tel. 802/928-3200. Double rooms from $58, including breakfast.

Situated on my favorite Lake Champlain island, Isle La Motte, the Ruthcliffe Lodge has been a summer hideaway since 1951. Seven of the nine guestrooms are on the lake, and canoes are available. Owner Mark Infante is a talented chef—the reason many locals consider Ruthcliffe's restaurant to be the best on the islands.

Burlington Radisson

Battery Street, Burlington, VT 05401. Tel. 802/658-6500 or 800/333-3333. Double rooms from $90.

If you plan on spending several days in Burlington, you can't go wrong with the Radisson. Ask for a room overlooking the lake and the Adirondack Mountains. The hotel is conveniently located across from the 8.2-mile Burlington bike path and down the road from sailboat rentals and scuba-diving charters.

Smuggler's Notch Resort

State Route 108, Smuggler's Notch, VT 05464-9599. Tel. 800/451-8752. Write or call regarding package deals.

Smuggler's Notch's reputation as one of the finest family-oriented resorts in the state is well-deserved. The resort is located at the foothills of Morse, Sterling, and Madonna mountains, just north of the notch. Families can cross-country or downhill ski the mountains in the winter, and mountain bike and hike on the trails in the summer. Climbing to the peak of Mansfield, canoeing on the Lamoille River, and good road biking are all in close proximity. The hodgepodge of accommodations range from studios with fireplaces to fully equipped five-bedroom condos.

Trapp Family Lodge

Stowe, VT 05672. Tel. 802/253-8511 or 800/826-7000. Doubles from $180 per couple, including all meals.

"The hills are alive with the sound of . . . cross-country skiers swooshing through snow" (I'd like to see Julie Andrews sing that line). Maria von Trapp, the woman who inspired *The Sound of Music*, is no longer with us, and the original building burned down in 1980, but Trapp Family Lodge endures. Set on a crest overlooking the Green Mountains, the new Austrian-style lodge has the same ole' stunning view. Members of the Trapp family are often found dining with guests and leading sing-alongs in the living room. The cross-country ski-touring facility offers some of the finest groomed and backcountry skiing in the country.

The Brass Lantern Inn

717 Maple Street, Stowe, VT 05672. Tel. 802/253-2229 or 800/729-2980. Double rooms from $80, including breakfast.

Located north of Stowe on State Route 100, far away from the traffic on Mountain Road, Andy Aldrich's nine-room inn is a cozy respite after a day on the slopes. At night, warm your body with a warm fire and, in the morning, warm your tummy with one of Andy's mouthwatering breakfasts.

Inn at Trout River

Main Street, Montgomery Center, VT 05471. Tel. 802/326-4391 or 800/338-7049. Double rooms with breakfast start at $72 per couple.

Built by a lumber baron over a century ago, the Inn at Trout River now features ten guest rooms, one suite, and a top-notch restaurant. The inn is located just down the road from Jay Peak and Hazen's Notch Ski Touring Center, in Montgomery Center. Along with her usual steak, chicken, and lamb dishes, owner and chef Lee Forman recently added a "Wholesome Choices" menu featuring low-calorie, low-cholesterol dishes. Try her zucchini and squash, some of the freshest vegetables I've ever tasted.

Inn on the Common

Craftsbury Common, VT 05827. Tel. 802/586-9619 or 800/521-2233. Double rooms with breakfast and dinner start at $169 per couple.

Driving into Craftsbury Common is like entering another century. I always expect the car radio to shut off, only to turn on again with Rod Serling's voice. "You are entering another time, another place. It's the mid-1800s and you've just arrived in Craftsbury Common, a town of gleaming white clapboard houses on a village green. A town where peace and quiet are not only attainable, but could be alarming to some. You are entering the Twilight Zone." To call Craftsbury Common sleepy is an understatement. This town has been slumbering longer than Rip Van Winkle.

The Inn on the Common, three stately houses just off the square, fits right into the scheme of things. Owners Michael and Penny Schmitt come from a time and place where service and comfort are of the utmost importance. The five-course dinner and breakfast are served in a luxurious setting overlooking the manicured English-style gardens. The inn is located near the cross-country and mountain-biking trails of Craftsbury Center.

Highland Lodge

Greensboro, VT 05841. Tel. 802/533-2647. Double rooms start at $87.50 per person, including breakfast and dinner.

Located in one of my favorite Northeast Kingdom towns, Greensboro, the Highland Lodge sits on a hill overlooking Caspian Lake. There are 11 rooms in the main inn and 10 cottages scattered about the grounds. The lodge is known for its extensive network of cross-country skiing trails in the winter. During the warm-weather months, fish and canoe on the lake or play tennis on the shores.

Mountain View Creamery

P.O. Box 355, East Burke, VT 05832. Tel. 802/626-9924. Double rooms with breakfast start at $90.

When I first laid eyes on the Mountain View Creamery, my jaw dropped. It was like walking onto the grounds of the Shelbourne Museum outside of Burlington. Set on a hill overlooking 440 acres of agrestic Northeast Kingdom scenery, the red-brick creamery is surrounded by four immense barns. The barns and the creamery were built in 1883 by Elmer Darling, owner of the elegant Fifth Avenue Hotel in New York. They were once used to house hundreds of cows, pigs, sheep, and Morgan horses. Today, the creamery functions as a 10-room B&B and the grounds are yours to stroll

upon. The inn is a5-minute drive from Burke Mountain and a 15-minute drive from Mount Pisgah and Lake Willoughby.

Blueberry Hill

Goshen, VT 05733. Tel. 802/247-6735. Rates per person start at $84 and include all meals.

Blueberry Hill is one of those secluded, intimate inns that you would never know about unless you read about it in a guide book like this. The eight-room inn is nestled in the foothills of the Green Mountain National Forest. Guests eat dinner together family-style at long tables, but you might not have any appetite after sneaking home-made chocolate chip cookies all day. The inn's cross-country ski center is one of the best and oldest in Vermont; 50 to 75 km of trails weave in and out of the forest. British-born owner Tony Clark is an avid traveler who knows from his own experience how to treat guests royally.

10

The White Mountains & Other New Hampshire Highlights

HEN THE REPUBLICAN PARTY PICKED NEW HAMPSHIRE AS the site for its first presidential primary, they didn't just throw darts at a map of America. New Hampshire has had the old Herbert Hoover "pick yourself up by your boot straps" slogan written all over it from its earliest days. The locals are strongly independent, rugged individualists who at times can be as hardened as The Old Man of the Mountain—the famous rock jutting out of Franconia Notch that resembles a stern male countenance. Other times, New Hampshirites are as gentle and inviting as the cerulean blue waters of the Lakes Region.

The state's diverse landscape definitely has an impact on the complex personality of its natives. The rolling green hills of the south give way to large lakes in the center of New Hampshire. It is the peaks of the impressive White Mountains in the north, however, that shape our image of this New England state and her people. Stunted trees border steel gray granite which has been carved by glaciers and ice beds into fantastic formations—the hand of nature's foray into abstract sculpture. At lower elevations, forests of firs and spruce hide ponds, streams, and hundreds of waterfalls. Mountains tower over 6,000 feet, including Mount Washington, the highest peak in the northeast, known for its fierce winds and weather that changes faster than Clark Kent turning into Superman.

Aside from poet Robert Frost, a noted New Hampshirephobe—who once said, "The only fault I find with New Hampshire is that her mountains aren't quite high enough"—most people walk away from the Whites awed and inspired. Tourists have been visiting the region since the early 1800s, when the Crawford family built inns and constructed bridle paths and hiking trails into the mountains. One of the trails, the Crawford Path, is the oldest hiking trail in the country. Most of these 30- to 40-room accommodations were simple, straightforward wooden structures built near a body of water. Visitors would go on guided hikes or horseback rides, usually around Mount Washington, and then return to the hotel for a copious meal.

In the 1850s, the Whites were home to the state's first art colony. Thomas Cole, Albert Bierstadt, and George Innes were just a few of the American landscape painters who devoted themselves to this enchanting scenery. By the latter half of the 19th century, two very different types of traveler emerged—the pampered urbanite and the able-bodied outdoorsmen.

Great rambling resorts like the Glen House, Crawford House, and Kearsage House were built in the 1870s and 1880s to provide sybaritic pleasures to those visitors seeking the solace of nature within a luxurious environment. They came on sleeper trains from Boston and New York, dined on gourmet food, took carefully organized excursions to the Old Man of the Mountain, the Flume, and other noted places of interest, and then returned to the hotel for tea in the manicured gardens. These comfortable resorts, like their counterparts in Europe, were created as healthy retreats

to revive the spirit. After 1869, when the Cog Railway was constructed to bring guests up to the peak of Mount Washington, fashionably dressed travelers could go on three-day excursions from the eastern cities at a cost of $17 per person. The journey included a train ride to one of the sumptuous hotels, a ride on the Cog Railway, a night in the summit hotel, and transfer by carriage down the eastern side of the mountain to the railroad line back home.

Another group from Boston was seeking to provide a much different type of shelter—small mountain huts that would lodge hikers or "trampers," as they were called in their day. In 1888, this small contingent of outdoorsmen built the Madison Spring stone cabin in the Presidential Range. The price for a roof over your head was half a dollar, and you were responsible for your own sustenance, blankets, and other basic needs.

Now, more than a century later, the exquisite Balsams in Dixville Notch is regrettably the only grand resort that still stands from the late 1800s in northern New Hampshire. The good news is that the small group of outdoorsmen who had the vision and willpower to provide shelter for America's early hikers is now the Appalachian Mountain Club, with more than 60,000 members nationwide and eight mountain huts. Best of all, the Whites and the state as a whole continue to entice and challenge every imaginable type of sportsperson, from rock climber to hang glider to canoeist to biker.

The Lay of the Land

The glacier that retreated 10,000-plus years ago to form the White Mountains seemed to have left in a hurry, without first smoothing the edges of the rocky detritus that remained. Narrow and steep mountainous passes, called notches, sharply cut through walls of granite that refused to budge. Gorges plummet to the forest floor, cliffs protrude from bare summits over 6,000 feet high, circular domes are not yet hewn, and massive boulders are found in the most absurd spots.

One-third of New Hampshire rock is granite, thus the nickname "The Granite State." This is the result of intense igneous activity—huge masses of molten rock welled up into layered rocks, where they solidified to form granite. Visitors from the west, who are used to viewing mountains twice this size, will inevitably find these unusual configurations dramatic. Unlike the Green Mountains to the west, which are smooth and form a narrow range running from north to south, the White Mountains are a chaotic group centered in the north-central portion of the state and straggling off in every direction. They venture into Maine and come within ten miles of Vermont and 50 miles of Quebec.

South of the White Mountains, New Hampshire starts to soften. Sharp-edged granite is replaced by blue waters the color of cobalt or slate; 273 lakes and ponds are found in the Lakes Region, an area that begins at the Maine border and spreads west, covering much of central New Hampshire. The largest and most popular body of water is Lake Winnipesaukee, bordered by more pristine Squam Lake. Lake Sunapee, a hidden gem, lies to the west. The larger lakes sit in broad, shallow basins that were scooped out by the overwhelming force of an ice sheet. Farther south, the state is quintessential New England, with undulating mountains of green, small towns, and covered bridges still standing from the mid-19th century. Then, of course, there's the ocean, and an 18-mile stretch of shoreline that connects Massachusetts to Maine.

Climate is not taken lightly in this part of the country. The highest winds ever recorded, 231 miles per hour, occurred atop Mount Washington on April 12, 1934. Every year, several people perish and hundreds more are saved by search-and-rescue squads in the Whites, because of the vast difference in weather between the bottom and the summit. Mark Twain's famous line about New England, "I have counted one hundred and thirty-six different kinds of weather inside of four-and-twenty hours" easily applies to the Whites. When taking hikes in the height of summer or the depths of winter, it is imperative that you know the weather atop the mountains.

The climate in the northeast is becoming increasingly hard to predict. Summers in New Hampshire range from 70° to 80°, winters from the teens to 30s (unless you're on top of Mt. Washington where the temperature can dip as low as –40°). If there's snow on the ground, late November and mid-March are my favorite times to ski. There are far fewer people on the slopes and the weather is reasonably warmer than the other winter months. Late August, when the humidity and bugs have vacated the countryside, is the perfect time to hike and bike. Leaf peeping is at its peak from late September through mid-October. Color starts to appear in higher elevations during mid-September, and gradually spreads south to the other parts of the state. I'd avoid Columbus Day Weekend since the traffic can be heavy and rooms are booked well in advance. The state maintains a **Fall Foliage Hotline** (tel. 800/258-3608) which provides updated conditions.

More and more moose are relinquishing their Canadian passports and traveling south into New Hampshire. Two of the best places to spot these large mammals is north of Berlin on Route 16, along the Androscoggin River, and

Route 26, east of Errol. The list of inhabitants include the occasional black bear and bobcat, deer, beaver, porcupine, raccoon, woodchuck, skunk, otter, and muskrat. There are close to 200 types of birds in the Whites, ranging from ruby-throated hummingbirds to eastern kingbirds to yellow-bellied flycatchers. Along the coast, black-crowned night herons, glossy ibises, snowy egrets, and other shore birds are commonly seen. The bird watching highlight is the pair of nesting eagles on Umbagog Lake.

Orientation

From the Canadian to the Massachusetts border, New Hampshire is almost 200 miles long. The northern tip is less than 20 miles wide, the girth at the base close to 100 miles. Travelers from Boston and other points east cruise up **I-93** past the state capital, Concord, to the center of the state. Visitors from the west and south take **I-89,** running from Lebanon to Concord, and **I-91,** following the Connecticut River along the border of New Hampshire and Vermont.

There are many scenic routes within the Whites, perhaps the most scenic being the **Kancamagus Highway** or "Kanc." A veritable corkscrew of a road, the 34.5-mile Kanc rises to 3,000 feet as it runs by rivers, waterfalls, mountains, and forests. The road starts in Lincoln and ends in Conway, heading west to east. Many of the easier hiking and cross-country routes in the Whites start from the highway.

U.S. 302, from Bartlett to Bretton Woods, is a spectacular drive through Crawford Notch. Mount Washington and the other high peaks of the Presidential Range are best seen from U.S. 302 or **Route 16** north of Jackson. There is also an auto road that climbs to the peak of Mount Washington, but we expect you

to do this on foot, skis, or crampons. In the Lakes Region, Route 109 borders the eastern half of Winnipesaukee from Melvin Village to Wolfeboro.

Right on the eastern shore of Lake Winnipesaukee, the town of **Wolfeboro** claims to be the oldest summer resort in the country. Pointed church steeples and quaint inns line the streets of this picture-postcard village. Wolfeboro's alter ego, **Weirs Beach,** is located on the western side of Winnipesaukee at the junction of Routes 3 and 11B. This is a raucous summer playland, where boardwalks and tacky amusements like go-carts, water slides, bumper cars, a large arcade, and miniature golf courses attract families.

Depending on your entranceway into the Whites, **Lincoln, Woodstock,** and **North Conway** are the best towns to stock up on food and water before you hit the trails. Lincoln and Woodstock are located in the western part of the White Mountain National Forest. North Conway, known for its long list of outlet stores, is the gateway to Mount Washington and Pinkham Notch.

Only 18 miles long, **New Hampshire's oceanfront,** accessible from U.S. 1 or I-95, is rarely seen by travelers heading north to the sprawling Maine Coast. What drivers miss is the historical seaside city of **Portsmouth** and lively **Hampton Beach.** Settled in 1630, Portsmouth was the colonial capital and an important seaport for more than 200 years. Today, Portsmouth's maritime heritage is present in the city's architecture, from the waterfront to its historical houses and inns. At the opposite end of the spectrum and seacoast is Hampton Beach, a popular hangout for New England families during the summer. The beach is covered with suntanners on hot weekend days, and the restaurants, arcades, and shops are packed during summer nights.

Parks & Other Hot Spots

The White Mountain National Forest

Headquarters: 719 Main Street, Laconia, NH 03247. Tel. 603/528-8721. Ranger Districts: Ammonoosuc RD, Trudeau Road, Bethlehem. Tel. 603/869-2626. Pemigewasset RD, Route 175, Plymouth. Tel. 603/536-1310. Androscoggin RD, Route 16, Gorham. Tel. 603/466-2713. Saco RD, Kancamagus Highway, Conway. Tel. 603/447-5448. Pinkham Notch Camp, Route 16, Pinkham. Notch Tel. 603/466-2725. Evans Notch RD, Bridge Street, Bethel, Maine. Tel. 207/824-2134.

Occupying 11 percent of New Hampshire, this is the highest percentage of federal land in any eastern state. More than 3 million visitors annually come to test their muscle on 1,167 miles of grueling talus-covered and soft stream-laced paths, ski down some of the oldest trails in North America, cross-country ski through more than a hundred miles of backcountry woods, or hook a trout or bass in the numerous ponds and streams. The 798,305-acre forest is also attracting a new breed of hardcore adventurer. Mountain bikers are pedaling up and cruising down single-track ridge trails and rock climbers face the daunting task of ascending a sheer wall of rock. The region is so vast and complex that it's best to break it up into specific features:

Crawford Notch State Park

North of Bartlett on U.S. 302. Headquarters: Star Route, Bartlett, NH 03812. Tel. 603/374-2272.

This is one of two spectacular state parks surrounded by the National Forest. A highly popular route since the stage-coach days, this sinuous 6-mile mountainous pass goes through some of the most rugged terrain in the northeast. When the Crawford family began taking travelers to the Notch and advertising in the Boston papers, the tourism industry in the White Mountains blossomed. Ethan Allan Crawford, who operated the first inn here, has the oldest continuously maintained hiking trail in America named for him. First blazed in 1819, the Crawford Path begins near the old Crawford House and climbs above the treeline to Mount Washington.

Franconia Notch State Park

South of Franconia on I-93. Headquarters: Franconia, NH, by the entrance to the Flume. Tel. 603/823-5563.

Located on I-93, a half-hour drive to the west of Crawford Notch, this state park is extremely crowded during the high season. The stunning 8-mile long pass sits on the eastern side of the Whites between Cannon Mountain and the high peaks of the Franconia Range. The notch offers an incredible display of unique scenery. The Flume is an 800-foot long gorge with steep, moss-covered walls as high as 90 feet with a width as narrow as 12 feet. The Basin is a deep glacial pothole almost 30 feet in diameter that sits at the base of a waterfall. The Old Man of the Mountain is a 40-foot-high rock formation that looks like the chiseled face of a proud man. It was immortalized in the story, *The Great Stone Face*, by Nathaniel Hawthorne,

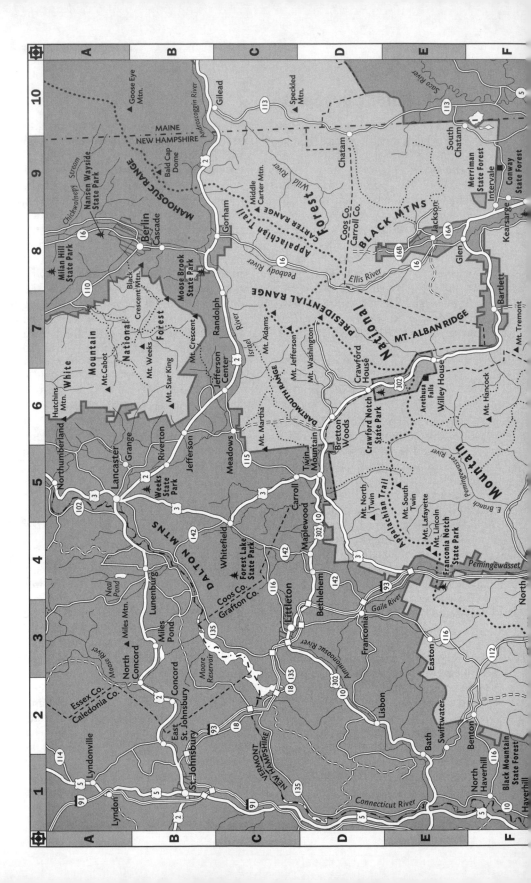

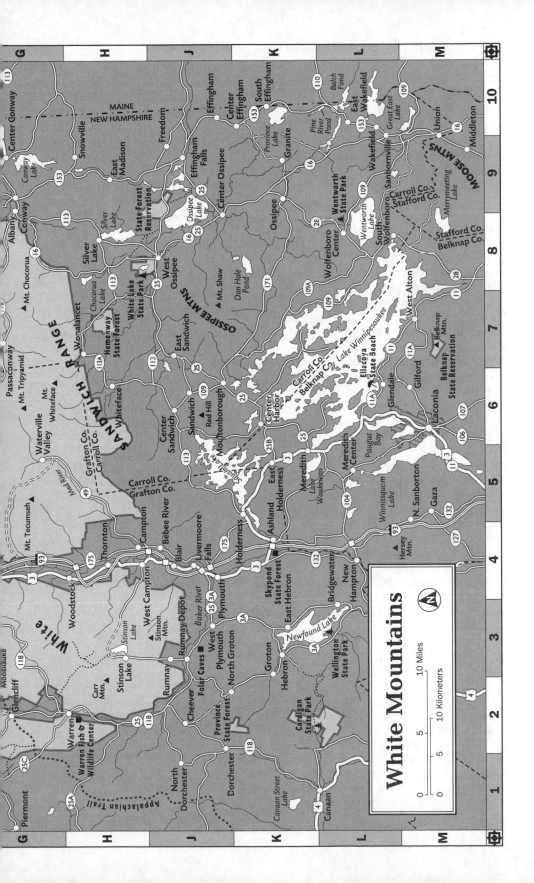

White Mountains

who wrote, "It seemed as if an enormous giant, or Titan, had sculpted his own likeness there upon the precipice."

Mount Washington and the Presidential Range

Standing 6,288 feet tall, Mount Washington is the highest peak in the northeast. The mountain is broad with three major ridges, numerous valleys, and two immense large glacial cirques, the renowned Tuckerman Ravine and Great Gulf. Similar to Crawford Notch, the mountain has attracted visitors for almost a century and a half. The Summit House was built in 1852, the toll road completed in 1861, the Cog Railway constructed in 1869, and the first weather observatory created in 1870. One of the wider New Hampshire notches, Pinkham Notch and the Appalachian Mountain Club's headquarters are located to the east of the mountain on Route 16. The surrounding mountains in the Presidential Range include six mountains over 5,000 feet, all offering sweeping views of the region.

Androscoggin River

Route 16. Contact the Northern White Mountains Chamber of Commerce, 164 Main Street, Berlin. Tel. 603/752-6060 or 800-992-7480.

Thirty-five miles long in New Hampshire, this river enters the state from Maine at Wentworths Location, and flows south through Errol, Milan, and Berlin, before turning sharply east and going back into Maine. Once used to float logs down to the paper mills, the river is now

one of the state's finest recreational locales. Fly-fisherman try their luck with the numerous trout, and canoeists come to paddle down Class II and III rapids. The Thirteen Mile Woods Scenic Area, just south of Errol, is the most splendid area of the waterway.

Umbagog Lake National Wildlife Refuge

5.5 miles north of Errol on Route 16. Tel. 603/482-3415.

Best known for its pair of nesting bald eagles, this largely undeveloped lake with roughly 60 miles of shoreline is home to a diverse array of wildlife. Loons, osprey, even raptors share the skies with the eagles. Moose are spotted regularly while bears have been seen infrequently. Situated on the Maine-New Hampshire border, the lake's canoeing and fishing are first-class. Anglers have been known to hook salmon, brook trout, brown trout, pickerel, and yellow perch.

Dixville Notch State Park

Route 26. Contact the Northern White Mountains Chamber of Commerce, 164 Main Street, Berlin. Tel. 603/752-6060 or 800/992-7480.

The narrowest notch in New Hampshire lies in the north across from the famous Balsams resort. Carved between Sanguinary Mountain and Mount Gloriette, the rocky cleft barely allows the two-lane Route 26 to squeeze through. The notch, once owned by Daniel Webster, is now part of a state park, replete with waterfalls, flume, and hiking trails. The short steep walk up to Table Rock leads to an exposed ledge that juts out over a cliff (see "Hiking," below).

Connecticut River

New England's longest river forms most of the border between New Hampshire and Vermont. As a general rule, the closer you get to the Canadian border, the more pristine and tranquil the Connecticut becomes. This is especially true of the Connecticut Lakes region at the Quebec border and the section of the river just north of Hanover. Blue-ribbon trout are found in the waterway between the Connecticut Lakes and North Stratford. Farther south, the river is known for its warmwater bass fishing.

The Lakes Region

Bordering the White Mountains, the hundreds of placid waterways that make up the Lakes Region are the perfect antidote to its rough-and-tumble neighbor to the north. The centerpiece is **Lake Winnipesaukee,** 28 miles long and 13 miles wide. The lake is known for its landlocked salmon and smallmouth bass, but anglers have to contend with pleasure boats for space and quiet.

People in search of a bit more peace head to **Squam Lake,** New Hampshire's second-largest lake, measuring about 5 by 7 miles. Much of the filming of *On Golden Pond*, the Academy Award–winning Fonda-Hepburn movie, took place here in 1981. Unfortunately, the lake has limited public access.

One of the best kept secrets of New Hampshire is **Lake Sunapee.** Remarkably clear, the lake is still a source of drinking water for the locals. You can swim at the beach at **Lake Sunapee State Park,** off State Route 103, 3 miles west of Newbury. Contact the Divison of Parks and Recreation, P.O. Box 856D, Concord, NH 03301 (tel. 603/271-3254), launch a boat onto the sparkling clean waters, or climb Mount Sunapee for the best views of the lake.

Mount Monadnock

Off Route 124, 4 miles north of Jaffrey. Monadnock State Park, Jaffrey Center, NH 03454. Tel. 603/532-8862.

Only 3,165 feet high, Monadnock just passed Mount Fuji as the most popular ascent in the world. Why is it so fashionable? Perhaps it's Monadnock's proximity to Boston (1 1/2 hours away) or the long history (hundreds of people from as far back as the early 1800s have inscribed their names in the boulders, prompting Thoreau, Emerson, and other writers to make the ascent). I think it has more to do with the geography of the mountain. The mountain is a monadnock, an isolated mountain on a plain; it offers expansive vistas of southern New Hampshire and northern Massachusetts.

What to Do & Where to Do It

BIRD WATCHING

Canoeing **Umbagog Lake** to view the only pair of nesting **bald eagles** in New Hampshire is a spectacle not to miss (see "Canoeing," below). **Herons, loons,** and **osprey** can also be found in the northern

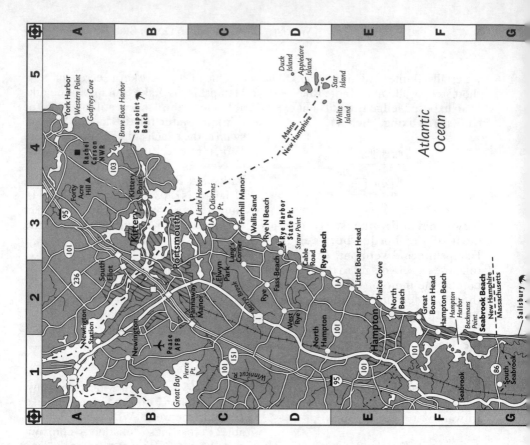

lakes. Farther south, in the Whites, the **Zealand Trail** (see "Hiking," below) is a good place to spot **warblers** and other colorful birds in August on their way south for the winter. AMC Naturalist John Green usually takes birders on a weekend tour of Zealand Valley during this time. Cost is $135 including instruction, lodging, and meals. Call 603/466-2727 for dates.

For a longer general discussion of the birds you're likely to see in the woods, on the lakes and riverbanks, and on the mountains of interior New Hampshire, take a look at the "Bird Watching" sections in the chapter on central and southern Vermont.

Cedar waxwings, bobolinks, and **American goldfinches** are some of the species found in the Lakes Region.

On the coast, State Route 1A from Seabrook to Newcastle harbors many tidal estuaries and saltwater marshes and, thus, migratory shorebirds. **Great and little blue herons, ospreys, ibises,** and **snowy egrets** have been spotted here, along with a variety of **ducks.** See the Cape Cod birding section in chapter 7 for more on birding in this kind of environment.

BOARDSAILING

Winni Sailboarder's School & Outlet, 687 Union Avenue, Laconia (tel. 603/528-4110) offer lessons and rentals on Lake Opechee. Mount Sunapee State Park, Route 103, Newbury (tel. 603/763-2356) gives instruction on the lake.

CANOEING

Most of the canoeing in New Hampshire occurs in short doses on the state's numerous lakes and ponds. If you want to canoe in the Lakes Region, I prefer

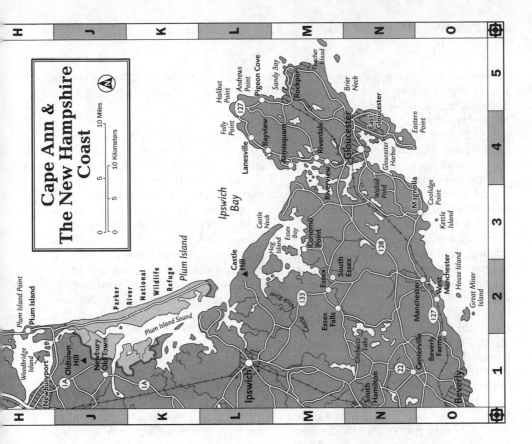

Cape Ann & The New Hampshire Coast

Squam Lake to its big brother, **Winnipesaukee.** Boat traffic, wind, and the sheer size of the lake create daunting situations at Winnipesaukee. Canoes can be rented on **Squam Lake** at the Sailing Center, U.S. 3, Holderness (tel. 603/968-3233). Three Legged Tours offers guided canoe, hiking, and biking tours in the Lakes Region. Contact Mike or Kicki Stecher (tel. 603/253-7635). For a longer paddle trip, try the Saco River.

DAY TRIPS

Saco River

From a 1-hour paddle to a 3-day trip. Class III–IV whitewater in reaches above Bartlett; mostly Class I–II whitewater from Bartlett to North Conway; quickwater below North Conway, quieting to placid, smooth current as river crosses into Maine. Put-in at Saco Bound outfitters for easy quickwater run:

From North Conway, take State Route 16 south to where U.S. 302 veers off to the east. River access is located 2 miles east of Center Conway on U.S. 302 (at old covered-bridge site, or Saco Bound Outfitters). Map: USGS Carroll County.

When your legs are weary from days of arduous hiking in the Whites, let your arms take over and canoe down the Saco River. The narrow waterway weaves from Crawford Notch in the heart of the White Mountains all the way through southeastern Maine, before emptying into the Atlantic at the city of Saco, south of Portland. The river rapidly changes character as it descends from Crawford Notch. It falls steeply at first—the Upper Saco is one of New England's more renowned whitewater runs. But by the time the river reaches North Conway, most of its fury has been dissipated. In the Conway area and east into

Maine, there's any number of access points and canoeing options along the Saco, from 3- and 6-mile day trips to a three-day, 40-mile canoe-camping journey to Hiram, Maine. There are a host of camping sites in the spruce forests that line the river.

One extremely hot summer afternoon I rented a canoe from Saco Bound outfitters and paddled for three hours and 6.4 miles to the put-out at Pigs Farm. Saco Bound's parking lot was packed, but I soon learned that the long stretch of river helps to keep you from playing bumper boats with other canoeists. Most boaters I passed were already entrenched in the sands, having a picnic on the shores, or keeping cool in the water. Shortly after entering my canoe, I passed a large flock of Canada Geese playing "follow the leader" by order of size: the little babies were struggling to keep up at the back of the line as they floated across the border into Maine. At the 3-mile mark, I passed under Weston's Bridge to find a town beach blanketed with suntanners. Views of the mighty Whites opened up to the west. I soon passed a girls' camp on the right, where instructions, amplified through the P.A. system, echoed in the surrounding forest. Far too quickly, I arrived at Pigs Farm, where the Saco Bound bus was waiting to pick people up. The river kept my hot skin wet for three cool hours—the small jaunt whet my appetite for a longer journey.

Umbagog Lake

Allow 4–5 hours. Easy paddling, though this is a large lake—be watchful of the weather, as winds and waves can make for dangerous conditions. Access: public boating access at southern end of lake, off State Route 26; at Umbagog Lake Campground, east of public boat access; at Androscoggin River (Errol) at northern end of lake, and at Magalloway River, off State Route 16 near the Maine border. Map: USGS 7.5 minute Umbagog Lake South, Umbagog Lake North.

Wildlife is abundant in the vast forests of northern New Hampshire and Maine—moose, white-tailed deer, red fox, beavers, and coyotes are common sightings. However, my wife Lisa and I weren't prepared for the extraordinary pair of birds we found nesting on a dead oak tree on Umbagog Lake. Northern Waters outfitters in Errol rented us a canoe and shuttled us to our put-in on Magalloway River. Loons were lounging on the glass waters, their call (the sound of laughter) echoed atop the spruce and fir trees. Many of the trees tilted toward the river, the result of hardworking beavers and the blustery winds of winter. We glided along the calm waters, following a great blue heron into a small channel which led into Umbagog. This vast lake, whose shores lie half in New Hampshire and half in Maine, is a National Wildlife Area, known for its exemplary landlocked salmon and trout fishing. Several islands dotted the western shores of the lake, one of which has the distinct honor of housing the only pair of nesting bald eagles in New Hampshire. We slowly paddled to our right, where we saw a large nest perched atop the highest branch of a leafless, dead tree. We drew closer to find the mother guarding her home, her pointed beak sticking out though the maze of twigs. The sight of her mate standing on the branch below was mesmerizing. His white head was cocked in a regal pose, his eyes aware of everything around him, hence the nickname "eagle eye." We skirted the island for a long time, fascinated by the awesome sight, before continuing on our 8.5-mile jaunt. Four immature eagles (in age, not attitude) learning how to fly hovered above as we turned right down the Errol river to the Errol Dam. This is where

Northern Waters picked us up to drive us back to our car.

For those who want to get out for a longer wilderness experience on Lake Umbagog, there are established campsites scattered all around the lake run by **Umbagog Lake Campground,** P.O. Box 181, Errol, NH 03579 (tel. 603/ 482-7795). Contact them for information about rates and maps of the location of sites.

OUTFITTERS & RENTALS

Saco Bound Outfitters, P.O. Box 119, Center Conway, NH 03813 (tel. 603/ 447-2177), rents canoes at their put-in, 2 miles east of Center Conway. The list of canoeing options they offer includes 3-, 6.4-, and 10.2-mile day trips, a 22-mile overnight jaunt to Lovewell Pond, and a three-day, 40-mile journey to Hiram. Saco Bound will pick you and the canoe up at a designated time. Cost for rental is $25.50 per day, including shuttle and parking.

Northern Waters, P.O. Box 119, Center Conway, NH 03813 (tel. 603/ 447-2177), is located on Route 16 in Errol, several hundred yards south of the intersection of Route 26. They rent canoes for day trippers and backcountry canoe campers heading to Lake Umbagog, and also offers whitewater canoe trips on the Androscoggin River's Class II and III rapids.

CROSS-COUNTRY SKIING

IN THE BACKCOUNTRY

Though my research was plagued by dismal weather, I somehow managed to ski all of the highly regarded cross-country routes in the Litchfield Hills, Berkshires, and Southern Vermont. But by the time I reached the northern reaches of New England in mid-March, New Hampshire was already undergoing a spring thaw. This is highly unusual for this part of the country. The end result was that I did not have the opportunity to try any of the routes recommended by park rangers, the AMC, local skiing outfitters, and friends who know the Whites intimately before this edition went to print.

However, I did have the chance to try many of the trails mentioned when I returned in the summer months. The **Zealand Trail** (see "Hiking," below) is a relatively easy trail that leads to one of two AMC huts open in the winter time. The hut is self-serve and can be downright chilly in the winter time, so dress appropriately. Since most of Zealand Road is unplowed in the winter months, the 6.8-mile ski trail is much longer than the hike. You must first take the 4.1 mile **Spruce Goose Ski Trail** to reach the Zealand Trail. Skiers staying overnight can ski back the next day or continue on the **Ethan Pond Trail** through narrow Zealand Notch to Shoal Pond or Thoreau Falls. The Carter Notch Hut is the only other AMC lodge open in the winter months. The **Nineteen-Mile Brook Trail** (also in "Hiking," below) to the hut is far more strenuous than the Zealand Trail, attracting hordes of snowmobilers and few skiers.

Two relatively flat mountain bike trails I tried would make excellent cross-country skiing runs in the winter—the former **railroad bed** that leads from Bradford to Lake Sunapee in the Lake Region and the **trail to Greeley Pond** in Waterville Valley (see "Mountain Biking"). The best way to reach the Greeley Pond Trail during snow season is from the Kancamangus Highway.

The following is a list of trails that were recommended to me but, unfortunately, were not attempted (the first four are easy/moderate routes; the last two are experts-only):

♦ The **bike path** in Franconia Notch;
♦ The **Wilderness Trail** in Lincoln, just north of the Kanc;

♦ The **Beaver Brook Ski Trail** in Bethlehem;

♦ The **Hayes Copp Ski Trail** north of Pinkham Notch;

♦ The **Wildcat Valley Trail** to the Jackson Ski Touring Foundation;

♦ The steep downhill run on the **Gulf of Slides.**

Even with the minute amount of snowfall when I was researching, there was one area that was still a white carpet—the legendary Tuckerman Ravine.

Tuckerman Ravine, Mount Washington

Allow at least 3 hours to climb. Experts only! This is a steep, mountainous wall. Access: trailhead behind the AMC Pinkham Notch Lodge, off State Route 16, between Jackson and Gorham.

Skiing Tuckerman Ravine is the most thrilling backcountry experience in the Northeast. This large glacial cirque or bowl, is on the southeast shoulder of Mount Washington. During the winter months, the ravine fills up with snow transported by intense winds from the mountain's summit. So, by springtime, this natural amphitheater is ready for you to cut your line down some of the steepest pitches in the country. Late March to mid-May is the best time to ski Tuckerman, but some years, people have skied here until the Fourth of July!

"Tuck" should only be attempted by expert downhill and telemark skiers! I can't emphasize this enough. Every year, someone dies on its slopes. A week before I arrived, a skier slid down a patch of ice on one of the runs, Hillman Highway, and slammed into the rocks. He simply became another statistic. That said, people have been skiing "the bowl" since 1926, when legendary AMC guru Joe Dodge and several of his cronies bushwhacked up the mountain and made their way down. During the 1930s,

the place became so popular that races were held from the top of the headwall all the way back to Pinkham Notch Lodge. That's a 4,200-foot drop in four miles.

In 1932, the U.S. Forest Service constructed a Fire Trail which is still the only way to get to Tuckerman today. Now called the Tuckerman Ravine Trail, it is an unrelenting, 2.4-mile, two-hour climb to Hermit Lake Cabin, or HoJo's, as the regulars call it. The trail is challenging enough without skis, but with full gear, be prepared to sweat. From HoJo's, the trail climbs steeply another 0.7 mile to the base of the ravine. Throw on a fresh pair of polypro so you don't freeze to death up top. Then decide your destiny.

There are no tow ropes, T-bars, or super quads here—just your two feet to hike up to the trail of your choice. Left Gully climbs to the lip just left of the main headwall. From here it's an 800-foot drop over a quarter of a mile. Right Gully is slightly shorter with less of a pitch. The longest run is Hillman Highway, a little over 0.5 mile. Pitches range from 35° to 55° depending on the trail you choose. It's wise to talk to other skiers to see which trail has the best snow and is the easiest to climb. When I went, I saw one fool take almost one-and-a-half hours climbing Left Gully only to have a horrible run on patches of ice afterwards.

On a sunny spring day, hundreds of spectators and skiers congregate on the Lunch Rocks. These large boulders on the lower right side of the headwall are the place to cheer other skiers on. But watch out for falling ice, which sometimes drops from the top of the headwall.

Don't worry about hiking the 2.4 miles down. You can ski on the John Sherburne trail, a sweeping downhill run that will have you back at the Pinkham Notch Lodge in less than 25 minutes.

NORDIC SKIING CENTERS

Combine all the ski touring centers in New Hampshire and you have more than 1,000 km of groomed trails. First and foremost is the **Jackson Ski Touring Foundation,** the largest cross-country skiing network in the Northeast. Over 154 km of trail (91 km groomed daily) escort skiers away from the country inns of this charming New England village high up into the mountains. Besides the challenging Wildcat Trail, try the Ellis River Trail, which hugs a small brook as it heads into the woods. For information contact Jackson Ski Touring Foundation, PO Box 2160, Jackson, NH 03846 (tel. 603/383-9355).

Situated in the western valley of Mount Washington, almost every trail in the **Bretton Woods Ski Touring Center** offers breathtaking vistas of the Presidential Range. There are 90 km of trails evenly split between beginner, intermediate, and expert. Contact Bretton Woods Ski Touring Center, Bretton Woods, NH 03575 (tel. 603/278-5181).

Known for its Alpine skiing, **Waterville Valley** also offers fine runs to cross-country skiers, including the Cascade Brook Trail. The White Mountain Criterion Trail is fun for skating. Waterville Valley, NH 03215 (tel. 603/236-4666).

If you can manage to get to Dixville Notch in the winter, you'll rarely find crowds at the remote **Balsams,** where 100 km of secluded trails reward the skier who journeys this far north. Contact The Balsams, Dixville Notch, NH 03576 (tel. 603/255-3400).

Gunstock Cross-Country Center (42 km) and **Nordic Skier** (20 km) offer groomed trails close to the shores of Lake Winnipesaukee. Gunstock Cross-Country Center, P.O. Box 1307, Laconia, NH 03247 (tel. 603/293-4341); The Nordic Skier, 19 North Main Street, Wolfeboro, NH 03894 (tel. 603/569-3151).

For New Hampshire cross-country ski conditions, call 800/262-6660.

DOWNHILL SKIING/ SNOWBOARDING

Looking for a nice cozy ski area where the sun shines daily and the snow is soft, cushioning every fall? Then beat it, buddy—head to Utah. Here, in the "Granite State," skiing is all about being outdoors and facing the elements—20° temperatures with swirling 20-to 30-mile-per-hour winds are considered a warm day. Hard-packed powder can change to ice at any given moment and stunted trees and submarine-gray skies provide little encouragement when you wipe out. This is the heart of New England, after all, the state that brought you Joe Dodge, where rugged individualism pervades every aspect of daily life, even the ski slopes. I'm not sure whether Gore-Tex has overtaken flannel and wool sweaters yet as the clothing of choice.

With so much of New Hampshire covered in rock, it's incredible that skiing exists at all. But you'll be surprised how good the trails are here, leaving you far more invigorated than battered. Let's start with the two granddaddies, Cannon and Wildcat—mountains that have been skied for over 60 years.

Cannon

Franconia Notch State Park, Franconia, NH 03580. Tel. 603/823-5563; snow report, tel. 603/823-7771. 35 trails (7 novice, 19 intermediate, 9 expert); 6 lifts including 2 quads, a triple, and 2 doubles, in addition to the tram; 2,146-foot vertical drop (the longest in New Hampshire, excepting Tuckerman Ravine). Full-day tickets $38 weekend, $31 weekday; Tuesdays $10 off.

Cannon is the home of the first ski trail in North America, the first ski school, and the first aerial tram, installed in 1938. The mountain is notorious for its tough trails, especially the ones facing the north which tend to be icy. One of its signature trails, Hardscrabble, is a challenging ride down a winding heavily moguled route. Zoomer's a classic New England bump run—in other words, a trail that will beat you to a pulp most times, if only to make your good runs seem more luminous. The short, steep, and bumpy Avalanche is another expert trail. Peabody's slopes have great lower-intermediate terrain, and Upper Canyon, Tramway, and Vista Way are free-flowing cruisers.

Wildcat

Jackson, NH 03846. Tel. 603/466-3326; snow report, tel. 800/643-4521. 29 trails (6 novice, 13 intermediate, 10 expert); 6 lifts which can handle 8,500 skiers per hour; 2,100-foot vertical drop. Full-day tickets $36 weekends, $19 weekday.

Another forbidding place to ski is Wildcat, first used in the mid-1930s when racers hiked up the mountain to compete on the original Wildcat Trail. Sitting on the wall of Pinkham Notch, the views of nearby Mount Washington and Tuckerman Ravine will take your visible breath away. Try to concentrate on your skiing, though—this is a big, rugged mountain that doesn't take well to a cavalier attitude among supplicants. Trails range from the slow-moving Polecat to the much steeper Lynx, a narrow route that falls through a succession of pitches and flats. Generally speaking, this is an expert's hill—there are just more choices and flavors here for strong skiers than newbies.

Waterville Valley

Town Square, Waterville Valley, NH 03215. Tel. 603/236-8311; snow report, tel. 603/236-4144. 53 trails (10 novice, 32 intermediate, 11 expert); 13 lifts including a high-speed detachable quad, 3 triples, and 5 doubles; 2,020 foot vertical drop. Full-day tickets $39 weekend, $34 weekday/weekend for adults; $28 weekday for teens, and $24 weekend; and $20 weekday for youths 6–12 years old.

Waterville Valley—like Loon, Attitash, and Cranmore—is one of the more modern White Mountain ski resorts. With sweeping runs like Upper Bobby's Run and Tippecanoe and the largest number of trails in New Hampshire, Waterville Valley is known as a great family resort. It's a lot like Stratton and Mount Snow in southern Vermont: a mountain within easy range of the big city (primarily Boston), and blessed with a bumper crop of fast-skiing, ego-boosting, wide cruising boulevards. Try the Tree Line/White Caps/Sel's Choice combo.

Loon

Kancamagus Highway, Lincoln, NH 03251. Tel. 603/745-8111; snow report, tel. 603/745-8100. 41 trails (10 novice, 22 intermediate, 9 expert); 9 lifts including a fast 4-passenger gondola, 2 triples, and 5 doubles; 2,100-foot vertical drop. Full-day tickets $39 weekend, $34 weekday for adults.

On the same side of the Kancamagus Highway, Loon Mountain attracts more skiers per year than any other New Hampshire ski area. However, its limited ticket policy ensures that lift lines are kept to 15 minutes or less. Loon's even more of a intermediate skier's cup of tea, with huge snowmaking and grooming operations and a plethora of wide cruisers. Loon's a little more homogenous—there's just not too much challenging skiing here.

Attitash

U.S. 302, Bartlett, NH 03812. Tel. 603/374-2368; snow report, tel. 603/374-0946. 28 trails (7 novice, 14 intermediate, 7 expert); 6 lifts including 2 triples and 4 doubles; 1,750-foot vertical drop. Full-day tickets are $36 weekend, $29 weekday for adults.

Attitash is known for having better weather and quieter winds than any other New Hampshire resort, but its low base elevation costs it the fluffier natural snow you find high in the Whites. It's the sort of rolling, unpredictably pitched ski mountain New England is famous for. Trails like Ptarmigan and Northwest Passage are moderately steep, if not quite long enough for my taste.

Mount Cranmore

North Conway, NH 03860. Tel. 603/356-5543; snow report, tel. 800/Sun-N-Ski. 30 trails (12 novice, 12 intermediate, 6 expert); 5 lifts including a triple and 4 doubles; 1,200-foot vertical drop. Full-day tickets $35 weekend, $19 weekday.

Another old-timer, Mount Cranmore was just bought out by the owners of Sunday River, so we can expect the mountain to compete with the other big boys in the future. At this point Cranmore's mostly a novice-to-intermediate hill.

Bretton Woods

U.S. 302, Twin Mountain, NH 03595. Tel. 603/278-5000; snow report, tel. 603/278-5051. 30 trails (9 novice, 13 intermediate, 8 expert); 5 lifts including a detachable quad, 1 triples, and 2 doubles; 1,500-foot vertical drop. Full-day tickets $36 weekend, $29 weekday for adults.

Bretton Woods is known for its calm wide-open style of skiing. Stunning views of the Mount Washington Resort and Hotel are found atop the mountain.

The Balsams

Dixville Notch, NH 03576. Tel. 603/869-5506; snow report, tel. 603/255-3400. 13 trails (4 novice, 6 intermediate, 3 expert); 4 lifts including one double; 1,000-foot vertical drop. Full-day tickets $25 weekend, $22 weekday.

If you're looking for a remote resort with rarely a line, head to one of the last grand resorts in the Whites, The Balsams in Dixville Notch. The skiing will strike not an ounce of fear into your heart, but that's not the point here. See "Resorts & Inns," below, for more information.

Mount Sunapee

Route 103, Mount Sunapee, NH 03772. Tel. 603/763-2356; snow report, tel. 603/763-4020. 36 trails (9 novice, 22 intermediate, 5 expert); 7 lifts including 3 triples and 3 doubles; 1,510-foot vertical drop. Full-day tickets $37 weekend, $31 weekday.

The finest ski area in the Lake Region is Mount Sunapee. Mostly intermediate skiing, but there are a few runs to test the restless.

FISHING

With so many lakes and ponds, the freshwater fishing in New Hampshire is superlative. In the Lakes Region, Lake Sunapee and Pleasant Lake are known for their abundance of lake trout, brook trout, and smallmouth bass. Anglers will find pickerel, bass, and perch in Perkins Pond and Otter Pond. The waters of Sugar River, Croydon, Long, and Lempster Ponds yield trout. Contact

Dickie's on Route 103 in South Newbury for other clandestine destinations (tel. 603/938-5393). Gadabout Golder Guide Service offers guided fishing trips. Contact Curt Golder at 603/569-6426.

In the western part of the state, brown and rainbow trout are caught in the Connecticut River. The White Mountain National Forest offers a guide to the best trout fishing in the Whites. Their headquarters are located at 719 Main Street, Laconia, NH 03247 (tel. 603/528-8721). Highlights include salmon fishing in Waterville Valley's Mad River, the East Branch of the Pemigewasset River near Lincoln, and the Saco and Swift Rivers close to Conway. North County Anglers, tel. 603/356-6000, offers trout and land-locked salmon tackle and information. They're located on Route 16, just north of North Conway.

Farther north, you're bound to see anglers fly-fishing or casting on the Androscoggin River, known for its abundance of trout. Lake Umbagog is good for brook trout and landlocked salmon.

On the coast, contact the Atlantic Fishing Fleet, Rye Harbor Marina, State Route 1A, Rye, NH 03870 (tel. 603-964-5220) to cast for saltwater fish. Anglers on their 70-foot party boat reel in cod, pollocks, and haddock. Around Hampton Beach, you can surfcast for blues and stripers.

GOLF

Consistently rated one of the top golf courses in the state by *Golf Digest* and other golfing publications, the Shattuck Inn Golf Course is situated on the mountainous slopes of Monadnock in the town of Jaffrey. All golfers, regardless of level, will find the par 71 course extremely challenging. Contact the inn in Jaffrey Center (tel. 603/532-4300). Here's a short list of other golf courses

in the state that Shattuck's pro, Lyman Doane, enjoys playing: the **Panorama Golf Course** (tel. 603/255-4961), located on the grounds of the Balsams in Dixville Notch. This course was designed by Donald Ross in 1912; the oceanside **Portsmouth Country Club** in Greenland (tel. 603/436-9719); the **Country Club of New Hampshire** (tel. 603/927-4246), a rarely crowded gem in North Sutton in western part of the state.

HANG GLIDING

Located on State Route 12 in western New Hampshire, just south of Claremont, Morningside Flight Park is the best place to learn how to hang glide in the Northeast. The 250-foot hill gently slopes to a big bull's-eye painted in the landing area, used for students to practice their spot landings. The hill is wide enough to accommodate 20 gliders side by side. Certified instruction is available by reservation only. Prices start at $85 for a four-hour bunny slope lesson. P.O. Box 109, Claremont, NH 03743 (tel. 603/542-4416).

HIKING

Time for a pop quiz. Don't worry, it's only one short SAT analogy question:

Hawaii: surfing

A) Maine: swimming
B) Vermont: whale watching
C) New Hampshire: hiking
D) Rhode Island: rock climbing

If you chose C, you're correct. Please collect your grade of 1600 and proceed to Harvard. Hawaii is one of America's premier surfing spots, New Hampshire is one of America's premier hiking locales. (For those of you who thought the correct answer was A, we recommend that you collect your diploma at the University of Maine in Orono. B is incorrect since "Champ" is not a whale. If you thought D was the answer, you have rocks in your head.)

Maine has its share of challenging hikes, Vermont has the rolling Green Mountains, and the Berkshires have Greylock, but no New England state can match the spectacular mountain scenery found in the White Mountains, nor can they offer the wide range of hikes available to all levels of expertise. From 5,000-foot high ridge walks to quick mountain ascents to soft springy paths that climb along a waterfall, New Hampshire has it all. So pull on those dirty mountain boots and get those thighs moving!

DAY HIKES IN THE WHITE MOUNTAINS

Falling Waters Trail/ Franconia Ridge/Old Bridle Path

8.7 miles. Allow 6–8 hours. Strenuous. Access: From Woodstock, take I-93 North to the Falling Waters/Bridle Path parking lot. Start the trail directly behind the parking lot. Map: Available at the Ammonoosuc Ranger District.

Tumbling streams and waterfalls, steep ascents to three of the highest peaks in New England, a 1.7-mile ridge walk where the spruce-studded White Mountains stand below you in a dizzying display—this is the Falling Waters/ Franconia Ridge/Old Bridle Path loop. When I say that this 8.7-mile trail is easily one of the most spectacular hikes in New England, I'm not using hyperbole. I'm also being sincere when I tell you that this loop is both popular and rigorous.

Turn into the woods from the parking lot and I-93's traffic is quickly replaced by the sounds of rushing water. Follow the Falling Waters Trail and the soothing waters will be your companion through the forest and over the stream for the next mile and a half. Within a mile, you'll reach the first of three picturesque waterfalls. The walk to the waterfalls makes a great hike in itself. When the path leaves the stream for good, the trail becomes steep and rocky, leading high up the mountainside to an alpine forest of firs and spruces. As you approach the 4,760-foot summit of Little Haystack Mountain, views of Cannon Mountain and Lonesome Lake open up. The vistas only get better when you reach the top and start walking on the Franconia Ridge Trail to the peaks of Mount Lincoln and Mount Lafayette, 5,108 and 5,249 feet, respectively. Part of the Appalachian Trail, this above-tree-line path offers a stunning panorama of New England's highest summits, including Mount Washington.

Follow the Greenleaf Trail down the steep rocks for a little over a mile to reach the Greenleaf Hut. Run by the AMC, this is the only place to refill your water bottle on the loop and get lemonade for 25 cents a glass. Continue your descent on the section of the Old Bridle Path known as Agony Ridge. This is the steepest part of the trail, where you jump from boulder to boulder and slide down sheets of rock. It's astonishing to think that this was once a horse trail. I wonder how many dead horses surround the Greenleaf Hut? At the open ledges, savor your most recent accomplishment by looking up at the eastern flank of Mount Lafayette, Franconia Ridge, and Walker Ravine. After about a mile, the trail becomes less rocky and more gradual as you make your way back through the hardwood forest to the junction of the Falling Waters Trail. After such an arduous trek, plunging into the cool waters of the stream is the best way to end the day.

The Appalachian Mountain Club

No book on New England outdoor recreation would be complete without a worthy introduction to the Appalachian Mountain Club (AMC). In 1876, 39 outdoor enthusiasts met in Boston and formed an organization devoted to exploration of the White Mountains. Several of the members had visited Europe and knew firsthand about Alpine huts—mountain refuges that sheltered hikers. They wanted to build this form of accommodation for the growing legions of avid "trampers." Twelve years later, dreams became reality when the stone Madison Spring cabin was opened in the col between Mount Adams and Mount Madison. The cost was 50 cents a night and you had to bring your own food. Lacking backpacks, hikers wrapped food and clothing in a blanket which was tied from shoulder to hip.

Three huts replete with cooking facilities were added to accommodate the steady stream of climbers who were coming to the White Mountains. New trails were eventually blazed, but it wasn't until Joe Dodge's arrival in 1922 that the current AMC began to take shape. Hired as the Pinkham Notch Hutmaster, Dodge arrived in the White Mountains when the huts weren't much more than a small and loosely joined foursome of rustic refuges. More than 30 years later, he left a unified chain of eight tightly run hostels that stretched over 50 miles of rugged wilderness. A tireless devotee of the mountains and the AMC, Dodge's gruff manner was cherished and respected by all who came in contact with him.

Three years after Joe Dodge retired in 1958, the AMC went through a third phase of development. In August of 1961, *National Geographic* published a 35-page article on "The Friendly Huts of the White Mountains." Authored by none other than Supreme Court Justice William O. Douglas, the publication reached 7 million readers—mass exposure the AMC was not capable of handling. By the summer of 1962, far more people were coming to the Whites than the AMC could possibly accommodate. Aside from expanding facilities and maintaining trails, the AMC started to offer hiker information and education services; workshops in natural history; outdoor schools; research on endangered species and the impact of hikers on the fragile ecosystem; and search-and-rescue missions for lost or injured climbers.

Today, the AMC has more than 60,000 members in the Northeast and is heavily involved in research, conservation, and education. They keep watch on the environment, testing mountain air for ground level ozone, visibility, reducing pollution, and acidity in cloudwater. The AMC takes a leading role in conservation issues ranging from the White Mountain National Forest to the 26 million acres of Northern Forest in New England and New York. They also host hundreds of educational workshops in the White Mountains, Acadia National Park, the Berkshires, and the Catskills. Courses range from mushroom identification and foraging to wilderness survival to mountain biking clinics. It's incredible what 39 people can accomplish in a small room in Boston!

Mount Willard

2.75 miles (round trip). Allow 1–2 hours. Easy. Access: From North Conway, take Route 16 North to U.S. 302 West up though Crawford Notch. Park at the Crawford Notch Visitor Center just next to the AMC hut. Map: USGS 7.5 minute Crawford Notch.

Ideal for young children and inexperienced hikers, Mount Willard is one of the easiest climbs in the White Mountains. If the thought of mountain climbing makes you sweat long before leaving your car to start your ascent, wipe your brow and give Willard a try. In less than an hour, you'll make it to the peak where jaw-dropping views of Crawford Notch stand below you, a reward for your accomplishment.

The hike begins behind the Crawford Notch Visitor Center, which is the old Crawford railroad station used by tourists in the early part of the century. The trail starts off steep but becomes more gradual as you criss-cross through the forest of dense pines. Eventually, sunshine will seep into the woods and you'll reach a large opening which is indeed "the light at the end of the tunnel." You have reached the 2,804-foot rocky summit where the vista of the surrounding mountainside will inevitably make you gasp. The old railroad line can be seen carved into the mountainside, superceded now by the onslaught of cars that make their way through the narrow pass on U.S. 302. The paved road slices the mountainside in two, with rocky ledges and verdant hills on either side. Mount Willard sits slightly off-center, offering expansive views of the whole panorama. After you pat yourself on the back for climbing one of the White Mountains, stroll back effortlessly to the Visitor Center.

Welch/Dickey Mountain Trail

4.5 miles. Allow 3 hours. Moderate. Access: From I-93, take Exit 28 and go east on Route 49 towards Waterville Valley. Turn left approximately 6 miles later, crossing a bridge and following Upper Mad River Road for 0.7 mile. At Orris Road, turn right and go 0.6 mile to the parking lot. Map: USGS 7.5 minute Waterville Valley. Available at the Pemigewasset Ranger District.

The short summits (relative to the rest of the White Mountains) of Welch and Dickie Mountains offer such majestic vistas that friends of mine got married atop this trail last September. That's not to say this 4.5-mile loop is easy. The bride decided to forego her traditional wedding gown for T-shirt, shorts, and hiking boots, and the groom wore a tuxedo jacket over his shorts. The trail leaves the parking area and enters a forest of beeches, maples, and oaks, before turning sharply to the right to reach the southern ridge of Welch Mountain. At 1.3 miles, you reach a broad exposed ledge that offers panoramic views of verdant Waterville Valley and the miniature cars weaving their way through the mountains on Route 49. However, this ledge is deceptive. The summit is 0.7 mile away, up a sheet of steep rock and over boulders where twisted jack pines and dwarf birches have been stunted by their exposure to the extreme climate. The 2,605-foot peak is a good place to stop, enjoy the view, and have lunch. Then proceed down into the col and steeply up 0.2 mile to the summit of Dickey Mountain (2,734 feet). Here, you can see the mountains that form the Franconia Ridge. The exquisite views continue for the next mile as you walk down the exposed ledge through patches of scrub spruce. Eventually you enter the woods again, where the trail becomes gradual. Don't be surprised to find a wedding reception back at the parking lot.

Zealand Trail

5.4 miles (round trip). 3 hours. Easy. Access: The Zealand Recreation Area is located 2.3 miles east of Twin Mountain on U.S. 302. Turn right at the Zealand Campground and continue on the road for 3.6 miles to its end at the Zealand Trail parking lot. Map: Available from the Ammonoosuc Ranger District.

If the numerous children under age 12 were any indication, the Zealand Trail is a great hike for young families. The easy 2.7-mile climb (one way) starts at an elevation over 2,000 feet and rises gently over 700 feet to the AMC Zealand Hut at the trail's end. Leave from the parking lot through a hardwood forest of red maples, beeches, and white birches. Webs of extended roots cover a forest floor that was decimated at the end of the 19th century by logging and fires. The trail, lined with yellow and white wildflowers in the summer, weaves along a brook where families stop on the rocks to picnic and swim. After you pass several beaver ponds, the forest opens up to the expansive Zealand Valley and Notch. The vistas are much better after the arduous 0.2-mile climb up to the Zealand Hut. Whitewall, Carrigan, Lowell, and Anderson Mountains can be seen from the steps of the wooden hut, which was built by Joe Dodge and company in 1931. Nearby, a waterfalls drops down the mountainside, providing the perfect place to ruminate with a glass of lemonade. If you're fortunate, you've booked a bunk in these idyllic surroundings overnight. If not, you have to return via the same trail you entered by.

Carter Notch

Allow 5–6 hours. Moderate to strenuous. Access: From North Conway, take State Route 16 North several miles past Pinkham Notch to a small parking lot on the right-hand side of the road. If you reach the Great Gulf parking lot, you went too far. Map: USGS 7.5 minute Carter Dome.

The 19-Mile Brook Trail leads to Carter Notch, a col situated between the dramatic ridges of Carter Dome and Wildcat "A." Here, you can spend the night at the AMC's oldest standing hut, a stone building constructed in 1914, perched just above two glacial lakes. Chris Costello, a former AMC employee and now head of outdoor recreation at the Stonehurst Manor, accompanied me on this 7.6-mile round-trip hike to the hut. We headed in from Route 16 and started our uphill climb along the brook, soon reaching a small aqueduct a mile into the hike. Along the way, Chris pointed out several types of indigenous flora like the "Indian Pipe," a small white flower whose bulb has no chlorophyll, and the Clintonia, a green-leafed plant named after DeWitt Clinton, which sports blue berries in the summertime.

The trail splits at the 1.8-mile mark, veering left to the top of Carter Dome or straight to Carter Notch. We crossed the bridge and continued our ascent to the notch, the trail becoming steeper at the higher altitudes. The northern hardwood forest was soon replaced by a boreal forest of sweet-smelling spruces and firs. This is where Chris taught me one of the most important things I've learned since my father clued me into "Righty Tighty, Lefty Loosey" (the trick to screwing or unscrewing any cap). To tell the difference between a spruce and a fir, you have to shake its hand. "Spruces are spikey, firs are friendly" (soft to the grip). The final 0.3 mile of the trail snake down between the two ridges and the majestic glacial lakes to the old hut. Inside the cozy walls, several hikers who were walking the Appalachian Trail in its entirety were talking to each other in their own distinct language laced with hiker's nicknames.

"Have you seen Sam-I-Am, Trail-bunny, or Bushmaster," said one of the through-hikers, referring to three other ATers.

"I passed them back at Pinkham," replied another long-bearded and strong-legged climber.

We had a lunch of homemade dip, crackers, and brownies, before Chris took me on a side trip to the Rampart. Large rocks sit precariously atop Carter Dome, waiting to fall down the ridge to add to the pile of glacial detritus, a mass of boulders ideal for hopping and easy rock climbing. Eventually, we had to walk back down to Route 16, wishing we could spend an extra day at the hut to take some more hikes through this vast wilderness. The ATers were certainly in no rush.

Basin-Cascades Trail

2.5 miles (round trip). Allow 2 hours. Easy to moderate. Access: Take I-93 north of Woodstock and look for the signs to The Basin parking lot. Map: USGS 7.5 minute Franconia, available at the Ammonoosuc Ranger District.

One of the most meditative spots in New England is atop the Basin-Cascades Trail. Choose a rock in the middle of Cascade Brook and listen to the waters forcibly tumble, foam, and swirl down the mountainside. You reach this tranquil spot by walking along the rolling brook for a mile. Start with the crowds at the Basin down at the bottom. The Basin is a granite pool 30 feet

wide and 15 feet deep. Called a pothole by geologists, this strange cavity was formed by a melting ice sheet 15,000 years ago. When Thoreau saw the Basin in 1839 he stated that, "this pothole is perhaps the most remarkable curiosity of its kind in New England." Stroll uphill and you'll find the large sign for the Basin-Cascades Trail. A web of extended roots jutting out from hemlock, maple, beech, and yellow birch trees combine with the ubiquitous White Mountain rock to make maneuvering tricky at times. The trail meanders along the brook, passing Kinsman Falls, before crossing the rocks to reach the far side. Soon you'll reach Rocky Glen Falls and a chasm of rock that forms a chute up to the top of the trail. Here, the stress of modernity is flushed away with the falling waters. You can make a four- or five-hour loop by turning right and venturing to Lonesome Lake, continuing on the Lake Trail to Lafayette Campground, and turning right on the Pemi Trail back to the Basin.

Table Rock

Under 2 miles (round trip). Allow 2 hours. Steep, moderate-to-strenuous climb. Access: The steep 0.3 mile trailhead is located on Route 26, on the downhill portion of the Dixville Notch pass, just before reaching the Balsams from the east. The more gradual trail to the rocks is also located on Route 26, a half mile down the road on the left, just past the Balsams. Map: USGS 7.5 minute Dixville Notch.

If you're fortunate enough to be staying at the Balsams, the two trails that lead up to Table Rock offer exquisite views of this historic resort, manmade Lake Gloriette, and the sharp ledges and hills that form craggy Dixville Notch. I usually take the 0.3-mile trail straight up the rocky slope and come down on the more gradual path that leaves me a half-mile away from my car on Route 26. However, you should have good hiking boots since the trail up is an extremely steep, gravel-strewn path that tends to be slippery. You'll often have to grab on to tree roots to pull yourself up. Table Rock is a ledge that sits like a gangplank over the sheer walls of rock that form Dixville Notch. If you're not scared of heights, this is a good place to have lunch and peer over the cliffs to Route 26 below. To find the easy downhill path, simply go uphill a short way until you see a campfire site, turn right, and descend.

DAY HIKES IN THE LAKE REGION & SOUTHERN NEW HAMPSHIRE

Mount Monadnock

4 miles round trip. Allow 3 hours. Easy to moderate. Access: Follow State Route 124 West through Jaffrey Center and look for the signs for the Monadnock State Park headquarters. The trailhead is located in front of the visitor center. Map: Ask one of the rangers when you drive in to the state park.

Mount Monadnock has been a popular ascent since the early 1800s. Monadnock has recently surpassed Mount Fuji as the most hiked mountain in the world. The rocky summit can be as crowded as Hampton Beach on a clear day. Standing only 3,165 feet high, Monadnock is the perfect introduction to mountain climbing—high enough to give you a sense of accomplishment, short enough to inspire you to hike another New Hampshire peak.

The well-trodden White Dot Path rises above the tree line less than 45 minutes after leaving the State Park

visitor center. Southern New Hampshire and northern Massachusetts are a bed of green, accentuated by the sporadic hill or small pond. This sharply differs from Thoreau's view of endless pasture and little hardwoods when he made the ascent in 1858 and 1860. Leave the dusty trail behind and start to meander up Monadnock's rocky slope to the bald peak. The view from the summit is a spectacular panorama of New Hampshire's far less precipitous lower half. Thousands of names are inscribed in the summit rocks from as far back as 1801, representing one of the earliest examples of American graffiti. This abuse greatly annoyed Thoreau. "Several (visitors) were busy engraving their names on the rocks with cold chisels, whose incessant click you heard, and they had but little leisure to look off." However, this didn't stop Thoreau from writing in large letters atop a massive rock "H.D.T. ate gorp here, 1860." Just kidding. You can return on the same trail or try the steeper White Cross Trail to complete the loop.

Red Hill

3.5 miles (round trip). Allow 2 hours. Easy. Access: From Center Harbor on the northern shores of Lake Winnipesaukee, take Bean Road for 1.5 miles to the sign for Red Hill Forest. Turn right and drive for 1.25 miles to the parking area and trailhead. Map: USGS 7.5 minute Center Harbor.

The trail up Red Hill is rather plain and uninteresting. A former wagon trail, the dry, wide path is a steady uphill climb, slowly curving as you begin to reach the top. The surrounding red oaks are charred and leafless near the summit, a result of forest fires, the most recent in 1990. Thus, nothing prepares you for the sight you'll see 1.75 miles and less than

Bullwinkle and Company

All along the routes of northern New Hampshire, you'll see signs for moose crossings and other signs that state "Please Brake for Moose, 193 Collisions." At sunrise or sunset, seeing a moose is a definite possibility, especially near the Androscoggin River from Berlin to Errol. Surprisingly, you'll also see bumper stickers on cars and trucks that read, "Don't brake for moose, fill your freezer." This statement is referring to a law in New Hampshire that says if you hit a moose or deer on the road and the animal is killed, you are entitled to bring home the animal. That's one way to deal with road kill.

Well, as one local recounted to me, the police were called to an unfortunate accident between driver and deer. The unharmed driver, seeing that the deer was killed, asked the officer if he could drive the deer back to his home. Seeing that the driver was riding in a compact car, the officer inquired as to where he was going to put the deer. "In my back seat," the man responded as he started to drag the animal in. An hour later, another police officer responded to an accident and it just so happened that it was the same driver. The man had hit a tree and was knocked unconscious. The officer opened the back seat of the car, only to find scratches all over the interior, and the deer barely breathing. The animal was not quite dead after all.

Moral of story: Hitting a wild animal can have *deer* consequences! Drive with a degree of caution—a collision with a moose is often fatal to the driver—and if you do have the misfortune of hitting a deer or moose, don't take the supposedly dead animal home unless you have a truck.

an hour later when you pass the fire warden's cabin sitting atop the peak. The western shores of Lake Winnipesaukee gleam under the slopes of Mount Major and Belknap Mountain. Climb the four flights of stairs to the top of the fire tower, for, arguably, the most spectacular view of the Lakes Region. Winnipesaukee can be seen in its entirety. To your right, smaller Squam Lake sits below Rattlesnake Mountain. Behind you is the village of Sandwich and the Sandwich Range, the southernmost tip of the White Mountains. On your left are the mountains of the Ossipee Range. Everywhere you turn, each view of mountains and lakes seems more stunning than the last. Who would have thought that such a dull, short ascent would reward you with one of the most incredible views in New Hampshire?

Lake Solitude

4–7 miles round trip. Allow 3 hours. Easy. Access: From Newbury and the southern end of Lake Sunapee, follow Route 103 South for one mile to Mountain Road. Turn right for 1.2 miles; there's a small parking area and trail sign on the right. Map: USGS 7.5 x 15 minute Newport.

Lake Solitude is an apt name for the lonely lake that sits on the slopes of Mount Sunapee, isolated by a thick forest from the rest of the world. There are no crowded beaches here—just the occasional frog jumping from lilypad to lilypad. To reach the lake, you need to climb 2 miles on the soft, gradual An-drew Brook Trail. Beeches and birches soon give way to the fragrant smell of spruces and firs. Sun starts to seep through as the forest opens up onto the shores of this quiet lake. You can con-tinue around the lake and up the White Ledges on the orange-blazed trail to the peak of Sunapee. Add 3 miles and two more hours for this round trip. Since the aerial tram brings throngs of tourists to the summit, I prefer to stop at Soli-tude, cool off in the icy waters, and return on the same trail. The sound of one person swimming in a large lake is as peaceful as the sound of one hand clapping.

OVERNIGHT & LONG-DISTANCE HIKES

Vermont has the Long Trail and Maine has its Hundred Mile Wilderness, but if I wanted to backpack for a week or less, I'd choose the Whites. The expansive forest offers a diverse network of soft, spongy, and root-studded trails. Notches, those sheer walls of granite that rise sharply from the forest floor, form narrow gaps that dwarf the back-packer. Domes, gorges, and bald ridges offer hikers spectacular above-tree-line views.

Between Crawford Notch and the Franconia Range, miles of trails slice through the high mountains and remote ponds of the Pemigewasset Wilderness. The region is popular for three-to-five-day hikes. East of Gorham, the Appala-chian Trail crosses the New Hampshire border into Maine, offering strenuous backpacking through the Mahoosuc Range.

If you want to do some serious hik-ing in the day, but don't want to rough it at night, consider hut-to-hut hiking. The Appalachian Mountain Club operates eight mountain cabins—rustic accom-modations with crews that offer two hot meals a day. All you need to bring in the summertime are sheets or a lightweight sleeping bag. The huts are strung along 56 miles of the Appalachian Trail, a day's hike apart. For more information, con-tact the AMC, 5 Joy Street, Boston, MA 02108 (tel. 617/523-0636).

OUTFITTERS

There's no better scenario than having owners of an outfitter run trips in their own home town. That's exactly the situ-ation with Clare and Kurt Grabher, own-ers of New England Hiking Holidays, who happen to live in the midst of the White Mountains in North Conway. Clare and Kurt know the trails of the White Mountains better than most park rangers. If you are planning to book an outfitter in the finest region for hiking in New England, than look no further than New England Hiking Holidays, PO Box 1648, North Conway, NH 03860 (tel. 603/356-9696 or 800/869-0949). They also run a tennis school known as Tennis Holidays.

Walking the World 50 Plus offers an eight-day tour of the Whites for people over 50. I hope you had your Wheaties, because the trip includes a trek up to Mount Washington. P.O. Box 1186, Frot Collins, CO 80522 (tel. 800/340-9255).

HORSEBACK RIDING

In the White Mountains, the **Mount Washington Hotel**, U.S. 302, Bretton Woods (tel. 603/278-1000), **Mittersill Riding Stable,** Route 18, Franconia (tel. 603/823-5511), **Loon Mountain Park,** Kancamangus Highway, Lincoln (tel. 603/745-8111) and **Waterville Valley Resort** (tel. 603/236-8311) all offer guided rides and instruction. Contact **Castle Springs**, Route 171, Moulton-borough (tel. 800/729-2468) for horse-back rides in the Lakes Region.

ICE CLIMBING

Huntington Ravine, on the slopes of Mount Washington, is the most popular place to ice climb in New England. It's only a one-and-a-half hour climb with crampons to get to the base of the ravine. The rest is up to you and your winter mountaineering skills.

Rick Wilcox, owner of International Mountain Equipment, operates the biggest ice climbing and rock climbing school in the eastern United States out of North Conway (tel. 603/356-6316).

ICE FISHING

Favorite freshwater fishing holes in the summer are equally popular in the winter months (see "Fishing," above). You won't find locals wearing polypropylene, thinsulate, or Gore-Tex, but I'd highly recommend all three for a frigid afternoon on a pond.

KAYAKING

Tim Morrison and **Andy O'Shaughnessy** offer kayak rentals and instruction on the waters of Lake Winnipesaukee and other nearby lakes. They're located on Route 109 in Melvin (tel. 603/544-3905).

MOUNTAIN BIKING

Over the past five years, the phrase "mountain biking" has been used rather loosely. Any trail that is off-road, whether it be a wide dirt road or a double-track in a flat state forest, is suddenly termed *Mountain* Biking. Sorry to bust your bubble, but the word mountain implies that you are riding on a large hill that surges upward from the depths of the forest. This is what makes riding in the White Mountains so invigorating. Whether you are riding on a fire road over streams or on a single-track that skirts the ridge of a summit, the term is appropriate for the Whites. And believe it or not, riding in the hills can be much easier than riding through the notches on a road bike.

Bartlett Experimental Forest

Allow 2 hours. Moderate. Access: From North Conway, take Route 16 North to U.S. 302. Turn left onto Bear Notch Road and go uphill until you find two large boulders on the left hand side of the road. There's a small area to park here. Map: Available at Red Jersey Cyclery, U.S. 302, Glen (tel. 603/383-4440).

In a region where off-road riding excels, the trails that weave up and down the Bartlett Experimental Forest are the crème de la crème. Miles of trails which snowmobilers have created in the winter time are remarkably maintained by biking fairy godmothers come spring. Kevin Killourie, avid mountain biker and owner of Red Jersey Cyclery in Glen, recommended one particular trail he enjoys riding in these woods. I immediately understood why, once I parked my car at the boulders and cruised downhill across a shallow stream. Crossing water with a bike is comparable to viewing a shark when scuba diving—leaving in its wake a thrilling feeling of freedom and an adrenaline high for the rest of the day. The springy single-track trail gradually made its way downhill through the dense blanket of pines, crossing another stream, then veering right before the third stream. I followed the orange blazes for the reminder of the ride, an exhilarating run down the mountainside to U.S. 302. However, I now had to go against the laws of gravity and make my way back up. The going was slow, but not as strenuous as expected. I eventually made it back to my car and, for a brief moment, contemplated cruising down the trail once again. That was a very brief moment.

For you wimps who can't handle the uphill portion of this ride, Attitash will shuttle you over to the same trailhead where you can cruise back down to their ski area. Cost is $5 (tel. 603/374-2368).

Ridgepole Trail

Allow 2 hours. Strenuous. Access: From I-93, take Exit 25, veering left onto Route 175 North. About 5 miles later, you'll see a large bear in front of a gift shop. Turn right on Perch Pond Road and continue on the gravel road for 3.3 miles until you see a pond on the left. Park here. Map: USGS 7.5 minute Squaw Mountains, available at the Pemigewasset Ranger District.

Experienced fat wheelers will savor the opportunity to ride the Ridgepole Trail. Nestled in the Sandwich Mountain Range, this single-track offers some of the finest technical riding in the White Mountains. If you have never cruised down the side of a mountain with a relatively steep grade, I would not recommend this trail. Your lunch might consist of a dirt sandwich stuffed with dry rocks.

For the first 2.8 miles, I rode easily up and down Perch Pond's gravel road. At the bottom of a hill, I turned left onto Mountain Road for 0.2 mile. When the road veered right, I continued straight on the grassy double-tracks for a grueling half-mile uphill run. At the top of the slope, I turned left at a yellow sign indicating the Crawford Ridgepole Trail. Almost immediately this tough single-track tested my skills, slicing up and down the mountain over rocks, roots, and mud. Hairpin turns made maneuvering that much harder. At the 5-mile mark, the yellow-blazed trail cruised along a ridge offering spectacular views

of Squam Lake and the Red Hill fire tower in the distance. I got another sight of the lake a mile later, before the trail turned back to the alpine forest, weaving in and out of the firs and balsams; 1.1 miles after that (7.1 miles total), I veered left onto the blue-blazed Cascade Trail for one of the most thrilling and challenging downhill rides I've ever been on. I slid down sheets of rock, jumped extended roots that were impossible to avoid, and almost came to a complete stop in a mud basin as I was speeding down the mountain. Still in one piece, I reached a set of grassy double-tracks that led back to Perch Pond Road and the pond itself. I turned right to reach my car and complete the 8.6-mile loop. Caked in sweat, mud, and dry dirt, I entered the waters of the pond for a therapeutic bathing.

Boulder Path to Greeley Pond Trail

Allow 2 hours. Easy to moderate. Access: Start in Waterville Valley by the Base Camp. Map: Available at the Pemigewasset Ranger District.

The trail to Greeley Pond was suggested by one of my mountain biking buddies for novice riders. I cruised around the tennis courts and veered left onto Greeley Hill Road. This brought me to Snow Mountain's ski trails. I rode on several trails across the mountainside, slid through mud down a hill, and was suddenly at the rushing waters of a stream. A well-trod hiking and biking trail along the water led me to an immense boulder in the middle of the stream. I learned later that I was on the "Boulder Path." I crossed the stream onto gravel Livermore Road, turned left, and soon found the sign for Greeley Trail. This rocky and level double-track goes straight for 3 or 4 miles to a pond popular with fisherman. However, I soon grew bored with the trail's lack of incline and turned around. I made my way back to Waterville Valley the same way I came . . . or relatively close to it.

Bretton Woods Summer Park

Allow 45 minutes. Strenuous. Access: From North Conway, follow U.S. 302 North. The large sign for Bretton Woods is on the left-hand side of the road. Map: Available at the ski area.

Many of the ski resorts in the northeast are now offering mountain biking in the warmer months. I tried one of these runs at Bretton Woods, in the heart of the White Mountains. Going up on the lift with my bike, I glanced at the trail map and decided to check out "Two Mile Run," a trail that seemed to gradually slope down the southeastern side of the mountain. The lift left me off at the restaurant atop the mountain where I had incredible views of Mount Washington and the sparkling white Mount Washington Hotel nestled in the valley below. I cruised under the restaurant and started to pick up speed as I headed down to "Two Mile Run." Small gullies and large patches of mud kept me alert. I turned left on what I thought was "Two Mile Run"—suddenly I'm flying down the side of the mountain, my knuckles turning the color of snow as they clutch the brakes. Every now and then I would hit a gully and go airborne, praying that my Trek 950 would somehow manage to land upright and not leave me in a ditch. I had visions of my bike sliding down the mountain like one of those old Westerns, in which the horse returns to the lodge without the dead owner. I made it back to the base far quicker than on the lift up. This type of mountain biking is only for the intrepid.

Bretton Woods Ski Area, U.S. 302, Bretton Woods (tel. 603/278-5000).

Rob Brook Road

Allow 3 hours. Easy. Access: From Conway, take the Kancamagus Highway or Route 112 to your first right turn onto Bear Notch Road. Start going uphill; just past the houses, you'll see a sign for biking and hiking on the left-hand side of the road. This is Rob Brook Road or Fire Road 35. Park along Bear Notch Road. Map: Available at Red Jersey Cyclery, U.S. 302, Glen (tel. 603/383-4440).

Mountain biking is a far better choice than road biking in the White Mountains, especially for families. Traffic is unrelenting during high-peak season, and many of the long uphill climbs through the mountainous passes are a challenge to the most experienced biker. The fire roads in the hills above the Kanc offer children a chance to ride in the Whites. Rob Brook Road is a wide gravel road that rolls gently through the forest, eventually making its way to Swift River. Along the way, you'll have numerous opportunities to stop and take in the panoramic vistas of the verdant valley below.

Great Glen in Gorham (tel. 603/466-2333) also offers easy to moderate mountain biking on their network of paths, which resemble carriage path trails.

Sunapee Railroad Bed

7.2 miles. Allow 1–2 hours. Easy. Access: From the Rosewood Inn, turn right and drive for 0.9 mile on Pleasant View Road to South Road. Turn right and drive 1.3 miles, just past a group of boulders on the right. Park on the left-hand side just past the double-tracks.

This ride follows a former railroad bed carved out of the hills of the Lake Sunapee region. Park your car and look for a grassy double-track that leads straight through a forest of birches, beeches, oaks, and maples. You'll cross over several wooden bridges and fallen logs before continuing across a dirt road on the same trail. At the 1.5-mile mark, veer left onto a dirt road for another 1.1 miles. Blackberries were ripe for picking when I rode through here in August. You can still see walls of rock and cement pylons, remnants of the railroad that last traveled through here in 1961. Cross over paved Mountain Road and continue on double-tracks for the best part of the ride—a short cruise through a granite chasm of rock. Silver mica flickers in the darkness, guiding your way through the narrow tunnel. When the pass was blasted out with nitroglycerin in the 1870s, it took almost a year to finish. Continue for another half-mile past the lumber yard to reach the Lake Sunapee Trading Post and the southern shores of Lake Sunapee. Picnic tables overlooking the lake are a good place to indulge in the Trading Post's own brand of root beer and their specialty, Uncle Buck's Hickory Smoked Teriyaki Venison Jerky (low in fat). A couple strips of this and you'll be ready to return by the same route back through the narrow chasm to your car.

POWERBOATING

Wolfeboro Marina, Bay Street, Wolfeboro (tel. 603/569-3200), **Anchor Marine,** Winnipesaukee Pier, Weir's Beach (tel. 603/366-4311), and **Meredith Marina,** Bay Shore Drive, Meredith Bay, Meredith (tel. 603/279-7921) all rent motorboats on Lake Winnipesaukee. **Sargents Marine,** Route 11 (tel. 603/763-5032) rents boats on Lake Sunapee.

ROAD BIKING

The best road biking in New Hampshire is in the south near the Massachusetts border, or west near the Vermont border. The closer you get to the White Mountains, the more strenuous the riding becomes. Steep one- to two-thousand foot climbs are the norm, challenging the best-conditioned bikers. However, if you are still intent on riding in the mountains, I would suggest the 36-mile Bear Notch Loop.

Cyclists in Lake Winnipesaukee will often wake up at 6 AM and ride 31 miles around the lake to Weir's Beach. Here, they'll catch the M/S Mount Washington ferry back to Wolfeboro. Contact Nordic Skier Sport, Main Street, Wolfeboro (tel. 603/569-3151) for all your road and mountain biking information in the Lakes Region. If you're venturing to the western part of the state, try the Upper Connecticut River ride (see "Road Biking" in the Southern Vermont chapter).

RIDES IN AND NEAR THE WHITE MOUNTAINS

Bear Notch Loop

36 miles. Strenuous, with a fairly abrupt 1,400-foot rise in elevation. Access: Start on Main Street in North Conway, near Eastern Mountain Sports.

From Eastern Mountain Sports, turn left on River Road down to the Saco River. Just after you pass the river, River Road merges with West Side Road. Head north on this road for 5.6 miles, through Glen, to U.S. 302. Veer left (west) and ride for another 4.1 miles to the blinking light in Bartlett. Turn left at Bear Notch Road for your mountain climb. The road rises from 600 to 2,000 feet in approximately 5 miles before descending to the Kancamagus Highway. At the T-junction, turn left onto the Kanc and ride 6 miles to the covered bridge at Blackberry Crossing. Turn left through the bridge and then right onto Dugway Road for 6.1 miles. At the junction of

Allen Siding, turn left, cross the railroad tracks, and turn left again to meet up with West Side Road. Pedal 5.6 miles to River Road, veering right to return to North Conway.

Outer Conway Loop

Allow 2–3 hours. Moderate; hilly terrain. Access: From North Conway, take State Route 16 to the junction of State Route 153 in Conway. Turn left at Route 153 South and turn right almost immediately into the Pleasant Street Plaza parking lot. Park behind the bank.

As you approach the Maine border from Conway, rolling hills replace the towering heights of the Whites. Park your car and turn right onto Route 153 South, following a small brook to one of New Hampshire's many small lakes, Crystal Lake. Who would have known that a majestic swimming hole lies just minutes from the crowds of North Conway? Turn left at the beach on Brownfield Road, up through a forest of firs and spruces. You'll pass by several beaver ponds and Hart Brook Farm, whose picture-perfect barn stands alone amid thousands of acres of crops. Entering Maine, turn left at the sign for North Conway, just past the white house with red roof. Views of the White Mountains start to open up on the right as you approach the shores of Conway Lake on your left. Turn left on U.S. 302 to ride through the village of Center Conway. Continue west on State Route 113 to the junction of State Route 153 to complete this 23-mile ride.

RIDES IN SOUTHERN NEW HAMPSHIRE

Covered Bridge Loop

Allow 2 hours. Easy; relatively flat terrain. Access: From Keene, take State Route 12 South to State Route 32 South to Swanzey. At the junction of State Route 32 and Sawyers Crossing Road, park at either Mount Caesar School or the Monadnock Regional High School.

The southwest corner of New Hampshire is a relatively flat, very quiet place of woods, farmland, college towns, and most notably, covered bridges. These wooden relics of yesteryear still stand as testament to simpler times. This 18-mile loop rides through four of the covered bridges on quiet country roads. Head south on State Route 32 for 1.5 miles till you reach Carlton Road. Turn left and you'll soon pass through covered bridge numero uno. First built in 1869, the Carlton Road Bridge uses a lattice of X-shaped wooden crosses to hold the ceiling in place. Then, 1.1 miles from the junction of State Route 32 and Carlton Road, turn right at the T-junction onto Webber Hill Road. You'll swing downhill past the East Swanzey Post Office, where you'll meet up with State Route 32 again. Veer right for 0.1 mile to Swanzey Lake Road where you turn left. This 3.9-mile ride brings you past Swanzey Lake. For views of the water, turn right onto West Shore Drive; otherwise, continue straight between the houses, farms, and small towns to Westport Road. Turn left and ride 0.8 mile to a stop sign on Main Street. Another left will bring you to the junction of Route 10. Veer left for a mere 0.3 mile to reach Coombs Road, where you turn right for covered bridge number two. Built in 1837, the 118-foot Coombs Bridge spans the Ashuelot River.

Retrace your trail back to Main Street, turn right and go for 0.7 mile, bearing right again on Westport Road for an additional 2.4 miles. This brings you to a three-way stop at the intersection of Christian Hill Road. Turn left through the quaint village of West Swanzey to reach my favorite bridge on the trip, the

Thompson Bridge. One of the two sidewalks still remains from the original construction (1832). To reach the final bridge, turn right on Winchester Road immediately after the Thompson Bridge. At the junction of Route 10, turn right for 0.6 mile and be cautious of the traffic. A right turn on Sawyers Crossing Road will eventually bring you to Sawyers Crossing Bridge, the longest of the four bridges. Continue straight to a stop sign and turn left on Eaton Road. This will bring you back to the two high schools.

ROCK CLIMBING

With an official nickname like "The Granite State," you know New Hampshire has to be a popular rock-climbing destination. The Whites' numerous granite outcroppings and sheer faces of rock have steadily earned respect as one of the top rock climbing destinations in the country. Heights might not be as impressive as in the Western mountains, but the thrill of climbing a vertical ridge thousands of feet above the forest floor is just as exhilarating. Many of the climbs are only five or ten minutes from the road, making the sport extremely accessible. Cathedral Ledge, Whitehorse Ledge, and Cannon Cliffs are known to challenge even the most adroit rock climber.

If you have never rock climbed or would like to improve your level of competence, contact **Rick Wilcox** at **International Mountain Equipment Climbing School,** in North Conway (tel. 603/356-6316). Rick is legendary in these parts for his work on search-and-rescue squads and for accomplishing the mountain climber's ultimate goal, to reach the peak of Mount Everest. The school is the largest of its kind in eastern United States.

SAILING

The **Sailing Center** on Squam Lake, U.S. 3, Holderness (tel. 603/968-3654) rents Phantoms, Force 5s, and 17-foot Daysailers by the half day, day, or week.

SCUBA DIVING

Dive Winnipesaukee, Main Street, Wolfeboro (tel. 603/569-8080) offers daily two-tank dives around the lake. Unusual rock formations and wrecks are found 30 to 40 feet below the surface. One of the wrecks, *Lady of the Lake*, is a 125-foot steamboat that sank in 1894. Remarkably, the cold waters of the lake have even preserved the paint. On Fridays, there's a special $5 charter.

SNOWMOBILING

Hundreds of miles of snowmobile trails criss-cross the White Mountains all the way to Maine, Vermont, and Quebec. Popular areas include **Mount Clinton Road** near Crawford Notch, **Twin Mountain,** and **Zealand Road** in Zealand Valley. Snowmobiling is a way of life in northern New Hampshire, especially in the towns of **Colebrook** and **Pittsburg** on the Vermont border. Check with the **Trails Bureau,** New Hampshire Division of Parks and Recreation, P.O. Box 856, Concord, NH 03301 (tel. 603/271-3254) and the New Hampshire Snowmobile Association, PO Box 38, Concord, NH 03301 (tel. 603/224-8906) for detailed maps.

SNOWSHOEING

The **Nineteen Mile Trail** to Carter Notch will give you a good snowshoeing workout in the winter. There are also guided tours to **Mount Washington's** summit during the brisk winter months.

Call Rick Wilcox or Nick Yardley at **International Mountain Equipment**, North Conway (tel. 603/356-6316). For more information, contact the **White Mountain National Forest**, 719 Main Street, Laconia, NH 03247 (tel. 603/528-8721).

SWIMMING

The best remedy for an arduous hike is the crisp waters of a lake, pond, or stream. Any body of water will do. My favorite swimming hole in the White Mountains was **Perch Pond,** simply because it was sitting there after the I took the Ridgepole mountain bike trail. However, if you're yearning for sand, try **Ellacoya State Beach**, the only state beach in Winnipesaukee (Route 11, Gilford), **Sunapee State Park Beach** on the shores of the lake (Route 103, three miles west of Newbury), and **Wadleigh State Beach** on Kezar Lake in Sutton (just off Route 114).

The hundreds of swimming holes include **Profile Falls,** a small natural pool under a 40-foot waterfall (U.S. 3A, 2.5 miles south of Bristol), the rocks of **Lower Falls Scenic Area** on the Kancamagus Highway, and **Jackson Falls** in Jackson.

Campgrounds & Other Accommodations

CAMPING

The vast array of New Hampshire campgrounds ranges from primitive sites with few amenities to full-service areas with all the modern comforts of a hotel room. State and White Mountain National Forest campgrounds operate on a first-come, first-serve basis. However, several of the National Forest sites accept reservations 120 days or less in advance, but 14 days before arrival is the minimum time (tel. 800/280-2267). Those campgrounds are **Campton, Waterville,** and **Russell Pond** off I-93, **Covered Bridge** off the **Kancamagus Highway, Sugarloaf I and II** in Twin Mountain, **Dolly Copp** in Pinkham Notch, **Basins, Cold River,** and **Hastings** in Evans Notch, and **White Ledge** in Conway. For more information, write or call the **New Hampshire Campground Owners' Association,** PO Box 320, Twin Mountain, NH 03595 (tel. 603/846-5511) for their directory of 171 private, state, and national forest campgrounds.

Backcountry camping is permitted in most areas of the White Mountain National Forest; the usual exclusions are within 200 feet of streams, lakes, or trails, and within a quarter-mile of roads and designated campsites.

If you want to upgrade from tents to bunk beds, the **Appalachian Mountain Club,** P.O. Box 298, Gorham, NH 03581 (tel.603/466-2727) has two lodges in Pinkham and Crawford Notch, in addition to their eight high huts. The rustic **Pinkham Notch** facility accommodates 106 guests and offers family style meals in the Main Lodge. The **Shapleigh Hostel** in Crawford Notch accommodates 28 people and is replete with self-service kitchen. Bring sleeping bags or sheets and food.

Sugarloaf I and II and Zealand

Access: From the junction of Routes 3 and 302 in Twin Mountain, head 2.3 miles east on U.S. 302. At Zealand Recreation Area, follow signs for 0.5 mile. Tel. 603/869-2626. 73 sites. No hookups, tables, fire rings, or grills.

These campgrounds are conveniently located for hikers, snowmobilers, and cross-country skiers who want to venture into the Zealand Valley.

Dolly Copp Campground

Access: From the junction of Routes 2 and 16, go 6 miles southwest on Route 16. Tel. 603/466-2713. 180 sites, no hookups, tables, fire rings.

These sites are near the network of trails at Pinkham Notch.

Lafayette Campground, Franconia Notch State Park

Located off I-93, no northbound access. Exit at sign for Lafayette Campground. Tel. 603/823-5563. 97 sites are located in the heart of Franconia Notch. No hookups, handicap rest room facilities, public phone, limited grocery store, ice, tables, grills, wood.

This is good starting-off point for the Falling Waters and Basin-Cascades hikes.

Umbagog Lake

Access: From the junction of Routes 16 and 26 in Errol, head 7 miles southeast on Route 26. 60 sites, some on small islands which can be reached by canoe or boat. 30 sites with water and electricity, 30 with no hookups; public phone, limited grocery store, ice, tables, fire rings, and wood. $18–$22 per family. Umbagog Lake Campground and Cottages, PO Box 181, Errol, NH 03579 (tel. 603/482-7795).

This is one of the more peaceful spots in New Hamsphire (see "Canoeing").

Pillsbury State Park

Access: The park is located 3.5 miles north of Washington on U.S. 31. Tel. 603/

863-2860. 20 sites, no hookups, pit toilets, tables, fire rings, and wood. Daily fees for most of the campgrounds in the range of $7–$9 per person.

Located in the Lakes Region, on the shores of May Pond.

RESORTS & INNS

The Balsams

Dixville Notch, NH 03576. Tel. 603/255-3400. Rates start at $149 per night per person, including lodging, meals, and all sports amenities—even the golf course and skiing.

There are so many reasons why The Balsams is in a class by itself that I have to list them:

♦ **Location.** 15,000 acres stare up at jagged Dixville Notch, one of the most majestic sights in New England.

♦ **History.** The 131-year-old resort is one of the last Grand Dames in existence.

♦ **Sports.** The Panorama golf course, clay and all-weather tennis courts, and 75-plus km of ski trails all consistently gain high marks in sports magazines.

♦ **Food.** Rating four stars from the Mobil Guide, the food is exceptional, service impeccable. The copious amount of food includes a large breakfast, lunch buffets, and six-course dinners.

♦ **Grounds.** Manicured lawns and colorful gardens slope down to the swimming pool and Lake Gloriette. Hummingbirds whiz by on their way to the bird feeders.

I could go on and on, but that's another book. Mountain biking has just been implemented on the cross-country trails, the downhill slopes have few lines, the resort bottles its own spring water, and they even found a way to eradicate black flies to make hiking and biking enjoyable in the summer. Like a fine wine, this resort just gets better with time.

Stonehurst Manor

Route 16, North Conway, NH 03860-1937. Tel.603/356-3271. Costs for two nights, one day of hiking, including all meals and guide services, is $154 per person weekday, $164 weekend. Packages range from two to five nights. The two-night, one-day Mount Washington hike in winter costs $321 including all meals, guide, and equipment.

Stonehurst owner Peter Rattay has created a Great Outdoor Program that caters to outdoor enthusiasts who enjoy returning each evening to the comforts of a country inn. Guides escorts guests on daily hikes, bike rides or canoe trips in the summer months, depositing you back at the inn just in time to wash up and have dinner at Stonehurst's acclaimed restaurant. Pizzas cooked over wood fires are the restaurant's signature dish. Depending on your level of expertise and sporting interest, guides will sit down with your small group each morning for breakfast and discuss the options available. In the winter months, Peter has teamed up with International Mountain Equipment Climbing School for ice climbing expeditions and one-day winter mountaineering jaunts up Mount Washington. This is in addition to the 65 km of groomed cross-country ski trails, part of the Mount Washington Valley Ski Touring Center, that start in front of the main lobby.

Snowy Owl Inn

Waterville Valley, NH 03215. Tel. 603/236-2383. Rates for rooms start at $69 in the summer, $89 during ski season.

The game rooms, breakfast buffets, capacious rooms, and reasonable price make this an excellent choice for families traveling to the White Mountain area. The three-story hotel is centrally located, close to Waterville Valley's ski slopes and mountain biking paths.

Rosewood Country Inn

Pleasant View Road, Bradford, NH 03221. Tel. 603/938-5253.

Who says the Granite State doesn't have a soft, tender side? This hidden gem near the slopes of Mount Sunapee in the Lakes Region is one of the most romantic inns in New England. Formerly the Pleasant View Farm, the roster of names on the guest list from the early 1900s includes Gloria Swanson, Mary Pickford, Douglas Fairbanks, Charlie Chaplin, and Lillian Gish. Wake up to a breakfast of Belgian waffles topped with peaches, homemade maple syrup, and a hint of grand marnier. Then try to get your bloated body to go cross-country skiing on trails located across the street, or mountain bike down the road (see "Mountain Biking"). At night, the skies are so clear that you can see the Milky Way.

11

The Maine Coast

MAINE IS A MECCA FOR ADVENTURERS. SAILORS AND SEA kayakers come for the chance to find an unknown cove on one of the 2,000 pine-covered islands that lace the shoreline like an emerald necklace. Hikers venture here for the opportunity to climb the largest mountain on the East Coast. Bikers arrive on Maine's shores to loop around remote Penobscot Bay islands and the fingers of land that hang like icicles from the eastern shores. Walkers and bird watchers flock to the coast and its islands to spot herons, hawks, puffins, even bald eagles and peregrine falcons. Anglers are baited by the quantity and variety of clean fish, and golfers are hooked on the shoreline courses. Mountain bikers, rock climbers, and scuba divers are all challenged by Acadia National Park.

Home for several centuries to fishermen and shipbuilders who endured the long, bitter winters and avoided the deadly shoals, Maine's rough-and-tumble shores did not attract visitors until the late 1800s when Bar Harbor was discovered as a vacation spot. Perhaps no other person had a greater impact on the development of tourism in Maine than the artist Thomas Cole. Cole, founder of the Hudson River School, ventured to Mount Desert Island for inspiration once he had exhausted all the possibilities in upstate New York. Returning to New York, he wove rhapsodic tales about the coast's beauty to his affluent friends—Roosevelts, Morgans, Tracys, and the like.

Whenever he was at a loss for words, Cole would simply point to one of his freshly painted canvases. New York's upper crust took heed and soon ventured to Mount Desert Island.

It was an arduous journey from the East's big cities to Maine in the late 1800s, and when you finally reached the state, the trip to its more remote shores became even more grueling. Railroads and steamships could only get you as far as Portland, Bangor, or Ellsworth. From here, you had to take horse-drawn carriages to your final destination. Needless to say, when the high society from New York, Boston, and Philadelphia finally arrived on Mount Desert Island, they stayed for a significant amount of time. Large tracts of land were purchased and summer "cottages" were built—elaborate mansions staffed by the locals. By 1900, Bar Harbor rivaled Newport as the summer capital of the Northeast. In spite of their huge homes, the owners liked to call themselves "rusticators," emphasizing their desire to be in communion with nature. They would go on bird walks, collect flowers, pick berries, chop wood, and become knowledgeable in astronomy and horticulture. Often they would build little cabins in the backwoods of their estates to escape from their world of wealth to a more contemplative and spiritual state.

With the advent of the automobile after 1910, tourism filtered down to the lower classes. Bridges were built and car ferries developed to facilitate travel. However, the rusticators performed one final generous act that had a lasting impression on the landscape. Around 1910, two men from Harvard, Dr. Charles Eliot and George Buckman Dorr, were enraged that lumber companies were cutting down Mount Desert Island's first-growth forest. With the help of their wealthy friends, they solicited funds and succeeded in purchasing about 15,000 acres, or one-fifth of the island. Much of this endangered land encircled Cadillac Mountain. The rusticators then offered the land to the Federal Government to be used as the first National Park east of the Mississippi. Congress accepted in 1919, calling the land Lafayette National Park. In 1928, the name was changed to its current handle, Acadia National Park. Other wealthy patrons soon chipped in—John D. Rockefeller, Jr., donated 43 miles of bridle paths, and land owners on Isle au Haut contributed the southern half of the island in 1943 to make up the rest of Acadia's total of 35,000 acres.

Today, tourism is one of the state's most profitable ventures, hence the name "Vacationland" printed on every Maine license plate. Locals, ancestors of fishermen and farmers, have accepted this change begrudgingly. Their taciturn personalities are a far cry from the gregarious ways of city folk. On the contrary, many locals respond to questions with one-word answers. The old saw is that a typical question like, "Is this the way to Acadia?" might be answered with the word, "Nope," followed by a prolonged and deafening pause. Don't let the rough veneer of Mainers dissuade you from traveling to this unique region of the country. Simply think of Maine's ragged coast and inclement climate suitable metaphors for the tough shell and moodiness of its inhabitants.

"On the coast of Maine, where many green islands and salt inlets fringe the deep-cut shore . . . stood a small gray house facing the morning light," wrote Sarah Orne Jewett, author of *The Country of the Pointed Firs* and Maine's finest writer in the eyes of many locals. "All the weather-beaten houses of that region face the sea apprehensively, like

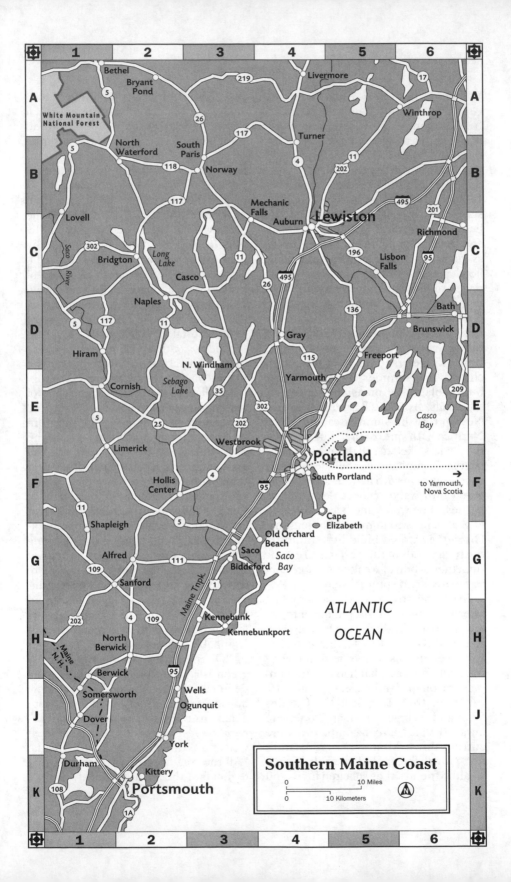

Southern Maine Coast

0   10 Miles

0   10 Kilometers

the women who live in them." Women and men, sailor or sea kayaker, we all approach the Maine coast with a degree of anxiety. Yet, when we finally face the elements head on, the wildness in them can bring on a great elation.

The Lay of the Land

The southern coast of Maine looks like most tourist destinations on the Atlantic seaboard: sweeping beaches and honky-tonk shops; long stretches of sandbars and silt brought down from the hills by rivers and spread out upon the edge of the sea. Rarely does a ridge jut out over the ocean.

Then you reach Cape Elizabeth, just south of Portland, and the sand is gone, replaced by a long stretch of Precambrian rock—grooved and roughened by the endless battering of surf and wind. This is the ragged and rocky Maine coast that has lured fishermen, shipbuilders, and artists to its shores for centuries.

In preglacial days, the coast of Maine measured less than 250 miles. Then the ice wreaked havoc on the land, resulting in more than 2,500 miles of jagged shoreline. When the last ice cap retreated, large bays, thousands of islands, coves, and inlets were created. Long fingers of the sea reached into narrow valleys and washed away the sunken coast. Pounding waves tore at the hills of bedrock, leaving jagged cliffs in their wake. Dangerous shoals fringed the islands. Geologists have a name for this highly unusual shoreline—the *Drowned Coast*.

Most startling is Mount Desert Island, now part of Acadia National Park. Solid granite mountains, rising 1,500 feet above the water's edge, were shaped from an 11-mile ridge that stretched east to west. The glacial upheaval rounded the summits and dug out the floors of the valley into U-shaped troughs. These basins now contain freshwater lakes and New England's only fjord, Somes Sound, which opens up onto the Atlantic.

For a long time, the glaciers left only barren wasteland standing above the sea—bedrock littered with rotting seaweed and other glacial refuse. Gradually, over the next four thousand years, lichens, mosses and other simple plant life covered the rocks with a thin layer of vegetation. Then the birches crept forward from the south, followed by pines, spruces, firs, and the slower-growing oaks and maples. Today, the northern Maine coast is a picturesque combination of forest and sea, unlike any other coastline in the East.

The weather in Maine is downright chilly, but along the coast you can expect it to be several degrees warmer than inland. The coast is known for its dense fog, which can cool things off to a degree in the summer and fall. The best time to visit Acadia and points north is mid-August, when the bugs are gone, the blueberries are ripe, and the weather is in the high 70s. Mosquitoes and flies are at their most predatory in June. If you plan to head to the beaches of the southern coast, it's almost impossible to avoid the crowds during Maine's short summer. Late July and early August are the warmest times.

In addition to lobster, the waters off the coast of Maine are home to a dazzling array of sealife, including harbor seals, porpoises, minke whales, and puffins. Inland, white-tailed deer, red fox, woodchucks, beavers, and snowshoe hares are common. The long list of migrating shorebirds include puffins, kestrels and storm petrels, razorbill auks, least terns, ruddy turnstones, sandpipers, and black guillemots.

Orientation

Don't underestimate the size of the Maine coast. Distances are long. Kittery to Eastport is 293 miles, but, adding peninsulas and shoreline that look like they were created from the scribbles of a five-year-old, and you easily have a seven- to eight-hour drive. **Interstate 95,** known as the Maine Turnpike, will take you as far as Brunswick before venturing inland. From here, you have to drive on **U.S. 1,** often a two-lane highway, as it meanders from seaside village to seaside village. If you're heading to **Acadia National Park,** many visitors avoid U.S. 1 by simply taking I-95 to Bangor to State Route 3 South. There are an incredible number of scenic drives, many of which head south from U.S. 1 to one of the peninsulas or islands. Indeed, one of the highlights of this region is getting off the main routes and exploring the small villages and ports on the lesser-known roads.

Heading south to north along the coast, this chapter takes in the **south coast,** the only part of Maine's coastline that looks like the rest of New England's coastline—long, sandy beaches lined alternately with summer homes and the midways and boardwalks common to more southerly beach destinations. North of Portland, the coast shatters into the ragged succession of estuaries and spits of rockbound land of the Mid Coast; this is where those lobstering and shipbuilding towns that grace the postcards are located—**Boothbay Harbor, Damariscotta, Pemaquid,** as well as **Thomaston, Rockport,** and funky **Belfast** along U.S. 1 on **Penobscot Bay.**

East of Penobscot Bay is the **Down East/Acadia** region, with Acadia National Park's grounds on **Isle au Haut** and **Mount Desert Island** getting the most attention in this book. Scattered about Mount Desert Island, **Bar Harbor, Northeast Harbor, Southwest Harbor,** and **Bass Harbor** are the four villages in which to find accommodations, restaurants, grocery stores, gas, and all other basic needs. Bar Harbor is by far the largest, with the widest selection of hotels. Southwest and Northeast Harbor, situated on opposite ends of Somes Sound, are far more intimate. Bass Harbor is the gateway to Swans Island.

North of Acadia is the **Sunrise Coast.** Traffic on U.S. 1 lessens and lobster buoys, traps, and weather-beaten fishing vessels thrive. This is the last stretch of untouched Maine coast—dotted with fishing communities, blueberry patches, and slick white lighthouses. It's also the easternmost part of the U.S., where the sun first makes its ascent in America. The peninsulas that jut out of the mainland are perfect for road biking, tranquil hikes, and bird watching. Machias Seal Island and Quoddy Head State Park are both accessible from U.S. 1 along the Sunrise Coast.

Parks & Other Hot Spots

Acadia National Park

Access: for Mount Desert Island section, take State Route 3 South from Ellsworth; for Isle au Haut section, take State Route 15 South from U.S. 1 to Stonington, passenger ferry from Stonington. Headquarters: P.O. Box 177, Bar Harbor, ME 04609; tel. 207/288-3338. Visitor Center: located at Hulls Cove; tel. 207/288-5262 or 207/288-4932. Camping at Blackwoods Campground (reservations required during summer) and Seawall Campground (closed winter). See "Campgrounds & Other Accommodations," below. Rest rooms; picnic areas; naturalist programs; foot, bike, and horse trails; fishing; tide pooling; bird watching; kayaking; cross-country skiing; snowmobiling. Park open year-round. Entrance fees $5 per vehicle, $3 per person without vehicle, $15 annual pass.

The Northeast's lone national park is a spectacular 35,000-acre playground for outdoor recreation. Located mostly on Mount Desert Island, Acadia is a compact mix of the Atlantic seaboard's highest mountains, seven major lakes and ponds, deserted offshore islands, and 41 miles of jagged coastline. There's more than 170 miles of hiking trails and carriage paths for walkers, bikers, and cross-country skiers, numerous kayaking tours, canoe rentals, rock climbing guides, even scuba diving charters. During the summer months, the roads can be congested, especially the 27-mile Park Loop, but it's still fairly easy to find secluded mountain trails with breathtaking vistas of the coast and islands.

One of the park's highlights is **Cadillac Mountain,** located on the Park Loop. The 1,530-foot-high mountain is the highest point on the eastern seaboard north of Brazil. Atop the rounded summit, one can view the hundreds of islands that dot Frenchman Bay. A spur road leads to the top, resulting in an overcrowded peak during high season.

Somes Sound, which is bordered on its west and east sides by State Routes 102 and 3, respectively, is a jaw-dropping fjord that almost splits Mount Desert Island in two, shaping the southern half of the island into two large crab claws. For exceptional views, take the short hike up **Acadia Mountain** (see "Hiking," below).

Eagle Lake is off State Route 233 west of Bar Harbor. Approximately 1¼ miles long, this hidden body of water is best seen from the seat of a mountain bike. Carriage path trails hug the perimeter of the lake (see "Mountain Biking," below).

Isle au Haut, 8 miles south of Stonington (70 miles southwest of Mount Desert Island) and accessible only by mailboat (call tel. 207/367-5193 for times) or your own boat, is a remote, much less visited part of the park. When you arrive, you'll find a remote, densely forested island 6 miles long and 3 miles wide. All of the island is private except for the 2,800-acre tract of land donated to Acadia in 1943. Numerous trails explore the rocky shoreline, bogs, marshes, and narrow lakes located on the southern half of the island.

Camden Hills State Park

Located on U.S. 1, north of Camden. Tel. 207/236-3109 or 207/236-0849. Camping, picnic areas, foot trails, biking, snowmobiling. Open May 15–Oct 15; day use and camping fee.

Not nearly as popular as its national park neighbor to the north, this 5,500-acre state park offers the same exquisite views of the coast. Hiking trails lead to Mount Battie and other small summits where vistas open up onto Camden, Rockport, and the Penobscot Bay islands. The heavily forested woods are a mix of northern red oak, red maples, spruce, ash, birch, beech, and at higher elevations, firs and white pines. The roads surrounding the park are known for their challenging biking.

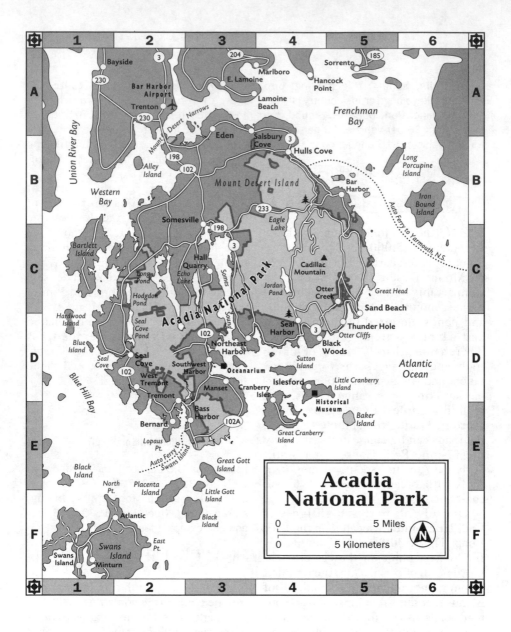

Acadia National Park map

Penobscot Bay

This is the premier sailing ground on the east coast, bar none. Hundreds of isolated coves are nestled on islands that only a sailor could possibly know.

The bay is also ideal for kayaking. Below is a list of favorite island destinations: North Haven, Islesboro, and Monhegan Island.

North Haven

In Penobscot Bay. Ferries leave from Rockland daily in the summer months. Contact the Maine State Ferry Service (tel. 207/596-2203).

The backcountry roads of this charming island brings visitors to expansive fields of wildflowers and pebble beaches with views of the bay. It's the perfect place to bike (see "Road Biking," below).

Islesboro

In Penobscot Bay. Ferries leave daily from Lincolnville Beach in the summer months. Contact the Maine State Ferry Service (tel. 207/789-5611 or 207/734-6935).

Another popular biking destination, Islesboro is a 10-mile-long island where every view of the bay seems better than the next. Summer homes the size of mansions line the small country roads (see "Road Biking," below).

Monhegan Island

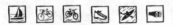

10 miles offshore outside Penobscot Bay, between Penobscot and Muscongus bays. Ferries leave from Port Clyde, Boothbay Harbor, and Damariscotta. From Port Clyde, contact the Monhegan Boat Line (tel. 207/372-8848); for Boothbay Harbor (tel. 207/633-2284); Damariscotta (tel. 207/677-2026).

As evidenced by the long list of artists who have painted Monhegan's dramatic cliffs, including Edward Hopper, Rockwell Kent, and George Bellows, the wild beauty of this island is a sight to behold. There are 17 miles of hiking trails, which wind through a forest of evergreens that border the 160-foot-high headlands.

The Sunrise Coast

The peninsulas that jut out of the mainland along the uncrowded Sunrise Coast are perfect for road biking, tranquil hikes, and bird watching. Machias Seal Island and Quoddy Head State Park are both accessible from U.S. 1 along the Sunrise Coast.

Machias Seal Island

At the mouth of the Bay of Fundy. Reached by charter boat from Cutler or Jonesport.

Only 25 acres, this small island is home to more than 800 pairs of puffins, 2,000 pairs of Arctic terns, and a host of other birds including razorbill auks and herons (see "Bird Watching," below). Offshore is a large school of harbor seals.

Quoddy Head State Park

From U.S. 1 in Lubec, turn left onto South Lubec Road and take your first left on Quoddy Head Road. You'll see a small sign and parking lot for Quoddy Head State Park. Picnic area, foot trails. Day-use fee charged.

Overlooking the Grand Manan Channel and New Brunswick, this park is the

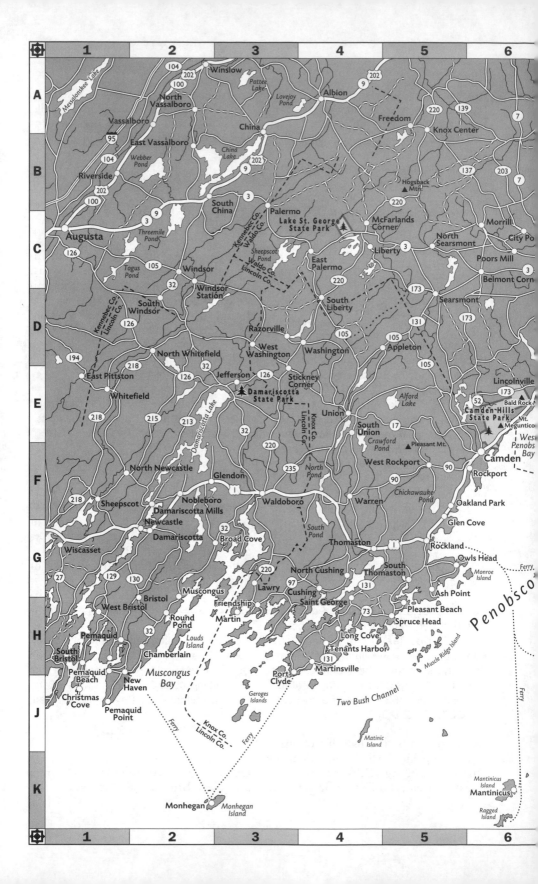

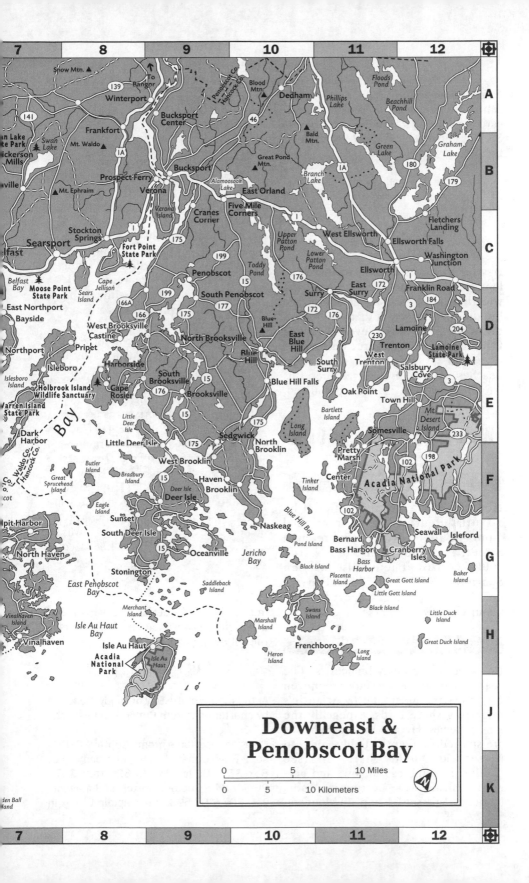

Downeast & Penobscot Bay

0   5   10 Miles

0   5   10 Kilometers

easternmost point in the United States. A boardwalk leaves from a picture-post-card lighthouse through peat bogs to 80-foot cliffs (see "Walks & Rambles," below).

The South Coast

If your idea of recreation consists of lounging on Maine's best beaches and wrestling with a lobster at one of the hundred lobster joints that line U.S. 1, this is the place to go. Seven-mile-long **Old Orchard** and three-mile-long **Ogunquit** are two of the more popular beaches. For the avid adventurer, this stretch of coastline is far too populated.

What to Do & Where to Do It

BALLOONING

Hot-air balloon rides are offered by a Portland outfitter with an original name—**Balloon Rides;** 17 Freeman Street, Portland, Maine 04103 (tel. 800/952-2076). There's also **Balloon Sports** (tel. 207/772-4401), **Hot Fun** (tel. 207/799-0193), and **Freeport Balloon Company** (tel. 207/865-1712).

BIRD WATCHING

Break out those dusty binoculars. The Maine coast and her islands are proven pit stops for most of the Atlantic's migrating shore birds, especially the larger species. **Herons** and **marsh hawks** are spotted frequently. **Bald eagles** can be seen at Quoddy State Park (see "Walks & Rambles," below) and **per-egrine falcons** were nesting in Acadia National Park (see Champlain Mountain

Blue in the Face

Maine is known for their abundance of blueberries, canned commercially since 1870. Indeed, more than 40 million pounds of blueberries are harvested annually from an estimated 25,000 acres. All of the sweet berries grow wild, and the only care given to them is to burn the fields every two to three years. This prunes the bushes, stimulating new growth, and induces a heavy crop of fruit.

If you happen to be on the Sunset Coast in early August, you'll inevitably see the large patches of blueberries and taste the luscious fruit. Don't miss the opportunity to stop for blueberry pancakes or pies at Helen's in Machias (they also serve their legendary, mouth-watering strawberry pie). In stores along this section of U.S. 1, you'll find blueberry jam, syrup, even blueberry wine. Lompoc Cafe in Bar Harbor has the best blueberry beer I've ever tasted on tap. It was also the only blueberry beer I've ever tasted.

in the "Hiking" section). However, the highlight for passionate bird-watchers is the following trip.

Machias Seal Island

At the mouth of the Bay of Fundy. Reached by charter boat from Cutler or Jonesport.

Charters available from: Captain Patterson, Bold Coast Charter Company, P.O. Box 364, Cutler, ME 04626 (tel. 207/259-4484); Captain Norton in Jonesport (tel. 207/497-5933); or Captain Wilcox in

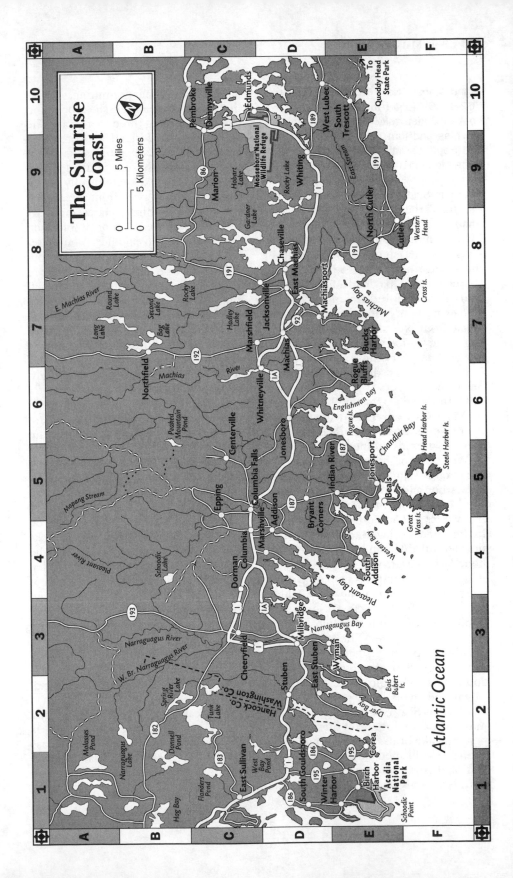

The Sunrise Coast

N

5 Miles

5 Kilometers

Atlantic Ocean

Grand Manan, New Brunswick (tel. 506/ 662-8296). To get to Captain Patterson's boat in Cutler, take U.S. 1 East to East Machias and turn right onto State Route 191 South to Cutler. Park across from the white Methodist church.

Machias Seal Island, way up near the mouth of the Bay of Fundy, is a tiny unspoiled sanctuary for a number of Maine's most noted marine bird species. I visited the island with the help of the charter boat operated by Captain Patterson. His payload of bird lovers that day included an older couple who own a farm in Pennsylvania, a journalist from New York whose carrying bags were stuffed with tripods and zoom lenses, and yours truly, with the requisite binoculars dangling from my neck. We arrived at 7 AM at the pier in Cutler, Maine, for the 9-mile cruise to Machias Seal Island on Captain Patterson's boat, the *Barbara Frost* (named after his mother).

We glided past the lobster boats and the circular salmon farming nets, out of the harbor, and into the Atlantic. This is the Maine shoreline north of Bar Harbor, where summer estates are replaced by lighthouses that warn boaters of its unmerciful tides and harsh coast. An hour later we arrived at a small, low-lying island. Hundreds of plump birds were whizzing over our heads searching the waters for breakfast. Some had hooded black heads that looked like Batman's disguise. These were the razorbill auks. Others had eyes the size of a parrot with beaks dotted red, black, and yellow—the bird we came all this way to see, the Atlantic puffin.

Machias Seal Island is the southernmost major nesting site of these stubby, penguin-like birds. Small colonies have been re-established farther south by the National Audubon Society, but those puffins can only be viewed from the sea.

At Machias, weather permitting, you can climb atop the seaweed-slick rocks and see puffins two to three feet away. The eastern part of the island is covered with Arctic terns. The razorbill auks might look like superheroes, but it is the aggressive tern that keeps deadly predators like seagulls away from the eggs of all the island's birds. Harassment by gulls has become a major problem on many of the puffin colonies. A puffin returning from his nest with several capelin dangling from its bill might be forced to drop the fish in order to save himself from further gull abuse. Gulls have also been known to eat chicks that stray too far from their parent's watch. But here on Machias Island, the puffins are greatly indebted to the terns. Stray off the island's main path and you might hear the irate click-click-clicking of a fearless tern one foot above your head. The paths lead to four blinds, where you can set up shop and watch the puffins return 15 to 20 minutes after your entrance. The day we stepped foot on Machias, we also found a yellow-crowned night heron and several swallows.

You are allowed up to three hours on the island. Captain Patterson then picks you up by skiff and ferries you back to the *Barbara Frost*. Before returning to Cutler, we glided around a small hump of land known as Gull Island. This is a playground for harbor seals, whose heads were seen bobbing up and down with the waves. The entire trip takes five or six hours and you should reserve well in advance, because there is a limit to the number of people allowed on the island. Cost is $50.

If you can't get enough of our winged friends, Captain Patterson also offers half-day and full-day trips to Cross Island Wildlife Refuge, an island outside of Cutler that is ideal for birding and picnicking.

BOARDSAILING

Portland windsurfers go to **Pine Point,** just north of Old Orchard Beach. Prouts Neck juts out of the mainland, forming a protected cove to sail. Follow State Route 9 North from Old Orchard Beach.

CANOEING

I'm a firm believer that one should kayak on the Maine coast. However, if you yearn for the tranquillity of still waters, there are many tributaries, ponds, and lakes several miles inland from the ocean. Starting on the easternmost coast, **Sunrise County Canoe Expeditions,** Cathance Lake, Grove Post Office, ME 04638, offers rentals and guided tours (tel. 207/454-7708). You can canoe on **Acadia National Park's** largest body of water, Long Pond, with the help of **National Park Canoe,** Pond's End, Mount Desert, ME 04660 (tel. 207/244-5854). Half-day rentals start at $18. **Maine Sport Outfitters,** U.S. 1, P.O. Box 956, Rockport, ME 04856 (tel. 207/236-7120) offers rentals in the Camden-Rockport area; Maine Guide **Mike Patterson** knows these waterways like the back of his hand, and thus is a worthwhile addition to any trip. He can be reached at Maine Sport Outfitters. **L.L. Bean Paddling Schools,** Freeport, ME 04033 (tel. 800/341-4341, ext.6666), offer whitewater and flatwater canoeing instruction. Both Maine Sport and L.L. Bean have guided canoeing trips to the Allagash and Moose Rivers, which are far better places to canoe (see chapter 12).

CROSS-COUNTRY SKIING

The mountains of the Maine coast provide cross-country skiers with the rare and exhilarating opportunity to ski with the ocean as a backdrop. Except for the Olympic Mountains in Washington, I can think of no other place in the contiguous 48 states that offers this memorable experience. At **Acadia National Park,** the same scenic Carriage Path Trails that are loved by bikers in the summer are cherished by skiers in the winter. There are 49 miles of trails, reserved only for skiers and snowshoers, which loop around Eagle Lake and Jordan Pond, continuing all the way to Northeast Harbor and the ocean. Smelling the heavy brine of the sea while gliding on snow is an unparalleled skiing thrill. The Park Service sets up a Winter Information Center and publishes a Winter Activities Guide. Both the Blackwoods Campground and the Atlantic Oakes (see "Campgrounds & Other Accommodations," below) stay open year-round, becoming the unofficial headquarters for the park in the winter. Since Acadia is surrounded by water on Mount Desert Island, snow covering here can be much lighter than in the rest of Maine. Call 207/667-8910 for conditions.

The trails weaving through **Camden Hills State Park** also offer spectacular views of the ocean. The routes are much harder than Acadia's wide carriage paths. Call 207/236-3109 for more information. Although you won't have a view of the Atlantic, the 10 miles of trails at the **Tanglewood 4-H** camp come without the hum and gaseous smell of snowmobiles. The ski area can be reached by taking U.S. 1 north from Camden to Lincolnville Beach; 0.8 mile north of the beach, turn left onto Ducktrap Road and go 0.7 mile to the first gravel road on the right. Travel 0.8 mile to the camp gate and parking area.

There are 16 miles of groomed trails available at **Val Halla Country Club,** Val Halla Road, Cumberland, ME 04021 (tel. 207/829-3700), near both Portland

Homer at Home

There is nothing more ominous than inclement weather on the coast of Maine. Bitterly cold gray seas crash against the shore's implacable granite ledges, uninvited waves flood the decks of small fishing vessels, the blinding fog is impenetrable. No one exposed these frightful scenes to the world's eye better than Winslow Homer. From his studio in Prouts Neck, a jagged sand barrier jutting out into the ocean, the artist had a perfect vantage point from which to view his favorite subject matter—man versus the chaotic forces of nature. Struggling fishermen, dramatic sea rescues, and surging waves crashing into huddled masses were some of Homer's favorite depictions during the 20 years he stayed at Prouts Neck.

Homer was just one of the many notable artists who have ventured to the shores of Maine since the late 1800s. Ten miles off mid-coast, Monhegan Island has been a prominent art colony since the 1870s. Robert Henri, Edward Hopper, George Bellows, and Rockwell Kent all painted Monhegan's 160-foot cliffs, meadows, and quaint fishing communities, all in their own unique styles. Georgia O'Keeffe, Marsden Hartley, and other early American abstractionists from Alfred Stieglitz's 291 Gallery joined John Marin to work at his summer cottage in Deer Isle. Impressionist Childe Hassam is best known for his colorful portrayal of a garden on Appledore Island. And contemporary artists like Jamie Wyeth are living proof that the alluring Maine coast is still inspirational to a new generation of artists.

and Freeport. **The Samoset Resort,** Rockport, ME 04856 (tel. 207/594-2511) offers 10 km of groomed trails right on Penobscot Bay.

DOWNHILL SKIING

Camden Snowball, P.O. Box 1207, Camden, ME 04843 (tel. 207/236-3438) is the only place to downhill ski and snowboard on the Maine coast. They have 11 trails, (one expert), 1 double chair and 2 T bars, a 950-feet vertical drop, and 40 percent snowmaking from top to bottom. Ski rentals and instruction are also available. Lift tickets cost $24 weekends, $14 weekdays.

FISHING

The cold, clear waters off the coast of Maine are loaded with saltwater fish. Go on a charter boat or surfcast from the shore

and you won't believe your luck. It's a rare occasion when you don't feel a bite, and more than likely, you'll come back with several "keepers" (or "keepahs," as they say in Maine). The main targets for deep-sea fishing are the wide variety of bottom fish found one to twenty miles from shore. **Cod** are the most common catch, ranging from a few pounds to the occasional 70-pounder. Then there's the sleek, silver-gray **pollocks** and the wide-eyed **haddocks.** Very often charter boats will go after the "trophy" fishes—giant **tunas,** weighing between 250 and 800 pounds, **halibut,** and **sharks.**

Surfcasting from the shore of the southern beaches is extremely popular. **Stripers** and **blues** (striped bass and bluefish) are the most sought-after fishes. Visitors to **Acadia National Park** will find **brook** and **brown trout, bass,** and **togue** in the island's more than 20 ponds and lakes.

FISHING CHARTERS

There are more than 50 deep-sea charters that run boats off the coast of Maine, and you probably won't go wrong with any of them. Those recommended to me were (starting from the South Coast):

◆ **Captain Tim Tower** offers full- and half-day trips on the *Bunny Clark*, P.O. Box 837M, Ogunquit, ME 03907 (tel. 207/646-2214);

◆ **Captain Barry Gibson** has full-day charters for up to six people, on *Shark IV*, Brown Brothers Wharf, Boothbay Harbor, ME 04538 (tel. 207/633-3416);

◆ **Captain John Earl** leaves from Rockland daily during the summer, P.O. Box 128, Spruce Head Island, ME 04859 (tel. 207/594-5411);

◆ **Captain Rick Savage,** on Mount Desert Island, offers private charters for up to 10 anglers. P.O. Box 321, Northeast Harbor, ME 04662 (tel. 207/276-3785);

◆ **Guide Ken Bailey** will meet you in Camden and Rockport and take you to his favorite fishing haunts inland in search of small and largemouth bass, brown trout, perch, and pickerel 15 Knowlton Street, Camden, ME 04843 (tel. 207/236-4243).

INSTRUCTION

Both **Maine Sport Outfitters** and **L.L. Bean** offer fly-fishing schools. Maine Sport Outfitters, U.S. 1, P.O. Box 956, Rockport, ME 04856 (tel. 207/236-7120). L.L. Bean Fishing Schools, Freeport, ME 04033 (tel. 800/341-4341, ext. 6666).

GOLF

With seven of its holes bordering Penobscot Bay, the **Samoset Golf Course,** Rockport, ME 04856 (tel. 207/594-2511), is coastal Maine's perennial favorite. Situated on the resort of the same name, the front nine make the most of the ocean view, while the back nine meander through woods, ponds, and gardens.

Hole number seven, the course's signature hole, is a par five dogleg left, that practically dares you to play over the ocean. Don't mind the brisk breeze.

The Samoset golf pros also recommended these other coastal courses: The century-old **Kebo Valley Golf Club,** Eagle Lake, Bar Harbor, ME 04609 (tel. 207/288-3000); **Sable Oaks Golf Club,** 505 Country Club Drive, South Portland (tel. 207/775-6257); the **Biddeford-Saco Country Club,** 101 Old Orchard Road, Saco, ME 04072 (tel. 207/282-9892); and **Cape Arundel Golf Club** in Kennebunkport, the course former President George Bush plays when he's in town, on Old River Road (tel. 207/967-3494).

HIKING

Maine's coastal mountains reward hikers with views of the surrounding hills, ocean, and lakes, in exchange for one or two hours of effort. All four of these hikes lead to perfect picnic spots on the peak (try saying that three or four times).

Acadia Mountain

2 miles (round trip). Allow 1–2 hours. Easy. Access: The trailhead is located 3 miles south of Somesville on State Route 102. Park at the small lot where the Acadia Mountain sign is clearly hung. The path is located across State Route 102. Map: Available at Acadia National Park visitor center.

Standing only 681 feet tall, the low summit of Acadia Mountain overlooks central and southern Mount Desert Island. The trail is situated on the island's far less popular western side, where you'll rarely see more than a handful of hikers even in the crowded months of July and August. The path weaves slowly through forests of birches and pines, before crossing a former road and continuing straight up the rocky path. The quick ascent to the peak begins here. A series of flat ledges overlook Echo Lake—each plateau offering a slightly better view than the last. Before you can swat that incredibly bothersome black fly, you're on top. As you meander over the rocks, the view becomes panoramic, from west to east. Fishing boats and yachts can be seen anchored in Southwest Harbor; the Cranberry Islands look more like green peas in the distance. Continue to the easternmost point of Acadia's peak for the best view: Norumbega Mountain practically plunges into Somes Sound, the only fjord on the Eastern seaboard. Now I can pat myself on the back for bringing that second roll of film.

Champlain Mountain

Allow 2 hours. Moderate. Access: From the Acadia National Park Visitor Center, take the Park Loop to the Bear Brook Trail sign. There are several parking places across the street. Map: Available at Acadia National Park visitor center.

The Bear Brook Trail to the peak of Champlain Mountain is one of those uphill climbs where you are constantly turning around to see the view behind you. In this instance, the view is the expansive Frenchman Bay. With every step upward, there seems to be another green dot beneath you joining a line of islands, another schooner slicing the waters with its two masts and full sails. Nevertheless, the climb to the summit at 1,058 feet is not easy. Your feet are climbing on rocks far more than on pine-strewn soil; 1.1 miles later, you're looking down at the small island in front of you called The Thumbcap, the lighthouse on Egg Rock, the town of Bar Harbor, and the petite pond to your left known as The Tarn. You'll notice that

the Precipice Trail to the summit is closed due to nesting peregrine falcons. However, you'll have a far better chance of spotting these swift birds from the Precipice Trail parking lot on the Park Loop, less than a mile from where your car is parked.

Maiden Cliff

2.25 miles (round trip). Allow 2 hours. Easy. Access: From Camden, take State Route 52 West, 3 miles from the intersection of U.S. 1. There will be a small parking area on the right-hand side of the road just before State Route 52 borders the lake. Map: Available from the ranger at Camden Hills State Park, U.S. 1, north of Camden.

You can add the word "manageable" to the list of adjectives I've used to describe the Maine coast. The mountains have short summits and the bike rides have subtle, rolling hills. A fine example is the climb up Maiden Cliff at Camden Hills State Park. The trail starts gradually, slowly climbing through the hemlocks until it reaches a junction at the half-mile mark. Turn right onto Ridge Trail and soon the ledges open up onto the waters of Megunticook Lake. The view only gets better when you turn left at the Scenic Trail and continue to climb to the summit. Camden and Penobscot Bay can be seen in the distance. However, this is not the Maiden Cliff. Walk downhill and follow the white blazes until you reach a junction where you'll turn right. A couple hundred yards later, you'll find a huge white cross at a point overlooking all of Megunticook Lake. The wooden cross marks the spot where 12-year-old Elenora French plunged to her death on May 7, 1864. She was running to catch her hat. This might be the fastest way down, but I suggest taking the Maiden Cliff Trail directly back to the parking lot.

Mount Battie

1 mile (round trip). Allow 1 hour. Moderate. Access: Take State Route 52 North from the intersection of U.S. 1 in Camden. Turn right on the first street from the intersection. Then take a left on Megunticook Street. There is a small parking lot at the top of the hill. Map: Available from the ranger at Camden Hills State Park, U.S. 1, north of Camden.

All I could see from where I stood
was three long mountains and a wood;
I turned and looked another way
and saw three islands in a bay.
So with my eyes I trace the line
of the horizon, thin and fine,
straight around till I was come
back to where I'd started from;
and all I saw from where I stood
was three long mountains and a wood.

Edna St. Vincent Millay wrote this first stanza from the poem "Penascence" at the young age of 18. The poem helped her gain admission to Vassar, after which she soon became one of America's finest poets. These lines are now engraved on a plaque atop Mount Battie, one of the numerous peaks in the Camden Hills that inspired her. The climb up to the summit of Mount Battie is only 20 to 30 minutes long, but you should wear good hiking boots and be in reasonably good condition. The trail climbs up slippery rocks for its entire length. Once on top, it's easy to see why Millay found the view enchanting. Camden's white steeples and schooners' masts surge toward the sky, surrounded by the ubiquitous pines. The island of North Haven lies straight ahead, Islesboro to the left, and Matinicus to the right in the distance. Climb up the medieval-looking tower to get an even better view and then make your way slowly back down.

Did They Get Bibs and Butter Sauce?

Lobster Pot, Lobster Hut, Lobster Wharf, Lobster Pound, Lobster in the Rough—it seems like there are more restaurants on U.S. 1 serving this tasty crustacean than all the McDonalds in the world. A boiled lobster is even on Maine's license plate. However, a hundred years ago, Maine's prisoners were so vehemently opposed to their steady diet of lobster tails that they rioted to protest. Lobster was only used as fertilizer, or food fit for the impoverished and imprisoned. Those poor, deprived tourists.

OUTFITTERS

You can take a five-day guided tour of Acadia National Park's best trails with **New England Hiking Holidays,** P.O. Box 1648, North Conway, NH 03860 (tel. 800/869-0949).

Hiking Holidays also offers a five-day guided tour of Acadia and the Maine coast. P.O. Box 750, Bristol, VT 05443 (tel. 802/453-4816).

Walking the World 50 Plus has an eight-day guided tour of the Maine coast including Monhegan Island, Mount Battie, and Acadia. As the name implies, walkers must be over the age of 50. P.O. Box 1186, Fort Collins, CO 80522 (tel. 800/340-9255).

HORSEBACK RIDING

On the South Coast just outside of Wells, the **Mount Agamenticus Riding Stables** offer one- to three-hour custom rides from their stables. Call 207/361-2840 for reservations. Farther north, **Long Horn Stables** offers trail rides near Old Orchard Beach (207/934-9578), and **Ledgewood Riding Stables**, near Boothbay Harbor, offers horses and trails for all levels (207/882-6346).

MOUNTAIN BIKING

The definition of mountain biking is that we can bike anywhere, even along the Maine coast.

Carriage Path Trails, Acadia National Park

Allow 2 hours. Easy terrain, with several hills. Access: Start at the visitor center off State Route 3. Map: Available at Acadia National Park visitor center.

The carriage path trails in Acadia National Park are hard to categorize. They are not mountain biking paths in the true sense of the word—no sweeping single-track rides down Cadillac Mountain. Instead, the trails are finely packed gravel roads, better suited for mountain bikes than road bikes since the rocks can get loose on some downhill runs. Financed by John D. Rockefeller, Jr., between 1917 and 1933, this 43-mile web of trails criss-crosses the entire eastern half of Mount Desert Island. They are off-limits to motorized vehicles and, thus, are the best way to see this part of Acadia by bike. The following 14-mile loop is a worthy introduction to these trails.

Start at the northern end of the visitor center parking lot, where there's a dirt path with a small bicycle sign. The next half-mile is the worst part of the entire ride, an unrelenting uphill climb. You can stomp on my book and say, "This sucks!" at the top of the hill. For now, keep riding. At signpost 1, bear left and take another left at signpost 3. This will bring you past placid Witch Hole Pond to a stone arched bridge high above roaring Duck Brook. Take a quick look from the overview, but continue riding along the same trail. Bear left at signpost 4 and ride downhill under a stone bridge to the shores of Eagle Lake—Acadia's second-largest body of water. Circle around the lake counter-clockwise under the forest of pines. The steady uphill climb at the southern part of the lake rewards you with a dramatic view of Cadillac Mountain as you speed downhill toward its eastern shores (now you know the reason why I like to ride this loop counterclockwise). At signpost 9, turn right under the stone bridge again and take a left at signpost 4. This will give you an even better view of Witch Hole Pond. Two more lefts at signposts 2 and 1 will bring you back to the visitor center parking lot. Be extremely cautious riding downhill on the same miserable hill you had to climb in the beginning. I'd like you to have a nice long life with numerous opportunities to throw down my book in disgust.

Pleasant Mountain, West Rockport

Time: Indefinite. Easy to moderate; hilly terrain. Access: From Rockland, take State Route 17 West to State Route 90 West and park at Bob's Variety Store, less than one mile from the intersection (you'll see the red Citgo sign). Be sure to ask Bob if you can park here. Bike across the street to the Volvo sign. Just past the sign is the dirt road.

Rain was drizzling lightly and the fog was rolling in from Penobscot Bay—a perfect morning for mountain biking on the Maine coast. I heeded the advice of one Jeremiah, local mountain biking guru at Maine Sport Outfitters, and hit the hills of Pleasant Mountain. I biked uphill on the dirt road from the "Hudson's Upholstery" mailbox and continued straight onto grassy double-tracks before the dirt road curved to a house and driveway. These paths are inundated with snowmobilers in the winter months. The rest of the year, they're ready to be tackled by mountain bikers. I followed the yellow snowmobile arrows and headed uphill above the treeline. Intermittent views of the valley appeared between waves of fog and the showers of mud my wheels were spraying into the air. I took a right onto one of the double-tracks that veer off the main snowmobile route and went cruising up and down hills. An hour later, I somehow managed to return to State Route 90, covered with more mud than a Marine in boot camp. Thank you, Jeremiah.

RENTALS, REPAIRS & SUPPLIES

Maine Sport Outfitters, P.O. Box 956, U.S. 1, Rockport, ME 04856 (tel. 207/ 236-7120). In Acadia National Park, **Acadia Bike** and **Bar Harbor Bicycle** both rent mountain bikes; located at 48 and 141 Cottage Street, Bar Harbor, respectively (tel. 207/288-9605 for Acadia and 207/288-3886 for Bar Harbor).

POWERBOATING

Explore the coastline of Acadia National Park on a 13- or 17-foot Boston Whaler. Boats, rented at Harbor Boat Rentals, Harbor Place, 1 West Street, Bar Harbor, ME 04609 (tel. 207/288-3757) or Mansell Boat Company, P.O. Box 1102, Main Street, Southwest Harbor, ME 04679.

ROAD BIKING

North of Portland, peninsulas protrude from the coastlike fingers stretching from a palm. Estuaries, coves, and fishing villages beckon bikers to the rugged coastline. Even more remote are the Penobscot Bay islands, reachable only by ferry. During the high season months of July and August, traffic here is barely a trickle.

Jonesport

Allow 3–4 hours. Moderate to strenuous; hilly terrain. Access: Take U.S. 1 North past Columbia Falls to a Rest Area. Park here. If you arrive in Jonesboro, you've gone too far. Any good road map will do.

Northeast of Ellsworth, U.S. 1 is the gateway to large blueberry patches and quaint villages where lobster and fishing are still more important than tourism. This is the Sunrise Coast, where the sun rises first in America. That's why I suggest taking this 30 mile loop early in the morning. Park your car at the Rest Area sign on U.S. 1 and take a right out of the parking lot. Be careful, since U.S. 1 is congested and there is no shoulder. At 2.7 miles, you'll see a sign for State Route 187 South. Take a right and begin a loop that will eventually bring you back to U.S. 1. This undulating road is lined with dark blueberry barrens and large stretches of farmland. Halfway down to Jonesport, views of the Atlantic start to seep through the mist. The water will keep you company all the way south to this quintessential Maine harbor. In the early morning light, the boats stand still, not daring to break the glassy surface of the water. Cross the bridge over to Beal's Island for the perfect "photo op." Stacks of lobster traps 15 to 20 feet high stand on docks next to tired fishing boats that look like they've gone out to sea daily for the past 30 years. If you want to expand the trip, you can continue all the way to Great Wass Island. Everyone else will want to turn around at the white Methodist church. Cross the bridge back to Jonesport and take a left onto State Route 187 again. The road back to U.S. 1 is hilly but just as rural as the other side. At U.S. 1, turn right to return to the rest area.

Southwest Harbor Loop, Mount Desert Island

Allow 3–5 hours. Moderate to strenuous; hilly terrain. Access: Start on Main St., Southwest Harbor, on State Route 102. Park Service map should do fine.

The eastern half of Mount Desert Island is extremely crowded in the summer months. If you prefer to bike in this area, I highly recommend renting a mountain bike and touring the carriage path trails, off limits to motorized vehicles (see Carriage Path Trails under "Mountain Biking"). For the avid road biker, an excellent alternative to Acadia's Park Loop is the loop around the western half of Mount Desert Island. This ride takes you along the Atlantic, past lakes, ponds, mountains of pine, and small fishing villages, each stop more picturesque than the last. Start in the village of Southwest Harbor, where shops selling lobster traps outnumber curios. Continue on State Route 102 South along the harbor and take a left onto State Route 102A. This is my favorite part of the trip. You cruise past Manset, known for its yacht-building facilities, and Seawall, where a natural stone seawall juts out over the Atlantic toward the Cranberry Islands. A great side trip is the 0.5-mile road to the left that brings you to the Bass Harbor Head lighthouse, built in 1858. Otherwise, proceed on State Route 102A into Bass Harbor, following the signs for the Swans Island Ferry. This slight detour will bring you to the ferry dock, which provides splendid views of the bobbing boats. If you want to make this ride an all-day affair, embark on the 40-minute crossing to Swans Island, which has about 7 more miles of paved road.

To get back on State Route 102A, simply ride downhill and take a left at the juncture. At the next intersection,

bear left at the sign to Seal Cove. The Harbour Dive Shop will be on your right. You are now on the westernmost part of State Route 102, heading north. Cruise past the towns of Bernard and West Tremont to the farming community of Seal Cove. This is the most grueling part of the ride, an up-and-down rollercoaster ride all the way to Pretty Marsh. You can comfort yourself with the sights of Seal Cove and Hodgdon Ponds, secluded bodies of water straight out of an Ansel Adams photo. Eventually, you'll arrive at the northern tip of Long Pond, the largest lake in Acadia National Park and a perfect picnic spot. If you want to give your legs a rest, you can always rent a canoe across the street and work on your arms. At the T-intersection, take a left to tour Somesville, the oldest community on Mount Desert Island, dating back to 1761. To get back to Southwest Harbor, simply turn around, heading south on State Route 102. The shores of Echo Lake are to the right of the road. Back in Southwest Harbor, take a left on Clark Point Road and head immediately to Beal's Lobster Pier. You deserve a meal of lobster and steamers after completing this 28-mile loop.

Rockport-Camden-Megunticook Lake

Allow 3 hours. Moderate to strenuous; hilly terrain. Access: From U.S. 1, veer east on Main Street to get to downtown Rockport. There will be a clearly marked sign. Any good road map will do.

The roads surrounding Camden Hills State Park are popular rides for local bikers, but be prepared. The gently rolling terrain can suddenly turn into steep uphill climbs that will have your thighs burning for the long downhill run. This 20-mile ride starts at Mary-Lea Park overlooking the quiet harbor of Rockport. Start on Central Avenue and ride up the hill, turning right on Russell Avenue.

Soon you'll see Lily Pond and strange black cows that have white, circular stripes across their bellies. These Oreo cookies of cows are better known as Belted Galloways. Rural Russell Avenue soon turns into congested Chestnut Street as you get close to downtown Camden. Bear left at the stone church and turn right onto U.S. 1, being cautious of the traffic. Take a quick left onto State Route 105 West for your first uphill battle. Megunticook Lake soon appears on the right with Maiden Cliff and others of the Camden Hills rising from the far shores. The ride continues around the translucent lake waters as you veer right onto State Route 235 North (Willey Corner Road). This shaded road passes through the small farming village of Lincolnville. Turn right onto State Route 52 South when you reach the stop sign. At Youngstown Inn, the road sweeps downhill, hugging the eastern shores of Megunticook. The trailhead for the climb up Maiden Cliff starts here (see "Hiking," above) if you want to get a bird's-eye view of the lake you just circumnavigated. Continue on State Route 52 South, bearing right on U.S. 1 to cruise through the heart of Camden. If you can tear yourself away from the galleries, shops, and chowder houses that line downtown, turn left on Chestnut Street and retrace your tire tracks back to Rockport.

Islesboro

Allow 3–4 hours. Easy to moderate; relatively flat terrain. Access: The ferry to Islesboro leaves from Lincolnville. Contact the Maine State Ferry Service (tel. 207/ 789-5611 or 207/734-6935).

Except for Manhattan, the islands off the Atlantic coast offer some of the best biking in the northeast. This is especially true when a ferry crossing is involved, because it keeps car traffic to a minimum.

When the ferry is small, like the one going to the island of Islesboro, bikers and walkers usually outnumber all other modes of transportation. This was the case the sunny Sunday my wife Lisa and I chose to make the 20-minute crossing from Lincolnville to Islesboro. Bikers of all ages were standing on the sides of the deck, ready and rarin' to go.

Of all the Penobscot Bay islands, Islesboro is best-suited for bikers. The island is relatively flat, yet hilly enough to offer majestic vistas of the bay; the ferry runs frequently, and the island is long enough to enable a 28-mile bike ride. We disembarked and rode straight on the only road from the ferry. Our first right led us to a T-intersection, where we turned right again. This is Main Street, which passes by the million-dollar mansions of Dark Harbor (so-called "summer cottages") on the way south to Pendleton Point. Here, the perennial battering of the surf has taken its toll on the beach. Long, striated rocks looked like rotted trunks of trees. Harbor seals and loons lounged in the water while we rested on the rocks. We turned around and made our way back to Dark Harbor, turning left on the road just before the general store, one of the few places on the island to buy lunch. This short road loops around secluded shoreside estates before turning left back onto Main Street. Heading north, the road narrows, offering views of Camden Hills State Park to the left and the numerous islands of Penobscot Bay to the right. We passed a small monument and plaque on the left-hand side of the road noting that on October 27, 1780, the first recorded observation of a total solar eclipse in America was made at this very spot. I felt privileged knowing that.

Main Street forks a half-mile after Durkee's General Store. We veered left and pedaled up a grueling hill from which sailboats could be seen hovering in the distant bay— only to zip downhill on an exhilarating run through an ocean seawall. The road loops around the northern tip of the island past small farms, eventually curving downhill to Durkee's General Store and Main Street again. We turned right just past the Islesboro Historical Society for more views of the shoreline before turning right onto Ferry Road. We had just enough time to stretch near the flagpole before the next ferry departed.

North Haven

Allow 3 hours. Moderate; hilly terrain. Access: The ferry to North Haven runs from Rockland. Contact the Maine State Ferry Service for times (tel. 207/596-2203).

North Haven's expanse of unspoiled hillside seems far less inhabited than Islesboro. The ferry from Rockland only leaves three times daily, so there is also less traffic. This 20-mile loop starts at the ferry landing, turning left onto Main Street and heading uphill past the Post Office. When the road forks 1.5 miles later, veer right onto South Shore Road (there are virtually no road signs on this island, but it's almost impossible to get lost). Wide-open vistas of this former sheep-grazing island stand before you. Fields of purple hyacinth were blooming when I was here in early June. Small gray shingled barns seem lost in the countryside, like the Olson House in Andrew Wyeth's *Christina's World*. The road curves around the eastern end of the island, where views of Penobscot Bay open up. Sailboats are anchored in a small harbor under a bridge. This is Pulpit Harbor, and you'll soon pass the Pulpit Harbor Inn where you turn right onto Crabtree Point Road. As you're cruising downhill look for the first paved road that veers right and try to make the turn; 0.3 mile later, take another left onto a dirt road where a forest of pines provide shade. I heard leaves rustling

when I biked through here, only to stop and find a baby doe the size of a puppy whimpering in the woods. Turn right onto Crabtree Point Road, which rolls downhill to a dirt path shortly after a rocky beach to your right. This is the turn-around point. The beach is a perfect spot to picnic, with views of the mountainous mainland in the distance and fluorescent yellow lobster buoys bobbing closer to shore. Venture back up Crabtree Point Road and take a right at Grange Hall. Another right on the next paved road will bring you back to Main Street and the ferry terminal.

OUTFITTERS, RENTALS, REPAIRS & SUPPLIES

Bicycles for the Southwest Harbor Loop can be rented at **Southwest Cycle,** P.O. Box 174, Main Street, Southwest Harbor, ME 04679 (tel. 207-244-5856). For the Camden/Rockport ride, bicycles can be rented at **Fred's Bikes,** Chester Street, Camden (tel. 207/236-6664).

Vermont Bicycle Touring offers three- to five-day guided tours to Penobscot Bay, Boothbay Harbor, and Acadia National Park; P.O. Box 711, Bristol, VT 05433 (tel. 800/245-3868).

Backroads features a five-day trip along the northern coast of Maine, including a night at one of my favorite inns, the Dark Harbor House in Islesboro; 1516 Fifth Street, Berkeley, CA 94710-1740 (tel. 800/GO-ACTIVE).

ROCK CLIMBING

Otter Cliffs in Acadia National Park is where serious vertical freaks congregate to rock climb. Granite rises from the ocean creating some of the only sea-cliffs in the U.S. Both **Atlantic Climbing** and **Acadia Mountain Guides** offer instruction and guided climbs. Atlantic Climbing, 24 Cottage Street, Bar Harbor, ME 04609 (tel. 207/288-2521).

We're Jammin'

If you want to taste the salt of the sea in the northeast's top cruising ground and you don't have the experience to charter a sailboat, try the next best thing—a windjammer. No, your faithful "off-the-beaten-track" outdoors writer hasn't sold out to mass commercialism. Unlike the rest of the wooden ships offering trips along the Atlantic coast, the majority of schooners docked in Rockland, Rockport, and Camden were legitimate working vessels in the early 1900s. Take, for example, the *Wendameen.* Built in 1912 for a wealthy socialite, this 67-foot yacht once entertained such notable guests as Eugene O'Neill and Katherine Porter. Then the Depression came and went, and by the late 30s, the boat was beached on the shores of City Island, New York, in a state of disrepair. Were it not for the incredible dream and determination of one Neil Parker, the *Wendameen* would have been laid to rest there. Parker fell in love with the *Wendameen* at age 17, and 14 years later, in 1986, he bought the heap of dilapidated wood. Miraculously, on July 1, 1990, the *Wendameen* sailed again for the first time in 57 years, completely restored to its original elegance. The boat accommodates 14 guests; the $143 fare is for an overnight stay, including dinner and breakfast. Rates for private charters start at $1,250 per day; P.O. Box 506, Camden, ME 04843 (tel. 207/236-3472).

The *Victory Chimes* offers longer cruises of three to six days, which is the requisite amount of time to see the splendor of Penobscot Bay. Built in 1900 in Bethel, Delaware, to carry lumber along the Chesapeake Bay, the 170-foot *Victory Chimes* is the only remaining three-masted schooner on the East Coast. Rates for the three-day cruise start at $400 per person, including all meals; P.O. Box 1401, Rockland, ME 04841 (tel. 800/745-5651).

More intimate than the Victory Chimes is the 22-passenger *Lewis R. French;* P.O. Box 482, Rockland, ME 04841 (800/648-4544). Launched in 1871, in Christmas Cove, Maine, this 64-foot boat freighted fish, coal, lime, and Christmas trees, before it retired to a life of leisure over a century later. The *Lewis R. French* and the *Stephen Taber* are the oldest windjammers in the fleet.

Further information can be obtained from the Maine Windjammer Association, P.O. Box 317, Rockport, ME 04841 (tel. 800/614-6380). ·

Acadia Mountain Guides, 137 Cottage Street, Bar Harbor, ME 04609 (tel. 207/288-8186).

SAILING

Maine's 2,500-mile stretch of granite coast is best suited for sailing. No other sport gives you the freedom to anchor in a secluded cove, hike on an anonymous island with few footprints, and sleep with seals by your window that evening. Some 2,000-plus pine-studded islands, more than in the Caribbean or Polynesian archipelago, entice sailors from around the globe. They come for the chance to test their acumen—to fight the fog, currents, wide tidal range, and cold waters, and to see the sun seep through and the waters calm upon their next tack. Maine's merciless shoreline and underwater rock ledges demand experience, patience, and well-maintained gear.

Only 250 nautical miles separate Kittery from Eastport, yet the majority of cruising is done between Penobscot and Frenchman Bay along the mid-coast. Here, one can sail from island to island, passing only the lone yachtsman or two. North Haven, Deer Isle, and Acadia's rarely seen sister island, Isle au Haut, are some of the popular anchorages. East of Mount Desert Island, places like Machiasport and Buck's Harbor are a throwback to a bygone era. Fishermen and sailors wave to one another like long-lost friends as they float by. There's rarely more than a handful of sailboats at each harbor.

If you plan to charter a boat without crew, you need to book well in advance and have two boating references. The minimum rental time for bare boats is a week. **Hinckley Yacht Charters,** Bass Harbor Marine, Bass Harbor, ME 04653 (tel. 800/HYC-SAIL) is based in a small fishing village on the southwestern shores of Mount Desert Island. They have 25 boats, ranging from a 34-foot Sabre ($1,775–$1,975 a week) to a 49-foot Hinckley ($3,775–$4,200). **Bay Island Yacht Charters** in Rockland (tel. 800/421-2492) offer 15 bare boats, from a 26-foot Nonsuch ($1,100) to a 43-foot Taswell ($2,950). They also offer American Sailing Association-accredited instruction. For day rentals, contact **Mansell Boat Company** in Southwest Harbor (tel. 207/244-5625); 19-foot Rhodes are available for $85/day.

SCUBA DIVING

Mount Desert Island's Harbor Divers goes on daily trips to the small islands and canyons in **Frenchman Bay** to view seals, porpoises, pink starfish, soft sponges, and other marine life that call the cool waters of Maine home; State Route 102A, P.O. Box 40, Bass Harbor, ME 04653 (tel. 207/244-5751). You can also dive with seals and find wrecks with **York Beach Scuba,** Railroad Avenue, P.O. Box 850, York Beach, ME 03910 (tel. 207/363-3330).

SEA KAYAKING

With hundreds of spruce-covered islands and numerous inlets in which to hide from rough waters, the coast of Maine is easily the top sea kayaking destination in New England. Add the Maine Island Trail to the picture (see the box below) and you have one of the foremost sea-kayaking ventures in the world. All along the coast, outfitters offer four-hour to four-day guided kayaking tours. Follow my lead and throw on a sea skirt. The crowded shops along the coast will soon be replaced by schools of harbor seals.

Frenchman Bay, Acadia National Park

Allow 4.5 hours. Access: Contact Coastal Kayaking in Bar Harbor.

One of the finest ways to see Acadia National Park in the summertime is from a distance, with your head and feet only inches away from the waterline. Sea kayaking around the phalanx of small islands that line Frenchman Bay is the perfect escape from the traffic jams at Bar Harbor. Many outfitters in town offer guided tours, but my wife, Lisa, and I chose Coastal Kayaking because of their 11 years of experience. We arrived at the store at 8:30 AM, met our guides Rob and Matt, and were fitted for life jackets, sea skirts, and booties. Our van soon arrived, six tandem kayaks hooked to the trailer on the back. The eleven of us piled into the van and headed for the "bar" of Bar Harbor, a sand spit that juts out of town

The Maine Island Trail

Few people outside the fortunate ones who live on the northern Atlantic coast know that there's an Appalachian Trail of the sea, the Maine Island Trail. The trail is a 325-mile-long waterway that hugs the Maine coast from Portsmouth to Machias. Designed specifically for kayaks and small sailboats, the Maine Island Trail cruises from pine-covered island to pine-covered island through salt water tributaries, picture-postcard bays, and secluded harbors. These 80 islands are rarely seen by the public, available only to small watercraft by permission of the state and private owners. Needless to say, this sea kayaking nirvana is the ultimate conquest in New England.

The trail has became a reality due to the efforts of the Maine Island Trail Association and Maine's Bureau of Public Lands. Working together, they designed the trail and created a guidebook. The guidebook and access to the privately owned islands are available only to MITA members at a cost of $40 per year. Avid kayakers usually take a month to complete the journey or paddle a small section at a time. The MITA can be contacted at P.O. Box C, Rockland, ME 04841 (tel. 207/596-6456).

at low tide. Matt and Rob unloaded the kayaks and passed out paddles, teaching us some basic strokes since only a few of us had ever stepped foot in a kayak before. We then got acclimated to our cubby holes, threw on our gear, and were pushed off by our trusty guides into the wide blue yonder.

Lisa took the helm in the stern while I provided the steady paddling in the bow. Needless to say, for the first several minutes Lisa steered us far away from the rest of the group while I thrashed my paddle like an injured bird trying to fly. We soon found our rhythm, however, and caught up with the gang as they made their way around the northern shores of Bar Island. Rob showed us several places where bright pink starfish were lying on rocks. As we continued around Sheep Porcupine Island, porpoises were seen jumping to our left and a young seal pup was playing with a buoy. We crossed the main boat passage in and out of Bar Harbor and made our way to Burnt Porcupine Island. Here, we glided past a small

inlet surrounded by steep cliffs called "The Keyhole." The hole was just big enough for a kayak and, at high tide, Rob told us he could coast right up to the small secluded beach behind the wall of rock. We continued paddling along the eastern coast of Long Porcupine Island, which, from a distance, looked more like a dolphin. Loons were lounging in the unusually calm waters of the bay. We stopped for a 15-minute break to stretch our legs at The Hop, a small island at the northernmost tip of Long Porcupine, before making our return trip back to Bar Harbor.

On the west side of Long Porcupine, the water was starting to get choppy, but soon flattened out when we made our run toward Burnt Porcupine. Black Guillemots, a cross between a penguin and a hummingbird, were divebombing their plump bodies into the waters around us. We crossed the main passage again and headed through the sight-seeing schooners and fishing boats toward the pier of Bar Harbor. We were all smiles when we disembarked at 1 PM, exhilarated and hooked on this graceful sport.

Coastal Kayaking is located at 48 Cottage Street, Bar Harbor, ME 04609 (tel. 207/288-9605). The cost for the half-day tour is $43 per person.

ADDITIONAL OUTFITTERS & SCHOOLS

So you want to go sea kayaking, but you have qualms about paddling through ocean swells? No problem. Simply contact Jeff Cooper, owner of **H2Outfitters,** P.O. Box 72, Orr's Island, ME 04066 (tel. 207/833-5257). Jeff and his fiancée, Cathy Piffath (who heads L.L. Bean's water sports programs) are the only two northeasterners who are certified to teach instructors, let alone beginners, in sea kayaking. Thus, if you want to learn from the best, call Jeff. He's already in such high demand for sea kayaking instruction that H2Outfitters courses are now being held in Kittery, Maine, Reading, Massachusetts, Old Saybrook, Connecticut, Riverhead, New York, and Brick, New Jersey. Still, if you can make it up to his home facility, an hour north of Portland, this is the place to learn.

Jeff and I went out one weekday last summer to go over his programs, and I instantly realized why he is one of the gurus of this growing sport. I wasn't pushing enough with my out-of-water hand and Jeff pointed out this weakness without hurting my sensitive writer's ego. Hiding behind his Grizzly Adams beard, he has an engaging wit that helps smooth out any kayaking flaw. No wonder he's called the Director of Fun. We paddled from Orr's Island, where Harriet Beecher Stowe's house still stands, across Harpswell Sound to Casco Bay. In the distance, Eagle Island, once home to Admiral Peary, could be seen. Maine's not quite as cold as the North Pole, but if you roll one of these kayaks in its frigid waters, you won't know the difference. That's why it's important to feel confident.

Besides instruction, Jeff also offers overnight tours along the Maine Coast. Cathy's in charge of L.L. Bean's Paddling School in Brunswick, Maine. Kayaking courses and trips to Penobscot and Muscongus Bays are on the agenda. **L.L. Bean Outdoor Discovery Program,** Freeport, Maine 04033, tel. 800/341-4341, ext. 6666. **Maine Sport Outfitters** also has intensive sea kayaking courses and trips. They teach their courses at the Outdoor School on an island in Muscongus Bay. Contact Maine Sport Outfitters, P.O. Box 956, U.S. 1, Rockport, ME 04856 (tel. 800/722-0826).

SNOWMOBILING

At **Acadia National Park,** you can cruise up the road to the peak of Cadillac Mountain. **Camden Hills State Park** offers 10 miles of groomed snowmobile trails through the woods with views of Penobscot Bay. The **Maine Snowmobile Association** represents 270 clubs and maintains a whopping network of over 10,000 miles (P.O. Box 77, Augusta, ME 04330, tel. 207/622-6983). They also have a trail condition hotline: 800/880-SNOW. For maps and additional information, contact the **Snowmobile Program,** Bureau of Parks and Recreation, State House Station 22, Augusta, ME 04333 (tel. 207/287-3821).

SNOWSHOEING

The 49 miles of trails open to cross-country skiers at **Acadia National Park** are also available to snowshoers. **Camden Hills State Park** also has good snowshoeing trails. See the "Cross-Country Skiing" section, above, for more information.

SWIMMING

Swimming? Let me get this straight. You want to go swimming in the Maine Atlantic? Are you insane? Locals describe the water as refreshing, but they were born here. I'd say it's bone-chillingly cold. You run in for three seconds, scream, watch your ankles turn blue, and then run out. However, the southern beaches are great for strolling and tanning. Long Sands Beach in York, Ogunquit Beach, Wells Beach, Goose Rocks Beach near Kennebunkport, Ferry Beach in Saco, and the legendary 7-mile-long and 700-foot-wide Old Orchard Beach arc all popular destinations. For a little more intimacy, try Fortune Rocks Beach near Biddeford Pool and Laudholm Beach off of Laudholm Road in Elms.

WALKS & RAMBLES

This is a small sampling of the many nature walks that line the coast and islands. Also recommended are **Scarborough Marsh** between Saco and South Portland, **Josephine Newman Sanctuary** in Georgetown, and **Isle au Haut's Western Head** and **Cliff** trails, part of Acadia National Park.

Quoddy Head State Park

Allow 2 hours. Easy. Access: From Lubec, turn left onto South Lubec Road and take your first left on Quoddy Head Road. You'll see a small sign and parking lot for Quoddy Head State Park on your right. Map: Available at trailhead.

Quoddy Head State Park lies on the easternmost point of the United States where Maine meets New Brunswick, Canada. The coastline of Maine might be rugged further south, but here cliffs rise 90 to 150 feet, carved by the battering surf below. Take the short trail to the left which leads to the red-and-white banded lighthouse built in 1858. Grand Manan Island's 12 miles of shoreline can be seen across the Lubec Channel. Return to the parking lot and continue straight to the Coastal Trail. This 4-mile (round trip) path meanders through the forest while hugging the rocky outlets that weave in and out of Maine's coast. While walking on the soft moss-lined trail, you breathe in the best air imaginable—the crisp, pine-filled smell of the forest and the salty sea mist from the pounding waves below. The first overlook is Gulliver's Hole, where the ocean waters surge upward and sound like a lion's roar. At High Ledge, the harsh winds shape the formation of the trees, creating the perfect perch for a bald eagle when I ventured here last. (I wonder if this majestic black and white symbol of America ever flies across the water to Canada?) Green Point is 1 mile into the hike, a picture-postcard lookout where the coastline fades into the horizon. The trail proceeds for another mile to Carrying Place Cove. Here you can return on Quoddy Head Road or simply take the Coastal Trail back. I'd choose the latter.

Monhegan Island, South Loop

2 miles (round trip). Allow 1–2 hours. Access: By ferry from Port Clyde, Boothbay Harbor, and Damariscotta. From Port Clyde, contact the Monheagan Boat Line; tel. 207/372-8848. Boothbay Harbor; tel. 207/633-2284. Damariscotta, tel. 207/677-2026. Map: USGS 7.5 minute Monhegan.

If you only have a limited amount of time on Monhegan, explore the southern part of the island, a region that has captivated artists for over a century. The trail begins at the Monhegan Spa, just above the docks. Walk through the small village and up a hill on a gravel road that eventually turns to grass. Above rocky Lobster Cove, where there are good views back to the mainland, a narrow path continues eastward. Huggingthe shoreline, the trail climbs slightly through a stunted forest of balsam firs and spruce. You soon reach the unusual rock formations in Gull Cove and the 160-foot-high cliffs known as White Head. The bluffs are a good place to picnic and take in the breathtaking views of the ocean. When you are finished, veer left onto the White Head Trail, a grass-covered road. On the way back to the spa, you'll pass the Mon-hegan lighthouse. If time permits, try the 1.75-mile northern loop.

Rockland Breakwater

Allow 0.5–1 hour. Access: From Rockland, take U.S. 1 North and take a right at Waldo Avenue. There will be a small sign for the Samoset Resort. Take a right on Samoset Road and park at the end.

The walk on the breakwater to the Rockland lighthouse is an ideal stroll at sunset. To your right, Rockland's noted schooners are docked in the harbor. To your left, the mountains of Camden Hills State Park stand watch over Maine's jagged coastline. Jeeps were once allowed on the stone jetty, resulting in large cracks, so be careful. Walk to the end of the breakwater on the far side of the lighthouse and see the boats glide in and out of the harbor. You'll feel like Columbus at the edge of the world.

Campgrounds & Other Accommodations

CAMPGROUNDS

Scarcely populated and virtually unspoiled, the camping facilities on the Maine coast rank as some of the top in the nation. This is especially true of the national and state park facilities. For further information on any of the state parks, contact the **Maine Bureau of Parks** and Recreation, Station 22, Augusta, ME 04333 (tel. 207/287-3821).

Blackwoods Campground, Acadia National Park

From the junction of Routes 3 and 233, head 5 miles south on State Route 3. 306 sites, no hookups, handicapped rest room facilities, sewage disposal, public phone, tables, fire rings, grills. Open year round. $14 per night. Reservations can be made at least eight weeks in advance from June 15–September 15 by calling Ticketron (tel. 800/365-2267). Otherwise contact the park at P.O. Box 177, Bar Harbor, Maine, 04609 (tel. 207/288-3338 or 207/288-3274).

Situated in a forest of spruce and shrubs, Blackwoods' 306 sites are conveniently located on the east side of Mount Desert Island, where trails lead up to the peak of Cadillac Mountain.

Seawall Campground, Acadia National Park

From the junction of Routes 102 and 102A, head 5 miles south on State Route 102A. 218 sites, no hookups, handicapped rest room facilities, sewage disposal, public phone, tables, fire rings, and grills. Open late May to late September. Campsites are handed out on a first-come, first-serve basis. Seawall ranges from $8–$12 depending on whether you're walking or driving up to the site. Contact the park at P.O. Box 177, Bar Harbor, ME 04609 (tel. 207/288-3338 or 207/244-3600).

Seawall is on the island's quieter west side. The 218 drive-up or hike-in campsites are linked to shoreline and self-guided nature trails.

Lamoine State Park, Ellsworth

From the junction of Routes 1 and 184 in Ellsworth, head 10 miles southeast on State Route 184. Tel. 207/667-4778. 61 sites, no hookups, pit toilets, and tables.

Situated across Eastern Bay from Mount Desert Island, Lamoine State Park is the best alternative if Blackwoods and Seawall are booked solid. Many of the sites are located on the water, only a few minutes walk from Lamoine Beach.

Isle au Haut, Acadia National Park

8 miles south of Stonington. Accessible by mailboat. Call 207/367-5193 for times. 5 Adirondack-style shelters at Duck Harbor that accommodate 6 people each. Available by reservation only. $25 to secure a site, but form should be sent back on time (April 1). Camping is permitted from mid-May through mid-October. In the shoulder season, you have to walk 5 miles from the town landing to Duck Harbor. Acadia National Park, P.O. Box 177, Bar Harbor, ME 04609 (tel. 207/288-3338).

Consider yourself fortunate if you've secured a spot in one of these lean-tos.

Camden Hills State Park, Camden

Located just 2 miles north of Camden on U.S. 1. Tel. 207/236-3109. 112 sites, no hookups, handicapped rest room facilities, flush toilets, hot showers, public phone, ice, tables, and wood. Reservations can be made by Ticketron. Cost ranges from $11.50 to $15 depending on whether you're a Maine resident.

Ideally located for hikes to Mount Battie and Maiden Cliff.

Warren Island State Park, Penobscot Bay

Tel. 207/236-3109. 10 campsites, 2 Adirondack shelters, a group campsite, fresh drinking water, and docking facilities are available. Cost ranges from $11.50 to $15 depending on whether you're a Maine resident.

This small state park is located on a 70-acre island in the heart of Penobscot Bay, only minutes away from Islesboro. There's one small hitch—you need your own boat to get here.

Cobscook Bay State Park, Sunset Coast

From the junction of Routes 1 and 86 in Dennysville, head 6 miles south on U.S. 1. Tel. 207/726-4412. 100 sites, no hookups, tenting available, pit toilets, hot showers, sewage disposal, tables, and wood.

Many of the sites in this state park have views of Casco Bay. The facility is close to Quoddy State Park and Cutler (see "Walks & Rambles" and "Bird Watching").

RESORTS & INNS

Micmac Farm Guesthouses

Machiasport, ME 04655. Tel. 207/255-3008. $50–$60 per night, $300–$375 per week.

Nestled deep within the woods, these rustic cottages overlook the Machias River. Borrow one of the owners' canoes and cruise down the waterway to fish for salmon. The gourmet restaurant occupies the main house, built in 1776. A great bargain.

Atlantic Oakes By-the-Sea

Bar Harbor, ME 04609. Tel. 800/33MAINE. Rates range from $59 to $146 depending on the size of room and season.

If you want to add tennis to the list of activities at Acadia, this is the place to go. All 150 rooms have ocean views at this former estate nestled next door to the Nova Scotia ferry. The copious amount of food served at the outdoor breakfast buffet will have you energized for the remainder of the day.

Samoset Resort

220 Warrenton Street, Rockport, ME 04856. Tel. 207/594-2511 or 800/341-1650. Rooms start at $120 in the summer, $100 in the winter.

Set on 230 acres of prime shoreline, the Samoset is easily Maine's finest resort. The 132 rooms and 18 suites all have balconies, most with views of Penobscot Bay. Aside from the highly respected golf course (see "Golf"), the resort also features an indoor golf center, indoor and outdoor tennis courts, racquetball courts and groomed cross-country skiing trails.

The Lime Rock Inn

96 Limerock Street, Rockland, ME 04841. Tel. 800/546-3762. Rates range from $85 to $160 depending on the room. The price includes breakfast.

Guests at the Lime Rock have the unique opportunity to climb aboard the owner's 36-foot yacht and sail around Penobscot Bay. Built in 1890 for Congressman Charles E. Littlefield, this eight-room mansion is exquisitely decorated with the finest mahogany furniture, rugs, and king-size beds the owners could find. Simple touches like bringing a jug filled with ice water to your room each evening and treating you to a cold drink upon arrival makes the stay extremely comfortable.

Dark Harbor House

P.O. Box 185, Main Road, Dark Harbor, Islesboro, ME 04848. Tel. 207/734-6669. Doubles are $95–$245 including breakfast.

If you feel like riding the Islesboro bike loop, but are in no rush to get back to the mainland, stay at the island's only accommodation. This elegant yellow-clapboard inn is a former summer cottage built at the turn of the century. Do the bike loop prior to having a meal at the inn's restaurant, or you might find yourself sitting on the front porch with a satisfied stomach and a content smile.

Bagley House

P.O. Box 249C, Freeport, ME 04078. Tel. 207/865-6566. The $95 price includes breakfast.

Whenever I'm in Freeport to pick up a new outdoor wardrobe at L.L. Bean or to attend one of their symposiums, I stay at this pre-Revolutionary War house. Located on the outskirts of town on a backcountry road, the inn overlooks acres of gardens and open fields. The owners, two former nurses from Boston, definitely know how to cater to the whims of their tired guests/patients.

12

The Maine Woods

NE OF THE MOST REMOTE, EXPANSIVE, AND UNDEVELOPED regions in the nation, the Maine Woods are a seemingly endless forest filled with mile-high mountains, large lakes, 100-mile-long rivers, and too many ponds to count. Canoeing and fishing the lakes and waterways of the Maine Woods, and climbing Mount Katahdin, are true wilderness experiences unlike anything else you'll find in New England. Whether you hike, bike, dogsled or ski, it's easy to find your own secluded spot in this immense region.

This vast tract of land has been treasured by outdoorsmen since Henry David Thoreau climbed Mount Katahdin in 1846. Others soon followed in his footsteps, visiting secluded log cabins to fish and hunt. Maine guides would pick their "sports" (guests) up in the towns of Rangeley and Greenville and canoe them to a rustic resort. Here, they could fish and hunt to their heart's content and be served three meals a day in a large lodge.

However, at the turn of the century, the timber industry changed the face of the landscape. Cooperative log-driving along the waterways soon turned to corporate deforestation in the small town of Millinocket. Charles E. Clark, author of *Maine, A History*, writes, "Millinocket sprang full-blown into being in 1899 and 1900. Where in 1898 there stood only a farm in a clearing, an army of workmen of a half-dozen nationalities created a town that by the fall of 1900 housed 2,000 people and a paper mill that was turning out 240 tons of newsprint a day."

If it wasn't for the generous act of one Percival P. Baxter, some of Maine's most precious scenery around Millinocket would have been drastically altered. Twice governor of the state and five times a member of its legislature, Baxter bought, with his own funds, 201,108 acres of wilderness around Mount Katahdin as a gift to the people, "forever to be held in trust in its natural wild state for the benefit of the people and as a sanctuary for the wild beasts and birds." The governor gave to his state the first portion of Baxter State Park in 1931. His final gift of 7,764 acres in 1962 brought the park to its present size.

Lately, timber barons and environmentalists have been engaged in a tug-of-war. The timber industry has made some concessions. In 1974, a paper company agreed to relinquish about 59,000 acres of wilderness lands around Baxter State Park and the new Allagash Wilderness Waterway. Yet, at the same time, other companies cut new swaths of land close to Moosehead Lake and the "Hundred Mile Wilderness" section of the Appalachian Trail. With increased tourism to the region, additional compromises will have to be made. For the time being, Maine's interior is unquestionably one of the major centers of outdoor recreation in the East.

The Lay of the Land

Not nearly as compactly bunched or as high as the Whites, the mountains of the Maine Woods are, nonetheless, geologically related. The **Mahoosuc Range** straddles the New Hampshire–Maine border, just north of U.S. 2; they're the most rugged range in all of Maine, strewn with glacial boulders and carved into steep cirques, with the ridge of the range cut periodically by precipitous "pinches" such as Mahoosuc Notch and Grafton Notch.

Northeast of Carrabassett, the mountain ridges become more irregular and a bit lower, before finally reaching the 5,200-foot monadnock known as **Mount Katahdin,** whose very name has a mythic feel. Lying 150 miles to the east of the Whites, the bedrock that forms Katahdin is gray and pink granite. Like Mount Washington's Tuckerman Ravine, Katahdin also has its share of cirques, including the Great Basin, regarded by many geologists as the finest example of mountain glaciation in the East. From Chimney Pond, steep headwalls ring the U-shaped cirque, forming a trough. The glacier's most distinctive mark on the mountain, however, is the "Knife Edge," a sharp ridge carved from the treeless alpine tundra on the south side of the summit. The glacier cut through the mountain flank like a steak knife, forming a precipitous headwall almost 2,000 feet high.

While the mountains at this end of the Appalachian chain are notoriously dry, both the highlands north of them and the lowland plain stretching off south toward the coast are scored and potholed by literally dozens of rivers and lakes. It's practically impossible to be out of sight of at least one arm of this complex web of waterways. **Moosehead, Rangeley, Sebago,** and the other large lakes lie in broad, shallow basins. The **Kennebec, Penobscot, Allagash,** and **St. John Rivers** tumble from the hills into the valley. And then there are the hundreds of anonymous ponds, strewn like broken glass on a plush green carpet. This is the legendary Maine Woods that Thoreau fell in love with in the 1850s, a vast forest of black, red, and white spruce mixed with stands of white pine, balsam fir, and occasional northern hardwoods—sugar maple, beech, and birch. There are bogs everywhere, overrun with Labrador tea and spaghnum moss, and swatches of alpine/arctic tundra top Katahdin and several other high Maine summits. Northeast of Baxter State Park, the expansive plateau of rambling forest falls away to Aroostook County's lowland at Ashland. The rolling fields here are known for their large harvest of potatoes.

The ten to fifteen million acres of forest provide more than ample space for the abundance of wildlife. Coyotes, red foxes, white-tailed deer, bobcats, black bears, and moose—everywhere—are free to roam wherever they choose. Beavers, otters, grebes, and loons are found lounging in or on the waters, along with schools of landlocked salmon, brook trout, and white perch. Eagles, hawks, ospreys, and peregrine falcons spread their large wings in the sky above.

Except for a small six-week period between July 1 and August 16, bikinis do not thrive in Maine. Summer days are commonly in the 70s, with very few days above 85°Fahrenheit. At nights, it can cool down considerably. Winters are long and cold. In January, the temperature averages less than 10°, and can occasionally drop to –30° below. Snow cover is continuous from Thanksgiving to mid-April and more than 8 feet of cumulative snowfall is not unusual. Dress appropriately and as the saying goes, expect the worst and hope for the best.

Orientation

Although I've dipped south of the north-easterly-tending chain of mountains that are the spine of central and northern Maine for a few special spots like Sebago Lake, most of the coverage in this chapter is in the mountains or the vast reaches of the "North Woods." The boundaries of this large tract of land are not easily definable, but people seem to agree that the North Woods lies west of I-95 and north of Greenville, all the way up to Allagash Village near the U.S.–Canada border.

Large parts the immense "working forest" of northern Maine present logistical problems to outdoorspeople that you don't encounter in any other area covered in this book. West of State Route 11, towns like **Millinocket, Greenville,** and **Jackman** are in effect the northernmost outposts of civilization, the last places you'll find all the conveniences we've come to expect wherever we go: paved public roads, easily obtainable supplies, Big Macs, and automatic tellers. Much of the land is privately owned by large timber and paper companies, and what roads there are through the woods are maintained under their auspices; most of these roads are open to the public for a fee.

It used to be that the many sporting camps spread throughout the woods on remote lakeshores were accessible only by floatplane, but many of them can now be reached by a long, jarring drive on the constantly evolving network of logging roads. The U.S. Geological Survey's topographic maps, such an essential everywhere else, can't always keep pace with the changes to this network of roads. DeLorme's **Maine Atlas & Gazetteer** does keep up-to-the-minute topo maps, and for this reason alone is an indispensable aid to trip planning in the North Woods. It's also loaded with recreational information and contact numbers for various Maine backwoods recreation ventures. DeLorme also publishes special map guides for canoe-camping trips, wildflowers and wildlife identification, fishing spots, even depth charts on rivers and lakes for fishing (contact DeLorme Mapping Company, PO Box 298, Freeport, ME 04032; tel. 207/865-0355).

North Maine Woods, P.O. Box 421, Ashland, ME 04732 (tel. 207/435-6213),

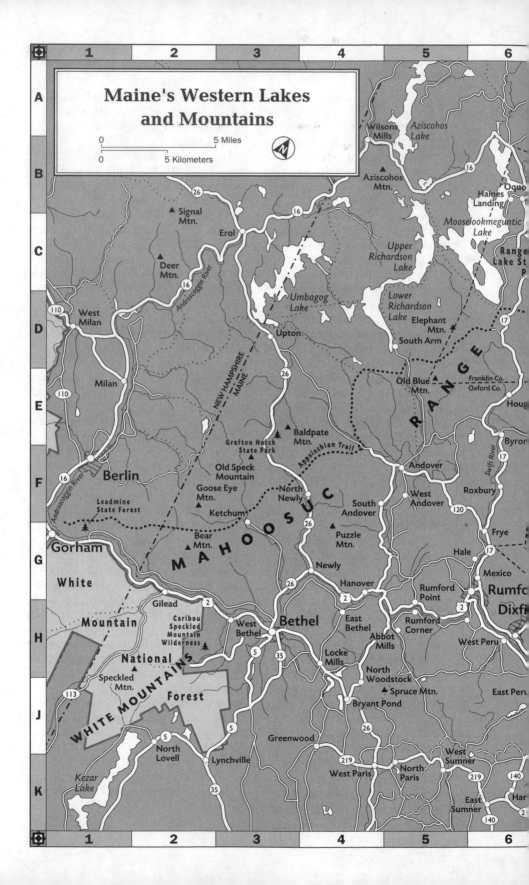

Maine's Western Lakes and Mountains

0 — 5 Miles
0 — 5 Kilometers

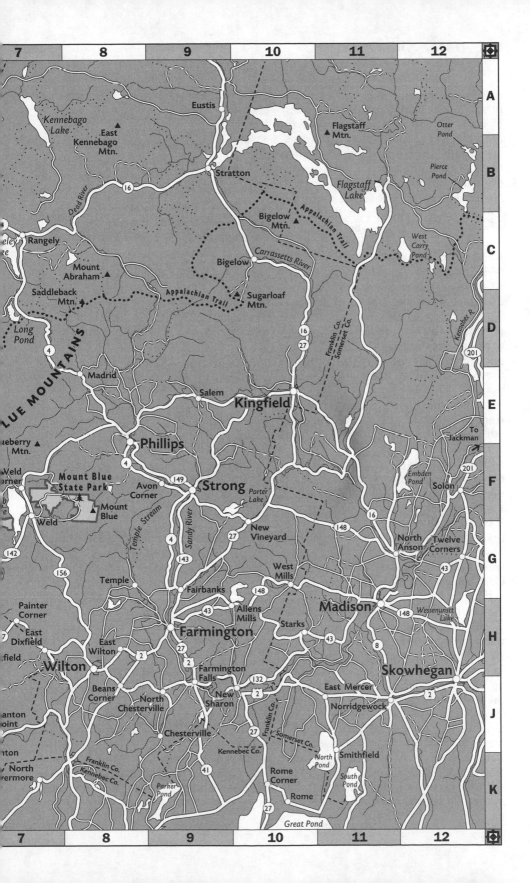

a private landholders' group, manages recreational use of several million acres of commercial forest in northwestern Maine, and publishes maps that are as up-to-date as you'll find for the logging roads, campsites, sporting camps, and outfitters servicing the North Woods.

Huge tracts of forest around Millinocket, Baxter State Park, and Chesuncook Lake are owned and operated by **Great Northern Paper,** One Katahdin Avenue, Millinocket, ME 04462 (tel. 207/723-5131, ext. 1229), which maintains endless miles of logging roads and hundreds of remote campsites. The company publishes a map guide to its lands, which is available by writing to the above address, care of the P.R. Department, or at the checkpoints onto those roads the company opens to the public.

The **Maine Sporting Camp Association,** P.O. Box 89, Jay, ME 04239, puts out a pamphlet listing all its members and their services.

If you're looking for a North Woods experience and don't necessarily want to go to the expense of hooking up with a sporting camp and float-plane service, **Baxter State Park** is probably the easiest place to reach. Simply take **I-95** or the Maine Turnpike to Exit 56 and drive west to Millinocket. Bethel, Rangeley, Carrabassett Valley, and Greenville take a little more imagination and time, depending on whether you're coming from the east or west. Many of the trailheads for hikes and boat launches are accessible only by logging roads not found on any other map. From Rumford on U.S. 2 to Rangeley, head north on **State Route 17,** a scenic drive through the mountains that will leave you breathless with its views of Mooselookmeguntic Lake to the left and Rangeley Lake to the right. At dawn or dusk, **State Route 16** east and west outside of Rangeley is known for its large share of moose sightings. From Greenville to Rockwood, **State Route 6/15** offers vistas of Moosehead Lake and Mount Kineo.

Parks & Other Hot Spots

THE WESTERN LAKES & MOUNTAINS

Sebago Lake State Park

Off U.S. 302 between Naples and South Casco. Tel. 207/693-6613 from June 20 to Labor Day, 207/693-6231 all other times.

Maine's second-largest lake is far more popular than the other waterways mentioned. That's due to its proximity to Portland. Swimmers, fishermen, canoeists, and campers congregate here.

The Rangeley Lakes Region

Accessible via State Route 16 from the east or west, State Route 17 from the south. Contact the Rangeley Lakes Region Chamber of Commerce, tel. 207/864-5364 or 800/MT-LAKES, for additional information.

Nestled between the mountains of spruce, 7 lakes and numerous ponds within a 20-mile radius of Rangeley village form the Rangeley Lakes Region. The area attracts fishermen and hikers in the summer, Nordic and Alpine skiers in the winter.

Carrabassett Valley

Access via State Route 16. For more information, contact the Sugarloaf Area Chamber of Commerce, RR 1, P.O. Box 2151, Carrabassett Valley, ME 04947 (tel. 207/235-2100).

Carrabassett Valley is home of Sugarloaf/USA, one of Maine's premier ski areas. The 17-mile-long valley also offers one of the top golf courses in the state, excellent cross-country skiing, and mountain biking.

Bethel

Access via U.S. 2 from the west, State Route 26 from the east. Contact the Bethel Area Chamber of Commerce for additional information; P.O. Box 439, Bethel, ME 04217 (tel. 207/824-3585 or 800/442-5826).

Only several miles away from Maine's portion of the White Mountain National Forest, this charming village has its own share of skiing and hiking. The Sunday River ski resort is only six miles to the north.

Mount Blue State Park

Off State Route 156. Tel. 207/585-2347.

This picturesque 6,000-acre park is rarely seen by anyone but locals. Hiking and backcountry ski trails traverse Mount Blue, and 6-mile-long Lake Webb offers good fishing and swimming.

THE NORTH WOODS & WATERWAYS

Large tracts of uninhabited forest surround lakes and rivers that are renowned canoeing and fishing spots. This region also includes the Hundred Mile Wilderness Trail.

Baxter State Park

Visitor center is 1 mile east of Millinocket on State Route 11/157. The actual park entrance is 18 miles north of Millinocket on the Golden Road to the Togue Park entrance. Headquarters: Baxter State Park Authority, 64 Balsam Drive, Millinocket, ME 04462 (tel. 207/723-5140).

This 201,018-acre state park is primarily known for massive Mount Katahdin, which stands 5,267 feet high in the center of the park. The mountain has been a popular ascent since Thoreau climbed it in 1846. Yet the park contains far more than Katahdin. The 178 miles of trails, including the first (or last) 10 miles of the AT, climb more than 46 peaks and ridges, 18 of which are higher than 3,000 feet. There are over 200 miles of streams but most aren't canoeable. Fishermen opt for the ponds, home to large numbers of brook trout.

Allagash Wilderness Waterway

Access via numerous lumber roads or by seaplane. Headquarters: Bureau of Parks and Recreation, State House Station 22, Augusta, ME 04333 (tel. 207/289-3821).

This 92-mile long chain of lakes, rivers, and ponds is a protected corridor

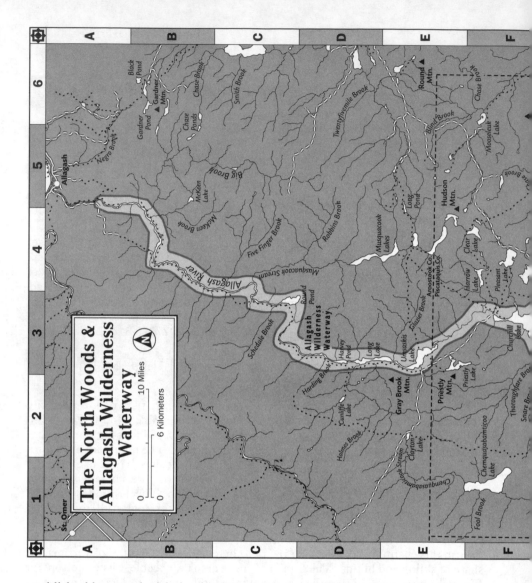

The North Woods & Allagash Wilderness Waterway

established by state legislation in 1966. Only canoes are permitted on this linear waterway, and a trip on it is one of the finest canoeing experiences in the country. Brook trout, togue, and lake whitefish are found in the waters.

Moosehead Lake

Access via State Route 6/15 to Greenville and Rockwood or by a network of lumber roads. For more information, contact the Moosehead Lake Region Chamber of Commerce, P.O. Box 581, Greenville, ME 04441 (tel. 207/695-2702).

At 30 miles long and 20 miles wide, Moosehead is Maine's largest lake. The immense body of water has been a famous resort for well over a century, known for its rugged scenery, including the cliffs of Mount Kineo. Anglers come for the brook trout, landlocked salmon, lake trout, and lake whitefish.

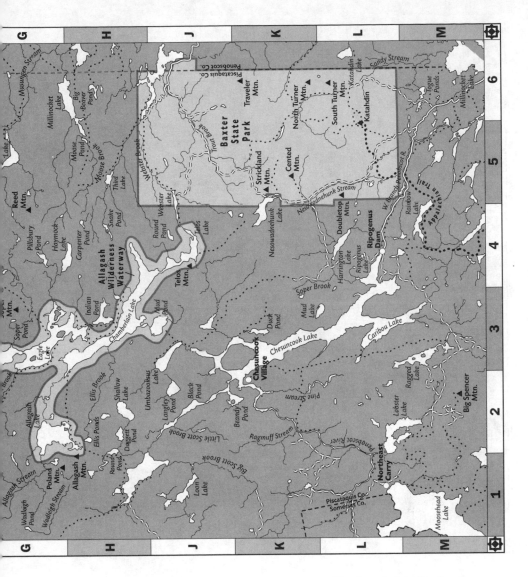

Chesuncook Lake

Accessible only by seaplane or canoe.

Since accessibility is limited, Maine's third-largest lake is rarely seen by anyone. Those who make the extra effort will find a tranquil retreat with Mount Katahdin looming large in the background. Wildlife run rampant through the outlying woods.

West Branch of the Penobscot

One access point at Abol Bridge, off Great Northern Paper's Golden Road out of Millinocket (not the regular town road to Baxter State Park).

West of Ripogenus Dam (which is about 10 miles west of the base of Baxter State Park), this serpentine waterway

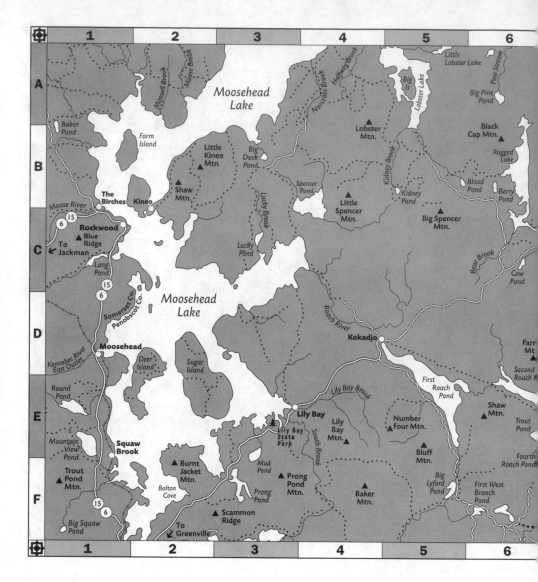

is a placid river that carries canoeists between the larger lakes. East of the dam, the Penobscot is a tumultuous waterway dropping more than 70 feet per mile, popular for whitewater rafting.

AROOSTOOK COUNTY

St. John River

Access via numerous lumber roads or by seaplane.

Almost 400 miles long, the St. John offers exhilarating whitewater canoeing or kayaking during May and June. The river is state property, but the land is privately owned, managed by the North Maine Woods, a consortium of private landowners consisting mainly of paper companies. Call the North Maine Woods (tel. 207/435-6213) or the Upper St. John District Headquarters, Maine Forest

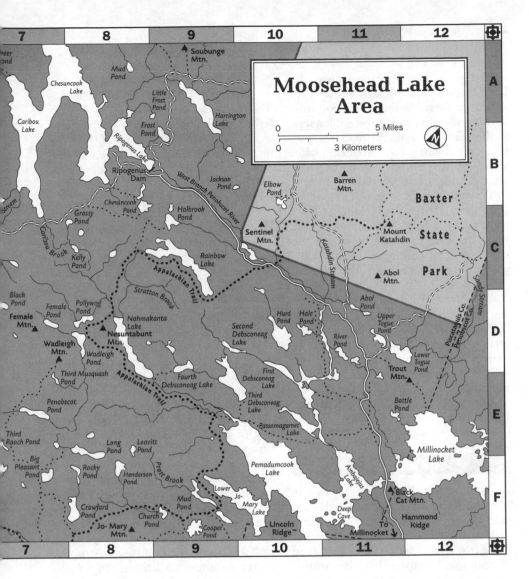

Service (tel. 418/244-6501) for river conditions.

What to Do & Where to Do It

BALLOONING

Lovell Balloon Works in Auburn (tel. 800/788-5562) offers hot-air balloon rides over the south-central part of the state. For rides further north, contact **Balloon** **Drifters, Inc.,** in Augusta (tel. 207/ 622-1211).

BIRD WATCHING

Just as exciting as the Maine coast, the North Woods has close to 200 species of birds. The range of inhabitants include **bald eagles, ospreys,** eight types of **hawks,** and **ravens** on high; **wood ducks,** 23 species of nesting **warblers** (including ovenbirds, black-throated blue warblers, and redstarts), **thrushes, juncos,** ruffed grouse and spruce grouse, the large, red-crested pileated woodpecker and little downy woodpecker, and owls in the spruce/fir forests; and goldeneyes, buffleheads, ruddy ducks, mallards, and, of course, loons on the woodland lakes and ponds. Though I'd spent years around birders, I myself didn't fully take to it until I spent a night camped on Rainbow Lake, off the AT about a day's walk south of Baxter State Park. There were several pairs of loons on the lake, and in the darkness their their loud, whinnying clarions were the wildest, most unearthly thing I've ever heard.

The North Woods are summer breeding grounds for countless species of birds, and with all that wild woods and water out there, you'd be hard put not to find yourself in view of birdlife. Even so, the Allagash Wilderness Waterway, Baxter State Park and the lake country just to its southwest, and the Rangeley Lakes Region are the finest birding locales.

CANOEING

A web of lakes and waterways is stretched across the North Woods, and many have names that bring a dreamy look to the faces of avid canoeists: the Allagash, the St. John, the Saco (see "Canoeing," chapter 10), the Androscoggin, Lake Mooselookmeguntic, the Moose River near Jackman, the West Branch of the Penobscot above Ripogenus Dam, the Fish River chain of rivers and lakes in the far northeast part of Aroostook County... the list just goes on and on, and what I've offered below is only a starting point. For more information regarding canoeing or camping on these majestic waterways, contact the Bureau of Parks and Recreation, State House Station 22, Augusta, ME 04333 (tel. 207/287-3821).

LONG-DISTANCE CANOE-CAMPING TRIPS

The Allagash, St. John, and St. Croix Rivers are legendary three-day to two-week jaunts that offer some of the best long-term canoeing in the nation. In the Northeast, only the Adirondacks in northern New York can compare for remote canoe-camping.

The 92-mile Allagash Wilderness Waterway takes 7 to 10 days to complete. Purchased by the state of Maine in 1966, the waterway is a collection of pristine rivers, lakes, and ponds. Development is prohibited within 500 feet of the corridor, and there are 65 authorized campsites within the zone. The put-in is Allagash or Chamberlain Lake. Take out is usually around the village of Allagash near the St. John River junction. Most of the water is flat, except for two Class II and III stretches known as Chase Rapids and Twin Brook Rapids. Chase Rapids is located at the beginning of the Allagash River. A ranger at Churchill Dam will truck you, your equipment, and your canoe around the rapids if you prefer not to paddle down the whitewater. Plan on spending about two-thirds of your trip on the lakes and one-third of your trip on the Allagash River. The last two weeks in August are probably the best time to go. At night the temperature can dip down to the low 40s, but the black flies and no-see-ums are long gone.

The St. John River, at the far northern reach of Aroostook County, is mostly Class II and III whitewater. Early May to mid-June are the only time to cruise down the rapids. By the end of June, the river might be too shallow. Remember to bring your bug repellent, since this is the heart of black fly season. The put-in for the 7- to 10-day St. John trip is Baker Lake. As on the Allagash trip, most canoeists end at Allagash Village.

However, it's possible to paddle into New Brunswick, Canada.

The **St. Croix River** is less turbulent than the St. John, but it's still predominantly rapids. The three- to six-day trip starts in Vanceboro, at the New Brunswick border in the far eastern corner of the state, and ends in Kellyland, northwest of Calais. Watch out for the wicked Class III drop near Loon Bay. You can paddle down this river all summer.

To some paddlers, even the Allagash is too crowded. Canoeists in dire need of seclusion create their own innovative itineraries. One of these "off-the-beaten-path" trips is a one- to two-week trip starting in **Lobster Lake** (just east of the north end of Moosehead Lake), weaving through the **West Branch of the Penobscot** to **Chesuncook Lake**. Here, one can travel to **Black Pond** and **Caucomgomoc Lake** or continue to **Mud Pond** for a grueling 1.7-mile portage to **Chamberlain Lake**. You're bound to see more wildlife than canoeists on these relatively uncharted bodies of water.

A DAY TRIP & AN OVERNIGHT

Chesuncook Lake

Can be a quiet retreat based out of Chesuncook Lake House, or part of a two-week, very remote canoe-camping trip. Access: for long trip, from logging roads near Lobster Lake (contact Great North Paper, address and telephone above), for short trip, by floatplane. Maps: USGS 30 x 60 minute Moosehead Lake, Millinocket, Chamberlain Lake, or Delorme's Maine Atlas and Gazeteer.

My vote for the most tranquil spot in the northeast goes to Chesuncook Lake. There are only two ways to reach this majestic spot—by canoe, or by floatplane from Greenville. Folsom's Air

Service (see below) will drop canoeists and canoes off anywhere in northern Maine. My wife Lisa and I, unfortunately, did not have time to canoe the route from Lobster Lake, so we opted for the floatplane option. It ended up being a wise decision. We spent two splendid mornings canoeing around the lake, passing only a few canoeists on our trips.

The first morning we rose early to watch mighty Mount Katahdin slowly disrobe its layers of cloud covering and strip down to its talus-covered summit. There was a slight current running against us as we paddled around Gero Island to an unnamed inlet at the northern part of the lake. The only sounds heard were the distinctive call of the loons echoing through the pines. In the distance, we saw movement along the shore, which on closer inspection turned out to be seven white-tailed deer feeding at the water's edge. One of the deer was a buck with a full rack of antlers. The skittish creatures soon noticed our presence and crashed off into the woods. We docked our canoe on the beach, only to see a furry head break the water's surface and show its buck teeth. Unlike most beavers, this one was not bashful. For the next 15 minutes, he showed us how well he swam, even slapping his strange circular tail on the water's surface. Leaving the beaver to his rounds, we found another deer feeding on the far shores, then we canoed with the current back to Chesuncook Lake House (see "Camping & Other Accommodations," below).

On the second morning, the sounds of coyotes howling in the wind replaced the loons' laughing. The lake was shrouded in a mysterious mist, but that didn't prevent us from seeing a red fox on the rocks of Chesuncook Village, the preserved 19th-century lumberman's hamlet that sits on the lake's northwest shore and is listed on the National Register of Historic Places. We paddled up Caucomgomoc Stream and saw one more deer and beaver to add to our list. The elusive moose was nowhere to be found, but it didn't seem to matter. Trivial worries and tensions slid off our shoulders into the clear water below. The hectic pace of modernity seemed like a distant dream, thankfully leaving these shores untouched.

Sunrise Canoe Trip, Kennebago River

Allow 3 hours. Access: State Route 16 West from Rangeley to Kennebago River bridge (Mooselookmeguntic Lake is to the south); or better yet, simply contact Rich Gacki (see "Outfitters," below). Maps: USGS 7.5 minute Kennebago, Kennebago Lake, Little Kennebago Lake, or Delorme's Maine Atlas & Gazetteer.

Registered Maine Guide Rich Gacki works odd hours. But if you want to see the vast array of wildlife that call Maine home, you have to wake up when the animals do. Rich brings paddlers on a unique adventure—a sunrise canoe trip. Every summer morning, he meets bleary-eyed guests at 5 AM on the steps of the Rangeley Inn to drive to the Kennebago River. Here, in the vast darkness, he gently puts the canoes in the still waters for one of the most serene outings in the Northeast.

Sunlight starts to slowly seep in between the branches as you wind down 3 or 4 miles of water in search of the animals. The first time I took this trip five years ago, we were paddling for less than 15 minutes before we heard the loud crunching of branches under hooves. We quietly stopped our canoes to see a large moose slurping the shallow waters of the river. This past time, we saw several beavers and a great blue heron. What makes this trip so exciting is the

unexpected—never knowing what Mother Nature has in store for you. The overwhelming sense of silence is broken only by the stroke of your paddle and the sounds of wakening wildlife. By the time this enchanting trip ends, you're as relaxed as a tall reed swaying in the wind. It's only 7:15, but you've already had an incredible experience before the rest of the world wakes up. What an eventful way to start your day.

GUIDES, OUTFITTERS & RENTALS, TRANSPORT, MAPS & ADDITIONAL INFORMATION

Folsom's Air Service in Greenville (tel. 207/695-2821) will transport you, your gear, and your canoe on seaplane to most destinations in the North Woods. They will also set a time to pick you up once you're finished. If you plan on driving to your put-in on the Allagash Waterway or the St. John River, **Norman Litalier** is a reliable person who will pick up your car and transport the vehicle to your final destination. Cost is $100. He can be reached at Pelletier's Campground, P.O. Box 67, St. Francis, ME 04774 (tel. 207/398-3187 or 207/834-6118).

There's a long list of rentals, shuttles, and guide services. **Allagash Guide Service** in Allagash (tel. 207/398-3418) rents canoes, paddles, and offers transport and car pick-up from the Allagash Waterway or St. John River. Others offering similar services are Maine **Canoe Adventures,** State Route 161, Allagash (tel. 207/398-3191), **Canoes-R-Us,** 2 Church Street, Soldier Pond, south of Fort Kent (tel. 207/834-6793), and **Allagash Wilderness Outfitters,** Star Route 76, Greenville (tel. 207/695-2821). Guides and canoe rentals are offered by **Allagash Canoe Trips,** Greenville (tel. 207/695-3668), **Wilderness Expeditions,** Rockwood (tel. 207/534-2242), and **Katahdin Outfitters,** Millinocket (tel. 207/723-5700). For guides, rentals, and other services on the St. Croix River, contact **Sunrise Canoe Expeditions,** Cathance Lake (tel. 207/454-7708).

Three Registered Maine Guides, Gil Gilpatrick and Alexandra and Garrett Conover, come highly recommended. 60-year-old Gilpatrick is author of *Allagash, The Canoe Guide's Handbook,* and *Building a Strip Canoe.* Gil also wrote DeLorme Publishing's *Allagash & St. John Map and Guide,* an indispensable aid to the trip (contact DeLorme Mapping Company, PO Box 298, Freeport, ME 04032; tel. 207/865-0355 for a copy). He has built hundreds of cedar-strip canoes and practically everything else he brings on his trips, including paddles, chairs, and axes. **Gilpatrick's Guide Service,** P.O. Box 461, Skowhegan, ME 04976 (tel. 207/453-6959).

The Conovers are also Registered Maine Guides, authors, and craftspeople. Garrett's first book, *Beyond the Paddle,* was published in 1991, and the Conovers' joint book on winter travel, *A Snow Walker's Companion,* was released in 1994. Both trained naturalists, the Conovers are now owners of North Woods Ways. The Allagash, St. John, and West Branch of the Penobscot are just a few of the waterways this dynamic duo visits (ask them about their 16-day trip to Grand River, Labrador). Alexandra carves paddles based on a pattern used in this region for over a century. **North Woods Ways,** RR2 Box 159A, Willimantic, ME 04443 (tel. 207/997-3723).

Maine Guide **Rich Gacki** (tel. 207/864-5136) runs the Sunrise Trip described above, which takes care of all the hard thinking and work you might not want to deal with at 5 AM The cost of the trip is $38 per person and includes an early morning snack and breakfast at the Rangeley Inn (see "Camping & Other Accommodations," below).

L.L. Bean Paddling School offers several canoe trips led by Registered Maine Guides. Two five-day trips head to the Allagash River, and two four-day trips go to Moose River in Jackman. They also offer instruction on the shores of Moose Pond, Bridgton. Contact L.L. Bean Paddling Schools, Freeport, ME 04033 (tel. 800/341-4341, ext. 6666).

Mike Patterson from **Maine Sport Outdoor School** offers customized trips on the Allagash, St. John, St. Croix, Penobscot, and Moose Rivers; Maine Sport Outdoor School, PO Box 956, U.S. 1, Rockport, ME 04856 (tel. 800/722-0826).

Northeast Ventures canoes the Allagash in June and July. Contact Northeast Ventures, PO Box 185, Newtonville, MA 02160 (tel. 617/969-7479).

CROSS-COUNTRY SKIING

IN THE BACKCOUNTRY

When you combine a long winter with a vast forest, you get an unlimited amount of cross-country skiing opportunities. Frankly, you can jump on any logging road and ski to your legs' content. Just be cautious of timber truckers, who tend to grin sadistically when they speed up behind you. **"The Maine Guide to Winter,"** published by the Maine Publicity Bureau, P.O. Box 2300, Hallowell, ME 04347 (tel. 800/533-9595 or 207/623-0363), lists all ski-touring operations. The **Maine Nordic Ski Council,** P.O. Box 645, Bethel, ME 04217 (tel. 800/754-9263), publishes its own guide and is the best source for backcountry routes.

The **Bureau of Parks and Recreation,** State House Station 22, Augusta ME 04333 (tel. 207/287-3821), has a guide to cross-country skiing on Maine state parks and public lands. Highlights include **Sebago Lake State Park,** where four and a half miles of trail hug the shores of Sebago Lake, **Bigelow Preserve** overlooking Flagstaff Lake, and the eight miles of trail at **Lake St.**

The Vanishing Wild Woods

The sobering impact of Maine's timber industry on Thoreau's "continuous . . . uninterrupted forest" came clearly into focus for me during my floatplane flight from Greenville to Chesuncook Lake. Like most Maine tourists, I had ventured down several logging roads and saw patches of recently cleared land where the trees were stacked at the side of the road. And of course, I soon realized that the hundreds of trucks loaded with large cargoes of spruce trees that barrel along narrow roads are right up there with moose as a Maine highway hazard. Yet nothing prepared me for the scale of the ruin below us.

Huge tracts of land were clear-cut, reduced to a scarred desert of dirt, tumbled trees, and an endless web of logging roads. Very little terrain was left unscathed. As far as I could see, this was the antithesis of "sustainable-use" forestry; it appeared that there'd been no selective cutting or reforestation. Just a vast wasteland of thin, spindly birches sprouting up where large forests of spruce and fir once stood. Situated so close to the shores of Maine's largest lakes, the clear-cuts were a haunting sight. As naturalist Bill McKibben noted in a recent *Atlantic Monthly* article, "millions of acres of Maine woods might be uninhabited, but don't mistake emptiness for wildness."

The effects of this unbridled timbering are evident throughout northern Maine, all the way to the Canadian border. Canoe the Allagash Wilderness Waterway and you'll camp under tall spruces and furs that line both sides of the river; a pristine corridor of water and trees hides the devastation that lurks less than a quarter-mile away from the river's edge. Maine environmentalists commonly refer to this sort of window-dressing as "beauty strips."

There's no doubt that a tragedy is taking place in the vast recesses of Maine's backcountry, but what to do about it is a many-sided issue and a very tough call. Suffering from a depressed, slow economy like all of New England, Maine needs the jobs and revenue the logging industry brings. Indeed, the forest-products sector still employs close to 100,000 people in northern New York and New England. But the overall revenue generated by the industry is deceptive—not all that much goes into Maine's pockets any more. Furthermore, many of the decisions being made by the logging industry cannot be described as anything other than short-term profit-taking. Maine's backcountry should be seen as a public trust, to be made use of responsibly. Legendary Maine governor Percival Baxter's vision of ·the Maine woodland, that it should be "forever left in its natural wild state, forever kept as a sanctuary for wild beasts and birds," is in serious jeopardy of being forever compromised.

While many advocates of the timber industry defend their practices by reminding all that deforestation has been going on for hundreds of years, it's only relatively recently that many of the largest timber operations have come under the control of international corporations, who care far more about immediate profit than long-term change to Maine's landscape. They cut down everything in their path and rarely reforest. Owners of Maine timber companies in the past would selectively cut down a section of the forest and then replant a new generation of fir or spruce. As one Mainer told me, today's timber companies are even chopping down precious cedar trees, one of the chief food sources for wintering deer—and a tree of no value to paper companies. They are simply letting these trees rot by the side of the road so that one day spruce and fir trees may rise in their places; and when those thickets of trees are gone, deer will continue to head south to find food in the orchards and groves of suburbia.

Another alarming turn occurred in the 1980s, when James Goldsmith, a British entrepreneur, bought the land and mills of Diamond International. He proceeded to split the large conglomerate into small parcels of land and sold them off to other companies. Prime lakefront property was sold to real estate developers. Though the remoteness and largely inhospitable climes of northern Maine would seem to be a formidable barrier to large-scale development, it can't be denied that condos and paved roads are yet another threat to Maine's wilderness.

It's likely that the best hope for compromise between those who would return the Maine Woods to their wild state and those who need to make money off the resources of the woods lies in protecting a good deal of the North Woods as parkland. A small Massachusetts-based group called RESTORE has proposed setting aside 3.2 million acres in the heart of the state as a new national park. The park would stretch 80 miles north to south, from Umsaskis Lake on the Allagash River to Sebec Lake, and 90 miles from east to west, from the East Branch of the Penobscot River to the Canadian border. The park would include the headwaters of the Allagash, Aroostook, Kennebec, Penobscot, and St. John rivers; Moosehead and many other lakes; the AT's Hundred Mile Wilderness; and Baxter State Park. Sporting camps and private roads could remain in the park, but logging and logging roads would be eliminated.

At first glance, the plan sounds admirable. The tourism industry makes far more money than the timber industry in Maine, and if the allure of the wild Maine Woods vanishes with the trees, people will venture elsewhere. This measure would give the scarred land time to heal and replenish, and there's good reason to think that the state of Maine will decide it needs to preserve such an important source of revenue. Money talks.

Even so, this plan for the North Woods makes me think of the world's many nearly extinct animals, beyond hope of reviving through breeding programs, merely playing out the strings of their species in zoos. The North Woods, for much of this century, has been the largest undeveloped tract of land east of the Rockies. As I think of it becoming another Yellowstone or Acadia, with visitor centers, paved park roads, and boundaries, I can't help but mourn. Generations of Mainers have ventured here to hunt, fish, and find ultimate freedom; sad to say, even if conservationists succeed in creating the new park, this land will never be truly wild again.

But that's life in the late 20th century. National park or not, the multitudes of lakes and rivers and trout streams; the high, blasted crags of the mountains; the frigid cold of winter and swarming blackflies of summer; the owls, eagles, moose, and loons—the stillness and quietude of the Maine Woods do yet exist, if not in as great a quantity, if not forever. We can only hope that the timber companies and conservationists work out a compromise so that this great tract of undeveloped land can be preserved for generations to come.

George State Park. For some reason **Baxter State Park** is not listed, but backcountry skiing is popular near Russell Pond and Chimney Pond.

Center Hill Trail, Mount Blue State Park

Allow 1–2 hours. Moderate; a steady climb. Access: From Wilton, go 10 miles north on State Route 156 to Weld and follow signs to park headquarters, to the Center Hill Road parking lot. Map: USGS 7.5-minute Weld.

The Center Hill trail is a relatively quick, 500-foot uphill climb to a dramatic lookout in the heart of Mount Blue State Park. Follow the winding, unplowed road to the picnic area. Here's where the fun begins. Take the Scenic Trail through red oaks, beeches, poplars, and the ubiquitous fir trees to the summit of the hill. This is an idyllic lunch stop. Mountains loom up in every direction; the 3,434-foot Little Jackson Mountain stands directly ahead of you. Saddleback and Sugarloaf mountains can be seen in the distance behind the deep blue body of water called Webb Lake. Do an about-face to see the mountain that gives the park its name.

The Scenic Trail curves around a small bog of blue flag irises, sedges, and sphagnum mosses—the likes of which you'll find everywhere in Maine, breaking up the monotony of the spruce/fir forests—before returning back to the unplowed road. From here, it's a quick run to the ranger station and your car. Check with the ranger for other exciting trails.

Rock Pond Loop, Saddleback Ski Touring Center

Allow 1.5 hours. Easy to moderate; gradual hills. Access: From Rangeley, take State Route 4 South to Dallas Hill Road. Take a left and at the fork, then take a right up to Saddleback. Map: Available in the lodge.

As the rain pelted my car window on the drive to Rangeley, I carefully considered my dilemma. Should I spend the day reading another electrifying Vietnam story by Thom Jones or start Sarah Orne Jewett's novella about late 19th-century Maine? There would be no skiing today. I was leaning toward Jones, but first I had a meeting scheduled with Greg Sweetser, Marketing Director at Saddleback, to find out his favorite downhill and cross-country runs. On the 7-mile drive from Rangeley to Saddleback Mountain, I learned something much more valuable—when Rangeley and the rest of New England are in spring thaw, Saddleback is still covered with snow. Instead of rain, beautiful white flakes were floating down to the snow-covered trails.

I told my editor that I would only feature backcountry runs where the trails are free. Well, I lied. At 2,750 feet, Saddleback is the highest cross-country touring center in New England and definitely worth a visit. For the price of a movie, you can ski on some of the most majestic trails in Maine, the best being the Rock Pond loop.

Narrow Trail 15 climbs gradually through the sweet-smelling spruces until you see a sign for Trail 16. Stay to your left and you'll shoot down a pass that leaves you at Midway Pond. Be careful here: the trails are supposedly groomed, but they are covered with moose tracks that make you feel as if you're skiing on moguls. (At nearby Sugarloaf Ski Touring Center, I skied round a loop that I'm sure is Bullwinkle's midnight jogging track.) The moose have good reason to come to Midway Pond. It's a frosted pearl in mountains gnarled as an oyster's shell. You'll want to take in the splendid view before continuing across the pond to the dense forest once again. Soon, you'll be at the even larger Rock Pond. Cruise across the ice to reach Trail 15 again and glide downhill to the lodge. Skaters will enjoy the wide three-hour trail around Saddleback Lake. If you don't have the energy to try this, at least take Trail 26 on a 20-minute ride to the lake's waters.

NORDIC SKI CENTERS

Yep. Maine's got plenty of them. From south to north:

A working farm in the summer, **Carter's** (State Route 26, Oxford, ME 04270; tel. 207/539-4848), is transformed into a ski touring center come winter. It has 20 km of gently rolling trails leading from the pasture down to the Andro-scoggin River.

Located in a valley near Bethel, **Sunday River Cross-Country Ski Center** (Sunday River Access Road, Bethel, ME 04217-9630; tel. 207/824-2410), has 40 km of groomed trails. The touring center is known for its diversity of terrain, guaranteed to challenge all levels. One of the trails leads to Artist's Covered Bridge. Built in 1872, this weathered town bridge was painted by numerous 19th-century landscape artists.

The **Bethel Inn**'s ski touring center (P.O. Box 49, Bethel, ME 04217; tel. 207/824-2175) is nestled in the foothills of the White Mountains. The stately inn's 25 km of trails cater predominantly to beginners and intermediates.

Opened in 1985 as a cross-country and fitness center, **Troll Valley,** on Red Schoolhouse Road, Farmington, ME 04938 (tel. 207/778-3656), is a former farm; its 25 km of trails wind through 300 acres of farmland.

The town of **Rangeley** maintains over 20 km of trails with set tracks and skating lanes. Contact Rangeley Parks and Recreation, P.O. Box 1070, Rangeley, ME 04970 (tel. 207/864-3326) for maps and more information.

With 85 km of trail, **Carrabassett Valley,** also known as Sugarloaf Ski Touring Center (State Route 27, Carrabassett Valley, ME 04947; tel. 207/237-6830), has Maine's largest touring network. Rarely crowded, the trails from the lodge roll gently into the woods, and over and under log bridges. For experts, it features some of the most challenging vertical drops. If you really enjoy your privacy, head across State Route 27 to the Carrabassett Trail. The path follows the northern edge of the Carrabassett River along the old narrow-gauge railroad bed (see "Mountain Biking," below).

Located on the shores of Moosehead Lake, **The Birches,** in Rockwood, ME 04478 (tel. 207/534-7305), gets the prize for the most remote ski-touring center in the Northeast. If you can somehow manage to get here, you're in for a treat: 40 km of groomed trails overlook Mount Kineo on the western shores of the lake. There's a multitude of backcountry skiing, including guided trips to Chimney Pond at Baxter State Park.

OUTFITTERS

Back Country Excursions, RFD 2, P.O. Box 365, Limerick, ME 04048 (tel. 207/625-8189), offers guided ski trips from their home base in Parsonfield.

Mahoosuc Guide Service, Bear River Road, Newry, ME 04261 (tel. 207/824-2073) offers guided overnight trips with dogsleds carrying your gear (see below).

DOGSLEDDING

Interested in doing some mushing? Well, the Maine Woods are the only place to try it in the Northeast. Polly Mahoney and Kevin Slater offer one-day or overnight trips from their base in Newry. The one-day jaunts head to the Maine shores of Umbagog Lake. They also offer two- to five-day tours in the northern regions of Maine. Depending on the size of the party, they use Cree-type toboggan sleds or traditional Inuit quimatik sleds blanketed with deerskins for warmth. Many of their dogs were born and raised in the Yukon and Alaska, and are veterans of the Iditarod and Yukon Quest dog races. Contact **Mahoosuc Guide Service,** Bear River Road, Newry, ME 04261 (tel. 207/ 824-2073).

Just north of Sugarloaf, Tim Diehl offers half-hour rides by his team of Samoyeds known as the "White Howling Express." All of his dogs were unwanted pets until Diehl adopted and trained them. Custom rides are also available.Contact **T.A.D. Dog Sled Services,** P.O. Box 147, Stratton, ME 04982 (tel. 207/246-4461).

Obviously, warm gear should be worn on these rides. Insulated boots, gloves, layered clothes, a hat, and scarf are essential. Protective eyewear is also useful, since the dogs kick up a lot of snow.

DOWNHILL SKIING

"Why go to Maine?" skiers ask me, unaware of their naïveté. "Vermont feels like the tropics compared to that place in the wintertime." First of all, Vermont feels just as cold as Maine when you're at 4,000 feet on a frigid January day. Second, if you haven't hit Maine's slopes lately, you're missing out on some great terrain. This hardscrabble land of tall spruces is home to the only tree-line-and-up skiing in the East—Sugarloaf, and Sunday River's wicked White Heat Run. Add little-known Saddleback and the mild slopes of Mount Abram, and you have four ski areas that provide long winters, mucho snow, and top-of-the-line services including hot tubs, fitness centers, and sumptuous accommodations. Oh, there's one other teeny weeny factor. The only line you'll encounter is the one at the microbrewery *after* skiing.

Sugarloaf/USA

Carrabassett Valley, ME 04947. Tel. 207/ 237-2000; snow report, 207/237-2000, ext. 6808. 107 trails (32% beginner, 33% intermediate, 35% expert), 14 lifts, including a high-speed detachable quad, a 4-passenger gondola, 2 regular quads, a triple, and 8 doubles; 2,820-foot vertical drop. Full day tickets $43 weekends, $36 weekdays.

The road up to Sugarloaf/USA is an impressive sight. This big, brooding mountain, Maine's second-highest peak, towers over Carrabassett Valley. Start with the three-mile long intermediate Tote Road, from which you can see Mount Katahdin and Mount Washington at the top. Once you've warmed up, throw your body down a seemingly endless twisting row of moguls known as the Bubblecuffer. For a finale, tackle the Skidder, an appropriate name for a run that's guaranteed to throw you on your ass.

Sunday River

Bethel, ME 04217. Tel. 207/824-3000; snow report, 207/824-6400. 110 trails (25% beginner, 40% intermediate, 35% expert), 16 lifts including 8 quads, 5 triples, and 2 doubles; 2,300-foot vertical drop. Full day tickets $43 weekends, $39 weekdays.

What Sunday River lacks in height, it more than makes up for in steepness and snow cover. If you don't believe me, try White Heat. Marketed as the "longest steepest, widest lift-served trail in the East," one side of the trail is groomed, the other all bumps.

@#*#$%*

Rangeley, ME 04970. Tel. 207/864-5671; snow report, 207/864-3380. 41 trails

(30% beginner, 35% intermediate, 35% expert), 5 lifts including 2 doubles; 1,830-foot vertical drop. Full day tickets $31 weekends, $17 weekdays.

Listen, I can't give away all my secrets!... Okay, fine, I'm talking about **Saddleback.** Located in the heart of the Rangeley Lakes region, this mountain is one of my favorite places to ski in New England. Listen, the base lodge at 2,450 feet is the highest in New England, so if there's snow anywhere in the Northeast, it's here. You're dreaming if you think I'm going to give away my favorite trails. I've said too much already.

Mount Abram

Locke Mills, ME 04225. Tel. 207/875-2601. 35 trails (25% beginner, 50% intermediate, 25% expert); 2 double chairs; 1,030-foot vertical drop. Full day tickets $28 weekends, $18 weekdays.

Almost on the verge of bankruptcy and closure, the lifts of Mount Abram have thankfully kept running due to the generosity of several locals. The mild-mannered mountain caters to young families and skiers who have no intention of becoming the next Jean Claude Killy.

FISHING

Let's summarize this chapter so far. Ballooning was so-so, cross-country and downhill skiing were well worth the effort to get here, canoeing was undoubtedly the best in the Northeast if not one of the top five destinations in the country, and now freshwater fishing. With rivers and lakes full of thriving wild **trout** and **landlocked salmon** and sporting camps catering exclusively to fishermen, the Maine Woods once again takes home first prize.

Move Over Milwaukee

Microbreweries and brew pubs are almost as prevalent as moose in the Maine Woods. Both Sunday River and Sugarloaf have their own brewing companies to chill you out after a frigid day on the slopes. There's also No Tomatoes (Great Falls Brewing Company) in Auburn, Lake St. George Brewing Company in Liberty, and a host of other small breweries. Indeed, Maine has more brewers per capita than any other state in the union. Let's face it, Mainers need some hobby in those long winter months. So sit yourself down on one of the stools and order a thirst-quenching Katahdin Red Ale, Black Bear Stout, or a Penobscot Pilsner.

Fishing for coldwater species like **brook trout** and **landlocked salmon** is best in May and June. The salmon are usually taken by surface trollers using streamer flies. Warmwater species like **bass, pickerel,** and **perch** are active during the summer months. There are hundreds of exceptional fishing holes; so many, in fact, that it's almost foolish to try to list the ones that are better than the rest. I'll mention the bodies of water that were recommended to me, but I highly recommend staying at one of the lodges or hiring a Registered Maine Guide.

The **West Branch of the Penobscot River** near Abol Bridge (near the south end of Baxter State Park, northwest of Millinocket) is a popular spot to lure landlocked salmon. Even farther north, in Aroostook County, salmon grow to unusually large sizes on the 80-mile, aptly named **Fish River** chain of lakes (Long, Eagle, and Square lakes). Two more hot spots for salmon and **brook trout** are **Moosehead Lake** and the **Rangeley Lakes region,** as evidenced by the number of lodges found there. **Nesowadnehunk Lake,** on the western edge of Baxter State Park, is also renowned for its brookie fishing. **Togue** are found in **Chamberlain Lake, large-mouth bass** on the **Kennebec River,** and the elusive **brown trout** has been hooked at **Androscoggin Lake.**

The **Maine Publicity Bureau,** P.O. Box 2300, Hallowell, ME 04347 (tel. 800/533-9595 or 207/623-0363) publishes a useful guide to fishing.

MAINE GUIDES & OUTFITTERS

If you're looking for a respected Registered Maine Guide in the **Carrabassett Valley** region, contact Steve Warren (tel. 207/246-4042). In **Rangeley,** contact Ned Stearns at Grey Ghost Guide Service (tel. 207/864-5314). At **Moosehead Lake,** contact Bob Lawrence (tel. 207/534-7709 or 800/346-4666). On the **Kennebec,** contact Caroll Ware (tel. 207/474-5430).

The **L.L. Bean Fly-Fishing School,** Freeport, ME 04033 (tel. 800/341-4341 ext. 6666), offers a five-day intermediate fly-fishing school at Weatherby's in Grand Lake Stream. Cost is $1,295.

SPORTING CAMPS

Other states, particularly out West, have their share of wilderness lodges, but very few places have the tradition and distinctive charm of the Maine sporting camp. These rustic retreats first started to appear in the late 1800s, when "sports" (city folk) were met by guides and escorted up the lake or river to a gathering of log cabins. Here, they could fish

and hunt to their heart's content and be served three meals a day in a central lodge. Many of these sporting camps still exist; nowadays, with access by floatplane and logging roads, you no longer have to rely on a guide to pick you up in Rangeley or Greenville. However, there are a slew of so-called sporting camps that are nothing more than log cabins. They leave you out in the middle of nowhere without a guide or advice on where to fish. In an article on sporting camps from a May 1992 *Yankee* magazine, writer Michael D. Burke discussed his criteria for finding the best sporting camps:

1. Peeled pine logs are essential and so are bare wood floors.
2. There must a minimum of ornamentation, and what there is must be appropriate, such as a clothes hook made from a tree branch.
3. It must be in an inspiring spot, preferably directly on a body of water.
4. It should be hard to get to, not directly off the turnpike.
5. A typical sporting camp provides a Registered Maine Guide for the guests.
6. A true sporting camp must have porches and rockers and come equipped with nearby loons to provide a mournful sound in the evening.

If you'd like a complete listing of Maine sporting camps, contact **The Maine Sporting Camp Association,** P.O. Box 89, Jay, ME 04239. If you'd like to own a sporting camp, contact Ron Masure at **Sports Real Estate,** Greenville, ME 04441 (tel. 207/695-2047).

My first and foremost criteria in evaluating camps is seeing that they have a long history of leaving customers satisfied. All the following camps can boast of this, and meet the above requirements as well:

Weatherby's

Grand Lake Stream, ME 04637. Tel. 207/796-5558. $80 per person double occupancy including all meals.

Fifteen log cottages surround the white lodge, built in 1870. Motorboats are $34 per day, guides $120 daily. The sporting camp is located at Grand Lake Stream near Calais.

Bald Mountain Camps

P.O. Box 332, Oquossoc, ME 04964. Tel. 207/864-3671. $95 per person, including all meals.

Some people might find this lodge too close to the main road, but it's just as quiet as the other camps. Built in 1897, the 15 camps are spread along the edge of Mooselookmeguntic Lake. The place is popular with children in the summer.

Grant's Kennebago Camps

P.O. Box 786, Oquossoc, ME 04964. Tel. 207/864-3608 or 800/633-4815. $92 per day, including all meals.

Only serious fishermen need apply. Grant's is located nine miles down a private dirt road on the intimate shores of Kennebago Lake. It's a fly-fishing-only body of water. The 18 camps, replete with dock and boat, were built in 1905 by Maine guide Ed Grant.

Bosebuck Mountain Camps

Wilson Mills, ME 04293. Tel. 207/243-2945 or 207/486-3238. $75 per person including all meals.

Located on the remote shores of Aziscohos Lake, these 11 camps can be reached by boat or via a 14-mile-long private road. The owners have access to Big and Little Magalloway Rivers, which are for fly-fishing only.

Tim Pond Wilderness Camps

Eustis, ME 04936. Tel. 207/243-2947. $98 per person including all meals.

In business since the 1860s, Tim Pond is billed as "the oldest continuously operating sporting camp in America." Fly-fishermen don't have to venture far from their log cabins to find the secluded waters of the pond.

Attean Lake Resort

Jackman, ME 04945. Tel. 207/668-3792 or 207/668-7726. $150 per person or $200 per couple, including all meals.

You can't get much more remote than this sporting camp, located on an island in Attean Lake. The 20 upscale camps (at least, by fishermen's standards) come with boats and canoes.

Tomhegan Wilderness Resort

P.O. Box 308, Rockwood, ME 04478. Tel. 207/534-7712. Moderate rates include all meals.

Built in 1910, these nine camps are located on the shores of Moosehead Lake. It's a 10-mile ride on a dirt road from Rockwood Village to get here. You can tell that Tomhegan is more interested in fishing than hunting by the tame deer that walk the grounds. Cross-country skiing and snowmobiling are available in the winter.

Nugent's Chamberlain Lake Camps

P.O. Box 632, Greenville, ME 04441. Tel. 207/695-2821. $22–$60 per person.

One of the newer sporting camps (1930s), Nugent's eight housekeeping cabins sleep 2 to 10 people. The camps are located on Chamberlain Lake, 50 miles north of Millinocket between Baxter State Park and Allagash Mountain. Leave the car in Greenville and take a seaplane (see Folsom's under "Canoeing").

Libby Sporting Camps

Drawer V, Ashland, ME 04732. Tel. 207/435-8274. $70 per person including all meals.

Family owned and operated for more than 100 years, Libby's guides will take you to one of 40 lakes and ponds from 8 outposts. The camp is located on the Aroostook River near Presque Isle.

GOLF

Ranked 1st in Maine and 63rd in the nation by *Golf Digest*, the **Sugarloaf/USA** course in Carrabassett Valley (tel. 207/237-2000) has no equal in the Maine Woods. Designer Robert Trent Jones, Jr., described Sugarloaf as "one of the most spectacular courses I've ever had anything to do with." With exquisite views of the mountain, the back nine features six challenging holes along the Carrabassett River, known as "the string of pearls." Golfers at the 11th hole tee off from an elevation of 200 feet across the river—the perfect water trap.

The **Golf School** offers weekend or midweek instruction. Two-day courses start at $439 per person, including accommodation. For more information, call 800/240-2555.

HIKING & BACKPACKING

The terrain in the Maine Woods is so diverse that some trails feel like the soft, springy hikes in the Berkshires, others like the impregnable granite of the Whites. Most of the climbs are rugged and challenging and offer exceptional views of the surrounding forests and lakes. However, there's one mountain that is unlike any other climb in the Northeast. It's called Katahdin.

DAY HIKES

Mount Katahdin, via the Helen Taylor, Knife Edge, Saddle and Chimney Pond Trails

9.8 miles. Allow 8–10 hours. Strenuous; steep, rocky, and mountainous. Access: The trailhead is located at the Roaring Brook Campground, 8 miles north of the Togue Pond Gatehouse in Baxter State Park. I would advise getting here by 6:30 AM, since the parking lot fills up rapidly and hikers are then turned away. Map: USGS 7.5-minute Mount Katahdin.

Mount Katahdin is a fitting end to a northbound Appalachian Trail end-to-end hike. Reaching the mass of rock atop the 5,267-foot summit is a challenge to the most experienced hiker, even the through-hiker who's spent the last 6 months racking up more than 2,100 rugged miles. Yet it's somewhat of a disappointment that the AT ascends Katahdin's broad mass from the west on the Hunt Trail, the easiest (if there's such a thing) and least spectacular path to the peak. For an unparalleled mountainous ascent in the east, you should not miss the Knife Edge. As the name implies, this 3- to 4-foot-wide granite sidewalk sharply drops off more than 1,500 feet on either side.

The best way to reach the Knife Edge is the Helen Taylor Trail from the Roaring Brook Campground. The parking lot at the campground only allows a certain amount of day passes, so it's imperative that you arrive early. Bring at least a gallon of water per person and lunch. The entire loop is approximately

10 miles and will take anywhere from 8 to 10 hours to complete. If the weather turns bad, however, you should not attempt to climb the Knife Edge.

All the ascents to Baxter Peak are a struggle. You start at about 1,500 feet and don't stop climbing until you run out of mountain. The Helen Taylor trail splits from the Chimney Pond Trail 0.1 mile from the campground. One mile later, you begin to climb more steeply as spruces and balsams replace the hardwood forest. After another mile, views of Pamola Peak, Chimney Peak, and the Knife Edge start to appear, daring you to set foot on them. You finally reach the 4,902-foot Pamola Peak 3.2 miles into the climb. Tiny Chimney Pond can be seen far below.

Bear left onto the Knife Edge Trail for a short descent into a gully between the peaks of Pamola and Chimney. On the right, you'll see the Chimney, a couloir climbed only by experienced rock climbers. Continue on the extremely steep trail to the summit of Chimney. Here's where the fun begins. The narrow trail drops off precipitously on both sides as it continues to climb. The east side plunges down to Avalanche Brook, the west side to the South Basin. The trail ascends South Peak first. In another quarter of a mile, you should congratulate yourself, since you are now at the summit of Baxter Peak, the top of Katahdin. Rest your weary legs and take in the spectacular views of northern Maine—Chesuncook Lake, the West Branch of the Penobscot River, Big and Little Spencer mountains, and all the peaks that form massive Katahdin.

As you descend the 2.2-mile Saddle Trail, you'll start to tire. Just remember this one item: Thoreau climbed this mountain when there was no trail. "The mountain seemed an aggregation of loose rocks, as if some time it had rained rocks, and they lay as they fell on the mountain sides," he wrote in his book,

The Maine Woods. "It was vast, Titanic, such as man never inhabits. Some part of the beholder, even some vital part, seems to escape through the loose grating of his ribs as he ascends." If you didn't feel your ribs cramping on the way up, you'll most definitely feel your legs sinking on the way down.

The Saddle Trail ends at the Chimney Pond Campground, a mere 3.3 miles from the Roaring Brook Campground. Think of the great pasta dinner you're going to have as your spaghetti legs continue descending the Chimney Pond Trail; 1.3 miles into this trail, you'll reach Basin Pond, a fine place to cool off. The final two miles feel like an eternity, but you'll eventually make it back to your car, and will feel proud of your accomplishment for at least as long as your legs are sore.

Gulf Hagas

Allow 7–8 hours. Moderate; terrain varies from rocky to flat. Access: 4 miles north of Brownville Junction on State Route 11, turn left at the sign for Katahdin Iron Works. Drive 6.5 miles to the Works, where you register and pay a day fee to the logging company. Also ask for a map. At the fork, bear right, and then left 3.4 miles later. Approximately 7 miles from the Works, you'll see a large parking lot. Maps: USGS 15-minute Sebec Lake; logging company's map (comes with day-use fee).

The people of Maine often refer to Gulf Hagas as the "Grand Canyon" of the state. There's nothing wrong with a little zealous pride, but Gulf Hagas is no Grand Canyon. However, it is one of Maine's most spectacular hikes. Hidden in the Hundred Mile Wilderness of the Appalachian Trail which extends from Monson to Abol Bridge, Gulf Hagas is a gorge carved by the pounding waters of the Pleasant River and the lumbermen's dynamite. A series of exquisite waterfalls form as the river drops nearly 500 feet in 2.5 miles through the narrow walls of the slate canyon.

A loop of little over 8 miles long, you should give yourself at least seven hours to enjoy the entire trek. Extended roots, large boulders, and sheets of rock make meandering slow, and you'll want to stop numerous times to gasp at the many breathtaking views, have lunch, and swim. Only 0.2 mile from the parking lot, you'll encounter your first obstacle, the West Branch of the Pleasant River. Either take your shoes off or bring a set of aquasocks in addition to your hiking boots to cross over the water. Bear right and follow the white blazes of the AT through the Hermitage, a grove of towering white pines preserved by the Nature Conservancy of Maine. At a junction, the AT bears right and continues up White Cap and Gulf Hagas mountains. You'll go straight, following the blue blazes across Gulf Hagas Brook to start the 5.2-mile circuit.

At the boulder inscribed with a bronze plaque, bear left for several hundred yards to view the first of many waterfalls. Called Screw Auger, the water plunges 26 feet down to the canyon rocks. Continue walking past the falls to a clearly marked sign indicating the Gulf Hagas Rim Trail (do not retrace your steps back to the large boulder). The Rim Trail offers many side trips to scenic overlooks perched high atop the canyon walls. The first detour is Hammond Street Pitch, where, unfortunately, trees obstruct the view of the rushing water 90 feet below. The next vista, Jaws, will not disappoint. Here, the chasm of rock is so narrow that the river surges upward to push through the small opening. Clamber over the large slabs of rock and jutting tree roots to reach the next highlight, Buttermilk Falls. The frothy white foam the river

produces as it cascades down the rocks justify the name. The river forms a watering hole just beyond the falls that is ideal for swimming. Under the sun's rays, your skin will turn the color of the water, auburn-red. Unfortunately, the sunlight doesn't keep the river warm. What do you expect in Maine?

Continue along the rim to another falls, Billing's, before you reach the Head of the Gulf. This is the beginning of the canyon, where you really sense the power of the river as it swirls around an island and falls down the rocky steps. The trail bears right and heads inland, completing the circuit on Old Pleasant River Road. Unlike to the Rim Trail, this path is easy and uneventful as it goes straight through a dense forest of maples, birches, and beeches back to the inscribed boulder. The tedium of the trail is only relieved by the occasional sight of colorful wildflowers. At the boulder, retrace your steps over Gulf Hagas Brook to the white blazes of the AT. This will bring you through the Hermitage once again, over the river, and back to the trailhead.

West Kennebago Mountain

Allow 3–4 hours. Moderate. Access: From the junction of Routes 4 and 16 in Oquossoc, travel west on State Route 16 for 4.9 miles. Turn right onto a dirt road, bearing right at 1.3 miles from State Route 16. 3.1 miles from State Route 16, turn right on Lincoln Pond Road, a large logging road. 5.4 miles along this road are places to park. The trailhead is located on the left-hand side of the road. Map: USGS 15-minute Cupsuptic.

To reach the West Kennebago Mountain trailhead, you first have to drive past this mighty mountain on a logging road. At just over 3,700 feet tall, the firetower on the summit stares down at you. To see this point close up is not an easy task. Contrary to the Maine Geographic Hiking Guide which I was using, the endeavor is not *slight* (unless you are the fire warden who lives in the cabin close to the peak). In fact, several people I met on the trail used the same guide and were not ready for the daunting task at hand. They turned back, having never reached the top.

The 2.25-mile climb is steep almost immediately. You climb rapidly through a hardwood forest, gradually leveling off as you reach the odoriferous pines. However, this part of the trail can be a struggle as well, since the path is not well-maintained. Numerous trees had fallen on the trail and over a brook, obstructing forward progress. Eventually, you reach the fire warden's cabin and continue up the trail on the right-hand side. The path gets steep again, climbing over rocks, as you approach the ridge of the summit. Here, vistas of the vast Rangeley Lakes region open up. The trail continues along the ridges for at least 15 minutes more, until you reach an open clearing. This is the best place to have lunch, since the views atop the summit are not above the tree line. The waters of the Kennebago, Cupsuptic, and Azicohos lakes add some vibrant color to the surrounding evergreens. This is but a small appetizer before the main course. Climb the last few steps to the summit and up the firetower. Every step higher offers better and better views of Maine's expansive mountains, lakes, and forests. It's like looking at a Chinese silkscreen on which vast layers of undulating hills fade into the horizon. Upon reaching the top, it's possible to see Mount Washington in New Hampshire, Mount Megantic in Quebec, and Katahdin in Baxter State Park. If the view leaves you gasping for air, there's a rocking chair in the room atop the firetower to sit in. You'll need the rest before you attempt the descent.

Bald Mountain, Rangeley Lakes Region (Oquossoc)

Allow 1.5–2 hours. Easy. Access: From Rangeley, take State Route 4 North to Oquossoc. Take a left turn on Bald Mountain Road and continue for 0.9 mile. A sign for the Bald Mountain Trail is displayed on the left-hand side of the road. Park here. Map: USGS 7.5-minute Oquossoc.

For a quick introduction to the splendor of the Rangeley Lakes region, hike up Bald Mountain. The trail ascends gently through a forest of firs and birches before coming to a small plateau about halfway up the hill. Take a quick right and continue up the path. Eventually, you'll make it to the rocky ledge of the mountain's summit. Standing 2,443 feet, there are fine views of Rangeley Lake to the east and the cerulean Mooselookmeguntic Lake to the south. Climb the firetower on a clear day, and you'll spot Saddleback and Kennebago mountains. Bald Mountain will whet your appetite for harder climbs and more spectacular vistas.

BACKPACKING

Perusing these pages, are you? Thought you'd just give this remote part of New England a quick look-me-over. Well, congratulations, you hit the jackpot! A long-distance tramp in Maine will keep you so far from roads, towns, the sounds of internal combustion, and all other signs of modernity that you may lose track of which century you're in. Maine's section of the Appalachian Trail wins two honors among those who know the length of the trail, which is no small thing, indeed: The **Mahoosucs** are pretty much universally held to be the most difficult section of the entire trail, Smokies and Whites included—it's a beautiful and varied ridge walk, but hellishly steep, strewn with boulders, and nearly totally dry to boot. I had time to walk only a few portions of the four-day, 30-mile-long stretch of the AT along the ridge of the Mahoosucs for this edition, but I'll get to it next time (gimme a break! I went through two pairs of boots researching this book as it is!). If you want the most rugged backpacking New England has to offer, the Maine Appalachian Trail Club's *Appalachian Trail Guide to Maine* will lay out the trip for you—and you'll get beautiful topo maps to the entirety of the AT in Maine to boot. Write to M.A.T.C., P.O. Box 283, Augusta, ME 04330.

As for the other honor, backpacking in central Maine is about as far as you can get from civilization on the entirety of the AT, not to mention New England. Please proceed to Shaw's Boarding House in Monson for a hot shower, dinner, and advice about tackling the wildest woods in the Northeast:

Hundred Mile Wilderness, Appalachian Trail

99.4 miles. Add another 14 miles if you plan to climb Mount Katahdin as the grand finale. Allow 10 days to 2 weeks. Strenuous. Access: Located in central Maine, between Monson on the south and the south end of Baxter State Park on the north. For the south-to-north hike, begin at the junction of the AT and Maine Highway 15, near the Spectacle Ponds, 4 miles north of Monson and 10 miles south of Greenville. The trail ends at the West Branch of the Penobscot River, at a Georgia-Pacific logging road near Abol Bridge. Maps: MATC's Appalachian Trail Guide to Maine (see above).

The Hundred Mile Wilderness is the northernmost stretch of the 2,135-mile Appalachian Trail. This section of Maine encompasses some 10 million acres of virtually uninhabited Maine forest (if you don't take the timber industry into account). Allow me to reiterate myself— *10 million acres.* That's the equivalent of five Yellowstones with a Yosemite thrown in for good luck. But unlike Yosemite, Yellowstone, or Acadia, for that matter, the Hundred Mile Wilderness is not a National Park, not even a National Forest. There are no park loops, no visitor center, no condos, no resorts, no cars. Just layer after layer of forest, comparable to the woods of Alaska or Canada.

Much of the land looks remarkably similar to the woods Thoreau saw in the mid-1800s. However, there's one major difference. Thoreau did not have the luxury of a trail. The path was cut in the 1930s by two Mainers, Walter Green and Myron Avery, who were determined that the northern terminus of the new Appalachian Trail reside on the summit of Mount Katahdin, not New Hampshire's Mount Washington. Starting just outside of Monson, the 99.4-mile section heads north through a blanket of spruces and firs. Winding through a network of federal, state, and privately owned land, the trail skirts numerous swimming holes and climbs many mountains. Indeed, the elevation gain northbound is a thigh-burning 17,000 feet. Not surprisingly, many through-hikers say it's the most primitive land they've seen on the AT.

Walk the trail in late summer or early fall and you'll reap a number of rewards: beautiful forest scenery with just the first tinges of fall color (although this far north you won't find all that many hardwoods); more wild blueberries than you could possibly eat; warm days and cool nights; no blackflies; long, lonely views over endless forest and lakes from the open summits; and walks through cedar bogs, past innumerable beaver ponds, through steep-walled gorges. But the real treasure of the Hundred Mile Wilderness is the truly abundant wildlife—beavers, loons on every lake, white-tailed deer, the occasional otter, coyotes, red fox, and, of course, Bullwinkle. On any given day, you can spot up to 10 or 20 moose. And this is one section of the trail where you damn well better hang your food: There are definitely black bears around, and if one eats its way through your dinners, you're going to be mighty hungry by the time you can buy one of the lousy doughnuts at the campground store at Abol Bridge.

Shaw's Boarding House in Monson (tel. 207/997-3597) is a legendary overnight stop for through-hikers. Shaw's offers rooms, hot meals (the peach cobbler I had there lingered in my memory for days), and hot showers. The extremely amicable owner, an old Mainer, knows all there is to know about the region and takes a genuine delight in being an authentic institution among hikers. He also offers a shuttle service to pick you up at the end of the trail—and is your only option if you don't have time to walk the whole trail and want to arrange a pickup at the only point along the trail where you can cut your hike short, the Jo-Mary Road. This is expensive, but not so much so that you shouldn't consider it in a pinch. If you are planning to set up your own shuttle, leave your second car at the Abol Bridge Campground, P.O. Box 536, Millinocket, ME 04462.

OUTFITTERS

L.L. Bean offers one-day hikes to the top of Little Bigelow Mountain in Stratton and Tumbledown Mountain in Weld. Cost is $55. Contact L.L. Bean Outdoor Skills, Freeport, ME 04033 (tel. 800/ 341-4341, ext. 6666).

HORSEBACK RIDING

Registered Maine Guide Judy Cross offers a variety of rides, from one-hour to one-day to overnight treks in the heart of the Maine Woods. Contact **Northern Maine Riding Adventures,** P.O. Box 16, Dover-Foxcroft, ME 04426 (tel. 207/ 564-3451 or 207/564-2965). Day and overnight rides are also available at **The Birches** in Rockwood. Contact Moosehead Wilderness Trail Rides (tel. 207/ 534-7305). In south-central Maine, **Sunny Brook Stables** in Sebago offers trail rides for all levels (tel. 207/ 787-2905).

ICE FISHING

Start drilling those holes. Ice fishing is becoming increasingly popular in Maine (especially when you have a winter as long as they have!). **Landlocked salmon, trout, togue, cusk, smelts, lake whitefish,** and **white perch** can all be caught in cold-weather months. Salmon are usually found at depths ranging from just below the ice to 10 feet. Togues, cusk, and lake whitefish are taken near the bottom. Smelts have often been hooked in less than three feet of water.

The best summer fishing spots are adequate in the winter, especially the large lakes like **Moosehead, Chesuncook**, and **Mooselookmeguntick.** For more information, get the guide to fishing, published by the **Maine Publicity Bureau,** P.O. Box 2300, Hallowell, ME 04347 (tel. 800/533-9595 or 207/ 623-0363).

MOUNTAIN BIKING

Comparable to cross-country skiers, mountain bikers can pick any logging road and ride for miles. On the other hand, good single-track and double-track were nowhere to be found. Fortunately, I stumbled upon this one route:

Carrabassett River

Allow 1–2 hours. Easy; flat terrain. Access: From the Sugarloaf Ski Area, turn right on

State Route 27 South for approximately 5 miles. A half-mile past the Sugarloaf Information building on the left, turn left at the Carrabassett Valley Town Office sign. Cross a bridge and turn left on Huston Brook Road. Park on the left after the last ski chalet. Map: USGS 7.5-minute Sugarloaf Mountain.

There's nothing like a cool stream to wash your dusty body off after a mountain-bike ride. Near Sugarloaf Mountain, a former railroad bed lines the Carra-bassett River, providing an ideal trail for the novice mountain biker. Start the ride on Huston Brook Road after parking your car just past the last ski chalet. Bear left at the fork 0.7 mile later for a 5.5-mile ride along the river. In the winter, the relatively flat trail is crowded with cross-country skiers. In summertime, the leaf-laden trees block the sight and sound of State Route 27's traffic. Sheets of bedrock form pools of water in the river that, in typical Maine fashion, range from refreshing to frigid. You can stop anywhere along the route for a dip before continuing straight or heading back to your car on the same trail.

OUTFITTERS & RENTALS

Cliff Krolick, owner of **Back Country Excursions of Maine,** RFD 2, P.O. Box 365, Limerick, ME 04048 (tel. 207/625-8189), has created a mountain biking playground called the "Palace." The 4,000-square-foot garden has over 100 tons of stones, log-packed trailways, bridges, and stairs, all situated in a natural half-pipe. Once you tire of this, you can take one of Krolick's guided tours through 60 miles of connected trails. Road biking and canoeing are also available. He's located in Parsonfield, west of Sebago Lake, near the New Hampshire border. A two-day tour including two nights lodging, breakfasts, lunches, and pot luck dinners costs only $100 per person!

Bigelow Bike Tours, P.O. Box 75, Stratton, ME 04982 (tel. 207/246-7352), near Sugarloaf/USA, offers half-day and full-day bike tours through the mountains bordering Carrabassett Valley. Cost is $25 per person half-day, $45 per person full-day. They also offer six-day bike camps.

The Birches Resort, P.O. Box 41, Rockwood, ME 04478 (tel. 800/825-WILD or 207/534-7305), offers 50 miles of trails and rentals.

Rangeley Region Sport Shop, Main Street, Rangeley (tel. 207/864-5616), rents mountain bikes.

POWERBOATING

Many of the sporting camps I listed (see the box below) offer boat rentals. In addition to these, there are more than 50 boat rentals in the Maine Woods. For complete listings, contact the respective region listed below: the **Bridgton-Lakes Region Chamber of Commerce,** P.O. Box 236, Bridgton, ME 04009 (tel. 207/647-3472); the **Rangeley Lakes Region Chamber of Commerce** (tel. 207/864-5364 or 800/MT-LAKES); the **Sugarloaf Area Chamber of Commerce,** RR 1, P.O. Box 2151, Carrabassett Valley, ME 04947 (tel. 207/235-2100); and the **Moosehead Lake Region Chamber of Commerce,** P.O. Box 581, Greenville, ME 04441 (tel. 207/695-2702).

ROAD BIKING

Except for the southernmost part of the state, road biking in the Maine Woods is far too hilly. Even finding a bike loop is hard, since paved roads are few and far between, and they're often crowded with timber trucks. South of Bethel the terrain is flatter, and there are simply more roads. Also, check out the Center Conway, New Hampshire-Fryeburg, Maine loop in chapter 10.

Norway Loop

Allow 3 hours. Moderate; rolling terrain. Access: The loop starts from the junction of Routes 117 and 118 in Norway. Map: any good state road map.

An hour inland from the hustle and bustle of Freeport, 200-year-old villages, lakes ponds, and short hills greet the biker who retreats to these backroads. The south-central region of Maine is a favorite haunting ground for bikers who live in Portland and other areas of the coast who want to escape the endless summer traffic on U.S. 1.

This 29-mile tour starts in Norway in front of the Guy E. Rowe Elementary School, at the junction of Routes 118 and 117. Follow the combined routes through town toward East Waterford. You'll soon approach the shores of Norway Lake with the mountains of pine on the far side. When the routes split, continue on State Route 118 around the lake and up a hill. Norway Country Club's golf course appears on your left, Little Pennesseewassee Pond to your right. Follow the forest-lined road over Crooked River past the few farms to the junction of State Route 37. Turn left onto State Route 37 and cruise downhill to the historic village of Waterford. Several picturesque country inns, clapboard houses, and a steeple, dating from as far back as 1775, surround the triangular village green. Veer left onto State Route 35 as it hugs the waters of Keoka Lake on the way to South Waterford. Sneeze and you'll miss seeing this small village. State Route 35 continues past serene Bear Pond and the rugged mountain of the same name as it approaches Harrison. This is the only place to stop for lunch on the tour. You can picnic on the benches of Long Lake Park, or opt for a sandwich at Caswell Restaurant House. Once you've attained your necessary protein, veer left on State Route

117 North back to Norway. Yet another body of water, Crystal Lake, appears on your left. Continue on this route for 10 miles, past corn fields, farmlands, and small creeks. Eventually you'll meet up with the junction of State Route 118 again, where a right turn will take you back through the village of Norway to your car.

OUTFITTERS

L.L. Bean Cycling Schools, Freeport, ME 04033 (tel. 800/341-4341, ext. 6666), offers two-day bike weekends from Bethel. Cost is $295 including meals lodging, and maps.

SAILING

Did you take a wrong turn in Portland? I said Penobscot Bay, not Penobscot River (see chapter 11). Oh, I see, you can't handle the ocean breeze. You want a nice small lake like **Moosehead** or **Mooselookmeguntick.** Rentals are available at **Bald Mountain Camps,** Bald Mountain Road, Oquossoc (tel. 207/864-3671); **Dockside Sports Center**, Main Street, Rangeley (tel. 207/864-2424); **The Birches,** Rockwood (tel. 207/534-7305); and **Salmon Run Camps,** State Route 15, Rockwood (tel. 207/534-8880).

SNOWMOBILING

Here's a few tidbits from the Maine Tourism Office:

◆ There are 10,500 miles of snowmobile trails in the entire state.

◆ Maine has 270 local snowmobile clubs.

◆ It is possible to travel from one end of the state to the other on a snowmobile.

Needless to say, snowmobiling in Maine is not a sport, it's a way of life. Aroostook County alone has 1,600 miles of groomed trails connecting Quebec,

Do You Know the Way to Moosehead Lake?

Throughout this chapter, I have sprinkled names of Registered Maine Guides. There are more than 1,000 guides registered with the state who have passed a strict qualifying exam. Standing in front of three to four people who work for a variety of state agencies, including the Department of Inland Fisheries and Wildlife and the Bureau of Parks and Registration, applicants face a barrage of questions. First and foremost, can you read a map and use a compass correctly? If you fail any of these initial questions, you're immediately shown the exit. However, if you make it through the map portion of the test, you next have to contend with a wide range of questions pertaining to specific sports like "Which fly do you use when you're fishing for salmon?" Other questions test your knowledge of nature or basic common sense. A friend of mine was asked, "Someone wants to pick fiddleheads in the summer for their dinner that evening. Is that all right?" The answer is no. Fiddleheads can only be eaten in May. They're poisonous the rest of the year. Other people I know were asked if it's okay to bring cans of soda on a fishing trip in summer. The simple answer is yes, but always check your open cans for bees.

The typical Maine guide in the past was a man wearing a pair of soleless moccasins and a worn felt hat pinned with numerous fishing lures. Times have changed. Fishing and hunting guides now share the spotlight with canoeing, snowshoeing, even dogsledding guides. For a complete list of all the guides available, contact the **Maine Professional Guides Association,** 18 White Street, Topsham, ME 04086 (tel. 207/785-2061).

Maine, and New Brunswick. *Snow Goer* magazine, a national snowmobile publication, rated Aroostook County the best in New England and the third best in the country. Jackman and the Forks area are also known for their extensive network of trails. Northern Outdoors' whitewater rafting center on the Kennebec becomes a snowmobile resort in the winter; contact **Northern Outdoors,** P.O. Box 100, U.S. 201, The Forks, ME 04985 (tel. 207/663-4466).

For more information, contact the **Maine Snowmobile Association,** P.O. Box 77, Augusta, ME 04330 (tel. 207/622-6983). The Bureau of Parks and Recreation has a detailed map of the state's trails; write to Snowmobile Program, State House Station #22, Augusta, ME 04333 (tel. 207/287-4957).

SNOWSHOEING

Registered Maine Guide **Carroll Ware** (tel. 207/474-5420) brings visitors snowshoeing to 90-foot high Moxey Falls, just north of the Forks, near the Kennebec River. Cost is $150 per couple, including a steak lunch and transportation. Available from December to mid-March, providing there's snow on the ground.

For individuals who prefer to go on their own, simply throw on a pair of snowshoes and head north. You'll reach Canada in no time.

SWIMMING

With hundreds of crystal-clear lakes, ponds, and streams, you don't need me to tell you where to swim. Simply change behind the closest bush and jump in. Believe it or not, these bodies of water are much warmer than the ocean in Maine. If you're looking for a beach, here are the best choices: **Sebago Lake State Park,** off U.S. 302, between Naples and South Casco; **Lake St. George State Park,** off State Route 3; **Lake Webb** in Mount Blue State Park, off State Route 156; **Rangeley Lake State Park,** between State Route 17 and State Route 4; **Cathedral Pines** on Flagstaff Lake, off State Route 27; and **Lily Bay State Park,** 8 miles north of Greenville on Moosehead Lake.

WALKS & RAMBLES

Angel Falls

Allow 1 hour. Easy. Access: From the junctions of Routes 4 and 17 in Oquossoc, drive south on State Route 17 for 17.9 miles. Turn right on a dirt road over a bridge and continue around a bend. 3.6 miles from State Route 17, park on the left-hand side of the road and search for a dirt road that leads down to a gravel pit. This is the start of the trail. Map: USGS 7.5-minute Houghton.

The hardest part of the Angel Falls Trail is finding the trailhead. Once you've found the proper parking spot, you're in for a special treat. Get ready to follow an easy trail across several streams to one of the largest single water drops in Maine. Stroll downhill past the gravel pit to a fork. Bear left on a grassy trail to rock-hop across your first body of water, Berdeen Stream. This crossing is a mere warm-up for things to come. The soft, springy forest path soon arrives at Mountain Brook, where you clamber atop the rocks to the other side. Young children especially enjoy this part of the trail,

which is more a mental challenge than a physical challenge, since you create your own path across the rocks. You'll cross the stream three times, following the red blazes, before you reach the waterfall, where a deluge of water falls 30 feet down a chasm of rock. For those of you without a heart condition, try swimming in the icy pool below the cascading water. Others will be content to simply look up at the two rock formations that look like an angel's wing and face, hence it's name. It's hard to leave the mesmerizing sound and sight of the falls, but once you've made that choice, simply hop back to your car.

WHITEWATER RAFTING

It was in the spring of 1976 that crazed adventurer Wayne Hockemeyer and a group of his buddies braved the tumultuous Kennebec River in a 20-foot raft. Prior to that time, the Kennebec was known solely for its fishing and the logs that went hurtling down the river to the mills below. When the Maine legislature quickly passed a law prohibiting transportation of logs and pulpwood down the Maine rivers in that fateful summer, Hockemeyer opened Northern Outdoors, a whitewater rafting outfit. Jim Ernst, a whitewater-rafting guide on the Colorado and Salmon Rivers, followed Hockemeyer's cue and opened Maine Whitewater. Another expert guide, from the swirling rivers of West Virginia, John Connelly, opened Eastern River Expeditions. They created a phenomenon.

Twenty years later, whitewater rafting is one of the most popular sports in Maine. Drive north on the **Kennebec River** on U.S. 201 from Bingham to West Forks, and you'll soon realize that there are as many whitewater outfitters in Maine as there are coffee shops on the Upper West Side of Manhattan. More than 60,000 people every summer participate in the sport, ranging in age from 8 to 80, and they all walk away exhilarated from an adventurous day. People are thrown off the rafts, but rarely does anyone get hurt (just wet).

No longer is the Kennebec the only river to raft down in Maine. Operations have moved to the raging **Penobscot** and **Dead Rivers**. Daily water releases from dams ensure high water from May to October. However, there are only six big water releases on the Dead, in May, June, September, and October. No matter which river you choose, after the ride, your adrenaline will be flowing just as fast as the rapids.

The West Branch of the Penobscot River

Access: Take exit 56 off I-95 to State Route 157 West. Go straight through Millinocket and follow signs to Baxter State Park. Northern Outdoors is located at the Penobscot Outdoor Center, 15 miles from Millinocket, and 5 miles past the North Woods Trading Post.

The 14-mile stretch of the West Branch of the Penobscot River from Ripogenus Gorge to Baxter State Park is a turbulent waterway that drops over 70 feet per mile through a narrow, granite-walled canyon. The strong surge of river is created by a dam and power station that releases water down to the mills in Millinocket. Lumber companies used to employ daring boaters to drag their timber down the river. Unfortunately, many of those men died en route. Today, Bowater/Great Northern Paper Company still owns over 2.2 million acres of land surrounding the Penobscot, but the only people crazy enough to go down the river and face the Class III and IV rapids now are whitewater rafters.

There are numerous rafting companies offering their services, but my wife Lisa and I chose Northern Outdoors for their 20 years of experience and excellent reputation. We met the other rafters at 6 AM for breakfast at the Penobscot Outdoor Center. After breakfast, some rafters rented wet suits and others watched in confusion wondering if they, too, needed these outfits. There should have been an announcement regarding the weather and the need for wetsuits and, comparable to other whitewater rafting trips I've been on, the cost of all gear should have been included in the overall price. Fortunately, the weather was perfect, and that was Northern Outdoors' lone flaw of the day. The only clothes we needed were a bathing suit, shirt, and shoes we could get wet.

At 7 AM, we grabbed our helmets, paddles, and life jackets and boarded the buses for a guided tour to the put-in. Since Great Northern Paper still owns this land, Northern Outdoors has to pay for every rafter using their logging roads to get to the river. We arrived at a parking lot, where the large group was taught various paddling techniques, like how to float downriver when knocked out of a raft. On average, 10 percent of the rafters are bumped into the water during every trip. We split into small groups and descended with our rafts down to the power station. Lisa and I were paired with a group of six guys from New Jersey including Phil, a Tom Selleck look-alike; the joker Jim, a veteran of Vietnam and 17 whitewater expeditions down the Penobscot; and Stephen, whom we would soon find out, loved to throw people in the water during the quiet spots on the river. Our guide, Greg, had four years of experience of leading tours down the river and, thus, was given the helm of the lead boat—the first boat down the river.

According to Greg, it was going to be a good day for rafting, since the water was bursting out of the power station at approximately 2,200 cubic feet per second. Within moments of leaving the put-in, we cruised over our first set of rapids, the Exterminator. Under Greg's keen guidance, none of us even got wet. That would soon change as we zipped by Troublemaker, a series of small rapids, and over Cribworks, the most ferocious rapid of them all. The morning became an exhilarating blur of running over these step falls, and screaming as our raft bent, twisted, and turned backwards with every succeeding drop. At points where the hydraulics sucked the boat into a rapid like the flush of a toilet, Greg showed us how to stay atop the water and "surf" the raft. We never tipped over, but we were drenched by the time we slowed down and stopped for our lunch of salmon, teriyaki chicken, or steak. The fish was probably caught on the lower part of the river, known for its large schools of landlocked salmon.

Hearts racing, we all tried to relax before we jumped back into our rafts for the afternoon's events. I almost lost my lunch on the first rapid, Nesowadnehunk Falls. The water shoots over the rocks for a thrilling free-fall. Many of the other rafts fell into the water, but Greg gracefully maneuvered us over the falls and then paddled back so we could disembark the boat and crawl on rocks under the spray of water. I didn't stay long—the sound of the falls crashing on the rocks was deafening. We then went through a slow stretch of the Penobscot, where we had water fights with other rafts (the boats came with buckets), Stephen threw my wife into the deep, and Jim, never at a loss for conversation, discussed his fetish for ruby red lipstick. Needless to say, he was the next one to be thrown in the water, followed by me. Floating swiftly downstream with my lifejacket and watching the land go by gave me a sense of what it's like to be in orbit. Mighty Mount Katahdin stood in the background while ospreys and great

blue herons flew closer to shore. We crawled back into the boat, just in time for the last two rapids. It was 4 PM by the time we arrived back at the Penobscot Outdoor Center, but judging from everyone's ear-to-ear grin, the fun-filled day went by far too quickly.

Contact **Northern Outdoors,** P.O. Box 100, U.S. 201, The Forks, ME 04895 (tel. 207/663-4466). They also host trips to the Kennebec and Dead Rivers. Cost is $75 weekdays, $95 weekends. They also offer accommodations at the Penobscot Outdoor Center and The Forks Resort Center.

OTHER OUTFITTERS

Aside from Northern Outdoors, **Eastern River Expeditions,** P.O. Box 1173, Moosehead Lake, Greenville, ME 04441 (tel. 800/634-RAFT), **Maine Whitewater,** P.O. Box 633, Bingham, ME 04920-0633 (tel. 800/345-6246), and **New England Whitewater Center,** P.O. Box 21, Caratunk, ME 04925 (tel. 800/766-7238) are regarded highly. For more information, contact **Raft Maine** (tel. 800/RAFT-MEE) for a listing of nine whitewater-rafting outfitters and their accommodations.

Campgrounds & Other Accommodations

CAMPGROUNDS

Sebago Lake State Park

Located off U.S. 302, between Naples and South Casco. Tel. 207/693-6613 between June 20 and Labor Day, 207/693-6231 all other times. 250 sites on 1,300 wooded acres, flush toilets, group campsite, fresh drinking water, hot showers, and guided nature hikes.

The sites are located in a dense 1,300-acre forest on the shores of the lake.

Evans Notch, White Mountain National Forest

These 5 campgrounds, operated by the White Mountain National Forest, are located to the west of Bethel. Basin has 21 sites, Cold River 12 sites, Crocker Pond 7 sites, Hastings 24 sites, and Wild River 11 sites. No hookups. Tables, fire rings, and grills. For reservations, call 800/280-2267, or contact the Evans Notch Ranger Station (tel. 207/824-2134).

Chances are you'll find a spot at these campgrounds, located in a rarely seen section of the Whites.

Rangeley Lake State Park

Can be reached from Rumford via State Route 17 or Farmington via State Route 4. Tel. 207/864-3858. 50 sites, no hookups, group campsites, handicapped rest room facilities, sewage disposal, hot showers, public phone, ice, tables, and wood.

Located on the southern rim of Rangeley Lake in an forest of spruces, these well-spaced sites are known for their privacy.

Mount Blue State Park

Situated 10 miles from Wilton off State Route 156 in Weld. Tel. 207/585-2347. 136 sites, no hookups, pit toilets, sewage disposal, public phone, ice, and tables.

Located on the shores of Lake Webb, this beachside facility is the State Park's best-kept secret.

Lily Bay State Park

Located 8 miles north of Greenville. Tel. 207/695-2700. 93 sites, no hookups, pit toilets, sewage disposal, public phones, tables, and wood.

Camping doesn't get any better than this serene locale on the shores of Moosehead Lake. The sites are well-spaced. Also in the area, the Maine Bureau of Forestry and Bowater/Great Northern Paper Company offer numerous sites in the North Woods, including islands on Moosehead Lake. Contact the Maine Bureau of Forestry (tel. 207/695-3721) and Bowater (tel. 207/723-5131) for more information.

Baxter State Park

Visitor Center is 1 mile east of Millinocket on State Route 11/157. The actual park entrance is 18 miles north of Millinocket on the Golden Road to the Togue Park entrance. Choices are virtually unlimited. They include 10 campgrounds accessible by road, 2 more hike-in campgrounds, and over 20 single backcountry sites or lean-tos. Russell and Chimney Pond, near the base of Katahdin, are extremely popular. Kidney Pond and Daicey Pond offer rustic cabins with beds, gas lanterns, table, chairs, and firewood. Summer reservations, May 15–October 15, can be sent by mail, with the fee enclosed, after December 26. Tent and lean-to prices are $6 per person, minimum $12 per site. Bunkhouses are $7 per person. Cabins at Daicey and Kidney Pond start at $17 per person. Send to Baxter State park, 64 Balsam Drive, Millinocket, ME 04462 (tel. 207/723-5140).

Not surprisingly, these sites fill up well in advance. Make a reservation months before you arrive!

Aroostook State Park

Located on U.S. 1, 4 miles south of Presque Isle. Tel. 207/768-8341. 30 sites, pit toilets, public phone, tables, and wood.

If you make it to the heart of Maine's potato country, you earned a spot in this

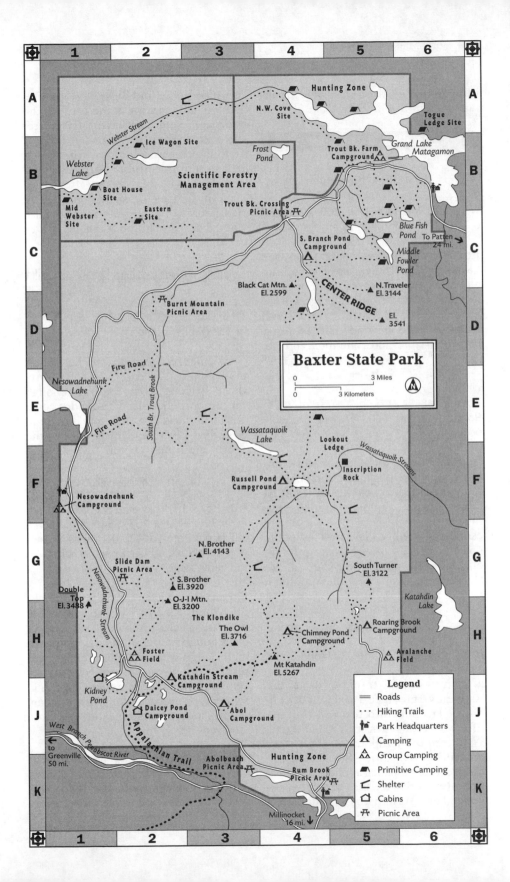

campground. Hike on Quaggy Jo Mountain or trout fish on Echo Lake.

INNS & RESORTS

Lake House, Waterford

Waterford, ME 04088; tel. 800/223-4182 or 207/583-4182. Rooms start at $79.

Found on the Norway Bike Loop (see "Road Biking"), the Lake House is an elaborate old stagecoach inn. The inn is located on Waterford's vintage village green, across the street from Lake Keoka. There are five guest rooms, a two-room suite, and a one-room cottage.

Bethel Inn

Bethel, ME 04217. Tel. 207/824-2175. Rooms start at $70 per person double occupancy.

Built in 1913 by a millionaire, this rambling, yellow clapboard mansion was initially intended to be a health resort. It still serves the salubrious-minded. Tennis courts, an 18-hole golf course, and canoeing on Songo Pond are a few of the options. In the winter, cross-country ski on 25 km of trails. There are also hot tubs, saunas, and a year-round outdoor heated pool (91°).

Rangeley Inn

Rangeley, ME 04970. Tel. 207/864-3341.

Not much has transpired at the Rangeley Inn since President Eisenhower strolled into town in the late fifties to try his luck with rod and reel. Walk into the lobby of the three-story inn and you'll notice the designs on the pre-Ike wallpaper, a collection of historic Revolutionary sites like Independence Hall, Washington's headquarters at Valley Forge, and Betsy Ross's house. Peeled and cracking at the corners, the wallpaper seems to have a far greater history than the places depicted. Indeed, Rangeley's classic lobby with stained oak columns, antique furniture, and grand piano is a cozy respite after a hard day of fishing or skiing at nearby Saddleback. Their restaurant/bar is also one of the best in the Rangeley Lakes region.

Sugarloaf/USA Condominiums, Carrabassett Valley

Carrabassett Valley, ME 04947. Tel. 800/THE-LOAF or 207/237-2000. Rates start at $110 for a studio.

Conveniently located near the slopes, cross-country ski center, and golf course, these spacious rooms are large enough for the entire family. The condos come with a full kitchen. Ask for a condo in Sugarloaf I or II, which are close to the sports and fitness center.

The Birches Resort, Rockwood

P.O. Box 41, Rockwood, ME 04478. Tel. 800/825-WILD or 207/534-7305. Rooms in the lodge start at $76 double occupancy with breakfast, $17 per person per day in the cabin tents.

Situated in a thicket of birches overlooking Mount Kineo on Moosehead Lake, the Birches caters to families who can't get enough of the outdoors. There's a main lodge with 12 "cabin tents" scattered through the resort. The list of sporting options is impressive—fishing, canoeing, horseback riding, boardsailing, sailing, mountain biking and, in winter, cross-country skiing.

Chesuncook Lake House

P.O. Box 656, Greenville, ME 04441. Tel. 207/745-5330 or c/o Folsom's Air Service,

207/695-2821. $85 per person, including three meals in the inn. Cabins cost $35 per day per person, 3 days minimum. $65 per day per person MAP. There is no charge for the Cushing's Landing boat trip for parties staying 3 days or more at the inn.

There are only three ways to get to Chesuncook Lake House—seaplane, canoe, or drive 30 to 40 miles on a logging road to Cushing's Landing, where owner Bert McBurnie picks you up by boat for an 18-mile trip to Chesuncook Village. Native Bert and his French-born wife, Maggie, make up half of the year-round permanent population in the village. Their small inn and cottages sit on the shores of Chesuncook Lake, with mighty Mount Katahdin peering down from afar. This is the place to catch up on your reading, watch the humming-birds fly in and out of the bird feeder, and enjoy Maggie's hearty cooking, much of which comes from her own garden. The inn also serves as solace and repose for the year-round outdoor recreationist. In the spring, fish for trout and salmon in the large lake. In summer and fall, canoe in the early morning to find a multitude of animals (see "Canoeing"). In the winter, stay in one of their warm cottages and snowshoe or cross-country ski.

Index

◆ A ◆

Abol Bridge Campground, 367
Acadia Bike, 327
Acadia Mountain, 15, 313, 323–24
Acadia Mountain Guides, 32, 330–31
Acadia National Park, 9, 11, 14, 15, 18, 23,
    27, 30, 31, 128, 309, 311, 312–13,
    319, 321, 322, 323–24, 325, 326, 327,
    328, 330, 334, 335, 355, 366
  camping, 336–37
Acadian Sporting Goods Store, 116
Action Outfitters, 253
Adventure Learning, 32, 134
Adventure Sports, 84
AJ's, 253
Aldworth Manor, 170
Alexander Lake, 70
Allagash Canoe Trips, 352
Allagash Guide Service, 352
Allagash River, 10, 27, 30, 321, 340, 350,
    353, 355
Allagash Wilderness Outfitters, 352
Allagash Wilderness Waterway, 10, 340,
    345–46, 350, 352, 354
Alpine Shop, 253
American Expeditions, 259
American Legion State Forest, 40, 43, 52
Anchor Marine, 302
Androscoggin Lake, 360
Androscoggin River, 275, 280, 290, 297
Andy Lynn Boats, 127, 134
Angel Falls, 371
Appalachian Gap, 178, 207, 208, 227
Appalachian Mountain Gear, 115
Appalachian Trail, 3, 6, 7–8, 16, 39, 40–42,
    45, 48, 49, 50, 99, 100, 104, 108, 109,
    111, 207, 291, 292, 295, 298, 333,
    340, 345, 350, 355, 362, 363, 364,
    365, 366
Arcadia Management Area, 19, 79, 81,
    82, 89
Arnold Arboretum, 135
Aroostook State Park, 374–76
Ascents of Adventure, 21 32, 116
Ascutney Mountain Ski Area, 201
Ascutney State Park, 184–85
Ashley Hill, 102–3
Atlantic Climbing, 32, 330–31
Atlantic Fishing Fleet, 290
Atlantic Oakes By-the-Sea, 338
Attean Lake Resort, 361
Attitash Ski Area, 288, 289
Audubon Shop, 63

◆ B ◆

Back Beach, 135
Back Country Excursions, 29
Back Country Excursions of Maine, 357
Backroads, 29, 114, 161, 215, 251, 259,
    264, 330
Baer's River Workshop, 80, 88–89
Bagley House, 338
Bailey, Ken, 323
Bailey's Beach, 89
Bald Mountain, 365
Bald Mountain Camps, 361, 369
Balloon Drifters, Inc., 349
Balloon Hollow, Inc., 42
Balloon Rides, 8, 319
Balloon Sports, 319

Balloon Squire, A, 42
Ballston Beach, 162, 166
Balsams, The, 274, 280, 287, 289, 290, 295, 306–7
Bantam Lake, 42
Bar Harbor Bicycle, 327
Barn Island State Management Wildlife Area, 63
Barnstable Harbor, 152
Bartholemew's Cobble, 99, 116–17
Bartlett Experimental Forest, 18, 299–300
Bartlett's Falls, 267
Barton River, 254
Basin Campground, 305
Basin-Cascades Trail, 295, 306
Basin Harbor Golf Club, 204, 262
Battenkill Anglers, 32, 204
Battenkill Canoe Ltd., 29, 192–93
Battenkill River, 13, 27, 174, 177, 182–83, 190, 191–92, 203, 236
Battenkill Sports Bicycle Shop, 215
Baxter State Park, 6, 30, 340, 341, 344, 345, 350, 355, 356, 359, 360, 362, 365, 374
Bay Island Sailing School, 22, 32, 332
Bay Island Yacht Charters, 332
Bay State Cruises, 144
Bay Voyage Hotel, 92
Bear Mountain, 39, 49–50
Bear Notch Loop, 302–3
Beartown State Forest, 94, 98–99, 100, 101–2, 105, 113, 116, 118
Beaver Brook Ski Trail, 286
Beavertail State Park, 23, 27, 79, 81, 89
Becket Road, 103–4
Beech Forest Trail, 150
Bell's Beach, 163
Benedict Pond, 99, 100, 101, 107, 118
Bennington-Pownel Loop, 211–12
Berkshire Balloons, 42
Berkshire Hiking Holidays, 29, 108, 112, 210
Bethel, Maine, 345
Bethel Inn, 357, 376
Biddeford-Saco Country Club, 323
Big Averill Lake, 244, 254, 255, 260
Big Equinox Pond, 186
Big Trees Nature Trail, 216
Bigelow Bike Tours, 32, 368
Bigelow Preserve, 353
Bike and Ski Center, 253

Bike Vermont, 29, 215, 264
Billington Sea Watercraft, 134
Birch Meadow Trail Rides, 229
Birches Resort, 357, 367, 368, 369, 376
Bird Watcher's General Store, 150
Black Gum Swamp, 186
Black Pond, 351
Black River, 192, 254–55
Blackwoods Campground, Acadia National Park, 336
Block Island, 21, 85–86
Block Island Club, 32, 88
Blue Hills Ski Area, 127
Blue Hills State Reservation, 125, 129
Blueberry Hill, 250, 252, 272
Bluff Point Coastal Reserve, 60, 63, 71
Bobby's Ranch, 128
Boland Balloon, 8, 217
Bolton Ski Touring Center, 11, 249
Bolton-Trapp Trail, 11, 249
Bolton Valley Ski Area, 233, 250, 254
Bolton Valley Walls, 233
Bomoseen State Park, 183–84, 235
Bonkers Board Room, 200
Boots & Boards, 253
Bosebuck Mountain Camps, 361
Boston Harbor Islands State Park, 138
Boston Harbor Sailing School, 32, 133–34
Boston Sailing Center, 32, 134
Boulder Path, 300–301
Boulders Inn, 55–56
Bourne Bridge, 144
Bousquet Ski Area, 106
Bowdish Reservoir, 80, 81, 91
Bradford Ski Area, 127
Branch Pond, 191
Brandon Gap, 178
Brant Rock Public Beach, 134
Brass Lantern Inn, 271
Brattleboro Bike Shop, 213
Breakheart Pond, 81, 82
Brenton Point, 81
Bretton Woods Ski Area, 289
Bretton Woods Ski Touring Center, 287
Bretton Woods Summer Park, 301
Brewster Flats, 150
Brewster River Gorge, 267
Briggs Ltd., 226
Briggs Riding Stables, 128
Brighter Skies Balloon Company, 62

Brighton State Park, 269
Bristol Falls, 267
Brodie Mountain Cross-Country Touring, 106
Brodie Mountain Ski Area, 106, 114
Bromley Mountain, 187, 207
Bromley Ski Area, 176, 180, 199
Brookside Angler, 32, 204, 226
Bruce Trail, 11, 12, 248–49
Buckley Duntan Lake, 100–101, 107
Bucksteep Manor Cross-Country Ski Center, 106
Bullock Woods, 117
Burke Mountain, 244, 256, 261
Burke Ski Area, 254
Burlingame State Park, 89, 91
Burlington Community Boathouse, 32, 265
Burlington Radisson, 270
Burr Pond State Park, 43, 44, 54, 55
Burrows Sports Shop, 200
Buttermilk Falls, 216
Butternut Basin Ski Area, 107
Button Bay State Park, 262, 268
Buzzard's Bay, 161

◆ **C** ◆

Cadillac Mountain, 14, 309, 313, 326, 336
Cahoon Hollow, 163
Calf Pasture Beach, 42
Calvin Coolidge State Park, 184, 235
Cambridge Stables, 260
Camden Hills State Park, 16, 313, 321, 328, 329, 334, 336, 337
Camden Snowbowl, 322
Camel's Hump, 15, 178, 185, 187, 206, 208, 227, 228–29, 249, 252, 256, 257, 258, 262
Camel's Hump Forest Preserve, 185
Camel's Hump Nordic Center, 249
Campton Campground, 305
Cannon Ski Area, 12, 287–88
Canoe Adventures, 352
Canoe Meadows Wildlife Sanctuary, 99, 117
Canoes-R-Us, 352
Canyon Ranch in the Berkshires, 36, 37, 110, 119
Cape Ann, 25, 120, 122, 124, 126, 134, 136, 138

Cape Ann Divers, 134
Cape Ann Loop, 131–33
Cape Arundel Golf Club, 323
Cape Cod Canal, 129
Cape Cod Country Club, 154
Cape Cod Divers, 161
Cape Cod National Seashore, 25, 145, 148, 155, 163
Cape Cod Rail Trail, 21, 148, 158–59
Cape Cod Waterways, 152
Cape Pogue Wildlife Refuge, 149, 151, 153, 159
Captain Barry Gibson, 323
Captain Bill Gould, 81
Captain Bill's, 127
Captain Bud Phillips, 81
Captain Frank Blount, 81
Captain Jack Cagnon, 81
Captain Jim Korney, 81
Captain John Boats, 127, 137
Captain John Earl, 323
Captain John Wadsworth, 63, 64
Captain John's Sport Fishing Center, 63, 64
Captain Rick Savage, 323
Captain Tim Brady & Sons, 127
Captain Tim Tower, 323
Captains Golf Course, 154
Carrabassett River, 357, 367–68
Carrabassett Valley, 11, 32, 33, 344, 345, 357, 358, 360, 368
Carriage Path Trails, Acadia National Park, 18, 313, 321, 326
Carroll and Jane Rickert Ski Touring Center, 250
Carter Notch, 294–95
Carter's Ski Touring Center, 357
Caspian Lake, 242, 254, 251, 260
Castle Springs, 298
Castleton River, 203
Catamount Family Center, 249, 260
Catamount Ski Area, 107, 109
Catamount Trail, 11, 193, 194, 196, 220, 249, 251, 252
Cathedral Pines, 371
Caucomgomoc Lake, 10, 11, 351
Cavallaro, Michael, 50
Cedar Brook Cross Country Ski Center, 46
Cedar Tree Neck Sanctuary, 25, 151, 166–67

Center Hill Trail, Mount Blue State
  Park, 356
Central Branch YMCA, 138
Chamberlain Lake, 350, 351, 360, 362
Champlain Mountain, 319, 324
Chance Hill Equestrian Center, 51
Chappaquiddick Island, 21, 148–49,
  159
Charles River, 125, 134
Charles River Bike Path, 129
Charles River Canoe and Kayak Center,
  32, 126, 134
Charlestown Breachway (State Camping
  Area), 91
Charlie's Northland Lodge, 255, 262
Chestnut Hill, 51
Chesuncook Lake, 10, 11, 30, 347, 344,
  351–52, 363, 367, 377
Chesuncook Lake House, 351 376–77
Chimney Pond Campground, 363
Chimon Island Nature Center for
  Environmental Activities, 42, 54
Chittenden Reservoir, 184
Chittenden Brook, 220
Circle K Ranch, 260
Cisco Beach, 163
Clark Art Institute, 112–13
Clarke Outdoors, 32, 43
Classic Fly Fishing, 226
Classic Outfitters, 226
Clear River, 81
Clearwater Sports, 29, 248
Cliff Walk, 25, 84, 90
Climb High, 233
Clyde River, 254
Coast Guard Beach, 145–46, 153, 164
Coastal Kayaking, 332, 334
Coastal Sailing School, 32, 134
Coastline Sailing School, 32, 68
Cobscook Bay State Park, 337
Cockaponset State Forest, 61, 66, 70
Cold Hollow Mountains, 240
Cold River Campground, 305
Cold Storage Beach, 163
Colt State Park, 89
Concord River, 120, 124, 125–26, 131
Connecticut River, 21, 31, 57, 59, 60–61,
  63, 64, 66–67, 70, 71, 174, 175, 176,
  177, 179, 183, 186, 190, 192, 203,
  215, 226, 231–32, 237, 238, 245,
  246, 247, 248, 255, 256, 267, 281,
  290, 302
Connecticut River Safari, 193
Coop's Bait and Tackle, 154
Corporation Beach, 163
Cortina Inn, 234
Country Club of Barre, 255
Country Club of New Hampshire, 290
Country Inns Along the Trail, 29, 210,
  259–60
Country Walkers, 29, 210
Courageous Sailing Center, 32, 134
Coventry Meadows, 65
Coventry Riding Stables, 65
Covered Bridge Campground, 305
Covered Bridge Loop, 303–4
Craftsbury Center, 29, 242, 261–62
Craftsbury Common, 19, 242, 251,
  261, 264
Craftsbury Nordic Ski Center, 251,
  252, 260
Craigville Beach, 162, 163
Cranberry Valley Golf Course, 154
Crane Beach, 135
Cranwell Resort, 119
Cranwell Resort Golf Course, 107, 119
Crawford Notch State Park, 277
Crescent Beach, 86, 89
Crystal Lake, 260, 303
Crystal Lake State Beach, 267
Cupola, The, 200
Cutting Edge North, 213, 215
Cuyler, Lewis, 32, 116
Cycle-Inn-Vermont, 213
Cycle Loft, 53
Cycle Shop, The, 158
Cycle Works, 157

◆ **D** ◆

Dark Harbor House, 330, 338
Dark Side Snow Board Shop, 201
Dartmouth Co-op, 225
Day Pond State Park, 61, 70, 71
Dead Creek Wildlife Management
  Area, 245
Dead River, 26, 372
Deer Leap Mountain, 233
Deerfield River, 26–27, 34, 107, 118, 194,
  195, 203

Devereaux Beach, 135
Devil's Hopyard State Park, 61, 73
Dickie's, 290
Dive Winnipesaukee, 304
Dixville Notch State Park, 280–81
Dockside Sports Center, 369
Dolly Copp Campground, 305, 306
Dolphin Fleet Boats, 168
Dolphin Fleet Whale Watching, 168
Dorset Quarry, 216
Double-track biking, 17, 18, 19, 51–52,
    65, 66, 114, 129, 156, 231, 261, 300,
    302, 327
Doubletree Islander Hostel, 91
Down River Canoes, 29, 63
Downhill Edge, 222, 225, 253
Duxbury Bay, 9, 125
Duxbury Beach, 125, 135

◆ **E** ◆

Eagle Lake, 313, 321, 326
East Bay Bicycle Path, 84
East Beach (Charlestown), 89
East Beach (Martha's Vineyard), 163
East Burke Sports, 261
East Island Route, 159
East Matunuck State Beach, 89
Eastern Mountain Sports, 162
Eastern River Expeditions, 371, 373
Easton Beach, 89
Eastport Resort, 113
Echo Lake, 260
Edgartown Great Pond, 152, 153
Edson Hill, 250
Elizabeth Islands, 22, 161–62, 166
Ellacoya State Beach, 305
Elmridge Golf Course, 64
Emerald Lake State Park, 183, 216
Equinox, The, 37, 236
Equinox Pond, 186
Equipe Sport, 200
Essex Marsh, 126
Essex River, 124
Essex River Basin Adventures, 32, 134
Esta's Bike Shop, 86
Ethan Pond Trail, 285
Evans Notch, White Mountain National
    Forest, 374
Exeter Country Club, 82

◆ **F** ◆

Falling Waters Trail/Franconia Ridge/
    Old Bridal Path, 291, 306
Farm Neck Golf Club, 154
Farmington River, 33, 40, 43, 47–48, 52, 54
Farmington River Tubing, 24, 54
Fenton River, 64
Fish River, 350, 360
Fisherman's Beach, 163
Fisherman's Memorial State Park, 91
Fisherman's World, 48
Fitch House, 74
Flame Stables, 210
Flanders Nature Center, 42
Flax Pond, 152, 158
Floating Bridge, 234
Fly Fish Vermont, 32, 255
Flyer's, 157, 161, 163
Folsom's Air Service, 351, 352
Foot Brothers Canoe Rentals, 126
Foot of the Notch Bicycles, 264
Force 5 Watersports, 152, 161, 162
Forest Beach Road, 151
Fort Hill Trail, 25, 164
4 Seasons Touring, 29, 210
Fourth Cliff, 127
Franconia Notch bike path, 285
Franconia Notch State Park, 277–80, 306
Frasers' Mountain Shop, 200
Fred's Bikes, 330
Freeport Balloon Company, 319
Frenchman Bay, 23, 313, 324, 332–34
Front Beach, 135
Fuller Pond, 45
Fun Seekers Inc., 162

◆ **G** ◆

Gacki, Rich, 352, 353
Galeforce Bike Rentals, 158
Gaspee Point, 89
Gay City State Park, 63
Gay Head Cliffs, 20, 25, 139, 144, 148,
    159–60, 167
George Washington Management Area,
    80, 91
Georgetown Rowley State Forest, 122
Gilpatrick's Guide Service, 29, 353
Glacial Park, 58, 72
Glen Lake Trail, 186

Gleneagles Golf Course, 204
Globe Corner Bookstore, 34, 134
Gloucester, Massachusetts, 122
Goddard State Park, 81
Golf School, The, 33, 362
Gone With the Wind, 33, 42
Good Harbor Beach, 134
Goodwin's Guide Service, 226
Goose Hummock, 33, 152, 162
Goose Hummock Shop, 157–58
Gooseberry Beach, 89
Governor Bradford Motor Inn, 138
Grafton Loop, 213–14
Grafton Ponds Cross-Country Ski
    Center, 197
Grand Isle State Park, 269
Grant's Kennebago Camps, 361
Great Brook Farm Ski Touring Center, 127
Great Glen, 301
Great Island, 25, 146
Great Island Trail, 25, 154–55
Great Marsh, 144–45, 150, 152
Great Meadows National Wildlife Refuge,
    122, 124, 125, 126, 136
Great Misery Island, 135
Great Outdoors Trading Company, 22, 200,
    201, 246
Great Point, 151, 153
Great Swamp Management Area, 80, 83–84
Greeley Pond Trail, 285, 300–301
Green Falls Campground, 73
Green Mountain Adventures, 24, 213, 216
Green Mountain Marine, 213
Green Mountain National Forest, 11, 14,
    16, 21, 31, 173, 174, 175, 176, 177,
    180–81, 182, 183, 184, 185, 190, 193,
    194, 195–96, 197, 204–5, 206, 212,
    216, 217, 220, 215, 227, 233, 237,
    240, 241, 242, 249, 258, 267, 268
    camping, 234, 235
Green Mountain National Forest Road No.
    10, 212
Green Mountain Outdoor Adventures, 226
Green Mountain Touring Center, 221
Green River, 203
Green River Reservoir, 10, 246–47
Green Trails Inn, 221
Green Valley Country Club, 82
Greenduck Snowmobile Tours, 215–16
Greenway Trail, Block Island, 25, 89–90

Greystone Farms, 65
Grinnell's Beach, 89
Griswold Inn, 75
Grout Pond Recreation Area, 182, 191,
    195, 216
Guided Snowmobile Tours, 215
Gulf Hagas, 363–64
Gulf of Slides, 286
Gunstock Cross-Country Center, 287

◆ H ◆

Hadley Harbor, 161
Half Moon Pond State Park, 184, 186,
    191, 216
Halibut State Park, 25, 121, 122, 124, 125,
    133, 135–36
Hamilton Falls, 217
Hammonasset Beach State Park, 60, 63,
    70, 73
Hampton Beach, 276
Hapgood Pond Recreation Area, 183,
    216, 235
Harbor Boat Rentals, 327
Harbor Divers, 332
Harmon Hill, 181, 205
Harold Parker State Forest, 122, 137
Harriman Reservoir, 174, 179–80, 181, 184,
    194, 203, 211, 252
Harvey's Lake, 267
Hawk Ledge, 187
Hawthorne Farm, 65
Hayes Copp Ski Trail, 286
Hazen's Notch Ski Touring Center,
    251, 252
Healing Springs Nature Trail, 186, 216
High Country Snowmobile Tours, 29,
    215–16
"High Huts," 8
Highland Links Golf Club, 154
Highland Lodge, 251, 271–72
Hiking Holidays, 29–30, 113, 210, 259, 325
Hilltop Haven Bed & Breakfast, 56
Hinckley Yacht Charters, 22, 332
Hog Island, 124, 134
Hoosic River, 174, 203
Hopeville Pond State Park, 63, 64
Horses for Hire, 210
Hot Fun, 319
Hotel Manisses, Block Island, 92

Housatonic Meadows State Park, 40, 47, 43, 54, 55
Housatonic River, 26, 39, 40, 43, 45, 47–48, 49, 50, 53, 54, 55, 56, 94, 98, 99, 100, 107, 112, 116
H2Outfitters, 30, 32, 70, 334
Humarock Beach, 127, 135
Hundred Mile Wilderness, 6, 31, 298, 340, 345, 355, 363, 366–67
Huntington Ravine, 16, 299
Hyannis Harbor, 162

◆ I ◆

Idle Times Bike Shop, 157
Inn at Castle Hill, 92
Inn at Longshore, The, 56
Inn at Mystic, The, 74
Inn at Round Barn Farm, 221, 238
Inn at Trout River, 271
Inn at Windsor, 237
Inn on the Common, 271
Interlaken Inn, 56
International Mountain Equipment Climbing School, 16, 21, 33, 299, 304, 305
International Sailing School and Club, 33, 246, 265–66
Ipswich River, 126
Ipswich River Sanctuary, 122, 124
Island Sport, 33
Island Windsurfing, 80
Isle au Haut, Maine, 22, 332, 335, 337
Isle de Motte, 241, 242–44, 263, 266
Islesboro, Maine, 20, 314, 315, 329–30, 337

◆ J ◆

J World, 22, 33, 88
Jack's Boat Rentals, 152
Jackson Falls, 305
Jackson Ski Touring Foundation, 11, 286, 287
Jamaica State Park, 183, 216, 235
Jay Mountain Trail, 260
Jay Peak, 7, 228, 240, 244, 251, 252, 255, 257, 259
Jay Peak Ski Area, 13, 253, 254
Jeffersonville Loop, 21, 263–64
Jetties Beach, 163

Jiminy Peak Ski Area, 106, 114
John Drummond Kennedy Park, 113–14
John Wing Trail, 165–66
Jonesport, Maine, 327–28
Josephine Newman Sanctuary, 335
Jubilee Yacht Charters, 48
Just Do It Too, 154

◆ K ◆

Kalmus Beach, 9, 151, 162
Kancamagus Highway Campground, 305
Kat Balloons, 42
Katahdin Outfitters, 352
Katama Beach, 163
Kebo Valley Golf Club, 323
Kedron Valley Stables, 16, 30, 210
Kennebago River, 352
Kennebec River, 13, 26, 340, 355, 360, 370, 371, 372
Killington Mountain Bike Center, 212
Killington Peak, 187, 207, 257
Killington School for Tennis, 33
Killington Ski Area, 13, 177, 180, 198, 201–2, 222
Kimberly Farms, 211
Kingdom Tele Boys, 251
King's Landing Marina, 126
Kingston Balloon Company, 80
Knight's Island State Park, 269
Kripalu Center for Yoga and Health, 37

◆ L ◆

Lafayette Campground, 306
Lake Bomoseen, 177, 184, 186, 203, 211, 213, 216
Lake Champlain, 10, 21, 22, 27, 32, 33, 34, 174, 215, 239, 240, 242–44, 245, 246, 255, 257, 260, 262–63, 264–65, 266–67, 268, 269
Lake Champlain Islands, 31, 242–44, 147, 263
Lake Dunmore, 211, 233, 255
Lake Dunmore Kamperville, 213, 215
Lake Fairlee, 226, 260
Lake Front Restaurant, 213, 215
Lake Groton, 267, 269, 270
Lake House, Waterford, 376
Lake Memphremagog, 244, 246, 254

Lake Morey, 226, 232
Lake St. Catherine Inn, 237
Lake St. Catherine State Park, 177, 183,
    186, 203, 211, 213, 214–15, 216,
    235, 237
Lake St. George State Park, 353–56, 371
Lake Solitude, 297–98
Lake Sunapee, 275, 281, 285, 302
Lake Sunapee State Park, 281
Lake Tashmoo, 152
Lake Waramaug, 43
Lake Waramaug State Park, 44, 54, 55
Lake Webb, 345, 356, 371, 374
Lake Willoughby, 15, 241, 242, 244, 254,
    256, 260, 261, 269
Lake Winnipesaukee, 22, 34, 275, 276, 281,
    283, 297, 299, 302, 304, 305
Lamoille River, 10, 31, 190, 244, 246,
    247–48, 255
Lamoine State Park, 30, 337
Laura Cowles Trail, 256–57
Ledgewood Riding Stables, 325–26
Ledyard Canoe Club, 248
Lee's Riding Stable, 50–51
Lenox-Stockbridge Loop, 115
Leonard, Larry, 204
Libby Sporting Camps, 362
Lighthouse Inn, 74
Lily Bay State Park, 371, 374
Lime Rock Inn, 338
Lincoln/Concord/Carlisle Loop, 20–21,
    130–31
Lincoln Gap, 178, 207, 227, 228, 255
Lincoln Guide Service, 126–27, 133
Lincoln Woods State Park, 89
Litalier, Norman, 352
Little Averill Lake, 244, 255, 260
Little Compton, Rhode Island, 85
Little River, 226
Little River State Park, 269
Livingston Balloon Company, 42
L.L.. Bean Outdoor Discovery Program, 30,
    324, 367
L.L. Bean Paddling, Fly-Fishing and
    Cycling Schools, 10, 14, 33, 321, 323,
    334, 353, 360, 369
Lobster Lake, 10–11, 351
Lobsterville Beach, 163
Long Beach (Gloucester), 135
Long Beach (Rockport), 134, 135

Long Point Beach, 163
Long Point Refuge, 151
Long Trail, 3, 6–7, 15, 173, 174, 178, 180,
    181, 182, 183, 184, 190, 204, 206–9,
    212, 227, 228, 255–56, 257, 258, 298
Longnook Beach, 164
Longshore Sailing School, 33, 53
Loon Mountain Park, 298
Loon Ski Area, 13, 288
Lovell Balloon Works, 349
Lower Falls Scenic Area, 305
Lucy Vincent Beach, 164
Lyman Orchards Golf Course, 64

◆ **M** ◆

Macedonia Brook State Park, 40, 55
Machias Seal Island, 8, 315, 319–20
McKibben Sailing Vacations, 262, 265
Mad River, 226, 234, 248
Mad River Bike Shop, 33, 230, 231, 233
Mad River Glen Ski Area, 178, 198, 222,
    224–25, 233, 238
Madaket, Nantucket, 151
Madaket Beach, 163
Mahoosuc Guide Service, 12, 30, 357, 358
Mahoosuc Mountain Range, 8, 298,
    365, 366
Maiden Cliff, 16, 324, 329, 337
Maidstone Lake, 260
Main Stream, 33, 43–44
Main Street Sports & Leisure, 101, 114
Maine Island Trail, 23, 332, 333
Maine Sport Outdoor School, 33, 334, 353
Maine Sport Outfitters, 10, 30, 321, 323,
    326, 327, 334
Maine Sporting Camp Association, 344, 360
Maine Whitewater, 373
Maine Windjammer Association, 30, 331
Manchester Sports, 200
Mansell Boat Company, 327, 332
Mansfield Hollow State Park, 62, 63, 64,
    65–66
Maple Ridge Sheep Farm, 19, 231
Marconi Beach, 150, 163
Marina St. Catherine, 216
Martha's, 159
Martha's Vineyard bike trails, 159–60
Martha's Vineyard State Forest, 17,
    148, 157

Mary's Boat Rentals, 129
Mashpee River Woodlands, 156
Mattabesett Trail, 62
Maudslay State Park, 19, 122, 128
Melville Ponds Campground, 91
Menemsha Beach, 163
Merck Forest & Farmland Center, 193–94,
    205–7, 216–17
Meridith Marina, 302
Merrell Hiking Center, 210
Metacomet Trail, 62
Mettawee River, 203
Miacomet Beach, 164
Micmac Farm Guesthouses, 337
Middlebury College Snow Bowl, 178, 222,
    223, 253
Middlebury Gap, 178
Middlebury Gorge, 267
Miles Pond, 267
Mill River, 191, 203
Minute Man Bikeway, 129
Missiquoi National Wildlife Refuge, 245
Missiquoi River, 190, 244, 246, 255
Mittersill Riding Stables, 298
Mohawk Mountain Ski Area, 47
Mohawk Mountain State Park, 40, 49,
    50, 54
Mohawk State Forest Loop, 45–46
Molly Stark State Park, 179, 235
Monhegan Island, 25, 31, 314, 315, 325,
    335 36
Monomoy National Wildlife Refuge, 8, 23,
    27, 148, 150–51, 161
Montague Golf Course, 227
Monument Mountain, 108–9, 110
Moon Sporting Goods, 107
Moose Bog, 246
Moosehead Lake, 22, 340, 344, 346, 351,
    355, 357, 360, 361, 367, 369, 370,
    371, 374, 376
Mooselookmeguntick Lake, 350, 367, 361,
    365, 369
Morningside Flight Park, 14, 33, 290
Morrison, Tim, 299
Moshup Beach, 163
Mount Abraham, 208, 221, 228, 233
Mount Abram Ski Area, 358, 359
Mount Agamenticus Riding Stables, 325
Mount Ascutney, 185, 187, 237
Mount Battie, 31, 313, 325, 337

Mount Blue State Park, 345, 356,
    371, 374
Mount Clinton road, 304
Mount Cranmore Ski Area, 288, 289
Mount Equinox, 174, 187, 236
Mount Everett, 7, 49, 94, 99, 109,
    110–11, 117
Mount Greylock State Reservation, 8, 14,
    15, 16, 23, 94, 95, 96, 97–98, 105,
    108, 110, 111, 114, 116, 118, 291
Mount Hope River, 64
Mount Hunger, 16, 240, 251, 256,
    257–58, 269
Mount Katahdin, 6, 14, 15, 339, 340, 341,
    345, 347, 351, 358, 362–63, 365, 366,
    373, 377
Mount Mansfield, 11, 16, 21, 27, 29, 32,
    187, 206, 207, 208, 228, 244, 248–49,
    250, 251, 252, 256–57, 258, 264,
    267, 269
Mount Mansfield Cross County Ski
    Center, 250, 260
Mount Misery, 62, 71–72
Mount Monadnock, 14, 281, 290, 296
Mount Pisgah, 15, 228, 256, 261
Mount Snow, 19, 187, 195, 216, 236
Mount Snow Golf Club, 204
Mount Snow Golf School, 33, 204
Mount Snow Resort Mountain Biking
    Center, 33, 212–13
Mount Snow/Haystack Ski Area, 13, 176,
    180, 196, 198–99, 200, 288
Mount Southington Ski Area, 47
Mount Sunapee Ski Area, 289
Mount Tabor Road Trail, 195–96
Mount Tom State Park, 44, 54
Mount Washington, 11, 16, 27, 273–74,
    275, 276, 280, 286, 288, 299, 301,
    304–5, 358, 366
Mount Washington Hotel, 289, 298, 301
Mount Washington State Forest, 99, 116
Mount Willard, 293
Mountain Goat, 114, 115
Mountain Meadows, 197, 252
Mountain Ridge Ranch, 260
Mountain Top Ski Touring Center,
    197, 252
Mountain Top Stables, 211
Mountain View Creamery, 272
Mud Pond, 351

My Fair Lady, 48
Myles Standish State Forest, 122, 129, 138
Mystic Cycle Center, 68
Mystic River Balloon Adventures, 62
Mystic Seaport, 58, 59, 68
Mystical Balloon Flights, 62

◆ **N** ◆

Nahant Island, 125
Nantasket Beach, 134
Nantucket, 9, 21, 160–61
Nantucket Boat Rental, 157
Nantucket Harbor Sail, 161
Narragansett Bay, 22, 27, 77, 79, 80, 83, 84, 86–88
Narragansett Bay National Estuarine Sanctuary, 79
Narragansett Town Beach, 80, 89
Narrow River Kayaks, 80, 89
Nashoba Valley Ski Area, 127
Natchaug River, 64
Natchaug State Forest, 70
Natchaug Trail, 62
National Park Canoe, 321
Naugatuck State Forest, 54
Nauset Beach, 145, 162–63, 164
Nauset Light Beach, 150
Nauset Marsh, 145–46, 150, 164
Nauset Sports, 33, 151, 162, 163
Naushon Island, 22, 161, 152
Navajo Farm, 229
Nebraska Notch Trail, 249
Nelson's Riding Stable, 155
Nepaug State Forrest, 40, 51
Nesowadnehunk Lake, 360
New England Aquarium, 137
New England Hiking Holidays, 30, 113, 259, 298, 325
New England Whitewater Center, 373
New Life, 36, 37
Newcomb Hollow, 163
Newport, Rhode Island, 78, 84–85
Newport Diving Center, 88
Newport Equestrian Center, 82
Newport Marina, 262, 266
Nicholas, Rob, 48
Nichols Snowmobile Rentals, 234, 267
Nickerson State Park, 146–48, 150, 153, 155, 158, 169

Nineteen-Mile Brook Trail, 285, 194, 304
Ninigret Pond, 80, 81
Nipmuck State Forest, 70, 72
Nipmuck Trail, 62, 72–73, 74
Nordic Adventures, 30, 197
Nordic Skier, 287
Nordic Skier Sport, 287 302
Norman Bird Sanctuary, 81
Norm's Bait & Tackle, 107
North American Canoe Tours, 44, 63
North Atlantic Scuba, 134
North Beach Park, 267
North County Anglers, 290
North Course (Stow Acres Country Club), 128
North Cove Outfitters, 70
North Haven, Maine, 314–15, 325, 330, 332
North Hero State Park, 269
North House, 200
North Monomoy Island, 148, 150, 162
North River, 125
North Shore Charters, 154
North Springfield Bog, 186
North Star Canoes, 193
North Wind Touring, 30, 210
North Woods Ways, 30–31, 353
Northeast Corner. *See* Quiet Corner
Northeast Kingdom Llama Expeditions, 260
Northeast Ventures, 30, 353
Northern Lakes, 244
Northern Maine Riding Adventures, 30, 367
Northern Outdoors, 370, 372, 373
Northern Pines Health Resort, 36, 37
Northern Ski Works, 201
Northern Vermont Llama Treks, 260
Northern Waters Outfitters, 284, 285
Northfield Dam Recreation Area, 54
Northland Trout Tours, 33, 226
Norwalk Islands, 39, 42, 54
Norwalk Sailing School, 53
Norway Loop, 369
Norwich Inn and Spa, 36, 37, 74
Norwich Municipal Golf Course, 64
Nota Boat Livery, 107
Notchview Reservation, 98, 104–5
Nugent's Chamberlain Lake Camps, 361–62

◆ O ◆

Ocean Beach, 70
Ocean Edge Resort, 169
Ocean Edge Resort Golf Course, 14, 154
Oceans & Ponds, 81, 89
October Mountain State Forest, 94, 98,
    100, 101, 102, 103, 104, 106, 113,
    116, 118
Off-Shore Yachts, 53
Ogunquit Beach, 319, 335
O'Hara's Landing Marina, 48
Okemo Ski Area, 176, 180, 198 199–201
Old Orchard Beach, 319, 321, 325
Old Riverton Inn, 56
Old Tavern, 214, 215, 236–37
Olde Barnstable Fairgrounds Golf
    Course, 154
Ole's Cross-Country Center, 222
Omer & Bob's Sport Shop, 225
Ompompanoosuc River, 226
Onion River Sports, 178, 225, 231,
    233, 234
Onset Beach, 135
Orvis, 14, 33, 182
Osgood Brook Culvert, 234
O'Shaughnessy, Andy, 299
Otis Ridge Ski Area, 107
Ottaquechee River, 226
Otter Creek, 174, 177, 183, 190, 191,
    203, 262
Outdoor Bound of Vermont, 31, 251
Outer Conway Loop, 303
Overton's Boat Livery, 48

◆ P ◆

Pachaug State Forest, 18, 62, 65,
    70, 73
Pachaug Trail, 62
Pamet Cranberry Bog Trail, 166
Panorama Golf Course, 290
Park Pond, 54
Parker River National Wildlife Refuge,
    8–9, 124, 125, 135
Pathfinders, 50
Patterson, Mike, 321
Pawcatuck River, 81
Peak Performance, 201
Pemigewasset Wilderness, 8, 15, 298

Penobscot Bay, 16, 22, 30, 31, 308, 312,
    313, 314, 321, 323, 326, 329, 330,
    332, 337, 338, 369
Penobscot River, 11, 13, 26, 30, 340,
    347–48, 350, 351, 353, 355, 359,
    363, 369, 372–73
Peoples State Forrest, 40, 43, 52, 54
Perch Pond, 300, 305
Pico Peak, 177, 187
Pico Peak Ski Area, 13, 177, 180, 201,
    202–3, 212
Pillsbury State Park, 306
Pine Knob Loop, 50, 56
Pine Mountain Ski Touring Center, 46
Pine Point, 321
Pinkham Notch, 276, 280, 288, 305,
    306
Pinnacle Ski & Sports, 253
Pittsfield State Forest, 113, 116
Pleasant Mountain, West Rockport,
    326–27
Pleasant Valley Trout Farm, 255
Pleasant Valley Wildlife Sanctuary, 98, 99
    trails, 110–11
Plum Island, 8–9, 120, 122, 124, 125, 126,
    127, 135, 136
Plymouth Beach, 135
Plymouth Bristol Charters, 133
Plymouth Parasail, 129
Pocha Pond, 152, 153
Point Judith, 81
Points North Outfitters, 107
Pond Hill Ranch, 211
Pootatuck State Forest, 54
Portsmouth Country Club, 290
Poultney River, 203
Powder Ridge Ski Area, 64
Presidential Mountain Range, 274,
    280, 287
Profile Falls, 305
Pro-motions, 127
Prospect Rock (Johnson), 258–59
Prospect Ski Mountain, 196–97
Prouty Beach, 267
Province Lands, 21, 146, 150, 158
Prudence Island, 22, 77, 79, 82–83, 88
P'town Bikes, 158
Pulaski Memorial State Park, 81, 89
Punkhorn Parklands, 156–57
Purple Alpine Outfitters, 200

◆ Q ◆

Quaddick Pond State Park, 63
Quechee Gorge, 234
Quiet Corner, 61–62, 65, 67–68
Quimby Country's Lodge, 255
Quinebaug River, 63
Quinebaug Valley Ski Touring Center, 64
Quoddy Head State Park, 25, 312, 315–19, 335, 337

◆ R ◆

Race Brook Lodge, 119
Race Brook Trail, 109
Race Point Beach, 153, 158, 163
Raft Maine, 373
Rail Trail Bike Rentals, 157
Ralph Waldo Emerson Inn, 138
Ram Pasture, 149, 167
Randall's Ordinary, 74–75
Randolph, Vermont, 20, 232–33
Rangeley Inn, 352, 353 376
Rangeley Lake State Park, 371, 374
Rangeley Lakes region, 14, 30, 340, 344, 350, 357, 359, 360, 365, 374
Rangeley Region Sport Shop, 368
Red Hill, 296–97, 300
Red Jersey Cyclery, 299
Reel Thing, 48
Rexhame Beach, 135
Rhododendron Sanctuary, 62, 71–72
Richter Park Golf Course, 48
Ricker Pond Campground, 269–70
Ride Snowmobile Tours, 234
Ridgefield Golf Course, 48
Ridgepole Trail, 18, 300
River Excitement, 204
Riverrunning Expeditions, 43
Roaring Brook Campground, 362
Roaring Brook Stony Ledge Loop, 16, 111
Rob Brook Road, 301
Robert Frost Interpretive Trail, 25, 267–68
Rock Pond Loop, Saddleback Ski Touring Center, 356–57
Rock River, 216
Rockland Breakwater, 336
Rockport, Massachusetts, 122
Rockport-Camden-Megunticook Lake bike ride, 328–29

Rockwell House Inn, 92
Rockwell Road, 105
Rocky Neck State Park, 60, 70, 73
Rodney's Surf & Turf, 89
Roger Wheeler State Beach, 89
Rohan Farm, 260
Rolling Green Ski Touring Center, 127
Roseland Acres Equestrian Center, 82
Rosewood Country Inn, 307
Russell Pond Campground, 305
Russell Yacht Charters, 53
Rustic Rides Farm, 82
Rustling Wind Stables, 51
Ruthcliffe Lodge, 264, 270
Rutland Country Club, 204

◆ S ◆

Sable Oaks Golf Club, 323
Saco Bound Outfitters, 284, 285
Saco River, 283–84, 290, 350
Saddleback Ski Area, 13, 358–59
Saddleback Ski Touring Center, 356–57
Sagamore Bridge, 144
Sail Newport, 33–34, 80, 88
Sailing Center, 283, 304
St. Croix River, 10, 351, 352–53
St. John River, 10, 30, 340, 348–49, 350–51, 352, 353, 355
Sakonnet Boathouse, 31, 34, 88
Sakonnet Point, 78, 81, 85
Sakonnet River, 79, 85
Salisbury Beach State Reservation, 135, 137
Salisbury bicycle loop, 52–53
Salmon River, 61, 64
Salmon River State Forest, 61, 70–71
Salmon River Trail, 62
Salmon Run Camps, 369
Samoset Golf Course, 14, 323
Samoset Resort, 321, 338
Sandy Beach, 54
Sandy Neck, 144–45, 152
Sanford Farm, 149, 151, 167
Sankaty Head, 153
Sargents Marine, 302
Satan's Kingdom Gorge, 54
Savoy Mountain State Forest, 19, 94, 97, 113, 114, 118
Saxton's River, 192, 203

Scarborough Marsh, 335
Schirmer's Fly Shop, 255
'Sconset Beach, 163
Seaside Cycle, 133
Seawall Campground, Acadia National
    Park, 336
Sebago Lake State Park, 340, 341, 353,
    368, 371, 373–74
Second Beach, 89
Sew'N So Shop, 67
Seymour Lake, 244, 254, 260
Seymour Lake Lodge, 255, 267
Shadow Lake Beach, 267
Shaffer's Boat Livery, 64
Shaffer's Marina, 64
Shaftsbury State Park, 181–82, 186, 216
Shake-a-Leg Sailing Center, 34, 88
Shapleigh Hostel, 305
Sharon Audubon Center, 42
Shattuck Inn Golf Course, 290
Shawne Crowell State Forest, 169
Shaws Boarding House, 366, 367
Shelter Harbor Inn, Westerly, 92
Shenipsit State Forest, 70
Shenipsit Trail, 62
Shennecosset Golf Course, 64
Sherwood Island State Park, 39, 42, 54, 56
Ship's Bell Inn, 169–70
Ship's Knees Inn, 169
Shrewsbury Peak, 184, 187
Siasconet Cranberry Bog, 151
Silver Lake State Park, 185, 226, 229,
    234, 235
Silver Maple Lodge, 217, 232, 238
Singing Beach, 135
Single-track biking, 17, 18, 19, 51, 65, 66,
    82, 114, 129, 156, 212, 231, 261,
    299, 300
Sitzmark Lodge, 216
Sitzmark Ski Shop, 225
Skaket Beach, 163
Ski Shack, 201
Ski Sundown Ski Area, 47
Skihaus of Vermont, 253
Skytop Trail, 249
Slab City Bike & Sports, 231, 233
Slater Memorial Park, 81
Small Boat Shop, 34, 53–54
Smuggler's Notch, 208, 244, 255, 260
Smuggler's Notch Canoe Touring, 248

Smuggler's Notch Resort, 270
Smuggler's Notch Ski Area, 222, 254, 258,
    260, 264
Smuggler's Notch State Park Campground,
    257, 269
Snow Job, The, 253
Snowy Owl Inn, 307
Somerset Reservoir, 174, 181, 182, 184,
    186, 190, 195, 203, 211
Somertime Charters, 48
Somes Sound, 15, 311, 312, 313, 324
South Bay Wildlife Management
    Area, 245
South Bridge Boat House, 126
South Trail, 165–66
Southwest Cycle, 330
Southwest Harbor Loop, 328
Spa at Grand Lake, 37, 75
Sperry Campground, 118
Spindrift Charters, 161
Spoke, The, 115
Sports Odyssey, 200
Springweather Nature Area, 187
Spruce Goose Ski Trail, 285
Squam Lake, 18, 22, 275, 281, 283, 300
Squibnocket Beach, 163
Squibnocket Pond, 152
Stacy Ann, 48
State Beach, 163
Steamline, 226
Steep Rock Loop, Steep Rock
    Reservation, 46
Steppin' Up Balloons, 42
Stepping Stone Ranch, 82
Sterling Pond, 228, 258
Sterling Yacht Charters, 68
Stillwater Campground, 269
Stockbridge, Massachusetts, 115
Stonehurst Manor, 294, 307
Stonyside Farms, 51
Stowe Golf Course, 255
Stowe Mountain Resort Ski Touring
    Center, 250
Stowe Recreation Path, 267
Stowe Ski Area, 13, 198, 222, 240, 244, 249,
    251–52, 253
Stoweflake Resort, 217
Stratton Golf School, 34, 204
Stratton Mountain, 182, 187, 190, 209, 252
Stratton Mountain Golf Course, 204

Stratton Mountain Ski Area, 176, 180, 198, 199, 200, 212, 288
Stratton Pond, 182, 208–10, 228, 252
Strictly Trout, 204
Stumpf Balloons, 80
Sugarbush Golf Course, 204, 227
Sugarbush Ski Area, 13, 178, 198, 221, 222, 223–24, 233, 238
Sugarloaf I & II campgrounds, 305–6
Sugarloaf Ski Touring Center, 356, 357
Sugarloaf/USA Condominiums, 376
Sugarloaf/USA Golf Course, 362
Sugarloaf/USA Ski Area, 13, 345, 358, 359
Suicide Six Ski Area, 223
Sunapee Railroad Bed, 301–2
Sunapee State Beach, 305
Sunday River Cross-Country Ski Center, 357
Sunday River Ski Area, 13, 345, 358, 359
Sunken Ship, 161
Sunny Brook Stables, 367
Sunrise Canoe Trip, 352
Sunrise County Canoe Expeditions, 321, 353
Sunset Ledge, 227–28
Sunset Ridge Trail, 256–57, 269
Sunsplash Boat Rentals, 129, 133
Sure Strike Charters, 255
Surfside Beach, 163
Swan Pond, 152
Swift River Inn, 106, 119

◆ **T** ◆

Table Rock, 295–96
Taconic Golf Course, 107
T.A.D. Dog Sled Services, 12, 358
Tangled Line, 204
Tanglewood 4-H camp, 321
Tarpaulin Cove, 161
Tashua Knolls Golf Course, 48
Teardrop Trail, 11, 248–49
Telemark skiing, 11, 12, 193, 250, 251, 286
Ten Mile Hill, 48–49
Ten Speed Spokes, 86
Texas Falls/Hancock Branch Brook, 221
Third Cliff Beach, 127
Thomas Mott Homestead, 264, 270
Three Legged Tours, 283
Three Stallion Inn, 238

Tim Pond Wilderness Camps, 361
Tisbury Great Pond, 152–53
Tiverton, Rhode Island, 85
Tomhegan Wilderness Resort, 361
Topnotch at Stowe, 37
Topnotch Stables, 260
Topnotch Touring Center, 250
Totem Pole, 200
Town Beach, 153
Trail of Tears, 155–56
Trapalanda Stables, 64–65
Trapp Family Lodge, 11, 248, 250, 252, 270–71
Triggs Memorial Golf Course, 82
Troll Valley, 357
Tuckerman Ravine, Mount Washington, 11, 12, 280, 286, 288, 340
Tudhope Sailing Center and Marina, 34, 266
Twin Mountain, 304, 305
Twin Ponds Farm, 113

◆ **U** ◆

U-Drive Boat Rentals, 116
Umbagog Lake Campground, 285, 306
Umbagog Lake National Wildlife Refuge, 9, 10, 30, 280, 281, 284–85, 357
Umiak Outdoor Outfitters, 24, 34, 248, 251, 259, 267
Underhill State Park, 268
Undermountain Farm, 113

◆ **V** ◆

Val Halla Country Club, 321
Valley View Horses and Tack Shop, 210–11
Vermont Bicycle Touring, 31, 115, 161, 215, 264, 330
Vermont Bound, 226
Vermont Fly Fishing School, 34, 226
Vermont Horse Park, 260
Vermont Icelandic Horse Farm, 16, 31, 229
Vermont Institute of Natural Science & Raptor Center, 217
Vermont North, 225
Vermont Voyager Expedition, 248, 251
Vermont Walking Tours, 259
Vermont Waterways, 31, 246, 247, 248
Vernon Black Gum Swamp, 179

Victory Bog, 245–46
Viking Biking, 213
Viking Center, 197
Village Inn, 197, 252

◆ **W** ◆

Wachusett Mountain Ski Area, 127
Wadleigh State Beach, 305
Wadsworth Falls State Park, 63, 70
Wahconah Country Club, 107
Waitsfield, Vermont, 18, 230, 233
Waitsfield-Warren Loop, 233
Walden Pond State Reservation, 21, 120,
    124–25, 127, 130, 131, 132
Walking-Inn-Vermont, 31, 210
Walking the World 50 Plus, 31, 90–91,
    298, 325
Walking Tours of Southern Vermont, 31,
    210, 211
Walloomsac River, 203
Wantastiquet Mountain, 187
Wardsboro Brook, 192
Ware, Carroll, 370
Warren Island State Park, 337
Wasgue Point, 153
Wasque Reservation, 149, 151
Waterbury Trail, 257
Waterfront Diving Center, 34, 266, 267
Waterhomes, 213, 215
Watershed, The, 34, 89
Watershed Balloons, 42
Waterville Campground, 305
Waterville Valley Resort, 298
Waterville Valley Ski Area, 287, 288
Wauwinet Inn, 161, 170
Weatherby's, 361
Webb's Camping Area, 169
Weirs Beach, 276, 302
Welch/Dickey Mountain Trail, 16, 293–94
Wellesley College, 135
Wellfleet Audubon Sanctuary, 150
Wellfleet Bay Wildlife Sanctuary, 8, 25,
    146, 148, 164–65
West Hill Shop, 213
West Kennebago Mountain, 364–65
West Mountain Inn, 236
West River, 26, 177, 183, 190, 192, 203,
    216, 217, 235
West River Lodge and Stable, 210

West River Stables, 210
West Rutland Marsh, 186
Weston Ski Track, 127
White Crest Beach, 162
White Elephant, The, 170
White Hart Inn, 53, 56
White House Ski Touring Center, 196,
    236, 252
White Ledge Campground, 305
White Memorial Foundation &
    Conservation Center, 41, 42, 44, 55
White Mountain National Forest, 7, 11, 14,
    16, 18, 21, 273, 276, 277, 283, 284,
    290, 293, 295, 299, 300, 301, 305,
    345, 357, 362
  camping, 374
White River, 31, 178, 207, 226, 234,
    247, 248
White Rocks Trail, 209–10
Wild Bird Center, 220
Wild Earth Adventures, 31, 50, 113, 259
Wild Wings Ski Touring Center, 197
Wildcat Ski Area, 12, 287, 288
Wildcat Valley Trail, 286
Wilderness Trail, 285
Wilderness Trails, Inc., 225
Wildwater Outfitters, 118
Williams River, 192, 203
Williamstown Loop, 114
Williamsville Inn, 119
Willimantic River, 10, 63
Willoughby River, 254
Willowdale State Forest, 128–29
Winchester Lake, 43
Wind Touring, 197
Winding Trails Cross Country Ski
    Center, 46
Winds of Ireland, 22, 265
Wind's Up on the Vineyard, 152, 153,
    161, 163
Windsurfing of Watch Hill, 34, 80
Wingaersheek Beach, 135
Winhall River, 192
Winni Sailboarder's School & Outlet,
    34, 282
Winnipesaukee Kayak Company, 34
Winooski River, 31, 190, 208, 226, 234, 244,
    246, 248, 250, 255
Winter Island Park, 137
Wolfeboro Marina, 302

Womanship, 34, 88
Women's Sailing Adventures, 53
Wood River, 81
Woodbury Ski Area, 47
Woodford State Park, 181, 184–95, 235
Woods, The, 149, 167
Woodstock Acres Riding Stable, 64
Woodstock Country Club, 14, 204, 227
Woodstock Golf Course, 64
Woodstock Hill Riding Academy, 65
Woodstock Inn & Resort, 223, 237–38
Woodstock Ski Touring Center, 221
Worcester Mountain Range, 240
Worden Pond, 80, 81
World's End, 120, 121, 136–37

◆ Y ◆

Yankee Clipper Inn, 138
Yankee Fishing Fleet, 127
Yankee Whale Watching, 137
Yawgoo Valley Ski Area, 81
Yellow Bog, 246
YMCA Marina, 101, 116
York Beach Scuba, 332
Young's Bicycle Shop, 159

◆ Z ◆

Zealand Campground, 305–6
Zealand Road, 304
Zealand Trail, 15, 282, 285, 294
Zoar Outdoor, 26, 34, 118

FROMMER'S COMPLETE TRAVEL GUIDES

(Comprehensive guides to sightseeing, dining, and accommodations, with selections in all price ranges from deluxe to budget)

Acapulco/Ixtapa/Taxco, 2nd Ed.
Alaska, 4th Ed.
Arizona '96
Australia, 4th Ed.
Austria, 6th Ed.
Bahamas '96
Belgium/Holland/Luxembourg, 4th Ed.
Bermuda '96
Budapest & the Best of Hungary, 1st Ed.
California '96
Canada, 9th Ed.
Caribbean '96
Carolinas/Georgia, 3rd Ed.
Colorado, 3rd Ed.
Costa Rica, 1st Ed.
Cruises '95-'96
Delaware/Maryland, 2nd Ed.
England '96
Florida '96
France '96
Germany '96
Greece, 1st Ed.
Honolulu/Waikiki/Oahu, 4th Ed.
Ireland, 1st Ed.
Italy '96
Jamaica/Barbados, 2nd Ed.
Japan, 3rd Ed.

Maui, 1st Ed.
Mexico '96
Montana/Wyoming, 1st Ed.
Nepal, 3rd Ed.
New England '96
New Mexico, 3rd Ed.
New York State '94-'95
Nova Scotia/New Brunswick/Prince
　Edward Island, 1st Ed.
Portugal, 14th Ed.
Prague & the Best of the Czech Republic,
　1st Ed.
Puerto Rico '95-'96
Puerto Vallarta/Manzanillo/Guadalajara,
　3rd Ed.
Scandinavia, 16th Ed.
Scotland, 3rd Ed.
South Pacific, 5th Ed.
Spain, 16th Ed.
Switzerland, 7th Ed.
Thailand, 2nd Ed.
U.S.A., 4th Ed.
Utah, 1st Ed.
Virgin Islands, 3rd Ed.
Virginia, 3rd Ed.
Washington/Oregon, 6th Ed.
Yucatan '95-'96

FROMMER'S FRUGAL TRAVELER'S GUIDES

(Dream vacations at down-to-earth prices)

Australia on $45 '95-'96
Berlin from $50, 3rd Ed.
Caribbean from $60, 1st Ed.
Costa Rica/Guatemala/Belize on $35, 3rd Ed.
Eastern Europe on $30, 5th Ed.
England from $50, 21st Ed.
Europe from $50 '96
Greece from $45, 6th Ed.
Hawaii from $60, 30th Ed.

Ireland from $45, 16th Ed.
Israel from $45, 16th Ed.
London from $60 '96
Mexico from $35 '96
New York on $70 '94-'95
New Zealand from $45, 6th Ed.
Paris from $65 '96
South America on $40, 16th Ed.
Washington, D.C. from $50 '96

FROMMER'S COMPLETE CITY GUIDES

(Comprehensive guides to sightseeing, dining, and accommodations in all price ranges)

Amsterdam, 8th Ed.
Athens, 10th Ed.
Atlanta & the Summer Olympic Games '96

Bangkok, 2nd Ed.
Berlin, 3rd Ed.
Boston '96

FROMMER'S COMPLETE TRAVEL GUIDES

(Comprehensive guides to sightseeing, dining, and accommodations, with selections in all price ranges from deluxe to budget)

Acapulco/Ixtapa/Taxco, 2nd Ed.
Alaska, 4th Ed.
Arizona '96
Australia, 4th Ed.
Austria, 6th Ed.
Bahamas '96
Belgium/Holland/Luxembourg, 4th Ed.
Bermuda '96
Budapest & the Best of Hungary, 1st Ed.
California '96
Canada, 9th Ed.
Caribbean '96
Carolinas/Georgia, 3rd Ed.
Colorado, 3rd Ed.
Costa Rica, 1st Ed.
Cruises '95-'96
Delaware/Maryland, 2nd Ed.
England '96
Florida '96
France '96
Germany '96
Greece, 1st Ed.
Honolulu/Waikiki/Oahu, 4th Ed.
Ireland, 1st Ed.
Italy '96
Jamaica/Barbados, 2nd Ed.
Japan, 3rd Ed.

Maui, 1st Ed.
Mexico '96
Montana/Wyoming, 1st Ed.
Nepal, 3rd Ed.
New England '96
New Mexico, 3rd Ed.
New York State '94-'95
Nova Scotia/New Brunswick/Prince
  Edward Island, 1st Ed.
Portugal, 14th Ed.
Prague & the Best of the Czech Republic,
  1st Ed.
Puerto Rico '95-'96
Puerto Vallarta/Manzanillo/Guadalajara,
  3rd Ed.
Scandinavia, 16th Ed.
Scotland, 3rd Ed.
South Pacific, 5th Ed.
Spain, 16th Ed.
Switzerland, 7th Ed.
Thailand, 2nd Ed.
U.S.A., 4th Ed.
Utah, 1st Ed.
Virgin Islands, 3rd Ed.
Virginia, 3rd Ed.
Washington/Oregon, 6th Ed.
Yucatan '95-'96

FROMMER'S FRUGAL TRAVELER'S GUIDES

(Dream vacations at down-to-earth prices)

Australia on $45 '95-'96
Berlin from $50, 3rd Ed.
Caribbean from $60, 1st Ed.
Costa Rica/Guatemala/Belize on $35, 3rd Ed.
Eastern Europe on $30, 5th Ed.
England from $50, 21st Ed.
Europe from $50 '96
Greece from $45, 6th Ed.
Hawaii from $60, 30th Ed.

Ireland from $45, 16th Ed.
Israel from $45, 16th Ed.
London from $60 '96
Mexico from $35 '96
New York on $70 '94-'95
New Zealand from $45, 6th Ed.
Paris from $65 '96
South America on $40, 16th Ed.
Washington, D.C. from $50 '96

FROMMER'S COMPLETE CITY GUIDES

(Comprehensive guides to sightseeing, dining, and accommodations in all price ranges)

Amsterdam, 8th Ed.
Athens, 10th Ed.
Atlanta & the Summer Olympic Games '96

Bangkok, 2nd Ed.
Berlin, 3rd Ed.
Boston '96

FROMMER'S BEST BEACH VACATIONS

(The top places to sun, stroll, shop, stay, play, party, and swim, with each beach rated for beauty, swimming, sand, and amenities)

California
Carolinas/Georgia
Florida
Hawaii

Mid-Atlantic from New York to
Washington, D.C.
New England

FROMMER'S BED & BREAKFAST GUIDES

(Selective guides with four-color photos and full description of the best inns in each region)

California
Caribbean
Great American Cities
Hawaii
Mid-Atlantic

New England
Pacific Northwest
Rockies
Southeast States
Southwest

FROMMER'S IRREVERENT GUIDES

(Wickedly honest guides for sophisticated travelers and those who want to be)

Amsterdam
Chicago
London

Manhattan
New Orleans
San Francisco

FROMMER'S DRIVING TOURS

(Four-color photos and detailed maps outlining spectacular scenic driving routes)

Australia
Austria
Britain
Florida
France
Germany
Ireland

Italy
Scandinavia
Scotland
Spain
Switzerland
U.S.A.

FROMMER'S BORN TO SHOP

(The ultimate travel guides for discriminating shoppers from cut-rate to couture)

Great Britain
Hong Kong

London
New York

FROMMER'S FOOD LOVER'S COMPANIONS

(Lavishly illustrated guides to regional specialties, restaurants, gourmet shops, markets, local wines, and more)

France
Italy